SIDNEY LANIER

Sidney Lanier. Marble bust in the Washington Memorial Library, Macon. Modeled by Gutzon Borglum from the ambrotype portrait of 1857.

SIDNEY LANIER

A BIOGRAPHICAL AND CRITICAL STUDY

BY

AUBREY HARRISON STARKE

"For until the Song of the Poet is heard
Ye do not live, ye cannot live."
  —*The Song of Aldhelm.*

NEW YORK
RUSSELL & RUSSELL · INC
1964

811.3
L287зо

TO MY GRANDMOTHER

MARTHA A. TURBEVILLE WATKINS

AND IN MEMORY OF MY AUNT

MARY LORENZO MORGAN

LIFE AND SONG

If life were caught by a clarionet,
*   And a wild heart, throbbing in the reed,*
Should thrill its joy and trill its fret,
*   And utter its love in love's own deed,*

Then would this breathing clarionet
*   Type what I would that I might be;*
For none o' the poets ever yet
*   Has wholly* lived *his minstrelsy,*

Or wholly sung his true, true thought,
*   Or utterly bodied forth his life,*
Or made what God made when He wrought
*   One perfect self of man and wife;*

Or lived and sung, that Life and Song
*   Might each express the other's all,*
Careless if life or art were long
*   Since both were one, to stand or fall.*

So that the wonder struck the crowd,
*   Who shouted it about the land:*
His song was only living aloud,
    His work was a singing with his hand!

—Sidney Lanier. 1868

PREFACE

ALTHOUGH the present volume offers a more detailed account of the life of Sidney Lanier than has previously been published, it was planned less as a biography than as a critical study, and therefore an attempt has been made to discuss the entire body of Lanier's work, collected and uncollected, inspired poems, scholarly lectures, and prose pot-boilers. But even in this critical study I have tried to present Lanier less as a poet, musician, or man of letters than as a man having greater social significance than is usually recognized. It is as a man whose greatness is not limited to his achievement in any one field that I think of Lanier; it is as an American hero with a message peculiarly worth listening to in the present period of economic and social unrest that I wish to present him.

In the Bibliography to this volume are listed the chief printed sources of information concerning the life of Lanier and the more important of the critical studies of his work, on all of which I have drawn freely. I wish, however, to mention here more specifically four earlier studies of Lanier, which are the most important of many published, and to acknowledge my own indebtedness to them. They are that of William Hayes Ward (1884), issued as a memorial in the collected edition of Lanier's poems; that of Professor Morgan Callaway, Jr. (1895), the most scholarly study of Lanier's work yet published; that of William Malone Baskervill (1897), rich in sympathy and understanding; and that of Professor Edwin Mims (1905), the only book length biography of Lanier, one based on material to which no other biographer has had access, the most complete of all studies of Lanier previously published and one which must serve as a standard by which all other studies—biographical or critical—are to be measured.

Much interesting and significant material concerning Lanier and his work was not reprinted in any of these four major studies, however, and much new material has been made available since the last of them (Professor Mims's biography) was published.

Furthermore, in no previous study of Lanier has any great amount of his uncollected prose and poetry been reprinted or even noticed, and yet there is a considerable body of such material which is extremely important for the light it throws on Lanier's better known work, and for the gaps it fills in his biography. There is also available now a certain amount of unpublished material, letters written by Lanier and contemporary letters concerning him, and written reminiscences of him. All this material I have endeavored to incorporate—in full or in part—in the present study.

To make more easily available, though to a necessarily limited extent, certain other material, I have adopted the somewhat uncritical procedure of quoting Lanier's poems in the first published—and often inferior—versions. (His later revisions of most of these poems are given in the volume of his collected poems [1884; latest revised edition 1916]. Save in the case of "The Song of the Chattahoochee" the early versions of the poems that Lanier revised have never been reprinted.) By means of such material one is enabled to trace and measure Lanier's development as an artist.

In quoting from Lanier's letters I have quoted exactly from the sources indicated, the manuscript originals or the best published versions. Inconsistency in spelling and punctuation has resulted, but I did not care to check or correct the spelling and punctuation of a few of the published letters with the manuscript originals without doing likewise for all, and the holograph manuscripts of many of the letters are not at present available for study. On the other hand, I wished to reproduce as accurately as possible the text of letters here published for the first time.

In similar fashion I have not attempted to impose consistency of spelling on quotations from Lanier's published work, and I have even allowed his various spellings of Shakspere's name to stand as he wrote them, though for greater consistency elsewhere I have adopted Dowden's spelling, adopted by Lanier himself after 1879.

I have omitted source notes wherever the text or the accompanying Bibliography, makes clear the source of my material, but I have given in notes bibliographical information concerning the separate poems and essays of the collected editions, to correct the often erroneous previously published ascriptions; and a certain amount of information that did not seem appropriate to the text proper. I have also given in notes a number of cross references to Lanier's work, hoping by such notes to indicate the pleasure to be derived from a comparative study of his varied work, and the wealth of material available for analytical studies of Lanier's character and of his thought.

Finally, I have throughout emphasized Lanier's importance as a national figure and his relations with men of national reputation. Professor Mims's biography makes beautifully clear the relation of Lanier to the South, but the time has come, I feel, for us to see Lanier first of all as a southerner who grew beyond all sectional limitations.

My own interest in Lanier grows out of the gift of a copy of the collected *Poems* made me years ago by my father, who in making the gift merely thought to add to my shelf of books another book by a southern poet. It was ten years before the interest in Lanier then aroused had crystallized into a desire to make a critical study of his life and work. That the study was even then begun is due chiefly to the encouragement given me by my friend, Dr. Thomas Ollive Mabbott.

In the course of my study and investigation I have consulted or corresponded with a great number of people to many of whom I was a stranger. Their kindness in furnishing me with the information I requested, in intrusting to me valuable documents and in putting themselves to considerable trouble to further my work, I regard as evidence of the hold Lanier still has on the hearts of those who have come in any way into contact with him. I wish that I might thank each and every one publicly for the assistance that has made this work possible, but the list of names is too long to be printed in full. The assistance of certain people has been so great, however, that I must, in courtesy, make public acknowledgment of it. Dr. Jay B. Hubbell, editor of *American Literature*, gave me encouragement and aid, gave my work generous publicity in the pages of his magazine, and put important material at my disposal. Mr. Henry W. Lanier early expressed sympathy and interest that have proved a constant stimulus, and cheerfully answered all questions put to him. Mr. E. R. B. Willis, of the Cornell University Library, furnished full information concerning manuscript letters in his library which I was unable to consult. Dr. John C. French has answered innumerable questions concerning Lanier material in the Johns Hopkins University Library and has been exceedingly helpful

in securing for me photographic copies of manuscript material,
Dr. H. W. L. Dana assisted in my attempt to gather full evidence
of the connection between Lanier and Longfellow by opening
the collections at Craigie House to me and by going through
them with me. The late Vachel Lindsay allowed me to copy
from a manuscript diary a record of his visit to Macon in 1906
and of C. E. Campbell's reminiscences of Lanier which he then
collected. The Lindsay record has been graciously supplemented
by Mr. Campbell's daughter, Miss Louise Weed Campbell. Mrs.
C. N. Hawkins and Mr. Ephraim Keyser wrote for me their
reminiscences of Lanier, not previously published. Dr. Waldo
Selden Pratt supplemented the account of his friendship with
Lanier written for Professor Mims in 1905 and sent me important
unpublished letters. Mr. Sidney Lanier Eason allowed me to
use a collection of papers pertaining to his cousin. Interesting
information concerning Lanier's life was gathered for me by
Mr. Oliver Orr—indefatigable in his work to extend Lanier's
fame—and supplied also by Miss Jennie Fleetwood Westfeldt,
Mrs. G. V. Cate, Mrs. K. G. Berrie (of the Brunswick, Georgia,
Board of Trade). Mrs. H. D. Allen, Sr., and several residents of
Macon, Georgia, who knew Lanier personally—chiefly Mrs. J. W.
Nisbet, Mrs. James Blount, Mrs. Granville Connor, and the late
Mrs. W. A. Hopson—to whom I was introduced by Miss Sally
M. Akin, librarian of the Washington Memorial Library, Macon.
My great-great aunt, Mrs. G. A. Hankins, prepared for me a
sketch of Lanier's war-time sweetheart, Virginia (or Ginna)
Hankins.

Permission to publish Lanier manuscript material in the present
volume has been given by the librarians or trustees of the Harvard
College Library, the Yale University Library, the Henry E.
Huntington Library and Art Gallery, the Johns Hopkins University Library, the Duke University Library, and the Washington Memorial Library; by Mrs. C. S. Hayden, Dr. W. S.
Pratt, Dr. T. O. Mabbott, Mr. Sidney Lanier Eason, and Dr.
H. W. L. Dana. Some of the manuscript material used is from
my own collection.

For permission to use quotations from Lanier's collected prose
and poetry I wish to thank Mr. Henry W. Lanier (as representative of the Lanier family) and the firm of Charles Scribner's Sons,
publishers of the collected *Poems*, *The Science of English Verse*,
The English Novel, *Music and Poetry*, *Retrospects and Prospects*, *Bob:*

The Story of Our Mocking Bird, and the four books for boys, the *Froissart,* the *King Arthur,* the *Mabinogion,* and the *Percy;* and Doubleday, Doran and Company, Inc., successors to Doubleday, Page & Co., publishers of *Shakspere and His Forerunners,* edited by Mr. Henry W. Lanier. For permission to use quotations from various letters by Lanier and other matter I wish to thank Professor Edwin Mims and the Houghton Mifflin Company, publishers of Professor Mims's biography, *Sidney Lanier;* Professor George Herbert Clarke and the J. W. Burke Company, Macon, publishers of Professor Clarke's pamphlet, *Some Reminiscences and Early Letters of Sidney Lanier;* Mrs. Laura Stedman Gould, co-author of *The Life and Letters of Edmund Clarence Stedman;* Dr. Fabian Franklin, author of *The Life of Daniel Coit Gilman;* and Miss Ada Sterling, compiler of *A Belle of the Fifties: Memoirs of Mrs. Clay, of Alabama.* The letters from Lanier to Northrup, which appeared in an article contributed to *Lippincott's Magazine* for March, 1905, are reprinted here by permission of the J. B. Lippincott Company, Publishers, and Mrs. M. H. Northrup, Sr. Mr. Stephen Vincent Benét has kindly consented to my use of four lines from his poem *John Brown's Body.*

For permission to publish pictures used as illustrations to this volume or for assistance in securing them (quite aside from other services rendered) special thanks are due to Mr. Henry W. Lanier, Mrs. H. D. Allen, Sr., Miss Katherine Carnes, Miss Sally M. Akin, Dr. John C. French, Mr. W. H. Stanard, Mrs. K. G. Berrie, Mr. John Voorhees, Mr. Sidney Lanier Eason, Miss Grace Turnbull, Dr. H. W. L. Dana, Miss Alice Northrup, and Mr. Kenneth Rede.

But I cannot conclude this preface without at least mentioning the names and acknowledging the kindness of certain other people who have been of great assistance to me in my search for material or in the preparation and publication of my manuscript: my father and mother, Mr. and Mrs. C. M. Starke, Miss Emily V. D. Miller, Dr. and Mrs. W. F. Ogburn, Dr. Howard W. Odum, Miss Parmelee Cheves, Mr. R. P. Eckert, Jr., Mrs. Theodore Gerould, Miss Ethelwynn Manning, Mr. John Russell Hayes, Mrs. W. P. Coleman, Miss Louise Hill, Mr. Paul M. Paine, Mrs. William McKay, Miss Lena E. Jackson, Mrs. Frederick J. Cooledge, Mrs. Alice T. Paine, and Mr. John J. Parish.

October 7, 1932   AUBREY HARRISON STARKE.

TABLE OF CONTENTS

LIST OF ILLUSTRATIONS

(With the exception of the title-pages, the illustrations face the pages indicated.)

PART I

Oh Georgia . . . Georgia . . . the careless yield!
The watermelons ripe in the field!
The mist in the bottoms that tastes of fever
And the yellow river rolling forever. . . !

Stephen Vincent Benét, *John Brown's Body.*

CHAPTER ONE

MACON, GEORGIA

§ 1

SIDNEY LANIER died September 7, 1881, under circumstances so pathetic that even the most outspoken of the literary journals promptly forgot the acrimonious criticisms of his work they had been publishing for six years and spoke of the loss to American literature occasioned by his death. For instance, the *Nation*, which in 1876 had called his Centennial cantata text "a communication from the spirit of Nat Lee, rendered through a Bedlamite medium," failing in all "the ordinary laws of sense and sound, melody and prosody," now spoke of him as "a poet and man of letters of much promise and considerable accomplishment" who was "to an appreciable degree of dignity and excellence" in advance of the magazine poets of the day whose fame was almost greater than his own; and in November, 1881, the *Nation* gave generous publicity to the fund being raised to provide for Lanier's family.

Almost immediately he was admitted to the select company of inheritors of unfulfilled renown. William Hayes Ward, the editor of the *Independent*, asserted without reservation that his place was with "the first princes of American song." The cultivated citizens of Baltimore and his colleagues at Johns Hopkins who had been his friends became so extravagant in their devotion to his memory that a visiting English critic, Edmund Gosse, complained that the only crumple in the rose-leaf of his visit to Baltimore was "the difficulty of preserving a correct attitude toward the local deity." And in Boston Thomas Wentworth Higginson turned from the task of grooming Emily Dickinson for posthumous fame to the preparation of a series of articles extravagant in praise of this "Sir Galahad of American letters."

But such unbounded posthumous acclaim was more tragic—and more unfortunate for Lanier's reputation—than the neglect and the critical mockery he had suffered during the brief years

of his career as a poet. His admirers forgot—and soon even dis-
passionate critics forgot—that Lanier had written humorous dialect verse as well as verbal symphonies on religious themes, that
in his poetry he had not only sung out in praise of his Lord the
Sun and the Crystal Christ, but had spoken encouraging words
to his trade-ridden fellow men, and that his début as first flutist
in the Peabody Symphony Orchestra had preceded by only a
year his first success as a poet, with the publication of "Corn,"
which is—whatever its beauty and its final fame as poetry—a
little treatise on agricultural economy, far-sighted and sound.

Naturally enough, then, the generations that followed have
taken limited interest in him, and as no revaluation of his work
was attempted the old labels have become fixed and we remain
in ignorance of the variety and the catholicity of Lanier's themes.
Sir Galahad has been allowed to ride upon his unearthly quest,
and from other poets have been sought the songs of nationality
and of brotherhood, the chants for the new day that Lanier had
sung when the day was only at dawn. To our generation Lanier
as a social revolutionist, who protested, as even Whitman did
not, against the modern economic system, is as unthinkable as
Joshua's miracle. Even academic scholars—who should know
better—have accepted the hastily formed opinion of Lanier's
contemporaries, and have assumed that the final estimate of his
work was made[1] and the complete biography written in the
timid, generalized sketches that the first quarter-century after his
death saw published. The legend of his life has grown without
interference from authority as the popular beatification of the
man has proceeded.

But all the while a different portrait has been in existence, even
showing through the over-painting of idolatry. In the poems—
which were his very life's breath, in the prose—which was bread-
and-meat labor to keep his body alive, but journalism of a high
order, and in the personal letters—which are his inviolate heart,
we have a portrait of a man we can all admire, a portrait of a very
human Sidney Lanier, who hated but forgave and loved, who
was reviled and ridiculed, who labored greatly, suffered greatly,
doubted and faltered, but who died victoriously in the certitude
that the assurance of achievement gives.

It is this Sidney Lanier that we need to know, and when we
have come to know him we shall rescue him from the slough of
half-neglect in which he has too long been allowed to remain,

and elevate him to the ranks not necessarily of the first princes of American song but of great critics of the American spirit and keen-eyed interpreters of America's achievement. Lanier, like Whitman, who rebelled against tradition—the traditions that bind not merely verse but thought, and belief, and action—and hated, as Lanier did, all shams and injustice and hypocrisy, Lanier like Walt Whitman we shall call national, proud that ours is the heritage of the forces that molded such a man.

But though he was a national poet whose poetry lacks all marks of narrow sectionalism, we must begin our understanding of Lanier by understanding the region out of which he came, and by seeing him as the product of that region, a section in which local feeling has always been intense. A Georgian, as Professor W. P. Trent[2] reminds us, is distinguished by moral earnestness and a love of virtue in action, by geniality like that of the Virginian, and by love of comfort, but above everything else by an "honest and hearty and not unfounded pride in Georgia, and a sort of masonic affiliation with every person, animal, institution, custom—in short, *thing*—that can be called Georgian." Lanier's poetry, in its chivalrous sentiment, its breadth and hospitality, and its patriotic fervor, is the sort of poetry one would expect a gifted, cultivated, American-minded Georgian to write; and Lanier himself, though he revolted against the proud conservatism of southern ways, was throughout his life unmistakably a son of that Georgia in which, at Macon, chief city of the central part of the state, he was born on Thursday, February 3, 1842.

§ 2

MACON was, however, even in 1842, not the dreamy, romantic southern town of legend but a town of commercial importance. Incorporated in 1823, it had soon become an important point on the stage-coach line between New York and New Orleans, and by 1826 it had a population of eight hundred people. The first steamboat had come up the Ocmulgee in 1827, and from that time Macon had been a cotton concentration point for middle Georgia; the bags—later bales—of cotton were carried by boat from Macon to the sea. In 1838 the first locomotive had run between Macon and Forsyth, twenty-five miles away. By the time of the Civil War Macon had grown to be one of the important industrial cities of the South, a far more important city than the younger Atlanta, and in the Confederacy it became not only a concentration point for food supplies and ammunition but also for treasury deposits. In 1850—when Lanier was eight years old—the population was made up of 3,323 whites and 2,352 blacks. Before the outbreak of the Civil War the population had been increased by more than two thousand people. Today the town, still thriving, still industrial, has a population of some 72,000.

The cultural and intellectual life of the town reflected in Lanier's day the creeds of several Protestant sects, of which the Baptists were the most numerous. In later years they were to bring Mercer University to Macon, but several years before Lanier's birth the Methodists of Macon had secured for their town Wesleyan Female College, said to be the first college ever chartered to make possible higher education for women. Less numerous and perhaps less influential than Baptists or Methodists, the Presbyterians were important as a sect and as individuals, and dominated the intellectual and social life of the town; if they were served by a clergy better educated than that of the Methodists and Baptists, it was nevertheless by a clergy equally conservative in theology. Baptists, Methodists, and Presbyterians were united on such questions as the morality of slavery, the need of conversion, and the efficacy of revival meetings; and though the Christianity they encouraged was largely emotional, they succeeded in creating a way of living and an attitude toward life that can only be described as Puritan. It was this Puritanism—with its distrust of change, its emphasis on virtue but on sin also, and its encouragement of graciousness and dignity in living—that colored the life of the town.

But to understand Lanier's Macon background we must understand more than the religious attitude of the Maconians. Though there was to be found in Macon then as now a kind of hospitality and a way of life that is generous and seems even lavish from certain points of view, society in Macon was not—as a common delusion concerning the ante-bellum South would lead us to believe—agrarian, and the lavish hospitality of the plantations was hardly imitated in this industrial, commercial town. The aureate accounts of life in Macon, recorded in later years by people who had visited there before the war, are, we must remember, memories—facts colored by the passing of time. There is in most towns at some time a leisure class of some sort, if only of college students home on vacation, and the "continual round of entertainments, musicales, and evening parties, . . . horseback rides and boat rides during the day and piano-playing, singing, fluting and impromptu cotillions and Virginia reels in the evening" mentioned in his autobiography by Joseph Le Conte, in later years professor of geology and natural history at the University of California,[3] and cited by other writers as evidence of the gayety of life in Macon, were admittedly the amusements of young collegians—and at that not very expensive amusements. The citizens of Macon were, as a group, probably sober-minded and industrious, given neither to prodigal living nor ostentatious display. And though certain wealthy citizens of Macon had handsome neo-classic houses set high on the hills of the town, their social superiority to the professional men and men of the middle class who lived on the slopes of the hills and in the lower city was chiefly one of altitude, their way of living less restrained only in that they felt less the want of ready money.

For various reasons middle Georgia was one of the most democratic sections of the old South. It was, in the 1840's and '50's, still new territory, still welcoming immigration, and the boast of heraldry meant little because there were few who could justly claim heraldic arms. Athens, the seat of the state university, with its ægis of Yale traditions, stood for education and culture, but Macon, in spite of the presence of Wesleyan Female College, stood for something more practical and more mundane. Social life in Macon was always simple, and no hard and fast social distinctions were made. As in the towns of the older Puritans, good breeding counted socially for more than money or ancestry.

§ 3

UNDOUBTEDLY little different from the majority of the citizens of Macon, in their backgrounds, their points of view, and their ambitions, were Lanier's parents, Robert Sampson and Mary Jane Anderson Lanier. The mother, who seems to have influenced Lanier the more, though the record of his father's influence on him is the fuller, was a native of Virginia, the daughter of one Hezekiah R. Anderson of Nottoway County, an interesting man of Scotch parentage of whom some slight account survives.[4] It is said that Anderson hated his own Biblical name to such an extent that he named four of his five sons after characters in the Waverley novels—Melvin, Waverley, Halbert, and Clifford. But the romanticism of his nature, which led him to choose such

names for his sons, was expressed even more definitely in the
faith he had in the integrity of his friends. His impoverished
financial condition at the time of his death in 1845 had been
brought about by the loss of his wealth in meeting the indebtedness of a friend whose notes he had indorsed. He left his children
little besides his good name and faith in the Biblical virtues
which he had not neglected to give them in refusing to give
them Biblical names.

Mary Jane Anderson Lanier inherited from her father a certain
romanticism of temperament—expressed chiefly in a love for
poetry and music—and a religious nature. She was a member of
the Presbyterian church—a church whose theology is essentially
that of the New England Puritan churches—and she was remembered as being "peculiarly though not narrowly" religious.[5] She
seems to have been an industrious woman who cared little for
social life but much for her church, and she brought up her
children in the practice of the strictest Christian creed. At her
solicitation her husband, Robert Sampson Lanier, left the
Methodist church, the family church of the Laniers, to become
identified with the Presbyterian. So it was in a home of undivided
religious affiliation that Sidney Lanier was brought up, and even
though in later life he fell away from the practice of his mother's
religion and evolved for himself a philosophy far from orthodox,
he remained as truly a Puritan as Emerson, and his poetry is
distinctly—often didactically—religious.

That the father, Robert Sampson Lanier, should have yielded
as willingly as he seems to have done to his wife's ideas of Christian
behavior and domestic deportment, would seem to show not only
that he was devoted to his wife but also that he was himself
something of a Puritan at heart, and a study of his background
and character and the descriptions of him as a "gentleman of
the old school" strongly suggest his innate Puritanism. He came
of a family of Virginia farmers of ancient Huguenot origin who
had prospered and made good marriages. His grandfather, Sampson Lanier, bred horses and fox hounds,[6] and lived, if not like
an English country gentleman, at least as a Virginia one. His
own father, Sterling Lanier, emigrated to Georgia from North
Carolina (whither Sampson Lanier had transported his family
and his hunting horses and his wealth), and in Georgia prospered
as a hotel proprietor. He was an ardent Methodist and a liberal
supporter of the institutions of his church. His daughters were

educated at the Wesleyan Female College of Macon, his son
R. S. Lanier—and probably other sons as well—at Methodist
Randolph-Macon, in Ashland, Virginia.

It was at Ashland perhaps, certainly in Virginia, that R. S.
Lanier met and became engaged to Mary Jane Anderson.[7] They
were married in 1840, soon after R. S. Lanier's graduation from
college, and R. S. Lanier went into the law office—in his home
town of Macon—of his wife's brother, William Henry Anderson,
who seems to have emigrated to Georgia some time before the
other members of his family. R. S. Lanier was twenty-one at
the time, his wife not yet eighteen.

Robert Sampson Lanier was never a very successful lawyer,
but he was fortunate in his legal partnerships. After the death
in 1850 of William Henry Anderson, a man of considerable ability
as a lawyer, R. S. Lanier took into the office (later into the firm)
his younger brother-in-law, Clifford Anderson, a man of excep-
tional talents, who was admitted to the bar in 1852 at the age
of nineteen, and who afterwards became judge, a member of the
Confederate Congress, and attorney-general of the state of
Georgia.[8] As a lawyer, R. S. Lanier is remembered chiefly for
his industriousness and his methodical handling of routine
matters.[9] His lack of real success in the practice of law was
probably due less to a lack of ability than to a lack of interest in
his profession. His sympathy for his son Sidney in that son's
desire for an intellectual life and the fondness for literature
revealed in his letters indicate that as "a man of considerable
literary acquirements and exquisite taste" (for thus his son wrote
of him[10]) Robert Sampson Lanier, like so many lawyers of the
old South, might have preferred a literary career to a legal one,
that had he been so fortunate as to have grown up under a
different order of society he might never have studied Blackstone.
His fate was that which his son but narrowly escaped, and he
satisfied his tastes for literature and romance with a library that
included the works of Shakspere, Addison, and Sir Walter
Scott— the conventional literary favorites of his generation—and
probably also poetry by first-rate contemporary poets.

Fortunately for the parents of Sidney Lanier, there was "money
in the family," available for them. Sterling Lanier, father of
R. S. Lanier, was reputed to be, and probably was, wealthy.
In 1844 he had sent his son Sidney, uncle of the poet, to Europe
to travel for his health, but undoubtedly too to make the grand

tour of the continent, a privilege that lingered in the minds of southerners of the period as the prerogative of a gentleman. He owned, besides the Lanier House of Macon, a hotel in Montgomery, Alabama, where his daughter Jane, Mrs. Watt, was one of the social leaders; and there was a third hotel belonging to Sterling Lanier, at Montvale Springs in Tennessee. He was undoubtedly perfectly able to contribute to the support of R. S. Lanier for some time after his marriage, and this we must assume he did. Since R. S. Lanier was not admitted to the bar until 1850 his work during the first ten years of his marriage must have been confined to routine matters, and his earned income could not have amounted to very much.

§ 4

DESCRIPTIONS of the house in which Sidney Lanier was born[11] confirm our impression of the somewhat straitened circumstances of the Robert Sampson Lanier family at the time of this first child's birth. It was a small cottage containing but four rooms and a central hall, with a small front porch that extended a few feet on each side of the door. If the kitchen was separate from the house, as in most southern homes of the period, there were probably two bedrooms, a dining-room, and a parlor in the cottage. But simple as it was, it was not unattractive: it was painted white, with green blinds, and the yard was full of trees and flowers.[12] Nor would it—in the place and the period—have been considered humble, for it was a typical home of the poor but well-born white people of the ante-bellum South; and undistinguished by any architectural design or refinements though it was, it had a southern spaciousness of proportion, a comfortableness that high ceilings give. The location on Second Street, near the business district, was not very desirable, however, and Robert Sampson Lanier and his wife must have dreamed, in spite of their Puritan idealism, of the time when they could move up the hill into a more attractive residential district.

The children born to Robert Sampson and Mary Jane Anderson Lanier were three: the first born, christened Sidney Clopton in honor of R. S. Lanier's brother and Judge David Clopton, a distant relative and friend of the family and classmate of R. S. Lanier at Randolph-Macon College; a second son, named Clifford Anderson for the maternal uncle, and a daughter, Gertrude. The second son, born the twenty-fourth of April, 1844, was, it

is true, born not at Macon but at Griffin, Georgia, where—
though exactly why is not known—the R. S. Laniers lived for
a few years, until 1846;[13] but Gertrude was born in Macon, in
1848, and probably in the house on High Street pointed out
today as the Lanier home, a house differing little from the cottage
on Second Street, but perhaps somewhat more substantially built
and certainly better located.[14] It is this house on High Street
that was the scene of the happy home life that has often been
described. Here, as Clifford Lanier has testified, Mrs. Lanier's
Scotch thrift enabled the family to live "comfortably, if narrowly."[15]

There seems to have been in the Lanier family what Mrs.
Sidney Lanier, studying the history of her husband's forebears,
called "a family talent for deep and tender love and home happiness."[16] Illustrative of this inheritance is the unusual friendship
that existed among the three children. Throughout their lives
Sidney and Clifford Lanier bore each other a love that resembled,
as we shall see, the extravagant, romantic friendships of medieval
literature, and no less romantic was the knightly devotion that
the brothers gave their sister. Clifford Lanier, writing after his
brother's death, recalled how as a child he stood always in awe
of his but two years older brother.[17] Sidney Lanier, writing to
Clifford, adopted always the tone of a loving father, calling his
brother his "darling boy"; and there has been printed a reference
made by Sidney Lanier in his maturity to his "vestal sister, who
had, more perfectly than any star or any dream," represented to
him "the simple majesty and the serene purity of the Winged Folk
up Yonder."[18] This mutual love was probably also inspired and
encouraged by the parents, and with the parents genuinely and
deeply devoted to each other and their children, and with such
an attitude as these quotations reveal existing among the children,
the life of the home must have been not merely gracious, affectionate, harmonious, and close; it was probably characterized by an
excessive display of emotion and expression of sentiment.

It is probably as a result of these earliest influences that Lanier
revealed in the poetry and lectures as well as in the personal
letters of his maturity a sentimentality that cannot be laughed
away with most of the sentimentality of the period, but that
confuses us and even embarrasses us, as if we had overheard the
most intimate of confessions. Beautiful and charming as the life
in the home must have been, it is doubtful if the influence was,

in the strictest sense of the word, wholesome. The wholehearted-ness of Lanier's devotion to his relatives, to his wife, to his children, to his friends, to his ideal of the poet's function, is his finest and most admirable characteristic, but it sometimes seems insincere because of the peculiar, overwrought, strained, and exaggerated expression of it. One feels that, for the sake of his poetry at least, young Lanier should have been taught reticence in the expression of emotion, if only verbal reticence in the description of emotions he so genuinely felt.

§ 5

OF LANIER's education outside the home we know little. We may be sure that as a Presbyterian child he was sent to Sunday school, and there is indeed a record, in the Macon *Telegraph*, May 2, 1854, of a Sunday school picnic held on April 29 by the Sunday schools of the various Protestant denominations, at which Master Lanier, age twelve, delivered an address as representa-tive of the Presbyterian Sunday school. We may be sure too that R. S. Lanier and his wife made possible for all their children what secular education was obtainable in the town, though this we know to have been meager enough.

In the days of Lanier's youth public schools were almost un-heard of in the South, but in Macon there were not even parochial schools for elementary secular education and no well organized elementary schools of any sort. In 1831, according to *Niles'* *Register* of August 27, that year, when the population consisted of nearly three thousand inhabitants, there was in Macon not one schoolmaster. Later, schoolmasters did come to Macon, and we are told that Lanier was schooled "in small private one-roomed establishments,"[19] perhaps longest in the Bibb County Academy presided over by George H. Hancock and P. A. Strobel. This "Academy" was conducted in the remodeled stable of Mr. Strobel on First Street, a fairly adequate building, pleasantly and ap-propriately located in a grove of oak and hickory trees.

Lanier is said to have been an accurate and persevering pupil, but fond of frolic and of informal sports, perhaps chiefly of sports that he could pursue alone. The trees in the 'Cademy yard were a source of great interest to him: it was fun to climb them, and in their branches lived flying squirrels, "dainty half-angel, half-animal" creatures that fascinated him.[20] The description of the squirrels, written years later, is his brother's, but even in his childhood Sidney Lanier probably thought of them thus himself, for already his poetic imagination and his talent for writing poetry were developing. It was in the 'Cademy that he wrote his first poems, much to the embarrassment of his desk-mate, Charles Wiley, and to the amusement of other boys who thought he could spend his time better at games. The poems have not been preserved, and if they had we should probably not find them very interesting, but the fact that he wrote them emphasizes the most significant trait in his character, his difference from other boys. The impression of this difference is the strongest impression of him that lingers to this day in Macon.

The difference, so those who knew Lanier insist, was chiefly that he was, to a very unusual extent, what one of his schoolmates called him years later, "a knightly and clean-tongued boy."[21] He himself tells us that as a child he was thought to be "a model for the Sunday-school children of all times."[22] He is said to have been singularly attractive, "not so much in physical appearance as in an indescribable air of gentlemanhood."[23] "Not good looking in the least" emphatically asserts one who knew him, whenever she speaks of him, but she adds quickly that he had charm even as a boy, and inspired love and admiration.

§ 6

AN IMAGINATIVE boy, Lanier liked imaginative games such as that of "cotton merchant," which he probably invented. He and Charles Wiley would play they were cotton dealers and take turns in being buyer and seller. The warehouses were tunneled out of the red clay sides of a deep gully that ran alongside of the main highway leading to the business section of the town. Most of the cotton that entered Macon passed over this road, and the boys would jump out of the ditch and grab handfuls of fresh cotton off the wagons and store it in their "warehouses." Hickory nuts served as money, though sometimes—when raids of another sort were successful—they used pins. The cotton was weighed carefully on the simplest of scales, in the palms of the boys' hands. The picture of this muddy, enthusiastic boy, sliding in and out of a red clay gully and pirating cotton, is in pleasant contrast to the picture of the Sunday school orator and the boy at the 'Cademy desk writing poetry. It is, of all the records of his school days, the most human, boyish picture that his school friends have left us.

His keenest delight was, like Wordsworth's, in being out of doors. In the woods on the other side of the Ocmulgee from Macon nuts and haw-apples were to be gathered in the fall; and sometimes on their excursions thither the boys were so lucky as to find Indian arrow heads. At tin.es they fished, with crude fishing poles. Lanier, we are told, was particularly fond of fishing, and we may be sure that as he sat quietly on the river bank his ears were alert to catch the sounds of the birds and of all the creatures of woods and water, which even as a very young child he had tried to imitate on his flute. Indeed, his childhood—in the legend that has grown up about it—suggests the childhood of Pan himself; and, Pan-like, he is said to have improvised a flute from a river reed when he was only seven years old, though it was certainly not on this crude instrument that "he made his first effort at music," as the legend has it,[24] for it was in his own home that Lanier learned to play.

Unlike New England Puritanism, southern Calvinism did not, as a rule, banish music from religious worship, nor the enjoyment of it from the Christian's pleasures. Mrs. Lanier played the piano well and taught her children in their earliest childhood to sing hymns and simple songs, so that from the first the children were not only accustomed to music, with its molding influence, but were disciplined in the performance of it. When but a few years old Sidney Lanier was given at Christmas time "a small yellow one-keyed flageolet-like flute" made in Germany on which he practised "with the passion of a virtuoso."[25] When, around the age of five, he displayed an aptitude for musical time by beating in accompaniment to the piano playing of his mother, his own education in music was begun with his mother as his teacher.[26] Later he is said to have learned to play the guitar, violin, and organ—the violin so well indeed that his father, fearing the strange effect violin playing seems always to have had on his son, discouraged it and encouraged him to take up the flute instead. It was as a professional performer on the flute that Lanier, later in life, earned the living that poetry alone would have denied him.

Neither in his youth nor later did his father give Lanier much sympathy in his writing of poetry, but he did sympathize with his son's musical ambitions and took much interest in his musical talents, as did also other people of Macon. There seems to have been in ante-bellum Georgia a deep and general appreciation of

The Lanier home on High Street, Macon, where Lanier spent his early years.

music, whatever the lack of interest in the other arts. In his study of Augustus Baldwin Longstreet, the author of *Georgia Sketches*, Professor J. D. Wade asserts that "In Georgia, a remarkably large number of people could play upon flutes and various stringed instruments,"[27] and he emphasizes the fact that Longstreet, a typical Georgian and a thoroughly practical man, had a sincere love for his flute and for flute music: he took great delight in playing for the students of the college of which he was president. Lanier's father encouraged every refining tendency, and he certainly encouraged flute playing, but just as, in encouraging Lanier to love poetry, he discouraged the writing of it, so also he warned his son constantly against making a profession of music. In ante-bellum Georgia it was part of the education of a gentleman to be able to perform on a musical instrument, but the ability, like the ability to produce what passed for literature, was meant to be regarded as only incidental.

Lanier "played directly and naturally from the first as one hardly conscious of effort or obstacle,"[28] but C. E. Campbell and C. K. Emmell, two music-loving young men of Macon somewhat older than Lanier, took him in hand as a boy and gave him lessons. Campbell has told of being with him when he bought his first "real" flute, "a humble but reasonably effective instrument," which cost $1.25.[28] On this flute Lanier practised diligently and became so proficient that he was made Corypheus of a children's amateur minstrel band of Negro mimics and musicians. He is said, too, like Schumann, to have organized an orchestra among his friends and playmates.

But a certain incident of his childhood came near ruining for all time Sidney Lanier's hopes of becoming a musician. "A heavy window-sash slipped from its button-fastening and fell . . . fortunately taking off a half-inch only of a middle finger. I remember"—it is his brother Clifford who records this incident—"his endurance, his fortitude while we ran screaming for help, and that he, unable to keep back the tears, yet uttered no cries. The finger was quietly held in cold water till a surgeon could be brought to dress it."[29]

While such fortitude, like much of his love of the out-of-doors, of music, and of poetry, was an element in his character, it may very well have been encouraged by his boyhood reading. In his father's library Lanier read the novels of Scott and, as he later recalled with particular pleasure, of Bulwer, the chronicles of

Froissart, and the adventures of Gil Blas. On such literature the ideals of southern chivalry were founded, and on such literature Lanier, in a more personal way, seems to have founded his own ideals, retreating from gay company to spend hours alone with books. Later, at the very end of his life, when he came to prepare for other boys editions of some of these authors whom he had read as a boy, he emphasized repeatedly the lessons in knightly conduct that they teach.

It is Lanier's own knightly conduct, his revival of medieval chivalry in an intimate and individual way, that explains best his difference from other boys. Toward his brother and sister and toward older people especially he constantly exhibited this chivalry, this affectionate gentleness. On the only occasion when he and his brother fought, he merely held Clifford in his grasp until the anger which had prompted the attack had passed. Here, of course, he had the advantage of physical strength to support him; but his brother also describes a different sort of fight in which his conduct was equally manly. It was a school-boy fight in which his opponent drew a "barlow" knife on him. Lanier "rushed straight, blindly in the face of the bloody menace, clasping his antagonist to continue the struggle despite such unexpected odds . . . instinctively, confusedly, the onlookers closed in and, disarming the infuriated [attacker], separated the schoolboy 'Sullivans' before the knife could descend in Sidney's breast."[30]

So in his childhood there was fighting as well as flute-playing and poetry-writing, and day-dreaming in the woods or on the banks of the Ocmulgee, and as the love of the flute and of poetry and of the out-of-doors increased, and never left him, so a good fight of whatever sort never failed to interest Lanier. In *Tiger-Lilies* and in other of his prose writings there are references to well known prize-fighters of the day, to Heenan and Mike McCoole; and in the last year of his life, in describing the unequal fight between himself and the disease that was killing him, he wrote courageously in prize-fighting language "I think I will manage to take the belt, yet."[31]

§ 7

IT WAS as a lover of battles and of manly military conduct such as Froissart described so vividly that Lanier, when he was some-what past fourteen, organized a military company, armed his men with bows and arrows, and drilled them according to ancient practice. There were about fifty boys in the company, between the ages of fourteen and sixteen. For uniforms they wore white trousers and a blue cambric blouse or jacket trimmed in white, and a sort of military cap adorned (according to the Macon tradition) with a white plume. The bows were of hickory, polished. On the march they "hung over the left shoulder, while the quiver of arrows hung diagonally across the back of the youthful archer."[32] The manœuvers were according to Hardee's *Rifle and Light Infantry Tactics*, published only the year before, the manual that Lanier was soon to study again as a Confederate soldier.

On parade days of the militia—usually the patriotic holidays— the boy archers were allowed to drill in battalion formation with the Macon Volunteers and the Floyd Rifles, companies which had seen service in the Mexican War and in Indian wars, and which were to see service in the war between the states as part of the Second Georgia Battalion with Captain Lanier of the Macon Archers become a private in the Macon Volunteers. But in those early days there was little thought of actual war in Lanier's mind. When black Charlie Bayer, big, fat, and perspiring, blew the fife like a cyclone, and John Tyner and Andrew Taylor—other loved Negroes—beat time on the kettle- drums, while the crowds cheered and the Macon Archers proudly led the march of soldiers, Lanier probably thought of himself less as a soldier of the present than as one of the brave English bowmen of Crécy or as some knightly hero of older legend, marching not through the streets of Macon but through the pages of ancient chronicles.

And it was as a knight of old that Lanier found himself con- stantly in love. "He was always very fond of the girls and carried on a lot of foolishness to amuse them. He loved to gather a crowd of boys and serenade the girls. That was a very popular custom. . . . And if a boy was not talented in music, he would often get a musical friend to serenade his sweetheart for him. Sidney was very much in demand with his flute—and he loved it too";[32] and sometimes he fell in love with the lady whom he had been only hired—as it were—to serenade. One who knew him said, in a romantically mixed metaphor, that he had "as varying symbols of a higher than human romance, 'a sweetheart in every port.' "[33] At fifteen, during his first term at college, he wrote to

2

his aunt, Mrs. Annie Anderson, protesting against the cruelty of a "beautiful Macon damsel" who had confessed that for him she had only a "sort of sisterly regard!": "The shock has almost been too much for me. I am in an agony of doubts and perplexities and do not know what to do, or which way to turn. Write me very soon and tell me whether I must continue hopelessly in love, or must endeavor to eradicate love from my heart, for, as to loving another, I do not believe that is possible."[32]

Writing of Lanier a few years after his death, Paul Hamilton Hayne cited Lanier's early reading as the cause of a certain quaintness, amounting almost to an affectation of archaism, in his literary style, a quaintness apparent even in his most casually written letters. "He had steeped his imagination from boyhood in the writings of the earlier English annalists and poets,—Geoffrey of Monmouth, Sir Thomas Mallory, Gower, Chaucer, and the whole bead-roll of such ancient English worthies. . . . [He quoted naturally] from 'Piers Ploughman,' and scores of the half-obsolete ballads of the English and Scottish borders."[34] But it was not only the books in his father's library that were responsible for the romantic conduct of his daily life. There was the heritage from his grandfather Hezekiah; and there was music which his father had taught him to love but the influence of which he had taught him to fear; and there were the Georgia woodlands, in which, as much as in the house on High Street, Lanier was at home. "In truth," he was to write twenty years later, "a certain sense of exile—which I feel would seem maudlin to most people and which nevertheless grows stronger with me every day—makes me prize any words from the dear old Macon hills. It seems a particularly hard cross-purpose that I—who love them surely better than any other of their children—must remain away from them in order to sing about them."[35]

And so, to the end of his life, he remained, in the religiosity of his disposition, in the exuberance of his song, in his passionate devotion to his native soil, in the romanticism of his most commonplace actions, in the loyalty of his devotion to an order which had passed but which he loved none the less for its passing, a son of the ante-bellum Macon in which he lived until at the age of fifteen he left for college. If we are to understand his poetry or his prose we must remember him in this environment. Later we shall find him, in the bitterness of his struggle to turn poetry into bread, hating the Macon in which he then lived and fleeing from it; but the Macon in which he found little friendship, or sympathy, or encouragement, was not the ante-bellum Macon of his youth, which survived for him indeed only in its influence upon him—and as a memory.

CHAPTER TWO

NOCTES AMBROSIANÆ

§ 1

IN 1854 an enforced change had taken place in Lanier's schooling. Mr. George Hancock, part owner and principal of the Bibb County Academy, had accepted an appointment as professor at the Wesleyan Female College, and the Academy had been closed. Macon had been left without an elementary school, and for three years Lanier and his brother, with other former Academy pupils, had studied with local teachers in private classes.[1] One who knew them at the school conducted by the Reverend Mr. Danforth has described the Lanier boys as "immaculate . . . always . . . in their dress and appearance betokening the gentlemen, and very studious, standing high in their classes. Of quiet and dignified manner, they did not indulge in the rougher sports of the boys, but they were not too proud to participate in their recreations. Courage was a predominant trait in their characters, while gentleness dominated their dispositions."[2]

§ 2

IN 1856 Lanier's parents decided that he should be sent to college. The college Mrs. Lanier chose was not the alma mater of her husband, Methodist Randolph-Macon in Virginia, but a staunch Presbyterian school not very far away. This was Oglethorpe University at Midway, two miles from Milledgeville, then the capital of Georgia. Macon friends, already students at Oglethorpe, accompanied him on the journey to Milledgeville, but Lanier probably never felt more lonely or unhappy in his life than on Monday, January 6, 1857, when he matriculated at Oglethorpe, separated for the first time from his family. The Georgia landscape is bleak and desolate in January, and the few scattered college buildings must have seemed as uncheering as the rest of the world he looked out upon the next morning as he made his way to his first classes. But the excitement of new studies, of a new life, probably dispelled his sadness quickly. Lanier wrote his father that night: "We were admitted into our classes, I into 'Soph,' Will[3] into Junior. I have just done studying tonight my first lesson, to-wit, forty-five lines of Horace, which I 'did' in about fifteen minutes."[4]

Such colleges as Oglethorpe (and Emory of the Methodists and Mercer of the Baptists) existed in Georgia chiefly because parents demanded for their children orthodox religious education and the cultivation of a strong, unassailable religious faith at institutions not too far from home. The more aristocratic state university was non-sectarian, and, for the son of Mrs. Robert Sampson Lanier, therefore out of the question. The students at Oglethorpe—a comparatively new college founded in 1835—were almost without exception of Presbyterian families; and, since the college belonged to the synods of South Carolina and Georgia, many of the faculty were ordained Presbyterian ministers.

Midway, where the college was located, was a small community situated on a plateau that overlooks Milledgeville. Both towns were very different from Macon. Milledgeville was known for its immorality and corruption, but Midway was, after all, two miles away, and its atmosphere was considered moral and safe. Furthermore it was forbidden by law for anyone to "establish, keep, or maintain any store or shop of any description for vending any species of merchandise, groceries or confectioneries within a mile and a half of the University." The boys at Oglethorpe were supposedly protected against contaminating influences of any sort.

A description of the college buildings, written by the president, accompanied a rather elaborate engraving in *Georgia Illustrated*, published by William C. Richards of Penfield, Georgia, in 1842.[5] The main building was "a brick structure, painted white, two stories high, beside a basement . . . constructed after the Grecian-Doric order, without and within." In it was the chapel, and in the wings were the offices and the classrooms. On either side of the campus was a row of six wooden dormitories one story high. Later there was erected Thalian Hall, a brick building three stories high, and the only building of the group that remains. In one of the rooms of Thalian Hall Lanier lived for at least part of his college course.[6] Slightly to the north of the college was the Academy, a preparatory school for younger boys, also owned by the synods and connected with the college.

In 1842, the year Lanier was born, and the fourth year in which the college functioned, there were seventy-five students in the Academy, and fifty in the college. Eighteen years later, when Lanier was graduated, the enrollment of the college (or "University") had probably not more than doubled, for Lanier's graduating class numbered only twenty-one.

The president of Oglethorpe was, and for fifteen years had been, the Reverend Samuel K. Talmage, D.D., an uncle of the more famous Dr. DeWitt Talmage. He was a native of New Jersey, and he had been educated at Presbyterian Princeton, where he had also spent three years as tutor, but his long, active life in the South had won his devotion to that section, and Georgia, in turn, acknowledged his wisdom and eloquence.

The names of only a few of the members of the faculty in 1857 have been preserved, but we know that Lanier studied mathematics with Professor Charles W. Lane, "the sunniest, sweetest Calvinist that ever nestled close to the heart of Arminians and all else who loved the Master's image when they saw it. His cottage at Midway was a Bethel; it was God's house and heaven's gate."[7] Undoubtedly the other members of the faculty were also very religious, though not necessarily, of course, of such sweet character.

The pervasive atmosphere of conservative piety at Oglethorpe was, as President Snyder remarks, "one which no impressionable young man could breathe for three years and afterwards depart far from its fundamental religious ideals."[8] What a thorough young Calvinist Lanier was at the time is revealed in a letter to his father in which he confessed that he had violated one of his father's commands by borrowing money from a college friend. "My father," he wrote, "I have sinned. With what intensity of thought, with what deep and earnest reflections have I contemplated this lately! My heart throbs with the intensity of its anguish. . . . If by hard study and good conduct I can atone I shall not be found wanting. . . . Not a night passes but what the supplication, God bless by parents, ascends to the mercy seat."[9] Even Lanier's enthusiasm for study partook of the nature of religious zeal. At the beginning of his second year at Oglethorpe he wrote: "I feel quite enthusiastic on the subject of studying. . . . The very name of Junior has something of study-inspiring and energy-exciting to me."[9]

§ 3

A SCHOOLMATE, J. O. Varnedoe, who met Lanier about this time (in January, 1858) has left an excellent description of him and of his character, confirmed photographically by the familiar ambrotype of Lanier taken during the previous year.[10] Varnedoe had been invited by Lanier's roommate Le Conte (a younger cousin of Joseph Le Conte and a brother of Ophelia Le Conte, one of Lanier's boyhood sweethearts), to hear some music. Lanier played the flute of course, Le Conte the guitar. "I was at once impressed with Lanier's personality," Varnedoe recalled. "Apart from the culture and moral refinement, which his face and manner indicated, there was a quiet dignity strangely unusual in one of his years. . . . [He was not austere, however.] On the contrary, he was always polite and affable, though never seeking promiscuous companionship nor courting popularity. Fair hair, parted on one side, was always brushed back behind his ears. His clothes were of good quality, always neat but never ostentatious. He carried himself easily and naturally, with just a suggestion of stoop in his shoulders. His gait was usually brisk. He showed no taste for athletics,—was seldom seen at the gymnasium. Music and books were his dearest companions. . . . [He was] not conspicuous as a debater, and yet what he attempted was always good and creditable. Among ladies his manner was easy and faultless; but he was not what the students called a lady's man." (Varnedoe, of course, did not suspect the passions that gnawed Lanier's heart!)

In a sort of diary note-book that he had begun to keep Lanier wrote: "Liberty, patriotism, and civilization are on their knees before the men of the South, and with clasped hands and straining eyes are begging them to become Christians."[11] It is not surprising to find Lanier uniting himself with the Presbyterian church during his junior year. He was never a very active member but, asserts Varnedoe, "he was carefully observant of the vows he had assumed, and his conduct was above reproach. Lanier never participated in any of the pranks indulged in by some students; nor was he addicted to any of their vices." At college, as he had been at Macon, Lanier was distinguished by a difference; and he seems to have taken himself very seriously.

He was not, however, without a sense of humor, though it

was of an amazingly childlike and innocent sort. "While uniformly dignified he would exhibit at times a jauntiness in singular contrast with his habit," Varnedoe continues. "With companions of his choice he was jolly and bright, enjoying a joke thoroughly and participating in friendly repartee." He loved puns with an Elizabethan ardor, and most of the humor of the prose works which he published later consists of them. To a time about ten years later belongs the reminiscence of Mrs. W. A. Hopson (née Connor), the wife of his college friend, Will Hopson. "One day when Mary Lou Lamar, Mary Day, my sister and I were over at Gussie Lamar's house . . . Sidney came over with a new joke he wanted to spring on us girls. It was the joke of how the tomato got its name. Sidney said that when the tomato was new as a food someone gave one to a Jap to eat to see if he liked it. When the Jap had finished eating, someone asked him how he enjoyed it and he replied with great relish, 'To ma toes.' And from that the tomato got its name."[12] Lanier was then about twenty-five, but humor of this sort was not, in the fifties and sixties, considered childish: the southern journals and newspapers of the day are especially full of examples of it. A critic writing on Lanier in 1877 cited as an example of the "sallies of wit" in Lanier's book on Florida the sentence "Woman, though younger than man, commenced to handle fruit sooner."[13] Such humor seems of course trite and dull at the present day, but the display of it at Oglethorpe gave Lanier a reputation for cleverness.

Though Lanier never bore a nickname other than that of the abbreviation Sid, there was undoubtedly about him something of the quality that won for young Milton at the same age the epithet "the Lady of Christ's"; and, knowing the ways of college boys, one wonders if it were not just this quality that incited the attack in the early schoolboy fight described by his brother and in the college fight recorded by Varnedoe. He had been misunderstood and denounced as a liar—and Lanier struck immediately. The student who had provoked the attack pulled his knife and stabbed Lanier in the left side. A surgeon had to be called; the wound when examined was found to be an inch deep. But it healed quickly, and Lanier was able to attend classes again in two weeks.[14] Though different from other boys he was thoroughly manly and no coward; in nothing that he ever did did Lanier lack personal bravery.

Sidney Lanier in 1857. From an old ambrotype in the possession of the family.

His studies at Oglethorpe he pursued with zeal and success. He read the usual Greek and Latin classics; he led his class in mathematics, taking in that subject the interest so often characteristic of the musician; he became interested in philosophy and science. In one letter to his father he requested copies of Olmsted's *Philosophy*, Blair's *Rhetoric*, Cicero's *De Oratore*, and an analytical geometry, mentioning the fact that he already had some Greek tragedies which he was to study. He joined a secret literary society, the Thalian, of which he wrote to his father: "I have derived more benefit from that, than from any one of my collegiate studies. We meet in a nice room, read compositions, declaim, and debate upon interesting subjects."[15]

T. F. Newell, the roommate of Lanier's junior year, has also left a description of Lanier at this period: "I can recall my association with him with sweetest pleasure, especially those Attic nights, for they are among the dearest and tenderest recollections of my life, when with a few chosen companions we would read from some treasured volume, it may have been Tennyson or Carlyle or Christopher North's 'Noctes Ambrosianæ,' or we would make the hours vocal with music and song. . . . On such occasions I have seen him walk up and down the room and with his flute extemporize the sweetest music ever vouchsafed to mortal ear. At such times it would seem as if his soul were in a trance, and could only find existence, expression, in the ecstasy of tone, that would catch our souls with his into the very seventh heaven of harmony. Or in merry mood, I have seen him take a banjo, for he could play on any instrument, and as with deft fingers he would strike some strange new note or chord, you would see his eyes brighten, and he would begin to smile and laugh as if his very soul were tickled, while his hearers would catch the inspiration, and an old-fashioned 'walk-round' and 'negro breakdown,' in which all would participate, would be the inevitable result. At other times, with our musical instruments, we would sally forth into the night. . . . And then on Saturdays we would walk through the groves and the 'gospeling glooms' of the woods, where every sound was a joy and inspiration. I have never seen one who enjoyed nature more than he. And his love for her was so intense that I have sometimes imagined he could hear the murmur, the music, that springs from the growing of grass."[16]

§ 4

NEWELL was not the only one of Lanier's college companions who spoke of the trance-like state in which Lanier played his flute and in which he sometimes seemed to hear music when he was not playing at all. Still another companion has written: "I shall never forget those moonlight nights at old Oglethorpe, when, after study hours, we would crash up the stairway and get out on the cupola, making the night merry with music, song, and laughter. Sid would play upon his flute like one inspired, while the rest of us would listen in solemn silence."[17] And Ward, on the evidence of unpublished letters of Lanier, asserted: "It was the violin voice that, above all others, commanded his soul. He has related that during his college days it would sometimes so exalt him in rapture, that presently he would sink from his solitary music-worship into a deep trance, then to awaken, alone, on the floor of his room, sorely shaken in nerve."[18]

To many, of course, these trance-like states seemed only periods of day-dreaming, indulged in too often by an overly poetical young man. A Mrs. Mattie Montgomery, of Montgomery, Alabama, whom Lanier first met during a summer vacation, has described how he would ride out to the plantation of which she was mistress, tie his horse, and wander off alone. "Often when I saw his horse tied in the grounds below the house, I went out in search of him. In some arbor I was sure to find him, or under the branches of some spreading shade trees, prone upon his back, gazing up through the leaves, lost in reverie.

" 'Well, son, what is it?' I would ask.

" 'O little mother!' he would exclaim, 'isn't it superb? Listen to their music'; at which I would chide him for his vain dreaming and laughing, would say that I should not be surprised at any time to see him vanish from my sight, and be lost in the depths of the sky into which his fancy so often soared."[19]

In the ante-bellum South such moods had their recognized place, but their place was in the romantic atmosphere of flower-scented moonlight, and Lanier indulged in these reveries at all hours of the day. But on such a night as Lorenzo searched for words to describe, with the parlor windows thrown open to admit the breeze that cooled the warm summer air, and with only the moon to furnish light by which to read the notes of music, even the "little mother," playing the accompaniment for his flute, would weep because of the tension that came of the "intensity of yearning, of hope and of aspiration, [which] he breathed from beneath his marvelous fingers."

It was music that possessed him; his poetic talents were not yet developed. Varnedoe writes: "Of his devotion to music, his fondness for letters, and his diligence along all lines of research, together with his high character and attractive personality, he had furnished ample evidence"; but as yet he had given no evidence "of the poetic fires that must have been smouldering in his soul. . . . Music, rather than intellectual affinity, was the potent influence that determined the choice of his comrades," with whom he lived in "an atmosphere of ardent and loyal friendship."

§ 5

IN LITERATURE his delight was, as one would suspect, in the quaint and curious, the romantic and the verbally musical, the sentimental and the idealistic. His taste was still unformed, and highly eclectic. The list of his reading furnished by his schoolmates and by the evidence of *Tiger-Lilies* is a varied one: Burton's *Anatomy of Melancholy;* Jeremy Taylor; Keats's "Endymion"; the poetry of Chatterton, Shelley, Coleridge, and James Hogg, the Ettrick Shepherd (particularly the poem "How Kilmeny Came Hame"); Tennyson's "Locksley Hall," "In Memoriam," and "Maud"; Carlyle's *Sartor Resartus, Heroes and Hero-Worship, Past and Present,* and his essays, particularly those on Burns, Jean Paul Richter, and Novalis. Names not found on this list but learned from other sources are those of Byron and Wordsworth;[20] another is that of Ruskin, a favorite author of Lanier's, often quoted, a writer with whom Lanier had much in common. In *Thorn-Fruit* Clifford Lanier quotes from Ruskin a maxim that Sidney Lanier may well have taken as the motto for his life: "Man's use and function is to be the witness of the glory of God, and to advance that glory by his reasonable obedience and resultant happiness." There can be no doubt, however, that Lanier read Ruskin quite early, as he did Wordsworth and Byron.

No adequate study of Lanier's early reading and of the influence of his reading on his thought has yet been made. In the present volume the influence of other poets on his work will be mentioned briefly from time to time. Here it may not be amiss to point out, though even more briefly, sources for some of Lanier's ideas. Many of these sources are to be found by tracing quotations in *Tiger-Lilies*, his early novel—a sort of literary note-book of college and war years, and in *Thorn-Fruit*, the companion novel of his brother. References, for instance, to *Festus*, the curious, romantic theological poem of Philip James Bailey, point to such a passage as:

> We live in deeds, not years; in thoughts, not breaths;
> In feeling, not in figures on a dial.
> We should count time by heart-throbs. He most lives
> Who thinks most—feels the noblest—acts the best.
> Life's but a means unto an end—that end,
> Beginning, mean and end to all things—God,

a passage Lanier may well have starred and underscored, and recollected in many a poem. From Mrs. Browning, too, he seems to have derived a great deal. In *Aurora Leigh*, for instance, there is much talk of love, and God, and the force of poetry in life, and the high nobility of art, and one passage in particular that Lanier must have taken to heart:

> But poets should
> Exert a double vision; should have eyes
> To see near things as comprehensively
> As if afar they took their point of sight
> And distant things as intimately deep
> As if they touched them. Let us strive for this.
> I do distrust the poet who discerns
> No character or glory in his times,
> And trundels back the soul five hundred years
> Past moat and drawbridge, into a castle-court,
> To sing—oh not of lizard or of toad
> Alive i' the ditch there,—'twere excusable.
> But of some black chief, half knight, half sheep-lifter,
> Some beauteous dame, half chattel and half queen,
> As dead as must be, for the greater part,
> The poems made on their chivalric bones.
> And that's no wonder: death inherits death.[21]

The poem which Lanier himself was, as we shall see, planning during his college days, was a story of medieval life, but the men and women were to be depicted as real characters, and the theme was to be a dateless one—the power of love.

His favorite poet, no matter how frequent the quotations from Shakspere and Keats, was surely Tennyson, Tennyson who wrote of the chivalric ages as he himself intended to, but wrote still of the present day, reconciling science and religion, glorifying the power of love, paying high tributes to music, reiterating his faith in the existence of God. His favorite essayist was surely Carlyle. The influence of Carlyle is apparent in Lanier's work in many ways: there is the influence of his vocabulary, actual phrases from Carlyle's works turning up long afterwards in Lanier's;[22] there is the influence of separate ideas—the identity of music and poetry, the maternal and divine aspects of nature, the dignity of labor; and there is the influence of his general thought—his stern creed of anti-industrialism and his positive transcendental faith, his idea of the necessity of heroes and of hero-worship to society, most of all his doctrine of the Everlasting No and the Everlasting Yea—"Love not Pleasure, love God."

But Carlyle's greatest service to Lanier was in revealing to him the world of the German romantic writers,[23] a territory that was ever afterwards Lanier's spiritual home.[24] How well Lanier read German and how widely he read in the works of the writers introduced to him by Carlyle—in Richter and Novalis especially— we do not know. But in Carlyle's writings are to be found the characteristic bits from these authors quoted by Lanier time and again for the rest of his life. "Ere long, he no more saw anything alone," wrote Novalis of his pupil; nor did Lanier, who loved the phrase,[25] see anything alone, but as a symbol or the complement of something else. With Lanier as with Novalis "the old hostility to matter" disappeared, and Nature became "the voice with which Deity proclaims himself to man."[26] The idea of the changing moods of nature from "geologic time to the modern period," expressed in the Shakspere lectures,[27] comes undoubtedly from early reading of Novalis or of Carlyle's essay on him; and if Lanier's idea of the centrifugal force of love does not come from Novalis, Novalis at least confirmed Lanier's idea. Like Novalis Lanier "sometimes seems to represent the Primeval essence of Being as love."[28]

That Lanier assimilated to himself what he read, making the thought his own and not remembering the words merely for the felicity of expression or the music of the phrase, is proved by the fact that few of the many quotations from other authors, with which his prose abounds, are exact. The lines

> or Lady of the Mere
> Sole-sitting by the shores of old Romance,

from one of Wordsworth's least known poems—one of the "Poems on the Naming of Places"—become in *Tiger-Lilies*

> or Lady of the Lake
> Lone sitting by the shores of old Romance.[29]

Two sentences from *Heroes and Hero-Worship*[30]—"Who is there that, in logical words, can express the effect music has on us? A kind of inarticulate unfathomable speech, which leads us to the edge of the infinite, and lets us for moments gaze into that,"—are shortened considerably and made to read thus: "Who shall say what music means in his soul? It leads us to the verge of eternity and lets us gaze on that."[31] Other quotations are, as a rule, as little exact. Lanier's was no martinet's memory, but a memory of the deep, germinating order of Coleridge's. What he read during his college days dropped, as it were, "into the deep well of unconscious cerebration,"[32] to come out later transformed, shining with the clear water of his own personality, made wholly his own.

§ 6

AT THE end of Lanier's junior year, his father, feeling that seventeen was too young an age for graduation, removed Lanier from college and secured for him a position as clerk in the post-office at Macon. Perhaps an important reason for this interruption in his college course was his father's persisting fear that his son would wish to make music his profession. But many a father, particularly in the South, has distrusted college education and college recreations with the Puritan's distrust of worldly pleasure and the practical man's distrust of the intellectual and artistic life, and has insisted upon his son's having some practical experience. Lanier's experience proved, fortunately, to be not unpleasant, for it brought him into contact with a great variety of people and stimulated his love of merriment. Throughout that year "he kept the supper table at home in a roar by mimicry of the funny speech of the middle Georgia Crackers, the country people applying for letters," his brother remembered;[33] and from this experience perhaps as much as from any other came the excellent dialect poems which Lanier at one period seemed so fond of writing.

Probably to this year belongs an amusing incident which Lanier himself related with laughter. One extremely cold winter night he went with a group of fellow musicians to serenade the daughters of Major John Lamar, and with benumbed fingers they went through their usual program. The door of the house was opened, as usual, and they started toward the parlor where they expected to find refreshments and the objects of their serenade, but the old darky butler announced that "Marsa an' de young ladies done been down to de plantation 'bout a week."[34]

His year of practical experience over, Lanier returned to college in the fall of 1859 as a member of the class that had been below his when he left. Most of his friends had been graduated and he probably felt the loss of their companionship keenly, though his brother Clifford was now at Oglethorpe, and he and John A. Weems roomed with Lanier.[35] He was in a state of mind, therefore, to welcome and to appreciate the friendship of an older man, a member of the faculty. To Lanier's senior year belongs the beginning of this, the most important friendship of his Oglethorpe days, his friendship with Professor James Woodrow, which was to be one of the determining influences of his life.

Woodrow was at the time about thirty-one, and fourteen years older than Lanier.[36] He had been born at Carlisle, England, but had been brought to America at an early age by his clergyman father, and educated at Jefferson College, in Pennsylvania, where he had been graduated in 1849. The summer of 1853 he had spent at Harvard, studying with Agassiz in the Lawrence Scientific School, and from Harvard he had gone to Heidelberg, in Germany, where he had taken the degree of Doctor of Philosophy *summa cum laude* in 1856. He is said to have been offered at that time a full professorship at Heidelberg. Before studying at Harvard and at Heidelberg he had been "principal of academies in Alabama" and his graduate work seems to have been undertaken with the definite purpose in mind of fitting himself to serve as professor of natural science at Oglethorpe, to which he had come in 1856, only a semester before Lanier. At Harvard and in Germany he had acquired some ideas of a liberal theology and training in modern critical thought, and at the time Lanier came under his influence he had already begun to formulate for himself ideas on evolution as the mode of creation of which the book of Genesis records the fact, departing in this from the teaching of Agassiz, who opposed any suggestion of evolution.

Woodrow's ideas on evolution, expressed in an address delivered May 7, 1884, and published in the July, 1884, issue of the *Southern Presbyterian Review*, precipitated a widespread controversy that led to a request for his resignation as "Professor of Natural Science in Connection with Revelation" in the Columbia (South Carolina) Theological Seminary, to which he had gone in 1861. In 1888 he was tried for heresy before the General Assembly of the Presbyterian church and condemned as a heretic in spite of his insistence upon his full belief in the Bible and his acceptance of the Presbyterian creed. For Woodrow there was no conflict at all between science and theology and nothing inconsistent in his action in having himself ordained a minister of the Presbyterian church soon after coming to Oglethorpe. In fact, as a minister he hoped to reach even more young people, of whom he was naturally a leader, than he could reach as a teacher. Even after his resignation from the theological seminary, even after he had gone into banking and had become president of the Central National Bank of Columbia, he maintained his status as a minister, and continued to edit a quarterly and a weekly religious journal. Long prominent in the South (he died in 1907, at the age of seventy-nine) as an educator, scientist, and leader of the Presbyterian church, he never became nationally known, nor did he become an original worker, possibly because his interests—he served the Confederacy as a chemist and his own wealth was derived from ownership of a successful publishing house which he also managed—were too varied. He was, however, a thorough scholar who kept abreast of the knowledge of the subjects that interested him, and he remained far ahead of his times in Georgia and South Carolina. Among other reasons for his being remembered is the fact that through his sister he was uncle to Woodrow Wilson.

He seems typical of modern academic thought at its best, liberal and tolerant; what he as a teacher most desired was to develop in young men a sense of responsibility for their own opinions and a capacity to form them intelligently. To young Lanier he opened a new world of scientific speculation in which he was for the rest of his life to be an enthusiastic explorer and to him Woodrow revealed (something that was to set Lanier apart from most of his southern contemporaries) the meaning of genuine scholarship. It is interesting to consider the influence he may also have had in stimulating in Lanier the burning desire to formulate the laws of the science of poetry and to reduce language to a series of musical notations.

To Lanier's classmates it seemed surprising that in spite of his passion for music and his love of nature and art, he was "a persistent student, an omnivorous reader of books, and in his college classes . . . easily first in mathematics as well as in his other studies,"[37] but Lanier had a burning curiosity concerning all the affairs of men. Under the influence of Woodrow this curiosity found intelligent direction, and Lanier began at this time to develop what he later called "the bent student's habits."[38] He threw himself more eagerly than ever into his studies and easily maintained the leadership of his class. At Commencement, however, there was a tie in class rank, and the "1st Honor" of his class of twenty-one members was divided: instead of the usual one there were two valedictories at the Commencement exercises, held on Wednesday, July 18, 1860.[39]

The two valedictorians, as it happened, represented respectively the literary societies of the college, between which there was a spirited rivalry, Lanier the Thalian and E. F. Hoge the Phi Delta. The addresses were chosen by lot and Lanier gave the first—"To the Community, Trustees, and Faculty." His subject was "The Philosophy of History," and he began with a quotation from Landor.[40] The second honor, the Latin salutatory, fell to John M. Goetchius, who was to go to his death three years later at Gettysburg. There was besides an "address before the literary societies," by John B. Gordon, Esq., afterwards a distinguished soldier and statesman but then a young lawyer of twenty-eight, though already enjoying some local reputation as an orator. It is interesting to note that in 1860 Gordon was practising law with his brother-in-law, Judge Logan E. Bleckley, who at a critical time in Lanier's career (1874) was to give him sympathy, encouragement, and helpful criticism.

3

§ 7

LANIER's undergraduate days were over, but his future was not
undecided, for Professor Woodrow, in friendly interest, had secured for him an appointment as tutor in the university. So,
with the knowledge that he was to return to Oglethorpe in the
fall, Lanier left Midway to spend the summer vacation of 1860
at Montvale Springs, in the mountains of Eastern Tennessee,
where his grandfather, Sterling Lanier, had acquired a large
estate and operated a beautiful hotel. Montvale Springs was a
fashionable resort to which came delightful and distinguished
people from all the southern states. Even without them, however,
Lanier could hardly have wanted for company, for most of Sterling Lanier's children and grandchildren—some twenty-five in
all—usually managed to spend part of the summer with him.[41]

Lanier responded enthusiastically to the pleasures of Montvale Springs, hunting, fishing, and social life. "What an assem-
blage of facilities for enjoyment I have up here in the mountains,"
he wrote in a letter to a friend. "Kinfolks, men-friends, women-
friends, books, music, wine, hunting, fishing, billiards, ten-pins,
chess, eating, mosquitoless sleeping, mountain scenery, and a
month of idleness; shades of Apicius and Heliogabalus!" But the
Puritan spirit manifested itself, and he added: "Not finding my
delight in life increased, I am come to the conclusion that the
luxuries of this world are humbugs and the idea that they are
essential to happiness a most magnificent absurdity."[40]

The summer spent in the Smoky Mountains gave him other
pleasures which he was not to appreciate fully until years later.
He carried from Montvale Springs memories that were to return
and fill his mind during campaigns in Virginia and to grow
eventually into *Tiger-Lilies*, in which, in spite of the intervening
experiences of war, he reproduced the life of Montvale Springs
in rich fullness and with an undampened youthful enthusiasm.
"Can I forget," he wrote there,[42] "the mighty hunter of the
black eye and beard whom in solemn convention we did dub
(it was the time of the Japanese invasion!) the Grand Tycoon;
or the six-footer uncle whom, being unfamiliar with the Japanese
gradations we assigned him as Deputy Tycoon; or old Ned, the
French cook, whom the Deputy touched off; or Cricket, the dog,
who climbed on old Ring's shoulders and stole the meat one
night, as Ned averred? Can I forget how, one divine morning,

The room in Thalian Hall (Old Oglethorpe), occupied by Lanier as a college student.

when we had just returned to camp from the killing of a buck, and were taking our several ease (as Lorrie said), *recubans sub tegmine* of certainly the most *patulæ fagi* any of us ever saw, the Grand Tycoon, in his lordly way, suddenly exclaimed, 'Get out of the way, old Ned, with your French fripperies; hand me the side of that buck, there!" and how the Grand Tycoon did then purvey him a long beechen wand with a fork on the end thereof, did insert the same in the ribbèd side of the deer, and did rest the whole upon a twig deftly driven in juxtaposition with a bed of glowing coals of the wood of hickory; and how the Grand Tycoon did stand thereover with his muscular right arm outstretched, like Hercules over the Lernean Hydra, save that our Hercules held in his right hand a bottle of diabolical hue wherefrom he ever and anon did drip upon the crisping ribs a curious and potent admixture of butter, hot-water, lemon-juice, mustard, pepper, salt, and wine; and how, presently, the Grand Tycoon came to me and said, 'Try that rib—!' and how I took hold of the rib with both hands, it being long as my arm, and near as large, and did forthwith, after the hyena fashion, bite into the same; and how as the meat, with its anointments and juices, did fare slowly down the passage appointed for such, the titillation thereof upon the uvula or palate was so exquisite that the world grew brighter upon a sudden, and methought even the brook that ran hard by did murmer [*sic*] a stave or two from the Drinking Song of Lucrezia?"[43]

And years later still, a professional musician in Baltimore, he was to remember another experience of this same summer and write to his wife: "Last night we gave a magnificent concert. The house was crowded. . . . The orchestra was inspired, the 'Symphonie Fantastique,' as difficult and trying a piece of orchestration as was ever written, was played to a marvel. . . . Then, the 'Hunt of Henry IV.!' . . . It openeth with a grave and courteous invitation, as of a cavalier riding by some dainty lady, through the green aisles of the deep woods, to the hunt—a lovely, romantic melody, the first violins discoursing the man's words, the first flute [which Lanier played] replying for the lady. Presently a fanfare: a sweet horn replies out of the far woods; then the meeting of the gay cavaliers; then the start, the dogs are unleashed, one hound gives tongue, another joins, the stag is seen—hey, gentlemen! away they all fly through the sweet leaves by the great oaks and beeches, all a-dash among the brambles, till presently, bang! goeth a pistol (it was my veritable old revolver loaded with blank cartridge for the occasion, the revolver that hath lain so many nights under my head), fired by *Tympani* (as we call him, the same being a nervous little Frenchman who playeth our drums), and then the stag dieth in a celestial concord of flutes, oboes, and violins. Oh, how far off my soul was in this thrilling moment! It was in a rare, sweet glen in Tennessee, the sun was rising over a wilderness of mountains, I was standing (how well I remember the spot!) alone in the dewy grass, wild with rapture and with expectation—yonder came, gracefully walking, a lovely fawn. I looked into its liquid eyes, hesitated, prayed, gulped a sigh, then overcome with the savage hunter's instinct, fired; the fawn leaped convulsively a few yards, I ran to it, found it lying on its side, and received into my agonized and remorseful heart the reproaches of its most tender, dying gaze."[44]

It had proved, indeed, a delightful and important summer. Lanier was rested and happy, and eager to return to Oglethorpe for a year of hard work. In the letter quoted above which he had addressed to his predecessor in the position he was to fill he had written: "Write me a summary of your experiences condensed into aphorisms, that I may have a pocketful of them ready to profit by on all occasions. . . . I tremble when I think of tutorship (by the way, my rightful title of tutor here has, owing to my exhibition of talents as a flutist, been corrupted into 'tooter,' it being considered that the last mentioned word euphoniously expresses whatever distinctive cognomen I ought to possess in the exercise of my two professions.)" He was, of course, only eighteen, and one of the subjects in which he was to tutor, Greek, he had never mastered; he trembled, naturally.

§ 8

AT OGLETHORPE again, his friendship with Professor Woodrow increased. Together they took long rambles through the woods and over the hills about Midway, observing and studying the objects of nature, and talking about everything under the sun. On Saturdays and Sundays Woodrow preached to small and struggling congregations—"in school houses, court houses, and private houses"—within a radius of forty miles or so of the college, and frequently Lanier would make the week-end journey with him. Often they drove late on Sunday night to be at Oglethorpe for their college engagements on Monday. "During such drives we were constantly engaged without interruption in our conversation," wrote Woodrow. "In these ways, and in listening frequently to his marvelous flute-playing, we were much together. We were both young and fond of study."[45] Years later Lanier referred to Woodrow as "the strongest and most valuable stimulus" of his youth.[46] Woodrow's liberating influence on Lanier can hardly be overestimated, but his service was especially this: that he stimulated in Lanier a deep reverence for science, while inspiring him with a fervent religious faith and a broad, liberal outlook on life, emphasizing not any agreement between science and the Bible, but an absence of contradiction. The sweep and the vigor of Lanier's poetry is the broadness and the catholicity of Woodrow's own wholesome attitude toward life.

Lanier described himself at this period as "a spare-built boy, of average height and under-weight, mostly addicted to hard study, long reveries, and exhausting smokes with a German pipe."[47] But boy though he was, he had that distinction of manner that inspires the confidence of other boys. It is said that even before the title of tutor had given him prestige, his fellow-students as well as the boys of the lower classes looked up to him with respect and regarded him as a being quite apart.[48] His brother Clifford, who returned to Oglethorpe with him, records his salient characteristics as "an intensity of spirit, a vivid realization of life, an eager looking out for and quick apprehension of impressions; he was now and always a much-alive personality."[49] According to his brother also, Lanier did much miscellaneous reading in the time left him from his duties, probably reading much history (which he seems to have neglected before this) and "began to jot down some hints and fragments of a poetical, musical conception that seems to have haunted his short after-life, clamoring for embodiment. This was a longing to put into something like music-drama the elements of the medieval peasant uprising in France, called the *Jacquerie*." But probably no part of the fragmentary poem was written at this period; it is more likely that at Oglethorpe Lanier merely brooded over the subject and planned the general arrangement of the poem.

What poems Lanier did write at this time were remembered by his brother as "*Byronesque*, if not *Wertheresque*, at least tinged with gloominess." These poems Lanier did not preserve, "perhaps because they were not hale, hearty, breathing of sanity, hope, betterment, aspiration." When we realize that of the one hundred and twenty finished poems by Lanier that have been published only sixty-nine were published before his death, and by him, we realize that Lanier was a severe self-critic. He dealt with his poetry as severely as Thomas Jefferson dealt with his architecture and Monticello, suppressing, revising, reworking old ideas and improving the form given them, refining constantly. His development as a man, and in his poetry, was dynamic. And if we do not have the poems that he wrote during this period, the loss is not to be lamented, for the energy of his culminating poem, "Sunrise," was generated at Oglethorpe, in reveries, in his studies, in his wanderings about the Georgia hills, in the long drives with Woodrow.

The year as tutor at Oglethorpe brought into his life another interesting friend besides young Dr. Woodrow, Milton Harlow Northrup. Northrup was only a year older than Lanier, a native of New York State and a graduate of Hamilton College, in the class of 1860. At Hamilton he had won membership in the Phi Beta Kappa fraternity. He had come to Midway to conduct the Oglethorpe Academy for boys. In later life Northrup was to win some distinction as a newspaper correspondent, especially for his letters from Washington in 1868 recounting scenes in Congress during the impeachment proceedings against President Johnson, published in the New York *Express*. His work as secretary to the House committee appointed to settle the Hayes-Tilden election controversy, was highly commended by Samuel S. ("Sunset") Cox (whose biography Northrup was later to write) in his book, *Three Decades of Federal Legislation*. A Democrat always, he held office only under Cleveland: during each of Cleveland's administrations he served as postmaster of Syracuse, New York, in which city he made his home from 1861 until his death—in a street-car accident—in 1906. For twenty years he was both editor and owner of the Syracuse *Courier*. His interest in literature and history, his gentle personality and keen sense of humor would have combined to make him attractive to Lanier.

In Midway, in 1860, Northrup and Lanier occupied adjoining rooms at Ike Sherman's boarding house (for with graduation Lanier had relinquished his room in Thalian Hall) and ate at the same table. There was a bond of sympathy between the two which quickly ripened into friendship. Northrup described Lanier in a letter of January 1, 1861, as "young and very intellectual,"

CHAPTER THREE

WAR'S RUDE SURGE

§ 1

LANIER'S questionings about his future were soon to be answered for him, but in a way neither wished for nor expected. Agitation for secession from the federal union had been wide-spread in the southern states for some months prior to the election of Lincoln in November, 1860, but it had been chiefly as a threat used against his candidacy. With Lincoln president-elect, southern leaders insisted that the threat be given meaning. On November 8, 1860, the people of Lanier's own town of Macon, recalling Revolutionary precedents, passed a declaration of independence setting forth their grievances against the northern states. South Carolina actually seceded from the union about six weeks later, on December 20. And on January 19, 1861, the secession of Georgia was voted by the state legislature at Milledgeville, only two miles from the scene of Tutor Lanier's academic engagements. The calm of Oglethorpe was from that moment definitely disrupted. The sleepy little dream world of Midway, where young eyes looked love and young lips sang soft songs to the music of the flute, had come suddenly to life. And Lanier, though not at first a secessionist, caught the contagion from the air he breathed. War of course did not seem imminent, but if Georgia's action meant war, then was he not ready to fight, he the brave soldier of Froissart?

It is the state of public mind in the spring of 1861 that he describes in *Tiger-Lilies:* "An afflatus of war was breathed upon us. Like a great wind, it drew and blew upon men, women, and children. Its sounds mingled with the solemnity of the church-organs and arose with the earnest words of preachers praying for guidance in the matter. It sighed in the half-hearted words of sweethearts conditioning lovers with war-service. It thundered splendidly in the impassioned appeals of orators to the people. It whistled through the streets, it stole in to the firesides, it clinked glasses in bar-rooms, it lifted the gray hairs of our wise men in conventions, it thrilled through the lectures in college halls, it rustled the thumbed book-leaves of the schoolrooms.

"This wind blew upon all the vanes of all the churches of the country, and turned them one way—toward war. It blew, and shook out, as if by magic, a flag whose device was unknown to soldier or sailor before, but whose every flap and flutter made the blood bound in our veins.

"Who could have resisted the fair anticipations which the new war-idea brought? It arrayed the sanctity of a righteous cause in the brilliant trappings of military display; pleasing, so, the devout and the flippant which in various proportions are mixed elements in all men. It challenged the patriotism of the sober citizen, while it inflamed the dream of the statesman, ambitious for his country or for himself. It offered test to all allegiances and loyalties; of church, of state; of private loves, of public devotion; of personal consanguinity; of social ties. To obscurity it held out eminence; to poverty, wealth, to greed, a gorged maw; to speculation, legalized gambling; to patriotism, a country; to statesmanship, a government; to virtue, purity; and to love, what all love most desires—a field wherein to assert itself by action.

". . . if there was guilt in any, there was guilt in nigh all of us, between Maryland and Mexico; . . . [and] Mr. Davis, if he be termed the ringleader of the rebellion, was so not by virtue of any instigation of his, but purely by the unanimous will and appointment of the Southern people."[1]

In this passage Lanier described as well as it is possible to describe the state of mind produced by war, which existed in both North and South that tragic spring. From his list of virtues stimulated by the new war-ideas, it is easy to select the virtues to which at that time it must have appealed in Lanier. As the wars of the Commonwealth seemed to Milton, so seemed this to him a holy war; and he was encouraged in this by the clergy who were, as usual at such times, belligerently patriotic. Furthermore, had not such an ardent opponent of secession as Alexander H. Stephens of his own Georgia, close friend of the respected president of Oglethorpe,[2] thrown in his lot with the newly formed Confederacy, written its constitution and become its vice-president? Patriotism demanded allegiance to his state and to the new union which it had helped to form, even if allegiance led to battle. Though Lanier wrote later in *Tiger-Lilies* of "the blood-red flower of war" as "a species of the great genus, sin-flower . . . whose roots are in hell,"[3] in the spring of 1861, after the establishment of the Confederacy and the beginning of war with the firing on Fort Sumter, Lanier, remembering Froissart and the manœuvers of the Macon Archers, was probably as martially minded as anyone; and like many another southerner who loved learning and chivalry he dreamed that "the new Confederacy was to enter upon an era of prosperity such as no other nation, ancient or modern had ever enjoyed, [and that] the city of Macon, his birthplace and home, was to become a great art-centre. Its streets were to be lined with marble statues, like unto Athens of old."[4]

Also, as he admitted with bitterness in an unpublished essay written in 1867, he had become "convinced of his ability to whip at least five Yankees. The author does not know now and did not know then, by what course of reasoning he arrived at this said conviction; in the best of the author's judgment he did not reason it out at all, rather absorbed it, from the press of surrounding similar convictions. The author, however, was also confident, not only that he personally could whip five Yankees, but *any* southern boy could do it. The whole South was satisfied it could whip five Norths. The newspapers said we could do it; the preachers pronounced anathemas against the man that didn't believe we could do it; our old men said at the street corners, if they were young they could do it, and by the Eternal, they believed they could do it anyhow (whereat great applause and 'Hurrah for ole Harris!'); the young men said they'd be blanked if they couldn't do it, and the young ladies said they wouldn't marry a man who couldn't do it. This arrogant perpetual invitation to draw and come on, this idea which possessed the whole section, which originated no one knows when, grew no one knows how, was a devil's own bombshell, the fuse of which sparkled when Mr. Brooks struck Mr. Sumner upon the head with a cane.

"Of course we laugh at it *now*,—laugh in the hope that our neighbors will attribute the redness of our cheeks to that and not to our shame. . . . The conceit of an individual is ridiculous because it is powerless. . . . The conceit of a whole people is terrible, it is a devil's bombshell, surcharged with death, plethoric with all foul despairs and disasters." "What fools we were!" he

said in after years to Northrup, who, suspected of being a Northern
spy, had made his way North in 1861 only with the greatest
difficulty, "What fools we were!"

§ 2

BUT IN this conceit, and full of zeal, Lanier volunteered for
military service in June, 1861, soon after finishing the year's
work at Oglethorpe. He was sent at once to join the Macon
Volunteers, who had left Georgia for Virginia the nineteenth of
April as a part of the first battalion to go out of the state. The
company—which included his old friends C. E. Campbell, C. K.
Emmell, C. M. Wiley, Granville Connor, and W. A. Hopson,
friends whose presence made much music possible[6]—was stationed
at the time near Norfolk, encamped on the Norfolk fair grounds,
"amongst the marshes of Sewalls Point, Virginia, immediately
opposite Fort Monroe"; and here, for the rest of the year, they
played "marsh-divers" and "meadow-crakes." But the war was
still a kind of picnic: there was an abundance of food from the
near-by market gardens, and the principal duty of these soldiers
was to picket the beach.[7] For "pleasures and sweet rewards-of-
toil" there were, Lanier tells us, "agues that played dice with
our bones, and blue-mass pills that played dice with our livers."
But there were also furloughs in Norfolk, where, almost oblivious
to the war that had not yet touched him, Lanier enjoyed a kind
of social life not unlike that to which he had been accustomed
in Macon.

When furloughs were not granted there was still a way of
gaining the city. Between the camp and Norfolk lay a cemetery,
and in this cemetery was a receiving vault with an unlocked
door. Of the vault the soldiers made a dressing room, changing
here to civilian clothes, in which they entered Norfolk unde-
tected. Here of course the civilian clothes were kept when they
were not being worn.[8] Lanier, considering the whole affair as
a grand lark, probably felt no more squeamishness in using a
cemetery vault as a dressing room than any other soldier did.

In April, 1862, the company of which the Macon Volunteers
had become a part was ordered to Wilmington, North Carolina,
but the change, Lanier records with his persistent facetiousness,
was chiefly "in style of fever." For two or three months they
indulged "in what are called the 'dry-shakes of the sand-hills,'
a sort of brilliant tremolo movement, brilliantly executed upon

Music for three flutes. Used by Lanier, Emmell, and Campbell in camp near Norfolk, Virginia, in 1861. Courtesy of Mr. John Voorhees.

'that pan-pipe, man,' by an invisible but very powerful performer." At Wilmington, where they were engaged in building Fort Fisher, they made friends in the city, however, and Lanier with his flute was the object of much feminine adulation. A northerner who escaped from the Confederacy by running the blockade carried away memories of the finest flute-playing he had ever heard, and Milton Harlow Northrup, overhearing his description of the music, asked if the name of the player was Lanier. It was. This, during the long four years of war, was the only news that Northrup had of his Oglethorpe friend.

From Wilmington the company was sent back to Virginia, and to Drury's Bluff, about seven miles south of Richmond on the James River. About this time Lanier was joined by his brother Clifford, who had left Oglethorpe and enlisted in Macon for the same regiment. One who knew them during the war has described the brothers as "inseparable; slender, grey-eyed youths, full of enthusiasm, Clifford grave and quiet, Sidney, the elder, playful with a dainty mirthfulness. . . ."[9] And in *Thorn-Fruit*, Clifford's confessedly autobiographical novel, Clifford describes the essential difference between them in saying that "In the character of his brother, the Ideal and the Real were twin rulers. Himself was a dreamer."[10] But he emphasizes their mutual devotion: "The constancy of the brothers had been remarkable. At school they had no feuds. No anger had thrown the fire-brand of fraternal war in their close companionship. If they were for a time separate, Mark's [Sidney's] address to Lee [Clifford] was 'My sweetheart brother!' If Mark commanded, Lee might resist a little; in the end he obeyed with a smile. 'Mark and I are two halves. Both of us make one.' "[11] It is easy to believe the statement that Lanier consistently refused promotion in order that he might remain with this younger brother whom he adored.

On May 15, 1862, there was some fighting at Drury's Bluff. The Monitor advanced up the river and fired on the small fort that Lanier's company was defending, but without success. The episode was probably Lanier's baptism of fire. But his regiment was next ordered to the Chickahominy, where it participated in the seven days' fighting around Richmond (June 26-July 2, 1862), and Lanier experienced warfare at its worst. Just before the battle of Malvern Hill (July 1) the men marched all night through drenching rain, over torn and swampy roads—a very different experience for Lanier from picketing the Norfolk beach or even the more arduous labor of building Fort Fisher. The battles of these seven days were the first battles of importance in which Lanier took part. Perhaps a sentence in a letter of later years— "Did you ever lie for a whole day after being wounded, and then have water brought you?"[12]—is an allusion to a real experience, but of his experiences in battle we know nothing definitely.

Soon after the seven days' fighting Lanier was "in a little gunboat fight or two" on the south bank of the James River. A soldier comrade has testified that "Lanier exhibited the courage, patience, endurance, and all the other high qualities of the martial spirit; steady adherence to discipline, as well as the bright *insouciance* characteristic of the American citizen-soldier."[13] Perhaps, indeed, it was not his experiences in battle but the more terrible experiences in prison and the disillusion following defeat that caused the great hatred of war which he exhibited later, but the *"insouciance,"* we may be sure, covered deep emotions— emotions which he dared not trust himself to express.

On August 26, 1862, Lanier's regiment was ordered to Petersburg to rest, and while there Lanier, his brother Clifford, and two friends obtained a transfer to Major Milligan's battalion of the Mounted Signal Service, at the time considered the most efficient in the southern army. The proficiency of the four Georgians and their expert horsemanship attracted the attention of the commanding officer, who formed them into a field squad and attached them to the staff of Major General S. G. French. But other qualities attracted the attention of that officer, and often in the evening Lanier and a friend would go on invitation to General French's quarters and pass the evening in music.[14] In a letter to his father Lanier tells of four Georgia privates with one general, six captains, and one lieutenant, in the democracy in the practice of art, serenading the city.[15] Almost always when one hears of Lanier as a soldier, it is as a flute-playing, singing soldier whose fortunes were as romantic as those of any hero of *opéra bouffe* (though for him the opera was to have a miserable ending). Once as he played on the streets of a small town beneath the windows of the Philharmonic Club, the orchestra in rehearsal upstairs ceased playing and the members came downstairs to listen and to grant him the honorary freedom of the town; and once, in another town, Lanier was given a flute by the proprietor of a music store after he had asked to see one and had played a strain upon it.[16]

At Petersburg there was a small public library and Lanier seized gratefully the opportunity to continue the literary studies which he had pursued even in camp. Reading of Carlyle had kindled in him a desire to know more of the German language; so with a glossary and a little volume of German poetry he was studying diligently, still dreaming, perhaps, of two years of study at Heidelberg. As part of his study he attempted verse translations of Heine, Goethe, and Schiller, working late at night after he had curried and fed his horse, and in the intervals of duty as a mounted signal scout detached for outpost service.[17] "For all knowledge," the comrade already quoted said of him, "he had an unappeasable hunger: in all odd moments, with every chance acquaintance, gaining something."[18] The war had interrupted his academic life, but it could not interrupt his pursuit of knowledge. Nor did it interrupt the serious, diligent, though always unguided study of music. For his flute he tried to compose some songs, and he set to music some lyrics by Tennyson, among them (his brother tells us) "The Song of Love and Death" from "Lancelot and Elaine."[17] Possibly it was at this time also that he composed music for "Love that hath us in the net," from "The Miller's Daughter," one of the two compositions by Lanier that have been published.

It was probably during the winter of 1862-63 that there occurred two of the few incidents of Lanier's army life that have been remembered. One, recalled by his friend Campbell,[16] tells of Lanier's coming in from sentry duty in the snow and finding his companions boiling a pasty mess that he supposed to be oyster stew. Tired, but even more hungry, he hurried away for spoons and saucers—and when he returned had to endure the jibes and laughter of his mates, for what they were cooking was paste to fill and patch the cracks of the cabin in which they were quartered. Lanier, Campbell also recalled, "didn't lose his temper."

The other incident, preserved in a sonnet by Clifford Lanier written some years later, is of another sort. They were on an all-night march, and Clifford—only nineteen years old and physically somewhat inert,[18] as well as exhausted from lack of sleep—soon appeared too weak to go on. To keep him from sinking Lanier, marching at his side, encircled him with his arm, and bore him up for miles, Clifford's tired feet going on without conscious volition, for he was in a stupor of sleep. Such experiences as recorded in these episodes may have proved Lanier's fortitude, but they also proved dangerous to his health. Ward, indeed, asserts that "at Petersburg . . . he began to feel the premonitions of that fatal disease, consumption, against which he battled for fifteen years."

§ 3

IN THE spring of 1863 both Sidney and Clifford Lanier were granted furloughs to visit their parents in Macon. The spring that year was unusually lovely, and in Macon food was plentiful, though already in Richmond there was serious want and in some camps the men were starving. Here, for the first time, Lanier met Miss Mary Day, whom he was later to marry, at the home of their common friend, Miss Gussie Lamar, with whom Lanier loved to play flute and piano duets, or for whose singing he would play the piano accompaniment. Mary Day, a tall, slender girl of delicate beauty, with large, dreamy black eyes, was the daughter of Charles Day, a successful jeweler of Macon, who was of northern parentage. Before the war she had been in the North, studying music in New York, and visiting at West Point and Saratoga, and she had returned to Macon only at the outbreak of hostilities to be with her father, who had cast his lot with the Southern Confederacy. She too played the piano. It is said that the first introduction took place at the meeting of a music club sponsored by Mrs. John Lamar—mother of Gussie Lamar—which met regularly in spite of the war. Certainly with music, and gay war-time flirtation, and such excursions on the water as Clifford describes in *Thorn-Fruit*, the ten days' furlough passed swiftly.

On their return to the Virginia battlefields in April, the Laniers escorted Mrs. Clement C. Clay, wife of the distinguished senator from Alabama, and her sister-in-law, Mrs. Hugh Lawson Clay. The ladies had been visiting Mrs. Hugh Clay's father, Major Anderson Comer, in Macon, waiting for the summons to join their husbands in Richmond. From Richmond Senator Clay—now serving as Confederate senator—wrote that food was as scarce as lodgings were difficult to obtain, but in the lunch basket packed for the long trip there the ladies carried "broiled partridges, sho' nuf sugar, and sho' nuf butter, and spring chickens, quality size."[19] Mrs. Clement Clay's account of the three days' journey is an interesting picture of war-time travel.

"The aisles of the car were crowded. At many stations, as we came through North Carolina, women entered the car with baskets of 'big blues,' the luscious native huckleberries, with full deep bloom upon them; these and other tempting edibles were brought aboard at almost every station along the way. When our pleasant party separated at Lynchburg, and the youths sat alone in their tents, they recalled in pages truly characteristic the memories of that long journey, in which, like tired children, they had sometimes fallen asleep, Clifford's head upon my sister's shoulder, and Sid's upon mine."

Lanier's "pages truly characteristic," written from the theater of war, from their camp near Suffolk, on April 6, read: "Have you ever, my Two Good Friends, wandered, in an all-night's dream, through exquisite flowery mazes, through labyrinthine grottoes, 'full of all sparkling and sparry loveliness,' over mountains of unknown height, by abysses of an unfathomable depth, all beneath skies of infinite brightness caused by no Sun; strangest of all, wandered about in wonder, as if you had lived an eternity in the familiar contemplation of such things? And when, at morning, you have waked from such a dream and gone about your commonplace round of life, have you never stopped suddenly to gaze at the Sun and exclaimed to yourself, 'What a singular thing it is up there; and these houses, bless me, what funny institutions, not at all like my grottoes and bowers, in which I have lived all eternity; and those men and women walking about there, uttering strange gibberish, and cramming horrid messes of stuff in their mouths, what dear, odd creatures; what does it all mean, anyhow, and who did it, and how is one to act under the circumstances?' . . .

"If you have dreamed, thought and felt so, you can realize the imbecile stare with which I gaze on all this life that goes on around me here. Macon was my two weeks' dream. I wake from that into Petersburg, an indefinitely long, real life. . . ."[20]

And in camp, in spite of such a diversion as the visit of Mrs. Clay and her sister-in-law on April 10, the business of this real life seemed to move relentlessly on. General French pressed the men to get into position guns of sufficient range to destroy the advancing gunboats. Foraging parties and immense wagon trains were sent out for provisions. "Instead of living that we may fight, we are fighting that we may live," Clifford wrote Mrs. Clay; probably to this period belongs the incident remembered

4

by Campbell of harnessing himself with Lanier to a wagon to haul goods and food for the soldiers,[16] doing without complaint work for which there were no horses.

On May 2 began the two days' battle of Chancellorsville, at which almost one-quarter of the Confederate force of 41,000 men was lost; and the regiment of which the Laniers were members was engaged in the battle. When the fighting was over Lanier, almost in rags, passed the corpse of a Federal private, clothed in a clean new shirt which caught his eye. "He hesitated for a moment, but quickly deciding that he could not take the shirt, moved on. Within a few minutes he had repented his squeamishness, reminding himself of his sore need of a whole garment, and urging upon himself the strong probability that the Federal would not, under the circumstances, begrudge the transfer. By the time he had returned, however, he found to his chagrin that a less tender-conscienced mate had dexterously captured the shirt."[21] The grotesque humor of similar situations lightens the heavy sentimentality of *Tiger-Lilies* more than once: Lanier might have written a realistic novel of the Civil War, had not experiences more terrible still made him want to forget it entirely.

After Chancellorsville, the Laniers were ordered to resume their scouting activity and to proceed to "The Rocks" (Fort Boykin), a point on the James River near its mouth, opposite Newport News. Here they remained over a year, until August, 1864, acting as scouts and transmitting the information they gathered across a signal line which extended up the river to Petersburg. The duties were oppressive, and there was constant danger of being captured, but in this work of hard riding and dangerous living Lanier displayed a cool and collected courage. He was untiring in his energy, patient and cautious.

And with the danger there was, properly enough for a soldier of Froissart, romance: "Our life, during this period, was as full of romance as heart could desire. We had a flute and a guitar, good horses, a beautiful country, splendid residences inhabited by friends who loved us, and plenty of hairbreadth 'scapes from the roving bands of Federals who were continually visiting that Debatable Land." He could, he wrote Northrup in later years, forgetting the danger and remembering the romance, "look back upon that as the most delicious period of [his] life in many respects," and he loved to talk with his brother "of the beautiful

women, the serenades, the moonlight dashes on the beach of
fair Burwell's Bay (just above Hampton Roads), and the spirited
brushes of [their] little force with the enemy."

§ 4

LANIER was always in love, and the still remembered names of
his youthful sweethearts are many. Those not won by the charm
of his personality and his poetic ways were inevitably won by
the music of his flute. Mrs. Clay speaks of a sweetheart in Macon
in the spring of '63 who may have been Gussie Lamar and may
have been Mary Day, whom he had only then met; but in the
summer and fall of '63 his sweetheart was one not so far away.
She was Ginna (or Virginia) Hankins, the daughter of Mr. John
Hankins, whose home, historic Bacon's Castle, so called because
it had been held and fortified by the rebel Nathaniel Bacon in
1676, was close to Fort Boykin where the scouts were stationed.

In *Thorn-Fruit* Clifford Lanier described her home as a rambling affair, a brick nucleus with wooden "improvements," but
large and spacious. Here the Hankinses, a family consisting,
besides the parents, of several children, of whom Virginia was
the only daughter, lived in comfort even in the days of the war.
The friendship of the Laniers with the family began in characteristic cavalier fashion. One morning Miss Hankins found
tied by a guitar string to her front door a torn piece of a Confederate paper on which was written:

Porch, Saturday morning, 1 o'clock.
Did *all* that mortal men *could* to serenade you—failure
owing entirely to "inclemency of the weather."
FIELD CORPS.[22]

An introduction followed, and after that there were serenades,
rides together, and much talk of poetry and of books. The Laniers
and Will Hopson became intimates of the household. Together
Lanier and Ginna Hankins would pace the long galleries of her
home or ride through the green woods of the estate. And at
Bacon's Castle there was food to be had such as they never saw
in camp. If we are to believe the evidence of *Tiger-Lilies*[23] and
of *Thorn-Fruit*[24] luxuries of the table were not uncommon: there
were "Virginia biscuits and spring-chickens and ham and eggs,"
and, when they spent the night at Bacon's Castle, mint-juleps

served by a faithful slave before they were out of bed—the last an incident well remembered and recorded in both novels!

Lanier was writing poetry now, probably at first merely continuing to translate poems from his German anthology but later—quite definitely—writing original verse. Sometimes he would read his poetry to Ginna Hankins. She was not so pretty as handsome, but a smart and witty girl of his own age—or a year or two younger—whom Lanier found congenial company, and who was well enough educated to appreciate his poetry and to discuss it intelligently with him.[25] In *Thorn-Fruit* Mark Wilton, who is Sidney Lanier disguised in little except name, translates for Lucy Pegram "some of the beautiful [German] poems her old library furnished in the original. Schiller's 'Des Mädchens Klage,' Heine's 'Du bist wie eine Blume,' and 'Die Nähe des Geliebten' of Goethe were rapturously applauded by his fair auditor."[26] Miss Hankins herself remembered his playful assertion that poetry was now his vocation. Once as he was reading to her a poem he had written, a grasshopper lit on his arm. He brushed it away, saying "Grasshopper, fly thou away, and know that once in midst of summer's greenness thou didst light on the hand of a poet!"[22] Certainly there was about him the air of a poet. " 'He was slight—so slight that he seemed to have grown out of air.' "—Miss Hankins, describing him years later, quoted "E. Berger's" description of the young Mendelssohn in description of him.—" 'He was young, so young that he could not have numbered twenty summers, but the heights of eternity were foreshadowed in the forehead's marble gleam.' "

He was at work, too, on *Tiger-Lilies*, the novel that had had its conception at Montvale Springs during that happy summer vacation of 1860. Possibly, indeed, he had begun in the summer of 1860 those disconnected first chapters descriptive of the life in the Smoky Mountains, but it is certain that he was working on his novel in 1863-64, and when he was ordered from Fort Boykin he left the manuscript with Ginna Hankins, who probably figures in the novel as Rebecca Parven. But the only literary work completed in this period is the poems that Lanier addressed to her.

The poem that Mark Wilton inscribes to Lucy Pegram in *Thorn-Fruit*[27] is probably by Lanier. Though Clifford Lanier himself might easily have written the verses, it would have been like him—and appropriate to the scheme on which the novel was

Bacon's Castle, Surry County, Virginia. The home of Mr. John Hankins, in which Lanier visited during

written—to have used here an early composition of his brother's; and this he might have possessed, for he preserved poems that Lanier himself discarded.[28] "Scribbled about a week ago, on the shore of Burwell's Bay, by moonlight," explains Mark in the novel, "like a lecturer interpreting a panorama"; and Lucy exclaims "Glorious! Glorious!" as she reads:

Now bends the lily, like a nun at prayer;
    The maiden-flowers let fall their dewy hair;
And on their dreams that do perfume the air,
    Thou floatest there.

Now falls old ocean's roar to monotone;
    Thinking of thee his caves forget to moan,
And whisper in a low, sweet undertone
    Of thee alone.

Now flutter down the yearning stars, to pair
    With sisters in the lake, all twinned so fair;
My heart's a lake, and covets thee, Sweet, there—
    Oh! rest thou there![29]

The poem is amateurish and conventional, with little original in it except the metaphor of the last stanza—and that a metaphor spoiled as most of Lanier's metaphors are spoiled by overstatement, and also by the unpoetic participle "twinned"; but it is written in a stanzaic form that Lanier was later to use with complete success in "Nirvâna" and it contains images that were to reappear there, beautifully polished. Moreover the poem possesses charm, if only the charm of graceful amateurishness—and of youthful dreams.

Either at this time or, more probably, a little later (after he had left Burwell's Bay), Ginna Hankins asked Lanier in a letter if he remembered the "Brown Bird" in Mrs. Browning's *Drama of Exile*, which they had read together, the bird "whose song, as he sat on his tree in Paradise, was the last sound heard by Adam and Eve as they fled along the glade. So, friend," she wrote, "do I send my cry . . . across these broad stretches of moonlight. . . ."[30] To her letter Lanier replied with a poem, a copy of which he sent, with charming lack of self-consciousness or conceit in doing so, to his friend Will Hopson.

To G. H.

Thou most rare Brown Bird on thine Eden-tree,
All Heaven sweet to me
Cometh thy song of love's deep loyalty
And love's high royalty
And love's sweet-pleading loneliness in thee.

Our one Star uttereth forth her light,
Her silver call to night,
Who, wavering between Dark and Bright,
Oncometh with timid flight,
Like one who hesitateth 'twixt wrong and right.

O, never was a night so dark as I!
But thou hast sent a sigh
Of love, as a star would send a beam, to fly
Downward from out the sky,
And light a heart that's dark enough to die.

And so, O Bird, and so, thou Silver-Beam,
Let me forever dream
That I am Night, and thou a Star, whose stream
Of light like love shall seem—
Whose Love-light through my Dark shall ever gleam![31]

Amateurish this poem also is, but it reveals more than the one previously quoted a genuineness of feeling for life and nature that is a characteristic of Lanier's best poetry, expressed in a kind of irregular musical verse that was to become the medium of his happiest expression. The metrical effectiveness of the alternating long and short lines and the musical effectiveness of the repeated phrases and the quintuple rhyme make the poem far more pleasing and more characteristic of Lanier than the more familiar poem also addressed to Ginna Hankins which appears in the collected poems as "To———"[32] The latter poem ends with a stanza that Lanier appended to the copy of "To G. H." which he sent to Hopson:

So Boyhood sets; comes Youth,
A painful night of mists and dreams,
That broods, till Love's exquisite truth,
The Star of a morn-clear manhood, beams![33]

Just why Lanier appended this stanza is something of a puzzle. One may guess, if one chooses, that the quotation but reveals the more the genuineness and seriousness of his love for Ginna Hankins.[34]

A copy of the poem "To ———" Lanier had already sent to Hopson, characterizing it as "a little poem which sang itself through me the other day. 'Tis the first I've written in many years."[35] And if it does indeed antedate "To G. H." and the poem given in *Thorn-Fruit* we are correct in assuming that these poems represent, no matter how brief the time that intervened between the writing of "To ———" and them, a growth in the facility and freedom with which Lanier composed. Although "To G. H." lacks the greater human truthfulness of "To ———," the technical ability displayed in it, and in the unnamed poem, is greater. But it must be admitted that Lanier's inventiveness during this first period of poetic composition was extremely meager, for in each of these three poems addressed to Ginna Hankins, the same figure, the figure of love as a star piercing the black night of human life, appears. The figure, of course, was the only one he had thus far found to express an idea that was to reappear constantly in most of his poems. This idea, the importance and the significance of love, will finally dominate his poetry and his thought. At the beginning of his career we find love figured as a star piercing the night; at the end of his career, less than twenty years later, we shall find the conception of love enlarged, and the figure intensified to become the great, primeval symbol of life itself, the sun, breaking through life which is death to illuminate death, which is the release into the greater life.

But Lanier preserved his sense of merriment and of humor, and not all the verses he wrote were melancholy or particularly serious. In a little verse given in a letter to Hopson dated September 15, 1863,[36] we have another idea that is to reappear often in Lanier's poetry and letters to be treated both seriously and lightly, but always with the brave assurance apparent beneath the flippancy here:

"I should have answered your kind letter long ago, but I have been indulging so liberally in chills and fever that I have had little leisure to devote to anything else. Your touching allusion to your own experiences in the chill line affected me almost to tears: I sympathized with you. Friend, when *thou* shookedst, *I* trembled; when *thou* wast feverish, *I* also burnt; and when *thou* perspiredst, *I*, in that selfsame moment (mine generally came about 11 A. M.) did sweat like the d———l. Verily, I have an idea of handing down to late posterity some fine dishes of juicy soul-meat, upon a poem for a dumb-waiter, the top shelf of which should be constructed 'thus':

> Oh, Life's a Fever and Death's a chill!
> 'Tis a disease of which all men are ill;
> Earth for a Hospital surely was given—
> Hell's an eternal relapse: Health is Heaven! !

etc., etc., etc. And I *would* do it, by the Nine! only it looks menial and low to be shoving dumb-waiters up and down; even for Posterity, who, for all they say he's going to be so rich and lordly and refined, and all that, may, after all, turn out but a scurvy fellow that eats with his fingers; no better, if the truth was told than we poor cooks and waiters of the present century. . . .

"Ginna H. and I have become firm Soul-friends. She is a noble creature, and has the best cultivated mind I've seen in a long time. I've initiated her into the beauties of Mrs. Browning and Robert B., together with Carlyle and Novalis; whereat she is in a perfect blaze of enthusiasm. She desires me to remember her very warmly to you, and to express to you her gratification that your only friend in Franklin[37] of the female persuasion is cross-eyed and otherwise personally deficient; since so (she added) you will have less temptation to forget your friends in Surrey. Five young ladies visit the castle shortly, to remain some time; among them, Miss Alexander, the intimate of Ginna, reputed a perfect paragon of all that is lovely, etc. We anticipate a good time, and wish that you were here, very much, to make it better."

§ 5

THE ATMOSPHERE of love and music and romance, the interlude of gaiety between battles, the free life of the saddle, under the stars, was, however, suddenly interrupted. There were only eighteen men in the signal corps, but the enemy landed a regiment of two or three hundred a mile above and around the bay and some below to capture the signal men and break up the signaling of secret news to Confederate headquarters. "Woodley's scouts were alive by the first hint of dawn lighting the dark mark of Fay's Point, [filed out] of the proposed trap, and [marched in double-quick time to a small] lunette (abandoned the previous year) whence, if driven, there was escape toward the nearest Confederate post on the Blackwater." So Clifford Lanier described the beginning of the attack, and continued: "Lanier was directed to take two men, C—— and E——, and fly to Smithfield Ferry to guard against surprise from the direction of Suffolk. A wise disposition; but when all the next day they returned not, nor any tiding came save distant rifle-shots, and [their comrades, among them Clifford himself,] heard that a small gunboat had steamed up Smithfield Creek, the hearts of those skirmishing under W—— with the main body were low in their breasts having little hope of seeing the detachment of S—— again. A brilliant passage of arms, this eighteen trying to snatch victory from three hundred and making such obstinate show that the three hundred, with some loss, got no farther than a mile from their transport, fighting all day for this, and kept ignorant of the smallness of the force that stubbornly contested every yard through the woods, and finally made successful head behind the mill-dam, wherefrom the enemy thought discreet to retire.

"So spirited an affair was noted in orders and W——'s men were esteemed thereafter as fighters as well as 'waggers' of their heads and signal flags."[38]

Late the next day Lanier and his comrades returned to camp. They had repulsed a boat's crew and prevented it from landing. The next morning the surviving Federals took ship and departed. Not one of Woodley's scouts had been lost, but the enemy had taken their clothes, their cooking utensils, their cots, and—worst of all, for Lanier—their dozen or so precious books, among them a volume of Heine's poems, Mrs. Browning's *Aurora Leigh*, Hugo's *Les Misérables*, Augusta Evans' *Macaria*,[39] a volume of poems by Coleridge, Shelley and Keats, and a German glossary. The lost clothing and camp equipment could be, and eventually was replaced, but books were another matter; as the war progressed they became more difficult to obtain, and to Lanier they were absolutely essential. He wrote to his father to "seize at any price" editions of the German poets, Uhland, Lessing, Schelling, and Tieck.[40] His flute went with him everywhere, in his haversack, and so, fortunately, had not gone the way of the books.

With more books he resumed his studies. Music became more and more a recreation, and to literary pursuits he gave the greater amount of time. To his father, to whom now and always he confided his ambitions, he had written: "Gradually I find that my whole soul is merging into this business of writing, and especially of writing poetry. I am going to try it; and am going to test, in the most rigid way I know, the awful question whether it is my vocation."[41] Only three years before he had written similarly of his talent for music, and now with his Puritan and southern distrust of art as a profession he sought to deny the rightfulness of this newly realized talent for poetry also.

But he enclosed for his father's criticism a number of poems, saying "I have frequently noticed in myself a tendency to a diffuse style; a disposition to push my metaphors too far, employing a multitude of words to heighten the patness of the image and so making of it a *conceit* rather than a metaphor, a fault copiously illustrated in the poetry of Cowley, Waller, Donne, and others of that ilk."[41] This self-analysis is excellent criticism of the poems we have examined, and a wholesome sign in a young poet, but one wonders at the self-assurance and at the tactfulness of his writing thus to his father. Something had happened, however, to stir poetic fires, and to give him this assurance and courage.

What had happened was the result, in part, of the war, in part of his love for Ginna Hankins and the determining influence of a woman—though of a woman no older than himself—who could not only share with him but perhaps, in some measure, direct his reading, and appreciate his compositions; and it was also in part the result of his reading, particularly of Shelley and Carlyle, the former with his high sense of the nobility, even the usefulness, of the poet's calling, and the latter with his many quotations from the German romantic writers and his high sounding phrases about the poet as hero.

§ 6

WITH THIS period of the war, a period of the greatest importance in the development of Lanier's literary powers, both *Thorn-Fruit* and the second part of *Tiger-Lilies* begin. In *Tiger-Lilies* Lanier's first picture of war is an account of a little band of signal scouts rescuing a family from death and assault at the hands of Negro guerillas. As Mrs. Parven says good-bye to her rescuers and

invites them to ride up frequently to dine with her, she thinks
to herself "God help us! It is but the beginning of the raids;
next time, the raiders will be more infuriated, and we may have
no friends at hand." Written before such episodes in fiction
about the Civil War had become conventional, the passage is
probably a description of a real, and brutally unpleasant, experience.

The advance of General Butler upon Petersburg in May, 1864,[42]
broke up the signal line, but Lanier's party was ordered to
remain, and act as scouts in the rear of Butler's army. By dint of
much hiding in the woods and much hard running from lair
to lair they managed to hold their position and to render valuable
service, keeping General French informed of the enemy's movements. Finally, however, they were forced into Petersburg, where
Lee was fighting to hold the city. Here one Sunday Lanier had
the opportunity of seeing General Lee, the idol of his soldiers,
whom Lanier revered as one of the greatest of men. At a memorial
meeting held in Macon a short time after Lee's death in October, 1870, Lanier described the scene, a peaceful interlude in a
week of terrible experiences, with the distant thundering of the
guns playing in sober overtones:

"The last time that I saw [General Lee] with mortal eyes
. . . was at fateful Petersburg on a glorious Sunday morning
whilst the armies of Grant and Butler were investing our last
stronghold there. It had been announced to those who happened
to be stationed in the neighborhood of General Lee's headquarters
that religious services would be conducted on that morning by
Major General Pendleton of the artillery. At the appointed time
I strolled over to Dunn's Hill where General Lee's tent was
pitched and found General Pendleton ensconced under a magnificent tree, and a small party of soldiers with a few ladies from
the dwellings near by, collected about him. In a few moments
General Lee appeared with his camp chair and sat down. The
services began. That terrible battery, Number Five, was firing
very slowly, each report of the great gun making the otherwise
profound silence still more profound. Even Hoke's line was
quiet. I sat down on the grass and gazed with such reverence as
I had never given to mortal man before, upon the grand face
of General Lee.

"He had been greatly fatigued by loss of sleep. As the services
progressed and the immortal words of Christian doctrine came

to our hearts and comforted us, sweet influences born of the liberal sunlight that lay warm upon the grass, of the waving leaves and trembling flowers, seemed to steal over the General's soul. Presently his eyelids closed and he fell gently asleep. Not a muscle of him stirred, not a nerve of his grand countenance twitched, there was no drooping of the head nor bowing of the figure, and I could not have been sure that he really slept had I not observed that a venturesome fly crawled unheeded upon his brow. As he slumbered so, sitting erect with arms folded upon his chest in an attitude of majestic repose such as I never saw assumed by mortal man before: as the large and comfortable words fell from the preacher's lips; as the lazy cannon of the enemy anon hurled a screaming shell to within a few hundred yards of where we sat, as finally a bird flew into the tree overhead and sat and piped small blissful notes in unearthly contrast with the roar of the war engines; it seemed to me as if the present earth floated off through the sunlight and the antique earth returned out of the past and some majestic god sat on a hill sculptured in stone presiding over a terrible yet sublime contest of human passions."[43]

§ 7

THE SCENE of the drama changes with the suddenness of a bursting shell. Lanier was plunged into the fighting at Petersburg of which, in *Tiger-Lilies*, he gives a description comparable in effectiveness with Whitman's lyric drum-taps: "They heard the sound of a cannon booming in the direction of Richmond. Another and another followed. Presently came a loud report which seemed to loosen the battle as a loud thunder-peal releases the rain, and the long musketry-rattle broke forth.

" 'Haygood's having a rough time of it. Let's get there, hearties! It'll be three more of us, anyhow,' said the major, sticking spurs to his horse.

"They approach the outskirts of the storm of battle.

"There lies a man, in bloody rags that were gray, with closed eyes . . . his lips are moving—he is praying.

"The wounded increase. Here is a musket in the road; there is the languid hand that dropped it, pressing its fingers over a blue-edged wound in the breast. Weary pressure, and vain,—the blood flows steadily.

"More muskets, cartridge-boxes, belts, greasy haversacks, strew the ground.

"Here come the stretcher-bearers. They leave a dripping line of blood. 'Walk easy as you kin, boys,' comes from a blanket which four men are carrying by the corners. Easy walking is desirable when each step of your four carriers spurts out the blood afresh, or grates the rough edges of a shot bone in your leg.

"The sound of a thousand voices, eager, hoarse, fierce, all speaking together yet differently, comes through the leaves of the undergrowth. A strange multitudinous noise accompanies it,—a noise like the tremendous sibilation of a mile-long wave just before it breaks. It is the shuffling of two thousand feet as they march over dead leaves. . . .

". . . The rags have rallied. Their line is formed, in the centre floats the cross-banner, to right and left gleam the bayonets like silver flame-jets, unwavering, deadly; these, with a thousand mute tongues, utter a silent yet magnificent menace.

" 'Charge! Steady, men!'

"The rags flutter, the cross-flag spreads out and reveals its symbol, the two thousand sturdy feet in hideous brogans, or without cover, press forward. At first it is a slow and steady movement; stately in the mass, ridiculous if we watch any individual leg, with its knee perhaps showing through an irregular hole in *such* pantaloons!

"The step grows quicker. A few scattering shots from the enemy's retiring skirmishers patter like the first big drops of the shower.

"From the right of the ragged line now comes up a single long cry, as from the leader of a pack of hounds who has found the game. This cry has in it the uncontrollable eagerness of the sleuth-hound, together with a dry harsh quality that conveys an uncompromising hostility. It is the irresistible outflow of some fierce soul immeasurably enraged, and it is tinged with a jubilant tone, as if in anticipation of a speedy triumph and a satisfying revenge. It is a howl, a hoarse battle-cry, a cheer, and a congratulation, all in one.

"They take it up in the centre, they echo it on the left, it swells, it runs along the line as fire leaps along the rigging of a ship. It is as if some one pulled out in succession all the stops of the infernal battle-organ, but only struck one note which they all speak in different voices.

"The gray line nears the blue one, rapidly. It is a thin gray wave, whose flashing foam is the glitter of steel bayonets. It meets with a swell in the ground, shivers a moment, then rolls on.

"Suddenly thousands of tongues, tipped with red and issuing from smoke, speak deadly messages from the blue line. One volley? A thousand would not stop them now. Even if they were not veterans who know that it is safer at this crisis to push on than to fall back, they would still press forward. They have forgotten safety, they have forgotten life and death: their thoughts have converged into a focus which is the one simple idea,—to get to those men in blue, yonder. Rapid firing from the blue line brings yelling from the gray.

"But look! The blue line, which is like a distant strip of sea, curls into little waves; these dash together in groups, then fly apart. The tempest of panic has blown upon it. The blue uniforms fly, flames issue from the gray line, it also breaks, the ragged men run, and the battle had degenerated to a chase."[44]

From this confusion Lanier has his hero, Philip Sterling, rescued by capture and imprisonment, but Lanier's own military experiences were to last a little longer before he was to undergo the imprisonment that for him proved more terrible than dying and more fatal than war. In August, 1864, Major Milligan informed the scouts that he had been ordered to send five of them to Wilmington for duty as signal officers on blockade runners. "No more pork and hard tack. Two hundred dollars a trip in gold—in gold; think of that! And cotton to make money on hand over fist—worse'n h——l beating tanbark!" Thus Clifford Lanier reports him as saying in *Thorn-Fruit*,[45] and proceeds to describe the pleasures reported of the blockade runner's life, the enjoyment of which they too could anticipate with all reasonable expectancy. "Could any more abrupt, more pleasing transition have occurred to a Confederate soldier? Here was no guard duty, no march, no winter-bivouac, no bed of slushy red clay, no Greek fire of mortars. Here was almost absolute quiet; instead of miserable rations, the most delicate viands, seasoned with wines from the world's vintages."[46]

The scouts chosen for blockade duty reported to Richmond and from the Secretary of War received instructions to report to Major General Whiting at Wilmington, the scene, late in the war, of the most brilliant successes of the swift Confederate blockade runners, a port that resisted successfully almost to the end of the war the strenuous efforts of the blockaders.[47]

But before being assigned to naval duty the scouts were stationed near General Beauregard's headquarters above the city,
and saw some service in the trenches. Hopson was encamped
about eight miles from Wilmington, and occasionally Lanier and
his brother could ride out to see him. Other comrades who had
been at Burwell's Bay were close by, and they could drink a
toast "to the beloved friends whose affection formed a common
tie" between them.[48] Letters came from Ginna Hankins, with
whom, indeed, Lanier was to correspond until the end of his
life; and friends in Wilmington whom he had known in the
early months of the war helped to make life pleasant. Lanier
still played the troubadour, singing his way through the war.

On August 24 he wrote to his friend Will Hopson from Smith-
ville, at the mouth of the Cape Fear River: "Ten or twelve
Blockade-runners came into Port within a day or two after our
arrival here, and were immediately placed in strict quarantine,
it being reported that the Yellow Fever was raging in Bermuda,
and even that there were cases on board some of the vessels.
This proceeding somewhat damped our hopes at first, as we did
not like the prospect of being assigned to duty in the forts protecting this harbor, and awaiting the coming of Frost before
we could proceed on our voyages. But the vessels having developed no serious cause of alarm after riding out a Quarantine
term of fifteen days, are being released and allowed to discharge
cargo and re-load. . . . It is reported that there are a number
of new blockaders in foreign ports awaiting Signal Operators to
bring them in; and it is probable that, in the course of two or
three weeks, a large majority of our party will sail from the
Port for that purpose.

"I had a letter from that blessed Brown-eyed child yesterday, which I verily believe to be more beautiful than anything
of the sort I ever saw. The letter was forwarded to me by Benson
from Petersburg, she supposing me still there. I transcribe a
part of it for your edification: 'I am glad that *you* see Mr. Hopson;
but I do not forget that the moving of the Signal Corps pre-
cludes all hope of *my* soon seeing him again. I do not know how
he regards it, but it is a very pleasant fact to me, as you know,
Mister Sid. By the way, did you deliver to him the package
I sent, together with the *big* bundle of kind messages? etc., etc.'
Certainly I did; didn't I, Hoppy?

"With my usual good fortune, I have met here several of the kind friends that I made two years ago in Wilmington. They are spending the summer here, and have introduced me to all the nice people in this truly pleasant village. Insomuch that every day since I have been here various servants, bearing white-covered dishes of delicacies, or fruit, or books, with notes of compliments from the ladies, 'might have been seen' wending their way toward the Signal Quarters where I reside. I'm keep-ing up the Troubadour wandering about the world with a sword at my side, and a lute (or flute) slung on my back with the ribbon of my ladye-love!"[49]

Soon, in spite of protests, Sidney and Clifford Lanier were separated, Clifford being given the first assignment to duty on a blockade runner. October 21 Lanier wrote again to Hopson, this time from the Marine Signal Office at Wilmington:

"I wish I knew how to thank you for this good letter that you send me, and which is the best I've ever seen from you. I could not help airing some of its beauties, and so sent copious extracts from it to our friend Ginna Hankins. I've been waiting to hear from her, that I might send you her comments thereon; but the diabolical mails are so slow that I cannot wait any longer, for fear you might think me under the waves.

"Cliff sailed last night on the Steam Ship 'Talisman' for Nassau. Telegrams from below this morning state that the vessel ran safely through the blockading fleet. She is owned by the 'Albion Trading Company,' E. Solomon, of New Orleans, partner and resident agent at this place. He was very intimate with our cousin, Major Lanier, of New Orleans, and entrusted to Cliff's care a large amount of bonds, besides giving him letters of introduction sufficient to insure his being well taken care of while at Nassau.

"I do not know what time I shall leave here. The imminent prospect of an attack on this place by the Yankees will probably induce the Blockading-firms to keep their vessels in port on the other side of the water, as far as possible. Were it not for this, I should get out very soon, in a week or so; since large numbers of new vessels are waiting at Nassau, Halifax and Bermuda for Pilots and Signal Officers. . . .

"Could you, by any possibility, run down here for a day or so? I have something very particular to consult you about. Oh, Himmel! If you knew!—You'd come. Don't make yourself uneasy trying to guess it; you couldn't do it in a million years.

"I haven't the remotest idea where you are, and so shall send this to Benson. Write me as soon as you receive it, addressing 'care of Lt. Wilmer, Marine Signal Office, Wilmington, N. C.' I am staying in the Office, as clerk, with Frank Hyman, being invited to do so by Lt. W. who is a magnificent fellow."[50]

Clifford Lanier made three exciting trips from Wilmington to Nassau and back, but was wrecked on the last voyage and rescued by a Federal schooner just before his own boat went down. In some way he escaped to Bermuda, and was on the point of sailing for Wilmington as signal officer on the "Maude Campbell" when, hearing of the capture of Wilmington, he went to Havana; and thence—after several weeks of opera and pleasures in that city—to Galveston. From Galveston he walked to Macon, arriving there on May 19, 1865.

§ 8

MEANWHILE, Sidney Lanier had been given an assignment to the "Lucy"[51] and on November 2, a stormy night, he ran the blockade successfully. But fourteen hours later the "Lucy" was captured in the Gulf Stream by the Federal cruiser "Santiago-de-Cuba." Just before the capture the English captain of the "Lucy" ordered Lanier to distribute the ship's money among the crew, which he did. Finding that an old tar had been over-looked, Lanier gave him all his own share except a twenty-dollar gold piece. He refused to don the uniform of his fellow officers and declare himself an Englishman, as he had been urged to do,[52] and submitted to capture. He was carried first to Norfolk, long since fallen to the Federal army, thence to Fortress Monroe (of which he leaves a revolting description in *Tiger-Lilies*), then to Camp Hamilton, and finally to Point Lookout, Maryland, where he spent three months of death in life.

The months of November and the winter were of course the most terrible of all to spend in prison, and Point Lookout was as unpleasant and unhealthy a place as any of the prisons of the Confederacy upon which Walt Whitman cast such burning strictures. When Lanier attempted a description of it in *Tiger-Lilies* he veiled the horrors with an account of the recreations and amusements of prison life, but this account only emphasizes the horrors. His beloved flute, smuggled into prison in his sleeve, was with him, fortunately, and gave some solace to him and to his fellow prisoners. One of them has left a memorable picture of Lanier standing in the cold twilight and playing such notes that the men wept to hear him and for a time forgot their captivity. "The night sky, clear as a dew drop above us, the waters of the Chesapeake far to the east, the long gray beach and the distant pines, seemed all to have found an interpreter in him."[53]

Surrounded by foul disease and awful despair, amid conditions so terrible that Father Tabb, who endured them with Lanier, could never forget them and the war, and could never forgive his enemies, Lanier was to his fellow prisoners a comrade of patience and good cheer. His was the only flute in prison, and he played it almost constantly. As winter progressed and conditions grew worse he still helped to keep up the courage and morale of the men.

The officer in direct charge of the prisoners, Major Brady, Tabb described as "an unprincipled, infamous character." The guards were Negroes, "who stopped at nothing to insult and torture" the prisoners.[54] There was a "lack of food, clothing, proper shelter, hospital accommodation, and sanitation. The camp was nothing but a collection of A-tents and Bell-tents covering about 20 acres, and surrounded by palisades and a heavy guard."[55] The floors were the damp ground: there were no planks, no straw; there was no dry place to sleep on, and no wood was allowed for fire.[56] And because of the infamous retaliatory measures, the prisoners suffered for rations. Almost every prisoner was ill. In an official report of July 1, 1864, Surgeon C. T. Alexander, U. S. A., admitted that the tents at Point Lookout were "old and worn," with six to sixteen men to a tent. The water was bad, his report added, and there was much diarrhœa, dysentery, and typhoid fever, scurvy and itch. The mortality was ten per cent.[57] There is no evidence that in the fall and winter conditions were any better. Tabb himself suffered for two months with diarrhœa, and here definitely began the illness that, aggravating the ill health caused by the hardships of army life and exposure—by James River agues and fevers and winter chills—was to send Lanier home ill beyond the help of doctors and to an early grave. Men died at Point Lookout at the rate of fifteen to twenty a day.[55]

But in this "hell-hole," as Father Tabb himself described it, began a wonderful friendship. Tabb, ill with fever, heard the distant notes of a flute from the opposite side of the camp and resolved to find the player. As soon as he was out of bed he began searching until he found him, and from "that happy moment" until Tabb's release in January, 1865, Tabb and Lanier were almost constantly together. Sometimes they admitted to their company a Polish doctor, an exile from his country and a fellow prisoner, who sang well and talked earnestly on subjects dear to the heart of Lanier—of classical literature and operas and art.

Lanier, convinced at last of the province of poetry in the economy of the world and aware of the inevitability of his vocation, was writing poetry even in the adverse and terrible conditions of Point Lookout prison. Here he made his translations of Heine's "Ein Fichtenbaum steht einsam" ("The Palm and the Pine")[58] and Herder's "Frühlings Grüss" ("Spring Greeting").[59] As translations they have the virtue of being literal, if not smooth. The first stanza of "The Palm and the Pine" is better than the second, which is spoiled by the awkward phrase "a most sad calm" and the harsh sound of the first foot of the last line, "Midst of," which is trochaic and not iambic, the predominating measure of the poem. "Spring Greeting" suggests Tennyson's "Lady of Shalott," with all its immaturity, and the onomatopœic effects of Poe's "Bells," imperfectly understood, more than it does Herder's German lyric.[60] It must be said, however, that the version which Lanier published in 1866 is superior in one line to the version given in the collected *Poems:* there the inclusion of an extra syllable, "e'en," in the fifth line of the second stanza spoils the meter, whereas an extra syllable in the last line would make for smoother reading; and in the first version we do indeed find this extra syllable, "Tell her" appearing there for the monosyllable "Say" of the second version. Probably the fact that he was translating limited and defined his ability, but amateurish as the two poems are, there is something fresh and charming about them, something that comes as much from Lanier's English words as from the original German.

§9

LANIER's physical health had never been robust. Now, weakened by the hardships and exposure of camp life, he quickly succumbed to the conditions by which he was surrounded, developed lung trouble and contracted fever. Finally, toward the end of February, 1865, after almost four months of imprisonment, he was

released, but he was more dead than alive. Some gold which
a friend had smuggled into prison in his mouth is said to have
obtained the release of both. "I made my way home by a long
and painful journey," Lanier wrote briefly to Northrup, but the
journey, coming after the long illness, was more than painful:
it was almost the death of Lanier.

His clothing was too thin to keep out the bitter cold of early
spring during the first part of the trip, the sea voyage, to City
Point, Virginia. For three days the cold was so intense that the
ship was frozen fast in the river, and Lanier with the other
wretched prisoners lay huddled in the hull of the ship, shivering
with cold. On the ship however, as if by the intervention of the
gods who love poets, there happened to be an old friend, the
"little mother" of the Alabama plantation where he had passed
many a day in pleasant summer revery. She had been in New
York for a time during the war, and was then returning with
her daughter Ella—who had long ago learned to call Lanier
"Brother Sid"—to Richmond. The child, playing about the ship
on one of the days when the boat was locked fast in the ice of
the river, heard the notes of a flute, and in childish curiosity
called down to a friend she had made among the prisoners to
ask who was playing.

" 'I was,' he replied, 'but I can't play for shucks. You just
ought to hear a fellow we've got down here, who can play sure
enough. But you'll never hear him: he's dying.'

" 'What's his name?'

" 'Lanier.'

" 'Lanier? What's the rest of it?'

" 'Sidney.' "

It was her Brother Sid! Even her childish mind grasped the
significance of what the man had said: Lanier was down in the
hold of the vessel, dying.

Ella herself won permission from Colonel Mulford, the officer
in charge, to have Lanier taken to her mother's cabin, and she
and her mother hurried below. There, in the rude stalls provided
for cattle, but crowded now with human wretches, they found
him, wrapped in an old quilt, his thin hands tightly clenched,
his eyes fixed and staring, and his wasted body shivering in
spasms of pain. There was no sign of recognition in his eyes,
nor did any response come when they called his name. Brandy
did not revive him, but gurgled down his throat as they poured

it: he was so unconscious that he made no effort to swallow. Several times the stimulant was repeated before Lanier revived, and then, as consciousness came back slowly, he turned his eyes about until he saw his friends. "Am I dead?" he asked. "Is this Ella? Is this heaven?"

His fellow prisoners crouched low and passed him over their heads, for they were so crowded together that it was impossible for them to make room for him to be carried through. In the cabin his friends wrapped him in clean blankets, and moved him near the fire, but he cried out in pain when the warmth of the fire reached him. Hot soup and brandy finally comforted him and he lay quietly until midnight. Then he asked for his flute and began to play.

The notes penetrated to the hull below, and from the shivering prisoners there came a yell of joy. For the first time they were sure that their comrade lived. About him in the cabin sat Mrs. Montgomery and her daughter, and the colonel and his wife, the women weeping softly as the music came in liquid notes from his magic flute.

When the time came for the prisoners to be landed, and he with them, in spite of his condition, Lanier carried his flute to Mrs. Montgomery. His name had not been on the list of prisoners to be exchanged, he said, but a friend, knowing that it meant certain death for him to remain longer in prison, had succeeded in having it added. He was afraid now that the list might be revised, and he be sent back—to die. Would she take the flute, and carry it to Clifford?

Either the list had not been revised, or the officers were merciful, or indifferent, as the other prisoners sought to push Lanier through, but he went ashore. Mrs. Montgomery gave the flute to another prisoner who passed it on shore to Lanier. He waved good-bye, and his friends watched him move away, a pitiful figure wearing an old slouch hat, battered, torn and faded, over the long, thin hair that fell, curling slightly, to his shoulders, and a coat of Confederate gray, given him in pity by some larger and stronger comrade, which fell loosely about his body and "afforded no protection to anything but the insects congregated in the seams of the same."[61] His feet showed bare through tattered shoes, and he walked feebly, but he was alive, and free.[62]

Then began the slow journey through the Carolinas, a painful journey made chiefly on foot though aided once at least by a farmer who, charmed by Lanier's flute playing, hitched up a team to drive him and a companion to an encampment of Georgia cavalrymen.[63] He reached Macon March 15, 1865, utterly exhausted. "Immediately upon my arrival," so he wrote Northrup, "losing the stimulus which had kept me going so long, I fell dangerously ill and remained so for three months—delirious part of the time." After this he was never again to know health or release from the suffering of disease.

CHAPTER FOUR

LITERARY SKIRMISHES

§ 1

MACON, in March, 1865, was crowded with refugees from the regions of Georgia devastated by Sherman on his march to the sea. Food was exceedingly scarce, though the warehouses of the Confederate government—and some of them located in Macon—were well stocked. Everywhere was suffering, illness, want. And worst of all for Lanier, his mother was on the point of death, finding strength to live only in her strong conviction, which she expressed repeatedly, that both her boys would return to her before she should die.[1]

Tuberculosis seems to have occurred frequently in the family. Mrs. Lanier's brother, William Henry Anderson, had died of it; she herself was dying of it; and her son was in the first stages, though the illness that almost brought him to death that spring was erysipelas. In his volume on Florida Lanier confessed that with him consumption "had everything in its favor at the start —the prestige of inheritance on both sides and the powerful reinforcement of a bent student's habits"; but it is noteworthy that neither there nor elsewhere except very rarely in personal letters did Lanier refer to the military experience which was so largely responsible for his own impaired health.[2]

Late in April, just as the immediate crisis in his illness passed and Lanier had begun to convalesce, General Wilson attacked Macon. There were only "inmates of hospitals, boys, old men too helpless to walk, decrepit with age and infirmity, riding in buggies,"[3] to oppose him, and capture was easy. Macon surrendered on April 20. It is not likely that Lanier was among those who attempted to prevent the inevitable. After the surrender the warehouses and commissaries were opened and food was distributed to the delicate ladies, gentlemen, and children who stood in line with the humblest of the citizens to receive the necessities of life from the hands of military agents, who were their enemies. Only a few days more, and the cause had become a lost one.

President Jefferson Davis, fleeing with the Confederate treasure train, surrendered to Federal troops somewhat west of Macon and was brought to Macon and taken to the Lanier House, where General Wilson made his headquarters. It was from Macon a few days later that he started, with Senator C. C. Clay, on the painful journey that led to Fortress Monroe and the long imprisonment. "The hearts of the Southern people bleed," wrote Lanier in *Tiger-Lilies*, "to see how their own act has resulted in the chaining of Mr. Davis, who was as innocent as they, and in the pardon of those who were as guilty as he! All of us, if any of us, either for pardon or for punishment: that is fair, and we are willing."

Now there was peace, "bitter, terrible peace. The last suns of April shone pleasantly on the smoking homesteads of the conquered and the glittering bayonets of the conquerors, to grieved and exultant hearts; on soldiers reveling in camp, other soldiers tramping wearily home; on illuminated cities and darkened villages; on one section jubilant with victory, the other silent with defeat; on demoralization, triumph, woe, want, and death; pomp and misery, laughter and tears."[3]

Clifford arrived in Macon May 19, two months almost to the day after he had left Havana, and penciled the entry in his diary: "Macon. Thank God!"[4] Three days later Mrs. Lanier died. Then, as Lanier wrote Northrup, "we looked about, over the blankest world you can imagine, for some employment." This Clifford found as book-keeper in the Lanier-owned Exchange Hotel of Montgomery, Alabama, but Sidney Lanier's precarious health made any sort of employment impossible for the present, and the summer months of 1865 he passed in Macon with his father and sister, who with many other citizens of Macon were, for mutual comfort and protection and for the sake of economy, boarding at Wesleyan College, which but for these civilian boarders must have closed its doors.

Here, among the boarders at the college, Lanier again met Mary Day. They were thrown much together, but Lanier still saw a great deal of his old friend Gussie Lamar, with whom he passed many hours in music. Macon tradition has it that during the summer of 1865 Lanier was very much in love with her. What the history of that love may have been we can only imagine,

Wesleyan College (Wesleyan Female College), Macon, as it appeared when the Days and the Laniers boarded there for a time after the War.

or guess from one of his poems, for that fall—on September 19—
Gussie Lamar was married to Mr. James Monroe Ogden, a
man of wealth some years older than she.

§ 2

IF LANIER's poem "The Wedding"[5] was written at this time,
as a footnote in the collected edition of his poems suggests, it is
possible that it expresses, though in decidedly overwrought and
poetically conventional language, Lanier's grief. The effect of the
poem as a whole reminds one of certain poems of Poe and even
more of medieval ballads on similar themes, but the figures of
Goodman Death, Groomsman Grief, and Bridesmaid Pain suggest
the old moralities and *Pilgrim's Progress*. Curiously enough, either
because he wrote in passion and carelessly, or simply because
the mixed metaphor did not offend him, Lanier makes himself
speak in the last line of the poem not as a man but as a woman:
"O Death, I am true wife to thee!" But the most interesting
question suggested by the poem is one not to be answered: what
had happened to his affection for Ginna Hankins?[6]

The happier "Wedding-Hymn" grouped with "The Wedding"
on the first publication of the two poems in 1884[7] is almost surely
in honor of Gussie Lamar's marriage. (A footnote to the poem
in the 1884 volume of collected *Poems* reads "Macon, Georgia,
September, 1865.") If both poems were inspired by that occasion,
the first was undoubtedly a private poem and the second was
probably presented by Lanier to the Ogdens as an epithalamium.
This tranquil "Wedding-Hymn" is the more characteristic of
Lanier, and is filled with evidence of his authorship. The first
stanza states his strong, and often repeated, faith in the divinity
of human love; the second stanza anticipates both "Nirvâna"
(1869) and "Opposition" (1879), two of his best poems; the
third stanza recalls the poems addressed to Ginna Hankins; the
poem as a whole may well be compared with "My Springs,"
which, though longer and a more mature piece of work, is not
more expressive of Lanier's high ideal of wedded life.

Of other poems that he may have written at this time, only
"The Dying Words of Stonewall Jackson" can on any evidence
be assigned to the period.[8] This is an excellent poem, in execution and conception perhaps the best Lanier had yet written,
and one cherished in the anthologies of southern poetry, for it
is not so much an elegy for Jackson as for the South. Lanier's

tone here as elsewhere is not one of bitterness but of resignation
and hope. The war had ended; no more battles were to be fought,
and those that had been fought were to be forgotten; but there
is in the poem a hint of the terrible suffering from which there
seemed to be no escape. Its weakness is that some of the phrases
are suggestive of other authors—as is so often the case in the
work of young poets—and that it is also suggestive of almost
every other poem by Lanier that preceded it, and of many that
were to follow. The first line of the second stanza, for instance,
is a paraphrase of the first line of "To ———," the lines

> The Day was dying; his breath
> Wavered away in a hectic gleam;

becoming "And so the Day, about to yield his breath." Both
this line and the first line of the first stanza, "The stars of Night
contain the glittering Day," anticipate "Night," written the
following April, which in turn anticipates the "Evening Song"
written in 1876. But of the three poems, the exquisite "Evening
Song" is by far the best.

§ 3

IN THAT same month of September, 1865, in which Lanier turned
once more to poetry, he took a position as tutor on a large plantation nine miles from Macon, resuming the career of teaching
which the war had interrupted. "I'm busy with brain," he
wrote, " . . . have little leisure . . . thirty classes a day . . .
and failing health prevents sitting up late at night. It almost
maddens me to be confined to the horrible monotony of Tare
and Tret (it should be swear and fret) when my brain is fairly
teeming with beautiful things. . . ."[9]

But relief came quickly. His health proved unequal to the
strain, and the doctor ordered fresh air and rest. From the uncongenial atmosphere of the classroom he escaped to Point Clear
on Mobile Bay where, in the home of an uncle, he spent the
first part of the winter of 1865, living out-of-doors and in the
pine forests as much as possible. As soon as his health improved,
however, it was necessary to seek employment again, and in
January, 1866, Lanier went to Montgomery to join his brother
as bookkeeper and clerk at the Exchange Hotel. This occupation was less confining than that of tutoring, and so for the

present at least the problem of living and of a livelihood seemed adequately solved.

His dreams of Heidelberg and the professorship were over. Northrup, eager to resume the friendship which the war had interrupted, wrote, reminding him of their days together at Midway and their plans for study in Germany, but Lanier knew that such plans belonged to the irrecoverable past. There was even a symbol of his own fate in the dreams that Northrup's letter called up. He was lost in the general wreck that had overtaken Oglethorpe also. President Talmage was dead: the outbreak of hostilities between the North of his birth and the South of his adoption had caused him such mental torture that toward the end of the war his reason had given way and he had died on September 2, 1865, soon after commitment to the insane asylum at Milledgeville. The college, closed during the war, had reopened in 1865, but its existence was precarious, so precarious that even in 1866 the demise which was to occur in 1872 could have been foretold.[10] As for Lanier himself, there was no money for study in Germany or elsewhere, not even for the leisure to give himself wholly to poetry as Paul Hayne was doing in his little shack at, Copse Hill.

But the letter from Northrup called up happy memories, as well. Lanier's answer is dated May 12, 1866: "So wild and high are the big war-waves dashing between '61 and '66, as between two shores, that, looking across their 'rude, imperious surge,' I can scarcely discern any sight or sound of those old peaceful days that you and I passed on the 'sacred soil' of M[idway]. The sweet, half-pastoral tones that should come from out that golden time float to me mixed with battle cries and groans. It was our glorious spring; but, my God! the flowers of it send up sulphurous odors, and their petals are dabbled with blood.

"These things being so, I thank you more than I can well express for your kind letter. It comes to be like a welcome sail, from that old world to this new one, through the war-storms. It takes away the sulphur and the blood-flecks, and drowns out the harsh noises of battle. The two margins of the great gulf which has divided you from me seem approaching each other: I stretch out my hand across the narrowing fissure to grasp yours on the other side. And I wish with all my heart that you and I could spend this ineffable May afternoon under that old oak at Whittakers[11] and 'talk it all over.'

"You must know that Clifford and I lost all we had, and have been compelled to go to hard work for our living. We have, however, through kind friends, obtained positions with good salaries, so that we are free, at least, from the pressure of immediate want. In the moments that we can spare from business we continue our studies, with even more ardor than while we had plenty of time to devote to them. Cliff has finished a novel, written entirely during intervals snatched from business, and I am working upon one which I hope to finish ere long.

"We also hope to get out a volume of poems in the fall written by both of us conjointly. You will laugh at these ambitious schemes when I tell you that we have not yet offered for print a single thing. But we have no newspapers here with circulation enough to excite our ambition, and, of course, the Northern papers are beyond our reach. Our literary life too is a lonely and somewhat cheerless one; for beyond our father, . . . we have not been able to find a single individual who sympathized in such pursuits enough to warrant showing him our little productions,—so scarce is 'general cultivation' here,— but we work on, and hope to become at least recognized as good, orderly citizens in the fair realm of letters yet. There's so much to tell you and so much to hear from you!—Our adventures (I say 'ours,' for Cliff and I were by each other during all the war) would fill, and possibly *will* fill, a volume.

"I'm thirsty to know what is going on in the great art world up there: you have no idea how benighted we all are. I've only recently begun to get into the doings of literary men through the *Round Table*, which I've just commenced taking.

"Write me soon, and believe that I am always
"Your friend,
"SIDNEY LANIER.

"Clifford sends regards. Many of your old friends at the College were killed in battle. Will particularize some other time."

The *Round Table*, the New York literary weekly to which Lanier had subscribed, was infinitely superior to the pretentious magazines and journals that even in the hard times that followed the war sprang up all over the South, and superior to many of the contemporary magazines published in New York and

Boston. The editors, Dorsey Gardner and Henry Sedley, were not men of prominence, but Howells, Aldrich, Stedman, and Stoddard—men whose names were to be reckoned with throughout Lanier's lifetime, whatever we may think of their abilities now—were regular contributors. Foreign letters came from the best correspondents. The book reviews were excellent, and the editorials on current events were sane, fair, and broad in point of view.

Its attitude toward contemporary politics and reconstruction in the South was evidence that there were in the North people magnanimous in their attitude toward southern problems and willing to stretch out their hands in friendship as Lanier himself was eager to do. One editorial on "The Duties of Peace" in the issue for July 7, 1866, is said to have appealed particularly to Lanier[12] as "the most sensible discussion" he had seen of contemporary problems.

This paper influenced Lanier greatly, not only because it recognized his talent and published the poems he soon began to send to it, but because it helped to develop and make coherent his own attitude toward reunion and national life. And this attitude of nationalism and friendliness the editors of the *Round Table* extended to literary questions. To a young, unrecognized poet, clerking in a Montgomery hotel, the editorial in the issue for May 12, 1866—the very day that Lanier wrote his letter to Northrup—must have seemed an invitation: "In fact the literary field was never so barren, never so utterly without hope or life. . . . Who will waken us from this sleep? Who will first show us the first signs of a genuine literary reviving?"[13]

§ 4

LANIER HAD promptly accepted this invitation, and in the issue of the *Round Table* for July 14, under "Literariana: American" appeared a brief note: "The translations from the German below, selected from a number sent us, appear to be very well done. The name of the original author is not stated."—followed by "Spring Greeting," the "Frühlings Grüss" that Lanier had translated in prison, and "To J. L———," an original poem, not a translation, which does not, however, appear with Lanier's collected poems.

To J. L——

A kind war-wave dashed thee and me together;
So we have drifted to the shores of peace,
A wintry shore, attained in wintry weather.
    Must here our loving cease?

Ah, was not ancient Love born of the ocean?
And is not *our* Love a tempest child
That rose from out the seething war's commotion
    And blessed it, as she smiled?

The buffets of this storm I have forgiven,
And all its drunken, rude barbarity,
Aye, I have begged a blessing on't from heaven
    Because it brought me thee!

My soul doth utterly refuse to render
Back to the waters of forgetfulness
This sister-love of thine, that grew more tender
    The greater my distress.

Shall, then, our wave-born love by waves be swallowed,
And foam to foam, as dust to dust, return?
Not so! I never cease to hold it hallowed,
    Nor cease for thee to yearn.

Never cease we, while on this side we wander,
To go like children singing hand in hand,
Until our Father smiles, and calls us yonder
    Into the home-like land.

Who J. L. was has never been told.

In this particular period of Lanier's poetic career the ocean seems to have had an unusual fascination for him. The figure of the waves and the surge of the ocean turns up often not only in the early poems but in *Tiger-Lilies* and in the repeatedly used quotation, the "rude, imperious surge" of war.[14] Perhaps, of course, the ocean had some other significance for Lanier, for some of his happiest and most exciting moments, and some of the most terrible, had been spent near it and on it. Seven years later—ten years after the happy days with the Hankinses at Burwell's Bay—he received from Ginna Hankins a spray of sea-weed and wrote to her in reply: "It is like a wave of the fair blue Southern Ocean, of a far off happy time, this wave that swells with round ripple and delicate murmuring to my strand and lays thereon a serrated leaf and a lock of green sea-hair. How serene must be the bay shore to-day, curving about the waters!"[15] But undoubtedly his literary devotion to the ocean was in part conventional: the ocean is the blood-stream of English poetry.

This fondness for the ocean and a general similarity in style and imagery to poems previously discussed, to "In the Foam," published a little over a year later, and to the sunset poems— "Night," "Evening Song," and "Night and Day"—lead one to believe that another poem, which appeared in the *Round Table* for September 8, 1866, though unsigned and without comment, is also by Lanier.

SEA-FOAM

The Sun is a golden goblet,
    Upflung by the reveler, Day—
How the red wine glows and sparkles
    As he reels on his bacchanal way.

And the mermaids rise, to greet him,
    Up from the coral caves,
And they chant him a chant of welcome
    That sounds like the plash of waves.

They leave the mermen lonely,
    Far down in their dim sea-hall,
And they fawn at the foot of the fair young Day,
    Those fond mermaidens all.

Their passionate, pale faces
    Are upturned pleadingly,
And their shining tresses fall and rise,
    Wreathed with the foam of the sea.

But weary of wine and wassail,
   The Reveler sinks to sleep,
And the wine from the falling goblet
   Pours purple over the deep.

And lo! those sad mermaidens
   Shriek wildly in despair,
And dash white breasts on the cruel rocks
   Among the breakers there.

Then up the mermen swarming
   Laugh loud in scornful glee,
And drag the shining corses
   Far out along the sea.

Their passionless, pale faces[16]
   Are upturned mournfully,
And their trailing tresses fall and rise
   Floating like foam on the sea.[17]

About this time was also written another uncollected poem which Lanier is definitely known to have written for Ella Montgomery, the "little mother's" daughter, and set to music carefully scored for her childish treble.

Her bright soul burned in her dusky eye
Like a silver star in the morning sky,
And my heart, all tired of life's lone night,
Like a bird sang songs to morning light.

As soft as the passion of flowers for dew,
As wild as the waves when tempests woo,
As high as a lark's flight up the blue,
As fair and pure and sweet as you,
   As you, as you, as you.

Oh, exquisite rare!
Oh, past compare,
Was that young star-soul shining there,
In an eye that gleamed dark bright like dawn,
When dews first sparkle on the lawn!

As soft as the passion of flowers for dew,
As wild as the waves when tempests woo,
As high as a lark's flight up the blue,
As fair and pure and sweet as you,
As you, as you, as you.[18]

Though this is probably the least pleasing of all his uncollected poems, it is interesting to study the lines and the musical rhythms in the light of the theories Lanier was to expound later in *The Science of English Verse*, to note the varying lengths of the lines, the musical rests, and the flute-like quality of the refrain. And if we had also the musical accompaniment composed for it we might learn much of Lanier's theory of the relation of poetry and music.

§ 5

WITH LITERARY success of a sort now achieved, with poems accepted and published, Montgomery seemed less dreary. Stirring with ambition, Lanier filled his notebooks with more poems. Moreover, he was also finding outlets—and appreciation—for his musical talents. Once, in a sudden emergency, he had taken the place of the organist in the Presbyterian church and after some demur had accepted the invitation pressed upon him to retain the place. He was as untaught in playing the organ as in playing the flute, and there was little time for practice; furthermore, the choir gave little coöperation; but the work brought its rewards, and alone in the church he would improvise little melodies, sometimes settings for the poems he had written. When the social life of Montgomery with which their aunt, Mrs. Watt, sought to beguile her nephews grew dull, there was the literary club which the Laniers had at last succeeded in organizing to give them not merely social life more congenial to their tastes but an audience, no matter how limited, to hear and comment upon their poems and essays.

Near Montgomery lived Mrs. Mattie Montgomery and her daughter Ella, and at Tuskegee not far away lived other friends and near relatives, the Cloptons and Mrs. Clopton's family, the Ligons. Lanier had been named for Judge David Clopton, and in Judge Clopton's home he and his brother were always welcome.[19] Describing a visit to these good friends in September, 1866, Lanier wrote to his sister: "I have just returned from Tuskegee,

6

where I spent a pleasant week. . . . They fêted me to death, nearly. . . . Indeed, they were all so good and so kind to me, and the fair cousins were so beautiful, that I came back feeling as if I had been in a week's dream of fairyland."[20]

But if fairyland, then only in a dream; for the cruel days of reconstruction had already begun in the South, and in Montgomery the civic stagnation which unjust laws and corrupt government produced was already felt. "You are all so alive, up there," Lanier wrote Northrup,[21] "and we are all so dead, down here. . . . There's not enough attrition of mind on mind, here, to bring out any sparks from a man." And a few years later he wrote of these days to Bayard Taylor as days of living death: "Perhaps you know that with us of the younger generation of the South, since the war, pretty much the whole of life has been merely not dying."[22]

To Northup he wrote again at this period: "I despair of giving you any idea of the mortal stagnation which paralyzes all business here. On our streets Monday is very like Sunday: they show no life, save late in the afternoon, when the girls come out, one by one, and shine and move, just as the stars do an hour later. I don't think there's a man in town who could be induced to go into his neighbor's store and ask 'How's trade?' for he would have to atone for such an insult with his life. Everything is dreamy and drowsy and drone-y. The trees stand like statues; and even when a breeze comes the leaves flutter and dangle idly about as if with languid protest against all disturbance of their perfect rest. The mocking-birds absolutely refuse to sing before twelve o'clock at night, when the air is somewhat cooled and the fire-flies flicker more slowly than I ever saw them before. Our whole world here yawns in a vast and sultry spell of laziness. An 'exposition of sleep' is come over us, as over Sweet Bully Bottom, and we won't wake till winter.

"It is possible that Cliff or I may go North in the fall, with bloody literary designs on some hapless publisher. I anticipate much pleasure in meeting you, if it should be my lot to go. Write me often. Your letters always wake me up from that sleep which I share with my torpid fellow-citizens here."[23]

The description of the apathy that had descended on the South is not exaggerated. Everything had been lost. The lovely estate at Montvale Springs no longer belonged to Lanier's grandfather; members of the Lanier family "who used to roll in wealth

Sidney Lanier in 1866, wearing the uniform of a Confederate soldier. From a carte de visite photograph sent to his friend, Milton Harlow Northrup.

are, every day," he wrote, "with their own hands ploughing the little patch of ground which the war has left them, while their wives do the cooking and washing."[24] His father had had to take up the practice of law from the start. The old civilization had passed away, and the new civilization which was to take its place had not yet been born. "The reign of law . . . was at an end. The civil powers of the states were dead. The military power of the conquerors was not yet organized for civil purposes. The railroad and the telegraph, those most efficient sheriffs of modern times, had fallen in the shock of war. All possible opportunities presented themselves to each man who chose to injure his neighbor with impunity. . . . Never had crime such fair weather for his carnival."[25] The prospect was not realized; the crimes were not committed; but the fear prevailed. The apathy that had settled over the South was one of complete despair.

And with Lanier, as with so many others, it was not only the material losses that mattered. It became increasingly evident that war had robbed him of strength which even the strongest will to live, and do, needs for its support. In July, 1866, he suffered a relapse, and for weeks he was seriously ill, "too ill to think, much less to write. . . . You'll pardon a poor letter"—he is writing again to Northrup[26]—"no bone in me but aches, no nerve but tingles when I cough, shaken by that old bronchitis I caught in your inhospitable Point Lookout prison, there." But in the fall his health was better, and he resumed his literary work.

§ 6

FORTUNE seemed to have turned when, in the early spring of 1867, there came one day into the Exchange Hotel a man whom Lanier recognized from his signature on the register as the Rev. W. J. Scott, editor of *Scott's Monthly*, a magazine of some merit, the publication of which had been begun at Atlanta in December, 1865. (It did not last beyond the decade, for publication ceased with the fourth volume and with the issue for December, 1869.) It was a magazine made up chiefly of reprints of articles from other magazines, or contributions from wholly unknown people, but Hayne and Timrod, recognized as poets of importance even before the war, contributed sometimes to it, as did Bayard Taylor once, and on the whole its make-up was able and dignified.

Scott was the first editor of a magazine of any importance

whom Lanier 'had met, and it seemed to Lanier as if fate had sent him to the Exchange Hotel. "I dread rejection like a mad lover," he had confessed to Northrup,[26] but he advanced bravely and introduced himself to Scott. He had read his magazine, he said, and liked it; he was, he added, in answer to Scott's inquiry, the son of R. S. Lanier of Macon, and a grandson of Sterling Lanier, whom Scott knew and admired as a loyal member of the denomination of which he was an ordained minister. He assured Lanier of his interest in him. So Lanier told more about himself, of college and the war, and then—it is easy to imagine the excitement which he felt—he confessed that he was "an occasional writer of prose and verse," and had even written a novel. Twenty years later in recounting the incident Scott wrote: "I confess that I was charmed, not more by the evidence of his varied accomplishments than by the frankness of his whole personal bearing, and expressed my willingness to secure a contribution for *Scott's Magazine.* On the next day, before leaving the city, I accompanied him to the third floor of the hotel, and, unlocking his trunk, he submitted to me a number of manuscripts—among them a prose article entitled 'Three Waterfalls,' which struck me as being a masterpiece of wit and humor." Scott left the hotel with the manuscript in his possession, and Lanier descended to the hotel desk knowing in his heart that the days of his hotel clerkship were at an end.

Tiger-Lilies was also finished; but to find a publisher Lanier should, he knew, go to New York. So he gave up his work in Montgomery, visited friends in Alabama and Georgia for a while, stayed a few weeks with his father in Macon, and then in April, 1867, moved on to New York and took a room at Number 7 Great Jones Street, just off lower Broadway. On April 11 he wrote to Northrup: "I have serious designs against the publishers here, but as yet have only skirmished afar off, without making any direct attack. Do you know any of them personally?"

Clifford Lanier's *Thorn-Fruit*, which as a novel of plot is far superior to *Tiger-Lilies*, appeared as No. 3 of Blelock's "Library of Select Novels by Southern Authors," a little paper-bound book which sold for fifty cents. The copyright was in the name of Blelock & Co., and the novel was issued by them from their publishing office at 453 Broome Street, New York, some time during 1867. It is quite possible that publication had been arranged for by correspondence. If so, it is also possible that Lanier, either by correspondence or through personal interview, sought to have Blelock & Co. publish his novel, and that it was rejected either because it in some ways duplicated *Thorn-Fruit* or because it was considered an inferior piece of fiction—both valid reasons.

Tiger-Lilies was copyrighted by Lanier in his own name, in the Clerk's office of the District Court for the District of Georgia. Professor Mims states that Lanier "was enabled to publish his book by the generous help of [a distant cousin,] Mr. J. F. D. Lanier."[27] That Lanier himself bore part of the expense of publication—possibly with money borrowed from or donated by Mr. J. F. D. Lanier—seems certain from a letter dated Macon, Georgia, August 21, 1867, addressed to Hurd and Houghton of New York, the publishers who issued *Tiger-Lilies* later that year:

"D'r Sirs:

"Your favors, containing receipt for my draft and announcing arrival of my MS. came promptly.

"I am also in receipt of y'r Mr. H. O. H[oughton]'s letter advising against appointment of Agents: which advice I of course will regard as conclusive.

"Circumstances render it necessary for me to change one or two sentences in the 'Dedication'[28] of my book: and I trust this is the only alteration I shall have to make. Please forward proofs to me at this place.

"If I had y'r Announcement, I could have it extensively noticed by editors South.

"What will be the trade-price of 'Tiger Lilies'?
                    "Very truly, &c.
                              "SIDNEY LANIER."[29]

So Lanier's "serious designs" against the New York publishers seem to have come to nothing. Considering that he visited New York in April and that the manuscript was not sent to the publishers until August, it is quite possible that his efforts to publish in the more usual fashion had been even more prolonged and more discouraging than we know. But certain it is that *Tiger-Lilies* owes its typographical superiority to *Thorn-Fruit* and its attractive binding to the fact that whereas Clifford Lanier found a publisher, Sidney Lanier hired one.

§ 7

BY FAR THE most important result of this visit to New York
was the connection which Lanier then established with Mr.
J. F. D. Lanier and his family. James Franklin Doughty Lanier
had been born in North Carolina in 1800 but had emigrated
to Indiana in his early youth. As a lawyer he was successful
but his fame came as a banker and financier. As early as 1849
he had left Madison, Indiana, where his stately home still stands
—maintained by the state as a memorial to him—and established
an office in New York. At the outbreak of the war he had made
a personal loan of $25,000 to the state of Indiana without stipu-
lation as to interest or the time in which it should be paid. Later
he had made a loan of about $400,000 more to equip Indiana's
first six infantry regiments; and, before the war was over, $640,000
for civil purposes. He had played a prominent part in the development of the railroads of the West, and he had served as
financial adviser to President Lincoln. The friendship with Sidney
Lanier, begun probably at the time of Lanier's visit to New
York in 1867, was destined to last. "He was of genuine help . . .
at critical times in [Sidney Lanier's] life," Professor Mims asserts,[30]
on the basis of information supplied by the Lanier family, and
his son, Mr. Charles Lanier,[31] became a close friend of his distant
younger cousin and, after his death, donated bronze replicas of
Ephraim Keyser's bust of him to Johns Hopkins University and
to the Washington Memorial Library of Macon.[32]

In New York these northern Laniers received their southern
cousin cordially, and for all that Lanier did not like New York
and the spiritual barrenness of the city, he could write in typical
good humor to his father: "The grand array of houses and
ships and rivers and distant hills [seen from Trinity Church
steeple] did not arrest my soul as did the long line of men and
women, which at that height seemed to writhe and contort
itself in its narrow bed of Broadway as in a premature grave.
. . . I have not seen here a single eye that knew of itself to be
in front of a heart—but one, and that was a blue one, and a
child owned it. 'T was the very double of Sissa's eye, so I had
no sooner seen it than I made love to it, with what success you
will hear. On Saturday I dined with J. F. D. Lanier. We had
only a family party. . . . Last and best little Kate Lanier, eight
years old, pearly cheeked, blue eyed, broad of forehead, cherried

i' the lip. About the time the champagne came on I happened
to mention that I had been in prison during the war.

" 'Poor fellow!' says little Katie, 'and how did the rebels treat
you?'

" 'Rebels,' said I, 'I am a rebel myself, Kate!'

" 'What!' she exclaimed, and lifted up her little lilies (when
I say lilies I mean hands), and peered at me curiously with
all her blue eyes astare. 'A live Reb!'

"This phrase in Katie's nursery had taken the time-honored
place of bugaboos, and hobgoblins, and men under the bed.
She could not realize that I, a smooth-faced, slender, ordinary
mortal, in all respects like a common man, should be a live
reb. She was inclined to hate me, as in duty bound.

"I will not describe the manner of siege I laid to her: suffice
it that when I rose to take leave, Katie stood up before [me],
and half blushed, and paused a minute.

"With a coquetry I never saw executed more prettily, 'I
know,' she said, 'that you are dying for a kiss, and you're ashamed
to ask for it. You may take one.' . . . And so in triumph, and
singing poems to all blue eyes, I said good night."[33]

During the summer of 1867 Lanier saw at least two more
of his poems in print: the first part of "The Tournament" was
published in the Round Table for June 8, the first of his poems
to appear other than anonymously, and the second part appeared
in the issue for July 6. His name as he signed it to these poems
is simply Sidney Lanier. The middle name, Clopton, had been
dropped, probably for the sake of euphony. He never used it
again, not even on his marriage license, nor was he to use again
even in personal letters the more familiar signature of Sid Lanier.
Sidney Lanier, poet, had arrived quite definitely on the literary
scene. His formal début as a writer of fiction—a rôle he was to
play but seldom—he made that fall with the publication of "The
Three Waterfalls" in the August and September issues of Scott's
Monthly Magazine.

That a living was not to be earned from publishing subsidized
novels, short lyrics, and an occasional story, Lanier perfectly
well knew, however, and a living wage was essential, for he was
already engaged to be married to Miss Mary Day. But having
no desire for a career as hotel clerk or even proprietor, and no
preparation for the practice of law, there seemed but one thing
for him to do—to resume the profession of pedagogy. Hearing

that the chair of metaphysics in the University of Alabama was vacant, and to be filled, he decided to present himself as a candidate for it. The first thing to do, of course, was to make his candidacy known and to enlist assistance for it. He wrote, therefore, on August 6 to his friend of '63, Mrs. C. C. Clay, whose husband—released sooner than President Davis from his imprisonment—was again in Alabama, and, though taking no part in public life, still a person respected throughout the state and able to wield some influence in Lanier's behalf.

The letter Lanier wrote[34] is amazingly juvenile, as ornate and absurd rhetorically as the worst passages in *Tiger-Lilies*. With its allusions to the journey from Macon to Virginia in '63 and to the tragic failure of their hopes, it reads like the fantastic production of a nightmare—and Lanier lived of course in a nightmare which was far from ended. What system of philosophy he had been studying he did not say, and what the system was that he had "dug up toilsomely in [his] cave" we can only surmise from *Tiger-Lilies*, but the tone of the letter convinces one—and the conviction is strengthened by *Tiger-Lilies*—that his philosophy was, unlike the philosophy of his later years, with its courageous acceptance of opposition, what we should today call a philosophy of escape. *Tiger-Lilies* is, by and large, an account of a land of legend, a Valley Beautiful where Music is God, and love creation's only law. Such a philosophy as Lanier had evolved would surely have suited badly "the needs of practical men," whatever comfort it may have brought to a few troubled souls in those troubled days. But present himself as candidate he intended to do, and if *Tiger-Lilies* was published in time he would offer it, with its "popularized metaphysical discussion," as evidence of his fitness for the desired chair. Failing the availability of his book for the purpose, he planned to publish in pamphlet form a metaphysical essay which he had written, and to distribute copies where they would do the most good in advancing his candidacy.[35]

The subsequent history of his candidacy is unknown. Lanier took for the winter a position in a large academy at Prattville, Alabama, with eighty-six pupils to teach and two assistants under him. " 'T is terrible work, and the labor difficulties, with the recent poor price of cotton, conspire to make the pay very slim," he wrote the sympathetic Northrup.[36] "I think your people can have no idea of the slow terrors with which this winter has invested our life in the South." But the life that gained for Lanier the title of professor, a title he never altogether lost, was more congenial than work in the hotel at Montgomery.

In November, or early December, *Tiger-Lilies* appeared, its publication, announced as early as September, having been delayed, and was enthusiastically received in Macon if nowhere else. Lanier was proud and happy. It meant a great deal to have a book in print and one's name on Hurd and Houghton's list of new books with that of W. D. Howells, the rising young author whose *Italian Journeys* was then first published, and something more to have one's name included with the celebrated names of Mrs. Margaret Preston, Paul Hamilton Hayne, Henry Timrod, Father Ryan, John Reuben Thompson, John Esten Cooke, and William Gilmore Simms as that of a contributor to the new *Southern Society*, of Baltimore. But it was a sign both of Lanier's independence and of his clear-headedness, his complete lack of the sectional pride that has vitiated so much of the literary work produced in the South and has dulled the critical acuteness of its citizens, that he could write of this magazine to Northrup "What a horribly jejune and altogether pointless affair is the *Southern Society* of Baltimore. My name was published as a contributor, but I shall certainly send nothing."[36]

CHAPTER FIVE

THE WAR IN RETROSPECT

§ 1

THE ITALICIZED "will" in Lanier's letter to Northrup of May 12, 1866—"Our adventures . . . would fill, and possibly *will* fill, a volume"—was significant. Lanier, with the reticence and unwillingness to discuss his work characteristic of young authors, was disguising his present activity with a future verb. Their adventures, however, filled two volumes, not one; and it seems almost as if there had been a well understood agreement, a division of adventures as well as of labor.

Of the two novels, *Tiger-Lilies* and *Thorn-Fruit*, Clifford Lanier's *Thorn-Fruit* is the more literally autobiographical in spite of the romantic plot imposed upon actual adventures. The dedication is "To Sidney Lanier"; and in the Preface Clifford wrote: "Here are some men and women as they appeared in '64 and '65 to two human eyes that endeavored to see simply what *was*. That his many faults in art may be traced to an earnest striving after that simplicity of plot and character, which in these days is so beautiful in the best of lives and so rare in the best of novels, is the great hope of The Author." And at the end of Chapter XIX he made an interesting digression: "The author, as he ends this chapter, wishes to speak briefly of his authority. This is partly a story of real character and real events; and, as there is a fancy somewhere of modest sculpture, to the effect that the beautiful figures of Praxiteles and Thorwaldsen are only released, like spirits, from their entombment in the shapeless block of marble, so the author has not built up, like the architect—has hardly used the brush of the painter—has rather chiseled off, like the sculptor." The character of Mark Wilton, moreover, is described in terms that describe Sidney Lanier exactly. We are therefore justified in reading details of Sidney Lanier's military experiences in his brother's novel. For a record of his inner life we must turn to his own novel, a very different sort of book, in which the plot

TIGER-LILIES.

A NOVEL.

BY

SIDNEY LANIER.

For mine is but an humble muse,
And owning but a little art
To lull with song an aching heart,
And give to earthly Love his dues.

Tennyson

NEW YORK:

PUBLISHED BY HURD AND HOUGHTON,

459 BROOME STREET.

1867.

Title-page of "Tiger-Lilies," Lanier's first published volume.
Courtesy of the Library of Congress.

is unimportant but the long discourses of the characters are of
the greatest interest.

Tiger-Lilies begins with an exclamation on the part of Paul
Rübetsahl: *"Himmel! Cospetto! Cielo!* May our nests be built on
the strongest and leafiest bough of the great tree Ygdrasil! May
they be lined with love, soft and warm, and may the storms be
kind to them: Amen, and Amen!" But there follows immediately
a digression on villainous lodging-houses, particularly those of
clay in which the children of Adam live, the tri-daily repairs
of which inevitably limit an author and prevent his plunging
into his beloved music. The digression includes an apostrophe
to one G. Percymon, grocer, who is held before the reader as a
sort of chief vice in the drama, who sees not "the tie betwixt
mess-pork and poetry" and knows not that there is no great
difference "betwixt cutting down the salary of [his] pale book-
keeper, and cutting up the coat of him for whose garments
they cast lots." The opening chapter, which might better have
been made a preface or an allegorical prologue, interpreted
literally seems to be not only a perfectly frank confession of
Lanier's actual poverty but a statement of his belief in the dignity
of the artist's function. Rübetsahl (Rübezahl) is a German word
meaning mountain-sprite. Lanier's Rübetsahl is a haunter of
mountains, a free spirit, and Lanier's transcendental ego.

Chapter II begins with a florid and artificial description of the
scenery of eastern Tennessee where, in Blount County, at the
junction of the Little Tennessee and Holston rivers, on the last
day of September, 1860, Paul Rübetsahl is standing. Philip
Sterling, hunting near by in the company of the mountaineer
Cain Smallin, drops behind his companion and pauses to solilo-
quize. He is overheard by Rübetsahl, who comes forward with
open hand extended and with a quotation on his lips: " 'Life is
too short to be long about the forms of it.' My name's Paul
Rübetsahl." Philip, with "a *penchant* for the love-at-sight theory,"
welcomes Rübetsahl immediately as his friend. The penultimate
paragraph of the chapter is a brief essay on friendship, written
in the spirit and style of Emerson. But Philip Sterling has found
in the mountains, not a friend, but himself.

Both Rübetsahl and Sterling are to be taken as delineations
of Lanier—one of the man most interested in the Ideal, the other
of the man interested in the Real.[1] But both are idealized conceptions: there is a swagger to Sterling that Lanier may at times

have affected but that was not an essential trait of his character, and there is lacking from Rübetsahl's character the sense of merriment and humor so characteristic of Lanier. Of the two characters Sterling is, of course, the more likeable and the more real; and even if his account of his college career is not an uncolored account of Lanier's college career, we are certainly to take it as evidence of the essential manliness—the normal, healthy life and ideas—of a young poet whom sickness had not yet cut off from the affairs of his fellows, making him more and more into a Paul Rübetsahl.

Chapter III introduces us to Philip's father, John Sterling, his guest, John Cranston, who trembles at the mention of Rübetsahl's name, and the Indian, Jim Skaggs. These men, with Cain Smallin (who is to prove the most interesting character in the book), and Philip Sterling are engaged in a deer hunt, but during Philip's meeting with Rübetsahl the deer has been killed, and they arrive just as it is being bled. Sterling leads his guests toward his home, Thalberg, and Lanier interrupts the narrative to recall "that jocund party of friends" in the passage quoted in the second chapter of this book. The description ends with an apostrophe: "Alas, and alas! O jocund hunters of the fall of '60, how hath the 'rude imperious surge' of the big wars tossed us apart, hither and thither! The Grand Tycoon is sunken; he hath gone into a wood contract with railroads, and old Ned languisheth. The Deputy beareth scar of Gettysburg, and yet deeper scars beareth he; I scribble; and poor Lorrie, the ever-genial, went, I hear, at Shiloh, to the happy hunting-grounds!" But the account of these mountains and of the pleasures enacted there is not colored by any sense of loss; the characters move through no aureate mist of nostalgic longing.

Sterling, we are told, had labored unsuccessfully at the law and had longed to live in the mountains, until a rich uncle of his wife's had died, leaving his wealth to her. With this money the Sterlings were able to build Thalberg on a level shelf of one of the Great Smoky Mountains, a house where music is a religious ritual and the spirit of music a household god, making "even the dumb walls eloquent with the harmonies of fair colors."[2] Sterling's guests pause, as they enter the house, to look down over the Valley Beautiful.

Chapter V begins as Chapter II had ended, with a brief essay on friendship, which for Lanier is indistinguishable from love.[3]

In one beautiful sentence he sums up his philosophy of love, which permeates all his poetry, all his critical studies, all his life: "I am quite confident that Love is the only rope thrown out by Heaven to us who have fallen overboard into life." And that love is the theme of *Tiger-Lilies* Lanier makes clear in the Preface and even on the title-page, where he gives a stanza from *In Memoriam*,

> For I am but an earthly Muse,
> And owning but a little art
> To lull with song an aching heart,
> And render human love his dues,

strangely misquoted thus

> For mine is but an humble muse,
> And owning but a little art
> To lull with song an aching heart,
> And give to earthly Love his dues.[4]

At the end of his life, almost at the end of the last lecture of his last lecture course, on The Development of Personality in the English Novel, Lanier speaks to the young artist: "Is it not clear that in the minds of these serious thinkers truth, beauty, wisdom, goodness, love, appear as if they were but orators of one and the same essential God?" How far the implications of his theory extend Lanier suggests even here. "Inasmuch as we love, in so much do we conquer death and flesh," Lanier writes in *Tiger-Lilies*, "by as much as we love, by so much are we gods. For God is love; and could we love as He does, we could be as He is." Lanier's theology is not orthodox, but his faith in love enriches and ennobles life. "And somehow it did not seem strange to anybody at Thalberg that Philip should have found this man wandering among the mountains at sunrise, in that lonely country. For Rübetsahl talked of mountains as he would talk of absent friends; he seemed to have peered into their ravines and nooks as if he were studying a friend's character, and to have slept upon them as on a friend's bosom." The realist will protest of course that this is sheer romantic transcendentalism, the result of too much early reading of Carlyle's essays on the German romanticists. But it is only a slight advance from this

youthful transcendentalism to the Franciscan sense of kinship
with nature that Lanier expressed in his maturity.

"All Mr. Lanier's characters," observed a contemporary critic
in reviewing *Tiger-Lilies*, "are musicians and German scholars."[5]
The nights at Thalberg are filled with music: John Sterling
leads his guests in chorus; Philip plays the flute, his sister Felix
the piano, Rübetsahl sings, and Cranston—the villain of the
piece—is allowed to play Lanier's best loved of all instruments,
the violin. All quote liberally from the romantic essayists—Richter,
Novalis, and Carlyle, and from Shakspere, Wordsworth, Tennyson, and Mrs. Browning, as well as from many half forgotten
poets. But this first night has a strange ending, one almost foretold by Cranston's weird, diabolical playing: Rübetsahl, after
some words in German with Cranston, strikes him with his open
palm, and Cranston falls to the floor, stunned. Philip and Felix
assert their faith in Rübetsahl and implore their father not to
order him away. Before morning comes Cranston has disappeared.

Chapter VI contains a description of John Cranston and something of an apology for his evil ways. It also contains the only
jesting remark about sex that Lanier ever put into print: "When
John C., senior, went about to beget John C., junior, that worthy
and prudent man probably embarked in the only enterprise of
his life in which he could not see his way clear from beginning
to end." This sentence is followed by Prince Rasselas' remark
that "The world must be peopled by marriage, or without it,"
and the reply of the Princess Nekayah: "How the world is to
be peopled is not my care and need not be yours. I see no danger
that the present generation will omit to leave successors behind
them!" a remark Lanier naïvely pretends to believe indicative
of "a cold-blooded shrinking of manifest responsibility." The
digression is as curious and as remotely connected with the main
story as are most of the digressions in *Tiger-Lilies*, but it is the
only one of its kind. The point of the digression is to make clear
that John Cranston grew from the beginning without direction,
and that, therefore, his life at Frankfort-on-the-Main, where
people said he was like Goethe, was, through no fault of his
own, undirected and dissipated; it is most significant in its
revelation of a fundamentally human quality in Lanier.

At Frankfort Cranston had seduced one Ottilie, the fiancée
of Paul Rübetsahl, who, feeling herself disgraced and unworthy
to remain longer in Germany among her friends, took ample

funds and her maid Gretchen and set out for America. Why
she left New York for the wilds of Tennessee we are not told,
but perhaps she was drawn there by love of the mountains. On
the precipitous road between Knoxville dépot and the city,
the horses of Ottilie's hack became unmanageable, and Ottilie
and Gretchen were saved from death by the Indian, Jim Skaggs,
whom Ottilie promptly renamed Chilowee, after the mountain,
thinking his own name too prosaic for so romantic a creature.
Chilowee, we are asked to believe, fell in love with Ottilie at
first sight, and through the rest of the book he hovers about
her like a protecting spirit.

In a little cabin in the mountains to which they were guided
by Chilowee, Ottilie and Gretchen live, communicating with no
one but the neighboring mountaineers, from one of whom
Gretchen learns of the masquerade to be held at Montvale
Springs and learns further that a Mr. Cranston, who is said
to be engaged to Miss Sterling, is to be there. Without telling
Ottilie all that she knows, Gretchen persuades her to attend
the masquerade, and she sends by Chilowee an anonymous note
to Cranston inviting him to an adventure. At the end of Chapter
X we are back where we were at the end of Chapter V: Cranston
left Thalberg on the receipt of Gretchen's note which she had
signed insinuatingly "Frankfort."

Chapter XI introduces us to three new characters who are to
figure more prominently in the second part of *Tiger-Lilies*.
These are B. Chauncey Flemington, John Briggs, and Alfred
Aubrey, who, dressing for the masquerade that evening, discuss
good-naturedly Alfred's courtship of Miss Rebecca Parven and
the plans he has made for Mrs. Parven's costume. The chapter
contains a little real humor but more humor of a cruder, "slap-
stick" variety, as does the description of the ball in the succeeding
chapter. Lanier's sense of humor was seldom subtle: he liked
puns, and minor physical discomfiture amused him tremendously;
the most amusing part of the description of the ball is ridiculous
to the point of utter improbability. It is equally improbable
that Rübetsahl, attired as King Arthur, and Cranston, who
impersonates Lancelot, should fight a duel which almost ends
in the death of Cranston while the spectators look on thinking
it only part of the masquerade.

On the way home from the ball Ottilie, overcome by the
excitement of the evening, faints, but conveniently near Flem-

ington, Briggs, and Aubrey—out to enjoy the night air—and near the road too, a convenient place for John Sterling to discover her. Sterling insists upon taking the ladies to Thalberg, and Philip Sterling invites the three friends—college mates of his—to spend a week with him there. And so once more we are back at Thalberg, with the group larger than before, and the conversation even more rhapsodical and transcendental. Like the "wild disputants" of Novalis' *Heinrich von Ofterdingen*, from which Lanier quotes often,[6] they are under the spell of their surroundings and discuss the effect of nature on human life.

It is John Sterling who expresses Lanier's own attitude toward nature: "Nature is nothing as an end; . . . Nature is everything as a means. Nature is finite in herself; she is infinite in her suggestions. We must not fly to her but to the great Christ she helps us see. Perhaps the mysterious idea of Divinity is like a sentence written backward; we make it out easiest by reflecting it in a mirror. As such a mirror, Nature is a glorious revealer to the sorrowful soul; an infinite-tongued preacher of the Son who is our Father. I do not know the metaphysics; but as a practical man, hunting something to live by through day and night, Sundays and all, I do not want other proof of Christ and his purifying faculty through love, than that fair pageantry [of the brilliant west] out yonder." And to Ottilie's reasonable protest that man reads in Nature what he chooses to read, interpreting it variously to suit various moods, he answers: "I think, through all phases of wavering distortion, the heart will find behind Nature love as well as terror, and will spring to the most powerful of these, which is love."

This, as we shall see, is almost the central idea of the lectures on Shakspere that Lanier delivered in the winter of 1878-79. In similar fashion Philip Sterling anticipates the central, integrating idea of another series of lectures, on the English novel: "And so," he cries, "who can believe all this humbug of Macaulay, that the advance of imagination is inverse to the advance of reason, and that poetry must decline as science flourishes? It is true Homer was at one end, and Newton at the other, of a time. But how long a time intervened between Humboldt and Goethe; how long between Agassiz and Tennyson? Moreover and what is more, one can scarcely tell whether Humboldt and Agassiz were not as good poets as Goethe and Tennyson

were certainly good philosophers! And nothing surprised me
more than that even fine Jamie Hogg must needs fall into this
folly and say, 'Let philosophers ken causes, poets effecks.' " In
the first of the lectures of his last course Lanier refuted at length
the contentions "that Science will destroy all literary art; . . .
that art is to advance by becoming democratic and formless;
and . . . that the future novelist is to enter the service of science
as a police reporter in ordinary for the information of current
sociology."

The essential value of *Tiger-Lilies* is not that it is Lanier's first
book, or his only effort in an art he never again sought to practise, or a fairly close autobiographical record of five years of
his life, but that, as a schoolboy essay on all that seemed to
Lanier most important, it enables us to discover the embryo
form of the ideas we find in his later poetry and prose, to recognize the unfaltering continuity of his development, and to estimate
the influence of the friendship of Professor Woodrow, who initiated
him into the study of science. "Today's science bears not only
fruit, but flowers also!" Flemington remarks. "Poems, as well
as steam-engines, crown its growth in these times." Lanier's
dream was of a time when the flower should be recognized as
quite as essential to life as the fruit, and the poem as the steam-
engine.[7] His point of view, always a catholic one, was as broad
as his interests were varied: no man in America has sought
more voraciously to explore the realms of knowledge to their
furthest limits, to see all things, to understand all things, and
to reduce all things to an intelligible unity, than Sidney Lanier.

And it is not the desire but only the expression of it which
we shall find difficult to comprehend. Lanier creates confusion
by constantly expressing this desire in terms of musical aspiration, believing implicitly that music is the greatest of modern
arts, "in common life what heat is in chemistry, an all-pervading,
ever-present, mysterious genius," without which life itself seems
unconsciousness. He believed that all that poetry and science
had to say, could be said as well or even better in music, and
that as poetry and science seek to reveal the existence and bene-
ficence of God, music should be always an act of worship.
Chapter XV, which is the final chapter of the first part of *Tiger-
Lilies*, ends with music, "a glorious thing of Chopin's," arranged
by Philip Sterling not for an orchestra of instruments but for
an orchestra of voices, though there were no words.

"The whole piece was like life and its end. It started with human yearnings and human failures; the second part brought religion, and the third part spoke of heaven.

"And so, the last notes floated out over the rocks, over the river, over the twilight, to the west. The echoes liked the music, and long after it was over, kept humming little snatches of it, calling to each other to admire, and answering with tiny bravos.

"A breeze came like a courier and told all the trees and the river that the great Night would shortly pass that way; whereat the leaves did stir a moment, and the waters ruffled, as making ready for the King.

"Who came, and sat, and administered his tranquil reign over quiet mountain and quiet valley; and over Thalberg House, not quiet, being full of young and passionate hearts of men and women, some sleeping, some waking, all dreaming."

Thus the idyll of the late summer of 1860 ends. In it we have been given the answer to the question that young Lanier recorded in his college notebook: "Question here: 'What is the province of music in the economy of the world?' " And the answer is the reasoned answer of his maturity—the full maturity that had come in the seven years between, the seven years of contact with a world as real and as bitter and as disillusioning as any poet ever knew.

§ 2

THE SECOND part of *Tiger-Lilies* begins with a chapter on "the blood-red flower of war," a chapter headed by three quotations printed thus:

"Thou shalt not kill."
"Love your enemies."
"Father, forgive them; they know not what they do." *Christ.*

War is described as a strange, enormous, and terrible flower, "a species of the great genus, sin-flower, which is so conspicuous in the flora of all ages and all countries, and whose multifarious leafage and fruitage so far overgrow a land that the violet, or love-genus, has often small chance to show its quiet blue." "It is supposed by some," Lanier writes, "that seed of this American specimen (now dead) yet remain in the land; but as for this author (who, with many friends, suffered from the unhealthy odors of the plant), he could find it in his heart to wish fervently that these seed, if there be verily any, might perish in the germ, utterly out of sight and life and memory and out of the remote hope of resurrection, forever and ever, no matter in whose granary they are cherished!"

It is thus that *Tiger-Lilies* is in no real sense a war-novel, for Lanier would not have glorified war by writing an account of it, and he shrank even from recalling in minute detail the horrors necessary to an indictment of it. An allegorical account in one chapter and in another a confession of sins and a brief defense of Jefferson Davis (suffering, at the time *Tiger-Lilies* was written, in a prison where Lanier himself had been confined): that is all. Though the scenes of the second part of *Tiger-Lilies* are laid in war-stricken Virginia, the war serves only to add further adventures to the lives of the characters previously introduced, and curiously enough the tone here is much less serious than that of the first part. Particularly in the scenes in which Cain Smallin figures is there genuine humor, and the characters behave more like real men in a real world than they ever have before. The novel, as Professor Pattee remarks, "comes suddenly to life. The hero enters the war and all at once there is realism."[8] But as fiction the two chapters that make up the episode of Gorm Smallin's desertion are the best in the book, and almost a short story in themselves—a very real and moving short story in which Lanier, long before Mary Noailles Murfree (Charles Egbert Craddock) used the Tennessee mountaineer, his dialect and his background, with dramatic effectiveness. Cain Smallin, shamed to the heart at the conduct of his brother, says to him: "Hit don't make much diff'ence to me now, whether we whips the Yanks or they whips us. What good'll it do ef we do conquer 'em? Everybody 'll be a-shoutin' an' a-hurrahin' an' they'll leave *us* out of the frolic, for we is kin to a deserter! An' the women'll be a-smilin' on them that has lived to git home, one minute, an' the next they'll be a-weepin for them that's left dead in Virginy an' Pennsylvany an' Tennessy—but *you* won't git home, an' *you* won't be left dead nowher; they cain't neither smile at you nor cry for you; what'll they do ef anybody speaks yer name? Gorm Smallin, they'll lift their heads high an' we'll hang our'n low. They'll scorn ye an' we'll blush for ye." The rhythm of Smallin's speech is, one should note, similar to the rhythm of such beautiful prose as that found in the plays of Synge.

The fighting at Petersburg, Sterling's capture, the dungeon at Fortress Monroe, Gorm Smallin's return to Tennessee, and the prison at Point Lookout—these are well described, and the incidents are treated dramatically, with dramatic effectiveness. One turns from them with regret to Thalberg where Ottilie and Gretchen and Felix and Mr. and Mrs. Sterling have remained during the war. The episode of Gorm Smallin's return and discovery that his cabin has been burned and his wife has died is, however, almost as powerful as the previous scene between Gorm and Cain: Lanier understood the true temper of the common people of the South and their attitude toward the war, intelligently emphasized by recent historians. Smallin's murder of the Sterlings is grim tragedy, understandingly motivated, though the effect is spoiled by Sterling's sermon on music and the religious life, which is as out of place artistically as the "Amen" which he speaks the moment before Gorm's bullet enter his heart.

Part III of *Tiger-Lilies* takes place in the last days of March and the first days of April, 1865. There are only three brief chapters. Ottilie, Gretchen, and Felix are in Richmond, and from Ottilie and Felix, the old love and the new, Rübetsahl in camp at Petersburg receives letters. Flemington, strolling about the desolate city, overhears Gorm Smallin's boasting account of his murder of the Sterlings and witnesses his destruction by a Yankee shell, the falling of which signalizes the beginning of a new bombardment, and the last. Late in the night of the first Sunday of April, Sterling, who has escaped from prison, Cranston, Rübetsahl, Flemington, Aubrey, Briggs, and Cain Smallin, start for Richmond. It is the night of the burning of Richmond, and women they reverence or love are there. And there the characters are paired off as successfully as in a modern musical comedy. Neither Rübetsahl nor Cranston gains Ottilie: she falls to Philip Sterling, who has previously manifested no great interest in her. Aubrey and Rebecca Parven are united, as are Felix Sterling and Paul Rübetsahl. Briggs has disappeared from the story, but Flemington and Cain Smallin grasp hands—to bring the rest (save Gretchen!) to the front of the stage in pairs for the final curtain. Nothing, in comparison with the burning of the city which illuminates for us even this little scene, could seem more trivial. The final sentence is grammatically misleading, for the real subject of the verb is carried to the end, and the subject seems to be Flemington, who has last spoken: " *'Cielo!'* Then, looking down into the deep gray eyes that yearned upward passionately into his own, 'I, the wanderer among mountains, pray: may we build our nests upon the strongest bough of the great tree Ygdrasil, and may love line them soft and warm, and may the storms be kind to them! Amen, and Amen!' said Paul Rübetsahl."

§ 3

ON DECEMBER 16, 1867, Lanier wrote to Northrup: "*Tiger-Lilies* is just out, and has succeeded finely in Macon. I have seen some highly complimentary criticisms in a few New York papers on the book, and what was written in illustration of a very elaborate theory of mine about plots of novels has been mistaken for the 'carelessness of a dreamy' writer: I would I knew some channel through which to put forth this same theory." What this theory was is not easy to say. In a letter to his father of July 13, 1866, Lanier had written: "I have in the last part adopted almost exclusively the dramatic, rather than the descriptive, style which reigns in the earlier portions, interspersed with much high talk. Indeed, the book which I commenced to write in 1863 and have touched at intervals until now, represents in its changes of style almost precisely the change of tone which has gradually been taking place in me all the time. So much so, that it has become highly interesting to me: I seem to see portions of my old self, otherwise forgotten, here preserved."[9] In the light of this admission, made almost a year before *Tiger-Lilies* was offered to a publisher, it seems even useless to attempt to recover the theory. *Tiger-Lilies* is a sort of spiritual autobiography, a continued journal of personal experiences, and the plot was determined by the events of Lanier's own life. Change of events brought a change in the plot. But in the second and third parts there is, strictly speaking, no plot at all.

Lanier's statement of purpose in writing *Tiger-Lilies*, expressed in the Preface to the book, holds, however, for the first half as well as for the second half of the novel: "This book declares itself an unpretending one, whose interest, if it have any, is not a thrill of many murders nor a titillation of dainty crimes. That it has dared to waive this interest, must be attributed neither to youthful temerity nor to the seduction that lies singing in the grass of all rarely-trodden paths, but wholly to a love, strong as it is humble, for what is beautiful in God's Nature and in Man's Art.

"This love . . . begs that the following pages may be judged only as registering a faint cry, sent from a region where there are few artists to happier lands that own many; calling on these last for more sunshine and less night in their art, more virtuous women and fewer Lydia Gwilts,[10] more household sweetness and less Bohemian despair, clearer chords and fewer suspensions, broader quiet skies and shorter grotesque storms." It is in the romantic "high talk" rather than in the story that this cry is made audible. And if Lanier's theory about plots of novels was that the plot should be made subservient to the high talk of the author's didacticism, then we must conclude that Lanier was mistaken in his attempt to write a novel, and should have been writing essays—as we shall soon find him doing. But the truth probably is that Lanier wrote *Tiger-Lilies* as most first novels are written—out of a burning desire to express in one book all that an aspiring author has to say. Judged artistically, therefore, *Tiger-Lilies* is a failure.

For one thing, the book is so crowded with quotations that it is almost a literary scrapbook. The men of the book, said the reviewer of the *Round Table*,[11] "perform prodigies of valor, whiskey drinking, and quotation." Part of this at least is true. In *Thorn-Fruit* the quotations are no more numerous than in the average Victorian novel, but in *Tiger-Lilies* the quotations are so numerous that they interfere with the plot, make the characters seem foppish, and stamp the book as a whole as a product of the college class-room. But these quotations give information concerning Lanier's thought and his reading. The Italian, French, German, and Latin phrases are affectations; the quotations from Shakspere, Tennyson, and Lanier's beloved Carlyle are not. It was chiefly through Carlyle that Lanier knew German literature; it was in part under the influence of Carlyle that Lanier developed his own religious philosophy and his appreciation of the function of poetry; and the quotations from Carlyle, Richter and Novalis are very blood and sinew of the book, while the quotations from Shakspere and even from the contemporary Tennyson are perfectly natural in a book by one with Lanier's heritage.

In his delineation of character—except in the case of the Smallins—Lanier was not successful, but when we seek the reason for this we find the characters are not really conceived as men and women but as personifications, like the characters in a morality play. Rübetsahl, about whom Felix twines her arms "with a yearning smile as of a lost goddess finding heaven," and Ottilie, for instance, are both to be understood as Germany, the country on which Lanier had centered all his dreams of study and music and literature and philosophy. Rübetsahl is also, as we have seen, Lanier's transcendental self. Neither character once appears real, and no characters in the book—with the exception of the Smallins—appear real throughout the length of it. Even the four college friends remain always types.

That Cranston, the villain—though a fairly virtuous one at that—is made a northerner is not to be taken as an expression of Lanier's attitude toward the North. Cranston is not the personified North, but the product of Bohemianism and of Trade, which seemed to Lanier the sources of all evil, and he is made a northerner only because he personifies qualities found more frequently in the North than in the South before the Civil War. Curiously enough, however, Cranston, like Milton's Lucifer, becomes almost the hero of the piece. In the second part of *Tiger-Lilies* he ceases to be a personification and becomes for a while a real, understandable man.

§ 4

To THE critics who examined the book when it first appeared, a first novel by a young and practically unknown poet, it must have seemed a curious puzzle indeed, and it is remarkable that any of them made anything at all out of it. But unpretentious as the volume was, even the *Atlantic Monthly* (then under the editorship of James T. Fields)[11] gave a half page to a review of it. The reviewer felt that Lanier was "saturated with Richter, and redolent of him; and worse still, he has touches of the musical madness which has in these times afflicted persons of sensibility," but considerable promise he did find in it. After a rather facetious summary of the plot he concluded: "The story is full of the best intentions and some very good performances. The author has a genuine feeling for Southern character, and we see some original poetry and natural traits in his people, in spite of Richter and music. But as a whole 'Tiger-Lilies' will not do, though we are not sure that Mr. Lanier will not succeed better in time. There is every element of romance in the life of the South, and he has a clear field before him. There are rogues at the North, too, and he need never be at a loss for villains. If only he will write us a good novel, he may paint us as black as he likes."

But of the reviews, the longest and certainly the best was that which appeared in the *Round Table* for December 14, 1867, which—appearing in the magazine which had already shown him such favor—Lanier must have read with considerable interest: "As the author of some quaint and graceful verses published from time to time in *The Round Table* Mr. Lanier comes to us not unfavorably known. His novel goes far to confirm the good opinion which his poems suggested. We have, indeed, seldom read a first book more pregnant with promise or fuller of the faults which, more surely than precocious perfection, betoken talent. . . . His errors seem to us to be entirely of youth and in the right direction. If we have to complain that Mr. Lanier sometimes forgets he is writing prose, that his characters garnish their talk with more tropes and metaphors than is usual in this workaday world, that his dialogue reads too often like a *catalogue raisonné* of his library, that he offers us only frothy fancies where we look for substantial thoughts, it is still pleasant to find in these vagaries traces of a scholarly and poetic taste. Exuberance is more easily corrected than sterility; and time, which chastens and purifies the imagination, can scarcely supply its wants. When Mr. Lanier learns to 'bridle in his struggling muse' with whatever pain it may cost him, or at least to confine her curvetings to her legitimate province of verse, we hope to have from his pen a better novel than *Tiger-Lilies*—a better one, in fact than any Southern writer has hitherto blest us with. As it is, we are thankful for a Southern book which, without at all disguising its sympathies with the rebellion, is still unmarred by the bad taste of many of its contemporaries in fanning a senseless and profitless sectional rancor. The only chapter where Mr. Lanier strays directly into politics is marked by [his] manly utterance in behalf of Mr. Davis. . . .

"Most readers will find the ending rather abrupt, but it is not inartistic. There are some superfluous characters in the book whose business seems mainly to show the poetic and linguistic attainments of the Southern warrior, and no very original ones. There is, too, in the style a straining after novelty and an affectation of quaintness so marked as to be often unpleasant. But with all its faults the book has uncommon merit; there is a freshness in the treatment, a vivacity and vigor, and in the prison scene, especially, a sense of humor which gives it an honorable distinction from the mass of recent Southern literature. If Mr. Lanier will only remember that Mr. Charles Reade is an author whose faults are so much more easily acquired than his excellences as to make him, for a young writer, the worst possible model, and that long abstract disquisitions on metaphysics and music do not enhance the interest of a work of fiction, we do not hesitate to say that his next book will justify our prophecy of success."

Excellent as this review is, the comparison of *Tiger-Lilies* with the novels of Charles Reade is inept. The obvious master—if Lanier had one—is Jean Paul Richter, who served as master also for one whose own first novel is very blood-brother to *Tiger-Lilies*—Henry Wadsworth Longfellow, little known as the author of a prose "romance," *Hyperion*. Both *Hyperion* and *Tiger-Lilies* belong to the transplanted German romanticism fostered by Carlyle; both have characters named after Jean Paul, Paul Flemming in the one, Paul Rübetsahl in the other;[12] in both, as in the work of Richter, "the serious and the comic, the sublime and the grotesque, the pathetic and the ludicrous, are mingled together";[13] both are interesting in many ways, but both are, as novels, like the novels of Richter also, notable failures. However, the man who could create Cain Smallin was not without ability as a writer of fiction, and we must regret that Lanier did not take to heart the encouragement given him by such understanding critics as those who wrote for the *Atlantic Monthly* and the *Round Table*, and make other attempts at fiction.

In April, 1868, Joel Chandler Harris, then a young man of twenty, working on the Forsyth, Georgia, *Advertiser*, wrote to his brother: "Clifford [Lanier] is very young, but promises good things. Sidney is the cleverest, as you say—in fact, he is a man of genius. His novel, 'Tiger-Lilies,' is original and good. His poems, published from time to time in the 'Round Table,' *are* poems—quaint, unique, and characteristic."[14] Harris's opinion is probably typical of that of most southerners of the time. The publication of *Tiger-Lilies* had made Sidney Lanier's name known: there was even a possibility of a second edition; and he was, undeniably now, one of the rising literary figures of the South. More than this, his novel was an authentic voice from the new

South at a time when the names of Charles Egbert Craddock, Octave Thanet, Irwin Russell, George W. Cable, and Joel Chandler Harris were still unknown.

CHAPTER SIX

RECONSTRUCTION

§ I

THE BETROTHALS into which the war-time romances of *Thorn-Fruit* and *Tiger-Lilies* resolve were not paralleled by the events of real life, though about the time of the publication of their novels both Sidney and Clifford Lanier were married, Clifford on November 26, 1867, and Sidney on December 19. Clifford's bride was Miss Wilhelmina Clopton, daughter of Judge David Clopton, in whose home near Montgomery he and his brother had been frequent guests. Some time during the preceding year Sidney Lanier had described her in a poem[1] in terms that suggest either that hers was the typical Pre-Raphaelite beauty so admired at that period or that Lanier in 1866 was much under Pre-Raphaelite influence. Pre-Raphaelite atmosphere certainly suffuses the letter he wrote on the occasion of the wedding: "My campanulæ, my Bell Flowers, whose silent chimes ring me upward, grow till your top-bells get in among the stars and live on the fire of 'em for dew! My climbing-roses, love is a lattice, from here to Heaven; grow over it and shade the cottage of our life, climb till your sprays lean over by the great white throne and burst into blossoms there as white as Heaven! . . . and drop . . . cool dew of the upper Land upon my hot mouth, which . . . mutters always Blessings, God's Blessings, Dew-Blessings, Sun-Blessings, Rain-Blessings, and South-wind-Blessings upon you who have always been all these blessings to

"Your, S."[2]

There is humor in the letter, but the letter was not intended to be either humorous or facetious in style. Lanier himself must have been quite unconscious of the ridiculous sentimentality of it.[3] But if such his letter to his brother and his brother's bride, then how much more "poetic" (for so things sentimental were

Sidney and Clifford Lanier. A photograph made on Lookout Mountain in 1866. The ladies have been identified as Miss Carrie Lignon (later Mrs. Edward Varner), and her cousin Miss Wilhelmina Clopton (later Mrs. Clifford Lanier). From a magazine reproduction of 1895.

then called) must have been the letters he was writing at this same time to his own fiancée, Mary Day.[4]

One who knew her during this period wrote of her: "Mary Day was a queen! She always wore a long train, walked very slowly, and spoke most deliberately";[5] another has described her as "a tall, slender sweet-faced girl, musically inclined."[6] Hers certainly was the typical Pre-Raphaelite manner, and Lanier, dreaming of blessed damozels, and ladies of Shalott, had probably felt the charm of her presence at their first meeting. During the summer of 1865, when they were fellow boarders at Wesleyan College, their friendship had been renewed, and sometime before August, 1867, when Lanier began to look about for some permanent employment, they had become engaged.

Their courtship, like their marriage, was idyllic, unmarred by quarrel or disagreement. Though Lanier's letters to her written during the period of their engagement have, with a single exception,[7] not been published, a letter written by Mary Day on November 25, 1867, to her friend, Mrs. Cosby Smith, gives us some idea of them. Mrs. Smith was the wife of one of the professors at Wesleyan College, where the Days were still boarding; in November she was away from Macon, visiting elsewhere in Georgia. "Your disconsolate spouse," wrote Mary Day, " . . . desires me in pathetic tone to state that he has taken a new spell in loving you. Whereupon, I observe to him that the aforesaid fact is one of the marked advantages in going away from one's husband. In response he looks dubious and doleful—and sighs like a young lover. (Mine, for instance, bless his sweet heart!) Every letter I receive from Sidney is more and more beautiful and heart-satisfying, and if I had any time for day dreams I could dream over these precious letters all day long."[8] It was the approach of her own wedding day and the preparations for it that prevented day dreaming, for the date had been set and Mary Day was making her own trousseau.

Clifford Lanier, married now, continued as clerk in the Exchange Hotel of Montgomery, eventually becoming the proprietor and one of the successful business men of Montgomery. Not until the last years of his life was he again to find any considerable time for the literary pursuits which were his first real interest, though occasionally he collaborated with his brother in writing poems and he wrote a considerable number of poems alone. His talent for poetry was slight, and little that he wrote is of itself worth preserving, but in 1867 his literary future seemed quite as promising as that of Sidney Lanier, and his renunciation of a literary career was less the result of a realization of the true limits of his ability than a submission to the Course-of-Things to which Sidney Lanier himself for the next few years made almost complete obeisance.[9]

§ 2

IN LESS than a month after his brother's wedding, Sidney Lanier and Mary Day were married at Macon. It is said that Miss Day was an invalid before marriage who "on the doctor's advice took marriage as the remedy."[10] Curiously enough, her health, never strong, proved better than his, and finding strength in the great love she bore him she lived for fifty years after her husband's death,[10a] rearing their children and editing his works, keeping alive and nourishing his fame by her untiring efforts. But in the fourteen years of their married life there were recurring spells of her old malarial complaint, and often husband and wife were ill at the same time, sometimes forced by climates that affected them differently to live apart.

The wedding party gathered at Wesleyan College, and proceeded to Christ Church (Espicopal), of which Miss Day was a member, and there, at four in the afternoon of December 19, 1867, the wedding ceremony took place. Lanier's old friend Campbell procured the license and acted as groomsman, and Granville Connor served also in the wedding party; Hopson was absent in New York. It is said that during the ceremony Mrs. Lanier was so slow in rising from her kneeling position at the altar that she was thought to have fainted; and it is told that when the minister had Lanier repeat "And with all my worldly goods I thee endow," Miss Viola Ross (afterwards Mrs. Anderson Reese), well known as a wit, whispered to her companion, Mrs. Charles Mills, of Griffin, "There go the Tiger Lilies," and that the whisper carried farther than she intended and a titter passed over the congregation.

The wedding ceremony is still talked of in Macon, as is the reception that followed the wedding, held at the home of Mrs. James Monroe Ogden who, as Gussie Lamar, had only a few years before played duets with Lanier and had been supposed to be his sweetheart. At the reception the dress of one of the bridesmaids, a younger sister of Mrs. Ogden, caught fire from an open grate, and there was much confusion before the blaze had been extinguished. Mrs. Lanier had already withdrawn, tired and exhausted, and when the accident was described to her she was "still too weak to feel alarm"—so she wrote, years later—"or even to realize the cruelty of having that bright evening made a blank for me."[11]

That marriage was for him economically very daring Lanier perfectly well knew. Miss Ross's jest was a bitter one, however she may have intended it. But he had written his father: "Not even the wide-mouthed, villainous-nosed, tallow-faced drudgeries of my eighty-fold life can squeeze the sentiment out of me."[12] And the marriage proved to be as rarely beautiful as that of the Brownings. Through illness, poverty, and disappointments their love for each other persisted, prolonging Lanier's life if anything prolonged it, and ennobling them both as only perfect love can ennoble human beings. In his love for his wife, all the faith in Lanier's own heart centered. Their love became the symbol of the power of love everywhere to transform all men and all human experience. Their love so clarified Lanier's thinking that, if he could not always understand the confusions and contradictions with which life is filled, he could yet trust love to preserve her votaries.

This love he recorded in a series of poems—"Life and Song," "June Dreams in January," "In Absence," "Acknowledgment," "My Springs," "Special Pleading," "Evening Song," besides others which contain references to his wife. Reading these poems, imperfect as they often are in expression, one realizes that here for once was perfect love, love of a sort no other American poet has recorded. Such a love was not sentimentally romantic; it was sensual only in that it was complete. For Lanier it gave unity, wholeness to life, a philosophy to be used as a touchstone in the understanding of literature, and unfailing inspiration for the creation of poetry.

§ 3

THE HONEYMOON was brief, and spent in Macon. The wedding journey was a short one, to Prattville, Alabama, where in January Lanier began again the onerous duties of the class room at the Prattville Academy. Prattville was a newly founded manufacturing town with even fewer social alleviations than Montgomery offered; and it was an unhealthy place, for the town was built

on a filled-in quagmire; the climate was damp; and the room
Lanier and his wife occupied at the Mims Hotel could not have
been very comfortable during the winter months. Lanier's pupils
were unruly and his employers hard and exacting. From this
drudgery his persistent playfulness and the happiness of married
life were his only escape. "There is but one man in my school,"
he wrote, "who could lick me in a fair fight, and he thinks me
at once a Samson and a Solomon";[13] but the facetiousness does
not obscure the difficulties of the situation with which Lanier
was confronted.

The winter of 1867-68, moreover, was a severe one; and the
worst years of reconstruction in the South were just beginning. "I
think your people can have no idea of the slow terrors with
which this winter has invested our life in the South," he had
written Northrup only three days before his marriage. One of
the worst terrors was the danger to be feared from the Negroes
who were beginning to feel and to assert their new freedom.
In a letter to his father of January 21, 1868, he wrote: "There
are strong indications here of much bad feeling between the
whites and blacks, especially those engaged in the late row at
this place; and I have fears, which are shared by Mr. Pratt
and many citizens here, that some indiscretion of the more
thoughtless among the whites may plunge us into bloodshed.
The whites have no organization at all, and the affair would
be a mere butchery. . . . The Canton imbroglio may precipitate
matters."[14] From the laws recently passed by Congress there
had resulted, Lanier could state with truth, "such a mass of
crime and hatred and bitterness as even the four terrible years
of war [had] entirely failed to bring about."[15]

This is the period of political corruption that Mr. Claude
Bowers, in a recent study, has called the Tragic Era, and nowhere was the tragedy more immediate than in the South. In
Georgia, one of the states that suffered least under reconstruction, the carpet-bag government was bankrupting the state.
Public life was completely demoralized. Waste worse than any
that the war had produced was evident on every hand. Even
the whites, who had carried on the war so bravely and audaciously, seemed, as Lanier reported, paralyzed into inactivity.
Lanier now spoke out in disgust and indignation. The poems
that he wrote in voicing his protest are neither great nor particularly significant, but their vigor is undeniable, and they

reveal an ability greater than that of the early poems addressed
to Ginna Hankins and the poems of the Montgomery period.
They reveal, too, a talent that was soon to find full and powerful
expression in "Corn," "The Symphony," and "The Psalm of the
West," poems which are indeed much more closely related to
these little semi-political pieces than they are to the more pleasing
and more musical lyrics that Lanier had been writing only a
year before.

First of this group is "Strange Jokes," to which Lanier gave
the bitter subtitle "In a 'Whimsey-Mood.' "[16] It is an exhortation
to courage written in the fullness of Lanier's Christian faith.
But it was difficult to be brave when spring brought no warmth
but only prolonged the desolation of winter barrenness, and
"Spring and Tyranny"[17] is a far more typical expression of the
mood that lethargized the South. To the group belong beside
these two "Laughter in the Senate,"[18] "Our Hills,"[19] and "The
Raven Days,"[20] and an unpublished poem, "Steel in Soft Hands,"
from which Professor Mims quotes a stanza. The irony is that
one who was so willing to forget the past and work for a brighter
future had to face helplessly and quietly the fact that a condition
worse than any in the past prevailed, sanctioned and supported
by the government at Washington. But it is only in "The Raven
Days" that pessimism seems to have colored his mood completely:

> Dumb in the dark, not even God invoking,
> We lie in chains, too weak to be afraid.

In the other poems he expresses in full optimism the conviction
that

> The Dawn will meet us, face to face,
> For down steep hills the Dawn loves best to race![21]

The corruption of the period did not end in 1867, however,
nor during Lanier's lifetime. Indeed, though the Crédit Mobilier
was already an accomplished fact, and the Black Friday bloodshed had already occurred, Grant's eight-year administration
was not yet begun, and corruption had not as yet penetrated
the White House. Listing today the scandals of the decade—the
Salary Grab, the panic of 1873, the Whiskey Ring, the Boss
Tweed affair in New York—the idea of total national depravity

8

is so emphasized that it seems impossible for any legitimate enterprise to have existed, any justice to have been administered, any poet to have had any hope for a better day. That Lanier's literary career coincided with the period of greatest corruption in our national life, and that he constantly reaffirmed his faith in his vision and constantly labored to give the vision actuality, is proof of the high seriousness of his art and the greatness of his spirit.

§ 4

IN JANUARY, 1868, without any immediate warning, a hemorrhage occurred. Lanier's health had improved since the severe and persistent illness of '65, but it was apparent now that consumption had seized upon him, and though there were to be periods of improvement when health seemed restored, Lanier was never a well man again. He must have realized at this time that not only his wife but his health would need more money than he could make as a school teacher or as a writer, for, though he returned to his school in the fall of 1868, at the end of the year he left Prattville to enter his father's law office.

It seems indeed as if Lanier had long before had a presentiment that sooner or later this must be his fate, in common with hundreds of other southern young men of artistic natures. In *Tiger-Lilies* he had written: "Of course John Sterling studied law—what young man in our part of the country did not?"; and almost prophetic seems his further account of John Sterling's career, written many months before he himself was married: "John Sterling junior went forth and committed what may be most properly called a chronological error. He took a wife before he took any fees; surely a grand mistake in point of time, where the fees are essentially necessary to get bread for the wife! Nor was it long before this mistake made itself apparent. Two extra mouths, of little Philip and Felix Sterling, with that horrid propensity to be filled which mouths will exhibit spite of education and the spiritual in man, appeared in his household; outgo began to exceed income; clouds came to obscure the financial sky."

Even so, Lanier was slow in making submission to the apparently inevitable. As late as June 1 he wrote: "I shall go to work on my essays, and on a course of study in German and in the Latin works of Lucretius, whom I have long desired to study";[22]

and music, now as always, absorbed him, so that it seemed to him again, as to others, that music might in spite of everything be the profession that he should follow. In the letter to his brother of April, 1868, previously quoted, Joel Chandler Harris wrote: Sidney Lanier "is the most accomplished flute player in America. There is something weird and mysterious, ravishing and entrancing in his manner of playing. It is absolutely impossible for me to describe it to you. One of his descriptions of flute-playing in 'Tiger-Lilies,' comes near telling it, but you should hear him to appreciate. He is a good, modest, young man, charming in manner." And—Harris might have added—always willing to help fill a program with his playing. Lanier now appeared frequently in public as a soloist; there still exists a program of one concert, given at Wesleyan College July 13, 1868, at which Professor Sidney Lanier played a flute solo, "Sacred Memories."[23] In the economy of the world, the province of music, he must have reasoned, was far more important than the practice of law. Music, he had written to Mary Day, "will revolutionize the world, and that not long hence. . . . The Altar-steps [which lead to the Sanctuary of Music] are wide enough for all the world, and Music inquires not if the worshipper be Vestal or Stained, nor looks to see what dust of other shrines is upon the knees that bend before her. She is utterly unconscious of aught but Love, which pardons all things and receives all natures into the warmth of Its Bosom."[24]

When Lanier did finally submit to studying law—the fate his southern heritage carried, it was probably as the result of some pressure on the part of his father, sympathetic to his artistic interests but intolerant of his professional indecision, and probably also because in September, 1868, his first child, a son, was born. The fact of this child's existence—they christened him Charles Day Lanier, in honor of the maternal grandfather—changed many things. Lanier exhibited him with a naïve, incredulous joy, expatiating in glowing terms upon the delicate beauties of his form and features. To Northrup he described him as "a most rare-lunged, imperious, world-grasping, blue-eyed, kingly mani-kin";[25] and Northrup, traveling in Germany, he envied now not at all. With a happy heart and the desire above everything else to provide his wife and this princely heir with rich luxuries, he began in January, 1869, his work in his father's office.

The firm of Lanier and Anderson was one of the oldest in

Macon, and Lanier's future as a lawyer, both because of his legal heritagè and because partnership in the firm was assured, seemed promising beyond question. He was at first of course merely a hired clerk in the office, reading law in his spare time. By the middle of March he could report to Northrup that he was "well advanced" in his studies, and that he expected to be "admitted to the bar in May next."[26] But in taking up the study of law he had not escaped the suffering of the poet, as is made perfectly clear from a letter of a very different sort written that same day to Paul Hamilton Hayne, with whom he had begun to correspond the year before. "I would not have dared to write to any ordinary correspondent what I wrote you," he confessed, referring to a previous letter, "for I should very surely have been told that I was a lackadaisical fool who needed work and physic. These wonderful hells into which we descend, at such times— who will picture them to one who has not dwelt in them? . . . As for me, however, the good God has seen fit to arm me, very singularly, against the dark hosts of temptations that dwell in these places. The longing for stimulants, which I feel in common, I suppose, with all men of like nature, always defeats itself in my particular case, by awakening a certain *Pride of Pain*, a certain *self-gratulation of Sorrow* (how foolish this sounds!) which enables me to defy the whole damnable troop with a power which seems thoroughly anomalous, in view of the fact that, ordinarily, I do not think my *will* is very strong, because my *sympathies*, which *are* strong, easily override it."[27] However, during this same period of residence in Macon, he began setting his own poems to music—so we are told—simply to escape ennui.[28]

But with Lanier for the time being at work in his father's and uncle's office, hoping that summer might bring more leisure which he might devote to poetry, we may well pause to examine more carefully than we previously have the poetry and the prose (other than *Tiger-Lilies*) that he had already written and published, and at the beginning of his career as a lawyer form some estimate of him as an essayist and as a poet.

§ 5

IT IS THE YEAR 1869, and a convenient year to take as the limit of our survey, for toward the end of that year James Wood Davidson published that curious, frequently erroneous but still valuable collection of information which he called *Living Writers of the South.*[29] Among "the names of 241 writers—166 males and 75 females" contained in it, is that of Sidney Lanier—not of course because Davidson considered Lanier an important or more than usually promising writer, but simply because any living southern man or woman who had ever published a poem or an essay that had come to the notice of Davidson was included. Only three and a half pages were given to Lanier, though almost two pages were given to his brother Clifford, who had published only *Thorn-Fruit* and no poetry, more than eight and a half pages to Mrs. Ada Reedy Vance, ten to Harry Lynden Flash, and four or more to many completely forgotten dilettantes. Lanier's name was included in Davidson's list chiefly for the sake of completeness, but what Davidson had to say about him indicates that even among two hundred and forty-one writers of the South Lanier, though among the youngest, was becoming well known. It is ironic, however, that the one serious typographical error in the volume consists of the duplication of one page from the sketch of Mme. Le Vert in place of the third page of the sketch of Lanier, the writer of the greatest lasting importance to be listed by Davidson.

When Davidson prepared his sketch Lanier had published under his own name some dozen poems, but, except for some fugitive and perhaps lost newspaper letters, only one prose piece besides *Tiger-Lilies*, the story "The Three Waterfalls," which the Rev. Mr. Scott thought a masterpiece of wit. The poems which Davidson should have recognized as by Lanier were "The Tournament," Parts I and II, "A Birthday Song. To S. G.," "Barnacles," "In the Foam," "Spring and Tyranny," "Laughter in the Senate," "Life and Song," "Resurrection," "The Ship of Earth," and "The Raven Days." The first of Lanier's dialect poems, "Thar's More in the Man than Thar is in the Land," may not have been published before Davidson issued his volume. All of Lanier's poems, with the exception of "The Raven Days" and "Thar's More in the Man . . . ," had appeared in the *Round Table*, in which, however, no other poems by Lanier were to appear.

Of these poems Davidson reprinted "Barnacles," which he called a terse little poem "bearing . . . strong marks of the author's individuality," and "The Tournament," Part I, which he thought "really more in our poet's prevailing vein." Lanier's chirograph he analyzed as "rapid, light, and consistent,—indicating freedom from conventionalities of thought and a young man's irksomeness of restraint,—a passion for adventure, with marked self-possession,—a fondness for display, but a horror of humbuggery." And of *Tiger-Lilies* he wrote: "The author disclaims making the bloody sensational his style; and yet we have a little murder and some pretty melodramatic touches. . . . The story is entertaining, and the style lively. The latter is paragraphical and exclamatory; and in a remote way—in its mingling pedantry and raillery, grotesquely together sometimes—it reminds the reader, remotely and just a little, of the *Sketch-Book of Meister Karl*. Italian, French and German words and phrases abound throughout the work." That Davidson so early appreciated Lanier's talents and individuality and so justly estimated his work speaks well for a person about whom and his abilities it is difficult to say much in praise.

But besides the poems that Davidson might have seen in print and those other earlier poems that we have already examined, some thirteen poems by Lanier that were not published until later had been written before the end of the year 1869, and at least three essays, "Retrospects and Prospects," "Nature Metaphors," and the unpublished "Devil Bombs," and one address, delivered at the 1869 commencement exercises of the Furlow Masonic Female College, at Americus, Georgia.

All of Lanier's poems of this period are on serious, often melancholy themes. He had written to Mary Day in October, 1866, of the first prelude in "The Vision of Sir Launfal": "I, except in some supremely happy moment, could never write a piece like this, wherein one finds nothing of that sorrow-tone which forever winds like a black thread through the glittering brocade of Music." His Puritanical cast of thought, his experiences in the war, and his contemporary experience of a life even more terrible caused him to take very seriously indeed such a serious task as the production of poetry, and he was, we must not forget, in spite of his experiences during the war, still immature in many ways at the time most of these poems were written. His seriousness is still, in a measure, the seriousness of youth.

His favorite theme is of course love; of love he writes in terms of natural phenomena, and with a strong and often strained tendency to the personification both of natural phenomena and of abstractions. Both tendencies need be traced no further than to the influence of German poetry which he was so thirstily absorbing, to which influence must also be ascribed Lanier's characteristic and often unfortunate tendency to use compound nouns and nominal adjectives. Manhood is "morn-clear"; Ginna Hankins is called "all Heaven sweet"; night, in Germanic verbal fashion, "oncometh." But of these tendencies Lanier himself was perfectly aware, as we saw in the letter to his father of January 18, 1864. Metaphors, in his work, too easily become conceits, and his style is diffuse.

The poem "To J. L———." is the work of a somewhat more mature poet, but still of a poet whose greatest weakness is verbosity and what appears at first to be affectation. The line "Beat back the backward-thrusting sea" in the poem "In the Foam"[30] is certainly a bad line, as is the line "My lissome-armed sea-Britomart; and the phrase "the water-bass" in the same poem is not only confusing but ridiculous. And yet "In the Foam" is the sincere expression of an experience—separation—common to all poets and most men, and in a figure that is powerful and commands attention, although it is a curious poem for Lanier to have written December 10, 1867,[31] nine days before his wedding, to which the poem cannot possibly have reference.

The poem "Night,"[32] written, according to Mrs. Lanier, in April, 1866, though not published until 1884, illustrates still another tendency in Lanier's poetry, or rather the first stage in the development of a habit which was to become one of his chief characteristics, and something of an original contribution to the art of poetry. This is the use of an historic fact or character or, and more often, of an incident or character from Shakspere to give descriptive force to a natural phenomenon. The lines in "Night"—

> Like the round pearl that Egypt drunk in wine
> The sun half sinks i' the brimming rosy brine—

Lanier actually reworked. In the "Evening Song," written eleven years later, they became

> Now in the sea's red vintage melts the sun,
> As Egypt's pearl dissolved in rosy wine,
> And Cleopatra night drinks all.

In similar fashion Othello's slaying of Desdemona as a metaphor
of sunset is used in "Night and Day,"[33] written in 1866, and in
"The Dove," written in 1877; while in *Tiger-Lilies* the figure
had also appeared, though there it was varied somewhat, with
the moonlight upon the mountains described as Desdemona's
"dainty white hand upon Othello's brow." But Lanier at this
time, like most southerners, was using Shakspere chiefly for
decorative—or oratorical—purposes; the real appreciation of
Shakspere on the part of Lanier was to come much later.

The influence of Shelley, Keats, and Wordsworth is less apparent than that of Shakspere, but it is real, and we know that
Lanier was still reading the works of these poets. The contemporary poet who had the greatest influence on Lanier's early
poetry was Tennyson. Lanier had set songs by Tennyson to
music for his flute; from "The Idylls of the King" he quoted
often in *Tiger-Lilies;* and in "In Memoriam" he found a poem
appealing so greatly to him that he read and reread it and
absorbed the spirit of it. The opening stanza of the unfinished
poem "To J. D. H. (Killed at Surrey C. H., October, 1866)"[34]
seems almost a paraphrase, in spite of the slight difference in
stanzaic form, from Tennyson:

> Dear friend, forgive a wild lament
> Insanely following thy flight.
> I would not cumber thine ascent
> Nor drag thee back into the night.

Like most young poets Lanier liked to contemplate death,
and his elegiac poems are as unoriginal and as uninspired as
most of the memorial poems of the lugubrious period in which
his boyhood was passed. Even "A Sea-shore Grave,"[35] written
in memory of their mother by Sidney and Clifford Lanier, seems
uninspired and insincere. Rose Hill Cemetery in Macon, where
Mrs. Lanier is buried, is washed by the river, not by the sea;
the geographical error typifies the emotional falsification. The
poem as a whole is trivial and contributes nothing to Lanier's
reputation. The "yelling wave" is perhaps the least forgivable
of all Lanier's strained fancies, and one would like to excuse him
by blaming Clifford for it.

Better is the little uncollected "Song" which Clifford and
Sidney Lanier also wrote together, and probably at this time:

Day is a silver veil
God draws across the stars;
Night is a mourning-veil
The heavens wear for wars;
Life is a bridal veil,
Cross-wrought with gems and scars.

Day dazzles, and destroys
The mellow lights of truth;
Night blinds us to our joys
With tears for the day's ruth;
Life's cross-work vague decoys
The strong right arm of youth.

Ere long, through noon-day fire
Truth's stars burn all the time;
Ere long, the heavens tire
Of Night's sad pantomime;
Ere long, Life's veiled desire
In God finds rest sublime.

But this too is funereal and in the "In Memoriam" tradition.

Tennyson was, however, a favorite author not merely because he had written one of the most beautiful elegies in the English language, and had retold in dignified and often splendid verse the stories of the *Morte Darthur*, possibly already familiar to Lanier, but also because his emphasis on love and friendship appealed to Lanier's sentimental, affectionate nature. *Tiger-Lilies* is a glorification of love and friendship, and its philosophy, so far as Lanier may be said to have given his book one, is a philosophy of love. The golden rule becomes in such a philosophy an Emersonian injunction, and love for friends and love for wife and love for God become confused. "These three," we are told, "chime like bells in a steeple to call us to worship, which is, to work. Three notes to a full chord, say the musicians; and this is the three-toned harmony our world should make, in this immense musical festival of the stars." In "The Symphony" we shall find music defined as "Love in search of a word."

Understanding this, one understands better why Lanier's interests turned naturally to the life and literature of the Middle Ages, the period in which the greatest philosophical confusion of earthly and heavenly love took place. "The Tournament,"[36] for better reasons than Davidson perhaps guessed, is therefore typical of Lanier. But the inspiration for "The Tournament" need not have been solely literary. Before and even during the war, tournaments were held often in the southern states; men on horseback, armed with hickory lances, rode past posts from which rings were suspended, collecting the rings on the end of their lances for the glory of their ladies. Popular these tournaments were, and Lanier may well have witnessed several; but, if he did not, he could easily have called up from the remembered reading of his youth the vision of a medieval one. "Joust the First" of "The Tournament," published in the *Round Table* for June 8, 1867, was, according to Mrs. Lanier, written in May, 1862. But Lanier himself referred to a poem written for Ginna Hankins in 1863 as the first he had written in "many years," and this half of "The Tournament" has a simplicity and directness of statement, a smoothness and freedom of versification missing from his early work and from much of his later work, and a lucid objectivity that is truly medieval. "Joust the Second," written June 15, 1867, lacks, however, the qualities of "Joust the First," and it is, incidentally, twice as long. The story is less interesting and the poem is even more didactic, and to spoil it completely there is a moral tag. Nine years later Lanier incorporated "Joust the First" into "The Psalm of the West" as an allegory of the Civil War. This fact serves to emphasize the essential modernness of his medievalism; southern chivalry was with him no hollow phrase; the Civil War, rightly or wrongly, he invested with chivalric glories.

Out of his interest in the Middle Ages had come, during his college days, the conception for the long poem planned all his life as his masterpiece. Later we shall see that in spite of the medieval setting, the poem was to have modern implications: the theme of "The Jacquerie" was to be the relation of trade to chivalry and social unrest. But it is hardly likely that the didactic undertone had been thought of at the time Lanier began composing songs for "The Jacquerie." In "May the maiden," "The sun has kissed the violet sea" ("Betrayal"), and "The hound was cuffed"[37] there is at least no indication of this; instead of revealing a concern with social problems they reveal rather an interest in verse technique. They were undoubtedly composed for musical settings—which others besides Lanier have given one of them[38]

—and suggest the semi-operatic nature of Lanier's first conception of "The Jacquerie."

We have seen that Lanier wrote no poems on the war, unless "The Tournament" is to be understood as such; from the spiritual implications of war and battle, from the devastation that it wreaks on the human soul, he shrank with horror. We do not know what Indian philosophy Lanier had read at this time; it is even doubtful if he had as yet read Fitzgerald's translation of Omar Khayyám's "Rubáiyát"; but an oriental preoccupation with the problem of existence becomes apparent in his poetry. There is a subtle connection, for the full understanding of which we have not as yet sufficient evidence, between "Night," written in April, 1866, "A Birthday Song. To S. G.," published in July, 1867,[39] "The Ship of Earth," published in November, 1868,[40] and "Nirvâna," published in March, 1870. In "Night" the following stanzas seem most important, and—placed between the timidly conventional opening and closing stanzas—in curious company:

> Now the swift sail of straining life is furled,
> And through the stillness of my soul is whirled
> The throbbing of the hearts of half the world.

> I hear the cries that follow Birth and Death.
> I hear huge Pestilence draw his vaporous breath;
> "Beware, prepare, or else ye die!" he saith.

In the poem "A Birthday Song," addressed probably to the son of his sister, Gertrude Lanier Gibson, these stanzas are echoed, thus:

> For ever wave, for ever float and shine
> Before my yearning eyes, oh! dream of mine
> Wherein I dreamed that time was like a vine,

> A creeping rose, that clomb a height of dread
> Out of the sea of Birth, all filled with dead,
> Up to the brilliant cloud of Death o'erhead.

> This vine bore many blossoms, which were years.
> Their petals, red with joy, or bleached by tears,
> Waved to and fro i' the winds of hopes and fears.

Here all men clung, each hanging by his spray.
Anon, one dropped; his neighbor 'gan to pray;
And so they clung and dropped and prayed, alway.

The compliment paid to the newly born S. G. in the remaining
three stanzas, strained and uncertain though it is, is also oriental.
He is a "lately-opened bloom" whose "visible perfume" draws
the poet "Straight through the cloud of death, where men are
free," to a superior height. All that we can say for certain, however, of the subject matter of these two poems (both written, it
should be observed, in the same metrical and rhyming schemes)
is that they offer evidence that Lanier was, for a time at least,
fascinated by the parallel facts of Birth and Death—abstractions
from which he was never to escape—and genuinely interested in
Hindu literature.

In "Strange Jokes" he introduced the problem of Birth and
Death again, and with macabre effect: to Eve in Eden Death
talks of life:

—"Death, on Life"—
As if he knew!

And the poem becomes a gruesome pun:

Well: Death is a huge omnivorous Toad
.   .   .   .   .
Who fears the hungry Toad? Not I!
He but unfetters me to fly.
The German still, when one is dead,
Cries out "Der Tod!"
But, pilgrims, Christ will walk ahead
And clear the road.

The poem is effective enough—if one can forget the pun.

On the metrical side we have found Lanier seldom using the
same stanzaic form, but experimenting constantly with new
forms and variants of old forms. If we examine even superficially
the forty poems that may be said with some certainty to have
been written before the end of the year 1869 (two of which,
"Wedding Bells" and "Her bright soul burned in her dusky eye,"
are irregular in meter and in rhyme scheme), we find Lanier

using twenty different rhyme schemes and an even greater number of metrical schemes. Only six rhyme schemes does he use more than once and only two—a-b-a-b and a-a-a-b—more than twice. The rhyme scheme a-b-a-b he uses twelve times, but not always with the same metrical scheme: "The Palm and the Pine," "Resurrection," and "The Ship of Earth" are more different than alike. He uses, too, nine different varieties of the quatrain, which differ in rhyme scheme: a-b-a-b, a-a-b-b, a-b-c-b, a-b-b-a, a-a-a-A,[41] a-a-b-A, a-a-a-B, a-b-a-B, and A-b-b-A; and the poems written according to these schemes differ metrically also. Even in poems marked by regularity of rhyme scheme we find irregularity of meter, and often an extra, internal rhyme; sometimes the rhyme is buried. Our conclusion must, therefore, be that from the first Lanier displayed in his own poetic practice that boldness in the use of meter and of forms which in *The Science of English Verse* (1880), he was to justify and to advocate. The logical development is, of course, toward greater irregularity in rhyme scheme, meter, and stanzaic forms, and Lanier's early poetry points correctly the direction his development was to take.

But it is not this irregularity—whether of rhyme or meter—which, as some critics declare, is the essential weakness of Lanier. The weakness is that in his early poetry as in his scientific study of verse he too often forgets that sound is not to be divorced from meaning: when the sound is emphasized too much, as in "Night and Day," the effect is sing-song; and when the meaning of a stanza is unimportant, no matter how well handled the sound, the effect is trivial. "Spring and Tyranny," for instance, is a vigorous poem spoiled by a single stanza:

> Before your birth
> Burn up, O Roses! with your dainty flame.
> Good Violets, sweet Violets, hide shame
> Below the earth.

This is quite as bad as any of the conventional flower poetry of the period. Lanier mentions in all his poetry not more than a dozen flowers, but these repeatedly; and of these most frequently the rose, the violet, and the lily—the flowers of sentimentalism.[42] It is this sentimentalism in his vocabulary, and not an over-melodiousness in his verse, that vitiates so much of his poetry.

But "Spring and Tyranny" is not a sentimental poem; it is a

peculiarly bitter poem, and effective because of its bitterness.
There is bitterness too of a sort in "The Raven Days" and "Laughter in the Senate," though the tone is, on the whole, as Mrs.
Lanier pointed out,[43] one of anguished remonstrance. Tournaments are all very well as distractions, but in these poems Lanier
attempts no Cabellian escape from reality. If he did not write
poetry of the war, he wrote poetry of the period of reconstruction, and he is almost the only poet to have done do.

And out of these desperate years was to come one poem which,
though one hesitates to call it great, yet approaches greatness.
In "Life and Song,"[44] so often quoted in reference to his own
life and poetry, Lanier expressed with simple beauty and great
effectiveness an ideal of life born out of Christianity, and a love
of beauty, and the inexpressible joy of wedded life. One thinks
of Milton's splendid sentence "that he who would not be frustrate
of his hope to write well hereafter in laudable things, ought
himself to be a true poem." It is not merely a sentimental fancy
to feel that Lanier's own life from this time forward was to express
what he sang so well in this little song written almost at the
beginning of his poetic career.

Critics have almost without exception admired it, and antholo-
gists have reprinted it. Even at the time of its original publica-
tion it enjoyed definite popularity: printed in the *Round Table* for
September 5, 1868, it was reprinted in the October issues of
both the *New Eclectic Magazine* of Baltimore and *Scott's Monthly
Magazine* of Atlanta. Here was the fame that comes of approval.
In the popularity it gained, as well as in the ability it revealed,
"Life and Song" was the first success of Lanier's poetic career.

That all the succeeding poems do not come up to the standard
set by "Life and Song" is of course to be expected. "The Golden
Wedding,"[45] written for the fiftieth wedding anniversary of his
grandparents, Sterling and Sarah Lanier, celebrated in September, 1868, is, after all, "occasional verse," as is, in a sense "Baby
Charley";[46] and both are mediocre poems. "Resurrection,"[47]
though it recalls "Night" and has a pleasing, musical lilt in its
lines, is not much better. But "The Ship of Earth" is quite as fine
as "Life and Song," and very different. It is essentially one of the
political pieces, one of the flowers of the evil days of reconstruction, and as such it belongs with "The Raven Days," "Laughter
in the Senate," and "Our Hills," but it is better than any of
these. The figure of the ship leads one, of course, to think of

Tennyson's "Crossing the Bar," and of Whitman's "O Captain,
My Captain." It is as dignified as either, noble and vigorous.
As originally published the two stanzas given in the collected
Poems were preceded by two others, which make the figure even
clearer:

> Enough the earth has rested in the harbor of the night,
> With south winds blowing farewell kisses to one linger-
>   ing star,
> She drifts on tides that bear her to yon black-shored light
> Whose silver breakers flash and foam upon the eastern bar;
>
> To sway all day upon the buoyant playing of the sea,
> Or lie, when noon is high, a calmly undulating barque,
> Or sail before the gale of eve, that blows her fast and free
> Past the bright sunset-harbor lights into the peaceful dark.

The last lines even more strongly suggest Whitman's "O Captain,
My Captain," which Lanier, however, did not read until eight
years later, and emphasize the anguish that Lanier, and others
in the South, suffered in the uncertain days through which they
were then passing. In them he cries:

> A pilot, GOD, a pilot! for the helm is left awry,
> And the best sailors in the ship lie there among the dead!

Whether it was from such poems as these or from Lanier's
chirograph that Davidson gave his rather shrewd analysis of
Lanier's character, there was in existence even when Davidson's
book was published one poem which he could not have seen,
a poem not published until some time after Lanier's death,
which of all Lanier's poems best reveals his character, and comes
most directly from his heart. It is "June Dreams in January,"
written in January, 1869.[48] The first part, the description of a
June night, is a lovely, musical "Southern Night Song,"[49] containing some exquisite lines, but in comparison with the rest of
the poem it is unimportant; it is the second part, the sixty-nine
lines in blank verse, which really matters. That Lanier is here
telling a true story literally is not to be believed, but the poem
reveals accurately enough his poverty, and his ambitions, and
the place that poetry held in his heart.

"Read me," he cried, and rose, and stamped his foot
Impatiently at Heaven,—"Read me this!"
(Putting the inquiry full in the face of God.)
"Why can we poets dream us beauty, so;
But cannot dream us bread? Wh/, now, can I
Make, aye, create this fervid throbbing June
Out of the chill, chill matter of my soul,
Yet cannot make a poorest penny-loaf
Out of this same chill matter; no, not one
For Mary though she starved upon my breast?"

And then, when the poem, sent to an editor by an artist friend,
has been accepted:

the poet wept,
And Mary slept with happy drops a-gleam
Upon long lashes of her serene eyes,
From twentieth reading of her poet's news,
Quick-sent. "O Sweet, my Sweet! to dream is power;
And I can dream thee bread and dream thee wine;
And I will dream thee robes and gems, dear Love,
To clothe thy holy loveliness withal;
And I will dream thee here to live by me—
Thee and my little man thou hold'st at breast,
Come, Name, come, Fame, and kiss my Sweetheart's feet!"

Had Lanier written more often thus, his reputation would be
greater today, for there are qualities here to recommend the poem
to a generation that admires Robinson and Frost. The utter
reality of the poem is far removed from the Tennysonian echoes,
the Shaksperean metaphors, the oriental personifications of his
earlier verse. It is a poem that, like "Life and Song," promises
much; and Lanier, in his heart, must have known that his submission to the unavoidable necessity of making a living which
had taken him to the study of law was not surrender. He knew
that he was a poet, and that as a poet he must live.

§ 6

EXCEPT for the great happiness with which he must have taken
up the writing of *Tiger-Lilies*, it is doubtful if Lanier ever put
into the writing of prose the enthusiasm with which he com-

posed poetry. One finds but seldom in his prose—and only in the university lectures and some of the personal letters—that sense of joy in prose-expression which Lamb, Emerson, and other essayists have put into their work. Nor is the absence of this feeling of affection for the medium he is using to be attributed to any discouragement arising from the rejection of the volume of essays he had begun to write just after the war and had submitted to a literary agent in the spring of 1869. The very titles of the essays indicate that Lanier was a scientist and scholar possibly, but an essayist in the truest sense of the word never. These essays on "The Oversight of Modern Philosophy," "Cause and Effect," "Time and Space," and "The Solecisms of Mathematics,"[50] written by such an amateur could have been neither convincing nor very interesting: perhaps they were little more than the olla podrida of his college studies that could not be fitted into the scheme of *Tiger-Lilies*. "Devil Bombs," one of the early essays, of which a part has been printed by Professor Mims and already quoted here,[51] is indeed repetitious of *Tiger-Lilies*, as is "The Three Waterfalls," in a different sort of way. The essay suggests the allegorical chapter on the war; while the story suggests the absurd episode of Mrs. Parven's entrance at the masquerade, and the juvenile humor of the novel.

"The Three Waterfalls" as a story is negligible and somewhat confused, and the point of the whole piece seems to have been to make as many puns as possible. The three waterfalls of the title refer to the three breakings of the heroine's *chignon*, known colloquially as a waterfall. The opening sentence is characteristic of others: "An individual of renown, in ancient days, was lowered into his grave by a raisin in his throat." Most of the puns are far-fetched, but obvious: "A budding tree invariably brings a sense of releaf to my limbs"; "I would not like to see this volume bound in muslin, for I do not believe in muzzling the press." When the hero first encounters the heroine they engage in a veritable tournament of puns, but the worst come at the last: when the hero and heroine are brought together in the court-room we are told that "The minutes of the court were of but secondary importance, for the day was hours." "I am quite sure," wrote Scott years later, "that [this story] will be considered by the better class of readers as one of the finest specimens of classical punning within the wide range of American literature."

But times have changed, and unless changing times make puns once more in fashion and a pun a sign of wit, "The Three Water-falls" may well be allowed to lie decently interred in the dusty volumes of Scott's short-lived magazine.

"Retrospects and Prospects," which Lanier wrote sometime after his return from New York in the spring of 1867 and rewrote later when he prepared it for the *Southern Magazine* (the former *New Eclectic* of Baltimore), in which it appeared in the spring of 1871,[52] is perhaps typical of the essays in the rejected volume, and therefore of Lanier's early attempts at expository prose. The essay, as the title suggests, is a comment on the times, and Lanier attempts bravely to survey the progress of the world in the arts and sciences. The fundamental weakness of the essay is, accordingly, one against which every college freshman is warned from the beginning of his course in English composition, one that comes from failure to limit the subject. Lanier's mind, it is true, was encyclopædic in its interests, but not in wealth of information. When he discusses poetry and music he is sure of his ground, but his experience with architecture was limited, con-fined largely to picture books and the neo-classic buildings of the South, though he had of course been to New York, and seen Trinity Church, which he admired; and his experience with sculpture and painting was even more limited, and probably a vicarious experience derived from the reading of Ruskin.[53] Though the essay ends with a discussion of the contemporary political situation, not only of America but of the world, the central and major part of the essay is given to a discussion of music, which, as in *Tiger-Lilies*, Lanier exalts as the great modern art, the art that he expected to usher in the spiritual renaissance which seemed to him inevitable. His language here is hyperbolic and more than ecstatic. Even in "The Symphony" he showed more restraint. Comparing himself to a medical student and music to the student's sweetheart, he asks if he is to be expected to "strip off the pearly skin and dissect the dainty limbs, in order to improve his science?" But this is just what Lanier was to do with poetry ten years later, and, realizing this, one realizes that after all "Retrospects and Prospects" is only a youthful essay and that Lanier was yet to demonstrate the growth both in artistic power and critical perception which every true artist undergoes.

His discussion of politics in "Retrospects and Prospects" is in-

teresting. That Lanier in 1867 was able to perceive the "etherealization" (by which he meant the enlightened purification) taking
place in government, in spite of the check given national politics
by the politicians who were in control after the death of Lincoln,
is remarkable, and greatly to his credit. He speaks of the fear felt
in the South that the disastrous termination of the war would
demoralize the southern soldiers and make them a menace to
the country, a fear proved false when the soldiers returned
quietly to their homes and set themselves to the orderly tasks
of peace. It was indeed because the southern soldiers and citizens
had behaved so well that the mistaken policies of the reconstruction governments were so inexcusable. "Who," he asks, "will find
words to express his sorrowful surprise at that total absence of
philosophic insight into the age which has resulted in those
hundreds of laws recently promulgated by the reigning body in
the United States; laws which, if from no other cause at least from
sheer multiplicity, are wholly at variance with the genius of
the time and of the people . . . ?" There follows a denunciation
of war reminiscent of that in *Tiger-Lilies*. War is unnecessary
and unchristian, and it must soon be banished from the face of
the earth. Three brief paragraphs on the religious changes and
the religious uncertainties of the time end with the prediction
that "as the era just now closed was an era of political revolution, [so] the era just now opening [will] be an era of religious
revolution." But it is difficult to say definitely what Lanier
expected from the religious revolution that he predicted. Of one
thing, however, we can be certain—Lanier was convinced that
the revolution was to be ushered in by and to proceed to the
accompaniment of such music as the world had not yet heard.

"Nature-Metaphors," an essay written about a year later,
though not published until 1872,[54] is an adolescent, confused,
and not easily understandable statement of what is practically
the same doctrine; but though less readable than "Retrospects
and Prospects" it is a far more important piece of work, one
that repays study, for "Nature-Metaphors" is packed with many
interesting ideas that Lanier was to develop in later lectures and
other essays. A nature-metaphor (the definition is partially buried
in the essay, and may for convenience be put into bolder relief
here) is "a union of human nature with physical nature," of
spirit with matter, a union in which spirit gains form and matter
gains immortality. Nature-metaphors occur usually in the spon-

taneous expression of the poet, arising like vapors from his heart, not coming like ideas from his brain. But they are, nevertheless, often expressions of profound truths, and always, as evidence of man's broadened love for the universe, evidence of the "etherealization" of man. Lanier was well aware of the difficulty of expressing his idea in words in such a way that his readers might understand the idea and grasp the significance of it. "If indeed my words convey any trace of those ideas which are so intangible that they cannot be directly imparted but only chance-awakened by some happy suggestion" comes, almost at the end of the essay, as a sort of apology. Happily, however, Lanier has by his suggestions stirred the mind of the reader; and in spite of digressions and in spite too of the overly numerous quotations from the *Gita-Govinda*, the *Æneid*, and *The Tempest*, the reader follows Lanier's thoughts to the final explicit declaration that "in spite of the cries of the distressed theologians . . . that the . . . world is given over to materialism, the open-eyed observer of our era must decide that all those important institutions of society which depend for their well being on spiritual strength and knowledge and loving sympathy, are now far in advance of the best olden times." The superiority of modern nature-metaphors over ancient ones is but another proof of religious and spiritual progress—the only sort of progress that is of significance.

The digressions in the essay reveal Lanier as speculating already on the difference between classical quantity and quantity in English verse—speculation that will come to fruition ten years later in *The Science of English Verse*, and speculating also on the difference between the idea of marriage developed in Plato's *Republic* and the idea of marriage developed in Tennyson's "Princess"—speculation that reaches its fruition in the 1881 lecture course popularly known as "The English Novel." There are digressions, too, on form in art, which we shall want to remember as we read Lanier's elaborate defense of form in *The Science of English Verse* and those last lectures intended as lectures on English prose. But "Nature-Metaphors" is most interesting for the revelations it affords of Lanier's philosophy. As in *Tiger-Lilies*, it is a philosophy of love—love for God, and man, and nature; as in *Shakspere and His Forerunners* it is a philosophy rooted deep in nature, which is both creation and revelation of God. Nowhere else, however, does Lanier say as explicitly as he does here, "Indeed, the cries of the theologians in favor of idealims are based upon a mistaken notion, and are full of harm which it will be the province of our nature-metaphors in some measure to counteract. For idealism, as a sole theory of life, is no better than materialism, and each is bad if dissociated from the other."

Such a statement illustrates Clifford Lanier's remark that in Sidney Lanier the Real and the Ideal were twin rulers, and indicates the essentially practical, intelligent, and reasonable quality of Lanier's thinking—his essential common sense. It is doubtful if in the year previous, when he sought the chair of metaphysics at the University of Alabama, Lanier had arrived at any such definite philosophic conclusion. But in even a year's time he had grown intellectually as well as in artistic power; and he had begun to wake from the nightmare of reconstruction days. "Nature-Metaphors," in spite of digressions, is a better constructed piece of work than anything he had previously accomplished, and the tone is quieter. In *Shakspere and His Forerunners* he expresses the same ideas with more clarity, and with greater beauty of language, but in "Nature-Metaphors," written at least eight years earlier, he gives ample proof of having already evolved a philosophy to which he may cling, which will direct his intellectual, spiritual, and artistic development. Of all Lanier's essays it is the one that most surely merits preservation.

§ 7

WHEN WE turn from the poetry and the essays of this first period of Lanier's artistic development to the remaining body of his literary work, his personal letters, we find the same weaknesses of conception that we found in the poetry, the same peculiarities of style that mar *Tiger-Lilies* and the essays, but we also find a revelation of the man who somehow eludes us in most of his poetry, who is obscured by the thinker in the essays. The letters to Hopson and to Northrup and to his father already quoted give evidence of this, but fuller revelation comes in the better known series of letters to Hayne.

Paul Hamilton Hayne at some time before 1869 had seen a poem by Lanier which he felt to be "distinguished by a peculiar and scarcely definable quality of fancy," and had written a letter of appreciation which proved to be the beginning of a full and interesting correspondence. Hayne's characterization of Lanier's letters is most interesting. "Their quaintness of thought and phraseology," he wrote in 1886, "seemed at first to indicate affectation,—an affectation of archaism; but soon I learned to understand that this style was as natural to Lanier as breathing." This quality came, Hayne observed, from much reading "of the earlier English annalists and poets," but the chief defect of Lanier's style, whether in prose or poetry, he pointed out, was not merely a defect of phraseology: it was a "deep, over-refining intellectuality, with its searching introspections, German rather than English," and for this the reading of his college days, continued in the army, of Carlyle and the German romanticists, is not alone responsible. A keen mind, directed from youth in the ways of Calvinistic orthodoxy, was after all a ready vessel into which the brew of German ideas and Carlylean interpretations might be poured. The notable quality that the letters reveal as the poems do not is one of common humanity—seen in confessions of despair, in an admission of a longing for stimulants, and in a perfect frankness undisguised by pride.

The defects mentioned by Hayne, were, however, deeply rooted, and Lanier never rid himself of them completely, nor is there any evidence that he tried. Objectivity in his poetry is rare, and equally rare even in his letters. Serious as the business of life is, serious as it was for Lanier, we are forced to admit that in literary expression at least he took himself far too seriously. He lacked too much a sense of proportion and of appropriateness; and he lacked too, for all his sense of merriment, the kind of sense of humor that would have allowed him to smile at his own exuberance and extravagances. "Dear Mr. Hayne," he exclaims in an early letter to Hayne, written in praise of Hayne's poem "Daphles: An Argive Story," "thou hast here made Death *aainty!*"[55] And the later letters to Peacock, we shall find, reveal many of the defects of these early letters to Hayne, though the careful editing of William Roscoe Thayer has obscured the defects somewhat in the published versions.

In his poetry, as in his prose, Lanier yielded little to changing customs and took but seldom the advice of friends for changes in his poems. The truth is that though he sang in "Barnacles"[56]

> Old Past, let go, and drop i' the sea
> Till fathomless waters cover thee!
> For I am living, but thou are dead;
> Thou drawest back, I strive ahead,

and wrote in *The Science of English Verse* the boldest attack on conventional verse forms that had, at the time, appeared—not excepting Walt Whitman's—he loved outmoded forms of expression and he remained in his manner of writing almost as much a man of the past as a child of the future; it was only when he found in the mysterious way that is inspiration freedom from outworn poetic devices, not only from the old and rigid forms but from the archaic idioms and the conventionally musical sounds which in his heart he loved and only toward the very end of his life appeared consciously willing to surrender, that his poetry became simple and easy, natural and spontaneous, and achieved the beauty for which poetry is remembered.

CHAPTER SEVEN

A FALLOW FIELD

§ 1

IT IS, however, a man thoroughly alive to the present that
the year 1869 introduces to us. The typical note of his character is sounded clearly in a letter of November 19, 1869,
written to his brother Clifford, who had been urging him to go
into the cotton-mill business. "I have a far more feasible project,
which I have been long incubating," Lanier replied; "let us go
to Brunswick. We know something of the law, and are rapidly
knowing more; it is a business which is far better than that of
any salaried officer could be. . . . It is best that you`and I
make up our minds immediately to be lawyers, *nothing but lawyers*,
good lawyers, and *successful* lawyers; and direct all our energies
to this end. We are too far in life to change our course now; it
would be greatly disadvantageous to both of us. Therefore, to
the law, Boy. It is your vocation; stick to it: It will presently
reward you for your devotion."[1] The plan of going to Brunswick,
where Mrs. Lanier had relatives, did not materialize, but for
two years more Lanier remained in his father's law office at
Macon. His activity was confined to the office, and he never
practised in the courts, but his work is said to have been accurate
and carefully executed, and the abstracts of titles recorded in
his neat and careful hand still exist, a tangible record of four
dull and unrewarding years.

The business of the firm sent him to New York at least once,
in April, 1869, and he felt then, as he had felt at the time of his
first visit in 1867, a fascination in the hurry and rush of the city
which he was to recall nine years later when he discovered *Leaves
of Grass* and read Whitman's descriptions of Manhattan. His
cousins, the New York Laniers, received him as a lawyer as
cordially as—and perhaps more approvingly than—they had as
a novelist. He visited their country place on the Hudson, near
Poughkeepsie; and in the city there were, to absorb his time,

"teas, dinners, calls, visits, business."[2] The remark made in a letter to his father that he was beginning "to feel entirely unflurried in the crowd and to go about business deliberately" suggests that he was outgrowing the uneasy provincialism which had made him feel overly self-conscious before and that the urbanity of his nature was beginning to develop. In New York (where he remained almost a month) he could hear good music well performed, something for which his soul had hungered in vain in Macon, where the most music he had was in Tuesday night practising with Mrs. S. M. Boykin at the piano and Vincent Czurda, professor at the College, playing the violin.[3]

§ 2

ENCOURAGED by the sympathetic criticism of Paul Hamilton Hayne—the most notable southern man of letters of the period, and one of the purest spirits in American literature—Lanier continued to write poetry, though he published but seldom: two poems in 1870, three in 1871, and none at all in 1872 or 1873, though in these four years four prose pieces were given print, and others—not published until much later—were written. His major literary activity of this period—for with Lanier it was more literary than oratorical—consisted in delivering public addresses, of which five have been preserved and published.

The first of these is the uncollected commencement address delivered before the Furlow Masonic Female College of Americus, Georgia, on June 30, 1869. Stating as his subject "the present condition and future prospect of some great departments of life in that peculiar portion of the United States which we inhabit"— the South—Lanier boldly added that he had no intentions of flattering. Bright though the possible future of the South might be, he said, there was little cause for pride in her present condition, the blame for which could not be laid wholly to the recently ended war. The condition arose rather as the result of certain social problems, which he wished to discuss.

The first problem on which he spoke was the growing emancipation of women. "I hear certain deluded sisters of yours," he admitted with reluctance, "crying aloud that women must vote, that women must hold political office, that women must be lawyers and physicians and ministers. . . . But listen. On the instant, when this cause shall have attained its accursed object, . . . on that instant we will love you not. . . . As voters, we could not love you, for you would be no whit different from men, and men do not love men. As lawyers, as ministers, as physicians, we can not possibly love you; we ourselves are all these, and we want something *beside* ourselves; we want two in one, and not one in two.[4] . . . The question is simple: will you rule our votes, or rule our voters? At the ballot-box, you can control the votes; at home, you can control the voters."

Old-fashioned as this may seem, and wiser though it might be for a modern biographer to attempt no defense of Lanier's contention that women should keep out of politics, one must insist that Lanier's attitude was at least well reasoned and far from narrow-minded. He was not forgetting, he reminded his audience, that they were the sisters, the sweethearts, the wives, and the mothers whose heroic conduct had inspired the men of the South during the War for Southern Independence, "those faithful women who have so loved, who have so lost but who, thanks to Almighty God, have so survived the Southern Confederacy!" In urging women to reject female political suffrage he was not urging them to reject female influence in politics. "So far from that, you can not, if you would, abandon that responsible attitude which in all ages and in all nations women have maintained towards the State. Consciously or unconsciously, directly or indirectly, silently or loudly, you *must* be a political power. . . . I pledge you the faith of all history and all philosophy, if you keep the private house pure, then the State-house will never become hopelessly corrupt; if you exhibit to us lofty ideals of womanly dignity at home, then the national Senate will not go, as it has gone, mumming and capering in clownish follies, utterly unrebuked; if you deal with daily cares in candor and sincerity, then all the sooner will the nation abandon its shuffling diplomacies, to substitute the broad and winning integrities of honest statesmanship." It is a society in which men and women have mutually supplementary and complementary but never identical duties that Lanier envisaged. In "Life and Song" he had written "One perfect self of man and wife"; and in the fourth sonnet of "Acknowledgment," a little sequence addressed to Mrs. Lanier, he was to write five years later:

> By the more height of thy sweet stature grown,
>   Twice-eyed with thy gray vision set in mine,

I ken far lands to wifeless men unknown,
I compass stars for one-sexed eyes too fine.

Such an attitude as Lanier's is classical and antique, and perhaps
not in vogue at the present; but it cannot be dismissed as merely
old-fashioned.

All women, Lanier thought, should be as noble and cultivated
as Tennyson's Princess, and the women who had come to listen
to him deliver this address he complimented by proceeding to
speak to them of "those elements, either good or evil, which the
departing war left in our agricultural system." From the poverty
and desolation that came in the wake of war the South had
sprung, Phoenix-like, to a new prosperity; the dire prophecies
with which southern newspapers were filled after the war, to the
effect that the South would never, could never recover from the
blight of war, had been proved false. Everywhere heartening
results of new agricultural efforts, only four years old, were to
be seen. "But as we felicitate ourselves upon them," Lanier
added, "let us not forget to accept and digest the lessons which
they learn us. Let us not forget, for instance, to accept and
digest the unpalatable truth that we, here in the South, are
among the crudest theorizers in the world. We put together too
many unsubstantial hypotheses. Day after day our public journals
are filled with letters whose conclusions rest neither on logic nor
on fact. I fear we are inordinately fond of predicting, of supposing, of prophesying, in agricultural matters. Let us learn to delay
our conclusions until we have gathered together many facts,
until we have taken all large and many-sided views, and above
all, until we have actually tried them by material weights and
measures. . . . Do not announce your projects before they are
born; do not bury them before they are dead. Think, labor,
wait."

This was bold criticism, criticism the South is not yet willing
to hear. But Lanier went even further: "I cannot leave this
subject without referring, in sorrowful fashion, to a certain in-
sidious evil, which, especially since the war, has been the very
bane and poison of all our humble artistic endeavor here in the
South. I mean the habit of inviting purchasers to buy artists'
works, *simply* because they happen to be Southern artists. I mean
the habit of regarding our literature as *Southern* literature, our
poetry as *Southern poetry*, our pictures as Southern pictures. I mean

the habit of glossing over the intrinsic defects of artistic productions by appealing to the Southern sympathies of the artist's countrymen.[5] . . . The basis of all this is unsound, and if we erect any superstructure of Art upon it, the whole building will inevitably topple into disgraceful ruin. For, the basis of it is hate, and Art will have nothing to do with hate." There is in the history of our literature probably no criticism of a section more trenchant than this.

Four principles he stated as essential if one is to produce any art worth while: "First, Art is a genuine creation. Second, God is the first Creator, and therefore the first Artist. Third, God is Love, and Love only is creative, while Satan is Hate, and Hate only is destructive. Therefore, Fourth, every artist must be like God, that is, must be full of love, which is creative, and empty of hate, which is destructive." But this love is not, Lanier insisted, "a sentimentality." "It is the grand overmastering passion for all that is noble in human life, and for all that is beautiful in natural organism, which each man and woman of us brings, in more or less vivid brightness, out of childhood into later life. . . . If then we would be genuine artists, let us love true Love,[6] let us hate false Hate. If we sing, let us sing for the ear of the whole world; if we write, let us write for all the nations of all the ages; if we paint, let us paint for the eye of time; if we build, let us build for the cosmopolitan taste of the myriad diverse people whom destiny will speedily pour into the length and breadth of our land."

There is more, of course, in the address than this, but this much is central, and it is on this thought that the address also ends. We shall find the message repeated many times—not always, as here, in the surviving, high-flown, rhetorical style of antebellum oratory, but always with the certainty that had led him to assert in "Life and Song" that song must be only a living aloud and life itself a work of art.

§ 3

THREE MEMORIAL addresses by Lanier that have been preserved and printed fall somewhat below the standard of this commencement address, but only because Lanier spoke on set subjects that were less noble and less important than the subject of our national life; the subjects set he treated adequately, vigorously, and with much of the beauty of expression that characterizes the best parts of his published lectures. Like the collegiate commencement address (and the later Sunday school address) they are melancholy in tone, partly because they are memorial addresses, partly because of Lanier's own somewhat Jaques-like temperament, but partly too because, in spite of a firm determination to look to the future, with the bright promise it offered, it was impossible for Lanier not to reflect to some extent the attitude of the suffering of his people.

The "Confederate Memorial Address," delivered April 26, 1870, and printed the next day in the Macon *Daily Telegraph*,[7] is therefore, as we should expect to find it, mournful, somewhat exuberant in phraseology, and for the most part discreetly conventional, but it is also much more. Beginning with appropriate reference to the trees and the heavens and the Ocmulgee, winding placidly about Macon's Rose Hill Cemetery, where the address was made, Lanier proceeded to discuss the nobility of southern manhood and womanhood, and to pay tribute to the memories that "exhale from these graves to meet and greet the fragrance" of the memorial flowers brought to decorate them. For us the address is most interesting because of the references to Trade, against which Lanier was to inveigh more and more indignantly in his letters and in his poetry, and to the river, which moves unhastingly and yet unresistingly "onward to destruction." It is Trade that fills modern life with such noise and confusion that there is no quiet in which to think and ponder and grow in wisdom; as a result of which condition "Crudity, immaturity, unripeness, acidity, instability . . . characterize our laws, our literature, all our thought, our politics, our social life, our loves and hates, our self-development." The observance of Memorial Day should teach us the value of silence. The trees should in like manner teach us stateliness, "an antique virtue," rare these days; the heavens, tranquillity, though the land be "stung half to madness" by the conqueror's lash; and the river, patience in the face of the inevitable, and unselfishness in the performance of duty. (The lesson of the river, it will be observed, becomes the theme of "The Song of the Chattahoochee.")

There is, and notably, in this memorial address as in the commencement address, but more notably here because of the occasion, no rehearsal of buried issues. Professor Mims characterizes it well in saying: "Lanier is not yet national in his point of view, but he represents the best attitude of mind that could be held by the most liberal of Southerners at that time."[8] The key to the address is in the appeal to the men and women of the South to rise to the plane of tranquillity and magnanimity: "Who in all the world needs tranquillity more than we? I know not a deeper question in our Southern life at this present time, than how we shall bear our load of wrong and injury with the calmness and tranquil dignity that become men and women who would be great in misfortune. . . . Today we are here for love and not for hate. Today we are here for harmony and not for discord. Today we are risen immeasurably above all vengeance." But in the beautiful cadences of Lanier's well measured sentences there is a note of loving, forgiving grief, more noble than suffering melancholy; even in its printed form the "Confederate Memorial Address" has a moving power, which must have been infinitely greater on the occasion of its delivery.

About six months later Lanier was called on to give an address at a meeting of the citizens of Macon held to honor General Lee, who had died on October 12. "The calm grandeur of Lee," Lanier was to cite later as one of the essential attributes of a great artist, and to the "stateliness" of Lee he had paid tribute in the "Confederate Memorial Address." In this address he described simply the experience of 1864 when he saw Lee at Petersburg, paid tribute in felicitous phrases to the man whom he admired with an intensity that became devotion, and ended by suggesting a lasting memorial, in the erection of which all might share, to him who of all contemporary figures seemed to Lanier the good soldier, the shining knight of the old romances. This address, from which the description of Lee has already been quoted,[9] hardly warrants fuller discussion here.

The third of the memorial addresses is one delivered before the Macon bar in April, 1871, in commemoration of Judge Eugenius A. Nisbet, a distinguished and much loved citizen of Macon who had died March 18, 1871. But here, even more than in the others, the imagery is too unrestrained, the language too melancholy to suit the taste of the modern reader. In our memorial addresses our expression of grief is different, and what is essentially beautiful in these memorial addresses of Lanier seems to us a little—if only a little—forced and exaggerated. Of them all, however, the best is perhaps this on Nisbet, for though here too the mourner "lets fall his humble violet from the woods upon the glorified pile of homage," there is a certain objectivity in his style that indicates growth in power. This objectivity is well illustrated in a passage in which Lanier recalled an experience of his boyhood: "I remember full vividly a certain afternoon in my boyhood, when chancing to pass his office, he invited me in, specially. It was late of a Summer's day, and he seemed to be at leisure. He closed the door, sat down and commenced to talk with me, in the kindest manner, in reference to my future course in life.

"As his wise and gentle words flowed from his lips with that singular felicity for which he was always so remarkable, as his slight and graceful figure swayed easily to and fro with his gestures, as finally, one large ray from the setting sun slanted through the pane and wrought a golden glory upon his earnest and animated countenance, it seemed to my boyish imagination as if I had been suddenly transported back into that sweet primal age of the world when the tender and eloquent spirits of Heaven were accustomed to descend and instruct the sons of men in the mysteries of life and time. I have never forgot and will never forget the beauty nor the counsel of that hour."

§ 4

THE FIFTH of the addresses is one called "What I Know About Flowers." It was written by Lanier at the request of the Presbyterian minister of Macon for his young son William McKay, junior, to deliver at one of the May Day picnics of the Macon Sunday schools.[10] If Lanier remembered when writing it that at the age of twelve he too had been chosen to represent the Presbyterian Sunday school and deliver an address at the annual picnic he did not allow the memory of his own experience to influence him in preparing the address for Master McKay. There is little in the address which seems appropriate to a youthful speaker.

By flowers Lanier meant what he so often meant, something quite different, and, in this case, the boys and girls who attended the picnic. They are flower-like, with their "fair and happy faces, [their] unstained eyes and innocent brows of childhood," and should be flower-like also in "inward form and feature." In the address Lanier points out some of the lessons that boys and girls should learn from flowers: consideration for others, dignified behavior, and silence. But there is one most important lesson, saved for the last paragraph. It is the lesson of serene death. The address closes with an exhortation: "God grant our souls may gently be blown upward like odors of dying flowers greeting all heaven and its angels with the perfumed incense of hearts which have been made as pure as God's flowers by God's grace."

The tone of the whole address is paternal, even melancholy, and hardly suited to the speaker—Master McKay!—or the occasion or the audience, even though it was an audience of Sunday school children. The address reveals, as the introductions of the books for boys that Lanier published some years later also reveal, that in spite of his reciprocated love for children, Lanier failed pathetically to understand them. One feels sorry for poor Master McKay, who was probably forced to memorize the address and recite it, to the mystification and amusement of his Sunday school comrades, but more sorry for Lanier that he should have failed as he did.

§ 5

LOCAL popularity as an orator and as a flute player—for he still appeared frequently in charity concerts—could not have given Lanier so much encouragement as the intelligent sympathy of Hayne, whom he had not yet met in person but with whom he was corresponding fairly regularly. Hayne's encouragement at a time when Lanier was "just daring to think of making verses"[11] was of double importance, because it was the first encouragement Lanier had from anyone of literary reputation and because it came from one who understood his background and training and one who had himself dared to rebel against the deeply rooted southern distrust of the artist life and to give himself wholly to the writing of poetry. There was little sympathy in Macon for the young lawyer who published poems, and the contemporary opinion of Lanier as "a young fool trying to write poetry" is in Macon still repeated. The letters Lanier wrote Hayne during these four years he spent in trying to be a lawyer are full of expressions of his gratitude for the encouragement Hayne gave to his attempt to be also a poet.

In the letter of March 15, 1869, he had made a confession, already quoted, in which he revealed more of the poetic temperament than we find Lanier usually revealing, and it is out of such a mood—which was probably not solitary, but repeated, and out of his metaphysical consideration of the problem of Birth and Death, and out of the oriental studies which must have engaged him at some time before this, that there came one

Desk used by Lanier in his law office in Macon, 1869-1872. Now in the library of Wesleyan College, Macon.

of the finest of all Lanier's poems—"Nirvâna."[12] Exactly what
was in his mind when he wrote "Nirvâna" we cannot say, but
as we read it we feel that Lanier, as if by intuition, has caught
the essence of Buddhism. In this poem he gives us a superb
companion-piece to Emerson's "Brahma" (a poem he read with
deep appreciation later), one worthy of greater fame and consideration than have been given it. It is more restrained in
expression, more deeply wise, and more poetically imaginative
than anything he had previously written and much that he was
to write later.

That Lanier was actually drawn as a disciple to Buddhism is
probably unlikely. The lines of the poem

> A Lotus on a lake of balm, I lie
> Forever in Nirvâna

are, after all, but a rephrasing of the closing sentences in the
letter to Hayne referred to above: "I say to myself, where are
the strong arms in which I, too, might lay me, and repose, and yet
be full of the fire of life? And always, through the twilight, come
answers from the other world: Master, Master, Master; there is
one, one Christ: in His Arms we rest"; and they anticipate the
lines from "The Marshes of Glynn":

> As the marsh-hen secretly builds on the watery sod
> Behold I will build me a nest on the favor of God.

But the vocabulary of Buddhism offered the opportunity for the
expression in poetry of ideas otherwise hackneyed; and it is an
amazing fact that Lanier caught so successfully the impersonality
of Buddhism in a poem that is, without doubt, highly personal.

A veritable patchwork of ideas and phrases gathered heaven
knows where and used already in earlier poems, a restatement
in verse of much that he had already said in prose, "Nirvâna"
yet fails to appear derivative or repetitious because its scope is
so broad and the expression so vigorous. It is at once an expression of Lanier's attitude toward problems of the most personal
sort and toward problems of the nation and of the South. In
this respect it is the poetical counterpart of "Retrospects and
Prospects," the Furlow College commencement address, and
the "Confederate Memorial Address," as so much of Lanier's

10

poetry is a distillation of his prose. Metrically, too, it is more successful than anything Lanier had attempted except "Life and Song": there is not a false rhyme in it, though his later work—and in spite of his famous statement in *The Science of English Verse* that only perfect rhymes should be used—was to offer examples of many; and there is hardly a phrase that one would wish otherwise. The Buddhistic quality comes in the universal scope of the poet's survey, in the idea of "perfect superiority to all passions of men and all vicissitudes of Time" which dominates the poem.

The opening quatrain sets the note perfectly:

> Through seas of Dreams and seas of Phantasies,
> Through seas of Solitudes and Vacancies,
> And through my Self, the deepest of the seas,
> I strive to thee, Nirvâna.

And through all the varieties of human experience the poem sweeps on:

> I slew gross bodies of old ethnic Hates
> That stirred long race-wars betwixt states and states;
> I stood and scorned these foolish dead debates,
> Calmly, calmly, Nirvâna.

> I smote away the filmy base of Caste;
> I thrust through antique blood, and riches vast,
> And all big claims of the pretentious Past
> That hindered my Nirvâna.

Until, in the end:

> But I, with kingship over kings, am free.
> I love not, hate not; right and wrong agree:
> And fangs of snakes and lures of doves to me
> Are vain, are vain, Nirvâna.

.   .   .   .   .   .

> The storms of Self below me rage and die;
> On the still bosom of mine ecstasy,

A Lotus on a lake of balm, I lie
Forever in Nirvâna.

But the note that accompanied the poem on its first publication makes clear what, charmed by the subtle beauties of the
poem, one may easily overlook. The note, probably prepared
by Lanier himself, explains Nirvâna as "The Highest Paradise
of Buddha, attainable only by long contemplation, and by perfect
superiority to all passions of men and all vicissitudes of Time."
The phrase, "The Highest Paradise of Buddha," suggests that
Lanier failed to grasp the fact that Nirvâna is not a state of
ecstasy but a state of non-existence, of extinction. The poem
probably conveys to one acquainted with the principles of Buddhism and prepared to expect a correct definition of Nirvâna
an impression not actually present in the poet's mind: the note
compels us to admit that as a definition of Nirvâna, Lanier's
poem is sadly misleading.

The fact that Lanier addressed Nirvâna directly, as in the
fourth line of each stanza, especially of the first, also suggests
that his comprehension of Buddhism was verbal rather than
philosophical, and based on erroneous notions of a similarity of
Buddhism to Christianity: Christians are accustomed to address
heaven thus. But if we remember the tributes that Lanier paid
his wife in his poetry and elsewhere, and frequently in such
lovely figures as that employed in "My Springs," it seems likely
that Nirvâna is to be understood not only as "the end of all
hope" but also as Mary Day Lanier, and that the poem is to
be read as his epithalamium—for marriage to her more than
anything else in his life brought to Lanier the enraptured ecstasy
and the sense of escape from the terrors of contemporary events
which he so subtly conveys to us in this poem. Whatever the
meaning of "Nirvâna," and whatever the author's intention in
writing it, it has suffered more neglect than almost any other
of Lanier's better poems. Lanier himself, strangely enough, seems
to have thought little of it: in all his published work there is not
a single reference to it, and it was never reprinted by him.

It was probably "Nirvâna," nevertheless, that first brought
Lanier's name to the attention of Lawrence Turnbull of Baltimore, co-editor with William Hand Browne and part owner of
the *New Eclectic Magazine* in which the poem was published,
and so prepared the way for friendships of Lanier's later years

in Baltimore. It is said that Turnbull visited Lanier at Macon in the spring of 1871 and became much interested in him and in his work.[13] If Lanier did meet Turnbull at this time, then it is quite possible that Turnbull's presence in Baltimore, and his continued association with the *New Eclectic* (under its changed name of the *Southern Magazine*) until publication ceased with the year 1875, may have been one factor that attracted Lanier to Baltimore in 1873.

The other poem published in 1870—"Eternity in Time"[14]—is probably correctly dated by Mrs. Lanier as having been written in 1867. The subject does, it is true, suggest the metaphysical speculations of 1869-70, but the intricate metrical pattern of the poem is more like that of "Her bright soul burned in her dusky eye," and even earlier poems, than it is of the simpler, better poems of more recent date; and the figure of the mirrored star carries us back to "Now bends the lily like a nun at prayer." Furthermore, if the poem has any relation to events of Lanier's life—which, of course, it need not necessarily have—it must be to a period that preceded his marriage, or to a still later date, when more tragic separations than that memorialized here were to occur frequently. "Eternity in Time" appeared in print one month later than "Nirvâna"; but none of Lanier's poems is quite such an anti-climax. And it is not much improved in the revised version of 1879.

§ 6

THE OTHER poems of Lanier's Macon period are of a sort very different from "Nirvâna" or "Eternity in Time." As a boy, we remember, he took great delight in mimicking the speech of the Georgia crackers who lived in the country about Macon, especially in the adjoining county of Jones, about which he makes a joke in *Tiger-Lilies*, and more jokes, later, in his "Sketches of India." Residence in Macon brought the Jones County crackers once more to his attention, and observation of their shiftless, short-sighted ways inspired a group of dialect poems which are not only delightful in themselves as humorous pieces and as a sort of poetical counterpart of A. B. Longstreet's realistic *Georgia Sketches*, but are highly important as the background of "Corn," the poem that was to bring Lanier into something that resembled national prominence.

Lanier saw, as he stated some years later in his essay "The New South," that the outcome of the Civil War meant above everything else the break-up of the old plantations into small farms, and he was enough of a student of economics to know, as he convincingly demonstrated in his essay, that a group of successful small farmers is a group of contented men. The problem of the South, as he saw it, was to induce the poor whites to cultivate the land intelligently and with a view to economic independence of foreign markets: the over-production of cotton, then as now, was bringing bankruptcy on the South, and yet year after year men went on planting cotton. "Thar's More in the Man Than Thar is in the Land,"[15] the first of this little group of poems, is therefore both an essay in economics and a poem of patriotism. Henry Rootes Jackson had written "The Red Old Hills of Georgia" in praise of the homeland, but Lanier, by contrasting the hills with the character of the men who farmed them, not only honors them but humanizes them, as he did later in "Corn."

The story of the poem—for it is, after all, a narrative poem—is simple. Jones, a thriftless, money-borrowing farmer of Jones County, Georgia,

> swore that he'd leave them old red hills and stones,
> For he couldn't make nuthin' but yallerish cotton,
> And little o' *that*, and his fences was rotten,
> And what little corn he had, *hit* was boughten
> And dinged ef a livin' was in the land.

So he sold his land for a dollar and a half an acre to one Brown, and emigrated to Texas

> whar cotton would sprout
> By the time you could plant it in the land.

But five years later Jones returned on foot to Georgia, and penniless, to find Brown living prosperously and happily because he had planted corn and wheat.

> Brown he axed him in, and he sot
> Him down to his vittles smokin' hot,
> And when he had filled hisself and the floor

Brown looked at him sharp and riz and swore
That, "whether men's land was rich or poor
Thar was more in the *man* than thar was in the *land*."

The poem reveals an ability on the part of Lanier—equaled in certain passages in *Tiger-Lilies* in which Cain Smallin figures— that makes it regrettable that he did not develop more fully, in prose and verse, this genre writing which must inevitably have brought him not only popularity but high repute, as Pike County balladry was later to bring to others whose gifts for this sort of writing were in no way greater than Lanier's—Bret Harte and John Hay, for instance.

In "Jones's Private Argyment"[16] Lanier writes again of the thriftless Jones. Jones is loud in praise of the argument that the economic salvation of Georgia lay in the growing of corn instead of cotton, and swears

> for true
> To quit a-raisin' cotton!

But privately he reasons thus:

> "Hit's true;
> That Clisby's[17] head is level.
> Thar's one thing farmers all must do,
> To keep themselves from goin' tew
> Bankruptcy and the devil!

> "More corn! more corn! *must* plant less ground,
> And *mustn't* eat what's boughten!
> Next year they'll do it: reasonin's sound:
> (And, cotton will fetch 'bout a dollar a pound),
> *Tharfore, I'll* plant *all* cotton!"

But in "Nine from Eight"[18] the rascally farmer is one Ellick Garry who, by incorrect subtraction, tries to convince himself that he has settled his loan at the bank; and though the argument for raising corn instead of cotton is not stated explicitly here, the thriftless Garry, like Jones, is bankrupt because "he lived pretty much by gittin' of loans" and never raised enough cotton to cancel the debt.

§ 7

THE LAST published poem which we have of this Macon period, "The Homestead," published in the *Southern Farm and Home* of August, 1871, and never republished, is not in dialect but belongs by virture of its theme with the group of dialect poems. It is a conventional picture of an agricultural Utopia, in the meter of "Nirvâna" and in a manner that suggests the eighteenth century—poetry as uninspired as any that Lanier was ever to write. But it contains certain images and phrases that are to appear later in "Corn" and others that are reminiscent of "Nirvâna," "Night," and "A Birthday Song," and it is a sincere expression of what Lanier hoped to see occur, and believed thoroughly possible of occurrence, in Georgia. A few stanzas (there are thirty) indicate the scope and theme of the whole:

> The State spread out her arms and said:
> "My Children, Hate to-day is dead,
> And Love and Law, together wed,
>   Sit on the hills to rule you.
>
> I will that they with equal reign
> Shall keep your weal, and clear the strain
> Red war hath left on my domain,
>   And strengthen you and school you.
>
> .   .   .   .   .   .
>
> I know the large sweet sanctities
> That grow in homes, and unto these
> I add the might of my decrees
>   To make the home-strength stronger;
>
> .   .   .   .   .   .
>
> Build me my homesteads firmly then!
> Hew me, from mountain-side and glen,
> Stones that outlast the sons of men
>   To latest generations.
>
> .   .   .   .   .   .
>
> Set me my homes like diamonds large
> In the great grain-fields' golden marge,

That life's chief staff may have chief charge
Of Life's most worthy treasure.

Aye, gleam, my hills and fecund plains,
With wheat-spears and tall soldier-grains,
Whose serried stateliness constrains
The hunger-tyrant's pleasure!

.   .   .   .   .   .

From my home-yards let cheery cries
Of homely cattle upward rise,
What time the cock salutes the skies
With heartsome, bold good-morrow.

.   .   .   .   .   .

Then shall my homesteads light the land
With gem-rays warm on every hand,
Like red heart rubies in the sand
Of a fair country lying!

It is the same vision of the future that he had set in contrast
with the present in the Furlow College commencement address,
a vision of the South redeemed by agriculture that he was to
describe again, nine years later, in "The New South." "Surely,"
he wrote there, "along that ample stretch of generous soil, where
the Appalachian ruggednesses calm themselves into pleasant hills
before dying quite away into the sea-board levels, a man can
find such temperances of heaven and earth—enough of struggle
with nature to draw out manhood, with enough of bounty to
sanction the struggle—that a more exquisite co-adaptation of all
blessed circumstances for man's life need not be sought. It is
with a part of that region that this writer is most familiar, and
one cannot but remember that, as one stands at a certain spot
thereof and looks off and up and across the Ocmulgee River,
the whole prospect seems distinctly to yearn for men. Everywhere
the huge and gentle slopes kneel and pray for vineyards, for
cornfields, for cottages, for spires to rise up from beyond the
oak-groves. It is a land where there is never a day of summer
nor of winter when a man cannot do a full day's work in the
open field; all the products meet there, as at nature's own agricultural fair; . . . in short, here is such a neighborly congrega-

tion of climates, soils, minerals, and vegetables, that within the compass of many a hundred-acre farm a man may find wherewithal to build his house of stone, of brick, of oak, or pine, to furnish it in woods that would delight the most curious eye, and to supply his family with all the necessaries, most of the comforts, and many of the luxuries of the whole world. It is the country of homes." The description is the dream of a poet, but also of a far-sighted economist; but most of all it is Lanier's tribute of love, the southerner's devotion to the state of his birth, to Georgia, where, so it soon became apparent, for him there could be no home.

§ 8

THE MACON period was not, on the whole, one of literary activity. Few poems and essays appeared in print; only a few more were written. To Hayne Lanier once explained: "I've not put pen to paper, in the literary way, in a long time. How I thirst to do so, how I long to sing a thousand various songs that oppress me, unsung,—is inexpressible. Yet the mere work that brings bread gives me no time. I know not, after all, if this is a sorrowful thing. Nobody likes my poems except two or three friends—who are themselves poets, and can supply themselves!"[19] He was reading, of course, and trying to keep abreast of what was good in contemporary literature—in a long letter to Hayne he discusses *The Ring and the Book*—but the business of the law was exacting, and the recurrent note in Lanier's letters of this time is one of despair. It was not true, after all, as he had sung in "June Dreams in January," that

> to dream is power;
> And I can dream thee bread and dream thee wine.

Still, these years in Macon were not lost and infertile years, for the powers of the artist, which were to come to fruition in the seven years that followed his final escape from the law, were steadily maturing. "Day by day," he wrote to his wife, conscious himself in spite of his impatience that the time was not altogether lost, "from my snow and my sunshine, a thousand vital elements rill through my soul. Day by day the secret deep forces gather, which will presently display themselves in bending leaf and waxy petal, and in useful fruit and grain."[20]

It is in these years that some of his most interesting letters were written; in tracing the artistic growth of the poet we cannot neglect them. In them he embodied suggestions for poems—as later he was to record ideas hastily on scraps of paper as he found them at hand—and frequently the letter itself takes on the aspect of a poem. Graciousness of expression had come to him, to be ever at his need thereafter, and the letters that he now wrote are among the most charming of all poet's letters that have been given to the world to read. Take, for instance, his letter of March 3, 1870, to his wife: "If the year were an orchestra, to-day would be the calm-passionate, even, intense, quiet, full, ineffable *flute* therein. In this sunshine one is penetrated with flute tones. . . . To-day is a prophecy of the New Earth: as . . . Music is a prophecy of another life. To-day floats down Time, as one petal of a Lily on the bosom of a swift stream. Silently it tells, at once, of the gap it has left in the full Lily, and of the ocean whither it drifts to be engulfed, to die, and to live again in other forms."

Remembering the figure used there, with the curious economy of phrase and ideas that makes all of Lanier's work seem but the revision, the careful polishing of what had gone before, he wrote to Hayne six weeks later: "If the year were an Orchestra, to-day would be the Flute-tone in it. A serene Hope, just on the very verge of realizing itself: a tender loneliness, . . . the ineffable withdrawal-feeling that comes over one when he hides himself in among the trees, and knows himself shut in by their purity, as by a fragile yet impregnable wall, from the suspicions and the trade-regulations of men; and an inward thrill, in the air, or in the sunshine, one knows not which, half like the thrill of the passion of love, and half like the thrill of the passion of friendship:— these, which make up the office of the flute-voice in those poems which the old masters wrote for the Orchestra, also prevail through-out to-day.

"Do you like—as I do—on such a day to go out into the sunlight and *stop thinking*—lie fallow, like a field, and absorb those certain liberal *potentialities* which will in after days reappear, duly formulated, duly grown, duly perfected, as poems? I have a curiosity to know if to you, as to me, there come such as this day:—a day exquisitely satisfying with all the fullnesses of the Spring, and filling you as full of nameless tremors as a girl on a wedding-morn; and yet withal, a day which utterly denies you the gift of speech, which puts its fingers on the lip of your inspiration, which inexorably enforces upon your soul a silence that you infinitely long to break, a day, in short, which takes absolute possession of you and says to you, in tones which command obedience, *today you must forego expression and all out-come, you must remain a fallow field, for the sun and wind to fertilize, nor shall any corn or flowers sprout into visible green and red until tomorrow,*—mandates, further, that you have learned after a little experience not only not to fight against, but to love and revere as the wise communication of the Unseen Powers."

But the "spring-germs" brought days of suffering as well, and in the late spring and summer of this same year (1870) there came a more alarming illness than he had recently experienced, one which left him with a deep-seated cough. In July he went for his health to Lookout Mountain, in Tennessee; and there he remained some weeks with his wife, recalling undoubtedly the summer—ten full years before—he had spent in these same mountains of Eastern Tennessee, and the war that had taken his grandfather's estate from him, and the battle that had been fought on the very mountain where he was staying—memories made more poignant by the presence of Mr. Jefferson Davis on the mountain and sometimes, as a caller, in Lanier's cottage.[21] In August he went alone to New York for medical treatment, and remained through August and September. Into his letters there now come, to reappear constantly, references to his health which from this time on kept him constantly in search of an agreeable climate. "I am travelling for my health," he confessed to Hayne. "If you know what this phrase means, you know to what a melancholy state I am come. It would seem that the foul fiend, Consumption, hath me on the hip. Against him I still fight: but God knows the event thereof. . . . I do no work at all. I am too ill. This is Apollyon's unkindest cut of all. In this, he hath wounded my sword-arm."[21]

But if he could not write, he could listen to music. Theodore Thomas and his orchestra were playing in New York then, and Christine Nilsson was to be heard in concert. "Ah, how they have belied Wagner," Lanier wrote, after hearing Thomas's orchestra play the overture to *Tannhäuser*. "I would I might lead a so magnificent file of glories into heaven!"[22] And of Christine Nilsson (to whom he addressed a poem)[23] in a letter to his wife: "Mlle. Nilsson singeth as thou and I love. She openeth her sweet mouth, and turneth her head o' one side like a mocking-bird in the moonlight, and straight-way come forth the purest silver tones that ever mortal voice made."[24]

The treatments proved beneficial, and Lanier decided against a proposed trip to Minnesota, and in October left New York to return to Macon, breaking the trip with a visit in Orange, Virginia, with a friend, Charles Taliaferro. In Macon once more, the happiness that he felt in being again with his family—a second child, who inherited his name and, as time was to show, his delicate constitution, had been born in September—is charm-ingly revealed in an uncollected essay called "Peace," written about the middle of October. It is a burlesque essay, full of the facetiousness of his early prose, with the humor derived from the mock-serious tone. "My son is two years, one month and five days old," the essay begins. "My nephew is older; he is two years, one month and six days of age." Lanier—so he tells the story—volunteers to keep the two children while their mothers, his wife and his sister, go out. Giving the children things with which to amuse themselves, carefully chosen in relation to pre-conceived ideas of child psychology, he sits at his desk to write an essay on Peace (—Memories here of *Tiger-Lilies*, and hints of unpublished essays?—) in which he would demonstrate that "it was very wrong indeed to make wars." But there is no peace, for the children hurt themselves with the toys he had given them, attempt to secure possession of each other's toys, start to fight, and overturn Lanier's desk. The moral that he points is his own ignorance of child psychology, and he invites the reader to laugh with him at the inadequacy of his boasted knowledge.

But in Macon Lanier's health failed rapidly, and experiments with the various "cures" for tuberculosis then thought benefi-cial—the milk cure, the beef-blood cure, the grape cure, the raw-beef cure, the whiskey cure, and the health-life cure: he lists them all in *Florida*—brought no noticeable improvement. A year later, in the late summer of 1871, it was necessary for him to leave Macon again. This time he went, with Mrs. Lanier and the children, to Marietta, Georgia, but the slight change in climate brought no relief. He was so unwell that it was difficult to sleep at night, and he would get up and walk in the woods, playing on his flute. Years later Mrs. W. G. Solomon, who was at Marietta that summer, described the impression this nocturnal playing made on her, then a child of thirteen: "We would hear it at all times of night and I thought then it was the eeriest sound imaginable coming from afar off in the middle of the night. I know now he was trying to soothe his troubled spirits." During the day he rode a great deal on horseback, and sometimes with her. When they rode up Kennesaw Mountain he told her the history connected with the mountain, and she, remembering the incident, recalled his patience and his interesting way of telling such things, and wondered why he should give so much time to a child.[25]

That fall he went again to New York for treatment. His letters of this year, like the letters of the year before, are full of the joy of music. In a letter describing Thomas's opening concert at Central Park Garden he records such a mood as his classmates at Oglethorpe had seen descend upon him so often: "I plunged into the sea, and lay and floated. Ah! the dear flutes and oboes and horns drifted me hither and thither, and the great violins and small violins swayed me upon waves, and overflowed me with strong lavations, and sprinkled glistening foam in my face, and in among the clarinetti, as among water-lilies with flexile stems, I pushed my easy way, and so, lying in the music-waters, I floated and flowed, my soul utterly bent and prostrate."[26] Life with all its suffering offered this much, only there was suffering too in such beauty: after a private concert of organ and trombone music in St. Paul's Church, to which he went on invitation of the organist, Mr. John Henry Cornell, he wrote to Mrs. Lanier: "I mostly have great pain when music, or any beauty, comes past my way, and thou are not by. Perhaps this is because music takes us out of prison, and I do not like to leave prison unless thou goest also. For in the smile of love my life cometh to life."[27]

That fall, while Lanier was still in New York, the sensational Tweed ring exposure was taking place, and he thought regretfully of the corrupt government that still prevailed in Georgia. "Somehow this isn't a good day for thieves," he wrote. "Wouldn't it be a curious and refreshing phenomenon if Tweed, Hall, Bullock, and that ilk should all continue in the service of the State—only changing the scene of their labors from the office to the penitentiary."[28] But the terrors of reconstruction in Georgia, though the crisis was past, were not yet at an end.

In March, 1872, Lanier suffered another relapse which left him unable to carry on for long the "continuous and exhausting" business of his legal practice.[29] In July he went to Alleghany Springs, in Virginia, for treatment, but the only help he found there was help of a spiritual sort. With the fervency of the psalmist he expressed in a letter to his wife an idea that was to flower five years later in Florida into a poem, "From the Flats": "How necessary is it, dear Comrade, that one should occasionally place oneself in the midst of those more striking forms of nature in which God has indulged His fantasy!

"It is very true that the flat land, the bare hillside, the muddy stream come also directly from the Creative Hand: but these do not bring one into the sweetness of the heartier moods of God; in the midst of them it is as if one were transacting the business of life with God; whereas, when one has but to lift one's eyes in order to receive the exquisite shocks of thrilling form and color and motion that leap invisibly from mountain and groves and stream, then one feels as if one had surprised the Father in His tender, sportive, and loving moments.

"To the soul then, weak with the long flesh fight and filled with a sluggish languor by those wearisome disappointments which arise from the constant contemplation of men's weaknesses, and from the constant back-thrusting of one's consciousness of impotence to strengthen them,—thou, with thy nimble fancy, canst imagine what ethereal and yet indestructible essences of new dignity, of new strength, of new patience, of new serenity, of new hope, new faith, and new love, do continually flash out of the gorges, the mountains, and the streams, into the heart, and charge it, as the lightnings charge the earth, with subtile and heavenly fires. . . ."[30]

On his return from Alleghany Springs in the fall it was apparent that Lanier could not remain in Macon, and that he must seek permanent relief elsewhere, at a great distance if necessary from his Georgia home. Texas, which at the time was enjoying a vogue among consumptives, was finally determined upon, possibly at the advice of Clifford Lanier, who had been in Texas at the close of the war. But it was necessary that he go alone into that newly opened, unsettled country, and leave his wife and sons in Macon. So, sad in heart at this separation, more terrible in its significance than the others, Lanier set out, going from Macon to New Orleans by rail, and by boat from New Orleans to Galveston, where he arrived November 23, 1872. The journey to San Antonio was in those days a difficult one, and one certainly to tax his feeble health. An overnight rail trip from Galveston to Houston, and then another to Austin (where in the wait of an hour and a half he wrote to his father an account of the trip which, according to Professor Mims, contains sketches of "many types of characters and scenes—sketches that show at once his knowledge of human nature and his ability as a reporter"),[31] and finally the overnight stage for thirteen weary hours over the eighty-two miles to San Antonio where, on Monday, November 25, 1872, he took up his residence at the Menger Hotel.[32]

He was alone and unknown, in a country still but scarcely populated, which had but recently seen the last of the Indian raids, and he must have felt immediately that if health meant exile in Texas, then he would prefer a few short years of life elsewhere—in New York, most of all, where there was Thomas's orchestra, and men and books and the good things of art and science, and the activity of the city that is life and not mere living.

CHAPTER EIGHT

MUSIC

§ 1

IT IS A curious fact, not without significance, that the one surviving person who knew Lanier during the months he spent at San Antonio, a Mr. Karber, of Comfort, Texas, recalls him as "a Northern gentleman" who wrote poetry and played the flute.[1] But if Mr. Karber did not know Lanier well enough to learn that he was a native of Georgia, he recalls accurately his appearance and the charm of his presence, for he describes him as "a refined gentleman, handsome, of a French type, with black hair, black moustache and goatee," who "played the flute to perfection and showed slight signs of consumption. He was jovial and entertaining and *no prohibitionist.*" The latter fact, emphasized by Mr. Karber, Lanier would willingly have admitted, for in his letters there are frequent references to his delight in good wines and German beer.

The air of San Antonio proved beneficial. To his sister he wrote: "Today has been as lovely as any day can hope to be this side of the Millennium; and I have been out strolling morning and afternoon, far and wide, ever tempted onward by the delicious buoyant balm in the air and pleasantly surprised in finding what a distance I could accomplish without over fatigue";[2] and to his father: "I feel today as if I had been a dry leathery carcass of a man into whom some one had pumped strong currents of fresh blood, of abounding life, and of vigorous strength. I cannot remember when I have felt so crisp, so springy, and so gloriously unconscious of lungs."[3]

He took long walks about the city and to the park; he rode horse-back on "the undulating prairie"[4] that surrounded San Antonio, or out to the old mission of San Jose de Aguayo, to "dream back the century and a half of strange, lonesome, devout, hymn-haunted and Indian-haunted years," that had trailed past the ancient walls of the mission; he watched with interest "the

Mexican women on their haunches, by their flat stones, washing the family garments" in the San Pedro River, and—perhaps with envy—the members of the German *Turnverein* "twisting themselves among the bars, and playing leap-frog and other honest games" at San Pedro Springs Park; and, alone on the prairie and in his room at the Menger Hotel, he played his flute for the joy of it, and in the firm conviction that the exercise of playing was of great benefit to his lungs.

He planned a series of articles for one of the New York literary weeklies, taking F. L. Olmsted's books of travels as his model, but the only article that seems to have been completed, one dated "San Antonio, Dec. 9, 1872," was not published until forty-one years later.[5] It is a brief essay, slightly reminiscent of Hazlitt, but the humor it possesses is the typical punning humor of Lanier. He describes the companions of the stagecoach, for instance, as "a Michigoose, or female Michigander, with her daughter, a very sprightly little gosling indeed, going to San Antonio to set up in the millinery line." In this essay he reveals, however, that curious lack of reticence and lack of seriousness about his physical condition which one notices both in his personal letters and in *Florida* (1875). Here he describes himself as "travelling as valet to his right lung—a service in which he had been engaged for some years."

Delving into the history of the city, Lanier produced an article on "San Antonio de Bexar" (written in February, 1873) which a later historian of the city has called excellent and reliable; but this single essay, published in the *Southern Magazine* for July and August, 1873,[6] and the previously written newspaper letter are the only prose works that he composed in San Antonio. Probably not one of his published poems was written during his residence there.

He still cherished poetic ambitions, nevertheless, and became "a literary member" of the Alamo Literary Society, that he might have the use of the library. There he found Michelet's *Histoire de France*, which, he wrote, gives "the essence of an old book which I had despaired of ever seeing but which is the only authority extant—save Froissart and a few others equally unreliable; it is the chronicle of the 'Continuator of Guillaume de Nangis,'"[7] and this was important for his work on his long poem, "The Jacquerie," of which he had already composed an episode or two and the three delicately musical songs.

11

But it is not likely that he actually worked on the text of his beloved "Jacquerie" in San Antonio; most of his creative energy seems to have gone into the composition of music for the flute. "I have writ the most beautiful piece," he wrote to Mrs. Lanier on February 28, 1873, " 'Field-larks and Blackbirds,' wherein I have mirrored Mr. Field-lark's pretty eloquence so that I doubt he would know the difference betwixt the flute and his own voice." It was the piece he was to play only half a year later for Asger Hamerik in Baltimore when Hamerik "declared the composition to be that of an artist, and the playing to be almost. perfect."[8]

Lanier tells us in his essay that in 1873 the population of San Antonio was greatly mixed, Germans, Americans of native stock, and Mexicans being present in approximately equal numbers. The San Antonians whose hospitality and friendship Lanier enjoyed bore such Teutonic names as Thielepape, Mahucke, Herff, Scheidemantel, and Duerber, and the delight he had taken from his college days in all things German must have made San Antonio delightful to him and him popular with its citizens. He soon identified himself with the musicians of the city, and the most interesting letter of this period is one of January 30, 1873,[9] in which he describes for his wife the meeting of the Männerchor, which he attended with Mr. Scheidemantel, and the "long-necked bottles of Rhine-wine" and the "great pipes and cigars" of the musicians who sang old German lieder so beautifully under the leadership of the venerable Herr Thielepape that "imperious tears" rushed into his eyes. And it was with a "tumultuous, beating heart" that he lifted his "poor old flute" at their request and began to play, with neither confidence in the flute nor in himself, and awed by the audience, the most critical and intelligently appreciative perhaps before which he had ever appeared. "But, *du Himmel!* Thou shouldst have heard mine old love warble herself forth. To my utter astonishment, I was perfect master of the instrument. Is not this most strange? Thou knowest I had never learned it; and thou rememberest what a poor muddle I made at Marietta in playing difficult passages; and I certainly have not practised; and yet there I commanded and the blessed notes obeyed me, and when I had finished, amid a storm of applause, Herr Thielepape arose and ran to me and grasped my hand, and declared that he hat never heert de flude accompany itself pefore! I played once

more during the evening, and ended with even more rapturous
bravos than before, Mr. Scheidemantal grasping my hand this
time, and thanking me very earnestly."

Again, on February 13, he played at a private party, and with
such success that when the last note had died away there came
"a simultaneous cry of pleasure . . . that almost amounted to
a shout," and Lanier, deeply affected by his own playing and
by the appreciation of his audience, could only bow and smile
mechanically while his "heart worked falteringly, like a mouth
that is about to cry."[10] This was, after all, the success he wanted,
and he had found it not in his own Macon but in a little frontier
town of curiously mixed population. The whole world seemed
filled with song and he the instrument through which the heavenly
music should come to those listening. To his wife he wrote:
"Were it not for some circumstances which make such a proposition seem absurd in the highest degree, I could think that I am
shortly to die, and that my spirit hath been singing its swan-
song before dissolution. All day my soul hath been cutting
swiftly into the great space of the subtle, unspeakable deep,
driven by wind after wind of heavenly melody. The very inner
spirit and essence of all wind-songs, bird-songs, passion-songs,
folk-songs, country-songs, sex-songs, soul-songs and body-songs
hath blown upon me in quick gusts like the breath of passion,
and sailed me into a sea of vast dreams, whereof each wave is
at once a vision and a melody."[11] But San Antonio, which had
given him this taste of success, had, by its gift, destroyed its
hold on him. San Antonio might bring him health, and Macon,
where he could share the legal practice of his father and his
uncle, might bring him worldly wealth or at least assured comfort,
but when there were such songs to be sung could he dare refuse
to sing them or to go where his singing might be encouraged?
To Clifford he put the question: "When Life, Health, Passion,
Bent-of-Nature, and Necessity all grasp me with simultaneous
hands and turn my face in one direction, why should I hesitate?"
The answer, however, was already determined: "My hope and
plan is to get a foothold in New York."[12]

§ 2

So KNOWING perfectly well that his hold on life was but slight,
and that even that hold might be weakened by the step he was
taking, Lanier left San Antonio in April, 1873, determined to give

what few years might remain to music, and to poetry. He knew
that to succeed he must face even longer periods of separation
from his wife and his boys than he had previously endured, and
opposition from friends and relatives (especially from his father,
who had from his infancy taught him that music may be a
pastime with a gentleman but never a profession), and poverty,
perhaps, and suffering. But what did it matter, what did anything matter except that the world should have the songs for
which the world was waiting? "I've shed all the tears about
it that I'm going to," he wrote, "and am now pumping myself
full of music and poetry, with which I propose to water the
dry world. . . . God has cut me off inexorably from any other
life than this. . . . So St. Cecilia to the rescue! and I hope *God*
will like my music."[13] He returned to Georgia,[14] but only for a
few months in which to make necessary plans and to settle once
and for all affairs at the office in which he had worked so futilely.
And as if to assert his independence and to strengthen himself in
his determination, he stopped, on his way to Macon, in Atlanta
to take part in a public entertainment there.[15] It is said that
Clifford Lanier, assured of his own income from the Exchange
Hotel of Montgomery, now agreed to take care of the financial
problems of the family that his brother might devote himself to
his artistic career.

That Lanier's chief interest at this time was in music, to the
neglect of poetry, is attested by the fact that not one of the
published poems can be assigned to the years 1872 and 1873,
and by a statement in a letter to Hayne, written from Marietta
May 26, 1873: "I don't know that I've ever told you, that whatever turn I have for art, is purely musical; poetry being, with
me, a mere tangent into which I shoot sometimes. I could play
passably on several instruments before I could write legibly;
and since then, the very deepest of my life has been filled with
music, which I have studied and cultivated far more than
poetry."[16] When he went North in September it was with the
idea of making his living as a musician and not as a poet.

He stopped, on his way to New York, in Baltimore, possibly
to see his friend, Henry Clay Wysham, after whom Lanier's third
son, born in June, 1873, was named,[17] possibly also because
he hoped to make arrangements with Lawrence Turnbull for
the publication of further articles in the *Southern Magazine*, in
which practically all his recent work had appeared; for Lanier

knew that while he studied music an occasional prose article or two, sold at a proper price, might help his plans on considerably.[18] In Baltimore Wysham, a lawyer by profession but a great lover of the flute who sometimes played in public, invited "the great Mr. Hamerik, director of the Peabody Conservatory of Music,"[19] to his house to meet Lanier and hear him play.

Hamerik was at the time trying to persuade the trustees of the Peabody Music Fund to authorize him to organize a full orchestra, for the day of Italian opera (which Lanier particularly disliked) was almost over, and orchestral music was coming into great vogue. Hamerik was by birth a Dane, though he had received his musical education in Paris, where he became the *protégé* of Berlioz, who with Von Bülow had been his master. Lanier considered him, partly perhaps because of the enthusiasm that personal contact engendered, "one of the first composers in the world,"[19] and his "Nordische Suite," which Thomas had performed with success in New York, a splendid example of modern music. With full consciousness that he was for the first time playing before a musician of eminence, Lanier played the little piece he had composed in Texas, playing it with no accompaniment save one of his own devising, "a roll of deep arpeggios in the lower octave,"[20] and Hamerik listened with delight and promptly offered Lanier the position of first flutist in the new orchestra that he hoped to succeed in organizing. Then, after making Lanier play again the three main movements of "Blackbirds," he gave him a letter of introduction to Thomas, in New York, and left, reminding Lanier that he expected to have him in his orchestra in a few months.

Lanier's head was in the clouds. "Kind Heaven, how my heart throbbed with delight," he wrote Mrs. Lanier, "that I had received, finally, and without any more peradventure, the hearty recognition and approval, both for my composition and for my playing, of one who is regarded as a composer just below the classic Beethoven and Mozart, whose compositions are played along with those of the great masters, and who has been accustomed to hear, and to conduct, the finest music in the world." But even better was the future which Hamerik's approval seemed to inaugurate. "It is, therefore, a *possibility* . . . that I may be first flute in the Peabody Orchestra, on a salary of $120 a month, which, with five flute scholars, would grow to $200 a month, and so . . . we might dwell in the beautiful city, among the great libraries, and midst of the music, the religion, and the art that we love—and I could write my books, and be the man I wish to be. I do thank God even for this dream."[21]

To New York then, with the letter of introduction to Thomas, for two months of study and practice. He had been there before as a novelist besieging the publishers, and as a lawyer trying to sell land on which iron was supposed to be, and twice for medical treatment. Now he went solely as a musician.

§ 3

ALMOST immediately Lanier began to attract attention, and the professional and critical attention which he knew was necessary if he were to rise in the profession. Leading critics gave him private auditions and musicians of reputation spent whole afternoons playing duets with him. When he played at a small concert in Brooklyn, a concert of the sort not ordinarily noticed by newspapers, he played so successfully that the newspapers spoke of the concert as his *début*, though Lanier himself knew perfectly well that many months of study must be passed before he should be ready to make one. Miss Alice Fletcher, later to become known for her studies in the music of the American Indian, declared that he "was not only the founder of a school of music, but the founder of American music," and that his flute awakened in her heart a feeling of patriotism she had never known before. He played in fashionable homes and at church concerts; and A. G. Badger, who manufactured the best flutes made in America, wrote to a customer: "Lanier is astonishing. . . . But you ought to hear him play the bass-flute. You would then say, 'Let me pass from the earth with the tones sounding in my ears!' If he could travel with a concert-troupe, and play solos on the bass-flute, I would get orders for fifty in a month."[22]

Lanier's letters are full of feverish enthusiasm, and of repeated praises, but also of admirable common-sense. "Oh, how I can play, with a couple of months' practice!" he writes. "The instrument begins to feel me, to grow lithe under my fingers, to get warmed to life by my kiss, like Pygmalion's stone, and to respond with perfect enthusiasm to my calls. . . ." And again: "Mr. Y———, who has been playing in New York for years, among the very best professional flutists, and who is certainly the best reader I ever saw, says *I* am the best *he* ever saw—I, who surely

have scarcely read a half-dozen new pieces in any year of my
musical life, before this last month or so!"

He must have met Thomas and been received cordially by
him, for he writes: "When I am ready to come out, which will
be after I practise four months in Baltimore, I shall make my
début under the auspices of the Philharmonic or of Theo. Thomas,
or not at all." And if he did play for Thomas "Field-larks and
Blackbirds" or his other original composition, "Swamp Robin,"
we may well wish that we might know what Thomas, an appreciative critic of modern music, thought of these pieces that
invariably puzzled no matter how much they delighted the
audiences for which Lanier played them. But if the compositions
survive, they have not been published,[23] and we can only guess
at the charm and humor and beauty that these realistic transcrip-
tions of bird music must have contained.[24]

Late in November in Brooklyn, Lanier received a call from
Hamerik. The orchestra had been formed, Hamerik said, but
for four months only, and he could offer Lanier only half the
salary he had previously promised him, a mere $60 a month.
But he expressed his confidence in Lanier and his hope of being
able to offer more the following year, and he offered to do all
that he could to make Lanier's stay in Baltimore pleasant. So
Lanier "concluded an engagement with him as *Flauto Primo*,"
hoping to supplement the meager salary in different ways, and
aware of the fact that it might mean a stepping stone to something better, for the Peabody orchestra and library were supported
by the same foundation, and he had not altogether relinquished
his scholarly ambitions, or his dreams of finishing "The Jacquerie." In the last letter to his wife written from New York
before his departure for Baltimore, he wrote: "I can finish my
darling Jacquerie midst of the great libraries. I am overjoyed
at this prospect."

In Baltimore Lanier promptly sought pen, ink, and paper to
state explicitly his final renunciation of even the possibility of
material success unless it should come in his chosen way. Even
before the first rehearsal of the new orchestra he answered a
letter from his father, a letter in which his father once more
urged him, with something akin to the Christian's fear of the
devil, to change his mind, to give up his wild plans for a musical
career, to return to Macon and share the business and the income
of the family law office. In his reply of November 29, 1873,

Lanier wrote: "I have given your last letter the fullest and most careful consideration. After doing so I feel sure that Macon is not the place for me. If you could taste the delicious crystalline air, and the champagne breeze that I've just been rushing about in, I am equally sure that in point of climate you would agree with me that my chance for life is ten times as great here as in Macon. Then, as to business, why should I, nay, how *can* I, settle myself down to be a third-rate struggling lawyer for the balance of my life, as long as there is a certainty almost absolute that I can do some other thing so much better? Several persons, from whose judgment in such matters there can be no appeal, have told me, for instance, that I am the greatest flute-player in the world; and several others, of equally authoritative judgment, have given me an almost equal encouragement to work with my pen. (Of course I protest against the necessity which makes me write such things about myself. I only do so because I so appreciate the love and tenderness which prompt you to desire me with you that I will make the fullest explanation possible of my course, out of the reciprocal honor and respect for the motives which lead you to think differently from me.) My dear father, think how, for twenty years, through poverty, through pain, through weariness, through the uncongenial atmosphere of a farcical college and of a bare army and then of an exacting business life, through all the discouragement of being wholly unacquainted with literary people and literary ways—I say, think how, in spite of all these depressing circumstances, and of a thousand more which I could enumerate, these two figures of music and of poetry have steadily kept in my heart so that I could not banish them. Does it not seem to you as to me, that I begin to have the right to enroll myself among the devotees of these two sublime arts, after having followed them so long and so humbly, and through so much bitterness?"[25]

But this letter, as Professor Mims is careful to remind us,[26] needs to be read with some caution. The reference to Oglethorpe, for instance, as a farcical college is unfair; but the atmosphere of Macon was probably as uncongenial as Lanier states it to have been, for the South of Lanier's day was even more unsympathetic to artists than the ante-bellum South or the South of today, and more so than Professor Mims in 1905 was willing to admit. But Professor Mims is correct in insisting upon the fact that "the very struggle he had to maintain his ideal, and it will

not do to minimize this struggle, had strengthened and enlarged
his soul. . . . After the fortitude and endurance manifested in
this period of his life, his later sufferings were the more easily
borne." His father yielded, of course, and remained as devoted
as he had always been. And often during the next eight years
he joined Clifford in contributing money to provide the bread
and meat and doctor's care that kept alive the musician and
poet in Baltimore.

§ 4

ON DECEMBER 2 Lanier attended his first rehearsal—and so
made his first appearance as a professional musician with other
professionals, he the "raw player and . . . provincial withal,"[27]
uninstructed by any teacher, not even knowing the value of a
dotted note,[28] and but little practiced in his art. But at once he
attracted the attention of the patrons of the orchestra. The
Baltimore *Sun* of December 8, reporting the opening concert of
the preceding Saturday, December 6, spoke of Lanier's playing
as one of the features of the concert. Often during the next four
months—there was one concert weekly—he was to win the praise
of the critics, though we are told that in orchestral work he
never tried to express himself but to discover and aid in revealing
the composer's meaning, and to lose his own individuality in
the larger personality of the orchestra.[29] The opening concert
he himself described to his wife: "It was brilliant, and I failed
not—though half-dead with cold, and though called on unex-
pectedly. I am better today. The music lifts me to a heaven of
pain."[30] He was hardly out of his heaven again that winter: his
health was not good, and he sometimes attended rehearsals and
concerts with difficulty, but with the heedlessness of a drunken
man, so intoxicated was he with the music.

It is easy to trace in his letters the quick and sure development
of his musical taste. His likes and dislikes were, as Hamerik has
said, "intuitive and spontaneous," and neither well reasoned
nor always to be justified. In this respect—for as with music so
with literature—Lanier's method of criticism was impressionistic,
like that of Pater; in accepting his judgments one must always
make one's own judgment first. His passion for Beethoven and
Wagner, whom he had discovered only in his mature manhood,
for Chopin and Schumann, is greatly to his credit, but his characterization of Mozart's music as poor and bald is certainly not.

"Why," he asks, "do we cling so to humbugs?"[31] On the other hand, it must be admitted that the evidence of his dislike of Mozart's music is to be found in a letter written after a performance of *Die Zauberflöte*, and was conditioned by the fact that he disliked opera—a dislike frequently felt by people of cultivation who love music devoutly—and that the flute part of this particular opera seemed to him unworthy of the flute: the development of the flute and of flute music has been comparatively recent, and in his correspondence Lanier complains constantly of the dearth of satisfactory solo pieces.

"His attitude in listening," Wysham says, "was usually a bent, reverent posture, with folded arms and closed eyes—a study of profound meditation and absorption." But if the true musician is the artist who thinks and feels in terms of pure sound, then Lanier, as Professor Foerster points out,[32] was no musician, for always the sound evoked mental images. The effect of music upon Lanier Professor Mims describes most happily when he says "He saw music as he heard poetry."[33] Music not only brought to Lanier physical sensations but was for him actually a physical experience. "I am just come from Venice," he wrote after playing in the orchestra for a performance of Flotow's "Stradella";[34] and the music of Méhul's "Hunt of Henry IV" could transport him as on some magic carpet to the mountains of eastern Tennessee, and to a deer hunt there.[35] Music had, too, a religious effect on Lanier, and he never overcame the feeling that music's sole purpose is a religious one. Though he does not definitely say so in his published writings, one feels that the dignified ritual of the Catholic worship must have appealed greatly to him: he went often, we know, to the Episcopal churches of Baltimore, perhaps sometimes to the Roman Catholic. He writes thus of an *adagio patetico* which he and his friend Wysham, second flute in the Peabody Orchestra, played during the offertorium at St. Paul's "a wonderfully ritualistic church"; "as the . . . spirituelle silver tones [of the organ and flutes] went stealing and swelling through the great groined arches of the enormous church, I thought I had never heard flute-notes so worthily employed before."[36] After the Christmas (1873) service at the same church, in which members of the Peabody Orchestra participated, he wrote with indignation of the conduct of certain of his fellow musicians during the communion service: "Dash these fellows, they are utterly given over to heathenism, prejudice and beer—

they ought to be annihilated; if they *do* get control of the age, life will be a mere barbaric grab of the senses at whatever there is of sensual good in the world."[37] The Bohemianism of his associates and the loose moral life that is traditionally the artist's he thoroughly abhorred. "Bohemianism and compliments fill not my heart," he writes from Baltimore,[38] echoing John Sterling's remark in *Tiger-Lilies* that "the artist-life is not necessarily a Bohemian life, but . . . it may coincide with and *be* the home-life." Bohemianism seemed to Lanier philosophically an attitude of despair, and the persisting religious influence of his early home life made such an attitude untenable for him.

This same influence, persisting through various metamorphoses, determined also his attitude toward the daily business of life. In spite of his already changed ideas toward Christian theology, we find him constantly apologizing for playing in Sunday concerts or at Sunday rehearsals: " 'T is a charity concert, and are we not allowed to lift the poor out of the ditch o' Sundays?" he writes in justification of his conduct;[39] and after a Sunday rehearsal: "If the constituents and guardians of my childhood—those good Presbyterians who believed me a model for the Sunday-school children of all time—could have witnessed my acts and doings this day, I know not what groans of sorrowful regret would arise in my behalf."[40]

As for his playing, only the legend remains, and all too often the enthusiasm of the testimony impairs its value as evidence. "I have never cared for the flute," one who heard him is quoted as having said, "but, to me, Lanier did not 'play the flute'; I only heard a voice breathing unutterable longings and messages of joy and love and sorrow."[41] And Miss Spann, who heard him or talked with those who had, has thus described his playing: "He dispensed with accompanist, yet avoided the meagerness of a bare melody by weaving with it a wonderfully rich and varied sequence of harmonies, conveyed either by a running accompaniment of broken chords or by cadenzas as free and unexpected as those of a song bird."[41] He himself said that he was forever hearing a ceaseless flow of melody, so strong and beautiful that the difficulty was not to listen when external matters required his attention, and that to "play" he had only to utter this melody of tone.

But one tribute to his playing is unimpeachable evidence of the beauty of it—the tribute of Asger Hamerik, under whose baton Lanier played for seven years. For Hamerik, whatever his limitations as a composer, was a gifted conductor who organized in Baltimore an excellent orchestra, and gave concerts remarkable for their progressiveness. There is no reason for doubting that Lanier's playing was as fine as Hamerik said it was.

"In his hands," Hamerik wrote, "the flute no longer remained a mere material instrument, but was transformed into a voice that set heavenly harmonies into vibration. Its tones developed colors, warmth, and a low sweetness of unspeakable poetry; they were not only true and pure, but poetic, allegoric as it were, suggestive of the depths and heights of being and of the delights which the earthly ear never hears and the earthly eye never sees. No doubt his firm faith in these lofty idealities gave him the power to present them to our imaginations, and thus by the aid of the higher language of Music to inspire others with that sense of beauty in which he constantly dwelt. . . .

"His playing appealed alike to the musically learned and to the unlearned—for he would magnetize the listener: but the artist felt in his performance the superiority of the momentary living inspiration to all the rules and shifts of mere technical scholarship. His art was not only the art of art, but an art above art.

"I will never forget the impression he made on me when he played the flute-concerto of Emil Hartmann at a Peabody symphony concert, in 1878: his tall, handsome, manly presence, his flute breathing noble sorrows, noble joys, the orchestra softly responding. The audience was spellbound. Such distinction, such refinement! He stood, the master, the genius."[42]

§ 5

IT WAS about the time of Lanier's first appearances with the Peabody Orchestra, and possibly in connection with his work in the orchestra, that he had taken, by Kuhn and Cummins of Baltimore, the photograph which, reproduced as a wood engraving as early as June, 1877, and as a half-tone for the frontispiece of the 1884 edition of his collected *Poems*, has become the most familiar of the likenesses of Lanier. It is not a good likeness, for—according to Mrs. Lanier—it "quite misrepresents his physique; for it suggests a man heavy built about the shoulders—the effect of a double breasted coat of extraordinary thickness and other heaviest clothing—all worn to guard him from the rigor of the first Northern winter; while the attitude (inclining backward), in combination with this bulk of clothing, results in the wider discrepancy of an impression of portliness—the very opposite of his build and movement." But in spite of her objections to this photograph, Mrs. Lanier gave it her preference, because it reveals "the expressive nostril, the brow, the ear, the fall of the silken-textured hair," and more than any other it disclosed to her the spiritual man.[43]

To those of us who did not know him and never saw him it suggests little however of Mrs. Lanier's own description of him, or of Stedman's description of "the Southerner, nervous and eager, with dark hair and silken beard, features delicately moulded, pallid complexion, hands of the slender, white, artistic type";[44] or of Lowell's mention of "his shining presence."[45] And certainly as we come to know him through his poems and his letters we find the picture taken in 1870 and the bust made by Ephraim Keyser almost at the end of his life far more satisfying than this portly photograph.[46]

§ 6

THE PUBLISHED letters of this winter spent in Baltimore were written exclusively to Mrs. Lanier, and from them have been edited away almost everything except his "musical impressions." There are full and interesting accounts of many concerts—he was playing not only with the Peabody Orchestra but with several German *Männerchor* orchestras, the orchestra of the Concordia Theater, and in churches and private homes—and occasionally such a revealing confession as this from a letter of February 7: "How much I have learned in the last two months! I am not yet an artist, though, on the flute."[47] But there is only a single reference to his literary activity, and that to "My Springs," which he wrote in March.

One passage, in a letter of January 22, is most significant. It was after hearing two concerts given by Thomas's orchestra that he wrote: "I am beginning, in midst of the stormy glories of the orchestra, to feel my heart sure, and my soul discriminating. Not less do I thrill, to ride upon the great surges; but I am growing calm enough to see the star that should light the musician, and presently my hand will be firm enough to hold the helm and guide the ship that way. *Now* I am very quiet; I am waiting." This new and strange calmness preceded, as he knew, creation, and it meant, too, growth in intellectual power.

The winter of 1873-74 was perhaps his most active winter musically, as also his most productive one: he wrote this winter a "*Danse des Moucherons* (midge-dance)" for flute and piano,[48] and another piece which he called "Longing." And this winter preceded the full, bursting spring of his finest poetic achievements. For now, after a long wait, a new period of poetic activity was to begin. It is with his sudden but unquestioned success as a musician that the first period of his development as a poet—a period in which "music seems to have satisfied his deepest longings and highest aspirations"[49]—ends. In the second period— which he called, in speaking of Shakspere, the Real or Hamlet Period, which follows the Dream Period and precedes the Ideal— we are to see him less and less as a musician, and in this period he is to produce some of his most interesting poems. As effort was characteristic of the poetry of the first period, so ease is to be characteristic of the poetry of the second, as if in the discipline of work in the orchestra he had achieved a mastery over all his talents of expression. The poems are to come more from the heart and less from the head, like the metaphors that he praised in his essay, and they will seem less labored and more natural in expression, and the allegories will be clearer. Without breaking as yet with old forms he is to achieve originality and power, until in the third period there is to come, as the result of long brooding over the things that make for poetry, a body of work that is powerful, distinctive, musical, unconventional in form, and highly original. The first poem of this new, second period is an occasional poem, descriptive of a picture, "On Huntingdon's 'Miranda,' " published in the New York *Evening Post* of March 6, 1874,[50] but it is only the first faint showing of green in what had been a fallow field. It is with "My Springs" that the period really begins.

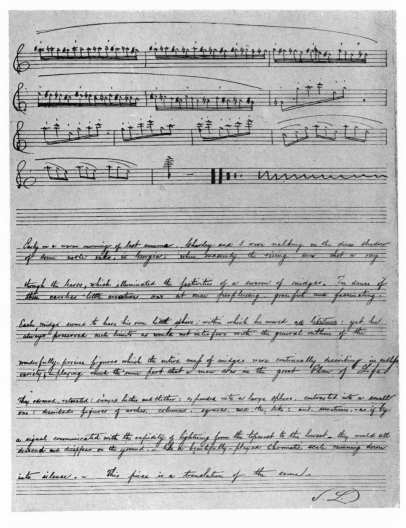

Second page of the "Dance des Moucherons (Gnat Symphony)," by Lanier, composed in December, 1873. "Which I think enough of to let it go forward as Op. I." Courtesy of Mr. Henry W. Lanier.

PART II

"He was a Southerner, always a Southerner. He loved the South, and the South loved and loves him. And in his day the spur of that glorious spirit, ever toiling, ever hoping, giving up all material success for the long pursuit of an ideal, was the very stimulus that the young men of the South needed above all others. Who shall say that the young men of the whole country do not need and cannot profit by it now?"

Gamaliel Bradford, "Sidney Lanier," *American Portraits.*

"His gospel was not one of denunciation, but of love, and gentleness, and beauty, and joy, and faith—and by this gospel he believed that a poet must first live, before he can teach—the holiness of beauty must be his chrysm."

Frances L. Turnbull, *The Catholic Man. A Study.*

CHAPTER NINE

POETRY

§ 1

IN MARCH, 1874, Mrs. Lanier was visiting at Sunnyside, a railroad-side hamlet, too small to be called a village, some sixty miles north of Macon, near Griffin, Georgia. She and her children were visiting there in the home of John McIntosh Kell. Years before, Kell had accompanied Perry on his famous expedition to Japan, and during the Civil War he had served as first lieutenant under Raphael Semmes on the famous Confederate warship "Alabama" which had carried the Confederate flag into every important port in the world. His wife was a poetess of minor importance but a person of great character and distinction. With the collapse of their fortune during the Civil War, they had taken refuge at Sunnyside with a little group of Mrs. Kell's relatives.

The house in which they lived was a delightful, two-story plantation home, surrounded by elaborate shrubberies. The parlor was adorned with rich Japanese objects and other souvenirs of Kell's visit to the Orient, but the beauty of the house came not so much from its furnishings as from the sense of the glory of an irrecoverable past and the graciousness of the life lived there; and it must have seemed to many in 1874 as it did to young Vachel Lindsay thirty years later "the most spiritually beautiful home I have ever entered." It is important thus to introduce the Kells at Sunnyside for we are to meet them again during the year. They were good friends to Sidney Lanier, and relatives of a sort to Mrs. Lanier, who was the god-daughter of Mrs. Kell's father, N. C. Monroe.

At Sunnyside Mrs. Lanier received one day from her husband in Baltimore a letter which she opened so hastily that she did not notice the enclosed sheet of paper that fell to the floor. She was constantly concerned about his health, and always eager to learn the condition of it, and she read through the letter while

little Tibbie Kell[1] patiently held out to her the paper that had
fallen to the floor.[2] Finally, the letter finished, she noticed the
child, took the paper, and read:

In the heart of the Hills of Life, I know
Two springs that with unbroken flow,
Forever pour their lucent streams,
Into my soul's far Lake of Dreams.

Not larger than two eyes, they lie
Beneath the many-changing sky,
And mirror all of life and time,
Serene and dainty pantomime!

   .   .   .   .   .   .

Always, when the large form of Love
Is hid by storms that rage above,
I gaze in my two springs and see
Love in his very verity.

   .   .   .   .   .

Always, when Art on perverse wing
Flies where I cannot hear him sing,
I gaze in my two springs and see
A charm that brings him back to me.

   .   .   .   .   .   .

O Love, O Wife, thine eyes are they,—
My springs from out whose shining gray
Issue the sweet celestial streams
That feed my life's bright Lake of Dreams.

   .   .   .   .   .   .

Dear eyes, dear eyes! and rare, complete—
Being heavenly-sweet and earthly sweet,—
I marvel that God made you mine,
For when He frowns, 'tis then ye shine![3]

In the letter with which the poem was sent Lanier had written:
"Of course, since I have written it to print I cannot make it
such as *I* desire in artistic design; for the forms of to-day require
a certain trim smugness and clean-shaven propriety in the face
and dress of a poem, and I must win a hearing by conforming
in some degree to these tyrannies, with a view to overturning
them in the future. Written so, it is not nearly so beautiful as
I would have it; and I therefore have another still in my heart,
which I will someday write for myself."[4] This poem, which he
called "My Springs," Lanier never published, however, and the
other was not, so far as we know, ever written; but the letter is
one of great significance, and for our study almost more important
than the poem. It reveals quite clearly that Lanier was already
dreaming of such a free and flowing poetic form as he was to
create for "Corn" that very summer, and for "The Marshes of
Glynn" four years later, and indeed of an entirely new school
of poetry. And this, perhaps we need to recall again, is but the
logical outcome of his practice of experimenting with poetic
forms. Simple as the stanzaic form of "My Springs" is, it is one
he had used but once before, and that in the single, burlesque
stanza sent in a letter to Hopson in 1863.

Though "My Springs" is, therefore, a compromise, and indicates a temporary submission to contemporary conventional
standards, it is one of the finest poems that Lanier ever wrote,
and one of three or four on which his fame rests. Upon the first
appearance of Lanier's collected poems in England the critic of
the London *Spectator* wrote of this poem: "There is here and
there a hint of the desire to say in a striking way what would
best have been said in a subdued way; and again we cannot
say that we like at all the

> high glory-loves
> And science-loves and story-loves.

But nothing could be more perfect than

> the whole sweet round
> Of littles that large life compound;

and the touch of wonder in the last two lines of the poem . . .
is as simple and exquisite as any touch of tenderness in our

literature." In it we find Lanier's typical weaknesses, but these are confined for the most part to three stanzas which are not the most prominent of the poem. In the poem as a whole we have Lanier at his best, writing verse that is technically clever but writing with a simplicity and directness of expression revealed but seldom before, and only faintly, in a few poems—"Life and Song," "The Ship of Earth," "Nirvâna" (of which there are echoes even in "My Springs") and the dialect poems, which, of course, represent an altogether different kind of writing.

§ 2

THIS WAS in March, and Lanier's Baltimore engagements were almost at an end. In the middle of April he took part in a concert at Wheeling, West Virginia,[5] but by May he was again in Macon, rejoined there by his wife and repeating to her, we may be sure, all that he had written during the past half-year of separation, telling her of the glories of the music he had heard, of the opportunities that Baltimore offered, quoting for her the little compliments and telling of the notices and events that confirmed his success, whispering again of the great longing he had felt for her, and the pain that absence had brought to his heart. Then, the excitement of the homecoming over, he wrote to Hayne, still the recipient of his confidences, summing up the events of the winter and stating his plans for the future.

"God only could express the delight and exultation with which I helped to perform the great works brought out by [the Peabody Symphony Orchestra] during the winter," he wrote. "Of course this was a queer place for me: aside from the complete *bouleversement* of going from the Court-House to the footlights, I was a raw player and a provincial withal, without practice, and guiltless of instruction—for I never had a teacher. To go, under these circumstances, among old professional musicians, and assume a leading part in a large Orchestra which was organized expressly to play the most difficult works of the great masters—was (now that it's all over) a piece of temerity that I do not remember ever to have equalled before. But I trusted in Love, pure and simple; and was not disappointed, for, as if by miracle, difficulties and discouragements melted away before the fire of a passion for music which grows ever stronger within my heart—and I came out with results more gratifying than it is becoming in me to specify. 'T is quite settled that I

cannot practise law: either writing or speaking appears to produce small hæmorrhages which completely sap my strength;
and I am going in a few weeks to New York—without knowing
what on earth I am to do there—armed only with a silver Boehm
flute, and some dozen of steel pens.

"Happy man—you who have your cabin in among the hills
and trees, you who can sit still and work at Home—pray a short
prayer once in a while for one as homeless as the ghost of Judas
Iscariot." But even the homeless wanderer had found a happiness he would not relinquish; in the same letter he wrote of
Hayne's poem "Cloud-Star": "To die, consumed by these heavenly fires:—that is infinitely better than to live the tepid lives and
love the tepid loves that belong to the lower planes of activity;
and I would rather fail at some things I wot of, than succeed
at some others."[6]

On Thursday, May 28, Lanier appeared in concert at Macon
with the local Harmonic Society. The Macon *Telegraph's* notice
of the concert tells us that "Mr. Sidney Lanier's solo was the
most exquisite music it has ever been our good fortune to hear
on the flute. Under his graceful and artistic management his
instrument becomes a human voice, most beautifully modulated,
with a tone and power such as we deemed impossible. An artist
in every sense of the word, Mr. Lanier held his audience in
rapt attention, and a persistent encore was the only means of
relieving everybody."[7] So in his own Macon, as in New York
and Baltimore, he was acclaimed for what Professor Vincent
Czurda, the director of the Harmonic Society, called "his match-
less warbling (nightingale-like) . . . on the flute."[8]

§ 3

LANIER did not go to New York in June, as he had planned,
possibly because ill-health interfered. After visiting Mrs. Lanier's
relatives in Brunswick, where the salt air was bracing and invigorating, he and Mrs. Lanier and the boys went to Sunnyside,
where they stayed first with the Kells and then near by, boarding
in the home of some country people, Grey by name. It was a
summer of happiness for the Laniers, a bucolic interlude, precious
to them because they were now constantly together. One feels
this happiness even in the answers Lanier set down to the stereo-
typed printed questions of a "character" album. His favorite
tree, he wrote, was the mimosa—the luxuriant, scent-laden

tree of the Atlantic coast; his favorite color, "the opal gray, which one sees on the horizon just after a gorgeous sunset"; his favorite musicians, Schumann, Wagner, Beethoven, Chopin; his favorite authors Shakspere, Chaucer, Robert Browning, Carlyle, George Eliot, and Elizabeth Barrett Browning; his favorite occupation, teaching; the quality he most admired in men "knightly magnanimity"; the age he preferred, "the Present"; his favorite amusement, "to be on a springy horse in a hilly country."[9] For the Lanier boys it was all a wonderful picnic, having their father with them again and being once more with their playmates, the young Kell children. A charming episode of that summer's holiday reveals Lanier—who would play his flute hours on end, at all times of the day and night—walking up and down the roadway that ran beside the railroad track, oblivious of everything, even of the young Kell boys who made flutes from swamp reeds and followed him, charmed children fascinated by the piper.[10]

Everywhere about the little cluster of houses at Sunnyside there were cornfields, filled with the lush, sweet corn of an unusually productive year, and through the fields there were paths that led as short-cuts from one house to another. Along these paths, through the rich fields of ripening corn, beholding the redeemed land of which he had long ago had a vision, Lanier wandered. Here was corn growing where cotton once had grown; here was prosperity; here was the new South. One day he came, musing thus, through the corn to the Kells' house, and going into the sitting-room dropped on the sofa and began to speak of how beautiful the corn was to him, and what the intense cultivation of it meant to the state, and the failure of so many farmers to realize that in the cultivation of corn lay their hope of economic salvation, and his longing to put such thoughts into a poem.[11] The rich corn pollen had quickened his imagination. Day after day after that he was to be seen sitting on a cross-tie of the railroad in sight of, almost surrounded by, the waving fields, writing on small scraps of paper which he held on his knee. But the poem—in the version that finally appeared in print—was not completed at Sunnyside, and Lanier carried the unfinished manuscript of "Corn" northward with him in September, knowing that if it was to express his thoughts clearly he must revise and polish it carefully, making it a worthy heir of his great vision.

§ 4

IN NEW YORK ("armed with a lot of poetry and music which I've written, and proposing henceforth to fight the Wolf in that way—though without any definite plans as yet"[12]) Lanier resumed the agreeable life of attending operas and concerts, but he practised feverishly, and gave a good deal of time to the "invention" of a long flute which would go to G below the staff, and which he hoped would eventually make possible as many flutes in an orchestra as there were violins. "And why should it not be so?" he asked. "What reason is there in the nature of things why the violins should be the orchestra, and the flutes and other instruments mere adjuncts? I say this not out of any foolish advocacy of the flute: thou knowest I love the violin with my whole heart. No, I speak in advocacy of pure music."[13] In literature and in music, in his ideas of the instruments of the orchestra as in his ideas of the technic of verse, Lanier was a revolutionary burning with a feverish desire to make the world—and his America first—understand that "old mouldy ideas" needed revision, and revision according to the principles of nineteenth-century science. Badger argued against his flute first on one point and then on another until "by good logic" and Lanier's unyielding persistence he was convinced that the long flute was a possibility. But this is the last we hear of the long flute in Lanier's published letters, and he turned with equal enthusiasm to his task of making the critical Badgers accept his theories of poetry.

He was again playing duos and quartettes with the leading musicians of the city, and he took lessons from Dr. Leopold Damrosch, the father of Walter Damrosch, who, though but recently come to America, was considered "at the head of fine music in New York." "Today," Lanier wrote his wife on October 29, "I played for the great Dr. Damrosch; and won him. I sang the 'Wind-Song' to him. When I finished he came and shook my hand, and said it was done like an artist; that it was wonderful, in view of my education; and that he was greatly astonished and pleased with the poetry of the piece and the enthusiasm of its rendering. He then closed the door on his next pupil, and kept him waiting in the front parlor a half hour, while giving me a long talk. I had told him that I wished to pursue music. He said: 'Do you know what that means? It means a great deal of work, it means a thousand sacrifices. It is very hazardous.'

"I replied, I knew all that; but it was not a matter of mere preference, it was a spiritual necessity, I must be a musician, I could not help it."[14]

Illness confined Lanier to his room during that fall, and then he took comfort in reading, for he had been ordered not to write. In Wasielewski's life of Schumann he found much of interest. A letter that Schumann wrote to his sister from Vienna described so perfectly his own loneliness in New York that he copied it at length in a letter to Mrs. Lanier. But in Schumann—for all his love for him—he found great weaknesses. Schumann's life was not great because his sympathies were not big enough: he did not care for his country, the poor, religion, or humanity; and Lanier felt, as George Eliot did, that art does nothing if it does not enlarge men's sympathies.[15]

§ 5

As EARLY as October 1, 1874, Lanier had sold to *Scribner's Monthly* "The Power of Prayer,"[16] a poem in Negro dialect which he had written during the summer with his brother, to whose inferior "Power of Affection" it serves as a sort of companion piece.[17] The poem has been almost completely ignored by biographers of Lanier and usually by historians of American dialect writing and of the Negro in literature,[18] and yet for Lanier may be claimed the honor of being one of the first to write in Negro dialect, and to record it correctly. The Negro and Negro dialect had appeared earlier in fiction, of course, and Stephen Foster had written songs supposed to be pictures of Negro life. Modern scholarship, however, insists that neither the words nor the music of Foster's songs came from the Negroes and that even the sentiments expressed in them are often alien to the race. To Irwin Russell, a little known but interesting poet of Mississippi, has been given the honor of the discovery of "the literary material latent in negro character and in negro dialect,"[19] and Thomas Nelson Page and Joel Chandler Harris, the leading exponents of the Negro character in American literature, have acknowledged his priority. But Russell's first published poem did not appear

"Wind Song," a musical manuscript by Lanier. Played by him for Dr. Damrosch on October 29, 1874. Courtesy of Mr. Henry W. Lanier.

until January, 1876, when "Uncle Cap Interviewed" appeared
in *Scribner's Monthly*, while "The Power of Prayer" appeared in
the same magazine for June, 1875; so Lanier's treatment of
Negro character preceded Russell's by half a year. It preceded
the first appearance of Uncle Remus by almost four full years.

"It is evident," wrote Professor C. A. Smith in the *Cambridge
History of American Literature*, "that Joel Chandler Harris came
at a time when the interest in the negro was at its height."[20]
Within a month after the appearance of "The Power of Prayer"
it had "gone all over the land," frequently returning to Lanier
in "heart-breaking yet comical disguises of misprints and dis-
figurements." "Tell me," he wrote Miss Cushman, "*ought* one
to be a little ashamed of writing a dialect poem,— as at least one
newspaper has hinted? And did Robert Burns prove himself no
poet by writing mostly in dialect? And is Tennyson's 'Death of
the North Country Farmer'—certainly one of the very strongest
things he ever wrote—not a poem, really?"[21] But Lanier's "The
Power of Prayer" is a poem, certainly, and it probably played
an important part in stimulating the interest in the Negro that
prepared the way for the immediate success of Harris's Uncle
Remus stories, which Lanier himself welcomed enthusiastically,[22]
and marked the beginning of the great artistic interest that was
to be taken in the Negro later. Certainly their success in selling
it encouraged Sidney and Clifford Lanier to write another
dialect poem, "Uncle Jim's Baptist Revival Hymn," which was
also bought by *Scribner's* and published in the May, 1876, issue
of the magazine.[23] "Lanier," as Professor Pattee remarks, "was
a pioneer in a rich field."

§ 6

LANIER's interest in dialect poetry was unquestionably sincere.
In the Macon *Telegraph* of October 29, 1874, appeared an uncollected poem called "Civil Rights," which, read with the
letter Lanier wrote the day of its publication in describing his
interview with Damrosch, will do as much as anything else to
set in bold and clear outline the truly catholic character of
Lanier and to reveal the difference in character between him
and such an artist as Schumann, for instance, whose sympathies
art had not enlarged. It was the year of agitation over the Civil
Rights bill, a year of great unrest in the South. The poor whites
resented what they considered an attempt on the part of Congress

to force the blacks and whites to live together on a basis of social equality; and there were, as a result, riots and frequent disturbances, and reconstruction was to drag on through many more terrible years in the South before the southern states were to be again truly free. Lanier's poem, written in the dialect of the Georgia crackers, is a vigorous statement of the attitude of the southern whites and a denunciation, as strong as that expressed in "Retrospects and Prospects," of the curious and incomprehensible blindness on the part of the North that had allowed such a condition to arise and still allowed it to continue. It is, moreover, the most bitter protest against the political situation that Lanier was ever to make, stronger by far than anything in his prose—in *Tiger-Lilies* or "Retrospects and Prospects," or even in the little group of political poems written in 1868.

The poem is long—twenty-eight couplets in iambic heptameter, a vigorous verse—and it is somewhat repetitious, but selected couplets give the spirit of it well enough. Uncle Johnny Stiles is talking to his friend Jeems, who reports Uncle Johnny's denunciation of the new laws.

"It *do* look like them Yankees is the curiousest set;
They *will* make treuble jest as sure as water'll make you wet!

"I jest was startin' out to learn to like 'em some agin;
And that was not an easy thing, right after what had bin!

. . . .

"But now, as I was sayin, when I jest had come to see
My way was clear to like 'em, and to treat 'em brotherlee;

"When every nigger's son is schooled (I payin' of the tax,
For not a mother's son of 'em has more than's on ther backs),

"And when they crowds and stinks me off from gettin' to the polls,
While Congress grinds ther grain, as 'twere, 'thout takin' of no tolls;

"And when I stand aside and waits, and hopes that things
    will mend,
Here comes this Civil Rights and says, this fuss shan't have
    no end!

"Hit seems as ef, just when the water's roughest here
    of late,
Them Yanks had throwed us overboard from off the Ship of
State.

"Yes, throwed us both—both black and white—into the
    ragin' sea,
Without but one rotten plank; while they, all safe and free,

"Stands on the decks, and rams their hands into ther pocket
    tight,
And laughs to see we both must drown, or live by makin'
    fight!

"For, Jeems, what in this mortal world of treuble *kin* be done?
They've made this Southern plank so rotten, it will not bear
    but one!"

.   .   .   .

(And here I'll say I've knowed him now for fifty year or
    more,
And never heerd him swear, nor cuss a single cuss before):

"I tell you, Jeems, I *kin* not help it—*maybe* it's a sin;
By God! ef they don't fling a rope, I'll push the nigger in!"

And yet the bitterness, if it was bitterness that prompted the
composition of "Civil Rights," was never a characteristic of
Lanier. In Wagner, as in all German poetry and music, he felt
that he detected the absence of "that . . . sentiment lying deep
in the heart of the author which would produce on his face a
quiet, wise smile all the while he was writing, a sort of consciousness underlying all his enthusiasms (which are not at all weakened
thereby), that God has charge, that the world is in His hands,

that any bitterness is therefore small and unworthy of a poet."[24]
The presence of the "quiet, wise smile" is not to be felt in "Civil
Rights," but there is in the poem the compassion of which such
a smile is the outward sign, and a note of human passion which
Lanier seldom sounded.

§ 7

MEANWHILE, Lanier had put the manuscript of "Corn" in such
form that he thought he could well submit it for criticism to
Judge Logan E. Bleckley of Atlanta, Chief-Justice of Georgia,
who during the summer had spoken encouraging words to Lanier
about his literary future, and of the faith he had in him. So on
October 9 he sent the manuscript of "Corn" to Bleckley with
the following letter: "I could never tell you how sincerely grateful I am to you, and shall always be for a few words you spoke
to me recently.

"Such encouragement would have been pleasant at any time,
but this happened to come just at a critical moment when,
although I had succeeded in making up my mind finally and
decisively as to my own career, I was yet faint from a desperate struggle with certain untoward circumstances which it would
not become me to detail.

"Did you ever lie for a whole day after being wounded, and
then have water brought to you? If so, you will know how your
words came to me.

"I enclose MS. of a poem in which I have endeavored to
carry some very prosaic matters up to a loftier plane. . . . Please
give me your judgment on my effort, *without reserve;* for if you
should say you do not like it, the only effect on me will be to
make me write one that you do like."[25]

Bleckley replied with a long letter full of many minute criticisms in which he suggested changes, some of which Lanier did
make. He ended his letter by giving a final impression of the
poem which is an excellent analysis: "You paint the woods, a
corn-field, and a worn-out hill. These are your landscapes. And
your portrait is the likeness of an anxious, unthrifty cotton-
planter who always spends his crop before he has made it, borrows
on heavy interest to carry himself over from year to year, wears
out his land, meets at last with utter ruin, and migrates to the
West. Your second landscape is turned into a vegetable person,
and you give its portrait with many touches of marvel and

mystery in vegetable life. Your third landscape takes for an instant the form and tragic state of King Lear; you thus make it seize on our sympathies as if it were a real person, and you then restore it to the inanimate, and contemplate its possible benefi- cence in the distant future. . . . As an artist you seem to be Italian in the first two pictures, and Dutch or Flemish in the latter two. In your Italian vein you paint with the utmost delicacy and finish. The drawing is scrupulously correct and the color soft and harmonious. When you paint in Dutch or Flemish you are clear and strong, but sometimes hard. There is less idealization and more of the realistic element—your solids predominate over your fluids."

Such an appreciation, however stilted and dilettantish it may appear to readers of today, was sincere and encouraging, and as honest and helpful criticism as anyone known to him besides Paul Hayne could have given Lanier. Encouraged, therefore, and rightly, by it, and believing that the poem, improved by the changes he had made at Bleckley's suggestion, was one he might offer without temerity to any editor and of which he might be justly proud, Lanier now entrusted it to M. M. Hurd, of the firm of Hurd and Houghton, which had published his *Tiger-Lilies* seven years before, and Hurd sent it with his com- mendation to William Dean Howells, editor of the *Atlantic Monthly*, which by this time had been acquired by the firm of Hurd and Houghton.

Certainly Lanier had every right to believe that a good poem, sent under such auspices, would be readily accepted for publi- cation by Howells. Excited by the expectation, and all the more by the feverish temperament of his disease, he was in a mood to be wounded to the quick by Howells's prompt rejection of "Corn." But more humiliating than the rejection was the way Howells had taken to let him know that he had not found the poem acceptable. "With every desire to like" the poem, Howells had politely written Hurd, he "did not find it successful"; he felt that readers would be mystified by it, that there was no "connection between the apostrophe in the beginning and the bit of narrative at the close," and "that neither was striking enough to stand alone." He ended by asking Hurd to show the letter to Lanier, which Hurd did in a most tactful way—by sending it through the mail.[26]

Months later, after "Corn" had been published and had made

his name famous, Lanier could still remember the terrible anguish the receipt of Howells's letter brought. Writing in April, 1875, to Edward Spencer, one of the many who had written him in appreciation of the poem, Lanier described the torture that he endured through one whole day, alone in his Brooklyn lodging house, and the beneficent calm that his suffering brought him: "I took the letter to my room,—it was a high room, in Brooklyn, N. Y., from whose windows I could see many things— and there, during a day whose intensity was of that sort that one only attempts to communicate to one's God, I led myself to an infinite height above myself, and meditated: and when evening came I found myself full of the ineffable contents of certainty and of perfect knowledge and of decision. I had become aware— not by reasoning, I could only reason about it afterwards, I know not what the process—that my business in life was to make poems. Since then, it has not occurred to me to doubt about my sort of work. Why should one disquiet oneself with asking whether one is to sing solos, or to come on only in the concerted parts? God must have his chorus."[27]

But most important of all, he now had an unassailable faith in himself. To Mrs. Lanier he wrote: "Know . . . that disappointments were inevitable, and will still come until I have fought the battle which every great artist has had to fight since time began. This—dimly felt while I was doubtful of my own vocation and powers—is clear as the sun to me now that I *know*, through the fiercest tests of life, that I am in soul, and shall be in life and utterance, a great poet. . . .

"Have then . . . no fears nor anxieties in my behalf; look upon all my 'disappointments' as mere witnesses that art has no enemy so unrelenting as cleverness, and as rough weather that seasons timber. It is of little consequence whether *I* fail: the *I* in the matter is a small business: '*Que mon nom soit flétri, que la France soit libre!*' quoth Danton; which is to say, interpreted by my environment: Let my name perish—the poetry is good poetry and the music is good music, and beauty dieth not, and the heart that needs it will find it."[28] "Corn" was a good poem, no matter if the editor of the leading literary magazine of the country had rejected it, and in this Lanier was and knew himself to be right.

The theme of "Corn" recalls the earlier dialect poems and "The Homestead," but metrically "Corn" is unlike anything

Lanier had attempted previously, a highly irregular poem in spite of the occasional regularity in rhyme and meter, with the musical irregularity of a Cowleyan ode but more like Lanier's own later marsh hymns than anything else. The normal line is iambic pentameter, but the beautiful rhythmic movement of the poem comes in part from the freedom with which Lanier broke the metrical uniformity of the line and in part from his use of lovely phrases and words that dissolve the steady iambic beat into irregular musical cadences.

The real success of the poem comes, however, from the atmosphere of reality—the reality of the immediate landscape—which, in spite of strained epithets and the presence of mythological figures, invests the poem from beginning to end. The poem has, as Bleckley suggested, the sharp, brittle reality of Flemish painting. There is no golden Venetian glaze here, nothing of the mist-veiled landscape backgrounds of Umbrian painting. There is here not even the mysticism of "The Marshes of Glynn," and no forest glooms but the bright, burning sunshine that ripens corn.

If the language is not always appropriate and felicitous, it is usually so.

> The leaves that wave against my cheek caress
> Like women's hands

is a beautiful sentence, embodying a beautiful figure, and one not spoiled by the unsuccessful figure that follows:

> The copse-depths into little noises start,
> That sound anon like beatings of a heart,
> Anon like talk 'twixt lips not far apart.

When Lanier speaks of his "sweetheart" nature in the terms of the acts of affection that human beings display toward one another, the result is not always happy; such uxoriousness is like the cinema kiss that provokes a laugh from the audience. Some of his phrases, however, such as "And ecstasy of burgeoning," are sturdy and virile in a way that recalls Chaucer and suggests the delight in the fullness of life which is the chief charm of Chaucer's poetry, as it is also of Lanier's. Such a figure as "the spacious foreheads of great pines" is characteristically weak, though not altogether unsuccessful because the personification of natural objects with Lanier is really an expression of his sense of kinship with them, and the emotion is noble enough to redeem the line from the weakness of expression. The description of the forest has something of the largeness of the forest: there is "beneath the restless striving for sensation and for expression . . . a strong deep love of trees such as one finds rarely in literature."[29]

Sometimes the felicities of sound weaken the sense, as when Lanier says that before his eyes

> Out of the silent corn-ranks rise,
>   Of inward dignities
> And large benignities and insights wise,
>   Graces and modest majesties.

But again the phrasing often contributes greatly to the strength of the idea, as in the two lines that follow:

> Thus, without tilth, I reap another's field;
> Thus, without theft, I house a wondrous yield,

which are suggestive of Emerson. Professor Foerster remarks that here, "as in most of Lanier's poetry, fancy tends to supplant imagination"—a remark that emphasizes the weakness of the conception of the cornstalks as soldiers, the corn-leaves as blades, and the hill as a "gashed and hairy Lear" that Spring, "the divine Cordelia of the year," cannot cheer. And yet such a fancy often leads to fine imaginative writing. The one stem of corn growing beyond the others typifies

> the poet-soul sublime
> That leads the vanward of his timid time
> And sings up cowards with commanding rhyme.

And the reference to Lear, in Lanier's characteristic manner of Shaksperean metaphor, inspires a lovely lyric, imaginative in conception and rich in sound, with which the poem closes.

The poem was revised meticulously before it was published, and even after the first publication in magazine form Lanier made other changes. Sometimes, as in the change of the lines

There, while I pause, before mine eyes
Out of the silent corn-ranks rise,

to

There, while I pause, my fieldward-faring eyes
Take harvests, where the stately corn-ranks rise,

the change is an improvement; but often, as in the change of
the lines

I hear faint bridal-sighs of brown and green
Dying to kindred silences serene
As dim lights melt into a pleasant sheen

to

I hear faint bridal-sighs of brown and green
Dying to silent hints of kisses keen
As far lights fringe into a pleasant sheen

bad lines are made worse. The figure of these lines is of course
a recollection of Poe's famous line, quoted in *Tiger-Lilies*, "The
murmur that springs from the growing of grass," but Lanier
seldom possessed Poe's faculty of saying a thing simply and
directly: the allusion to bridal-sighs and kisses complicates without
enriching.

The description of the cornfield is more successful than the
description of the woods: in the verse there is simple and dignified
music suggestive of Emerson's best verse, and there is something
of Emerson's philosophy, and of Carlyle's, in the description of
the poet.

But the description of the barren hill is best of all, and the
sudden change from a religious tone to one of vehement indignation, as if Lanier had lost all patience with the state and the
people who could blindly plant cotton year after year in constantly disappointed hope of sudden riches, is one of the most
effective things in the poem. Later, in "The Symphony," Lanier
was to denounce bravely the hold of Trade upon the land; his
denunciation here of cotton planting, and of cotton, sets Lanier
distinctly apart from other southern poets and southern senti-

mentalists who pay unquestioning homage to King Cotton. Corn would grow on the hillsides—and yet the hills were uncultivated! The pity that Lanier feels for the deserted hill is a human pity, deeper than Wordsworth's reverence for nature and more memorable than Wordsworth's respect for those who have learned nature's lessons and given her faithful service.

After the vigorous denunciation of the unthrifty Jason farmer who loses all in pursuit of "the Fleece," comes the splendid cry of sympathy for the hill, and however fanciful the reference to Lear, it gives to what is essentially a tragic theme a tragic dignity of human significance. The final stanza of the poem begins with the impassioned music of this cry, but it ends with music that is quieter, with the perfection of conscious art.

"Corn" cannot be called a great poem merely because it was a timely poem, presenting an important agricultural lesson for the South of forty years ago in effective verse. But that a poem written on such a topical theme, so timely in significance, should also achieve universality of significance is evidence of the essential truth of vision and of feeling on the part of Lanier. "Corn" has been disparaged, but far more often praised—and able critics have called it the most poetic of American odes, more beautiful and more American than any of Lowell's, and have pointed out resemblances to the best passages in the superb odes of Keats. There is, moreover, in "Corn" a little of that quality so lacking in most of Lanier's work, the quality that Matthew Arnold called "inevitableness of style," as if nature herself had written for the poet with her own bare, sheer, penetrating power. Than this nothing is more necessary in a nature poem. That it should be here is proof, of course, of true poetic ability on the part of Lanier, but proof also of the vitalizing power of his devotion to his native Georgia.

§ 8

How MANY editors rejected "Corn" we do not know, but enough certainly to cause Mrs. Lanier to doubt her husband's wisdom in attempting a literary career when he would not fit his wares to the taste of those who would buy. It was to comfort his wife, in this period of uncertainty, says Dr. Ward, that Lanier wrote on October 23 the letter of frankest confession previously quoted. Now, after other disappointments, he penned a denunciation of the "wooden-headedness" of some of the literary leaders:

Lanier at the age of thirty-two. From a photograph made by Kuhn and Cummins of Baltimore, January, 1874.

"I remember that it has always been so; that the new man has always to work his way over these Alps of Stupidity, much as that ancient general crossed the actual Alps—splitting the rocks with vinegar and fire—that is, by bitterness and suffering. D. V., I will split them. . . . The more I am thrown against these people here, and the more reverses I suffer at their hands, the more confident I am of beating them finally. I do not mean by 'beating' that I am aggrieved with them; no, they know no better, and they act up to their light with wonderful energy and consistency. I only mean that I am sure of being able, some day, to teach them better things and nobler modes of thought and conduct."[30]

But by the middle of November "Corn" remained unsold, and it was somewhat apologetically that Lanier wrote again to Judge Bleckley. The letter, however, is a remarkable one, and interesting for several reasons; one passage of it—on the need of a great man—has been printed repeatedly, but with the train of thought leading up to it not indicated. "I did not know," he wrote, "any method of showing you my thorough appreciation of your criticism on my 'Corn' better than sending you a printed copy of the poem, thoroughly amended and revised so as to avoid nearly all the flaws which you found in it; and I delayed answering your kind and valued letter in the hope of being able to do so.

"But things go slowly here in Babylon,—with all the hurry and bustle: and I have not yet made such arrangements for publication as I wish.

"My idea is first to get it printed in a magazine of influence, and then to issue it in the form of a small book.

"I have your cry of jubilation and it makes my heart light up all manner of torches. The War is over. What a fight it has been. We had to grip religious fanaticism and frantic patriotism for four years, and rascality for ten.

"If there are any other three Devils that are harder to wrestle with than these they have not yet made their appearance in terrene history. I have been wondering where we are going to get a *Great Man*[31] that will be tall enough to see over the whole country and to direct that vast un-doing of things which has got to be accomplished in a few years. It is a situation in which mere cleverness will not begin to work. The horizon of cleverness is too limited; it does not embrace enough of the heart of man to enable a merely clever politician, such as those in which we abound, to lead matters properly in this juncture.[32] The vast generosities which whirl a small revenge out of the way as the winds whirl a leaf; the awful integrities which will pay a debt twice rather than allow the faintest flicker of suspicion about it; the splendid indignations which are also tender compassions, and which will in one moment be hurling the money changers out of the Temple, and in the next be preaching Love to them from the steps of it:—Where are we to find these? It is time for a man to arise, who is a man. . . .

"My head and my heart are both so full of poems which the dreadful struggle for bread does not give me time to put on paper—that I am often driven to headache and heartache purely for want of an hour or two to hold a pen. I manage to get a little time tho' to work on what is to be my first *Magnum Opus*—a long poem, founded on that strange uprising in the middle of the 14th Century in France, called 'The Jacquerie.' It was the first time that the big hungers of The People appear in our modern civilization: and it is full of significance.

"The peasants learned—from the merchant-potentates of Flanders—that a man who could not be a lord by birth might be one by wealth: and so Trade arose and overthrew Chivalry. Trade has now had possession of the civilized world for four hundred years: it controls all things, it interprets the Bible, it guides our national and almost all our individual life with its maxims; and its oppressions upon the moral existence of man have come to be ten thousand times more grievous than the worst tyrannies of the Feudal system ever were. Thus in the reversals of time it is *now* the *gentleman* who must arise and overthrow *Trade*. That Chivalry which every man has in some degree in his heart; which does not depend upon birth but which is a revelation from God, of justice, of fair dealing, of scorn of mean advantages; which contemns the selling of stock which one *knows* is going to fall to a man who *believes* it is going to rise as much as it would contemn any other form of rascality or of injustice or of manners:—it is this which must in these latter days organize its insurrections and burn up every one of the cunning moral castles from which Trade sends out its forays upon the conscience of modern society.—This is about the plan which is to run through my book; though I conceal it under the form of a pure novel.

"I must beg you to pardon such a long sermon; it is not writ with malice prepense, only you seem to be an earnest man, and I know so few of them to whom one can talk of such things."[33]

§9

BEFORE Lanier returned to Macon, "Corn" was accepted for publication in *Lippincott's Magazine*,[34] the Philadelphia rival of Boston's *Atlantic;* so Lanier could face his wife with lighter heart and with some proof that he might make literature a paying profession. But before the year was over, at the Christmas season to which he had looked forward, there was to be another disappointment, bringing deeper humiliation, for the scene was Macon and the spectators of his chagrin were people who had known him all his life. Encouraged perhaps by the success of the concert in which he had appeared in May, and in need of funds, Lanier now planned a concert, the profits of which should be wholly his own. In the Macon *Telegraph* of December 20, 1874, under the heading "Sidney Lanier Concert," appeared the following notice: "Mr. Lanier leaves Macon on the 25th to remain in Baltimore the balance of the Winter, where he is to be engaged in completing his poem, 'Jacquerie' and in filling the position of first flute in the symphony orchestra of the Peabody Conservatory. He is also prosecuting some extensive experiments, designed to apply a modern musical invention to the purpose of greatly enlarging the powers and resources of the flute and all similar wind instruments.

"In order to accumulate a fund to defray the expenses of these experiments, he intends organizing a series of concerts in Baltimore, and will also give one in Macon, on Wednesday, December 23, at Harmonic Hall. He will be assisted by [various local artists]; and with this material will present an array of vocal and instrumental solos and concerted pieces, such as will certainly constitute a beautiful entertainment.

" . . . We earnestly hope to see Harmonic Hall crowded Wednesday night." On the day of the concert the *Telegraph* printed the program, calling it not the Sidney Lanier Concert but the Flute-Fund Concert. The pieces played were from the conventional repertoire of the day, chosen obviously with the Macon audience in mind, and tickets sold at a dollar.

But the concert was not successful. To his friend Mrs. Boykin Lanier wrote from Baltimore on January 3: "I intended to call and thank you in person for your exquisite flowers; but was

compelled to leave Macon early on Christmas morning in order
to meet my engagement here, and so could not possibly find
time, in midst of many delayed preparations for departure,
to carry out my wish in this regard. Your kindness was so particularly grateful to me on that funereal night, that I cannot
resist the temptation to send you this brief note, which shall
bear to you my sincere acknowledgments of your thoughtfulness."[35] The New Year, however, brought a sense of peace and
victory, and promises that he would not have to endure again
the suffering of the four months just past. In a little greeting
that he had sent to his wife on the first day of the new year,
there is a paragraph which seems almost a prayer for forgiveness
for any indignation against the blind farmers of Georgia, or the
blind legislators of the North, or unsympathetic editors of magazines, or fickle citizens of Macon, which he may ever have felt,
even in his secret heart: "Let us try and teach [our boys], dear
wife, that it is only the small soul that ever cherishes bitterness;
for the climate of a large and loving heart is too warm for that
frigid plant. Let us lead them to love everything in the world,
above the world, and under the world, adequately; that is the
sum and substance of a perfect life."[36]

He was a member once more of Hamerik's orchestra in Baltimore when this New Year's letter was written, happy to have
been invited to return and happy to help "to perform the great
works" of the masters. But the promise of the new year was
most splendidly fulfilled when, in the middle of January, there
appeared the issue of *Lippincott's Magazine* for February, containing his poem "Corn," which won an immediate and definite,
though limited, success, bringing him letters of appreciation and
congratulation from the very sort of people he wanted most to
know, for to a few of the nation's lovers of poetry at least "Corn"
was evidence that a new singer had appeared, capable of making
poetry out of matter too long ignored.

CHAPTER TEN

TRADE

§ 1

ONE OF the many who in reading "Corn" recognized immediately the ability of the "new" author was Mr. Gibson Peacock, editor of the Philadelphia *Evening Bulletin*. Peacock, a graduate of Dickinson College, was an educated, cultivated man who insisted upon treating matters of art in his paper as seriously and as gravely as he treated matters of political interest, as if his journal were a magazine and not merely a daily paper. So, with keen appreciation of the talent that Lanier's poem revealed, he printed a full and sympathetic review of it, calling it "the most American of American poems"; and, knowing the effect of encouraging an unknown author in a more personal way, he sent a note to John Foster Kirk, editor of *Lippincott's*, commending him for publishing the poem.[1]

But Peacock did even more. He read "Corn" to Miss Charlotte Cushman, the actress, who was then in Philadelphia, and asked her to seek out the author in Baltimore. Charlotte Cushman was not merely a great actress but a great woman, and one who appreciated poetry intelligently and befriended poets. Struck by the power revealed in "Corn" she hastened to write a note of appreciation to Lanier, which, with Lanier's reply, began a tender and intimate friendship which blossomed quickly and, nourished by their common devotion to music, lasted until Miss Cushman's death. Lanier's grateful appreciation of her kindness is clearly revealed in a little poem he sent to her on January 27 with a copy of the magazine containing "Corn."

O what a perilous waste from low to high,
　　Must this poor book from me to you o'erleap,—
From me, who wander in the nights that lie
　　About Fame's utmost vague foundations deep,
To you, that sit on Fame's most absolute height,
　　Distinctly starred, e'en in that awful light!

The day previous Lanier had written to Peacock a letter of gratitude, thanking him for his notice of "Corn" which had appeared in the Philadelphia *Bulletin* of January 16 and had been called to Lanier's attention by a Baltimore friend. The letter is overly long and, as Lanier perfectly well knew, somewhat too personal, but Peacock, who was almost twenty years his senior, must have realized that the author of "Corn" who expressed himself so humbly, with confusion and almost with embarrassment, did so only because he was truly a "new" author, and one to whom intelligent criticism meant much. To Edward Spencer, poet and man of letters, another of the new friends "Corn" had brought him, Lanier wrote: "Your letter, which crowns a very pleasant number of hearty recognitions with which 'Corn' has been honored, gives me great comfort at this point, and, with that comfort, much firmness of hand and humble piety for future work: and you can in this view understand an enthusiasm of thanks that might under other conditions appear to you as the effuse extravagance of one unbalanced by praise."[2]

So, early in 1875, Lanier, first flutist of the Peabody Symphony Orchestra, a musician so able and intelligent that the discriminating Hamerik cared to talk with him through the night until early morning,[3] had as a poet also won recognition, and as a poet appeared before an audience as large as the circulation of one of America's leading magazines.

His interests were, however, leading him into still other fields than those of poetry and music. Scientific interests, fostered by Professor Woodrow some twenty years previously, were, under the stimulus of his flute playing and the congenial atmosphere of Baltimore, developing rapidly. About this time, probably as the result of his attempts to perfect a long flute, he began to make plans for some lectures on the technic of music, hoping to give them under the auspices of the Peabody Library and Orchestra. These plans, though never perfected, were to lead to the lectures on the technic of verse which, delivered in the winter of 1879-80 at Johns Hopkins University, have proved a stable basis for his fame. But the success of "Corn" encouraged Lanier to give more time than he had previously to poetry, to the subsequent neglect of his career as a professional musician; and it is noteworthy that by the end of March he had ready for publication a poem even longer than "Corn," which he called "The Symphony."[4]

§ 2

AN IMPORTANT, though at first reading apparently unrelated, companion-piece to "The Symphony" is the essay on "Paul H. Hayne's Poetry" which Lanier published in the *Southern Magazine* for January, 1875, after working almost three years on it.[5] In a letter to Hayne of April 17, 1872—a letter written while Lanier was gathering strength for the rebellion against Macon and the law, he had written: "The review of 'L[egends] & L[yrics]' was particularly near my heart: for I was keenly desirous of pointing out, and dwelling upon, a certain rare and lovely feature in your writings, wh., in these days, gives me a world of pleasure. I mean the entire *absence*, in every thing you write, of *Trade* in any of its forms. Utterly *uncommercial:* that is glorious, my dear Friend, and that is the spirit of your writings.

"Trade, Trade, Trade: pah, are we not all sick? A man cannot walk down a green alley of woods, in these days, without unawares getting his mouth and nose and eyes covered with some web or other that Trade has stretched across, to catch some gain or other. 'T is an old spider that has crawled all over our modern life, and covered it with a flimsy web that conceals the Realities. Our religions, our politics, our social life, our charities, our literature, nay, by Heavens!, our music and our loves almost, are all meshed in unsubstantial concealments and filthy garnitures by it. . . .

"It is not necessary for me to explain, to *you*, what I mean by these hasty metaphors. You know what the commercial spirit is: you remember that Trade killed Chivalry and now sits in the throne. It was Trade that hatched the Jacquerie in the 14th Century: it was Trade that hatched John Brown, and broke the saintly heart of Robert Lee, in the 19th."[6]

A full year later, on May 26, 1873, Lanier wrote to Hayne for a second copy of the volume to replace one he had lost; and again on June 10, 1873, he wrote: "I entreat you, forget not to send me a copy of 'Legends & Lyrics.' " Sometime during the next year the review was completed, offered to *Lippincott's Magazine* and rejected, and finally accepted for publication by Browne of the *Southern Magazine*. It had become a review not merely of one of Hayne's volumes but a critique on his work as a whole, but it is noteworthy that in the printed article there is no praise of Hayne as a poet who ignored altogether the existence of

Trade and sang rather of the dream world of the past. Instead, Lanier took occasion to point out that Hayne was at his best when he escaped entirely from the enervating influence of Morris and followed the example of Chaucer, who wrote of the vibrant life about him. But this makes clear a fact about "The Symphony": it is not an appeal for a revival of antique manners and antique virtues in the present day. It is a warning that we must take a lesson from the past to correct the errors of the present, and a plea for us to do so. It is, thus, the distillation of the long narrative account of the Jacquerie, which Lanier still expected to complete and make his masterpiece. The theme of "The Jacquerie," as stated in the letter to Judge Bleckley of November 15, 1874, is in a sense a summary of "The Symphony." "The Symphony" was, then, no spontaneous growth of the two months that had passed since the publication of "Corn." The theme of "The Symphony" is the tyranny of Trade, the cruel, deadening spirit of commercialism, and for years Lanier had been protesting, in poetry and prose and in his personal letters, against that. The roots of "The Symphony" reach deep into Lanier's past.

§ 3

We MAY remind ourselves of some of these roots. In the first place, Lanier had much of the professional man's scorn for those in trade and of the southerner's traditional but inconsistent contempt for certain ways of acquiring money. Once—in boyhood or in youth—he had had a serious quarrel with his friend Campbell: Campbell's father happened to be in trade, and Lanier's was a lawyer. How the quarrel arose or ended we do not know, but Campbell insisted there was as much over-reaching in law as in anything else, and Lanier denied it.[7]

In *Tiger-Lilies* Lanier had pictured an Arcadia in which music dominated life and in which people lived pleasantly and beautifully and with no perception of the necessity of even the most elemental industry. The villain Cranston was described as a soul warped by the contaminating influences of Trade. Idealized and exaggerated out of all proportion to the civilization that Lanier sought to depict, the Arcadia of *Tiger-Lilies* is nevertheless the poet's dream of the ante-bellum South and of a condition of society that the war, though it did not destroy, had weakened fatally; and it was the poet's reality. The first reference to Trade

in his poems is not a bitter reference: in stanzas six and seven of
"Spring and Tyranny" he expresses regret that political conditions
interfered with the orderly and, to Lanier, natural activity of his
countrymen in manufacturing and in commerce. To one who
had grown to manhood in a town of commercial prosperity and
importance, trade, pursued within reason, did not seem altogether
ignoble.

Later, however, as husband and father, with a wife and child
to support, and totally unable in the maladjustments of society
and character that followed the war to do this adequately, he
began to realize what money can buy, and that, though the
pursuit of wealth was dangerous to the spirit, the lack of wealth
was dangerous to the body, and to the spirit too. The lines in
"June Dreams in January"

> And while soft Luxury made show to strike
> Her glovèd hands together and to smile,
> What time her weary feet unconsciously
> Trode wheels that lifted Avarice to power

express a personal indignation. But his distrust of trade was
becoming, though slowly, a reasoned indictment of it. In the
"Confederate Memorial Address" delivered in April, 1870, he
made his first public protest. He said then: "I tell you the world
is far too full of noise. The nineteenth century worships Trade;
and Trade is the most boisterous god of all the false gods under
Heaven. . . . Are not your ears fatigued with his loud bragga-
docio, with his braggard pretensions, with his stertorous vaunt-
ing of himself and his wares? . . . I know that there is an evil
in all this noise. Out of this universal hubbub there is born a
great wrong. . . . In these days there is so much noise that we
cannot hear ourselves think."

Professor Mims mentions a letter of April 16, 1874, written
from Wheeling, West Virginia, in which Lanier described indignantly "a city completely dominated by factory life."[8] His
indignation that trade should so possess the life of a people
suggests, of course, that of Ruskin—an analogy often noticed;
and his indignation at the blindness of the southern farmers who
planted cotton instead of corn is a part of his indignation against
the spirit of trade. All of these references reveal what was con-
tinuously in Lanier's mind. Even in a sonnet on Martha Wash-

ington, written in February, 1875,[9] he managed to introduce a
reference to the chilling effects of Trade upon the age. And "The
Symphony," growing out of this persistent indignation, and the
finest expression of it, is not the final denunciation of trade: we
shall see that even in books designed to be read by boys Lanier
took occasion to break a lance at the menacing black knight.

Early in March, 1875, in Philadelphia, Lanier met Gibson
Peacock and his wife. Peacock was deeply read in the best English
literature, and familiar with modern languages, a connoisseur
of art and a discerning critic of music and drama as well as of
poetry. His wife, the daughter of the Marquis de la Figanière,
at one time Portugese minister to the United States, was an
exceptionally lovely woman, as gifted and cultivated as her
husband. In the Walnut Street home of the Peacocks all the
prominent artists and literary people who lived in Philadelphia
or who visited Philadelphia were entertained. They were ideal
patrons for a young, unknown poet, patrons who could, and
did, do much for Lanier.

His first visit with the Peacocks was brief, though long visits
were to be made later. At this time—probably as a result of
repeated exposure during the winter, the severest known on the
North American continent since 1741—he suffered a slight
attack of the old bronchial trouble, which caused Mrs. Peacock
considerable alarm. In Baltimore, on March 24, writing to Peacock, Lanier referred to this attack, trying playfully to identify
it with the excitement of composition: "Pray tell your good
Mrs. Peacock that I am much better, and, though in daily fight
against severe pain, am hard at work. Four days ago, a certain
poem which I had vaguely ruminated for a week before took hold
of me like a real James River ague, and I have been in a mortal
shake with the same, day and night, ever since. I call it 'The
Symphony': I personify each instrument in the orchestra, and
make them discuss various deep social questions of the times, in
the progress of the music. It is now nearly finished; and I shall
be rejoiced thereat, for it verily racks all the bones of my spirit."
Not long afterwards the poem was finished, and Lanier sold it
promptly to Kirk, of *Lippincott's*, but he waited impatiently for
the June number of *Lippincott's Magazine*, the number containing
his poem, to appear. "It has so much of my heart in it," he
wrote, "that I feel a personal fate as inhering in it."[10]

§ 4

"THE SYMPHONY" is the first of the truly national poems that Lanier wrote, for his protest here is not against the evils in southern life, or in Georgia life, but in the national life—against, indeed, the whole spirit of the age in which he lived. With its fierce denunciation of industrial enslavement it suggests Mrs. Browning's "Cry of the Children" and Hood's "Song of the Shirt," but the protest is against no particular evil, in behalf of no one group. Lanier shows, as the English poets did not, the far reaching effects of industrial ills not merely on the industrial slaves but on the industrial slaveholders, the undermining of the whole of society by a social evil. In this his poem suggests *Piers Plowman*—a poem that Lanier loved, as we know from his later lectures, but which he may not have read before this time. It is not necessary, however, to assume that he had read it, in order to account for the similarity of feeling—a similarity noted by Professor Callaway, who also remarks upon the similarity to Ruskin's *Unto This Last*. The comparison with Ruskin is, indeed, more to the point, for as Ruskin united an interest in art with his zeal for social reform, so Lanier found the justification for his denunciation of Trade in music. "I have so many fair dreams and hopes about music in these days," he had written only a fortnight before he began work on "The Symphony." "It is a gospel whereof the people are in great need. As Christ gathered up the ten commandments and re-distilled them into the clear liquid of that wondrous eleventh—Love God utterly, and thy neighbor as thyself—so I think the time will come when music, rightly developed to its now-little-foreseen grandeur, will be found to be a later revelation of all gospels in one."[11]

The Trade of the poem is modern capitalism, which prevents harmony in national life. The voices of protest are the voices of orchestral instruments, which should be played in harmony, in a perfect symphony; the figure used is one Lanier loved and one particularly appropriate to the kind of national life of which he dreamed. The poem, however, reveals another conviction, a conviction concerning the function of art in social life. This Lanier ably expressed in a letter of February 12, 1876, to Edward Spencer. He wrote there: "I met with a line in one of Shakespeare's sonnets some time ago which seems to me so completely a nutshell judgment on my side as regards the possibility of interpreting—within limits—one sense by another through the forms of art that I can't help sending it to you. It is: 'To hear with eyes belongs to Love's fine wit.' In my 'Symphony' Love's fine wit—the love of one's fellow-men—attempts (not to hear with eyes, but precisely the reverse) to see with ears.''[12] Love, charitable love for our fellow-men, hearing the cries of the poor, perceives with clearer vision their terrible plight, and the poet, orchestrating these cries into a harmony, creates through music a realization of social injustice and of the evils of modern industrialism. Photography is not more candid nor experience more convincing.

The first voice of protest is that of the violins asserting "We're all for love." But soon all the stringed instruments of the orchestra are repeating the song of the poor, in protest against the hardness of their circumscribed lot. In their behalf the instruments ask:

> "Does business mean, *Die you—live, I?*
> Then 'business is business' but sings a lie:
> 'Tis only war grown miserly.
> If Traffic is battle, name it so:[13]
> War-crimes less will shame it so,
> And widows less will blame it so.
> Alas for the poor to have some part
> In the sweeter half of life called Art
> Is not a problem of head, but of heart.
> Vainly might Plato's brain revolve it:
> Plainly the heart of a child could solve it."

There follows a description of the music which, though an interruption of the main argument, is an effective contribution to it, for the description of the music of the strings, like the music itself, conveys an impression, creates a mood, into which there breaks naturally the voice of the flute.[14] The lesson of Nature, which the flute voice teaches, is the lesson of the majestic, sheltering tree, of the "one tall corn-captain" of "Corn." But this lesson, the poet goes on to say, was obscured in early times by the absurd invention of fauns and rascal gods and nymphs— "cold creatures of man's colder brain"[15]—and so lost until Christ taught us that we should love our neighbors, for then

man found neighbors in great hills and trees
And streams and clouds and suns and birds and bees,
And throbbed with neighbor-loves in loving these.

This nature love of Lanier is more akin to that of St. Francis than
to that of Wordsworth, just as in the lines that immediately
follow the tenderness is distinctly Christian:

> But oh, the poor! the poor! the poor!
> That stand by the inward-opening door
> Trade's hand doth tighten ever more,
> And sigh their monstrous foul-air sigh
> For the outside hills of liberty,
> Where Nature spreads her wild blue sky
> For Art to make into melody!
>
> .   .   .   .   .   .
>
> Trade! is thy heart all dead, all dead?
> And hast thou nothing but a head?

the flute voice asks, and is silent, but he has plead eloquently,
and the silence that follows his plea is "thrilling." Vague stirrings
are heard among the various instruments, and then there sings
out the soprano voice of the clarionet,[16] the voice of the eternal
Magdalen who knows the difference between the carnal love
that is bought and true love that is given. She knows all too well
the enervating effects of Trade upon the hearts and manners
of men, to whom women are likely to be only as other chattels,
and adds her cry of protest to that of the poor:

> Base love good women to base loving drives.
> If men loved larger, larger were our lives;
> And wooed they nobler, won they nobler wives,

she asserts, making a plea in behalf of the emancipation of
women from the only condition that has ever truly enslaved
them.

Her cause is espoused by "the bold straightforward horn"
who cries

Shall self-wrapt husbands aye forget
Kiss-pardons for the daily fret
Wherewith sweet wifely eyes are wet—
   Blind to lips kiss-wise set—
      Fair Ladye?

Shall lovers higgle, heart for heart,
Till wooing grows a trading mart
Where much for little, and all for part,
   Make love a cheapening art,
      Fair Ladye?

Shall woman scorch for her single sin
That her betrayer may revel in,
And she be burnt, and he but grin
   When that the flames begin,
      Fair Ladye?

The inconsistency in Lanier's longing for a return of medieval standards of chivalry and his plea for a single standard of morality is only apparent, not real. The horn continues:

Shall ne'er prevail the woman's plea,
We maids would far, far whiter be
If that our eyes might sometimes see
   Men maids in purity,
      Fair Ladye?

The ideal of this knight is to be like Sir Philip Sidney, "To fight like a man and love like a maid," and the horn protests that his
                        faith is bright
      That God doth right and God hath might,

in spite of human failures and weaknesses.

   The voice of the knightly horn is followed by the voice of the innocent child-like hautboy which sings out finally, with the eloquence and melodiousness of William Morris in "Love is Enough":

"Life! Life! thou sea-fugue, writ from east to west,
　　Love, Love alone can pour
　　On thy dissolving score
　　Of harsh half-phrasings,
　　　Blotted ere writ,
　　And double erasings
　　　Of chords most fit.
Yea, Love, sole music-master blest,
May read thy weltering palimpsest.
To follow Time's dying melodies through,
And never to lose the old in the new,
And ever to solve the discords true—
　　Love alone can do.
And ever Love hears the poor-folks' crying,
And ever Love hears the women's sighing.
And ever sweet knighthood's death-defying,
And ever wise childhood's deep implying,
But never a trader's glozing and lying.

"And yet shall Love himself be heard,
Though long deferred, though long deferred:
O'er the modern waste a dove hath whirred:
Music is Love in search of a Word."

And so, in praise of love, which is music, and music, which is
love—and both revelations of God, "The Symphony" ends. The
final definition is a spiritual gloss on Mme. De Staël's famous
definition, which Lanier had read as a youth: "Music is love's
only interpreter";[17] but it is religious as well. It recalls Lanier's
assertion, made nine years earlier, that "Music . . . is utterly
unconscious of aught but Love."[18] It recalls, too, the declaration
of Felix Sterling, in *Tiger-Lilies*, that "Music means harmony,
harmony means love, and love means—God!" This is the core
of Lanier's philosophy, and "The Symphony," though certainly
not the most effective nor the most beautiful of Lanier's poems,
is, for the revelation it makes of his philosophy, without doubt
the most significant.

Undeniably there are defects in "The Symphony," phrases
that jar as badly as anything in "Corn," an exaggerated use of
compound words—more than seventy different ones, whole lines

14

that one would wish omitted, epithets that are ridiculous, but "The Symphony" possesses a music more varied and more beautiful than that of "Corn," and a richness of imagery that comes from a close observation of nature unsurpassed by that of Marlowe or Shakspere or Keats for accuracy. Furthermore, in this poem Lanier "achieved the amazing *tour de force* of making real poetry out of the money question,"[19] and poetry that is truly symphonic. Even so, "The Symphony" is less important as poetry than as protest, the first full-voiced protest of an able poet against the economic tyranny that still keeps politically freed men enslaved.[20] With its evidence of Lanier's reaction against gross materialism and too pure transcendentalism, and his attempt to direct the attention of poetry to the practical problems of the world, it is the most succinct evidence we possess of Lanier's concern with the predominant movement of his century, the industrial revolution as social fact and as philosophic ideal. And in spite of its emphasis on spiritual values, Lanier's poem, it may be justly insisted, presents an intelligible program for social amelioration.

§ 5

"THE SYMPHONY" appeared in *Lippincott's* for June, 1875, and immediately the success of "Corn" was repeated. Peacock, even more enthusiastic about it than he had been about "Corn," brought it to the attention of Bayard Taylor, who was greatly impressed and wrote in praise of it a letter which Peacock hastened to forward to Lanier. Charlotte Cushman and others whose opinion Lanier valued congratulated him on his achievement; *Dwight's Journal of Music* reprinted the entire poem; newspapers throughout the South reprinted Peacock's notice of it in the Philadelphia *Bulletin;* Elizabeth Stuart Phelps, who herself had tried to make literature out of the industrial ferment of New England in *The Silent Partner* (1871), based on a quoted line from it a poem which appeared in the New York *Graphic*. Best of all, the aristocratic and scholarly George H. Calvert, a critic of wide sympathies and intelligent comprehension, wrote of it at length in the *Golden Age* for June 12, 1875, the first serious notice given Lanier's poetry outside of newspapers and reviews since Davidson's notice in 1869.

"What immediately seizes and holds the reader in new poetry," Calvert wrote, "(and little of that printed is new even when

first uttered) are fresh aspects of old things, glimpses into here-
tofore undivulged vistas, new affinities flashed into view by a
stroke of genius. The generative play of thought thus attested
is a primary token of poetic quality. [In] the poem 'Corn' . . .
do you not feel as though a breath of hitherto unfelt life had
blown upon you? . . . Upon the reader's mind is shed a new
light, as of dawn with horizontal play into sparkling dewy
distances.

"From this joy in things visible and audible, from this wealth
of sensuous appreciation, it were a mistake to infer that Mr.
Lanier is at all a polished pagan. The fineness of his sensuous
sight comes from spiritual insight. . . . A sympathetic humanity
interpenetrates and warms his whole thought.

" 'Corn' . . . [and] 'The Symphony,' . . . alike in spirit and
execution, are a deep basis upon which may be built up a great
reputation. . . .

"The poems write themselves out of an overflowing soul. Their
great thoughts come . . . from the heart. And thence the verse
has the springiness which is only the result of interior movement;
the undulation inherent in life is everywhere perceptible. Both
poems have their roots deep in the personality of the poet; not
a sentence in them is drawn from mere memory and fancy; his
themes are illuminated with soul. And his soul being aglow with
music, he is empowered, through warm, healthy sympathies, to
make each natural thing utter the music there is in it, he thus
becoming one of the enraptured spokesmen of man and Nature."

This criticism, which Lanier appreciated greatly, is extremely
penetrating; but that Calvert was able to criticize and to appreciate the poet so justly on the evidence of only two poems is less
a tribute to his critical ability—he was after all not a great
critic nor even one of lasting importance, and he recorded big
words perhaps more often than big ideas—than to the completeness with which Lanier wrote himself into every poem.

§ 6

WHEN "The Symphony" appeared, however, and the appreciations began coming in, Lanier was already out of Baltimore,
and in Georgia. The Atlantic Coast Line Railway had commissioned him to prepare a guide book to Florida, then just
beginning to achieve a reputation for climate and popularity as
a resort, in the exploitation of which the railroad was chiefly

active. For Lanier's health it would have been far better that he go to Florida in the winter time, but money seemed more important than health, and certain employment with its certain rewards was a golden gift. In April, at the conclusion of his engagement with the Peabody Orchestra, Lanier had left Baltimore to begin the travels necessary to the preparation of the book.

A few days in the middle of April he spent at Brunswick, Georgia, with his wife and children and brother Clifford. Here, where he was later to find the inspiration for his most famous poem, he had a poignant sensation of the charm of the southern way of life, of the inescapable appeal of the South, but, with his strong sense of duties to be performed, he was determined to be on guard against it. "I am convinced," he wrote Mrs. Peacock, "that God meant this land for people to rest in—not to work in. If we were so constituted that life *could* be an idyll, then this were the place of places for it; but being, as it is, the hottest of all battles, a man might as well expect to plan a campaign in a dream as to make anything like his best fight here."[21] Three days later he was on his way to Jacksonville, a lonely traveler on a lonesome journey which he would gladly have avoided had it not been perfectly apparent that prose could be made to pay when poetry couldn't, and that economic security was necessary if one were to make any headway at all in the unceasing fight to make the world accept one's art.

It would be possible, on the basis of the published book on Florida, to reconstruct fairly accurately Lanier's travels in that state. He was not in Jacksonville in January, in spite of the evidence of the title of Chapter IV, but he was in St. Augustine for a pleasant visit late in April, and his chapter on that town is, as might have been expected, the best in the book, much like his essay on San Antonio de Bexar in method and in style. He recalled an incident of his visit here in the lectures on Shakspere which he delivered several years later, and probably in the quiet, old-world town of St. Augustine and in the trip up the lucent waters of the Ocklawaha River he found the only peace the long journey offered. Jacksonville was his headquarters, and from Jacksonville he made trips in various directions over the state. Whether he actually visited Key West and Dade County (of which Miami, not settled until about 1895, is now the county seat) is doubtful, however, for at the time lower Florida attracted

The Lanier oak and memorial at Brunswick, Georgia. " 'Neath this gracious tree stood Sidney Lanier and under inspiration of the oak and the marsh wrote 'The Marshes of Glynn.' "

few visitors and offered practically no facilities for their entertainment. Though he included a brief chapter on this part of Florida in his book his employers would hardly have insisted upon or even encouraged a visit there.

§ 7

By the middle of June Lanier was in Brunswick again, and reading eagerly the pile of letters and critical notices of "The Symphony" and of "The Power of Prayer" which had been accumulated for him.[22] There was a letter from Miss Cushman, whom he had finally met in March.[23] Letters from Mr. and Mrs. Peacock were doubly welcome, for one enclosed the letter from Bayard Taylor to Peacock in which Taylor praised "The Symphony" and criticized it intelligently. Lanier had long felt "a longing after him" and now the possibility of a meeting in the near future was a bright reward for the long, tiring journeys. This was what he wanted most: communion and fellowship with his equals, with men who spoke his language and who might understand his songs.

June 18 he began his travels once more, going from Brunswick to Savannah and thence up the coast to gather material for the appendix on Georgia and South Carolina resorts for the Florida volume. His activity for the next six weeks he described as that of a shuttle knocked violently backward and forward in a loom, for after an interview with his employers in New York he found it necessary to go South again to collect additional material, and though the twice-used metaphor of the shuttle is somewhat exaggerated, his traveling was extensive enough to leave him at the end of that time exhausted physically. At the end of July he went to Philadelphia to confer with Mr. J. B. Lippincott concerning the publication of the completed book on Florida and of certain chapters of it in *Lippincott's Magazine*. Unfortunately he found the Peacocks out of the city, and so he was deprived of the happiness in being with them that he had anticipated, but in the package of letters left for him at Peacock's office there was one from Bayard Taylor that made the possibility of a meeting with him certain.

The arrangements for the publication of *Florida* were thoroughly satisfactory; it was something, too, to have two chapters accepted as articles for the magazine, for that meant more money—and money Lanier had never needed more. Moreover, he had other reasons for pride, for he had also sold four sonnets to *Lippincott's* which were to (and did) appear in the September issue. Miss Emma Stebbins, Charlotte Cushman's companion and friend, had given him a letter of introduction to her brother, the chairman of the Board of Trustees of the new College of Music in New York, whom Lanier hoped to interest in his plans for lectures on the Physics of Music, the course that he had not been able to persuade the Peabody trustees to sponsor. And except for the immediate drudgery of putting his Florida volume into final shape, a labor on which alone he spent a month, working in Brooklyn, his future seemed bright and life wonderful indeed. His interest in the performance of music as a profession seems to have diminished already, for in his letter of July 31 to Peacock he wrote of the proposed lectures: "I can scarcely describe to you how lovely my life would seem if I could devote the balance of it to such lectures as would properly belong to a professorship of this nature, and to my poetry." There is nothing in this letter, we observe, of helping to interpret the music of the great masters.

§ 8

TAYLOR had informed Peacock that he intended writing to Lanier, but the letter had not come, and so Lanier decided to anticipate his letter with one thanking him for his "full and generous" appreciation of "The Symphony" in the letter to Peacock. The letter that Lanier now wrote, like his first letter to Peacock, was formal and stilted, but amazingly personal, even though the fact be granted that Taylor was already well informed about Lanier through the Peacocks and that Lanier could honestly feel therefore that he was not writing to a stranger. And yet the student of Lanier must be grateful for the self-revelation that one paragraph contains, for in it Lanier expressed briefly and with the succinctness of which he was often capable what all the preceding chapters of this volume may not have adequately expressed. In it he wrote: "I could never describe to you what a mere drought and famine my life has been, as regards that multitude of matters which I fancy one absorbs when one is in an atmosphere of art, or when one is in conversational relation with men of letters, with travelers, with persons who have either seen, or written, or done large things. Perhaps you know that, with us of the younger generation in the South since the War, pretty much the whole of life has been merely not-dying."[24]

Remembered now chiefly as the author of an excellent translation of Goethe's *Faust*, Bayard Taylor was in his and Lanier's day famous as an original poet, an agreeable and successful lecturer, and a critic of sympathy and penetration. Those who knew him personally found him a widely traveled man of unusual charm. In his travels—which had carried him to Africa and the far North and to the Orient (whither he went with Perry on that epochal voyage in which Lanier's friend, J. M. Kell, had also participated)—and as chargé d'affaires of the United States legation at St. Petersburg, Taylor had met and won the friendship of many distinguished people; his New York circle of close friends included Stoddard, Stedman, Aldrich, most of the editors and publishers, and G. H. Boker, who frequently came up from Philadelphia. With all the other important literary men of his day in the United States he was on terms of friendliness. He was the typical, sophisticated, genial, cosmopolitan man of letters whom Lanier yearned to meet, and one who could give Lanier the boost with the editors that he needed.

Taylor responded to Lanier's letter with cordiality, welcoming him "to the fellowship of authors" and inviting him to attend the celebration of Goethe's 126th birthday in New York on August 28, a celebration at which Bryant was to give the address and Taylor himself the ode. There, Lanier knew, he might see gathered together those for whose companionship he longed. The matter of tickets and meeting necessitated the exchange of several letters: it is pleasing to observe the care with which Taylor endeavored to give Lanier full directions for reaching the Hippodrome, where the celebration was to be held, and to spare his feelings in the matter of a dress suit, which, however, as a professional musician Lanier of course owned.[25]

No letter by Lanier in description of the Goethe celebration has been published, but it is easy to imagine the sort of letter he must have written to his wife: his account of the large auditorium and the brilliant gathering which he observed carefully from his seat in Taylor's box; of Bryant's address and Taylor's fine ode, of his excitement that carried him as on a great wave through the evening; of the suffering of returning alone to his room in Brooklyn. And it is easy to imagine, too, his description of his visit with Taylor at his home on Sunday afternoon, and the long, long talk through supper and into the evening of poetry and art and music and religious faith, in the comfortable, book-filled library, with the window opening on Central Park, which represented the economic security, the domestic permanency, the scholarly achievement it seemed he himself was destined not to know.

The long talk that Sunday afternoon and evening of August 29, 1875, confirmed their friendship; the signed photograph that Lanier sent two days later was the seal. Almost all the important friendships of Lanier's literary life were begun in correspondence, but when meeting came, the mutual interest was deepened. Capable of the greatest personal devotion and of drawing people to him by sheer force of personality, Lanier in other circumstances would have won and held among the great of the day a host of friends. But the accidents of birth, poverty, ill-health, kept him away from New England and New York, and finally even from Baltimore, an exile just beyond the boundaries of the promised land. Yet before he died, only six years, almost to the day, from the date of his first meeting with Taylor and his initiation into the ranks of the literati he had met or corresponded with practically every literary man of importance in America in his generation: and he could number among his closest, most devoted friends Paul Hamilton Hayne, Gibson Peacock, Charlotte Cushman, and Bayard Taylor, who were great in their day, though they were not, we can now see, so great as he.

The day after that memorable Sunday afternoon Lanier sent to Taylor for criticism five sonnets, three of which were in continuation of the four that had appeared in *Lippincott's* for September under the title of "In Absence."[26] "They form the beginning of a series," he wrote, "which I will probably be writing all my life, knowing no other method of heart's-ease for my sense of the pure worshipfulness which dwells in the Lady they celebrate." And Taylor replied: "I can't tell you how rejoiced I am to find in you the genuine poetic nature, temperament, and *morale*. These are the necessary conditions of success (not in the lower popular meaning of the word)—of the possibility of steadily approaching one's ideal, for we never can, or ought to, reach it. All I can say is: 'Be of good cheer!' "

But the excitement of Saturday and Sunday, combined with the overwork necessitated by his promise to have the *Florida* ready for the printers by a set date, played havoc with his health. When Taylor's letter came he was suffering terribly, and was not allowed by his physician the privilege either of speaking or of writing. Hemorrhage followed hemorrhage, and when they stopped, weak though he was, he had to take up again the manuscript of *Florida* and work "the whole of each day and much of each night."[27] "I'm crawling back into life," he wrote Peacock, "and hope to be at work in a few days";[28] but from this time on the crawl back into life became a fall back into death.

When *Florida* was finally finished, by the middle of September, Lanier took it to Philadelphia to the publishers and for a few brief days rested at the home of the Peacocks before hurrying back to Brooklyn and the necessity of packing to move to the Westminster Hotel in New York. Taylor, informed of his illness by Peacock and finally by Lanier himself, hastened to write a note of sympathy, and to say that he too was changing his residence and would henceforth be at 143 East 18th Street, within two blocks of Lanier's hotel. On Saturday, October 2, he took Lanier to the monthly meeting of the Century Club, where Lanier met for the first time Whitelaw Reid, Stoddard, Stedman, and other members of the New York group of writers whom he had merely seen at the Goethe celebration. This was a group as important in the decade of the '70's as the Boston group had been in a previous one. "God be praised that you exist," Lanier exclaimed in a letter to Taylor a few weeks later.[29] It was Taylor more than anyone else who had brought him acquaintance "with literary people and literary ways." What the Century Club—to which Lanier was given a guest card signed by Taylor, Stedman, and Stoddard—itself meant is delightfully revealed in a long letter to Edward Spencer written some time later. Lanier's description of the club and its members, the generous hospitality, the brandy-and-soda ("the best tipple of that nature" he had ever known), the long smokes and conversations, and the lavish Saturday night suppers, reveals the connoisseur of good food and good company, the lover of life and urbanity that we are too likely to forget Lanier was.[30]

§ 9

A CURIOUS episode of these first meetings of Lanier with the New York literati that has been censored out of the collected letters reveals clearly, however, that Lanier was not humbling himself with Boswellian obsequiousness. It also reveals his utter lack of the cosmopolitan sophistication that was characteristic of most of the contemporary poets with whom he felt himself in competition, and his extreme sensitiveness. In November, 1874, he had sent a brief note to E. C. Stedman[31] asking for an appointment that he might present a letter of introduction from Dr. J. G. Holland of *Scribner's*.[31] What came of the interview (if, indeed, it ever took place) is not known, but after the meeting at the Century Club in October, 1875, we find Lanier writing exuberantly to Stedman: "Won't you sometime or other—if only for your sins —read my '*Symphony*' in the magazine sent herewith?

"Although written in a mere lawless gust—a sort of little whirlwind originating at a point where the passion of music and the passion of pity, blowing different ways, happened to converge— yet, since it has cooled a little, and I have called myself to account for it, so many and great extensions of the artistic principles underlying it occur to me that I feel a strong desire, in beginning to exemplify them in new works, to do so with at least the hope that better embodiments of them than this very crude one might find favor in the eyes of so keen a critical faculty as that which reveals itself in your '*Victorian Poets*.'

"When we meet again, which I hope may be soon, you shall abuse or praise my poem just as much as you like, knowing that in either case I'm going to remain

"Your friend

"SIDNEY LANIER."[32]

Sometime later at Taylor's house Lanier met Stedman again, and in a letter of February 7, 1877—a letter written in answer to one from Taylor in which the name of Stedman was briefly mentioned—Lanier confessed to a humiliating experience. "I was never able to *stay* angry in my life," he wrote, but he was angered in spite of his declaration by the memories which the mention of Stedman's name called up, and he continued: " . . . I should meet Stedman without ever letting him know how much pain he has given me. Indeed, he has quite forgotten the details; it was *not* at the Century, but on the night when we left your house together; and he did *not* speak 'harshly' or 'abruptly' to me—I fear the old Gascon Adam in me would have had an all-too-quick slap in the face ready for that:—but he *advised* me

in a friendly way, 'not to be asking poets to dinner lest I might
be thought to be pushing my way!' I fancy it only increased
the pain of the wound that it was given in this advisory way
which would have made me seem very truculent to resent it;
and there was nothing to do but get off into some brake of silence,
like a deer with a shot in his flank, and lick mine own wound.
This seems extravagant; but it is not, compared with the real
suffering; it was *such* a fall for my vanity; to think that any
human being could have dreamed me capable of such a thought
after having seen me twice."[33] Here is an excellent illustration of
the remark made of Lanier by his friend Wysham that he suffered "woman's tortures . . . of enduring agonies never to be
confessed."

Lanier was to meet Stedman again later, and on terms of
friendship, and after Lanier's death Stedman, through kind
offices as an anthologist and critic, did much to promote Lanier's
fame; but Lanier could never have felt toward Stedman as he
felt toward Taylor, no matter what kindnesses Stedman might
have done him. Indeed, Lanier never became intimate with any
of the New York circle of writers except Bayard Taylor; he knew
them little better than he knew, for instance, the Brownings,
of whom he heard so much from Taylor's lovely German wife
whom both Lanier and Mrs. Lanier soon came to know most
pleasantly.

Taylor's chief service to Lanier was not, therefore, in introducing him to men of letters but in giving him sound critical
advice. It is beyond doubt partly because of Taylor's criticism
that the four sonnets called "Acknowledgment," written at this
time in continuation of the "In Absence" sonnets, though not
published until a year later,[34] are so much better than the first
four. In them Lanier has not yet achieved the ease and natural-
ness of expression of the Columbus sonnets in "The Psalm of the
West," the best sonnets he was to write, but they do possess
something of the grace of Elizabethan sonnets, to which Taylor
may very well have directed his attention. Taylor probably
encouraged the writing of sonnets as an exercise in form and
because he felt that Lanier should attempt short "swallow flights"
as well as long symphonic composition. It is interesting to note
that in the first of the "Rose-Morals," which Lanier sent to
Taylor in October, he made a metrical correction suggested by
Taylor but he did not agree with Taylor's objection to the

repeated vowel sound in the line "Say yea—say yea." Taylor, in objecting to such a line—which follows shortly on another line, "As yon red rose, and dare the day," in which the same sound also occurs, defined one of the greatest weaknesses in Lanier's verse; and Lanier, in refusing to accept the suggestion, reveals that this overly-musical element in his poetry was to him a matter of pleasure and pride.

§ 10

IN OCTOBER it was necessary for Lanier to go again to Philadelphia to correct proof sheets and supervise the wood-cuts of *Florida*, which the publishers were rushing through in order to have the book on sale before the travel of winter visitors to Florida began. While he was there, staying in the home of the Peacocks, he received a letter from Charlotte Cushman inviting him with "lavish goodness" to visit her at the Parker House in Boston; and since the visit held out also prospects of meeting Longfellow and Lowell and Aldrich, to whom Taylor had already offered him letters of introduction, Lanier accepted her invitation, settled the problem of a new dress coat, and went, early in November, to spend a week there.

Unfortunately the references to this visit in Lanier's letters are meager indeed, and though certain bald facts concerning it survive, we miss his own account of his call on Longfellow, his afternoon with Lowell, and his meeting with other people of importance whose names had long been familiar to him. And somehow the impression arises that these meetings with the great of New England were disappointing to Lanier. Of all the New England writers of the time only Emerson, in many ways the most untypical of them all, seems ever to have held his interest, and personal contact with Lowell and Longfellow probably meant as little to Lanier—once it had come—as meeting him did to them. Longfellow, it is true, wrote Taylor that he "was much pleased with Mr. Lanier,"[35] and referred to him later as "the charming Southerner,"[36] but Longfellow was old, much older than Lanier; and there was too much difference in age, reputation, and temperament for them to have taken any real interest in each other. Upon his return to Baltimore Lanier sent to Longfellow copies of "Corn," "The Symphony," and the "In Absence" sonnets, but the letter that accompanied them is studiedly formal, in strange contrast with the warmth of the first letters that he

wrote to Peacock and to Taylor when he had never even seen
them.

"My dear Sir," he wrote: "I send you today by express three
magazines containing the poems you were kind enough to speak
of during my recent visit to Boston. I have the less hesitation in
submitting them to you since I know that upon your own theory
of criticism—as you expounded it to me—you will give yourself
no trouble to say anything about them in the event you shall
find them having no effect upon you as poems.

"Very truly yours,

"SIDNEY LANIER."[37]

And the letter, it is probably unnecessary to add, did not inaugurate a correspondence. It is not recorded in Longfellow's
letter book that it was even answered. "Corn" and "The Symphony" apparently had no effect on Longfellow as poems.

The letter of introduction by which Taylor recommended
Lanier to Lowell still survives.[38] In it Taylor calls Lanier "the
only poet of the younger generation whom the South has given
us. I need only say," he added, "that I find in him the true
instinct, gift, and culture, to assure him a kindly reception by
you." But Lowell responded less to the charm of Lanier's personality than his account of that afternoon, written thirteen
years later, would suggest. To President Gilman of Johns Hopkins
he wrote on the occasion of the celebration of Lanier's forty-sixth
birthday: "He was not only a man of genius, with a rare gift
for the happy word, but had in him qualities that won affection
and commanded respect. I had the pleasure of seeing him but
once, when he called on me 'in more gladsome days,' at Elmwood,
but the image of his shining presence is among the friendliest
in my memory."[39] "His shining presence" is one of the happiest
phrases ever spoken of Lanier, but the praise in Lowell's letter
is hollow. The brightest memory of his visit to Boston for Lanier
was undoubtedly that of his "good Charlotte Cushman," the
brave sufferer, the kind friend, whom he was never to see again.

§11

FROM BOSTON Lanier went to New York for a day, and then
directly to Macon for two weeks. To Taylor he wrote: "I had
a charming visit to Miss Cushman, and . . . each day was
crowded with pleasant things which she and her numerous

friends had prepared for me."[40] His stay in Macon, reunion with
his wife and his boys, meant far more, however, than all Boston,
and all the great and the near great he had met in this busy,
crowded year that had opened so auspiciously with the publication of "Corn." As he looked back upon the events of the past
eleven months he could smile with pleasure and satisfaction,
knowing that now he could dream his sweetheart bread and
dream her wine, for fame had come at last to him. And ever
grateful for past kindnesses he could write to Hayne: "all along
through these last three or four months when gratifying things
have been happening to me in connection with my little artistic
efforts, I have had constantly in mind the kindly help and
encouragement which your cheering words used to bring me
when I was even more obscure than I am now."[41]

But the struggle was not yet over, and separation from his
family was still necessary. On November 26 Lanier returned to
Baltimore to resume his old place as first flute in the Peabody
Orchestra, "though hoping all the time still to find some opportunity for getting [the] longed-for chair of The Physics and Metaphysics of Music established in some college or other";[42] but with
him he took young Charles Day Lanier, age seven, for he could
not endure to be separated from all his loved ones. There was
fresh excitement of the kind he had been knowing all that year
for three days, the 21st, 22nd, and 23rd of December, when Taylor
was in Baltimore, lecturing before the Peabody Institute. "Join
me at the hotel and go with me [to the opening lecture]," Taylor
had written. "We can then have a glass of punch together,
afterwards."[42] Five days later Taylor wrote from Philadelphia,
without having mentioned the subject previously, that it was
quite decided though not yet announced that Lanier would be
invited to write the cantata for the opening of the Centennial
Exposition in Philadelphia the following spring. The honor,
unexpected and unsought, was official recognition of Lanier's
fame.

CHAPTER ELEVEN

FLORIDA AND INDIA

§ 1

THE WAY in which fame, invoked so long before, had come to Lanier could hardly have been more gratifying, but the fame he had won was not the only fact on which Lanier, at the end of the year 1875, might congratulate himself, for his financial position was more secure than it had ever been previously. He was selling poetry now to *Scribner's Monthly* and prose and poetry to *Lippincott's Magazine*, both of which certainly paid better than the southern magazines in which his work had previously appeared. His position with the Peabody Orchestra, his pupils, and other musical engagements, he retained. And he now had an established reputation as a writer, which caused publishers to seek him out with commissions. Unfortunately these commissions were chiefly for prose: they paid well but they were difficult to execute and did not give him the joy in execution that he found in writing a poem. Upon the completion of them he was usually exhausted spiritually and physically, and such work was, with all its compensations, never truly congenial to him.

Two well paid prose works executed in this way in 1875 were the railway guide to Florida and a series of papers on India written for *Lippincott's Magazine*. It is significant, however, that into what was essentially hack-work, quickly done, Lanier could put so much of himself. Too much, indeed, some reviewers complained. A paragraph in the *Nation* for October 28, 1875, had caused Lanier considerable pain, for he had read: "In *Lippincott's* for November there is the usual strong proportion of sketches of travel, with and without illustrations. The paper on 'St. Augustine in April,' by Sidney Lanier, belongs in the former category, and the wood-cuts are very good indeed. It is more historical than descriptive, and Mr. Lanier's poetical licenses in prose are accordingly fewer than usual. He has an agreeable style when it is not surcharged with imagery. Even here his rhetorical-poetical foible of seeing 'God in everything' displays itself once too often, in the passage where he speaks of 'a morning which mingles repose with infinite glittering, as if God should smile in his sleep.' In a former paper of his, also on Florida, similes like this occurred several times, if we remember rightly. Mrs. Rebecca Harding Davis is a much more restrained and artistic writer, and her descriptions in 'Qualla' of the natural scenery of North Carolina are excellent in point of taste and effectiveness. . . ."

Lanier's indignation at this criticism burst forth in exaggerated terms in a letter to Taylor: "The [*Nation*] takes occasion to give me some pain, anent this poor St. Augustine article, by first making a statement which is grossly inaccurate, and next basing on it a criticism which would be unjust even if its foundation were not untrue, and finally dismissing the subject with a comparison of my merits and Mrs. [Davis]'s, which is as pure a piece of gratuitous ungentlemanliness as a vulgar soul could well devise. Not that I care in the least for the judgment, or that I shall change my 'foible'—foible! of seeing God in everything: but it may interfere with one's already very short allowance of bread, by making the magazines shy of giving employment to one who fails to please the [*Nation*]. . . . [My] indignation is wholly impersonal, and entirely due to that repugnance with which one sees a really strong newspaper turning over articles to be 'criticized' by persons who do not even understand the usages of gentlemen."[1] But this was extreme to the point of being ridiculous, and probably called forth entirely by the reference to his religious predilections, for Lanier, with his naturally religious temperament, conceived the function of both poet and prose-writer as essentially a religious one. The *Nation's* criticism was not unkind, and the statement that his "poetical licenses in prose are . . . fewer than usual" should have pleased Lanier, for it implied that the *Nation's* reviewer, unless indeed he was referring only to the previous Florida paper, "The Ocklawaha River," had taken notice of his articles in the *Southern Magazine*, for it was with the two Florida papers—chapters taken verbatim from the book, which was not yet published—that Lanier made his début as a prose writer in the northern press. The *Nation's* criticism, we must also admit, should have been helpful to Lanier;

FLORIDA:

ITS

SCENERY, CLIMATE, AND HISTORY.

WITH

AN ACCOUNT OF CHARLESTON, SAVANNAH, AUGUSTA, AND AIKEN, AND A CHAPTER FOR CONSUMPTIVES;

BEING

A COMPLETE HAND-BOOK AND GUIDE.

BY

SIDNEY LANIER.

WITH NUMEROUS ILLUSTRATIONS.

PHILADELPHIA:

J. B. LIPPINCOTT & CO.

Title-page of "Florida," Lanier's second published volume.

15

the reviewer had hit upon the essential weakness of his prose style—its sentimentality.

In November, 1875, the completed volume, *Florida: Its Scenery, Climate, and History*, appeared. The *Nation* does not seem to have noticed it, though the *Literary World* of Boston gave it a complimentary notice, and spoke of Lanier as "an easy and sometimes brilliant writer."[2] Lanier described it to Hayne as "a kind of spiritualized guide-book,"[3] and though it was designed for the practical purpose of luring visitors to the state and furnishing them with information concerning the best ways to reach and to tour it, it was inevitable that Lanier should have put much poetry and much of himself into it. Otherwise, indeed, the very composition of it would have been intolerable to him. To Mrs. Boykin, who had written him in praise of it, he replied: "The book has been like a wound to me ever since I was engaged to write it; for, aside from the inherent difficulties of the commission (my instructions from my employers were simply to write them a guide-book which should not be also a poem), I did not wish ever to appear before the public again save in the poetic character. . . . it is balm to my hurt when anybody finds poetry in the book—as your kind letter tells me you do; . . ."[4]

Lanier's prose style, seldom clear-cut and concise, and usually weakened, like his poetry, by the sudden interjection of an adjective or an epithet that seems almost effeminate and has the effect of startling the reader by the very inappropriateness of it, was hardly the style for a book of this type, and yet it must be admitted that Lanier did produce a thoroughly readable book on Florida which even the modern visitor to Florida would do well to pack in his hand-bag. What Lanier described he described accurately and well, and with a sprightliness not always spoiled by exuberance; and the development of Florida since his visit has produced few places of interest to call for comment in more modern guide-books—which make, indeed, certainly less pleasant reading. Except for the quaint town of St. Augustine there was little in Florida to attract the sightseeing tourist, Lanier knew, but his task was to make a land chiefly notable for its climate as interesting as possible for those whom the climate should attract, and this he did by giving detailed comments on the climate, with illustrative anecdotes, going into a long discussion of the Gulf Stream, the soil, and the fruits that the soil would bear, and the means of transportation, with descriptions of the hotels. But so filled is *Florida* with references to himself, so revealing is it of Lanier's own tastes and pleasures, that it is an interesting book of quite another sort for anyone interested in Lanier.

The efficaciousness of the climate in the treatment of various diseases he discusses, citing examples of cures, but the chief importance of Florida as a health resort, he perfectly well knew, was in the treatment of consumption. In this connection he discusses repeatedly his own personal experience with frankness and intelligence, but it is a little surprising to find him stating at the outset that he "used to be a 'consumptive,' " for certainly the occurrence of severe hemorrhages at the very time he was engaged in preparing the book for the press must have reminded him that his own illness was far from being cured.

Lanier even found in Florida a spiritual quality that seemed an antidote for the mercantile spirit of which he had sung so bitterly in "The Symphony." "The question of Florida," he wrote, "is a question of an indefinite enlargement of many people's pleasures and of many people's existences as against that universal killing ague of modern life—the fever of the unrest of trade throbbing through the long chill of a seven-months' winter." He found "rests and balms and salutary influences in the green leafage" and "the grave and stately courtesies of the antique Spaniard . . . in the profound reserves of its forests, in the smooth and glittering suavities of its lakes, in the large curves and gracious inclinations of its rivers and sea-shores." And he adds, with an almost exact echo of a letter he had written Hayne five years before: "Here one has an instinct that it is one's duty to repose broad-faced upward, like fields in the fall, and to lie fallow under suns and airs that shed unspeakable fertilizations upon body and spirit. Here there develops itself a just proportion between quietude and activity: one becomes aware of a possible tranquillity that is larger than unrest and contains it as the greater the less." Two methods, as he states in his introductory chapter, he had decided upon in preparing the book, one the practical, the other the poetical, but except in the appendices and a few brief chapters it is "the poetical or descriptive" method that predominates, as here.

The second chapter, an account of a trip up the Ocklawaha River, is a fair example of this method that so annoyed the *Nation's* reviewer. Lanier describes the day and the boat, the vegetation and trees that bordered the stream, the alligators that lived in it; he reproduces with exactness the dialect of the native whites and records in musical notes the tunes whistled by the Negro deck-hand, and slips into a discussion of whole tones and semi-tones, and the effects achieved by the use of whole tones alone in the singing of the Negroes and in works by Asger Hamerik and Edward Grieg—all of which is interesting and rather charming, but hardly exciting enough to make one wish to go to Florida to repeat Lanier's trip.

One paragraph of this chapter we should note, however, because we shall meet with it again in different guise. It is the brief account of the conjunction of the river with Silver Spring Run, and of the strange effect of the two streams, the one clear enough, the other so amazingly clear as to make the former seem muddy in comparison, flowing side by side, unmixing, for some distance. Twice later,[5] Lanier was to use this phenomenon to illustrate a fact about Chaucer's poetry—that it is no well of English undefiled but two streams flowing side by side and unmixing, the one French, the other English, and each clear and good of its kind. The trip up the Ocklawaha was an experience in Lanier's life which was unforgettable; in like fashion the visit to Silver Spring and to the similar Wakulla Spring gave him a simile for transparency and depth that he was to find useful in describing for boys the beautiful, frank work of Malory.[6]

The third chapter, on St. Augustine in April, contains good descriptions of old Fort Marion and other buildings of the town, an interesting account of the Indians,[7] and of Ponce de Leon's spring which is called The Fountain of Youth; and in it Lanier reprints extracts from various early documents of interest and importance in the history of St. Augustine, following the method employed in his earlier account of San Antonio de Bexar. But the long digression on love, and on the sea wall as an ideal promenade for lovers, with the quotation from Chaucer's catalogue of his early tales concerning lovers, is not merely sentimental and out of place: it is, one is tempted to say, actually in bad taste, and somewhat silly.

Florida appeared first in 1875, and again with numerous appendices in 1876; it was reissued in 1877, and again in 1881; and two chapters were included in Strahan's volume, *Some Highways and Byways of American Travel*, issued in 1878.[8] But one wonders if the various reissues of the book and two of its chapters indi-

cate a real popularity or merely the lack of other and better
guide-books to the state. Useful as it must have been, especially
in the second and subsequent editions, with its "railway guide,"
its "Gazetteer of Towns, Rivers and Counties," and its appendices on various topics concerning agriculture and horticulture
in Florida, written by experts on the different subjects, the main
body of the book must have seemed, even to the tourists of an
age more sentimental and less commercialized than our own, a
little incoherent, a little too literary for a guide-book. In Chapter
III, "Jacksonville in January," there is a rambling digression
on pine trees, with a long quotation from Ruskin and a moraliz-
ing paragraph on hill-pines and the pines of the plain. "The
pines of the plain," we are told, "have higher meanings if lower
sites;[9] theirs is the unwrinkled forehead of a tranquil globe; they
signify the mystery of the repose that comes only from tested
power and seasoned strength—a grandeur of tranquillity which
is as much greater than the grandeur of cataclysms as Chaucer
is greater than Byron, as Beethoven is greater than Berlioz, as
Lee's manhood is greater than Napoleon's." This is interesting,
for in it Lanier anticipates certain things he was to say later in
his letters, his poems, and particularly his Shakspere lectures,
but in a guide-book to Florida—? In the chapter on the coast
cities of South Carolina and Georgia Lanier, in mentioning the
poets of the various cities—Timrod, Hayne, Randall, and H. R.
Jackson—quotes poems written by them, but in the chapter on
Jacksonville he actually quotes a medieval Latin song in the
original language.

Three other chapters in the book call for special comment.
In Chapter XII Lanier discusses scientifically the climate and
the cause of it, the Gulf Stream, the Arctic Current, winds and
rainfall. In Chapter XIII he gives a brief history of Florida
from the discovery to the time at which he wrote. Lanier was
always an interested student of history, and when he undertook historical writings, as in the paper on San Antonio, this
chapter, and the Shakspere lectures, he investigated his subject
thoroughly, prepared his material carefully, and usually wrote
an interesting, readable paper. He never of course made any
original investigations, but there was scholarliness in his handling
of the investigations of others.

But Chapter XIV, "For Consumptives," is for the student
of Lanier perhaps the most interesting chapter in the book, a

sort of medical *apologia pro vita sua*, and in all Lanier's published work the clearest statement concerning his own illness. He begins the chapter with a paragraph that is amazingly frank, coming from one so reticent: "In the course of a desperate but to all present appearances successful struggle with a case of consumption which had everything in its favor at the start—the prestige of inheritance on both sides and the powerful reinforcement of a bent student's habits—this present author finds remaining prominently in his recollection a few cardinal principles of action in this behalf which may possibly be of practical service to consumptives. In view of such a possibility, one cannot hesitate upon the sacrifice of personal delicacy involved in referring to oneself. A pain that cures a pain justifies its being."

The principles that he presents are principles grounded in an invincible optimism which was perhaps of all Lanier's traits the one most characteristic. The first principle is: "Set out to get well, with the thorough assurance that consumption is curable." Not that he means, in the fashion of certain religious cults, to deny the existence of the disease, but to have faith in the possibility of a successful cure. His second principle is: "Give faithful and intelligent trial to every apparently reasonable mode of cure suggested for the disease," for Lanier realized that individual idiosyncrasies necessitated individual treatment. He discusses in this connection the use of stimulants (placing an importance upon the use of whiskey which would be questioned by medical men at the present time) and the exercise of the lungs, which he had found most helpful and most pleasant by the use of a Boehm flute.

The third principle is "Never get in the slightest degree wet, cold, or tired." It was this principle that Lanier himself found it impossible to obey, for tired he usually was from the unceasing battle with trade, and if, as an authority on consumption has recently stated,[10] emotions are dangerous for the consumptive, and among them the emotions of love and worry, Lanier was doomed by the very nature of his existence to succumb to the disease, which even as he was writing *Florida*—hurrying to send his manuscript to the printer that the book might be ready before the winter travel to Florida began—struck him a fatal blow.

It is a curious book, this *Florida*, as personal and revealing as anything Lanier ever wrote; for the general reader, an adequate account of an interesting state; for the student of Lanier a mine of information, a guide to Lanier's mental habits and interests, and with the Shakspere lectures, which it, curiously enough, resembles, a comprehensive picture of the man with his many varied interests; and for the tourist to Florida, a sort of week-end library of useful and pleasing information compressed into a small volume—a wealth of practical information, an anthology of poetry, a text-book of history, a guide to horticulture, and a "family physician."

§ 2

FROM WORK on *Florida* Lanier turned to similar work on a series of articles called "Sketches of India," which appeared anonymously in *Lippincott's Magazine* in four installments, during the first four months of 1876.[11] The information he gathered from books borrowed from the Philadelphia Free Library while he was in Philadelphia seeing *Florida* through the press, and the actual writing he began in Boston at the time of his visit to Miss Cushman. The articles are entertaining, and filled with correct knowledge of India, of Indian history and art, religion, customs, and industry, but it seems strange that *Lippincott's* should have cared to publish work that had no value as a first-hand report, should even have commissioned Lanier to prepare the articles.

The articles are written much in the discursive manner of the book on Florida, with Lanier "talking coolly of strolling about Bombay with a Hindu friend." The reason and justification for what was essentially a literary imposture Lanier himself explained in a letter to Peacock: "Bhima Gandharva . . . is only another name for *Imagination*—which is certainly the only Hindu friend I have; and the propriety of the term, as well as the true character of Bhima Gandharva and the insubstantial nature of all adventures recorded as happening to him and myself, is to be fully explained in the end of the last article. I hit upon this expedient, after much tribulation and meditation, in order at once to be able to make something of a narrative that should avoid an arid encyclopedic treatment, and to be perfectly truthful. The only plan was to make it a pure *jeu d'esprit;* and in writing the second paper I have found it of great advantage."[12]

In spite of the accuracy with which Lanier recast the material of books and articles on India by other writers, our interest in these papers must be considerably less than our interest in *Florida*, and limited almost entirely to the occasional revelations of himself which Lanier makes. Humorous references to himself and his American characteristics—he gives himself a "slightly nasal" voice, which he, a cultivated Georgian, did not have— and to his native "Jonesville," lighten the encyclopædia-like tone of the articles, but the humor is often ill-conceived as when, after quoting a magnificent passage from the *Bhagavad-Gita* listing the infinite aspects of Krishna, Lanier remarks: "When my friend finished these words there did not seem to be anything particular left in heaven or earth to talk about." References to indigo culture in Florida repeat information recorded in the Florida volume. A scheme that anticipates the modern city-manager plan of government suggests Lanier's disgust with the contemporary political situation in the United States. But one searches through the sketches with little success for information, for references that will throw light on "Nirvâna" and casual references to India in Lanier's earlier work: the "Sketches of India" represent an interest in India cultivated for financial reasons; there is in them no revelation of an appreciation of the Buddhistic philosophy and Brahmanic thought which at one time seem to have held Lanier's imagination.

These sketches are therefore unlike everything else that Lanier ever wrote in that they reveal so little of himself and bear so remote a relation to the body of his work, suggesting in style and method only a few passages in the Shakspere lectures. But in them, in spite of the imaginative conception of Bhima Gand-harva, Lanier writes with more restraint than usual, and there are fewer digressions and more unadorned facts. The "Sketches of India" are not, we may feel sure, the kind of sketch Lanier would have written had he actually gone to India and made first hand observations; on the other hand, they are not what they would have been had they been written any earlier in his career.

§ 3

FOR LANIER's prose style here is more objective, and it grows noticeably better from this time on, just as in his poetry, under the restraining influence of Taylor's experienced judgment and practice in the sonnet form, he also shows improvement. Indeed, nothing could have helped Lanier more at this time than the exercise of writing sonnets, and nothing measures his real growth in poetic expression more than the superiority of his later sonnets over his first ones. The first of the series of sonnets addressed to Mrs. Lanier, the first of the four called "In Absence," seems only a mechanic exercise, for the opening quatrain is a paraphrase of the first stanza of "In the Foam," written eight years previously, and there is little felicity of expression or metrical grace in the sonnet, save in the line, suggestive of Shakspere, "When lips draw back, with recent pressure pale"; on the whole it is immature, and like his first verses.

The second of the "In Absence" sonnets is better, and more suggestive of Shakspere's sonnets, which Lanier was obviously imitating, and the third and fourth are very good indeed—quite as good as the sonnets of Boker, who is generally considered the best of the American sonneteers of the century. But the four "Acknowledgment" sonnets are better still, and one, the third, beginning "If I do ask, How God can dumbness keep," is probably Lanier's best sonnet. The tone here is less Shaksperean than Miltonic; never altogether happy in putting into words for print his confessions of love, Lanier was often vigorous in administering rebuke, and Milton and Wordsworth (though Lanier would have denied this) were better masters for him than Shakspere. In spite, however, of good conception, expressive figures, and some memorable, well composed lines—such as the line "When life's all love, 'tis life: aught else, 'tis naught"—neither these eight sonnets nor the separate sonnets, "To Charlotte Cushman"[13] and "Laus Mariae"[14] are wholly successful; but they represent progressive improvement, and less than half a year later Lanier was to write for "The Psalm of the West" the very fine sonnet sequence of the Columbus episode.

The sonnets and the essay on "The Physics of Music," written about this time, indicate that for Lanier the year 1875 was a year of experimentation, and of research. The improvement in his prose and poetry, of the "Sketches of India" over *Florida*, of the later sonnets over the first, of "The Symphony" over "Corn," reveals that the year was also one of rapid artistic growth. Furthermore, success had given him courage. In the letter to his wife which accompanied "My Springs" he had complained that inasmuch as the poem was written for publication he had not dared to write as freely as he would have liked. But toward the end of 1875 he wrote of another poem, "Special Pleading,"[15]

"In this little song I have begun to dare to give myself some of the freedom in my own peculiar style, and have allowed myself to treat words, similes, and metres with such freedom as I desired. The result convinces me that I can do so now safely."[16]

The poem, read after this statement, is most disappointing: the figures are echoes from earlier poems; the rhyme scheme, though a new one (a-a-b-b-a), is less elaborate than ones he had used previously; the metrical scheme is less involved than that of "Rose-Morals," though the idea is too involved to be clear. But the musical effects are evident, and it was of course in the direction of greater and more varied verbal music that Lanier was striving. A magnificent opportunity to test his ability even more, to publish a poem that should embody his ideas of poetry and to publish also—as things were to happen—a clear statement in prose of those ideas before an audience that, officially at least, was the whole nation, came, as we have seen, at the very end of the year with the invitation to write the words for the Centennial cantata.

CHAPTER TWELVE

DEAR LAND OF ALL MY LOVE

§ 1

THE PLANS for the official opening of the centennial exhibition in Philadelphia in May, 1876, called for a hymn and a cantata, each to be written for the occasion by a poet of national prominence. Lowell was invited to compose the words for the hymn, and declined the invitation. Taylor was then asked, and accepted. Later Bryant, Longfellow, and Lowell in turn were asked to write an ode for the exercises on the Fourth of July, and each refused the invitation;[1] so—in March—Taylor was asked to write the ode and Whittier the words for the hymn. The music for the hymn was to be written by John Knowles Paine, the music for the cantata by Dudley Buck; and the music for both was to be played by Theodore Thomas's orchestra. The words for the cantata were to be asked of the poet who, after Bryant, Longfellow, Lowell, Taylor, and Whittier, seemed most important: E. C. Stedman. But Stedman had gone to Panama, and Buck was impatient to have the text in his possession that he might begin his work at once. In this dilemma General Hawley, president of the Centennial Commission, had asked Taylor "to name a poet *not* of New England,"[2] and Taylor had suggested a southern poet, and, specifically, Lanier.

So, feeling certain that Hawley would accept his suggestion, Taylor had written Lanier December 28, 1875, informing him what he had done and giving a little advice on the text which, he knew, Lanier would be only too glad to write. "I have just had a visit from Theo. Thomas and Mr. Buck," he added, "and we talked the whole matter over. Thomas remembers you well, and Mr. Buck says it would be specially agreeable to him to compose for the words of a Southern poet. I have taken the liberty of speaking for you, both to them and to General Hawley, and you must not fail me.

". . . It's a great occasion—not especially for poetry as an
art, but for Poetry to assert herself as a power." Lanier, rejoic-
ing in the honor and the opportunity and Taylor's goodness,
did not fail him. The official invitation from General Hawley
reached Lanier in Baltimore January 4, 1876, and he dispatched
his acceptance the same day. "This is very pleasing to me," he
wrote Mrs. Lanier, "for I am chosen as representative of our
dear South; and the matter puts my name by the side of very
delightful and honorable ones, besides bringing me in contact
with many people I would desire to know. . . . God is great."[3]
But his acceptance of the invitation was to precipitate a critical
controversy that makes an amusing chapter in American literary
history.

Taylor, as conscious of Lanier's poetical weaknesses as of his
true ability, repeated his advice: "you must not exceed fifty
lines; . . . 'Occasional' poetical work should always be brief,
appropriate in idea, and technically good. One dares not be
imaginative or *particularly* original."[4] With Taylor's advice in
mind Lanier produced the first version of the poem January 9,
and sent it that same day to Taylor for his criticism. The next
day, "being cool,"[5] he rewrote the poem, and sent the second
version with musical annotations also to Taylor.

Taylor, meanwhile, had received the first version and written
out his criticism of it. " 'Stairèd,' " he said succinctly, "will not
do, especially after 'hundred-*terraced*,' " and "stairèd" Lanier
changed to "towering." "Is 'balking' the best adjective?" Taylor
asked, but "balking" remains. It is quite evident that even in
asking Taylor's advice Lanier retained the privilege of his own
independent judgment. Taylor objected to the word "Lover" in
the last line of the cantata as "not true," and Lanier, accepting
the objection, changed the noun to "wisher," but in the final
version the poem, as published by Schirmer and presumably as
sung at the opening ceremonies, the original noun is restored,
and the line reads "And wave the world's best lover's welcome to
the world." "The plan," Taylor said in conclusion, "is entirely
poetical, and ought to be made very effective in music. I want,
for your sake, to have the Cantata universally liked, but you
will be sharply set upon if you use the words 'stairèd,' 'prescribèd'
and 'conscribèd,' and the line 'clothes for men,' etc. . . . Why
not yield that much, for this once? I also think that the sugges-

tion I make for the change in the stanza will make the whole piece more popular. There is both originality and lyric fire everywhere else."[6]

Lanier could be equally tactful, as he revealed in his answer to Taylor's letter. "I agree with your main points of objection," he replied, "and I will change the stanza about which you are most apprehensive. I'm particularly charmed to find that you don't think the poem *too* original. I tried hard to think—in a kind of average and miscellaneousness. . . .

". . . You see I had to compose for the musician as well as the country, and had to cast the poem into such a form as would at once show well in music (where contrast of movement between each adjacent part, in broad *bands of color*,[7] was, from the nature of the art, a controlling consideration) and in poetry. I wished indeed to make it as large as a Symphony of Beethoven's.[8] If it does not come up to this, I've failed; but your commendation confirms my own cool feeling about it, which is that it will do.

". . . Your criticisms on the piece are invaluable to me; for though I don't agree with all of them, the sharp re-examinations which they compel me to make develop many things which otherwise would not be developed."[9] The same day, before he could have received Lanier's letter, Taylor wrote, *à propos* of the second version: "If you doubt my judgment in the matter, consult Peacock also."[10] And so, through a series of letters, the discussion continued.

In Baltimore Lanier read and explained the poem to Theodore Thomas on January 12. Thomas praised the musical conception of the poem, and, while refusing to pronounce upon the poetic merits of it, pronounced the ideas "very beautiful."[11] But Thomas understood better than Taylor that the musical conception was most important, and that in the actual performance of the cantata the separate words of the text, indeed whole lines, would lose their identity and survive only "in broad bands of color." Taylor's criticisms on the text as a poem were excellent, but, considering the poem merely as a text for a cantata, unimportant. "I have had constantly in my mind those immortal melodies of Beethoven in which, with little more than the chords of the tonic and dominant, he has presented such firm, majestic, and at the same time artless ideas," Lanier wrote in a later letter.[12] It is perfectly clear that he was composing in sounds, and only secondarily in ideas. The whole discussion leads to the sweeping definition in *The Science of English Verse* that "The term 'verse' denotes a set of specially related sounds."[13]

On January 15 Lanier sent the complete text of "The Centennial Meditation of Columbia" with the musical analysis of each movement, or stanza, to Buck. Buck, who had been assistant conductor to Thomas in his concerts at Central Park Garden, was a musician of prominence and of real ability. A certain ecclesiasticism of temperament and long experience as a church organist—in Chicago (where he lost his valuable library in the great fire), in New York, and in Hartford—caused him to prefer to compose ecclesiastical music, and to color even his secular compositions with ecclesiastical themes. Both his temperament and his style were therefore congenial to Lanier, and probably no happier combination of composer and poet could have been achieved than the one that came about almost by accident. "God send you a soul full of colossal and simple chords," wrote Lanier, quite devoutly;[14] and Buck, probably also with a prayer began his work.

Buck seemed to be "immensely pleased"[15] with the text, and though all adjustments of music and words had to be made by letter, for Buck and Lanier had not yet met, they worked in "perfect harmony"; and within a few weeks' time the corrected text was ready for the printer and Buck's score was almost finished. But Lanier, who had been bravely indifferent to the criticism of his poems and had ignored Taylor's repeated warning to correct the text of the cantata with current fashions and public taste in mind, was, now that publication was imminent, overcome with fear and timidity. To Buck he wrote: "The truth is, I shrank from the criticism which I fear my poem will provoke,—not because I think it unworthy, but because I have purposely made it absolutely free from all melodramatic artifice, and wholly simple and artless; and although I did this in full consciousness that I would thereby give it such a form as would inevitably cause it to be disappointing on the first reading to most people, yet I had somewhat the same feeling (when your unexpected proposition to print first came) as when a raw salt spray dashes suddenly in your face and makes you duck your head. As for my own private poems, I do not even see the criticisms on them, and am far above the plane where they could possibly reach me; but this poem is *not* mine, it is to represent

1776—1876.

BY APPOINTMENT OF THE U. S. CENTENNIAL COMMISSION.

THE

CENTENNIAL

MEDITATION OF COLUMBIA.

A CANTATA

FOR

THE INAUGURAL CEREMONIES

AT

PHILADELPHIA, MAY 10, 1876.

POEM BY

SIDNEY LANIER,

OF GEORGIA.

MUSIC BY

DUDLEY BUCK,

OF CONNECTICUT.

NEW YORK:

G. SCHIRMER, 701 BROADWAY.

Title-page of "The Centennial Meditation of Columbia." Courtesy of the Library of Congress.

the people, and the people have a right that it should please
them."[16]

§ 2

WITH THE publication in the newspapers of the text without
music the attacks that Lanier dreaded commenced. Hardly a
newspaper or magazine failed to comment on the cantata, and
most of them repeated in varying tones a criticism of Lanier's
text that Taylor had tactfully made of the first version. For
instance, Hassard, the critic of the New York *Tribune*, wrote in
the issue of his paper for March 31, that the music was "simple
and clear in expression, while Mr. Lanier's language is sometimes obscure." The passage beginning with line 17 of the
published (fourth) version, "Jamestown, out of thee," he called
a "tough morsel"—one of the many pitfalls Lanier had set for
Buck which Buck however "escaped . . . with great skill"; and
he praised Buck's score generously. He gave no indication of
appreciating the fact that the words were inseparably a part of
the music, that the cantata was not a poem to be read but a
song to be sung; and of course Hassard could not know that
Lanier had had an important share in planning the music which
was, as he had wanted it to be, "clear and strong."

The Baltimore and the Philadelphia *Bulletins* rose, of course,
to Lanier's defense. Certain southern newspapers—out of sectional pride—answered the northern papers harshly without dis-
playing any real appreciation of the poem and, ignoring completely the compliment paid the South in Lanier's appointment,
accused them of condemning the poem purely on sectional
grounds. The discussion soon attained a vehemence and an
importance difficult to appreciate or to understand in days when
centennial expositions and matters connected with them attract
so little general interest.

To Lanier the notice in the *Tribune* seemed definitely to require
an answer, not merely because his artistic purpose had been
mistaken or his poem criticized but because the "attack" of the
critic seemed to him an attack on the sublime art of music and
poetry, and a "wrong on the public" for which he had written.[17]
Accordingly he prepared an answer which he intended offering
to the *Tribune*, first submitting it to Taylor and to Buck for
approval. But Taylor hastened to warn Lanier to be cautious:
"There are not fifty readers of the 'Tribune,'" he wrote "who

comprehend your annoyance sufficiently to sympathize with your rejoinder. Were it my case, my first thought would be to reply as you have done; my second thought would be, not to reply at all."[18] There was still time, he might have added, to profit by the criticism and make certain changes in the text.

Taylor's advice was sound. The publication of brief quotations in the *Tribune* article had been merely incidental to a discussion of the music, to which most of the article had been devoted and which had been highly praised. Buck, with admirable tact, replied to Lanier's letter in magnanimous terms. The "pitfalls" referred to by the critic had been "godsends," he insisted; it had been a pleasure to set the poem to music because he had taken a fancy to it. The effect of the poem on people of intelligence, he added, was cumulative: "Several have said to me 'these words grow upon me every time I read them.' . . . I think the intelligence of the country will be on your side, and about the rest I would not trouble myself. Be therefore comforted and write me a dramatic cantata!"[19]

But Lanier was not mollified. "I deem it of very great importance," he replied to Taylor, "that some intelligent criticism of my poem should appear in a journal of standing. . . . I am convinced that if one influential paper would take the initiative in judging the poem [in relation to the principles which guided its composition], all the loose opinions would crystallize about it, and, if not, I shall be cruelly misjudged and mistreated. . . . I feel as if the great wrong done me by Mr. [Hassard]'s criticism gave me a half-right and claim upon the paper." Then in a postscript he made this revealing confession: "I should like it to be stated that I have been a member of the Peabody Orchestra for three years, under Asger Hamerik."[20] His poems had been attacked as unmusical: his professional pride had been insulted, his poetic pride wounded to the quick.

Through Taylor's good offices, and with the sanction of Whitelaw Reid, the editor, the *Tribune* carried in the issue of April 12 the full text of the cantata—of which only quotations had previously been given—with a laudatory "explanatory introduction," written by Taylor himself. The cantata form, the reader was reminded, "presents a most ungrateful task to the poet who is not able to call up an attendant musical inspiration and persuade his conceptions to acknowledge the double sway. Mr. Lanier's verses, therefore, must be read with constant reference to the inevitable restriction of his task. . . . Contrasted with the Cantata written by Tennyson for the opening of the International Exhibition in London, its greater freedom and freshness are very evident, while in earnestness and absence of self-congratulation it will doubtless harmonize with the spirit of Whittier's hymn." This was gracious and generous: Taylor had written exactly what Lanier had requested.

§ 3

MEANWHILE other things had been happening which should have soothed Lanier's pride, both as musician and as poet. Thomas had invited him, at the suggestion of Wehner, his first flutist, to join his orchestra at the end of the summer for the concerts of the coming winter; Kirk, of *Lippincott's*, had commissioned him to write a centennial ode for the July number of his magazine; and in March Taylor had tactfully submitted to him for his criticism the hymn which he had written for the same opening ceremonies during which the cantata was to be performed. The hymn was withdrawn of course when Taylor was asked to write the ode, and Whittier was assigned the hymn, but the discussion of Taylor's hymn continued through several letters in which Lanier defended himself and his practice against Taylor's rejoinder that "you cannot apply the laws of Music to Poetry"[21] in a way that probably gave him much satisfaction.

Lanier's engagement with the Peabody Orchestra ended in March, and as he looked forward to playing with Thomas's orchestra the next season he prepared to leave Baltimore definitely. As soon as the Centenial ode commissioned for the July number of *Lippincott's Magazine* was completed, and necessary business had been attended to, he went to Montgomery, where his wife and boys had been staying with Clifford Lanier and his family, and then went on to Macon for a few days with his father. From here he wrote to Peacock: "The Southern people make a great deal more of my appointment to write the Cantata poem than I had ever expected, and it really seems to be regarded by them as one of the most substantial tokens of reconciliation yet evinced by that vague *tertium quid* which they are accustomed to represent under the general term of 'the North.' . . . The 'Tribune' notice of the Cantata has been copied by a great many Southern papers, and I think it materially assisted in starting the poem off properly; though the people here are so enthusiastic in my favor at present that they are quite prepared to accept blindly anything that comes from me. . . . The [Baltimore] 'Bulletin' represents 'The [Nation]' as saying that the poem is like 'a communication from the spirit of Nat Lee through a Bedlamite medium.' Nothing rejoices me more than the inward perception how utterly the time, and the frame of mind, are passed by in which anything of this sort gives me the least disturbance. Six months ago this would have hurt me, even against my will. Now it seems only a little grotesque episode."[22]

But in spite of his assertion that he had grown beyond being hurt by such attacks, he wrote to his father from New York ten days later the most confessionary and self-conscious of all his letters: "My experience in the varying judgments given about poetry . . . has all converged upon one solitary principle. . . . That principle is, that the artist shall put forth, humbly and lovingly, and without bitterness against opposition, the very best and highest that is within him, utterly regardless of contemporary criticism. What possible claim can contemporary criticism set up to respect—that criticism which crucified Jesus Christ, stoned Stephen, hooted Paul for a madman, tried Luther for a criminal, . . . drove Dante into a hell of exile, . . . reviled Shelley as an unclean dog, killed Keats, . . . and committed so many other impious follies and stupidities that a thousand letters like this could not suffice even to catalogue them?"[23] It is impossible to agree with Mr. Henry Lanier that the pain caused Lanier by "the criticisms and ridicule of the Centennial Cantata . . . was due . . . far less to personal sensitiveness than to the feeling that his critics were falsifying before the public principles of art which seemed to him vital."[24] A high sense of the duty of the poet to defend poetry against contemporary judgment Lanier did have, but in spite of repeated assertions to the contrary,[25] Lanier was far from indifferent to journalistic criticism of his own poetry. He would, indeed, have been unique among poets had he been as indifferent as he pretended to be.

§ 4

THE GRAND opening ceremonies of the Exposition were held May 10. The Emperor of Brazil, the governors of states, representatives of foreign nations, and an audience of fifteen thousand were present. Wagner's "Centennial Inaugural March," composed specially for the occasion, was played; Whittier's hymn was sung;

there were speeches by John Welch, President of the Centennial Board of Finance, General Hawley, and President Grant: and the cantata was performed by a chorus of eight hundred and an orchestra composed of one hundred and fifty musicians, with Myron Whitney of Boston as soloist for the Good Angel's song. It won the great crowd that neither the significance of the occasion nor the oratory, lost in the open air auditorium, had succeeded in stirring. "From the overture to the closing cadence," D. C. Gilman wrote[26] in describing the event, "it held the attention of the vast throng of listeners. The applause for Whitney's solo, 'Long as thine art shall love true love,' was so great that the chorus, already under way, was stopped that the solo might be repeated. When the Cantata was concluded loud applause rang through the air. A noble conception had been nobly rendered." Buck appeared and bowed his acknowledgment. The chorus rose and cheered. The enthusiastic approval of the cantata was surely a vindication of Lanier's text—or at least proof that the critics who had been so much disturbed about the effect of the words had been proved wrong. "Lanier had triumphed," Gilman added. "It was an opportunity of a lifetime to test upon a grand scale his theory of verse. He had come off victorious."

Instead, however, of accepting this popular approval of the performed work as a vindication, Lanier sent to the New York *Tribune* the letter that Taylor had previously advised him not to send, replying to all the criticisms made of the published text.[27] Lanier's letter is an interesting analysis of the cantata text and an able statement of the principles by which he had been guided in writing it, and, except for the final paragraph, in perfectly good spirit.

The chief note of the poem was one of reconciliation. Writing to Buck before the text had been published, while Congress still reverberated with the noise of opposition created by the Centennial bill, Lanier had said "All this will die out in a couple of months, and *then* everyone will be in a temper to receive a poem of reconciliation. I fancy that to print the poem *now* will be much like making a dinner speech before the wine has been around."[28] Lanier not merely ignored entirely—as a northern poet, for instance, would probably not have done—the Civil War; he was generous enough to praise Massachusetts before Virginia, appreciating the religious idealism of the Puritans and over-

looking the chronological precedence of the Jamestown settlers.
The Good Angel sings:

> Long as thy God is God above,
> Thy brother every man below,
> So long, dear Land of all my love,
> Thy name shall shine, thy fame shall glow.

Lanier had written Peacock from Macon: "any success seems
cheap which depends so thoroughly on local pride as does my
present position with the South." Now in his letter to the *Tribune*—and to the nation itself—he wrote: "Much of [the] praise
has come from the section in which [the author] was born, and
there is reason to suspect that it was based often on sectional
pride rather than on any genuine recognition of those artistic
theories of which his poem is—so far as he now knows—the first
embodiment. Any triumph of this sort is cheap because wrongly
based, and to an earnest artist is intolerably painful." It is the
protest he had voiced in the Furlow College commencement
address seven years previously, a protest against the sort of blind
chauvinism that, whether sectional or national, Lanier wished
above everything else to avoid in his poem.

The discussion of the cantata, given new impetus by Lanier's
defense, continued. On May 21 the *Tribune* carried an editorial
on the subject, expressing regret at the sectional antagonism
raised by it. "Whatever may be thought of his performance,"
the writer stated in reference to Lanier's letter, "he makes it
evident that he worked in accordance with a conscious, intelligent
system, and that, if he has failed, it was not through ignorance
or lack of honorable intention." But this was faint praise: Lanier's
letter had won him far less honor than the popular approval had
previously given him, and it actually provoked another attack
from the *Nation*, which had previously called on the commissioners
to "save American letters from the humiliation of presenting to
the assembled world such a farrago as this."

Quoting Lanier's statement that his work was "at all events
a faithful attempt to embody the status of poetry with regard
to the most advanced musical thought of the time, made upon
carefully evolved laws, and with clear artistic purposes," the
critic asserted: "This statement of his object indicates the defect
alike of his poem and of his letter. No one accustomed to use

of words with precise and definite meaning could speak of a poem as an attempt to embody the status of poetry with regard to musical thought or anything else. Mr. Lanier's poetic sensibility and serious purpose cannot make up for the lack of clear expression in his writing. This lack is the evidence not so much of want of practice in composition as of discipline in thought." The writer then proceeded to point out that music, contrary to Lanier's contentions, "is not capable of adequately expressing any strictly intellectual conceptions."

In spite of this Lanier felt that a reaction in his favor had set in. In a letter of May 23 to his brother he wrote: "I see that you have been annoyed by the howling of the critics over the Cantata. I was greatly so, at first, before I had recovered from my amazement at finding a work of art received in this way sufficiently to think, but now the whole matter is quite plain to me, and gives me no more thought at all.

"I enclose a letter of mine to *The Tribune*, which, by all accounts, leaves me master of the situation.

"I find I have sent away all the 'sweet voices' for which you ask, anent the Cantata. They were principally in *The Tribune*, the *Bo. Gazette*, the N. Y. *Evening Telegram*, the *Pha. Bulletin* and the Women's paper called *The New Century for Women* so far as I know besides the Southern papers. Mr. Taylor tells me that he knows of quite a reaction in my favor in New York; and my letter completely demonstrates that the whole body of absurdities called critics went off half-primed. The poem is not in the least ultimate danger and the snarls will have long been forgotten before it dies. It is really the first English poem written in such a way that the whole body of it could be genuinely set to music. . . .

"The whole agitation has been of infinite value to me. It has taught me, in the first place, to lift my heart absolutely above all expectation save that which finds its fulfillment in the large consciousness of faithful devotion to the highest ideals in art. This enables me to work in tranquillity.

"In the second place, it has naturally caused me to make a merciless arraignment and trial of my artistic purposes; and an unspeakable content arises out of the revelation that they come from the ordeal confirmed in innocence and clearly defined in their relations with all things. I do not hate the people who have so cruelly maltreated me; they knew not what they did; and my life will be of some avail if it shall teach even one of them a consideration that may bloom in tenderer treatment of any future young artist.

"The Columbus *Times* article which you had is very good. I had not heard that Randall[29] and Hope[30] were unfavorable to the Cantata. If it is so I am sorry for them; for wholly leaving aside all question of the truth of their criticism, their position as poets who have failed makes it unquestionably a thing of bad taste to say anything, if not something favorable, in such a case as mine.

"The commotion about the Cantata has not been unfavorable on the whole to my personal interests. It has led many to read closely what they would otherwise have read cursorily and I believe I have many earnest friends whose liking was of a nature to be confirmed by such opposition."[31]

To Mrs. Lanier he wrote on May 27: "The papers are wonderously more respectful in their tone toward me, and it really seems as if my end of the seesaw was now rising steadily. I think the business has been of great value to all my artistic purpose, just at this stage of it; I have been compelled to throw aside every adventitious thing in the way of inspiration. God has been good to show me at the outset in its most repulsive form the fatal figure of contemporary popularity, and to remind me how far apart from it were Shakespeare, Beethoven, and Bach. Hereupon I feel already resulting an immortal and unconquerable toughness of fiber in the strings of my harp, insomuch that if the world shall attempt to play me—as it *does* play all the popular men—it will only get its awkward fingers sore."[32]

But further criticism was forthcoming. Much of it, it is true, was as trivial as the complaint of "J. F. M." in the New York *Tribune* of June 24 that the cantata was "totally lacking in historical fidelity" because in it Lanier had made no mention of the Catholic settlers of St. Mary's, Maryland; much of it, however, was serious enough for Lanier to take it to heart. For instance, W. F. Apthorp, writing in the *Atlantic Monthly* for July on the performance of the cantata, said: "We must think that Mr. Buck has been unfortunate in the text to which he has written music" and proceeded to criticize not only Lanier's text, and the performance of the cantata, but his explanation of his musical theories, published in the *Tribune*. "Mr. Lanier," said Apthorpe in conclusion, "says that he saturated his mind with a theory and then waited for the poem to come. He would have done better to keep his mind clear from theories, and to have gone ardently and without prejudice in search of his poem." But criticism, favorable or unfavorable, painful to him or not, had brought Lanier one reward at least, a gift more valuable than fame, one that might make possible the accomplishment of the things he wished to do, and that gift was, to put it unequivocally, notoriety. Kirk, capitalizing on Lanier's new national prominence, made his Centennial ode, "The Psalm of the West,"[33] the feature of the July number of *Lippincott's*, printing in bold type across the front cover of the magazine the name of the poem and of its author.

§ 5

THE ODE had been composed under difficulties: in February the news of Charlotte Cushman's death on February 18 had been a shock, a sense of which Lanier gives in the poem "At First,"[34] written at this time. "It has been uphill work with me to struggle against the sense of loss which the departure of my beloved Charlotte Cushman leaves with me," he wrote Taylor. "She and you were the only friends among the Artists I have ever had; and since she is gone I am as one who has lost the half of his possessions."[35] In March Lanier was seriously ill for a week, and though he returned to his work with the orchestra, his health remained precarious. The engravers, who were to do the designs for "The Psalm of the West" wanted his text early in April. On March 24 he wrote Taylor that he was working on it night and day, but that it was only half finished. April 4 he reported "By the grace of God my Centennial Ode is finished. I now only know how divine has been the agony of the last three weeks during which I have been rapt away to heights where all my own purposes as to a revisal of artistic forms lay clear before me, and where the sole travail was of choice out of multitude."

In the Centennial cantata Lanier had written words for music. Now in accordance with his maturing poetic theories he attempted in "The Psalm of the West" to compose a poem which should carry or create its own musical accompaniment.[36] Taylor had objected to Lanier's criticisms of his hymn and his suggestion for a formal architectural structure as an attempt to apply the laws of music to poetry, and Lanier had replied that the weak-

ness in most of Taylor's poems was their "want of a proper con-
vergence of the components upon a single point." Taylor had
admitted the justness of the criticism. "The Psalm of the West"
Lanier conceived as a symphony, and he composed it in accordance with a strict architectural form, though the form is in no
way that of the classic Pindaric ode.

The West is America—the nation whose centenary of independence was being then celebrated; and Lanier tells in a beautiful
rhapsody of stirring lines the story of American independence.
The West is the Adam of lands, out of whose side was created
the Eve of independence and freedom. In knowledge of good
and ill, brought by freedom, there is peril and danger, but

> Weakness, in freedom, grows stronger than Strength with
>   a chain;
> And Error, in freedom, will come to lamenting his stain.
>
> .   .   .   .
>
> And Friendship, in freedom, will blot out the bounding
>   of Race;

and Science and Art shall turn to the knowing and loving and
serving of the Highest, and of each other. These magnificent
opening lines are not obscure: their idea (which is also the idea
of the closing lines of the Centennial cantata) is clearly presented,
and is a forceful one. The imagery, which seems forced in a
bald prose summary, seems particularly appropriate in Lanier's
poetry. Lanier, whatever the *Nation* may have thought, was
using words with precise and definite meaning to achieve a
definite effect.

In passionate, tremulous language the birth—and rebirth to
artistic consciousness—of the All-lover is told. He is the lark of
the dawn, and the song he sings is of all men and all things.
Violins and flutes speak softly together (as in "The Symphony")
as the God of the Artist speaks to this Son, promising to reveal
the Time gone by. The old dream of June (from "June Dreams
in January"), carefully revised and much improved, is introduced
as a lyrical interlude descriptive of the western Eden. The voyages
of the Northmen are ably charted in good ballad measure, but
suddenly the meter and form change and we are given the eight
splendid Columbus sonnets.

That Lanier himself thought highly of these sonnets we know

because four years later, when he was lecturing on the sonnet and reading sonnets to prove to his class that the sonnet is capable of sounding "the whole gamut of human emotion,"[37] he chose these Columbus sonnets, with an apology for doing so, to show the complete contrasts of moods capable of expression in the sonnet form. He had just been reading a complaining, amorous sonnet by Bartholomew Griffin, and the class must have been startled with delightful surprise as he began intoning the splendid lines of the Columbus sequence. The form Lanier uses is the Miltonic one, and like Milton Lanier achieves in the sonnet much of the dignity of blank verse.

Not only because of their subject matter (the series is essentially a dramatic monologue) or the phraseology, is the series suggestive of Tennyson's "Ulysses." For here is not only the spirit of Renaissance daring, which Tennyson recaptured also, but the steady, stately flow of idiomatic English transformed into poetry of high order and touched, occasionally at least, by that magic without which even the best of poetry must be called unsuccessful. We can be quite sure that Columbus did not feel the emotions Lanier attributes to him, but the final sonnet, in which the discovery of land is related, is splendid as poetry whatever the value it may have as an interpretation of an historic event:

> I marvel how mine eye ranging the Night,
>> From its big circling ever absently
>> Returns, thou large low Star, to fix on thee.
> *Maria!* Star? No star: a Light, a Light!
> Wouldst leap ashore, Heart? Yonder burns—a Light.
>> Pedro Gutierrez, wake! come up to me.
>> I prithee stand and gaze about the sea:
> What seest? *Admiral, like as land—a Light!*
> Well! Sanchez of Segovia, come and try:
> What seest? *Admiral, naught but sea and sky!*
>> Well! But *I* saw It. Wait! the Pinta's gun!
>> Why, look, 'tis dawn, the land is clear: 'tis done!
> Two dawns do break at once from Time's full hand—
> God's, East—mine, West: good friends, behold my Land!

The coming of the Mayflower pilgrims is next related. The colonial period is hurried over (Lanier gives no space to the settlement of Virginia and the Southern colonies), but the battle

of Lexington and the signing of the Declaration of Independence
are sung in effective, spirited verse and appropriate measure.
The Civil War, still too close to be described realistically, is
described as a Tournament: it is the old poem of the joust between Heart and Brain, written so long before, but a new quatrain is added:

> Heart and Brain! no more be twain;
> Throb and think, one flesh again!
> Lo! they weep, they turn, they run;
> Lo! they kiss: Love, thou art one!

The God of the Artist now interprets for the All-lover what
he has been shown: and the poem closes as it began, with a
prophecy of the future:

> Ah, name thou false, or tame thou wrong,
> At heart let no man fear for thee:
> Thy Past sings ever Freedom's Song,
> Thy Future's voice sounds wondrous free;
> And Freedom is more large than Crime,
> And Error is more small than Time.

> Come, thou whole Self of Latter Man!
> Come o'er thy realm of Good-and-Ill,
> And do, thou Self that say'st *I can*,
> And love, thou Self that say'st *I will;*
> And prove and know Time's worst and best,
> Thou tall young Adam of the West!

But "The Psalm of the West" is not to be understood as a
prophecy: the poem has no message save that of Lanier's own
devotion to the United States as a nation and as a land.

Even a superficial reading of the poem will reveal, of course,
typical defects. The imagination is often strained; the imagery
is frequently obscure; there are too many compound words,
which are usually forced in connotation, ineffective as poetry,
and uneuphonious as sound; and sometimes a good passage or
stanza is spoiled by one ludicrous phrase, as in the lines:

> O manful arms, of supple size
> To clasp a world or a waist as well!

But whatever the defects of "The Psalm of the West," it is a splendid national poem, a little epic not merely in architectural structure but in nobility of conception and in cosmopolitan breadth of sweep, fall though it often does from the epic pitch; and it is an epitome of American history. As in "The Centennial Meditation of Columbia," there is nothing sectional in this chant of the glory of freedom, while there is much that is noble, in noble words beautifully expressed.

§ 6

A just criticism on "The Psalm of the West" was pronounced by Orpheus Kerr (R. H. Newell) in the New York *Graphic* of January 22, 1877, when he wrote: "This vigorous strain of sympathy for the young life of our own great continent is novel and brotherly as coming from the lyre of a section hitherto best pleased with attempts to adapt Old World conceits and traditions to itself in numbers not more original. The tenderness, passion, and local sentiment of the South have been musically sounded by Timrod, Hayne, and Flash; but this new singer puts something of the straightforward spirit of the whole Country" into his poetry. Professor Mims has reminded us that it was at a critical time that "Lanier came forward . . . to express his passionate faith in the future of the American union."[38] The reconstruction governments of the South were still in power; the old sectional antagonisms were perhaps stronger than ever. Only a few leaders, men like Lamar of Mississippi and Wade Hampton of South Carolina, could forget the past completely in the earnestness with which they worked to relieve the conditions of the present and to create a united nation for the future: and with these leaders Lanier belongs. He was, like Wordsworth, a poet and teacher, but he taught something beyond Wordsworth, beyond, indeed, most of his generation. In this he reminds us of another southerner, who became a national—and international—leader, the nephew of Lanier's old college instructor Professor James Woodrow—Woodrow Wilson. It is a little ridiculous, even if it were not also uncritical, to think of Lanier as "a Southern songbird," or merely as a Georgia poet. He was, whether Whitman would have allowed him the title or not, a poet of democracy, singing in new measures to new music the song of the new nation and the nascent national spirit.

CHAPTER THIRTEEN

DREAR SAND-LEVELS

§ 1

LANIER'S illness early in March, 1876, was a warning he had ignored. He was overworked and exhausted: the writing of the difficult India papers, the Centennial cantata, and "The Psalm of the West," his regular musical engagements, work on various essays and several short poems, and the lengthy correspondence involved in the writing of the cantata and the defense of it, with the mental anguish that this caused—all had broken down his health and sapped his energy, but had also made him feverishly restless to work the harder, to write the more. "I am continually and increasingly amazed at the intense rate of life at which I have to live," he wrote Mrs. Lanier;[1] and to Judge Bleckley: "I have been working at such a rate as, if I could keep it up, would soon make me the proverb of fecundity that Lope de Vega now is. . . . As for me, life has resolved simply into a time during which I must get upon paper as many as possible of the poems with which my heart is stuffed like a schoolboy's pocket."[2]

But the work that had improved his financial condition considerably—"The Psalm of the West" alone was sold outright to *Lippincott's* for $300—and increased his reputation and given him greater prestige with the editors, had brought other gratifying rewards. "I suppose," Lanier confessed to Judge Bleckley, "that any man who, after days and nights of tribulation and bloody sweat, has finally emerged from all doubt into the quiet and yet joyful activity of one who *knows* exactly what his Great Passion is and what his God desires him to do, will straightway lose all anxiety as to what he is working *for*, in the simple glory of doing that which lies immediately before him."[2]

More than this, the nebulous questions concerning artistic form that had filled his mind were now finding their answers. His purpose, he could now declare in answer to the old question of

Oglethorpe days, was to preach a new poetic gospel, both of form and of matter. In the letter to Peacock written April 27, after describing the enthusiastic appreciation of his cantata in the South and the hold "Corn" had taken upon all classes, Lanier added: "in view of the long and bitter struggle which I must make up my mind to wage in carrying out those extensions of poetic Forms about which all my thoughts now begin to converge, it is pleasant to find that I have at least the nucleus of an audience which will be willing to receive me upon the plane of mere blind faith until time shall have given a more scientific basis to their understandings." And to his brother, as we have seen, he wrote that the agitation over the Centennial cantata had brought him faith in his art and in the sincerity of his intentions.

This new certainty concerning his artistic purposes Lanier explained briefly in the letters to Taylor which grew out of Taylor's rebuke, in reference to his criticism of Taylor's Centennial hymn, that "you cannot apply the laws of Music to Poetry." He wrote: "I see from what you say in reply to my letter on the Hymn, that my musical associations have put me under a certain suspicion with you, of a propensity to impart the principles of musical construction into poetry. But this was a principle far larger than any peculiar to music or to any one art. . . . Now it seems to me . . . that every poem, from a sonnet to Macbeth, has substantially these elements—(1) a Hero, (2) a Plot, and (3) a Crisis; and that its perfection as a work of art will consist in the simplicity and the completeness with which the first is involved in the second and illustrated in the third. In the case of a short poem the Hero is the central Idea, whatever that may be; the plot is whatever is said about that idea, its details all converging, both in tone and in general direction, thereupon: and the crisis is the unity of impression sealed or confirmed or climaxed by the last connected sentence, or sentiment, or verse, of the poem. Of course I mean that this is the most general expression of the artistic plan of a poem: it is the system of verses, which may be infinitely varied, but to which all variations may be finally referred. I do not think that there is, as you feared, any necessary reason why a poem so constructed should present 'a too-conscious air of design'; that is a matter which will depend solely upon the genuineness of the inspiration and the consummate command of his resources by the artist."[3]

This is a clear statement of the artistic thinking (not theory: "I hate theories," said Lanier[4]) that was to direct more and more the composition of his own poems, and it is, negatively, excellent criticism of all that Lanier had written previously, from the crowded, diffuse lyrics of Montgomery days, through "Corn" and even "The Symphony," the statement of a weakness from which not even "The Psalm of the West" is absolutely free. On the positive side, such discussion of artistic purpose and poetic composition leads directly to the little "Song of the Future,"[5] which Lanier wrote about this time, a song which, in spite of a weak, sentimental ending, is a song of courage, repeating once more the faith earlier expressed in "Barnacles" and in many letters, such a song as anticipates great achievement. But that Lanier should have been at such pains to justify his theories to Taylor suggests that they were not yet quite clear to himself. "I have seen Lanier recently," Taylor wrote Hayne on August 1.[6] "He is a charming fellow, of undoubted genius, and I think will make his mark. In him the elements are still a little confused, but he will soon work into clearness the power he has already." Taylor seems purposely to have dropped the discussion that Lanier seemed so eager to carry on, realizing the futility of it.

§ 2

LANIER, of course, felt sure of the correctness of his principles and he was eager to embody them in new poems. Unfortunately there was little time in the spring and early summer of 1876 for him to create new poems—except a few very short ones: the second of the "Rose-Morals"[7] and "To————, With a Rose,"[8] a graceful poem in the best *vers de société* tradition, written for the birthday of Mrs. Peacock, June 5, 1876. His first task in this period of new realization of the principles of art was to collect and revise poems he had already written and published for the volume that Lippincott & Co., capitalizing once more on his current prominence and increased reputation, now planned to issue.

The title-page of this, Lanier's third published volume but his only volume of poetry, reads *Poems. By Sidney Lanier. Philadelphia: J. B. Lippincott & Co.; London: 16 Southampton St., Covent Garden. 1877.* Professor G. S. Wills, who prepared an excellent bibliography of Lanier's published work for the Southern History Association in 1899, states that the volume appeared in October or November, 1876. A letter exists, written by Lanier to Dooley, a bookseller of Terre Haute, Indiana, in which he states under date of August 15, 1876, that "Messrs. Lippincott & Co. of Philadelphia inform me that they intend issuing a volume containing three poems of mine—*Corn*, *The Symphony*, and *Psalm of the West* during the coming fall."[9] But in a letter to Taylor dated July, 1876, Lanier refers to a copy of the volume "that Mr. Peacock bought [*sic:* brought?] up . . . yesterday which had been sent to the Bulletin Office, from which I presume that the book is now published." It would seem, therefore, that though the book might have been withheld from publication until late in the year—possibly to have it new for the Christmas trade— it was certainly in print before the middle of July, 1876. But it is curious that the Lippincotts should not have issued the book in the month in which, because of Lanier's connection with the Centennial and the publication of "The Psalm of the West," he was probably being most discussed, especially since, as Lanier himself afterwards complained,[10] the book was hurriedly made by the publishers, with little time allowed him for a revision of the contents.

The volume is a small quarto of ninety-four pages, and it includes, of the thirty-eight or more poems that Lanier had published in magazines and elsewhere, not a selection of the best but only the ten that had appeared in *Lippincott's Magazine:* "Corn," "The Symphony," "The Psalm of the West," "In Absence," "Acknowledgment," "Betrayal" (one of the songs for "The Jacquerie," published in November, 1875[11]), "Special Pleading," the sonnet "To Charlotte Cushman," "Rose-Morals: 1 and 11," and "To———, With a Rose." To these ten poems Lanier prefixed a graceful "Dedication"[12] to Charlotte Cushman. The ten poems which were brought together in this volume are, however, a satisfactory selection, representative of Lanier's several styles. And the selection, so fortuitously produced, expresses the poet's tribute, it should be observed, to three women who had influenced his growth as an artist or given him the appreciation that such growth required: his wife, Mrs. Peacock, and Miss Cushman.

§ 3

ANOTHER task that kept Lanier from working immediately on new poems was the commission given him by the Cushman

POEMS.

BY

SIDNEY LANIER.

PHILADELPHIA
J. B. LIPPINCOTT & CO.
LONDON:
16 SOUTHAMPTON ST., COVENT GARDEN.
1877

*Title-page of "Poems," 1877, Lanier's third published volume and the
only volume of poetry published before his death.*

family to prepare the official biography of Charlotte Cushman, with the assistance of her friend and companion, Miss Emma Stebbins, to whom alone a great mass of material was accessible. He is said actually to have made a contract with the publishers, Houghton, Osgood & Co., of Boston, successors to the firm that had published *Tiger-Lilies* for him,[13] and in this connection he probably made a trip to Boston late in May or early in June. The contract was probably signed at this time, but a severe return of illness prevented Lanier from beginning work on the biography immediately. In July he spent some days with the Peacocks in Philadelphia, too ill even to see his Philadelphia publishers. Meanwhile, however, he had made plans to bring his family North to rejoin him, for good and all, after almost four years of separation, which, though not unbroken, had become unendurable to Lanier. By the middle of July he was able to join them and possibly also his brother's family, at West Chester, Pennsylvania, where they boarded at the farmhouse of a Mr. Thompson and where Lanier expected to work on the life of Miss Cushman. The sequence of published letters to Mrs. Lanier now ceases altogether, for they were not separated again.

The commission meant eight months of steady employment, and relief for the time-being from the necessity of producing pot-boilers, and some peace of mind favorable to the writing of his own poems. "I can't tell you with what ravishing freedom and calmness I find myself writing in these days," Lanier wrote Taylor, "nor how serene and sunny the poetic region seems to lie, in front, like broad upland fields and slopes. I write all the time, and sit down to the paper with the poems already done. I hope to have out another volume soon of work which will show a much quieter technique than this one."[14] Not even the relapse which soon sent him to bed once more could dampen his enthusiasm or destroy the cheerful serenity which the success of the previous year and a half and the bright hopes for the future had given him.

But disappointing news came that on account of ill health Miss Stebbins could not fulfill her part of the contract, and that the biography of Miss Cushman could not be written, and Lanier's contract with the publishers had therefore to be cancelled. Suddenly and completely all his hopes were destroyed. The financial security he had anticipated had proved an illusion. Without a single commission on hand it looked indeed as if, in his own bitter jest, God intended him "to feed on blackberries all the summer."[15]

For the consumptive such disappointments as this are fatal, and that summer disappointments came to Lanier in rapid succession. Poems he had sent to editors were returned, rejected. Thomas's plan to have him in his orchestra fell through, possibly however on account of Lanier's ill-health. He went to Baltimore to discuss with Daniel Coit Gilman, formerly president of the University of California but now president of the newly-founded Johns Hopkins University, which began to function that September, the possibility of an appointment to the teaching staff of the university. Gilman, recalling the success with which the poet Edward Rowland Sill had taught at the University of California, was eager to attach Lanier to the faculty of Johns Hopkins, requested the interview with him, and encouraged Lanier to hope for the appointment, and the creation for him of a nondescript chair of "Poetry and Music," but nothing came of Gilman's efforts to persuade the trustees to share his views and his opinion of Lanier's ability. After the honors of the spring such disappointments, failures, rejections, seemed the more bitter. Lanier's health became increasingly worse.

We have practically no letters written in this period: three to Taylor in July, one each to Dooley, Hayne's bookseller friend,[16] and Edward Spencer in August, two to Taylor in September—and no more; we cannot know how terrible was Lanier's anguish nor how great his despair. "In the notes I received from him during [the last six years]," wrote Hayne, "his tone alternated between a certain feverish exaltation and a profound despondency. Never have I known him to complain—to 'wear his saddened heart' ostentatiously 'upon his sleeve;' but I could read between the lines even of his (apparently) more cheerful communications, and detect the slow, half-muffled throb of heart-break there! . . . he suffered a species of torture." What happiness the summer brought him was in quiet wanderings along the Brandywine, in companionship with those he loved most, his wife, his boys, his brother, brief visits with the Peacocks and once with Taylor, who spent a few days that summer at his home, "Cedarcroft," not far from West Chester, and in "friendship with the dead poets," with Chaucer, and Shakspere, and Keats—whom he was reading that summer with joy and a mournfulness of longing.

§ 4

THE NECESSITY of earning money caused him to take up once more the writing of pot-boilers; and his recent absorption in musical theory suggested the subjects he should write upon. To this period belong the essays "From Bacon to Beethoven"[17] and "The Orchestra of Today." The former begins with a quotation from Sir Francis Bacon to the effect that music is a useless and contemptible art. On the contrary, asserts Lanier, the time has almost arrived "when the musician will become quite as substantial a figure in every-day life as the politician." In the course of his argument Lanier asserts that "The Art of any age will be complementary to the Thought of that Age." When the thought is concerned with the unreal, and the unknown, the art will portray the real, the known; when the thought is concerned with the real and the known, the art will seek to portray the unreal and the unknown. The ancients and the men of medieval times knew little of the actual world and speculated unsuccessfully and fantastically concerning the unknown, the world of spirit: hence their arts were concerned with reality—and sculpture and painting portray reality. In an age of scientific achievement art will be less concerned with reality than with making an escape from it; and music, "being free from the weight and burden of realism [as Lanier had already demonstrated] . . . what more natural than that the spirit of man should call upon it for relief from the pressure and grind of Fact," and that it should become the characteristic art-form of the modern time?

But Lanier's argument, though developed with the logic of a syllogism, is open to attack from many points: it is not only based on an incomplete account of the relations of music and science, but it reveals on Lanier's part as much ignorance of sculpture and painting *as arts* as he had revealed nine years before in "Retrospects and Prospects." Music has, beyond doubt, reached its greatest development in modern times, but it does not follow that it is the characteristic art-form of the present; nor is music alone of all the arts the art that offers an escape from reality. Poetry may be equally well an avenue of escape.

The fundamental weakness in Lanier's argument lies in his assertion that the art of an age is complementary to the thought of the age. On the contrary, as Lanier himself implies in his later, unreprinted essay, "Mazzini on Music," art and thought reveal not complementary but the same characteristics. In an age of science music will not fail to reveal the influence of scientific thought. And so far from being the means of leading men's thoughts solely to the finite and God, music, as we have seen and as Lanier himself would have seen had he not mistaken contemporary music for the first music of a new age rather than understood it as the last music of a passing age, music may equally well direct men's thoughts to earth, and the finite pleasures of fleeting moments.

It is digressing to comment on the pleasure with which Lanier reported the popularity of piano music and the presence of pianos in so many homes, but one cannot fail to be struck by the fact that music has, through instruction in music in the public schools and by means of mechanical arrangements especially, become more and more a household art, or at least a household possibility. Lanier would undoubtedly have hailed with delight the development of the phonograph and especially of the radio. In spite of the fact that much of the music that comes through the air is cheap and vulgar, the radio remains an agent for good, and Lanier would have welcomed it as such and given his support to the sponsoring of better music.

The other essay written at this period, "The Orchestra of Today,"[18] is "a plain and untechnical account, for nonmusical readers, of the nature of orchestral instruments and the work of their players." There is in the essay little matter of a controversial nature, and time has proved the truth of Lanier's assertion that science would come to the aid of music in developing new instruments which would "indefinitely increase" the resources of the orchestra of the future. Elementary as such an essay is, it is still useful; a clearer popular account of the instruments of an orchestra and the function of the instruments is probably not to be had. And if Lanier's essay is amazingly naïve in part, it is the more delightful for being so. In his faith in what might be accomplished through music Lanier was always somewhat naïve.

§ 5

"From Bacon to Beethoven" was sent to *Lippincott's*, "The Orchestra of Today" to *Scribner's*. Although neither was published for some years, the latter not until 1880, the former not until 1888, Lanier probably received compensation for both in

1876. Still, the money received could not have been very much, hardly enough to raise his spirits or to break the mood of disappointment that had settled over him.

That the mood persisted—a mood caused not merely by disappointments but by much brooding over the literature of the past and perhaps also by lingering resentment of the treatment accorded his Centennial cantata by the newspapers and magazines—is indicated by a poem Lanier wrote that summer and dedicated to another poet who had been as severely treated by the critics as Lanier imagined himself to have been, and who had also struggled as unsuccessfully as it seemed to Lanier he was then struggling against ill-health and disappointments: it is the poem "Clover. Inscribed to the Memory of John Keats."[19]

The clover-stems with which the upland meadows about Chester were covered are men

> Whose loving service to the world has been
> In the artist's way expressed and bodied. . . .
> . . . . Dante, Keats, Chopin,
> Raphael, Lucretius, Omar, Angelo,
> Beethoven, Chaucer, Schubert, Shakespeare, Bach,
> And Buddha (sweetest masters! . . . . . .)
> . . . . bright throngs unnamable
> Of workers worshipful, nobilities
> In the Court of Gentle Service, silent men,
> Dwellers in woods, brooders on helpful art,
> And all the press of them, the fair, the large,
> That wrought with beauty.[20]

These the Course-of-things, figured as an ox, as in *Werther* and in Norse mythology, descends upon and destroys, and the poet asks the ancient question: to this end only, that they should be destroyed, did these sweet masters and brother artists live and play their part? But the clover men answer that they play a rôle more important than this:

> To quality precise is built for plans of His
> The general brawn . . . .
> Tease not thy vision with vain search for ends.
> The End of Means is art that works by love.
> The End of Ends . . . in God's Beginning's lost.

It is the only answer that brings comfort, and refuge from the stupidities of contemporary criticism and hasty judgments. Only faith can save us, faith and still greater faith, that we fulfill our purpose in the divine, eternal scheme no matter what our life here.

It is probably to this poem that Lanier referred in a letter of September 25 to the editor of *Scribner's Monthly:* "The enclosed grew out of a mood of solemn protest against the doctrine of 'Art for Art's Sake,' which has led so many of our young artists into the most unprofitable and even blasphemous activities."[21] But the poem was rejected, and Lanier's protest went unpublished, and the manuscript went the rounds of editorial offices for two years more.[22] And yet "Clover" is one of the best of Lanier's poems. It is written in blank verse—the first, presumably, that Lanier had written since 1869, blank verse of a quality that suggests that of the masters, Shakspere and Milton, but suffused with a warm morning atmosphere that suggests the poetry of him to whom "Clover" is inscribed, John Keats. If we wish other resemblances we shall find them in Emerson and Tennyson, but the poem is wholly Lanier's own, suggestive of the work of other poets only as friends close in spirit and association suggest each other.

In a volume that he was preparing for publication at the time of his death, Lanier gave "Clover" first place, grouping with it "The Waving of the Corn," another poem written at West Chester, and "The Song of the Chattahoochee"—three poems preaching a single lesson, less evident in "The Waving of the Corn,"[23] but expressed more clearly and simply in "The Song of the Chattahoochee" than elsewhere in Lanier's poetry: it is the lesson of duty and of purpose, taught by the large amiable trees and the hurrying river, a lesson Lanier had learned by his own sad experience and from the masters whose names he lists in "Clover." It is, in æsthetic theory, the lesson of art, not for art's sake but for the sake of love, art that is at all times moral, produced not necessarily under the most moral of conditions but growing out of fundamentally moral intentions.

§ 6

THE PRODUCTIVITY of Lanier's first weeks at West Chester had ceased entirely by September, however. Illness prevented all work with pen and ink, and the illness of one of the children had exhausted Mrs. Lanier, who had been a constant nurse.

Lanier in his loneliness was driven more and more to companion-ship with books. But in spite of illness he went to Baltimore to confer again with Gilman of Johns Hopkins.[24] Gilman was familiar with Lanier's literary work, his interest in physical experiments, and his desire to pursue the scientific study of the relations of poetry to music, and he sincerely desired his connection with the university; but the difficulty was to adjust the special work that Lanier wished to do with the existing scheme of the institution, and the conference in late September brought his connection with the university no closer.

The reversal of fortune made it necessary for him to plan to return to Baltimore and to the Peabody Orchestra for the winter, but his health made the wisdom of this doubtful. "A peculiar affection of the side" prevented any literary activity, though Lanier disobeyed the doctor's commands and wrote a letter to Taylor in appreciation of his review in the New York *Tribune* of Lanier's recently published volume of poems. He and his wife had left West Chester and were staying temporarily with the Peacocks, possibly for Lanier to be closer to his doctor, but Lanier could not face complete separation from his wife and sons for another winter, and it was decided that Mrs. Lanier and the boys should remain at West Chester, where they could live cheaply and be in easy access of him in Baltimore. To be near them was happiness, but Taylor's kind words of encouragement in November— "I see that you are finding quiet friends, genuine appreciators— therefore, *Sursum Corda!* All will be right in the end"—came at a time when Lanier had never needed encouragement more.

December 4 Lanier went to Baltimore to fulfill an orchestral engagement, made a business trip to New York, and was in Philadelphia again December 6, certainly none the better for his tiring journeys. The Peacocks, to whose home he had gone, were alarmed and summoned a physician, and Dr. Lippe, the physician, alarmed at "the gravity and persistence of his illness," summoned a specialist, Dr. Schell; and Lanier was ordered to leave immediately for Florida. He wrote jestingly to Taylor that he refused to be persuaded that any conceivable combination of circumstances could induce him to die before he had written and published five additional volumes of poems, but he was in a more serious condition than he knew. Plans had to be made hurriedly. The boys had to be placed somewhere, for it was impossible that they should be taken to Florida: Mrs. Lanier would need all her uncertain strength and all her time to nurse her husband. And, worst of all, money was scarce. But the Peacocks, with their great kindness, solved all the problems: the boys would stay with them for a while at least, and Mr. Peacock generously advanced money to cover the first expenses of the trip, and assumed charge of the necessary sale of some family silver. Finally, by Monday night, December 11, Lanier and his wife were ready to start.

Hardly a year before, in his book on Florida, Lanier had referred to his own consumption as a thing of the past, but now he was going to Florida to seek the cure he had recommended to others. The cardinal principles for the treatment of the disease which he had recorded he had not followed. Though still convinced that consumption, and his consumption specifically, was curable, he had failed signally to observe his second and third principles: he had brooded long over disappointments, and he was tired out. Florida promised sunshine, warm air, and a rest; and for a few dearly bought months escape from the struggle that increased his brooding. Perhaps it would also give the supreme gift, the strength to put on paper before he should die all the poetry and music of his teeming heart and brain. With a heavy blue blanket, the gift of Mrs. Peacock, to insure warmth on the trip, and with his wife beside him, he began the long journey south.

§ 7

IN THE appendix to *Florida* Lanier had given thirty-four possible rail and water routes to Florida, but the route they took was a different one still: a sleeping-car from New York to Danville, Virginia; another sleeping-car to Brunswick, where they may have broken the trip with a short visit with Mrs. Lanier's father and brother, who now lived there; a steamer from Brunswick to Fernandina; and at Fernandina the train again to Jacksonville and Cedar Keys, on the Gulf Coast; and finally another boat from Cedar Keys to Tampa, with a stop at Manatee. The last part of the journey—from Cedar Keys to Tampa—alone consumed thirty-six hours. They arrived at Tampa toward evening on December 21. The journey had lasted ten days.

Just why Lanier chose Tampa is uncertain. In 1876 it was not so well known or so interesting as other resort towns in Florida—if, indeed, it could then have been called either resort or town. It is doubtful if Lanier had even visited Tampa on his previous trip to Florida. They found it "the most forlorn collection of little one-story houses imaginable." The Orange Grove Hotel, "a large three-story house with many odd nooks and corners, altogether clean and comfortable in appearance, and surrounded by orange-trees in full fruit," was open, however, and there the Laniers secured a large second-story room which opened upon a wide balcony from which they could reach into the orange trees and pick the ripe fruit.[25]

The Peacocks' thoughtfulness had anticipated them. There was a long letter with news of the boys, who were getting on famously with Mrs. Peacock, and enclosed were other letters that had been addressed to Lanier at Philadelphia. H. M. Alden, the editor of *Harper's Magazine*, sent a check for "The Waving of the Corn"; George C. Eggleston, literary editor of the New York *Evening Post*, wrote a cordial letter concerning Lanier's volume of verse and his rich promise as a poet, a letter in which he also expressed sorrow at his illness; R. W. Gilder, of *Scribner's*, wrote concerning the essay "The Orchestra of Today," which had been purchased for his magazine; and Miss Stebbins wrote in friendly fashion explaining that the biography of Miss Cushman would, quite definitely, not be written at all—as if by the statement to relieve Lanier's jealous fear that the commission might be assigned to someone else.

Such letters from friends in the North brought pleasure, and almost immediately at Tampa Lanier made new friends. The proprietor of the Orange Grove Hotel took an immediate fancy to the Laniers and sent up roses and violets from the garden, and his wife was all kindness. Mrs. C. N. Hawkins, the young wife of the editor of the Tampa *Sunland Tribune*, sent to Lanier a little jar of marmalade that had come to her in a Christmas box.[26] To this courtesy Lanier replied with a verse, which, twice printed, has never been added to his collected poems, and which deserves to be better known than it actually is:

> How oft the answers to our passing prayers
> Drop down in forms our fancy ne'er foretold!
> —Thus when of late, consumed by wasting cares,
> "*Angels preserve us*" from my lips up-rolled,
>   I'm sure I pictured not—as thus I prayed—
>   Angels preserving me—with marmalade! ! ! !

The point of the verse, like the point of most of Lanier's attempts
at humor, is a pun, but the verse is graceful and it supplements
the impression that the letters give us of a very cheerful invalid
who, as he tells us more seriously in "The Stirrup-Cup," written
at some time during the Tampa sojourn, would face even death
with a smile.

The weather was "perfect summer." Escape from city air and
northern damp brought rapid improvement in Lanier's health
and a revival of his spirits, though Mrs. Lanier was disturbed
by the appearance of symptoms of her old malarial trouble.
Lanier had been in Tampa hardly a week when he began to
take daily rides on a shaggy gray mare through the great pine
forest that surrounded Tampa. A hoarseness remained to trouble
him and he was still forbidden the use of the pen, but he began
to compose poems and he wrote a few letters, nevertheless. "In
truth, I 'bubble song,' " he wrote Taylor.[27] Mrs. Lanier served
as amanuensis. Soon the climate and his happiness and Mrs.
Lanier's careful nursing were bringing visible rewards.

§ 8

IT WOULD be pleasant to imagine that Lanier composed the
"Evening Song," which appeared in *Lippincott's Magazine* for
January,[28] shortly after his arrival in Florida. The poem makes
use of a figure used ten years before in "Night," but this poem
is shorter, and more compact, and far more beautiful. Read as
a poem addressed to Mrs. Lanier (which, of course, it undoubtedly
is) composed as they walked along the beach at Tampa or at
Cedar Keys and watched the sun set over the Gulf, at a time
when the Florida sojourn still seemed a fight with death itself,
the poem seems exquisitely tender, infinitely pathetic. But Lanier
had hardly reached Florida before he began receiving complimentary notices concerning the poem. The January number of
Lippincott's had indeed reached him within ten days of his arrival.[29]
But whatever the inspiration, the "Evening Song," is one of
Lanier's best lyrics, an extremely beautiful song that has reminded more than one critic of the songs of Sappho.

By January 11 Lanier had finished a new poem, nevertheless,
and a long one. In a letter of that date to Taylor he enclosed
"To Beethoven," which Taylor sent to the *Galaxy*, where it
appeared in the March number.[30] Lanier described it as "a
poem which I have endeavored to make burn as hotly as, yet

with a less highly colored flame than, others of mine."[27] But later he admitted that it was too crowded, and certainly it is too long. "It is like reading the dictionary—the meanings presently become confused, not because of any lack of distinctness in each one, but simply because of the numerous and differing specifications of ideas," he wrote.[31] Such criticism of his own treasured work is the surest proof of what he might have achieved had he lived longer. Like Keats he was growing as definitely in critical ability as in creative ability at the time he died, and he knew what direction his work was taking.

In thanking Taylor for his notice of the volume of poems Lanier had written: "I was particularly pleased with the light way in which you touched upon my faults; and I say this not hastily. . . . I am convinced that every genuine artist may be safely trusted with his own defects. I feel perfectly sure that there are stages of growth—particularly with artists of very great sensibility who live remote from the business life of men—in which one's habitual faults are already apt to be unhealthily exaggerated from within; and the additional forcings of such a tendency from without, through perpetual reminders of short-comings, become positively hurtful, by proud-fleshing the artistic conscience and making it unnaturally timid and irritable. In looking around at the publications of the younger American poets I am struck with the circumstance that none of them even *attempt* anything great. The morbid fear of doing something wrong or unpolished appears to have influenced their choice of sub-jects."[32] In the poem "To Beethoven," written for the semi-centen-nial observance of Beethoven's death, Lanier attempted greatness.

The version of the poem that appeared in the *Galaxy* differs somewhat from the version printed by Mrs. Lanier in the collected poems. The second and third stanzas of the later version, which are the same as stanzas fifteen and sixteen, replace three of the first version; a stanza is dropped between stanzas eight and nine of the later version, and a rejected stanza appears in place of stanzas ten and eleven. There are a few linear and verbal changes which are, without exception, improvements. But with the verbal and metrical echoes of Tennyson (particularly of "In Memoriam") the poem seems unoriginal as well as too long. The best stanzas are the repeated two:

O Psalmist of the weak, the strong,
   O Troubadour of love and strife,
Co-Litanist of right and wrong,
   Sole Hymner of the whole of life,

I know not how, I care not why,—
   Thy music sets my world at ease
And melts my passion's mortal cry
   In satisfying symphonies.

The poem does, it is true, record many of the emotions that
Beethoven's stupendous music often rouses in the appreciative
listener and makes one aware of Beethoven's own words that
"Music is a loftier revelation than wisdom or philosophy," but
Lanier's own judgment of the poem may well remain our judg-
ment; it is useless to defend it against Lanier's condemnation.

Perhaps it was in an attempt to reduce the long, crowded
poem to unity and to give it coherence that Lanier wrote, probably
at this same period, the uncollected sonnet "To Beethoven"
which summarizes effectively the sixty-eight line lyric.

Sovereign Master! stern and splendid power,
   That calmly dost both time and death defy;
Lofty and lone as mountain peaks that tower,
   Leading our thoughts up to the eternal sky;
Keeper of some divine, mysterious key,
   Raising us far above all human care,
Unlocking awful gates of harmony
   To let heaven's light in on the world's despair;
Smiter of solemn chords that still command
   Echoes in souls that suffer and aspire!
In the great moment while we hold thy hand,
   Baptized with pain and rapture, tears and fire,
God lifts our saddened foreheads from the dust—
The Everlasting God in whom we trust!

But the sonnet is inferior of its kind, and less pleasing than the lyric.
   It should be noted that in both poems Lanier commends
Beethoven's message[33] and not his technic—the spirit of the

sonatas and symphonies, rather than their superb architectural form. Mr. H. C. Thorpe, writing of Lanier as a poet for musicians, takes this as evidence that "with Lanier the architectural element in music was entirely subordinate to the idea that music was a medium of expression and that what is said is more important than the particular form which is the vehicle of thought." Music was to Lanier the religion of the new age,[34] but Beethoven is praised not as a theologian but as a priest.

In all, at least eleven poems seem to have been written or planned in large part during the three months that Lanier spent in Florida, and, of these, seven appeared in print almost immediately. For "The Stirrup-Cup"[35] Scribner's paid "twice as much as ever before,"[36] which was encouraging. "Redbreast in Tampa,"[37] was bought by Lippincott's and published in the issue for March. Unrelated as the poems at first appear, they are together a statement of the poet's attitude toward death and life. In the second the poet, through the robin, avows his intention of singing blithely as long as life may last; in the former, speaking of Death, the "cordial old and rare," he says

> Then, Time, let not a drop be spilt;
> Hand me the cup whene'er thou wilt;
> If death such dear distillment be,
> I'll drink it down right smilingly.

Neither poem is as a poem particularly interesting; each is important in the study of Lanier's total work. The former possesses the added interest of listing together, as he was to do again, and with added names, in "The Crystal," David, Keats, Omar Khayyám, Chaucer, and Shakspere as men who wisely sweetened death with song. It is perfectly possible that the list reflects the study of Emerson's essays, which Lanier had undertaken in earnest, and that the list as well as the metaphor indicates his recent discovery of Fitzgerald's translation of Omar's rubáiyát. Mr. Bruce Weirick feels that in the poem Lanier caught something of the spirit of both, and he finds here "the tonic medicinable flavor of one of Emerson's epigrams in verse, combined with the richness of some exotic black and red wine, that drops with beauty and terror of blood."[38]

"The Bee,"[39] a poem Lanier had great trouble in selling, is, like "Corn," a poem of personal experience, such as Emerson might have written. Lanier, like the bee, will force his way into each "world-flower" to reach the honey and to achieve success. But the meaning is even more noble and less personal than this: Lanier, as the type *poeta*, knows that the service of the poet is not merely to make honeyed poetry but to communicate to others the rich lessons of life, to fertilize and to inspire them with the heaven-pollen which clings to him through no effort of his own. The thought, however, is perhaps more appropriate to a Maeterlinckian essay than to a poem. "The Bee" reveals the poetic idealism of Lanier, but not more definitely or more successfully than other poems do. The best parts of the poem as poetry are the lines that convey by rich suggestion the endless summer of Tampa and the appearance of the Florida forest: the live-oak trees, hung with gray moss and wrapped with bright sprays of the yellow jessamine which Lanier had loved from the days of his youth in Georgia.[40] Mention should also be made, however, of the masterly use of alliteration and syzygy for onomatopœic effect, as in the lines

> As some dim blur of distant music nears
> The long-desiring sense, and slowly clears
>   To forms of time and apprehensive tune,
>   So, as I lay, full soon
> Interpretation throve: the bee's fanfare
> Through sequent films of discourse vague as air,
> Passed to plain words.

How much concern the composition of the poem gave Lanier is indicated in a letter to Taylor (to whom he had sent the manuscript for Taylor to sell), requesting him to change "his" to "its" and "him" to "it" as he had just remembered that the worker-bees, formerly thought to be sexless, had recently been found to be imperfectly developed females. He was further concerned by his knowledge that the pollen used by the bee for food is carried in "pollen-baskets" on the legs, and that pollen used in cross-fertilization adheres to the body of the bee rather than to the wings.[41] Taylor must have laughed aloud when he received Lanier's letter. Certainly a smile is visible in his reply: "I shall make the changes you desire, although *je n'en vois pas la nécessité.*

You see, I admit your full right; but not one man in 10,000,000 will know enough about bees to notice any scientific mistake."[42] Lanier said of Poe that he did not know enough to be a great poet.[43] Sometimes one is almost driven to conclude that Lanier knew too much; at least he let scientific knowledge interfere with poetic imagination.

It is the scientific knowledge, for instance, that spoils for many readers the concluding couplet of the sonnet to "The Mocking-Bird."[44] From boyhood Lanier had been fascinated by the mocking-bird as English poets and their American imitators have been for centuries by the lark and the nightingale. In a college notebook, we will recall, he had recorded the observation: "A poet is a mocking-bird of the spiritual universe. In him are collected all the individual songs of all individual natures." But unfortunately Lanier as an amateur scientist was conscious of the fact that the bird sings only after it has eaten, and in the couplet this physiological fact is recorded:

> How may the death of that dull insect be
> The life of yon trim Shakespere on the tree?[45]

This is almost offensive.

"Under the Cedarcroft Chestnut"[46] possesses a certain similarity to these other poems written at Tampa in that the poet (*poeta*) is again compared with a natural object: and this time a chestnut tree. The spirit of the eight-hundred-year-old chestnut tree on Taylor's estate at Kennett Square is apostrophized and finally Taylor, whose generous, unselfish friendship had meant so much to Lanier, is compared to the tree. But the point of the poem is not the rhetorical prayer that Taylor might grow even more like the tree: the compliment, as Lanier intimated in a letter to Taylor, is in the implication, not in the literal meaning of the lines. For instance, the line "In soul and stature larger than thy kind" stands out more strongly as a quotation in a letter than as a subordinate clause in the poetic prayer.

Taylor was pleased, naturally, with Lanier's tribute; and *Scribner's*, glad to pay tribute to Taylor in accepting a poem by Lanier, published it a year later (January, 1878) with a drawing of the chestnut tree by Thomas Moran. But even in thanking Lanier for his tribute—and Taylor reminded him that his recognition of his "genius and character, and the purity of

the aims of both," conferred no obligation of any sort on Lanier[47]—
Taylor could wisely point out that to place certain stanzas in
italics was equivalent to the author's saying "Mark how fine
this is!" In the poem as published in *Scribner's Monthly* no italics
were used; but in the text given in the 1884 volume the fifth
and sixth stanzas and the first line of the seventh are printed in italics as Lanier intended them to be. Lanier, while not wishing to say
"Mark how fine this is," seems to have been constantly afraid that
without italics the moral of a poem might not be absolutely clear.

"From the Flats"[48] is a cry from the poet's heart. Four years
previously, on July 12, 1872, Lanier had written from Alleghany
Springs, Virginia, the long letter, already quoted at length,[49]
which is the prose counterpart of this poem. Three years later,
in reading the description of the happy land in *The Phœnix*
to his Baltimore class, he paused to say "Here, by the way, is a
curious contrast between the old English poetry and modern
poetry. Here we find that the mountain has not yet ceased to
be an object rather of dread than beauty. A modern poet would
never have described a Happy Land as an unbroken plain where
no mountains stand; the picture of a landscape without broken
ground is to our eyes intolerable."[50] And in July, 1877, he was
to write to Taylor, then at White Sulphur Springs, West Virginia:
"[May you] be drawing strength from the dear mountains, as
it were from the very breasts and big nipples of our Mother
Earth."[51] "From the Flats" is an expression in poetry of a mood
and a thought that were recurring; the poem expresses, however,
a longing for one place in particular, his beloved Georgia. It
also explains one reason why Lanier was eager to get away from
Tampa though he must have known that his health demanded
a longer residence there.

Lanier burned too feverishly with the flame of creation to
remain long in Texas or Florida or any place where he found
himself spiritually empty. And as in Texas so he had now again
become indifferent to his health. The posthumously published
poem "On a Palmetto"[52] is an expression of this same lethargizing
mood of impatience, and though given a later date by Mrs.
Lanier, it may have been written at this time. The lines

> Yon tall palmetto in the twilight stands,
> Bare Dante of these purgatorial sands

present so perfect a picture of a lone palm tree growing in a

18

sandy waste in the hot Florida climate that it recalls inevitably
the other poem, "From the Flats."

It is characteristic of Lanier, however, that he should have
followed these poems of protest with a poem in praise of the
very thing against which he was protesting—in this case the
spiritual deadness of Florida. The Catholic Man could not have
done otherwise. In "A Florida Sunday"[53] he states the lesson
that could be learned and understood even in "the drear sand-
levels." It is a restatement of something he may have read in
Emerson, but Lanier's interpretation of the mysterious unity of
nature is different from Emerson's. In "Each and All" Emerson
sought to show by a series of examples that

> All are needed by each one;
> Nothing is fair or good alone.

Lanier is most concerned to discover

> —How *All's in each, yet every one of all*
> *Maintains his Self complete and several.*

Emerson would have made of the question the problem of the
individual in society, but Lanier is more orthodox in thought
than Emerson and his approach is not philosophic but religious.
What he seeks to discover in the unity of created nature is God;
and having found Him through revelation he seeks to identify
his own soul with the great soul of God. His yearning is that of
the medieval mystic. In the lines

> All riches, goods and braveries never told
> Of earth, sun, air and heaven—now I hold
> Your being in my being; I am ye
> And ye myself; yea, lastly, Thee,
> God, whom my roads all reach, howe'er they run,
> My Father, Friend, Belovèd, dear All-One,
> Thee in my soul, my soul in Thee, I feel,
> Self of my self,

there is clearly distinguishable the echoing voice of the imitator
of Christ who cries "My God, my Beloved! Thou art all mine,
and I am all thine." "A Florida Sunday" is essentially a poem

of religious experience, and it foreshadows "The Marshes of Glynn" which was to be published only a year later, and the culminating poem, "Sunrise."

Whatever the poetical debt it owes to Lanier's new master, Emerson—and in the strictly American quality of the imagery one feels a debt as certain as in such phrases as "and each live whole in all" and "All's in each," and "mutual sea and shore"— "A Florida Sunday" owes more to Keats. The lines

> thou always fair,
> Still virgin bride of e'er-creating thought—

recall of course often quoted lines from the "Ode on a Grecian Urn." Indeed, the first part of "A Florida Sunday," like "Under the Cedarcroft Chestnut," is a sort of ode to tranquillity, which the "Ode on a Grecian Urn" is also. But the specific influence of Keats is to be traced more definitely still in the catalogue of the natural "riches, goods and braveries," the contemplation of which leads to the discovery of the unity of all, which is the moral of the poem. One thinks of the splendid list of sensuous delights in the "Ode to a Nightingale," though Lanier is of course less sensuous. Such lines as

> Pale in-shore greens and distant blue delights,
> White visionary sails, long reaches fair
> By moon-horn'd strands that film the far-off air

Keats, we may feel sure, would have loved, and might well have written. Here is to be found not only a Keatsian delight in color but also in music. The robins and mocking-birds

> all day long
> Athwart straight sunshine weave cross-threads of song,
> Shuttles of music—

and this too is Keatsian.

But the imagery throughout "A Florida Sunday" is so splendidly American that Keats, while he might have admired such lines, could never actually have written them. And whatever the similarity to the verse of others Lanier's may here seem to have, it is nevertheless original. Lanier can give freshness even to a figure from classical mythology, as in the line "The great bird Purpose bears me twixt her wings," a line followed by lines worthy of St. Francis:

> And I am one with all the kinsmen things
> That e'er my Father fathered.[54]

And it would be foolish to say that the lines are so good that another might have written them. They are good because Lanier did write them, and because he was a genuine poet. The committee that chose the first of these lines, "The great bird Purpose bears me twixt her wings," for inscription on the pedestal supporting Gutzon Borglum's bust of the young Lanier recently unveiled at Macon[55] chose wisely. It is as splendid a line as one will find among many splendid lines, and from boyhood until the end Lanier never forgot that his God had a purpose which it was for him to discover and having discovered to fulfill.

Reviews of his volume of collected poems began coming in in profusion. The *Nation* commented on "that convulsive and startling mode of utterance which amazed the nation in his Fourth of July ode"; and *Harper's Magazine*, though admitting genuine poetic genuis, suggested that his poems were far from clear— at least not clear on first reading. Some reviews were of course enthusiastic and laudatory, but Lanier accepted all comments with equanimity. He knew quite clearly now what his purpose in life was, and no critical attack could have stilled the voice lifted in God's chorus.

CHAPTER FOURTEEN

EPHEMERÆ

§ I

THE FIRST week in April, 1877, the Laniers left Tampa for Brunswick, where they spent a month with Mrs. Lanier's father and brother. Lanier's health was better, so much better that he could take long drives in a basket phaëton and soon could dispense with the carriage to ride horseback. Nor was there further prohibition on his use of the pen; he was writing almost constantly, but composing more poems than he could put on paper. "I have at command a springy mare, with ankles like a Spanish girl's, upon whose back I go darting through the green overgrown woodpaths like a thrasher about his thicket," he wrote Taylor. "The whole air seems full of fecundity; as I ride I'm like one of those insects that are fertilized on the wing,— every leaf that I brush against breeds a poem. God help the world when this now-hatching brood of my Ephemeræ shall take flight and darken the air."[1]

And this was no fleeting mood of inspiration, for one month later he wrote to Peacock from Macon, where the Laniers spent the month of May: "I'm taken with a poem pretty nearly every day, and have to content myself with making a note of its train of thought on the back of whatever letter is in my coat-pocket. I don't write it out, because I find my poetry now wholly unsatisfactory in consequence of a certain haunting impatience which has its root in the straining uncertainty of my daily affairs; and I am trying with all my might to put off composition of all sorts until some approach to the certainty of next week's dinner shall remove this remnant of haste, and leave me that repose which ought to fill the artist's firmament while he is creating. Perhaps indeed with returning bodily health I shall acquire strength to attain this serenity in spite of all contingencies."[2]

But except for his delight in the southern spring and the happi-

ness of creation—he was at least jotting down his "Ephemeræ"—
and of being with his relatives, Lanier could not have been very
happy either in Brunswick or in Macon. His future lay, he knew,
in the North, where the editors and publishers were; and no
matter how much he loved the Georgia marshes and hills, he
had long since outgrown the Georgia scene. From Macon he
wrote to Taylor: "The talk here is of the advance in corn, and
of the failure of our City Bank; and, so far as concerns any man
I have yet conversed with, there is absolutely nothing in heaven
or earth or the waters under the earth but corn and the City
Bank. Perhaps, if I had several thousand bushels of the former,
or a large deposit in the latter these topics might interest me
more. But I haven't; and when I think how I shall enjoy tackling
you about something or other—say Emerson, whom I have been
reading all the winter, and who gives me immeasurable delight
because he does not propound to me disagreeable systems and
hideous creeds but simply walks along high and bright ways
where one loves to go with him—then I am ready to praise God
for the circumstance that if corn were a dollar a bushel I could
not with my present finances buy a lunch for a pony."[3] The
sympathetic audience for his poetry which the excitement over
the Centennial cantata had created in Macon was not dis-
coverable now.

But the poems were good poems, whether there was an audience
ready for them or not, and they came in vernal profusion. To
this period belong undoubtedly a great number of those poetic
fragments from which Mr. Henry Lanier published in 1908 a
small selection in a volume called *Poem Outlines*. Of the fragments given in that volume the ones that date from this period
are probably neither the rough drafts for poems nor the fairly
well thought-out outlines, but the phrases, the couplets, the
poetic images that, like the ephemeræ, came suddenly and would
have disappeared as suddenly had Lanier not fixed them on
paper as they came.[4] Such fragments as

> Cousin cloud
> the wind of music
> blow me into wreath
> and curve of grace
> as it bloweth thee[5]

and
>   The black-birds giving a shimmer of sound
>   As midday hills give forth$\begin{cases}\text{transparent tremors}\\ \text{luminous}\end{cases}$
>   of heat and haze[6]

and

>   In a silence embroidered with whispers of lovers
>   As the darkness is purfled with fire-flies[7]

and "Star-drops lingering after sunlight's rain"[8] are not poem outlines but poem pollen, brushed from the boughs of the Georgia forest through which Lanier rode. Unused though they seem to have been, they are not, however, the wasted seed which nature, in her safe economy, so lavishly provides, for such fragments and thoughts impregnated Lanier's mind, and started the growth of poems he was to give out later. It is more than likely that in the spring of 1877 Lanier, visiting at Brunswick where the marshes are, had begun to plan his series of "Hymns of the Marshes," had actually begun to write "The Marshes of Glynn," though it is difficult to believe that "The Marshes of Glynn" in the published version of 1878 was written at this time, much less two years previously as the local Brunswick tradition asserts.[9]

§ 2

IN ADDITION to poems suggested by the immediate scene, there was also, and persistingly, in Lanier's mind at this time his long poem, "The Jacquerie," on which he had worked for almost ten years. It was the desire to finish it that prompted the wish expressed in a letter to Mrs. Peacock: "If Mr. Hayes would only appoint me consul somewhere in the south of France! ! !"[10] But there actually was under way at this time a scheme to secure for Lanier a political appointment that would give him a certain income and therefore repose from financial worries—two things he knew to be absolutely necessary to the fullest development, not of his talents, for by 1877 they had been developed, but of his ideas into poems.

While he was still in Macon his father, with his permission, undertook to secure letters from "persons of eminence" that would recommend Lanier to a position in the Treasury at Washington. J. F. D. Lanier, the financier, seems to have first suggested the possibility of the appointment; and why, with his influence, he was not able to secure an appointment immediately, is very strange. Sherman, Secretary of the Treasury, and Evarts, Secretary of State, both knew that Lanier would accept an appointment. His friends, Senator Lamar of Mississippi and Senator Morgan of Alabama, both urged it. J. F. D. Lanier's son-in-law, Judge Advocate General Dunn, and General Humphreys, Chief of the Engineer Corps, an old friend of Mrs. Lanier's mother, used their influence. Taylor, from whom R. S. Lanier solicited a letter of recommendation,[11] and who himself was appointed by President Hayes as Minister to Germany, lent what influence he had. The chief difficulty in securing the appointment was probably the fact that Lanier shrank from the publicity that would attend his seeking it in person, and failed, until it was too late, to make personal application for it.

A formal application for political appointment might of course have resulted in newspaper publicity. "I scarcely know what I should do if I should see my name figuring alongside of Jack Brown's and Foster Blodgett's and others of my native state,—as would quickly be the case," Lanier confessed to Peacock.[12] It had even taken a struggle to consent to his father's proposal that informal application be made. He had long since conquered his aversion to accepting loans of money from friends, but this was another matter. Still, he was willing to accept any position that gave him a regular salary. The service of poetry demanded the annihilation of the last vestiges of pride.

In June Gibson Peacock went to Washington to urge in person Lanier's appointment, and later in the month Lanier and his wife, who had now come north to Baltimore, spent a few days in Washington to pursue still further this distressing matter. Sherman gave orders that Lanier was to have the first vacancy (though Lanier did not learn this until some time later) but to Lanier the appointment seemed no nearer than it ever had been. In July he and Mrs. Lanier went on to Philadelphia, and to the boarding house in West Philadelphia where they had stayed during their visit to the Exposition the summer before. The last of the month they moved, with their boys, to Chadd's Ford, near West Chester, where they boarded with a Mrs. Caleb Brinton.

Lanier still worked on the magazine articles which paid—when they sold—better than poetry, but left him physically and creatively exhausted. He went to Baltimore to make personal application for any kind of clerical appointment, but without success. In September he was called to Washington in connection with the government appointment, which was still hanging fire. He borrowed fifty dollars from Peacock to make the trip, had to postpone it because of "a severe pleuritic attack," and when he did finally get to Washington he suffered a hemorrhage which prevented his attending to the business he had come on and kept him confined to his hotel room for several days.

But by October he had definitely given up all hope of securing any sort of favor from the government, and he again set out to find work elsewhere. And though his health was again so bad that he was unable to resume even his literary work, he set on foot another attempt to secure a place at Johns Hopkins University; he sought employment as an assistant at the Peabody Library; and finally he went back to the Peabody Orchestra, hoping to eke out his meager salary as first flutist by selling poems and articles to magazines.

§ 3

SUCH months of uncertainty and wretchedness were tragic and undid most of the good of the three months' carefree existence in Florida. On September 27 he wrote Peacock: "Altogether it seems as if there wasn't any place for me in this world, and if it were not for May I should certainly quit it, in mortification at being so useless." But even that was written partly in jest. In November, after a serious attack of his malady, he could write: "The hæmorrhage, however, which disabled me from work temporarily, has greatly relieved my lung, and I am now stronger than at any time in the last fifteen months. My whole soul is bursting with chaotic poems, and I hope to do some good work during the coming year."

In this year of uncertain income and no employment, Lanier's expenses were more than usually large, and that he was at all able to meet his debts and pay for his extensive traveling was due undoubtedly to the help of his brother Clifford, whose freely given checks were usually accompanied by a sonnet,[13] and possibly also to the assistance of his father. Peacock had made an anonymous gift of a five-hundred-dollar bill the preceding Thanksgiving; during the fall of 1877 Lanier borrowed fifty dollars

from him that is recorded and perhaps more. Miss Stebbins had
sent a fifty-dollar bill in the spring. And then of course some
money had been raised by the sale of family silver. Some way,
some how, money had been found to keep the wolf from the
door, but even so there were now, as until the end, great priva-
tions which Lanier kept proudly hidden, acknowledging with
shrinking delicacy the assistance offered by even his most devoted friends.

He had by October engaged rooms in Baltimore and moved
his family from Chadd's Ford.[14] Mrs. Lanier had not previously
lived in Baltimore with her husband, but gravely alarmed by
his continued ill health, she was in the future to remain constantly with him. Baltimore, quite definitely now, was home;
and in-Baltimore they drew around them an ever increasing
circle of friends, Mrs. Lanier winning as her own those who had
already been won by her husband.

§ 4

IN THE July, 1877, number of *Harper's Magazine* Lanier had
read a little poem called "The Cloud," signed with the name
John B. Tabb. It was the name of his friend of Point Lookout
Prison, whom he had supposed to be dead. A letter sent through
Harper's reached Tabb at St. Peter's Boys' School in Richmond,
where, after graduation from St. Charles's College, a Roman
Catholic school near Baltimore, Tabb was serving a sort of
novitiate, preliminary to taking up theological studies.[15] Shortly
afterwards Tabb returned to St. Charles's College as an instructor,
and in Baltimore he was reunited with Lanier.

Tabb—son of an old Virginia family, born and bred an Episco-
palian—had been received into the Roman Catholic church in
1872. He was not ordained to the priesthood until after Lanier's
death, in December, 1884, but during these years spent at
St. Charles's as a postulant for ordination his life was undoubtedly
circumscribed, and he and Lanier were not able to be often
together. But the friendship renewed, it was never again relinquished, and for the rest of Lanier's life they wrote letters characterized by mutual love and affection. Tabb, we are told,
was the only friend younger than himself that Lanier ever had.[16]
Both were loyal in friendship—like David and Jonathan, and
they actually called each other by those names. If Tabb exerted
any influence on Lanier and on his poetry, it is difficult to label

it. Lanier, however, exerted a perceptible influence on Tabb's style, possibly even giving Tabb the idea of describing nature in Biblical or liturgical terms, as Lanier does in the lines from "Sunrise":

> Peace to the ante-reign
> Of Mary Morning, blissful mother mild,
> Minded of naught but peace, and of a child,[17]

an idea which Tabb was to use so often and so successfully as to develop a new genre of nature poetry, as Lanier himself—with Tabb imitating him in this also—so developed the use of the Shaksperean or historical metaphor in description of nature as to create what is almost a distinct genre.

To Lanier Tabb dedicated his first important literary venture—a privately printed volume of poems, without dedication, had been issued in 1882—the collected *Poems* of 1894, and to Lanier he inscribed at least nine poems.[18] It is a great misfortune that Lanier's letters to Tabb were destroyed in the fire that in 1911 destroyed the buildings of St. Charles's College, and that Father Tabb's letters to Lanier, on account of his positive disapproval, may not be published. As a result, little is known of this strange, beautiful friendship. Tabb was sometimes with the Laniers in Baltimore, talking of poetry and music, of the children and Lanier's work;[19] his devotion to his friend is perhaps best expressed in a poem called "The Captives" (a poem suggested by his experience at Point Lookout where he heard Lanier's flute before he met the player) in which he told of two who

> lived and loved and died apart
> But soul to soul and heart to heart.

Long after Lanier's death Mrs. Lanier continued to correspond with Tabb, and in their letters they referred constantly to their lost David.[20]

Besides Tabb, another Baltimore friend, later to become a close friend of Tabb, was William Hand Browne. Browne was fourteen years older than Lanier, a man of charming personality, a musician, a painter, and a scholar. He and Lanier had first met some years before when Lanier contributed poems to the *Southern Magazine*, of which Browne was editor. Browne was now connected with the faculty of Johns Hopkins and he introduced

Lanier to his professional friends, to artists, and to others of the city.[21]

In Baltimore Lanier had again met Lawrence Turnbull, the publisher of the *Southern Magazine*, and the Laniers were now often with Mr. Turnbull and his poetic, music-loving wife, whose romantic idealization of Lanier has stamped itself unmistakably on Lanier's character as it appears through the aura of the Lanier legend, but who must be remembered as a real benefactor of Lanier's Baltimore days.[22] Among the men of letters whom Lanier knew in Baltimore was Richard Malcolm Johnston, in whose latent literary career Lanier played a helpful part by bringing his work to the attention of northern editors and by offering able criticism; among artists, John Tait; among musicians, Wysham and Frederick H. Gottlieb, who had taken Wysham's place as second flutist in the Peabody Orchestra. President Gilman of Johns Hopkins he now knew fairly well, and he may have met Alexander H. Stephens, now living in Baltimore and a friend of many of Lanier's friends.

An attractive glimpse of Lanier in Baltimore is afforded in a drawing by Dr. Volck, a dentist of Baltimore who had considerable artistic skill, published in the Wednesday Club Album in 1878. In a long sketch the members of the club as a whole are shown on parade, the music section first. Lanier is shown with his flute under his arm. The picture is the only evidence of Lanier's membership in the club, and it is quite possible that lack of time and money and health prevented his taking a very active part in it, but a member he was, and the fact of his membership in a club to which most of the distinguished musicians, writers, and artists—professional and amateur—of Baltimore belonged, defines the social position and importance of Lanier in his new home.

But not the friendship of Tabb or of the Brownes or of the Turnbulls or of all the people in Baltimore was so important as the fact that he had his wife with him. Years later Mrs. W. G. Solomon of Macon recalled entering the Laniers' apartment in Baltimore with a friend also from Macon, Mrs. Randolph Jaques, Sr., and finding Lanier standing at the window, in the glow of the sunset, his arm about his wife, his face transfigured. Mrs. Lanier, constantly watching over him like a guardian angel, held up her hand to motion the visitors to be silent. After a few minutes the trance passed, and Lanier greeted his Macon

The Musical Section of the Wednesday Club, as portrayed by Dr. Volck. Lanier is shown as No. 11, his friend Wysham as No. 2.

friends warmly. And that evening, though the Laniers were
poverty stricken, they entertained with joy and gaiety, and
played flute and piano duets; and their visitors returned to
Macon with an imperishable memory of a perfect love which
is epitomized in a phrase Mrs. Lanier used in a letter to a sister
of Mrs. Solomon: "This precious life, which I hold by so frail
a tenure."[23]

§ 5

IN POETRY and prose Lanier's accomplishment during the last
three quarters of 1877 was meager. In the May issue of *St. Nicholas' Magazine* appeared "The Story of a Proverb,"[24] delightfully
illustrated by E. B. Bensell, "an incongruous melange" such as
"one might 'make up as he went along' for a lot of children about
his knees,"[25] and filled with intentional incongruities. This story
had probably been written before Lanier went to Florida. The
story for which he received twenty-five dollars from *Lippincott's*
in September was a sequel to the first, another "Story of a
Proverb" but this time "A Fairy-tale for Grown People," as the
sub-title indicated.[26] The proverbs (both probably invented by
Lanier) were, of the first, "To him who wears a shoe, it is as
if the whole earth was covered with leather"; and, of the second,

> I was as a treasure concealed:
> But I loved, and I became known.

As stories, even though deliberately filled with incongruities,
both represent an improvement in the story-telling art over
"The Three Waterfalls," his only other published short story.
One or two touches in the first reveal delightfully what was in
the mind of the author. "I belong," says the young inventor of
shoes, "to the tribe of the poets—who make earth tolerable for
the feet of man." And his fault in making the invention is said
by the Scribes-and-Pharisees to be that he actually did "the
very best he could in the most candid manner; this is clearly in
violation of the rules of art—witness the artistic restraint of our
own behavior in this matter!" Obviously, "The Story of a Proverb" Lanier intended for his critics as much as for children.
And even more deliberately planned for his critics is the second
story. The poet, Genius, says of his enemies: "How can these
poor ones know Genius when they see him? Their eyes are hurt

with much work, with much error, with much wrangling, with little good, with ignorance. Unworthy, indeed, is that artist who allows himself to be long bitter against them." This, it should be noted, is a paraphrase of the first line of the Good Angel's song in the Centennial cantata, which was itself an echo of something he had said before in the Furlow College commencement address,[27] and elsewhere.

In July Lanier had taken the time to write for Mr. J. F. D. Lanier a long letter on the Lanier genealogy.[28] This letter appeared as an appendix to the second edition of the privately printed *Sketch of the Life of J. F. D. Lanier* which was issued that same year. In Baltimore Lanier had spent many hours in the Peabody Library searching for information concerning the English Laniers with which to supplement the traditions of his family. In April, 1879, Lanier wrote for J. F. D. Lanier a second letter on the same subject, in which he set forth the results of later researches and gave an account of Jerome and Nicholas Lanier, the musicians and court-favorites of Elizabeth and the first Stuarts, friends of and collaborators with Ben Jonson and Henry Lawes, and also of the musical Laniers whose playing put Pepys "in an exstasy almost," dubious progenitors to whom Lanier's biographers have been overly fond of tracing his ancestry. In this first letter, however, the chief boast that Lanier makes is that one of his ancestors married Elizabeth Washington, an aunt to George. This tradition has, since Lanier's death, been disproved, as his ancestress belonged to a different family of Washingtons, the Washingtons of Surry County, Virginia.

The attempt to trace Lanier's ancestry to Queen Elizabeth's musicians and to account thus for his lyric gift is as ridiculous as the claim to kinship with George Washington. Lanier's letter to his cousin gives reliable information concerning later generations of Laniers in America and the names of "living heads of families who represent widely distinct branches of the Laniers," but he was probably in error when he insisted that all of them derived from the same Huguenot stock, certainly in error in giving the name of his emigrant ancestor as Thomas instead of John (1633-1719), and, some genealogists are now inclined to believe, in insisting on a French rather than an Italian origin for his family. The name Lanier is a common one in the South; it is still known in Europe; J. F. D. Lanier had himself met Laniers from Cuba. It undoubtedly pleased Lanier to trace his ancestry to Jerome and Nicholas, and their qualities and virtues he seems to have possessed, whether by inheritance or not. But faults that we shall find apparent in his scholarly studies vitiated likewise Lanier's genealogical researches. Curiously enough, he seems to have overlooked entirely one fact which should have appealed to him, for he does not seem to have realized that the word "Lanier" in French means a falcon.

§ 6

ONLY FIVE poems besides those already discussed can be said with certainty to have been written by Lanier before the end of 1877. On August 7 he wrote "The Dove," but not the version that appeared in *Scribner's Monthly* for May, 1878.[29] That version, the second, is much better than the first, for in it he makes the improvement that he made when he reworked a stanza from "Night" in the "Evening Song," giving concreteness and the beauty of literary association to his figure. "If haply thou, O Desdemona Morn," is certainly as much of an improvement over "If thou, if thou, O blue and silver morn," as is "Dear Night, sweet Moor," over "Sweet Night, my Love!"

But we may well ask if the metaphor of Desdemona and the Moor should have been used at all. It gives to the first stanza an emphasis and a vividness which the final stanza and the title to the poem do not justify, for "The Dove" is not a description of daybreak. It is merely a poetic statement to the effect that morn mourning over the departed night, and spring yielding to summer, and the heart separated by death from its beloved, might sing together and yet not equal the "melodious art" that the "dim sequestered dove"—next to the mocking-bird, Lanier's favorite among birds—daily achieves. The poem, judged by the strict standards that Lanier recorded in discussing an equally brief and unimportant poem by Taylor (the unused Centennial hymn), is not a good one: the Ruling Idea is confused and obscured from the first.

In the November number of the *Galaxy* appeared "A Dream of the Age: To Richard Wagner," a poem which, shortened and with a new title, Lanier grouped with the "Street Cries" with which it appeared in the collected poems.[30] The original version is longer by four stanzas than the later version, but the omitted stanzas do not occur where the asterisks are in the 1884 version, as the reader might suppose: one is dropped between the first and second stanzas, three between the fifth stanza and the asterisks. The omitted stanzas are unimportant, for they do not convey any idea not expressed in the uncancelled stanzas, nor are they any more adequate as descriptions of Wagner's operas and of his mighty power than those that remain. One cannot easily guess why they were suppressed. The poem as a whole is a failure: shortening it does not improve it. Lanier deeply and intelligently appreciated Wagner's music at a time when it was new and not widely appreciated.[31] He understood too that the figures of the operas were, partly at least, symbolic, and that the effect of the operas should be to give new emphasis to the antique virtues. He saw Wagner as a musical prophet of a new age, an age of industry, more noble than an age of Trade, in which work should be performed to the sublime strains of divine music. More than this, Lanier saw that Wagner, in recreating figures from the past, had adequately expressed the spirit of the present; and in *Tannhäuser* especially, with its theme of the life-long antagonism of good and evil, he found an opera dear to his soul, the work of a brother artist. But Lanier's verse was no proper medium for interpreting the music of Wagner, just as it had proved unsatisfactory in interpreting the music of Beethoven. The line "A Swan soft floating tow'rds a magic strand" conveys little of the dignity and beauty of *Lohengrin;* the line "Valkyries, heroes, Rhine-maids, giants, gods!" is a weak-voiced and unimpressive roll-call of the inhabitants of Valhalla and their vassals. Lanier comes nearer Wagnerian mightiness and musical effectiveness when he makes no effort at imitation or at interpretation.[32]

We might assume that "A Puzzled Ghost in Florida" ("A Florida Ghost" in the collected poems[33]) was written during Lanier's residence in Florida, but the definitive note appended to the poem in the 1884 volume, "Chadd's Ford, Pennsylvania, 1877," is not to be ignored. It does not belong by mood with the other Florida poems, and nothing in it makes one feel that it must have been written in Florida; but it was certainly written when Lanier was in an extremely happy mood, for which there was little reason in August. It is neither so amusing as the poems on Jones of Jones, nor does it have the undercurrent of serious implication; but it is an amusing poem and it produced a check from the editor of *Appleton's Journal*, in the December, 1877, sisue of which magazine it was published. Most of Lanier's

dialect poems, like Tennyson's, were written out of a deep
interest in the dialect and in the lives of the men who used it.
But one suspects that this poem was written, as certain others
were, for the purpose it accomplished. When a man's wife and
boys need bread and the man himself needs medical attention,
who will demand that every so-called poem he produces be also
a true one?

Certainly mercenary was Lanier's purpose in writing "Hard
Times in Elfland," which appeared in the Christmas issue of
Every Saturday, an ambitious weekly recently started in Baltimore.[34]
In fact, Lanier, in discussing his plans for the future in a letter
to Peacock, cited his commission to write the poem with some
pride, and the pride is not so much that of the poet as of a wage-
earner. It is a long poem of 236 lines, written to be understood
and appreciated by children. Lanier makes the story interesting
for other children by introducing his own as characters in the
poem, as well as himself, his wife, and Fran, the Newfoundland
dog. The opening stanzas give a charming picture of the poet
and his family gathered round the fireside in their Baltimore
flat. The picture is indeed something in the Flemish manner,
and perhaps in writing it Lanier remembered the Flemish "Fireside Fancies" of Hayne which he had so enthusiastically admired.[35]
The actual domestic situation of the Laniers is not glossed over
or idealized: the story of the hard times in Elfland is told

> with inward purpose sly
> To shield my purse from Christmas trees
> And stockings and wild robbery
>
> When Hal and Nimblewits invade
> My cash in Santa Claus's name.

Hal, the four-year old, naïvely asks "Papa, is hard times
ev'ywhere?" The poem becomes a fantasy, for Santa Claus
suddenly appears in person. But it is an undernourished, pale,
and thin Santa Claus. The belly that once

> shook like a bowl of jelly fine:
> An earthquake could not shake it now;
> He *had* no belly—not a sign.

His emaciated condition and his poverty are the result of rash

19

investments in a celestial Grand Trunk Railway, designed to
carry the souls of the dead to heaven and the unborn babes to
earth and Santa Claus on his annual tour. The railroad was
never built: lawyers' fees, rights of way, injunctions, leases and
charters consumed all the capital. At the bankrupt sale Santa's
reindeer—he bursts into tears as he confesses it—were bought in
by the railroad president. Retrenchment was in order, and now,
Santa tells the children, he has to make his round of the house-
tops on foot, and he has developed a cough. Nevertheless, he makes
his round, distributing simple toys made in his own home; the
Christmas toy factory had been wiped out with the rest of his
assets. Leaving a bundle he says

> "Now, hoist me up; there, gently, quick!
> Dear boys, *don't* look for much this year:
> Remember, Santa Claus is sick!"

We may take the poem, if we like, as an allegory: Elfland is
the South, and Santa Claus is the southern planter who has
listened to the honeyed persuasions of the industrialist and the
stock-broker, and the lesson which Santa learns through bitter
experiences is a lesson the South must learn, for industrialization,
Lanier believed, and many now with even greater conviction
believe, has been the South's undoing. But Lanier may not have
intended it as an allegory, and if it became one in the writing
it is because in describing the hard times in Elfland he merely
described the hard times that he knew all too well. His boys
probably did not have to accept the story as an excuse for presents:
the poem probably made a difference. But certainly nothing
could be a more charming substitute for a Christmas gift. It is,
in every way, one of the most successful and delightful poems
that Lanier ever wrote, and one that all children should enjoy,
though strangely enough it seems never to have been reprinted
in any anthology intended for them. For the biographer and the
reader who would know Lanier as a man it is particularly important and interesting. It belongs with "June Dreams in January"
as a revelation of the poet at home and as an insight into the
poet's heart.

One other poem by Lanier may have been written in 1877,
"The Song of the Chattahoochee," a poem so successful in

onomatopœia that it early caught the popular fancy and has become perhaps the best known of all Lanier's poems. In the 1884 volume of collected poems Mrs. Lanier gives the date of composition as 1877, and in the table of contents notes the original publication as *"Scott's Magazine,* 1877." But *Scott's Magazine* had ceased existence in 1869. Inasmuch as the poem was printed in the *Independent* for December 20, 1883,[36] exactly as given in the collected poems, one might guess that the poem had not been published during Lanier's lifetime, and that the date of composition may well have been 1877. However, at least one poem, "A Song of Eternity in Time," was twice published by Lanier himself in only slightly different versions, in 1870 and again in 1881; so posthumous publication in the *Independent* is no proof of original publication. Furthermore, F. V. N. Painter gives in his little volume, *Poets of the South,* published in 1903, a version of "The Song of the Chattahoochee" that differs from the 1883 *Independent* version. The first stanza is not written in the first person, so that the poem is not, therefore, the song of the Chattahoochee but a description of the river with a transcript of its song. Painter states in a note: "This poem was first published in *Scott's Magazine,* Atlanta, Georgia, from which it is here taken. It at once became popular, and was copied in many newspapers throughout the South. It was subsequently revised. . . ."

But a careful search of files of *Scott's Magazine* has so far failed to reveal any version of "The Song of the Chattahoochee" or any poem by Lanier (or ascribable to Lanier) except those discussed in an earlier chapter.[37] Unfortunately there is absolutely no reference to the poem in any of Lanier's published correspondence or in any of the unpublished letters available, and all those who have written on Lanier except Painter (whose book, it should be noted, preceded the appearance of Professor Mims's official biography by two years) have accepted 1877 as the date of composition. It probably is the date of the revised version, and Lanier probably revised it for inclusion in one of the several volumes of poetry he was preparing for publication at the time of his death. This version shows a change from the third person to the first in the first stanza, a change in four lines of the fourth, and a few verbal changes elsewhere. The changes are with two exceptions improvements, but they are not drastic. The poem in the early version is essentially the same as the poem in the later version.

It is, surely, the most popular of all Lanier's poems but, as is so often the case, popularity is no sign of excellence, and "The Song of the Chattahoochee" is far from being a great poem. Still, like Tennyson's "Brook," with which it must inevitably be compared, it deserves a recognition greater than that accorded it by frequent inclusion in grammar school readers. Any child can hear in it the music of the water, but the child who has heard this too often, may fail later to note the varied meter of the poem, the use of short vowels, liquid consonants, alliteration, internal rhyme, and skillful repetition by means of which the music is recorded. Nor does early familiarity with the poem make for intelligent appreciation of its central idea, the river's swift answer to the call of duty.

But defects in the poem are numerous. The rhythm is monotonous; the music is not varied enough; the style is not always transparent, for some of the sentences are awkwardly constructed and some of the words—such as "brawl," in the fourth stanza—are used in an unfamiliar way; and the thought is not always clear; what, for instance, does the river mean in saying "I . . . flee from folly on every side"? Nor is the apparent fact of gravitation a fitting symbol of devotion to duty and of the sacrifice of individuality in merging it in a larger individuality. Still, without "The Song of the Chattahoochee" American literature would be the poorer, and the American literary landscape the less pleasing.

§ 7

ONLY FIVE poems were written by Lanier during 1877 after he left Florida, but when we make a year-by-year count of Lanier's poems and count the eleven that actually appeared in print in 1877 we find that, measured thus, the year marks the peak of Lanier's productivity. He had published seven poems in 1868, ten in 1876, and he published eight (besides a German version of one) in 1878; but the yearly average for the sixteen years of his literary activity is only four. In 1877, in spite of the discouragement of ill-health and poverty, Lanier was, as his own letters also testify, unusually prolific; and the eleven published poems probably represent only a small part of the "Ephemeræ" for which he made notes but which he did not live to develop. "I feel as if I could do the whole Universe into poetry," he wrote Taylor, "but I don't want to write anything large for a year or two, and thus I content myself with throwing off a sort of spray of little songs."[38]

In this year, too, many intelligent critical appreciations appeared, accompanied by gratifying recognitions of his talent. Previously Peacock had given him as many boosts as possible in the Philadelphia *Evening Bulletin*. The publication of the Centennial cantata had brought his name often into print. The earliest review of the 1877 volume of poems was probably that of Bayard Taylor, published in the New York *Tribune* for Tuesday, November 21, 1876. The Boston *Literary World* had carried a brief and favorable notice of the volume in the December, 1876, issue. The "Evening Song" was much copied. In January, 1877, a new edition of *The New Library of Song* appeared, carrying William Cullen Bryant's name as editor, and including Whittier's hymn, Taylor's Fourth of July ode, and Lanier's text for the cantata. In February, while he was still in Florida, Lanier had been cheered to receive a copy of the New York *Daily Graphic* for January 22, containing the elaborate notice of him by Orpheus Kerr (R. H. Newell), who, instead of ridiculing and parodying his verse as he might easily have done, wrote a full and dignified review of the 1877 volume of poems.[39]

The June number of the *Cottage Hearth* (in which his Centennial cantata had been reprinted a year before) carried a brief biographical sketch of Lanier with an engraving of the familiar portrait by Kuhn and Cummins of Baltimore, taken in the winter of 1873-74, and a facsimile signature. On the cover of the magazine also his picture and signature were reproduced. Lanier made a joke about the picture, writing to Taylor: "This, this is Fame: to have your 'visnomy' transformed into that of a keen blue-nosed New England manufacturer of shoe-pegs. I have not often seen anything more tragic than my wife's indignation over this wood-cut; nor have I succeeded in allaying her resentment by my sympathetic assurance that I think it the unkindest cut of all,"[40] but the reproduction of his portrait was a compliment and a tribute.

In the article that accompanied the picture Earl Marble attempted to criticize Lanier's poetry, but Marble's criticism of his poetry is less interesting than the opinion of Roland McDonald of the New York *Times* on Lanier's flute playing, which Marble quoted at length: "Mr. Lanier's peculiarities in flute-playing are his cultivation of the low tones, for which the Boehm flute is so admirably adapted, and of the *cantabile* style. Besides this, he is a thorough master of florid styles, executing the most brilliant passages with the utmost ease and grace. His facility in reading elaborate compositions at first sight is a marvel to all who have heard him. . . . His taste in music leads him to study the works of the classic composers, and his own compositions, while modeled on purely classical methods, are full of the sweetness and freshness of nature. Two or three that we have had the pleasure of hearing him play are remarkable for these latter characteristics. The 'Blackbirds' and the 'Swamp Robin' are compositions in which the notes of these birds are woven into melodies full of the coolness and the freshness of the woods. The 'Midge Dance' suggests the fantastic swirlings, minglings and sudden and unaccountable subsidings of a swarm of midges dancing in a cool spot in the woods, and in its light and brilliant structure rivals the famed 'Queen Mab' scherzo of Berlioz."

But this criticism of Lanier's flute playing and musical compositions is of other interest. "Mr. Lanier," Marble added, "seemingly writes poetry as he plays the flute." And in this contemporary account of his playing and of his music we perceive the close union in Lanier of what he considered but two aspects of one art, the art of sound, though we must go back to 1875, and to a letter of April 1, that year, to Edward Spencer for a clear statement from Lanier as to the distinction he made in sound-composition. "Things come to me mostly in one of two forms," he had written there, "—the poetic or the musical. I express myself with most freedom in the former modus: with most passionate delight in the latter. Indeed I ought to say that, *apud* me, music is, in my present stage of growth, rather a passion than a faculty: I am not its master, it is mine."[41] With two years of added experience Lanier had achieved full mastery in both forms of expression.

§ 8

IN DECEMBER Lanier, tiring of the small crowded flat, went house hunting, and found an eight room house with "many charming appliances"[42] near the outskirts of Baltimore and close

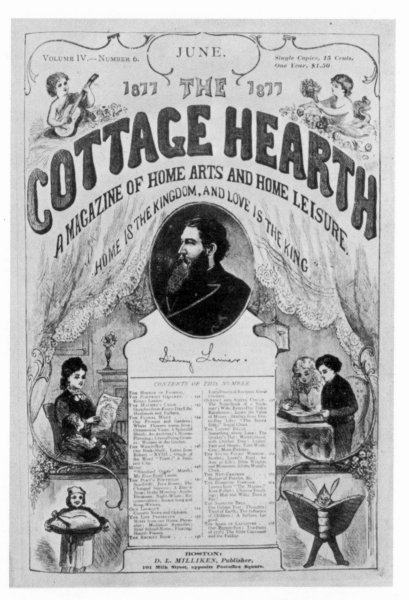

The first published picture of Lanier—"the unkindest cut of all." Courtesy of the Boston Public Library.

to the open fields, which could be rented for less than he paid for the four-room flat. So, just before Christmas, the Laniers moved again, though how they could afford either house or flat is something of a mystery. Half of the money borrowed from Peacock had been repaid with the money received from *Lippincott's* for "The Story of a Proverb" (which *Lippincott's* still held for publication), but in November Lanier was still unable to repay the rest of it. However, move they did, and the first letter of the New Year, written from the house at 33 Denmead Street, is a delightful one to Peacock, in which Lanier describes the move.

Although he yearned for a home, the picture of Lanier bargaining with, reproaching, and paying off white-washers, plumbers, locksmiths, gas-fitters, "stove-put-up-ers," car-men, pianomovers, and carpet-layers is an amusing and incongruous one. But the move had been accomplished successfully and a "colored gentlewoman" (the phrase is significant[43]) had been hired as cook and maid, and Christmas had been celebrated with a Christmas tree—as if prosperity had at last been achieved and the hard times in poetry-land dispelled for once and all. In the letter Lanier confesses his nervousness about the gas-bills, which were inevitable, the water-rates, and the taxes. "But then," he added, "the dignity of being liable for such things! is a very supporting consideration. No man is a Bohemian who has to pay water-rates and a street-tax." His delight in being a house-holder is almost naïve. Like the lords of old he would dispense hospitality lavishly and invite each poor soul in Baltimore, whether saint or sinner, to dine with him. "Good Heavens," he devoutly exclaimed, "how I wish that the whole world had a Home."[44]

PART III

Thus shall his songs attain the common breast,
*   Dyed in his own life's blood, the sign and seal,*
Even as the thorns which are the martyr's crest,
*   That do attest his office, and appeal*
Unto the universal human heart
In sanction of his mission and his art.

Henry Timrod, *A Vision of Poesy.*

For all the beauty that we know
*   Is pierced with a secret sense of pain,*
And not till the time-floods cease to flow
*   Can the sad and the sweet be cleft in twain.*

Richard Hovey, *The Laurel: an Ode.*
To Mary Day Lanier.

CHAPTER FIFTEEN

RESEARCH AND DISCOVERIES

§ 1

LANIER'S joy in being at last in possession of a house, in having his family with him in a home of which he was, if not the owner, at least the proprietor, knew no bounds. A recount of the rooms had revealed nine instead of eight, and the extra room was itself a source of pride. "When I am on the street," he wrote Taylor, "there is a certain burgher-like heaviness in my tread; why should I skip along like a bladdery Bohemian? I am a man of substance; I am liable, like you, for water rates, gas bills, and other important disbursements incident to the possession of two gowns and everything handsome about me. . . . Our new address here is—and God grant long may be, for we are *so* tired of moving!—33 Denmead St."[1] And so, having written Peacock and Taylor of his pride of possession, of this new joy that had come to him, on that Sunday night, the sixth of January, 1878, Lanier, like the honest burgher, retired to his bed feeling not only at peace with the world but suspecting in spite of himself that all was well with it.

The next morning he awoke with a raging fever which, growing worse, kept him confined to his bed for the rest of the week. It was his old foe, pleurodynia, and that meant a cessation of literary activity. At the end of the week he made a slight improvement, only to suffer a relapse. It was almost the end of the month before he could leave the house, or make any effort at work. Taylor, answering Lanier's letter, mentioned how much happier he himself was over his prospects for the future and the possibility of a diplomatic appointment, and added: "Keep up *your* spirits, also;—but I think you have the blessing of a good natural stock of them."[2] On this stock Lanier was to make increasingly great demands during the next few months.

It was necessary, no matter what the condition of his health to find work: he was still first flutist of the orchestra, but his only other source of income was from his writing, and it was, as he wrote Taylor, impossible to maintain the supplies of daily bread by poetry alone. He was of course working again on prose pot-boilers, but with little success and less interest than ever. Taylor suggested that he do literary reviews for the Baltimore newspapers, but it is doubtful if he did any. His only work for the Baltimore *Sun* (the leading local paper) seems to have been two articles on the Maryland Musical Festival which appeared in the issues of May 28 and 30, 1878,[3] work for which he would not have been paid much, if anything. For a while he considered borrowing money on a thousand acres of Georgia lumberland which had come to him by inheritance, and using the money to pursue a course of scientific study and to provide the free time necessary to the completion of "The Jacquerie," but his plans came to naught. There was no kind of "constant work," insuring a regular if meager income, to be found. It was probably as much to contribute to his pitifully small income as to benefit from his instruction that Mrs. Edgworth Bird, a Georgia lady in whose home at 40 Mt. Vernon Place Lanier had previously lived,[4] organized a class of men and women to meet in her parlor and listen to Lanier lecture on Elizabethan poetry.

These lectures, begun in March, were, according to Professor Mims, "attended by many of the most prominent men and women of the city."[5] Lanier had spoken in public often before, but this was the first series of related lectures he gave, and the experience was valuable to him in preparing his lecture courses the three following winters. Contact with the members of the class was helpful also and increased his reputation in Baltimore to such an extent that Gilman could persuade the trustees of Johns Hopkins to consider him again for appointment. But the lecture course did even more for Lanier, for, his interest stimulated afresh, he took up with greater zeal the scholarly study of literature. And whatever the fee paid by the members of the class, the money helped considerably in meeting the expenses of the house on Denmead Street.

§ 2

IN AN article contributed to the initial number of the *New Freeman*, Mr. Lewis Mumford refers to the period in American history from 1865 to 1895—Mark Twain's Gilded Age and Professor Parrington's Great Barbecue—as that of "the Buried

Renaissance," a period that "reversed every value, giving insignificant poetasters precedence over Emerson and Melville, distributing stones instead of bread, and wrapping in a shroud the newborn offspring of the mind," but still a period of promising fresh beginnings and of some great achievements. Though Mr. Mumford does not mention Lanier, either in this article or in his more recent study of the period, *The Brown Decades*, and states dogmatically that "there are, with the exception of Emily Dickinson, no poets that can even be placed near the earlier galaxy," Lanier is nevertheless one of the men of genius overlooked in the curious reversals of the period, lost in the shadow cast by the glare of Aldrich, Stedman, and Stoddard.

He reminds us, however, in the variety of his interests and in his eager desire to master all knowledge in one brief lifetime, not only of certain contemporaries of the Buried Renaissance but of the men of the Greek (or Humanistic) Renaissance; and though he lacked the genius of such a typical and masterly figure as Leonardo he possessed Leonardo's spirit of eager curiosity, and his work suffered, as did that not only of Leonardo but of many of Leonardo's contemporaries, from the diversity of his interests. Indeed, and in spite of his considerable achievement in poetry and his contribution to the science of verse and his success as a musician, one cannot help feeling that Lanier, without the dilettante's desultoriness, was nevertheless a dilettante in his dissipation of energy, in his overestimation of his own abilities, and in his failure to see things always in their proper light. He was bothered in writing "The Bee" by his knowledge of recent scientific discoveries, and now, in the last years of his life, he diffused his talents and wasted his ability in attempting scholarly work for which he lacked the proper preparation.

In November, 1880, a year before Lanier died, President Gilman wrote to him: "It is a wonder to me perpetually that you can complete so many good undertakings, and I hope you will have a life as long as you wish for, to devise and execute fresh enterprises."[6] But Gilman must have been astonished, to say the least, when he received Lanier's letter of September 26, 1877, the letter in which Lanier made application for a fellowship in order that he might pursue the study of "first, . . . the physics of musical tone; second, . . . a thoroughly scientific *general* view of Mineralogy, Botany, and Comparative Anatomy; third, French and German literature." "I fear," Lanier had

explained, "this may seem a nondescript and even flighty process;
but it makes straight towards the final result of all my present
thought, and I am tempted, by your great kindness, to believe
that you would have confidence enough in me to await whatever
development should come of it."[7]

Gilman must have seen—as the practical trustees very plainly
did[8]—that it was not at all predictable what would come of
such a course of study, even had he then had Lanier's assertion
that "You need not dream of winning the attention of sober
people with your poetry unless that poetry and your soul behind
it are informed and saturated with at least the largest final
conceptions of current science."[9]

Such a course Lanier did undertake, in a way, without the
aid of a Johns Hopkins fellowship, and with uncertain results,
lost in the future across which his untimely death drew a curtain.
We know, however, the aim of all Lanier's "present thought":
it was the relation of man to the universe, to the supernatural,
the natural, and to his fellow men, a subject he made the theme
of his last course of Shakspere lectures and pursued with the unbounded curiosity of Sir Francis Bacon, yearning for general
understanding in a period of specialized information.

§ 3

BUT THE studies listed in the letter to Gilman bore fruit, and
early fruit. A more thorough knowledge of French, of which
Lanier had already a smattering, seemed necessary to the completion of "The Jacquerie." The study of German—inspired
long ago by reading of Carlyle—was for a less specific purpose,
but it would enable him to read certain scientific books obtainable
only in that language. Lanier's proficiency in French was probably greater than his proficiency in German, but in March, 1878,
Lanier actually published a sonnet in German, addressed to
Frau Nanette Falk-Auerbach,[10] a pianist of Baltimore who
taught at the Peabody Conservatory. Taylor, an able German
scholar, to whom Lanier sent the German version of the sonnet,
which he also published in English, wrote: "Both my wife and
I find your sonnet quite remarkable for a neophyte in the
language. It moves stiffly and somewhat awkwardly, but it is
anything but absurd—on the contrary, informed with a distinct
idea, which, moreover, is German in its nature. You have

mastered the secret of the language already; now go on and master its literary treasures."[11]

The study of the purely scientific subjects was never pursued very far, for there was neither time nor money, but Lanier's interest in scientific investigation never lapsed, and his devotion to science amounted almost to reverence. It was, of course, as part of this interest that he made his careful studies of the science of music, producing an essay on the physics of music and, in the summer of 1879, his important work, *The Science of English Verse*.

Reading Lanier's life from his published work and available letters, however, one cannot fail to be struck by the fact that with the development of his interest in so many other subjects, his interest in music seems to have diminished greatly, though he remained a member of the Peabody Orchestra and continued to think of himself as first of all a musician. Whereas once he had hoped for nothing greater than to be flutist in Theodore Thomas's orchestra, his chief ambition from the fall of 1877 on was to study English literature and to become attached to the teaching staff of Johns Hopkins University. This change had not grown out of, nor did it produce any analysis and revision of, his estimate of his own talents: it came neither because he had not, for one reason or another, become a member of Thomas's orchestra, nor because the regular life of a university lecturer with its assured salary seemed to offer the maximum of leisure time in which to pursue other interests. There is, indeed, something childlike in Lanier's constant change of plans, his substitution of one ambition for another; but it is the childishness of an impatient, restless genius.

In a development so dynamic there is nevertheless logic. Though it was ostensibly in preparation for his lectures at Mrs. Bird's and the hoped-for appointment to a Johns Hopkins lectureship that Lanier, during the six months beginning with March, 1878, made an intensive study of Shakspere and pre-Shaksperean literature, he himself knew that reasons more eternally valid impelled him. Such study, of course, more than that of French, German, botany, anatomy, or mineralogy, could be and was of benefit to him in his work as a poet. The aim of all his study was the understanding of men, and where better than in the poetry of Shakspere could he find the elements of this understanding? In his studies Lanier learned a great deal about historical

English meters—enough to write a book on prosody and to make his own poems more richly metrical—but the important thing is that from this time on the quality of his poetry became deeper and purer. And whether out of knowledge or out of pain, but certainly out of the deepened understanding of human nature that the study of Shakspere had brought, Lanier seems suddenly to have found the inspiration for the truly great work of the final years, the poems on which his fame definitely rests.

§ 4

THE NUMBER of Lanier's published letters of these last years is small. For instance, no letters written to Gibson Peacock between January 30 and November 5, 1878, have been published and yet he must have written often to Peacock during this period. Taylor sailed for Berlin on April 11, having been appointed minister to Germany by President Hayes after six months of uncertainty, and Lanier hesitated to write, knowing that Taylor was far too busy with his new duties to have much time for personal correspondence. The letter he did write on October 20 was his last, and that was never answered, for Taylor died in Berlin in December, only a few weeks after the letter reached him. To his old correspondent Hayne, Lanier now wrote but seldom; indeed, from a remark in the letter to Hayne of November 19, 1880, we may assume that he had not written Hayne for three years at least. But as the record of his outer life becomes more meager, the record of his inner life, the volume of his literary work, grows fuller; and for our study of the last three and a half years of Lanier's life we have a body of work greater than that of all the preceding years put together. Our study now becomes almost exclusively an examination of this work.

We are to picture him spending most of his days in the library of the Peabody Institute, in Lanier's day one of the best research libraries in the United States, among the then but recently inaugurated publications of the Early English Text Society, the Chaucer Society, and the Percy Society, and the reprints of Elizabethan literature made by Grosart and Arber and other English scholars, working regularly every day with energy and unbounded zest. Lanier had certainly read Chaucer long before this time, quite possibly in college, but his interest in Old English grammar and his acquaintance with the work of Anglo-Saxon and Middle English writers other than Chaucer probably began at this time. It is more than likely that he first found the texts in the Peabody Library and then studied the grammar and learned to read the language with little scholarly aid. Yet within a year he was lecturing intelligently on these writers, in a way that revealed a grasp of the language, and pointing out the beauties of Anglo-Saxon and Middle English literature at a time when even the university scholars were just beginning to see the texts as something more than etymological records.

Handicapped by training and prevented by temperament, Lanier did not become an original scholar, and it may be that he would not have done scholarly work of importance had he been granted the opportunities, but he did make scholarly and intelligent use of the researches of others, curious and indefensible as many of his misstatements are; and his achievement in mastering the grammar and acquiring in so short a time his wide knowledge of early English literature is rather remarkable. He worked with the zeal of a discoverer, the feverish, untiring energy of an explorer. "I have been so buried in study for the past six months," he wrote in his last letter to Taylor, "that I know not news nor gossip of any kind. Such days and nights of glory as I have had!"[12] But even now when he seems so lost in the glories of the past, of the times of Shakspere and his predecessors, Lanier makes a discovery that brings him close to our own day and emphasizes his catholicity, for in the spring of 1878 the literary discovery that Lanier reported with most enthusiasm was the poetry of Whitman, the poet of all those writing to whom he himself was most akin.

Toward the end of January, 1878, in New York, Lanier called on Taylor who pressed upon him three books for immediate reading: *Among My Books* by Lowell—perhaps the second volume, published in 1876; *Atalanta in Calydon* by Swinburne; and Walt Whitman's *Leaves of Grass*, none of them new books but all presumably previously unread by Lanier. On Sunday, January 27, 1878, Lanier stayed in his room at the hotel, deeming it imprudent because of his recent severe illness to venture out more than necessary, and read through the three volumes. The next day he returned them, and but for the fortuitous happening of Taylor's being out when Lanier called and of the books' being left instead with a servant, Lanier's first impression of *Leaves of Grass* might not have been recorded. But deprived of the opportunity of seeing Taylor and telling him the joy with

20

which he had read Whitman's poetry, he wrote him a letter, and
though it was not written until a week later—he had returned
meanwhile to Baltimore—his enthusiasm had not waned. He
wrote: "upon a sober comparison I think Walt Whitman's
'Leaves of Grass' worth at least a million of 'Among My Books'
and 'Atlanta [*sic*] in Calydon.' In the two latter I could not
find anything which has not been much better said before; but
'Leaves of Grass' was a real refreshment to me—like rude salt
spray in your face—in spite of its enormous fundamental error
that a thing is good because it is natural, and in spite of the
world-wide difference between my own conceptions of art and
its author's."[13] The comparison, it is hardly necessary to point
out, is anything but sober: the praise is that of the convert, the
discoverer; but Lanier was sober enough to realize the irrecon-
cilable differences between Whitman and himself in their attitude
toward poetry and the art of poetry, and his unreserved praise
is, therefore, extremely generous.

Anyone who has ever found joy in a book and has wanted to
own a copy, though realizing perfectly well that purchase would
be an extravagance, and hesitated, and recalled the joy, and
hesitated again, and finally, being unable to forego the indul-
gence longer, has ordered the desired volume, will understand
how and why it was that three months later, on the fifth of
May, Lanier addressed to Whitman, from whom alone the then
current edition (1876) of *Leaves of Grass* was obtainable, the
following letter, in which he enclosed a bill for five dollars:

"My dear Sir:

"A short time ago while on a visit to New York I happened
one evening to find your *Leaves of Grass* in Mr. Bayard Taylor's
library; and taking it with me to my room at the hotel I spent
a night of glory and delight upon it. How it happened that I
had never read this book before . . is a story not worth the
telling; but, in sending the enclosed bill to purchase a copy
. . . I cannot resist the temptation to tender you also my grateful
thanks for such large and substantial thoughts uttered in a
time when there are, as you say in another connection, so many
'little plentiful mannikins skipping about in collars and tailed
coats.' Although I entirely disagree with you in all points connected with artistic form, and in so much of the outcome of
your doctrine as is involved in those poetic exposures of the
person which your pages so unreservedly make, yet I feel sure

that I understand you therein, and my dissent in these particulars becomes a very insignificant consideration in the presence of that unbounded delight which I take in the bigness and bravery of all your ways and thoughts. It is not known to me where I can find another modern song at once so large and so naive: and the time needs to be told few things so much as the absolute personality of the person, the sufficiency of the man's manhood *to* the man, which you have propounded in such large and beautiful rhythms. I beg you to count me among your most earnest lovers, and to believe that it would make me very happy to be of the least humble service to you at any time."[14]

It is, really, an amazing letter, "a florid, gushing letter," Whitman thought;[15] and when, ten years later, Whitman gave it to Traubel he chuckled over the inconsistency with which Lanier stated bluntly that he disagreed with him in all points connected with artistic form and then praised him as the master of modern song, of "strong and beautiful rhythms." "That hardly seems to gee," said Whitman. "I don't say I am one or t'other, but I know I ain't both."[14] Whitman was right, and the inconsistency cannot be explained away. But the praise is genuine, the enthusiasm sincere.

The phrase "little plentiful mannikins skipping about in collars and tailed coats" Lanier quoted twice elsewhere, in a letter and in the Shakspere lectures, and probably it is the key to his appreciation of Whitman. Lanier, like Whitman, had the utmost contempt for all that was mean and small, and Lanier's contempt extended also to that which was useless. The "bigness and bravery" of Whitman's ways appealed to him. Both, whether Whitman admitted it of Lanier or not, were national in their vision; both had a genuine, passionate love for the American soil; both—though Whitman denied it of Lanier—were striving for newer and freer forms of poetry; and each had a vision of a redeemed America, the one of an America singing his bold, brave songs, the other of an America consecrated to the love of which his poetry was the gospel.

Neither of course influenced the other, but it is curious to note that in some of the "poem outlines" which Lanier was still jotting down at this period, when his studies allowed him little leisure to develop ideas into finished poems, he actually achieved a form, determined solely by the "rhythm of idea," that somewhat suggests Whitman's finished work. The similarity to Whitman is suggested also by unpoetic—or at least not conventionally poetic—terms in much of Lanier's poetry, in "The Crystal" especially, the use of which suggests an attempt as deliberate as that of Whitman to enlarge the vocabulary of poetry and bring it nearer the everyday speech of the average man. Finally, there is a "bigness and bravery" in the poetry Lanier himself published from this time on which has no connection of course with his reading of *Leaves of Grass* but which indicates that in 1878 Lanier had reached the stage of spiritual development where he not only could appreciate Whitman's message of the "absolute personality of the person, the sufficiency of the man's manhood to the man," but could himself express the same message in beautiful and noble poetry.

An undated prose outline makes both these latter points perfectly clear. Lanier wrote in two paragraphs that contain the key to the doctrine developed in *The English Novel,* but with a different implication:

Lo, he that hath helped me to do right (save by mere information upon which I act or not, as I please) he hath not done me a favor; he hath covertly hurt me: he hath insidiously deflowered the virginity of my will; I am henceforth not a pure Me: I am partly another.

Each union of self and self is, once for all incest and adultery and every other crime. Let me alone. God made me so, a man, individual, unit, whole, fully-appointed in myself. Again I cry to thee, O friend, let me alone.[16]

It is further interesting to note that in this outline Lanier used terms from the vocabulary of sex with a freedom characteristic of Whitman but altogether uncharacteristic of Lanier. The central idea of the outline is, as we shall see, by implication the message of Lanier's poem "Individuality," a poem that lacks altogether the vigor of the outline but asserts clearly enough the same idea.

Interesting also in connection with the discussion of Lanier and Whitman is a passage in the prose piece, "Bob: the Story of Our Mocking-Bird," which Lanier wrote about this time. The story was undoubtedly written for children, but at the end Lanier draws a moral which children can hardly be expected to comprehend: Bob has lived in a cage almost from birth, and has never failed to sing sweet woodland songs. "I do protest,"

Lanier wrote, "that the greater the artist, and the more profound his piety toward the fellow-man for whom he passionately works, the readier will be his willingness to forego the privilege of genius and to cage himself in the conventionalities, even as the mocking-bird is caged. His struggle against these will, I admit, be the greatest: he will feel the bitterest sense of their uselessness in restraining *him* from wrong-doing. But, nevertheless, one consideration will drive him to enter the door and get contentedly on his perch: his fellow-men, his fellow-men. These he can reach through the respectable bars of use and wont; in his wild thickets of lawlessness they would never hear him, or, hearing, would never listen. In truth, this is the sublimest of self-denials, and none but a very great artist can compass it: to abandon the sweet, green forest of liberty, and live a whole life behind needless constraints, for the more perfect service of his fellow-men."

The paragraph is remarkably apt as a comment on the difference and likeness between Whitman and Lanier. Whitman's unconventionality of expression and of phraseology has too often prevented the essential message of his poetry from reaching those for whom he intended it, and yet the phrase of his own writing, "barbaric yawp," indicates what the story of his life reveals, that his unconventionality was cultivated and deliberate. With Lanier it was quite otherwise. He was as desirous as Whitman was of seeing a new school of poetry inaugurated, as eager that our national life should be purer, nobler, our actions freer, our individuality more reverently respected; yet, unlike Whitman, he deferred somewhat to public opinion in order that his poems might be published and his message broadcast, all the time hoping for the day when, his reputation achieved, and the public at last willing to listen, he might sing out the bolder song in the freer rhythm of which he knew the new age and America to be in need.

§ 5

THE FIRST poem by Lanier to be published in 1878 was "The Harlequin of Dreams,"[17] a fanciful sonnet, not unsuggestive of Shakspere's many allusions to sleep and in a way an epitome of them. Still experimenting with the sonnet form, stimulated to further practice of it by his scholarly studies, his second poem is also a sonnet, addressed to Frau Nanette Falk-Auerbach, which appeared simultaneously in an English and a German newspaper

of Baltimore. The English version[18] is less pleasing than the
German, as if the English were the translation rather than the
original. The third poem of the year is a sequence of three
sonnets, "To Our Mocking-Bird, Died of a Cat, May, 1878,"[19]
in which he sings of the bird that for six years had given him
so much pleasure, with tenderness which the fancifulness of the
second sonnet cannot obscure. (At some time before May, when
the bird was still alive, he must have written the prose piece
already referred to, "Bob: the Story of Our Mocking-Bird,"[20]
which has been published posthumously with interesting illustrations by Major A. Radclyffe Dugmore.)

The next poem of this period is distinctly a product of Lanier's
scholarly studies. The close attention to the older English prosody,
necessary to his study of the older English literature, had taught
Lanier some things about meters that he had not known before,
and among other things he had discovered that the English
dactyl is not the same as the classic dactyl, that Longfellow's
"Evangeline," for instance, is not written in the meter of the
Æneid but in logœdic dactyls. The meter that he himself had
used most often was the simple and regular iambic, though
he had introduced considerable variety of meter in "The Psalm
of the West" and "The Symphony"; and in "The Song of the
Chattahoochee" he had achieved an extremely effective metrical
irregularity. In 1878 he wished, however, to make an experiment
in composing a poem in logœdic dactyls, and for the purpose
he chose an incident related in a contemporary magazine novel,
William Black's *Macleod of Dare*,[21] of the revenge of a serf upon
his lord. Lanier's poem, the most ambitious narrative poem that
he ever completed, is "The Revenge of Hamish."[22]

The plot of the poem is identical with that of the tale told
in the novel, and the development of the plot is the same. But
instead of a dull prose narrative told with little imagination,
Lanier gives us a poem in which, by his simple, straightforward
telling of a gruesome incident of medieval life, and by the effective
metrical treatment, he recreates the atmosphere of the past and
restages the incident itself, achieving, for once, dramatic effectiveness hardly surpassed by Browning. One of the finest poems
Lanier wrote, it is also sufficient contradiction of Gosse's estimate
of Lanier's poetry as "never simple, never easy." In it he achieves,

better than William Black, what Black, speaking through his character, Macleod of Dare, called "the chief gift of a born narrator—an utter forgetfulness of himself." One of the simplest, most effective things conceivable is the ending of the poem. Hamish, brutally punished by his master Maclean for disobeying orders while hunting, seizes Maclean's child and threatens to drop it into the sea. He promises to spare the child if Maclean will accept ten blood-drawing strokes on his back, and Maclean, yielding to his wife's entreaties, takes them, and his wife reaches out her arms to take the child.

> In a flash fierce Hamish turned round and lifted the
>   child in the air,
>
> And sprang with the child in his arms from the horrible
>   height in the sea,
>   Shrill screeching "Revenge!" in the wind-rush; and
>   pallid Maclean,
>   Age-feeble with anger and impotent pain,
> Crawled up on the crag, and lay flat, and locked hold of
>   dead roots of a tree—
>
> And gazed hungrily o'er, and the blood from his back
>   drip-dripped in the brine,
>   And a sea-hawk flung down a skeleton fish as he flew,
>   And the mother stared white on the waste of blue,
> And the wind drove a cloud to seaward, and the sun began
>   to shine.

Here is the spirit of the old balladry, if nothing of the manner. In the complete detachment with which the incident is related, the poem is almost brutal, and though "The Revenge of Hamish" bears no relation to American life or to the main current of American literature it is one of Lanier's most successful poems, a triumph of narration and of art. Lanier, himself realizing the success of his achievement, and of his use of the simple, prose-like logaœdic dactyls, longed to write another poem in which he should make even freer use of this freest of English metrical feet. This he soon had an excuse for doing.

§ 6

Roberts Brothers, publishers, of Boston, had conceived the idea of a series of works to be published anonymously, helped to success by no well known name but by merit alone. The idea of this "No Name Series" would strike a publisher today as being economically unsound, but it was not motivated solely by a sound critical theory of the effect of a well known name upon the reception accorded a new work: Roberts Brothers expected the series to create discussion and induce among readers much guessing as to the identity of authors that should react to the publishers' advantage. The majority of the volumes of the series were, of course, novels, but a volume of poetry, to bear the title *A Masque of Poets* and to be edited—anonymously— by George Parsons Lathrop, was planned, and "famous poets," among them Stedman, Lowell, Helen Hunt Jackson, Louisa May Alcott, Aldrich, and Austin Dobson, had promised to contribute poems specially written for the volume, braving critical dissection of their creation under this anonymity.[23] Lanier was also invited to contribute, and accepted the invitation. Of the one hundred and seventy-five poems contributed, Lanier's, "The Marshes of Glynn," is Number 88, and, except for the novelette in verse, "Guy Vernon," it is the longest poem in the book.[24] It is also, of the one hundred and seventy-five poems of the volume, one of the two or three that have survived, and the only one that has become at all well known. "The truth is," wrote Lanier of the book, "it is a distressing, an aggravated, yea, an intolerable collection of mediocrity and mere clever- ness. . . . I could find only four poems in the book. . . . If these gentlemen and ladies would read the old English poetry— I mean the poetry before Chaucer, the genuine Anglish utter- ances, from Cædmon in the seventh century to Langland in the fourteenth—they could never be content to put forth these little diffuse prettinesses and dandy kickshaws of verse."[25]

The measure of Lanier's poem[26] is basically that of "The Revenge of Hamish," the logaœdic dactyl, but the treatment is freer than in the other poem, approaching almost the free rhythmic treatment of Whitman, especially in the last half of the poem. The general effect of the poem, to borrow a figure from another art, is that of a rich landscape tapestry, and this is indeed the effect that Lanier strives for consciously in his choice of verbs and adjectives:

> Glooms of the live-oaks, beautiful braided and woven
> With intricate shades of the vines that myriad-cloven
> Clamber the forks of the multiform boughs,—
> Emerald twilights,—
> Virginal shy lights.

An air of medieval mysticism, and of medieval piety in the realization that the God of men is the God of nature, pervades the first stanzas of the poem:

> Beautiful glooms, soft dusks in the noon-day fire,—
> Wildwood privacies, closets of lone desire,
> Chamber from chamber parted with the wavering arras
> of leaves,—
> Cells for the passionate pleasure of prayer to the soul
> that grieves,
> Pure with a sense of the passing of saints through the
> wood,
> Cool for the dutiful weighing of ill with good.

But "The Marshes of Glynn" represents no new mood in Lanier: here too is the protest, implied if not loudly voiced, against trade; the half uncertain assurance of "The Symphony" has grown to certitude, to a knowledge of his own wisdom. "The Marshes of Glynn" is the poem of Lanier's spiritual maturity, to which he has worked through all his other poems. He can assert

> I know that I know,
> And my spirit is grown to a lordly great compass within.

From the forest of live-oaks, the forest of dusks and doubts, the poet steps out to the "firm-packed sand" which stretches beneath the bright afternoon sun like a shimmering ribbon between the sea-marshes and the forest, and suddenly "From the weighing of fate and the sad discussion of sin" his soul seems free. He has won

God out of knowledge and good out of infinite pain
And sight out of blindness and purity out of a stain.

Two of the few changes that Lanier made in the version of
"The Marshes of Glynn" appearing in *A Masque of Poets* are
the changes of "favor" to "greatness"[27] and of "largeness" to
"greatness" in four lines of the following stanza:

> As the marsh-hen secretly builds on the watery sod,
> Behold I will build me a nest on the favor of God:
> I will fly in the favor of God as the marsh-hen flies
> In the freedom that fills all the space 'twixt the marsh
>   and the skies:
> By so many roots as the marsh-grass sends in the sod
> I will heartily lay me a-hold on the favor of God.
> Oh, like to the favor of God, for the largeness within,
> Is the range of the marshes, the liberal marshes of Glynn.

The change, which is from a subjective idea to an objective
one, is important. The phrase "the greatness of God" is simple
and completely awe-inspiring; no words could more perfectly
express the realization of God which the poet finds in his contemplation of the marshes, the sky, and the sea. In the mind
of the sympathetic reader, the stanza—one of the best passages
in all Lanier's poetry—cannot fail to create a sense of quietness
and of well-being. But suddenly, with the most remarkably
varied of rhythms, the mood of quietness is broken by the inflow
of the flood-tide and the whirr of the birds as they rush from
the marsh grass to the land. Then, the measure changing abruptly
once more,

> all is still: and the currents cease to run;
> And the sea and the marsh are one.

But even here, in this ecstasy, occurs a line that might have
been lifted from a prosaic hydrographical report: "The tide is
at his highest height." The final stanza, however, is beautiful
in language and in rhetoric, a Christian benediction pronounced
at the end of the service, even though it ends with an implied
question:

And I would I could know what swimmeth below when
the tide comes in
On the length and the breadth of the marvellous marshes
of Glynn.

The poet is successful, not only in describing beautifully the
forests and the marshes and the flood-tide that follows sunset,
but also in conveying to the reader the effect of the place on
him. To have described his emotion would have been something;
but to show the actual creation of the emotion, in a way that
creates the emotion in the reader at the same time is much
more. There is no one word that labels poetry of this sort; onomatopœia tells but half, for among the sounds that Lanier fixes
and recreates in "The Marshes of Glynn" are whispers audible
only to the soul. Quotation cannot suggest the magic of it, the
beauty of the long, intricate, musically patterned sentence composed of the first thirty-six lines of the poem, the cadences of
the symphonic structure, freer and more splendid than that of
"Corn" or of "The Symphony." But to point out only the varied
meters and the splendid metaphors, is to overlook the beautiful
nature pictures with which it is filled. For here is the tropical
exuberance of the southern sea coast, in strange contrast to the
more familiar nature pictures of New England.

Wordsworth, in his Tintern Abbey lines, has described the
healing effects of nature on the spirit of man; but in that poem
as elsewhere in Wordsworth's poetry, nature is the antithesis of
man, not the counterpart. With Lanier nature is humanized.
Indeed, since St. Francis, no soul has seemed so heavily over-
charged with a feeling of brotherhood for all created things, all
natural objects, and all natural phenomena. Lanier's love extends
even to the colors of the landscape:

O braided dusks of the oak and woven shades of the vine,
While the riotous noon-day sun of the June-day long did
shine,
Ye held me fast in your heart and I held you fast in mine.

But a similar sense of intimate companionship with nature is
of course to be found in most of Lanier's poetry.

An analysis of sense-words in Lanier's poetry made by Mr. J. S.

Snoddy has revealed the interesting fact that while most of Lanier's references to colors are to the characteristic colors of nature—green, blue, red, and gray—most of his pictures consist not of colors at all but of lights and shadows. It is hardly necessary to add that the lights predominate. As Keats was fascinated by the moon, so Lanier was fascinated by the sun. Whether he sang of sunset, as in "The Marshes of Glynn," or of sunrise, in the poem which could have no other title than the simple one of its subject, or of birds and trees which the sun warms and vitalizes, one feels that all his songs are hymns to the sun—and one wonders if there existed a subtle connection between this devotion to life-giving heat and his own tubercular condition. Lanier sometimes sings of night, the temporary eclipse of the sun, but never of winter, from whose chill he had suffered so much. No poem, unless it be "Sunrise," could be more typical of Lanier than "The Marshes of Glynn," which reveals in full measure his devotion to nature, his love of natural objects, and the invigorating quality of the sunshine that he succeeded in transfixing into verse.

A Masque of Poets, containing Lanier's "Marshes of Glynn," was published in November, and reviews appeared in the magazines shortly afterwards. No one seems to have suspected Lanier's authorship; and Howells, who had consistently rejected Lanier's poems sent to him—from "Corn," and several sonnets, to "The Bee"—and who continued to ignore his work as a poet,[28] was deceived into writing, in the course of a flattering review of the volume, "There is a fine Swinburnian study called The Marshes of Glynn, in which the poet has almost bettered, in some passages, his master's instructions."[29] Longfellow probably learned from the publishers the name of the author of "The Marshes of Glynn" for on the third of January he wrote Lanier requesting permission to include the poem in his collection of *Poems of Places*.[30] Lanier replied on the eighth: "I am glad you like my poem, and cheerfully consent to the arrangement you propose both as to inserting it in your volume and signing my name to it." So "The Marshes of Glynn" appeared in print a second time in 1879 in the volume of Longfellow's collection devoted to the southern states of the United States. Of all Lanier's poems, it and "The Song of the Chattahoochee" are the best known and the most frequently reprinted.

180 St. Paul St.
Baltimore, Md.
Jan. 8th 1879.

My dear Sir:

I am glad you like my poem, and cheerfully consent to the arrangement you propose both as to inserting it in your volume and signing my name to it. I suspect the publishers still control the entire matter, however, and you will doubtless confer with them about it.

I beg you will let me avail myself of this opportunity to send my respectful and cordial wishes that the New Year may bring you all that you desire, in health, wealth and art.

Very truly yours,
Sidney Lanier.

A letter from Lanier to Longfellow. From the original in Craigie House, Cambridge, Massachusetts.

§ 7

ONE OF the undated "poem outlines" may refer to a contemporary verdict on the poem. "Do you think," wrote Lanier, "the 19th century is past? It is but two years since Boston burnt me for witchcraft. I wrote a poem which was not orthodox; that is, not like Mr. Longfellow's."[31] But with success, limited though it was, and with poetic maturity—the consciousness of the ripening of his art—had come at last true indifference to contemporary opinion. This indifference, symbolized by the free rhythms of "The Marshes of Glynn," finds its most vigorous expression in "Remonstrance" (probably written in August, 1878).[32] It is a denunciation of the intolerance of the age as the "Acknowledgment" sonnets had been a denunciation of the scepticism of the age; and it is, in spite of the artificiality of the diction, an artificiality matched by the elaborately patterned rhyme scheme, a bold protest. Since Wagner confused his critics by writing *Die Meistersinger* in double counter-point there has been in art no more ironic triumph than this of Lanier in confusing the critics who condemned him for not writing verse conventional in form by denouncing them in a poem that is, in form and diction, highly conventional. But the protest is thoroughly vigorous and free. There is, as a matter of fact, little in Lanier's prose or poetry that is quite so outspokenly denunciatory: the poem almost qualifies for inclusion in an anthology of abusive and invective verse.

> Assassin! Thief! Opinion, 'tis thy work.
> By Church, by throne, by hearth, by every good
>   That's in the Town of Time, I see thee lurk,
> And e'er some shadow stays where thou hast stood.
>   Thou hand'st sweet Socrates his hemlock sour;
>   Thou sav'st Barabbas in that hideous hour,
>   And stabb'st the good.

> .   .   .   .

> —Thou base-born Accident of time and place—
> Bigot Pretender unto Judgment's throne—
>   Bastard, that claimest with a cunning face
> Those rights the true, true Son of Man doth own

By Love's authority—thou Rebel cold
At head of civil wars and quarrels old—
Thou Knife on a throne—

I would thou left'st me free, to live with love,
And faith, that through the love of love doth find
My Lord's dear presence in the stars above,
The clods below, the flesh without, the mind
Within, the bread, the tear, the smile.
Opinion, damned Intriguer, gray with guile,
Let me alone.

In a letter to Kirk, of *Lippincott's*, who had rejected the poem, Lanier wrote: "I rather expected the poem wouldn't do: though I thought perhaps there might be enough margin of obscurity in it to leave Orthodoxy in some doubt as to whether or not it was being abused."[33] There is in "Remonstrance" not the slightest margin of obscurity, or doubt that it is orthodoxy of opinion and of practice, in poetry, in politics, and in religion, that is being trounced. And nowhere in American literature has orthodoxy been more severely trounced than in this poem, unless it be in the prose of Emerson and Melville.

It is platitudinous perhaps to add that only in escape from servitude to the past does freedom in art lie, and yet the persisting vigor of academic forms and the consequent sterility of so much that passes for art is proof of the fact that the truth of the platitude is not generally realized. In Lanier's day new movements in art were under way, but they had not won their justification nor created the organized support that current movements, for example, have succeeded in winning. When we, through a successful effort of the imagination, see Lanier in his own decade—the decade of the seventies, a period of political corruption, industrial tyranny, and artistic sterility, we see that he not only was a progressive but even a radical who went unpersecuted only because of the indifference to poetry of the generation in which he lived. But "Remonstrance," the poem in which this radicalism is given its most vigorous expression, Lanier himself never saw published.

In an uncollected essay called "Mazzini on Music," which had been published in the *Independent* for June 27, 1878, Lanier had remonstrated with current orthodoxy of another sort. The essay is a sort of extended comment on an essay on music by Giuseppe Mazzini, with several digressions. The value of Mazzini's essay, Lanier asserted to be "derived from the lofty plane upon which he does it." There was little enough loftiness, Lanier thought, in contemporary art. The point of his essay seems to be, not the discussion of Mazzini's essay nor the discussion of the music of the new day and the effect such music might have on the lives of men, but the discussion of moral purpose in art. To the end that art may be spiritualized, he writes, "the artists must purify their hearts and exalt their lives. . . . Art is a means, it is not an end. Art exists that man may accomplish his destiny." In the poem "Clover," in this essay, and—most outspokenly of all—in the last lecture of the last lecture course, Lanier disputed the current conception of art for art's sake, asserting that "wherever there is a contest as between artistic and moral beauty, unless the moral side prevail, all is lost." It is, of all Lanier's remonstrances with the time in which he lived, the most significant.

§ 8

SUCH IDEAS of moral beauty in art as he set forth in this essay characterized undoubtedly the lectures on poetry which he had given in the spring of 1878, just as they characterize the lectures which a favorable turn of events made it possible for him soon to give before a larger audience than that which had gathered at Mrs. Bird's. For Gilman, still eager to have Lanier connected with Johns Hopkins but unable to secure an appointment for him, had arranged for him to join a number of Johns Hopkins professors in giving a course of lectures on Shakspere at the Peabody Institute.[34] The original plan seems to have called for twenty-four lectures by Lanier on the text of the plays and fourteen lectures on the background of the plays by Basil Gildersleeve, Ira Remsen, H. B. Adams, E. G. Daves, and R. M. Johnston.

To provide himself and his classes with a satisfactory textbook of matter supplementary to the plays, Lanier now planned a two-volume work to be called "The English Sonneteers, from Surrey to Shakespere," made up of critical accounts similar in tone to that of his paper on Bartholomew Griffin (a paper designed, as a matter of fact, as a chapter of the projected book) and numerous illustrative specimens. But the paper on Griffin—

with its surprisingly erratic judgments—and the projected volume were both turned down by the Lippincotts, although Lanier sought to convince Kirk that the book would be unique of its kind and should "soon become a favorite Reader, or Manual, especially in female schools."

The certainty, however, of his giving the course on Shakspere prevented his being too disheartened by Kirk's rejection of his projected book. He still hoped, to be sure, to persuade another publisher to bring out the book for him, and he had other plans on foot. The Scribners were considering his plans for an edition of Froissart's chronicles edited for boys, and had accepted for their magazine three papers on "The Physics of Poetry." These papers Lanier hoped to develop into a full volume on the subject of English prosody; and the possibility of seeing these volumes and a fourth, a book of original verse to be called "Songs of Aldhelm,"[35] soon in print made the future seem bright. Work on these volumes and on a number of essays on such subjects as "The Death of Byrhtnoth" and "John Barbour's Bruce"— both including literal translations and both apparently designed for young readers, as companion pieces to his *Boy's Froissart*—filled all his spare time, and provided him with material to be used in the coming lectures.

The essay called "The Death of Byrhtnoth"[36] reveals as fully as a letter might the attitude with which Lanier approached his studies. To him it seemed strange and deplorable that with all our boasting of Anglo-Saxon blood we take so little interest in our literary lineage, and remain even totally ignorant of it, while devoting so much time and attention to the study of Greek and Latin. He did not of course mean—he was careful to assert— that the intrinsic value of Anglo-Saxon literature is equal to that of the Greek and Roman classics, but that with our love for great poetry in general it is strange that we should not care more for the fine, vigorous poetry of our own forefathers. And, he asserted, "Our literature needs Anglo-Saxon iron; . . . we lack a primal idiomatic bone and substance; we have not the stalwart Anglicism of style which can tolerate [robustious individuality such as, for instance, that of Carlyle, over whom] we are as uncomfortable . . . as an invalid, all nerves, with a great rollicking boy in the room. . . . [Our modern tongue must] recur to the robust forms, and from these to the underlying and determining genius, of its Anglo-Saxon period.

"In other words . . . culture must be cited into the presence of the Fathers." The rest of the essay is devoted to a discussion and translation of the poem known as "The Battle of Maldon" or "The Death of Byrhtnoth."

Lanier's enthusiasm for Anglo-Saxon poetry is greater even than that of Tennyson; but it is so genuine that it does not strike us as being excessive. His enthusiasm for Anglo-Saxon versification is of course not so much enthusiasm as delighted surprise that Anglo-Saxon poetry should be metrical and not a rude barbaric chant. His enthusiasm for the spirit of the old poems and for the virtues and emotions described in them is that of the man of great soul for virtues whose genuineness and largeness he recognizes instinctively. "I have been studying Early English, Middle English and Elizabethan poetry, from Beówulf to Ben Jonson," he wrote to Taylor; "and the world seems twice as large."[37] Perhaps no greater tribute was ever paid the poetry of old England than this simple statement of Lanier.

"The Death of Byrhtnoth" (or "The Proper Basis of English Culture" as it was called upon first, though posthumous, publication) was written for immediate sale, as was "John Barbour's Bruce."[38] Lanier might reasonably have expected to sell the first, though he did not succeed in doing so; the second, which consists of a brief introductory account and long extracts from the poem with interlinear translation, was certainly beyond the interest of boys, and if submitted to editors must have been promptly rejected. But it was as necessary as ever to increase his meager income, so—the sale of pot-boilers falling off—Lanier now sought to commercialize in another way the fruits of his study, and he attempted to make arrangements to deliver the course of Shakspere lectures planned for the Peabody Institute before classes in Washington and Philadelphia as well as in Baltimore.

He had become convinced, as a result of his experience in lecturing to the private class in the preceding spring, that grown men and women are interested in pursuing subjects and attending courses of lectures after graduation from college. Indeed, the plan that he formulated and outlined in a letter of November 5 to Gibson Peacock is very similar to that of the extension courses given at present at Harvard, the University of Chicago, and elsewhere with such notable success. "The fault of the lecture system as at present conducted," Lanier wrote, "—a fault which must finally prove fatal to it—is that it is too fragmentary a mass—*indigesta moles*—of facts before the hearers. Now if . . . a scheme of lectures should be arranged which would amount to the *systematic presentation* of a *given subject*, then the audience would carry away some genuine possession at the end of the course. The subject thus systematically presented might be either scientific . . . or domestic . . . or artistic, or literary."[39] Lanier's scheme, as he further outlined it, is by implication a criticism of much of the work being done in universities at the time, and it anticipates with a close degree of accuracy the lecture system that, for better or worse, held undisputed sway in our colleges a few years ago.

On Saturday, November 2, 1878, at twelve noon, Lanier inaugurated his division of the Peabody Institute lectures,[40] making his first lecture a general discussion of form in poetry, or of verbal sound, as he considered that essential to a serious and profitable study of the literature of poetry. The plan for repeating the lectures in Philadelphia and Washington fell through, and the Baltimore course was not given without changes that resulted in a reduction of the number of lectures and the omission altogether of the lectures to have been given by the Johns Hopkins professors. But the excitement of giving the course was thrilling to Lanier. And when in December Charles Scribner's Sons agreed to publish his *Boy's Froissart* and decided to hold the three papers on "The Physics of Poetry" and to consider the projected volume on prosody which would replace them, it seemed to Lanier as if success were indeed crowning all his efforts. "I have reported progress up to date," he had written Taylor in October. "Who better than you—who looked so kindly upon my poor little beginning—has the right to know how far I've gone?"[41] But the greater success was yet to come, though it came too late for Taylor, who died in Berlin December 19, 1878, to be informed of it.

This was Lanier's appointment as lecturer in English literature at the Johns Hopkins University. The news of the appointment was communicated to Lanier by Gilman in a letter that reached him on his thirty-seventh birthday, February 4, 1879.[42] The appointment was to a position sought twice before in vain, and it meant the achievement of a goal toward which Lanier had been striving for twenty years. As he read the letter and comprehended the import of it his head dropped to his breast and he murmured "It is the first thing in all these years."[43] He was at last to take his place as a scholar among scholars in a university that had been founded to make possible in America intellectual training of an order higher than could at that time be obtained at Harvard, Yale, or any of the other universities of America, and without political or ecclesiastical interference. And the appointment had come directly as an appreciation of his Centennial cantata and his defense of it—which had won for him the admiration of Gilman—and of his growing importance in Baltimore, and of his increasing reputation as a poet. Gilman was an able administrator and a keen appraiser of men. He needed and wanted Lanier on the faculty of Johns Hopkins, to broaden the institution on the side where it was weakest, and he had at last brought the trustees round to his own point of view.

Lanier's course of lectures at the Peabody Institute lasted through the spring of 1879, unaffected by the appointment. The highest tribute paid these lectures was Gilman's suggestion that they be repeated as the lectures of Lanier's first public course at Johns Hopkins.

CHAPTER SIXTEEN

THE GOSPEL OF POETRY

§ 1

THE YEAR 1878 had been for Lanier essentially a year of intellectual growth. The Peabody Library of Baltimore had become the scholarly Germany of which he had dreamed in the old days at Oglethorpe, and much of his time this year—perhaps too much for the good of his health—had been spent in scholarly research there. One of the assistant librarians has recalled the regularity of his visits and the absorption with which he pursued his studies. When ill health prevented his visits to the library—as it did more and more—"he would write notes to the desk attendants asking them to verify some reference or copy some extract for him," or—and frequently—Mrs. Lanier would go to the library to secure the information.[1]

To Lanier scholarship was always a spiritual adventure, and the charm of his scholarly studies—as well as the weakness—results from the excitement of his own enthusiasm with which he never failed to invest even the most routine matters. This enthusiasm led him often to hasty conclusions, particularly in *The Science of English Verse*, or to uncritical esteem of such a minor poet as justly forgotten Bartholomew Griffin. It led him, too, to change abruptly the announced schedule of his courses, rearranging the Shakspere lectures that he might give five readings from Anglo-Saxon and Middle English poems and making the course on "The English Novel" a course not on the English novel but on the novels of one writer, George Eliot. Yet Lanier's scholarship is not to be despised. He always reveals a full knowledge of the bibliography of the subject he treats, and he attempted to keep informed of the latest studies and investigations of every subject that interested him—as when in the Shakspere lectures, written in 1879, he suggested the use, in experiments in the physics of sound, of the phonograph, the invention of which had been only that year announced. He knew the necessity of specialization and the importance of specialists. And he under-stood perfectly the attitude with which scholarly work must be undertaken. "Educate your intellectual powers," he had told the graduates of Furlow College in 1869. "Question unceasingly, question audaciously, all history, all science, all philosophy. Be content with no half answers. Be bold enough to accept any truth. Be wise enough to preserve from improper distortion, and to classify, in proper relation, every fact. Beware how . . . quick intuitions . . . hurry you on to erect isolated instances into general principles. Life and art and knowledge will cast upon you the necessity of drawing many grand conclusions. Let these conclusions be from large deductions, be slowly drawn, be care-fully weighed, be rigidly outlined." The difficulty was that Lanier did not, he could not, give to his work the painstaking care he knew to be so important. One life was too short, and there was so much that he wanted to know! Becoming interested in Helmholtz's recent discoveries in acoustics, he ransacked the Peabody Library for books on the subject and persuaded the librarians to admit him to the catalogue room where the latest were, not yet unpacked. The marvel is that working in haste and excitement his scholarship is as accurate as it is, that his notes, references, and citations are generally reliable.

The Johns Hopkins appointment was a recognition of his ability as a poet, a disseminating scholar, and a lecturer. President Gilman wrote: "we need among us some one like you, loving literature and poetry, and treating it in such a way as to enlist and inspire many students."[2] But it was particularly gratifying to Lanier for another reason. The Peabody Institute lectures had not proved at all successful in any popular sense of the word. The first seven lectures, Lanier stated in a letter written early in January, had been attended by an interesting class of twenty-five or thirty members, but so small a number did not produce sufficient income to meet the expenses of the course. The course was a languishing one, he had to admit. "My own lectures," he added, "will be delivered for nothing: with the best help there is not now the least prospect that I will raise even enough to pay the expenses of the course without adding from my own pocket."[3]

By the members of the faculty of the newly founded university, by such scholars and scientists as J. J. Sylvester,[4] the mathemati-cian, Gildersleeve and C. D. Morris, the classicists, Henry A.

Rowland, the physicist, Ira Remsen, the chemist, and H. B.
Adams, the historian, Lanier was probably not thought of as a
scholar but as a poet, fulfilling the poet's function of keeping
"the line of men touching shoulders with each other" and of con-
verting learning to wisdom.[5] "He was eager, receptive, reaching
out to all the knowable, transmitting all that he learned,"
Gildersleeve wrote of him.[6] The trustees in appointing him to a
lectureship rather than to a fellowship probably thought of him
as he thought of himself, not as an original investigator but as
"an enthusiastic interpreter,"[7] whose usefulness in an academic
capacity was to direct rather than to lead.

§ 2

BUT THE appointment was the achievement of a goal, and
it had the effect of turning Lanier's interest for the time almost
solely to scholarly matters. It is not surprising to find that he
published only one new poem in 1879, an elegy in honor of
Bayard Taylor, which appeared in *Scribner's* for March,[8] and even
it, one feels, in spite of its rich beauty, suffers as poetry from
having been written by a scholar; the difficulty of following the
involved sentences causes the reader's attention to relax, while
the references to other poets, the allusions to other poems, the
echoes of "Adonaïs" and other elegies, even the less distinct
echoes of Shakspere, and the Elizabethan phrasing, combine to
distract the reader's interest wholly from the main theme and
to turn it to the background out of which this poem grows.
One other poem by Lanier was published that year, in the
biography of Charlotte Cushman which Miss Stebbins had at
last prepared, but it was an old poem sent to Charlotte Cushman four years previously with a copy of "Corn." The composition of not more than five of the hundred and twenty
published poems by Lanier can be assigned with any certainty
to this year. Even more, perhaps, than in the preceding year,
his time was spent in study and in making plans for the next
winter's work.[9]

With a sentimental devotion to the dreams of his youth he
urged his brother Clifford, a successful business man of Montgomery, to come to Baltimore and resume his own literary
career. They could write together, and they would form a publishing house to issue the many books that Lanier looked forward
to producing with regularity, books on language and literature,

THE

BOY'S FROISSART

BEING

SIR JOHN FROISSART'S CHRONICLES

OF

Adventure Battle and Custom in
England France Spain etc.

EDITED FOR BOYS WITH AN INTRODUCTION

BY

SIDNEY LANIER

Illustrated by Alfred Kappes

NEW-YORK

CHARLES SCRIBNER'S SONS

743 & 745 BROADWAY

1879

Title-page of "The Boy's Froissart," Lanier's fourth published
volume. (In the original the initial letters of the main title
appear in red.)

books of verse and on the science of verse, editions of the classics for men and women and for boys and girls; at least two a year for the next ten years![10] Clifford wisely discouraged the scheme, but Lanier's enthusiasm was unabating. By the middle of July he had made plans not only for the lectures of the following winter but also for most of the texts that he considered so necessary to the success of his lectures. These plans he recorded in detail in two long letters to President Gilman.

In the first of the letters[11] he outlined only vaguely his scheme for the systematic study of English literature; but undeveloped as the outline is, it indicates a remarkably broad grasp of the place of education in life, as if in planning his course Lanier had taken the achievement of Matthew Arnold's definition of culture as his goal. By way of preparation for the fuller understanding of literature he would have students acquire "(1) A working vocabulary of idiomatic English words and phrases; (2) A working stock of illustrative ideas drawn from all those departments of learning which are within the range of persons of average culture; and (3) A working acquaintance with those peculiar forms of modern communication which have evolved themselves out of the special inward needs of our time, as, for example: (a) the lecture . . . ; (b) the magazine papers . . . ; (c) the newspaper leveler; (d) the sermon; (e) the novel; (f) the modern drama; (g) the address . . . ; (h) the poem; and other forms." His scheme Lanier seems to have planned as a three years' course, but it is obviously a course to be pursued through a lifetime. The second part alone, the acquisition of a "stock of illustrative ideas," involves the pursuit of all branches of learning, the reading of the classic works on all the arts and sciences: even the brief catalogue of such works as Lanier gives is that of a library hardly to be compressed into a five-foot shelf.

Ambitious as the scheme is, it is nevertheless fundamentally sound; that is, it is based on a full realization of the fault in current systems of education. His course was arranged, he explained, "with a primary view toward the practical outfit of every English speaking man" and "should, in its last stages be especially directed toward counteracting that very lamentable narrowness of range which seems peculiarly incident to the absorbed specialist in modern science and modern linguistics." Beyond this, the aim of the course was that of humanistic education from the beginning of time: "To this end the spiritual consolation and refreshment of literature . . . should be brought out, so as to initiate friendships between special students and particular authors which may be carried on through life."

Lanier, moreover, looked forward many years to a revolution in academic life: his course was admittedly somewhat theoretic. Immediately practicable plans he explained in the second letter to Gilman:[12] in his class work for advanced students he planned to have each student undertake a piece of work involving original research which would "if properly carried out—constitute a genuine contribution to modern literary scholarship." The class work was also carefully designed to supplement and make use of the work of the students in other courses, and, instead of having each student make a superficial investigation of a wide field, he planned to keep constantly before the student the moral aim— or at least the moral character—of all great art. But all this was to be centered about the study of certain plays of Shakspere. The plan meant in essence "the serious study of the poetic art in its whole outcome," in all its implications and ramifications.

The books on which he was at the time actually engaged he listed as *The Science of English Verse*, a treatise on prosody which he considered essential in clearing the student's path of the errors and confusion that obstruct and obscure the student's understanding and enjoyment of poetry, and two textbooks— an anthology of poetry from Cædmon to Chaucer and a book of selections from Chaucer—in which he planned to give the original texts with interlinear glossarial explanations which should facilitate the reader's understanding and immediate enjoyment of the poems as "pure literature." These, he wrote, he planned to print and sell himself "on the cheap plan which has been so successfully adopted by Edward Arber," and if they succeeded he looked forward to preparing three more volumes— a "Spenser," "The Minor Elizabethan Song-Writers," and "The Minor Elizabethan Dramatists." The scheme, it is hardly necessary to point out, anticipated the "Athenæum" series and other series since inaugurated for texts used extensively in American universities. But the ultimate object of the course, as of all Lanier's thought, was not merely instructive but moral: it was to make "a finer fibre for all our young American manhood by leading our youth in proper relations with English poetry."

What was probably intended as an introduction to the proposed "Chaucer" is preserved in part as a brief uncollected essay called

"How to Read Chaucer," which was either never finished by Lanier or has been shortened more in publication than the editorial note that accompanies it indicates. Repeating the idea, already asserted in "The Death of Byrhtnoth," that Chaucer is not a well of English undefiled but that he was fed by two streams of language which were still essentially distinct in many particulars, the one French and the other English,[13] Lanier asserted that in order to read Chaucer with pleasure we must read his language as he himself would have read it, not as modern English, understanding his Sense, his Rhythm and his Rhymes, and to do this we must prepare ourselves as carefully as we are prepared in school to read a foreign classic in the original language. Unfortunately, after this introduction, the article in its published version is cut off, with only a brief paragraph to suggest that Chaucer's "Sense" was to be determined by a careful study of his words—such a semantic study as Lanier was to suggest in the Shakspere lectures—and an editorial note stating that Lanier analyzed and compared passages from the Bible in Anglo-Saxon and in Wycliffite versions to point out how this should be done.

Lanier probably developed—or would have developed—in this essay an analysis of Rhythm and Rhymes in Chaucer as thorough if not as extended as that made for Shakspere in his coming lecture course, but as we have the gist of the matter in the discussion of Chaucer in The Science of English Verse[14] the loss of the second and third parts of the essay is not irreparable. The chief importance of the essay lies in Lanier's sensible insistence that we must not let our opinion of old writers be determined by the quaintness of spelling and the charm of tradition under the ægis of which the writer's works are presented to us. This statement defines clearly enough the genuineness of Lanier's own interest in the study of our English classics.

A phrase in Lanier's letter to Gilman, "of making a finer fibre for all our young American manhood," serves to emphasize once more the close touch that Lanier kept with contemporary events, the solid ground on which he stood as he reached to clutch a star. He continued to read southern newspapers and to follow important events in southern and in national development. Indeed, at the very time he was preparing the proposed outline of the academic course to be submitted to Gilman he paused to write to his brother a long letter in which he analyzed the contemporary political situation with the astuteness of a statesman, revealing in his letter little that marked the author as a poet.[10]

§ 3

LANIER, during the first few days of June and probably in another effort to find a publisher for the textbooks he wished to bring out, had made a trip to Boston.[15] That the trip proved unsuccessful is shown in his proposal to publish the books himself; but it gave him another opportunity for a call on Longfellow, which he made, not for any assistance that he hoped to receive now but because as a young poet who had won his laurels it was appropriate that he should call on him.[16] Upon his return to Baltimore he found a letter from Stedman asking for information to be used in his book on the *Poets of America*, then in preparation, and though the request was in the nature of a compliment Lanier, suffering still from the wholly unintended hurt Stedman had caused him several years previously, answered with some coolness, informing Stedman that the 1877 volume of poems was his only collected volume and that his Shakspere lectures had not been printed.[17]

At the end of July the Laniers with their younger boys went to Rockingham Springs, in the Shenandoah Valley of Virginia, Lanier carrying with him notes and illustrative material used in the lectures of the preceding winter and spring which he was already working into his manual of prosody, *The Science of English Verse*. The choice of Rockingham Springs as a place to do this work was probably due to the fact that Lanier's friend John R. Tait, the artist, and other citizens of Baltimore were accustomed to spend their summers there. Here Lanier stayed for six weeks, working systematically six hours a day, riding horseback in the late afternoon, and playing on his beloved Boehm flute before the assembled company of fellow visitors in the evenings. He is said to have done some sketching this summer—probably because of the encouragement of Tait—sitting on the bridge at McGaheysville, with Mrs. Lanier holding an umbrella over him. If this is true, it is interesting as the only record of Lanier's talent for sketching and of his practice of the art. Professor John Wayland, who has gathered all the available information concerning the summer and has printed it in an interesting brochure called *Sidney Lanier at Rockingham Springs*, has found a record in the *Rockingham*

Register, a weekly newspaper published at Harrisonburg, of a tournament held at McGaheysville on August 8, at which Lanier delivered the address to the knights. Bald though the newspaper account of the affair is, it gives us an attractive picture of Lanier standing on the verandah of a rustic cottage charging these Virginia knights to do after the good and leave the evil, and ever to live nobly in the service of their fair ladies. An equally romantic picture is the expected one recalled by Mr. G. T. Hopkins, owner and manager of Rockingham Springs, that of Lanier improvising on his flute late at night, on the upper porch of the cottage, singing his heart out in the full enjoyment of musical art.

The summer must have been a happy one. Before it was over big Charley, almost eleven, came to join his parents and eight-year-old Sidney and six-year-old Harry. Twenty years later he—Mr. Charles Day Lanier—was to recall how his father "loved to swing in full-muscled walks through the fields and woods; to take the biggest bow and quiver out of the archery implements provided for himself and his brood of boys, and with them trailing at his heels to tramp and shoot at rovers; to stride a springy horse and ride through the mountains and the valleys, noting what they were pleased to show of tree and bird and beast life."[18]

The happy mood of this summer finds expression in "Owl Against Robin," a gay, amusing poem written at Rockingham Springs in 1879, though not published until two full years later.[19] Inconsequential as the poem must appear to one who reads it expecting to find in it, as in most of Lanier's poems, a sense of moral purpose, a serious interpretation of nature, "Owl Against Robin" is one of the gayest, pleasantest nature fantasies conceivable, with the sage owl voicing the annoyance that human beings feel at the robin's persistent chirp, and rationalizing his command to stop. The last line, "O, irritant, iterant, maddening bird!" is a little *tour de force* of descriptive writing. Together with the sonnets on the pet mocking-bird, "Owl Against Robin" reveals an aspect of Lanier's talent not generally recognized, a sympathetic understanding of animal life. Had not the business of poetry seemed so serious to Lanier he might have written more of this delightful sort of light verse, but it was all too seldom that, as at Rockingham Springs, with his wife and boys, and with himself in fairly good health, life seemed such a happy

Owl Against Robin.

Frowning, the owl in the oak complained him
Sore, that the song of the robin restrained him
Wrongly of slumber, rudely of rest.
" From the north, from the east, from the south and the west,
Woodland, wheatfield, cornfield, clover —
Over and over and over and over —
Five o'clock, ten o'clock, twelve, or seven —
Nothing but robin-songs heard under heaven:
        How can we sleep ?

8

Be like the owl, scarce seen, scarce heard,
O irritant, iterant, maddening Bird!

                            Sidney Lanier.

Rockingham Springs.
Near McGaheysville.
    Virginia.

A Lanier manuscript. First and last pages of "Owl Against Robin." Courtesy of Mr. Kenneth Rede.

summer idyll—though to Mrs. Lanier, with her keen perception, even this summer idyll was only "a lull between storms."[20]

That summer Lanier accomplished a considerable amount of work, for when he returned to Baltimore he carried with him the nearly completed *Science of English Verse*, taking the heavy manuscript in a hand valise. His wife remonstrated at his carrying so heavy a bag, "but he solemnly declared," she wrote in an account of the episode, "that if anything should happen to that manuscript it would kill him: that he could never replace it; meaning, that there was no reserve of life left for the task."[20] His health, unfortunately, had not been greatly improved by the six weeks at Rockingham Springs, and though he was in no condition to resume work in the fall of 1879, he went back to his old place in the Peabody Orchestra, began classes in literature in several private schools,[21] and on Tuesday, October 28, began at Johns Hopkins his first series of sixteen lectures on "English Verse, especially Shakespere's," lecturing in Hopkins Hall toward the close of the afternoon to a class of about one hundred and fifty men and women.

It was during the next three months, when the pressure of professional engagements left him no leisure, and the fever of tuberculosis allowed him little peace, that *The Science of English Verse*, the first important offering of Lanier in his new academic rôle, was brought to completion.[22] Once again, in passing judgment on his work we must, in human kindness, temper our expectations with a realization of the difficulties under which the work was produced. Read sympathetically, *The Science of English Verse*, while it reveals errors of statement and of judgment, also reveals qualities that made its appearance significant and that make it still useful in the study of prosody.

§ 4

LANIER begins with a definition of verse, which he defines as "a set of specially related sounds," a definition easily accepted but not acceptable at all with the explanation that "when verse is repeated aloud, it impresses itself upon the ear only by means of certain relations existing among its component words considered purely as sounds, without reference to their associated ideas. . . . The ear accepts as perfect verse a series of words from which ideas are wholly absent, that is to say, a series of sounds." Lanier's fundamental proposition is undoubtedly an overstatement, inconsistent with his own practice of packing his lines tight with thought. Pushed to the logical conclusion, the proposition can be made to sanction the theory of the Dadaists, but Lanier would undoubtedly have been among the first to condemn the literary excesses of such theorists even on non-technical grounds. The exaggeration in his initial proposition arises, of course, from his desire to establish the sharpest distinction between verse and poetry—between technic and inspiration, as he already had done in three of the mottoes on the title-page. It in no way vitiates the principles of verse that Lanier proceeds to elucidate, but it should warn us to examine carefully his principles, his reasoning, and his conclusions, and to beware of other such exaggerations.

Sound for Lanier is "the real clew to the whole labyrinth of verse," and with a study of sounds, not of accent, the study of verse must begin. The appreciation of this fact (which is perhaps unchallenged today except by the academic conservatives) is, strange as it may seem, perhaps Lanier's greatest contribution to English prosody. Others before him, as he well knew, had advanced the idea, but Lanier first advanced it in such a way as to make it carry conviction and win popular approval. The laws of classical verse do not apply to English verse, but English verse as well as classical verse has quantity—no less definite for not being fixed—and it is the laws of English quantity that Lanier discusses. He goes too far, again, in insisting that "there is absolutely no difference between the sound-relations used in music and those used in verse" and it is to be questioned if the discussion of verse is simplified by discarding the old poetic terms iambic, trochaic, dactyllic, etc., and by adopting the terms of music and the musical method of the notation of sounds, of time, of rests, etc. But one agrees readily that "Sounds differ from each other in four, and in only four, ways: that is, they can differ (a) in Duration, (b) in Pitch, (c) in Intensity, and (d) in Color,"[23] and that sounds, whether musical or poetic, may be studied with reference to these four, and only these four, particulars. The real differences between the sounds of music and the sounds of verse lie in "(a) the generic and specific tone-colors of the human speaking-voice; and (b) the peculiar scale of tones used by the human speaking-voice." It is the latter difference particularly that renders "the tones of verse so much more subtle than those of music."

Lanier seems to have developed Poe's theory that verse might and should be based on the less regular and more nearly hidden rhythm of music, that poetry is melody in words just as music is melody in tones which singly are meaningless and even unbeautiful. But be that as it may, his preliminary discussion of sound makes it perfectly clear that the origin of his theories of poetry is to be found in his theories of music, and that the roots of *The Science of English Verse* lie in the rejected or held-over essays on music that Lanier had been writing for some four or five years. In the first of these, "The Physics of Music," written in 1875 but not published until after his death,[24] a not quite polite or well-poised rebuttal of arguments advanced by Richard Grant White in a contemporary magazine article on "The Science and the Philosophy of Music,"[25] Lanier had asserted "that music is an art which *does* involve both in its composition and its performance a precise knowledge of musical science." His position, in disagreement with White, is the modern one, that art, whether it be the art of painting, sculpture, or music, profits from the assistance of science, and that so far from murdering in dissecting we really understand and learn to create anew. For us this is the important point revealed by the essay: White's propositions are so obviously wrong that Lanier's earnest and indignant refutation of them is a little amusing.

Lanier had concluded his paper on "The Orchestra of Today," written in 1876 as a further contribution to the discussion of modern music precipitated by his Centennial cantata, with the prediction that science had great contributions still to make to the orchestra, through the invention of new instruments "indefinitely" increasing the resources of the orchestra of the future. The preceding statement, that "In the judgment of the writer, although the improvements of the orchestra have been very great in modern times, it is yet in its infancy as an adequate exponent of those inward desires of man which find their best solace in music," makes perfectly clear Lanier's conception of science as the servant of art, and art as the priest of religion, and prepares us for the assertion of Mazzini, quoted with approval by Lanier in his essay, "Mazzini on Music," that "Music is the religion of the entire world, of which poetry is only the philosophy." It is rhythm as the fundamental law of nature, and sound therefore as a revealer of God that Lanier is seeking ultimately to explain in *The Science of English Verse*. "It is through [the] relation of music to man," he had written in "From Bacon to Beethoven" in 1876, "that it becomes . . . a moral agent." And at the very end of that beautiful justification of the place of music in our daily life: "For as Shakspere is, so far, our king of conventional tones, so is Beethoven our king of unconventional tones. And as music takes up the thread which language drops, so it is where Shakspere ends that Beethoven begins."

§ 5

BUT IN *The Science of English Verse* Lanier seems to have forsworn his first fealty to music, and given it to verse, though his essential loyalty is explained by the oft-repeated assertion that language is a species of music—that the arts of music and verse are twin components of the art of sound. Accordingly, therefore, in *The Science of English Verse*, verse is explained in musical terms and as a kind of musical art. With the great interest in music today, which Lanier foresaw, and with the development of musical instruction in our public schools, Lanier's exposition of the science of verse should be even clearer to this generation than to preceding ones. And though the reader must be cautioned to remember that "the relative duration of sounds" includes "the correlative durations of *silences* between sounds, which are called 'rests' and which are quite as necessary to many forms of verse as are the sounds thereof," it is hardly necessary to simplify the elementary explanation of duration, intensity, pitch, and tone-color given by Lanier, who kept always in mind the fact that he was writing for the general reader, and who desired with religious fervor to win converts to the religion of poetry and to smooth the way to their conversion.

Of duration, intensity, pitch, and tone-color, the first, third, and fourth are the more important in verse, for "the art of tone . . . depends upon exact coördinations by the ear" and the ear "is not capable of exactly coördinating [sounds] with reference to . . . intensity." Rhythm depends primarily on duration, tone depends on pitch, and rhymes, alliteration and the other ornaments of poetry depend on tone-color; a secondary use of duration, pitch and tone-color involves, however, the use of intensity. "For the purpose of enabling the ear to make exact coördinations of a long and complex series of sounds with reference to their duration, it becomes convenient to arrange the sounds so that the whole body may be grouped by the ear into smaller bodies which can be, as it were, handled with more ease." These "smaller bodies" are the bars of music, and the feet of verse; but rhythm depends primarily on duration, not on intensity; and "time," therefore, "is the essential basis of rhythm."

In Lanier's detailed discussion of the rhythms, tunes, and tone-colors of English verse which follows, in *The Science of English Verse*, the fifty-eight pages of introductory matter, two hundred and two pages are assigned to rhythm, thirty-nine to tunes, and thirty-six to colors. Parts II and III are, of the three parts, the less important, the more easily accepted, and the less carefully written. As Mr. T. S. Omond observes, the last chapters—the five chapters of Part III on rhyme, syzygy, and alliteration—"show special marks of haste, as if time or strength failed their writer." It is startling for example, to find Lanier stating that "no rhyme but a perfect rhyme is ever worth the poet's while. . . . If the rhyme is not perfect, if it demands the least allowance . . . throw it away"; and it is also in Part III that Lanier, after identifying the author of *Reulis and Cautelis* correctly as James VI and I[26] confuses him with the fifteenth-century James I of Scotland. What he fails to discuss in Parts II and III is likewise significant: there is no mention of onomatopœia at all. It is in Part I that Lanier's best work is to be found, and it is for his original discussion of rhythm that *The Science of English Verse* has become known.

It is with the secondary rhythm of art, not with the simple primary rhythm of nature that his discussion is concerned, not with the steady "Tick-tick-tick-tick" of the clock but with the "Tick-*tack*, tick-*tack*" which, whether occurring or not, we imagine we hear, for "The tendency to arrange any primary units of rhythm into groups, or secondary units of rhythm, is so strong in ordinary persons, that the imagination will even effect such a grouping when the sounds themselves do not present means for it," and "it is this secondary rhythm which is usually meant by the term 'rhythm' in ordinary discourse." It is in determining this secondary rhythm that intensity (accent) plays its chief part in verse, but this secondary rhythm "necessarily presupposes a primary rhythm which depends upon considerations of time or duration," so "rhythm of any sort is impossible, except through the coördination of time." This point is made more clear by the summarizing statement that "the ordinary habit

22

of English utterance in current speech . . . associates primary rhythm with the separate sounds of words, and secondary rhythm with the words composed of these sounds." Phrases composed of separate words, marked off for the ear by the "rest," by the recurrence of the same tone-color (alliteration), or by the logical habit of emphasizing important words, create a tertiary rhythm "which agreeably breaks the uniformity of such *un*varying rhythms as that of the bar [or foot] and of certain larger groups." These larger groups Lanier considers as 4th, 5th, and 6th orders of rhythm: the fourth is the line and constitutes what is commonly called meter; the fifth is the stanza (commonly but erroneously called the verse); and the sixth is the final rhythmic group embracing all the others—in short, the poem.

Lanier's development of his subject is logical and orderly, but almost too much so, because the reader's progress is impeded rather than aided by the frequent summaries, placed like "Reviews" at the end of lessons in elementary school textbooks, and his patience is taxed by frequent repetitions, such as the repetition of references to the juba dancing of the Negroes. We may limit our study of Lanier's work to his significant discussion of primary and secondary rhythm, covering pages 97-232 of *The Science of English Verse*. His discussion of the phrase is brief and superficial; his discussion of the stanza is confined almost entirely to a discussion of the sonnet; and Chapter IX, "Of Rhythm Throughout All Those Motions Which We Call 'Nature,' " interesting though it is, is not essential to a formal discussion of rhythm at all. It is in these hundred and thirty-six essential pages that Lanier's really constructive work is done, with a thoroughness that commands praise, though Lanier modestly asks that his discussion "should not be considered exhaustive," but only as "an outline . . . to furnish the student with such an outfit of facts and principles as will serve for pursuing farther researches"; and elsewhere Lanier states that he intended by further research himself to gather facts for a future edition of the work.

The real difficulties in the book for the ordinary reader, even the typical reader who, as Lanier carefully explains, possesses a sense of rhythm and of time but who, nevertheless, may lack even the elements of a musical education, occur in Lanier's attempt to use the cumbersome system of musical notation to express with precision all the possible rhythmic relations of English verse-sounds. But Lanier explains carefully and simply, and careful reading must, even for the ordinary reader, bring understanding. Certainly the explanation of quantities and silences and time values in Tennyson's "Break, break, break" is easily understandable and an understanding of it makes intelligible the hundred and fifteen pages on secondary rhythm.

In a discussion of the types of rhythms, in which he discusses even the difficult rhythm of 5 against 7,[27] Lanier discards the old poetic terms, iambic, trochaic, dactyllic, anapæstic, and the like, and reduces the (secondary) rhythms of English verse to two, named from the typic number of time-units in the bar 3-rhythm and 4-rhythm, the first consisting of three subsidiary forms marked in music as $\frac{3}{8}$ time, the second, consisting of two subsidiary forms, as $\frac{4}{8}$ time. The two kinds of 4-rhythm are those known to us as the classic dactyl-spondee form and the amphibrach; the three kinds of 3-rhythm are the classic iambus, trochee, and the logaœdic dactyl.

Of the two rhythms, 3-rhythm is, as any student of poetry must have realized, the more popular in English, though perhaps it is an exaggeration to state, as Lanier does, that from Cædmon to Lanier's own time "every long poem and nearly every important short poem in the English language has been written in some form of 3-rhythm." As Mr. Omond remarks, criticism that finds identity of movement where most people feel diversity, asserting sameness of structure in the meters of Anglo-Saxon poetry, "Lhude Sing Cuccu," Piers Plowman, The Canterbury Tales, Shakspere's plays, "Endymion," "The Raven," "The Idylls of the King," "The Psalm of Life," "Brahma," and "Atalanta in Calydon," is criticism that misses its mark. Lanier himself states, however, that the "modern heroic measure" is "a very different form of 3-rhythm" from the "ancient heroic measure" as used in "The Battle of Maldon," and his insistence upon sameness of structure as more important than difference is merely an overstatement, revealing his desire to consider the present as the rightful heir of the past and English poetry and the English language developments as an unbroken continuity.

The typic form of 3-rhythm in Anglo-Saxon is an alternation of bars in the form $\frac{3}{8}$ ♩ ♩ ♩ | with bars in the form

$\frac{3}{8}$ ♩ ♪ |. The first bar is the logaœdic dactyl, characteristic of such a line as this from "The Battle of Maldon":

Brim-man-na bod-a, a-beod eft on-gean;

or these from Whitman's "Song of Myself":

I loafe and invite my soul;

. . . .

Walt Whitman am I, a kosmos, of mighty Manhattan the son.[28]

It is perhaps the simplest form of rhythm—essentially the basic rhythm of prose, and we are not surprised to find Lanier declaring that "prose, scientifically considered, is a wild variety of verse."

It is not necessary that every bar of a line follow the typic form of three eighth-notes, or one quarter and one eighth-note. In such lines as "Byrhtnoth mathelode, bord hafenode" and "All in the valley of death rode the six hundred" the bars "mathelode," "hafenode," and "valley of death" Lanier explains as consisting of two sixteenth and two eighth-notes, thus: $\frac{3}{8}$ ♪ ♪ ♪ ♪ though, he adds, they might be written $\frac{3}{8}$ ♪ ♪ ♪ ♪ the line above the bar indicating, as in music, that the four eighth-notes are to be played in the time of ♩ ♪. And he deprecates "the timidity of English poetry during the last two hundred years . . . to venture out of the round of its strictly defined iambics" and to vary bar with bar as in the Mother Goose rhymes "Peas Porridge Hot" and "One-a-penny, Two-a-penny," depending "upon the sense of rhythm which is well-nigh universal in our race" to account properly for the time measure in reading.

But the ordinary reader may well ask if it is not timidity on Lanier's own part that makes him find even this regularity in "The Charge of the Light Brigade." Instead of scanning the following lines

Half a league| half a league| half a league| on - ward |

In - to the | val - ley of death |rode the six | hun - dred |

as Lanier does, the ordinary reader may well consider them correctly scanned thus:

Half a league| half a league| half a league| on - ward |

In - to the | val - ley of |death | rode|the six | hun-dred|

for certainly logic demands an emphasis upon the word "death" and possibly also an emphasis upon the word "rode," and by all means a rest after "death." In like manner the opening line of Emerson's "Brahma" is not to be scanned

When me | they fly, | I am | the wings. |

but

When me | they fly, | I am | the wings. |

Again, Lanier's scansion of the lines from Morris's "Love Is Enough"

Love is e -|nough:tho'the|world be a -|wan-ing, And the |

woods have no | voice put the | voice of com -|plain -ing. |

must seem to the ordinary reader contrary to sense and unreasonable when the meter of the verse is satisfied perfectly by the scansion:

Love is e-nough: tho' the world be a-wan-ing,

And the woods have no voice but the voice of com-plain-ing.

Lanier's own careful explanation of the disputed line from *Measure for Measure*, Act II, Scene 2, line 117, "Than the soft myrtle; but man, proud man," as a line to be read thus:

Than the soft myr-tle; but man, proud man.

with a rest after myrtle, where the semicolon occurs, for emphasis and contrast, prepares the ordinary reader to expect more boldness elsewhere in Lanier's scansion of verse. Indeed, his discussion of feminine-ending lines in Shakspere, in which he makes the last syllable of the first line really the first syllable of the next with the bar thereby explaining abstrusely the opening bar which to the ordinary reader must seem merely a trochee, is extremely confusing. And when we are further told that "by writing blank verse with the first unaccented note as an anacrusis, thus:

Na-varre shall be a lit-tle Ac-a-deme,

we can bring the accented note to the first place in each bar, as customary in music," the ordinary reader must doubt greatly if the science of English verse is an exact science, for here our native iambics are made indisputably trochees. Lanier's knowledge of music here interferes seriously with his discussion of verse: he approaches verse almost entirely from the side of music, and in this lies his weakness as well as his strength.[29]

Mr. Paul Elmer More has pointed out that Lanier's study is one of ideal or model verse which fails to consider the variance between the *ideal* and the *actual* rhythm. Rhythm in verse is much less absolute and regular than rhythm in music, of which it is at its best only an approximation. "In the actual reading of poetry two distinct, even contradictory, impulses will be found at work—the rhythmizing instinct and the normal, unrhythmical enunciation of the language. The result is a compromise shifting toward one extreme or the other." Lanier's treatise would suggest that in reading poetry he himself shifted toward the extreme of music, but all accounts of his public readings of poetry indicate that he did not do this at all. Certainly, however, his scansion seems at times to approach nearer the rhythm of music than that of words, and results in eccentricity. But his tendency to deny strict rhythms and to prefer the freer rhythms of music leads also to his statement: "I am strongly inclined to believe that English poetry might be a great gainer if we would at once frankly recognize rhythmic but unmetric verse as a strictly rhythmized prose, and print it as such without the deceptive line-division." In his desire to reduce verse to a scheme of musical notation he often loses sight altogether of what verse is—specially related sounds recorded in words, and not in musical notes—and it is for principle and not for conclusions that his discussion of English verse is valuable. The text of *The Science of English Verse* is filled with inaccuracies; the line from *Measure for Measure*, "Than the soft myrtle; but man, proud man," is, for instance, given four times out of nine as "Than the proud myrtle; but man, proud man," and mistakes even more significant are numerous. One wonders, therefore, if Lanier scanned correctly the line from *Piers Plowman*

In a som -er se - son whan soft was the son - ne

placing the accent of the first bar on the third note instead of on the second.[30] Certainly too the typic[31] scheme

does not tell the ordinary reader how to read correctly the almost syncopated lines of "The Ballad of Agincourt," and the scheme given for Jean Ingelow's poem "Like a Laverock in the Lift" seems hopelessly unreasonable.

In his discussion of 4-rhythm Lanier does distinguish correctly the classic dactyl from the English logaœdic dactyl, which is a form of 3-rhythm and not of 4-rhythm at all, but surely the old

Scotch poem "Hame came my gudeman, an' hame came he" is not a good example of classic dactyllic verse. And Lanier's judgment of the 4-rhythm bar $\frac{4}{8}$ ♭ ♭ ♭ ♭ as "comic" indicates an incomplete examination of English verse. The opening lines of Meredith's "Love in the Valley" (published in 1851) should have given him an example of quadruple rhythm that is light without being comic; and it seems perfectly logical to scan Poe's "Raven,"

Once up - on a | mid - night drear - y, |

as I pon - dered | weak and wea - ry |

O - ver ma - ny a | quaint and cu - ri - ous |

vol - ume of for '- got - ten lore |

as Miss Harriet Monroe, in other respects a faithful follower of Lanier, does, rather than as Lanier does, as a perfect example of trochaic, 3-rhythm verse—scansion that does make the rhythm comic.

It was not, however, to defend himself against such charges of inaccuracy and carelessness and incompleteness as we have brought against him, but to define clearly his own attitude toward prosodic science that Lanier wrote in the final chapter of his treatise (which, with a reminiscence of the literary manners of the medieval philosophers he entitled "Of the Educated Love of Beauty, as the Artist's Only Law"): "And this sketch of the colors of English verse may now be closed with the statement already partly anticipated in several other connections, that the matters herein treated are only in the nature of hints leading to the widest possible views of poetic form, and by no means laws. For the artist in verse there is no law: the perception and love of beauty constitute the whole outfit; and what is herein set forth is to be taken merely as enlarging that perception and exalting that love.[32] In all cases, the appeal is to the ear; but the ear should, for that purpose, be educated up to the highest possible plane of culture." Lanier with his fondness for italics might well have put in italics the sentence: *"For the artist in verse there is no law."*[33]

It is not, then, as a manual of instruction for the young artist that *The Science of English Verse* must be considered. "As a point of fact," Lanier said, "a book of rules for making verses might very well be written; but then it would be a hand-book of the art of verse, and would take the whole science of verse for granted."[34] It was as a manual of instruction for the young scientist, the apprentice in the understanding of verse, the scholarly student of English poetry, that Lanier himself considered—and planned—his book. His own homely comparison makes this clear: *The Science of English Verse* is no more a collection of rules for making verses than "a work on the science of anatomy [is] a collection of rules for making bones or for procuring cadavers"; or than Huxley's treatise on the crayfish is "really a cookery-book, intended to spread intelligent ideas upon the best methods of preparing shell-fish for the table."[35]

CHAPTER SEVENTEEN

MUSIC AND POETRY

§ 1

BY THE middle of May *The Science of English Verse* was ready for distribution. Lanier presented copies to Longfellow, Hayne, Stedman, and others.[1] The publishers saw that copies reached the critics. Lanier waited impatiently for reviews and criticisms to come in.

In an admirable and sympathetic essay on Sidney Lanier the late John Macy charitably suggested that had Lanier been free to write poetry, he would not have written his book on prosody: "A professor cannot earn his salary by reading original poetry to a class, but he can earn it by lecturing on the science of verse." But we shall have misunderstood Lanier's passionate desire to find out truth, and have misread his own clear statements if we subscribe to Macy's theory. Lanier wrote *The Science of English Verse* partly, it is true, because he wished to appear in print and receive the rewards of the fame that attends publication, but he wrote it also because he had things that he wanted to say, which he earnestly believed needed saying. His attitude toward his book is expressed clearly in the letter that accompanied the copy of the book sent to E. C. Stedman.

"Some days ago," he wrote, "in searching for a special letter of our beloved Bayard Taylor, I came upon one which dwelt on you so much and so tenderly that I felt myself moved to snatch a moment from the frightful bread-and-meat work which has owned me so long, for the purpose of sending a line that might bring me some little word of your health and personal concerns. Herewith goes to you a copy of my 'Science of English Verse,' just published by Messrs. Scribner's Sons, which may interest you, since, in finding physical principles of classification for all possible phenomena of verse, it seems, to place these phenomena in their true relations,—for the first time, so far as I know. I hope you may find the book a sound one,—all the more because it was so indescribably irksome to write. To go back, and interrogate one's own artistic procedure, and formulate in cold propositions for the general mind processes which are so swift and instinctive as those of the poet's technic: none but the artist knows the appalling constraint of this task. Indeed, I could never have found the courage to endure it, save from the fact that in all directions the poetic art seemed suffering from the shameful circumstance that criticism was without a scientific basis for even the most elementary of its judgments, and I had some poems which I hope soon to print but which I could not hope to get understood, generally, without educating their audience. I will be very glad to know of your work and your welfare."[2]

Lanier's letter was written in a tone of affection very different from that of other recent letters to Stedman, and one that the rereading of Bayard Taylor's letter and an awakened appreciation of Stedman's generous attitude toward him must have induced. But Stedman's reply, written May 17, must have chilled again the friendly feeling toward him that was beginning to penetrate Lanier's heart. "Let me congratulate you, and all of us," Stedman wrote, "upon the heroic industry and the profound rhythmical analysis, which have enabled you to render so complete this most scientific—this wholly unique work. Of course it will be long before I shall have mastered it throughout—it is a kind of calculus brought to bear upon the art of verse. But I have already been able to study certain of its departments, with the greatest interest and with a necessary confession of their truth. . . . *You* seize, classify, analyze, combine, and have made the first grammar of English verse. But grammarians do not make language, nor do men become writers by aid of grammars. Hence I should much prefer recognizing the truth of your novel and wonderful analysis, in my own works, after having written them by instinct, than to attempt, *a priori*, to sing in accordance with laws which govern the poet willy-nilly. God made the world first, and then 'saw that it was good'—and saw the reasons why."[3] Stedman had been sympathetic but he had not revealed a real understanding of Lanier's purpose. And if Stedman persisted in taking "a work planned to be at once a popular treatise for the general reader and a manual for the academic student"[4] as primarily a book of rules and instructions for the closed and secret fraternity of poets, Lanier could hope for little better understanding on the part of the professional reviewers, and less able critics.

Peacock made a short statement of the book's appearance, complimentary in tone. But the critic of the New York *Evening Post* objected that the book had "a tendency . . . to exaggerate . . . the undue attention already given to . . . the pretty fripperies of ingenious verse-making." Impatiently Lanier exclaimed: "If the book has one tendency beyond another in this respect, it surely is . . . to make real artists out of those who study it, and to warn off all scribblers from this holy and arduous ground."[5] He did not, however, as he had once before, make an effort to defend his work publicly in the journals that revealed a misapprehension of it. He maintained his silence when the critic of the *Literary World* ended an otherwise appreciative review by insisting that the value of the work to students of poetry was like that of the lives of Jesus by Strauss and Renan to students of theology—negative rather than positive; and again when the critic of the *Nation*, reviewing the book in detail and at considerable length some months later, pointed out many errors and attacked Lanier's exposition of $\frac{3}{8}$ time. Perhaps, indeed, he made notes for the revised edition of the book which he had already announced.[6]

But in a letter to Mrs. James T. Fields of Boston—whom he had met some time before, probably through Bayard Taylor—he wrote: "I am astonished—and, I confess, a little taken aback— that you, and several others who have written me about my book, find it abstruse. Almost everyone refers to the 'patient scholarship' of it;—and you can fancy that this is perplexing, when I add that the book was planned and written from beginning to end during the five weeks of my last summer's vacation, in the mountains of Virginia, where I had no works of reference save what I carried in my trunk. I have no more claim to 'scholarship' than to the throne of England and you cannot imagine how it embarrasses me to find newspaper notices thus shoving upon me responsibilities I can never hope to support and am even unambitious to deserve. To be an artist and preach the gospel of poetry: that is the breath of *my* life."[7] And in the second lecture of his last course at Johns Hopkins, when in discussing the science of English prose he made a digression to discuss the misunderstanding with which his views on the science of English verse had been received, Lanier answered his critics decisively:

THE SCIENCE

OF

ENGLISH VERSE

BY

SIDNEY LANIER

So preye I God that non myswrite the,
Ne the mysmetere for defaute of tonge.
CHAUCER: *Troylus and Cryseyde.*

If . . . some perfect platform or Prosodia of versifying were . . ratifyed and sette downe. — WEBBE: *Discourse of Eng. Poetrie.*

A Poet, no industrie can make, if his owne Genius bee not carried unto it. . . . Yet . . . must the highest flying wit have a *Dedalus* to guide him. — SIR PHILIP SIDNEY: *Apol. for Poetrie.*

. . . Gif Nature be nocht the cheif worker in this airt, Reulis wilbe bot a band to Nature . . . ; quhair as, gif Nature be cheif, and bent to it, reulis will be ane help and staff. . . . — KING JAMES I.: *Reulis and Cautilis, &c.*

Poesie therefore may be an Art in our vulgar, and that verie methodicall and commendable. — PUTTENHAM (?): *Arte of Eng. Poesie.*

But the best conceptions cannot be, save where science and genius are. — *Trans. from* DANTE: *De Vul. Eloq.*

NEW YORK

CHARLES SCRIBNER'S SONS

743 AND 745 BROADWAY

1880

Title-page of "The Science of English Verse," Lanier's fifth published volume.

"nine out of ten [of the critical notices], even of those which most generously treated the book in hand, treated it upon the general theory that a work on the science of verse must necessarily be a collection of rules for making verse. . . . In point of fact, a book of rules for making verses might very well be written; but then it would be a hand-book on the art of verse, and would take the whole science of verse for granted,—like an instruction-book for the piano, or the like. . . .

"But even when the functions of form, of science, in literary art have been comprehended, one is amazed to find among literary artists themselves a certain apprehension of danger in knowing too much of the forms of art. A valued friend who has won a considerable place in contemporary authorship [and here Lanier was surely making reply to Stedman] in writing me not long ago said, after much abstract and impersonal admission of a possible science of verse—in the way that one admits there may be griffons, but feels no great concern about it—'*as for me, I would rather continue to write verse from pure instinct.*'

"This fallacy—of supposing that we do a thing by instinct simply because we *learned* to do it unsystematically and without formal teaching—seems a curious enough climax to the misconceptions of literary science. . . . For—to go no farther—the most poetically instinctive child is obliged at least to learn the science of language . . . before the crudest line of verse can be written; and . . . since every child has to learn from others every word it uses,—with an amount of diligence and of study which is really stupendous when we think of it—what wild absurdity to fancy that one is writing verse by instinct when even the language of verse, far from being instinctive, had to be painfully, if unsystematically, learned as a science.

"Once, for all, remembering the dignity of form as we have traced it, remembering the relations of Science as the knowledge of forms, of Art as the creator of beautiful forms, of Religion as the aspiration towards unknown forms and the unknown Form-giver, let us abandon this unworthy attitude towards form, towards science, towards technic, in literary art, which has so long sapped our literary endeavor.

". . . the genius, the great artist, is forever ravenous after new forms, after technic; he will follow you to the ends of the earth if you will enlarge his artistic science, if you will give him a fresh form. For indeed genius, the great artist, never works

in the frantic vein vulgarly supposed; a large part of the work
of the poet, for example, is reflective; a dozen ideas in a dozen
forms throng to his brain at once; he must choose the best; even
in the extremest heat and sublimity of his raptus, he must preserve
a god-like calm, and order thus and so, and keep the rule so
that he shall to the end be master of his art and not mastered
by his art."[8]

§ 2

WITH LANIER's defense of his own work we might well let
the matter rest. But something still remains to be said, questions
still remain to be answered. What light, for instance, does *The
Science of English Verse* throw on Lanier's contention that music
and poetry are one? What influence did Lanier's theories of
prosody have on his own work? What influence has his treatise
had on the work of poets who have come after him?

Lanier's own answer to the first question is that music and
verse are but two aspects of the single art of sound—the one
being sound expressed through mechanical instruments, the other
sound expressed through the natural instrument of the human
voice. "The art of sound must always be regarded the genus,
and music and verse its two species. Prose, scientifically considered, is a wild variety of verse."[9] Poetry is a word by which
we seek to label not the formal sound-patterns of verse but the
inspired content for which the words serve merely as a mechanical
recording, as the phonograph record without *being* music *contains*
the scientific reduction of music, which the phonograph—acting
in relation to the record as the eye, the intelligence, and the
vocal organs to the printed words—*turns into* music. What we
actually need, Lanier might have insisted, is another word to
replace "music" in common parlance and to stand for the
emotional-intellectual content of musical sound-arrangements as
poetry labels and stands for the intellectual-emotional content
of verse sound-arrangements. Lacking this new word we must
use the word music with the greatest care, letting sound take
the place of music as the word is commonly used.

With this distinction between music and poetry clearly defined,
we may answer the question of the relation between the two,
implicit in the question asked by Lanier himself in his Oglethorpe days, of the province of music in the economy of the
world. He had quoted with approval Mazzini's remark that

music is the religion of the world, of which poetry is the philosophy; and Lanier was, we know, enough of a child of the past to place religion higher than philosophy. Sometimes, indeed, music seemed to him a distillation of all the gospels. "Only think," he had written his wife in 1875, "how it is beginning to do the people's worship in the churches, here, of late! I was at one the other day where half of the service was music, and if the man at the organ had been at all a preacher in soul (alas! he was not), he would have dealt out the far heavenlier portion of the doctrine."[10]

But such a statement is, like music, emotional rather than intellectual. In the essay "From Bacon to Beethoven" Lanier had stated definitely and clearly that music, though it may lead man toward the infinite, is yet bound by limitations, and is incapable of intellectual statements—which are the province of words. Such clear, intelligent statements about music are less characteristic of Lanier, however, than emotional statements of what music meant to him. To him it meant what nature meant, or love, or religion—an escape from the unendurable reality of his sufferings.

He was not, we have seen, really interested in pure sound: in his poems to Beethoven it was Beethoven's message, not Beethoven's technic, that he praised. But some strange quirk impelled him to subject the other art of sound—poetry—to an analysis never given by him to the primary one—music: to judge from *The Science of English Verse*, at least, his interest in poetry was not in the matter but in the manner, not in the substance of the poem so much as in the poet's technic. Had Lanier himself been able to see the inconsistency in such an approach to music and poetry he might have saved himself from many pitfalls; but his inconsistency he seems never to have realized. As a result, for all his consideration of the two arts and the sciences of these arts, he never achieved even a working hypothesis of the essential differences: he never saw that while music may safely forego intercourse with the imaginative intellect, it is fatal for poetry to attempt to do so.

His own music was, the available evidence suggests, poetical: programme-music, descriptive and imitative, highly suggestive of the sounds of nature. His poetry is, in like manner, musical—not musical as Poe's is, simply and melodiously, nor yet as Milton's is, with organ-voice harmony, but symphonically, orchestrally musical. "In the Marsh Hymns," says Professor Foerster, "we hear, not one melody artfully varied, but a bewildering succession of winding and darting melodies; we are aware of a full, rich, complex background of sound, of crescendo and descrescendo restlessly alternating, of a rapid tempo bespeaking eagerness and wonder, relieved perhaps too rarely by a brief tranquil interlude; and everywhere words are poured out lavishly like so many notes, not so much expressing a meaning as illustrating it."[11] It is apparent that Lanier, equally gifted as poet and musician, no more made up his mind as to which he was or which he wished to be than he succeeded in defining the differences between music and poetry. His failure as an artist is, nevertheless, not without historic parallels. Neither Leonardo Da Vinci nor Michael Angelo nor Rossetti succeeded in carrying the methods of one art into the practice of another, in spite of definite mastery of several arts. As with them, Lanier's rich endowment was his own undoing.

§ 3

IT WAS by this confusion in point of view and by the richness rather than the meagerness of his endowment, not by his critical theories, that Lanier was hampered in his work as a poet. If we examine his poetry to discover the extent to which the rhythmical principles stated in *The Science of English Verse* are exemplified in Lanier's own work, we find several significant differences between theory and practice—even in the later poems. Indeed, almost the only significant agreement is revealed by his fondness for 3-rhythm. Miss Ruth Willcockson, who prepared a careful metrical analysis of Lanier's verse as a master's thesis at the University of Chicago, has pointed out that the change in the position of the rhythmic accent in Lanier's verse does not always appear near the beginning of the line, nor following a rest, as Lanier thought it should, but that by his very failure to follow the plan that he thought it best to follow, he achieved a variety in rhythm and an agreement between logical accent and rhythmic accent which makes his verse as agreeable to one's sense of fitness as to one's ear. Furthermore, his own practice in using the rest is much more conservative than his theory would lead one to suspect, for rests in his poems occur frequently at the end of a line, and often within a line, but rarely elsewhere, rarely even at the beginning. He did not always make clear the typic scheme of a poem at the beginning of the poem, and with the utmost freedom he introduced bars that do not follow the typic scheme: in his later poems the proportion of typical and non-typical bars is about equal. The triole, a form which he explained at length as helpful in analyzing a difficult passage, seems never to have been used by him. Indeed, after her exhaustive metrical analysis of Lanier's poetical work, Miss Willcockson was forced to conclude that the one stated principle that Lanier followed with any consistency was the principle of freedom in the following of principles. The apparent inconsistency of his theory and his practice is therefore an excellent illustration of the rhythmical freedom that Lanier advocated, and proof indisputable that his book was what he claimed it to be, a book for critics of poetry rather than for poets, and that he himself was not hampered in the least by scientific theories.

On the other hand, if we analyze Lanier's poems without regard to his theories, from the point of view of classical scansion, as Miss Pearl Brown of the University of Chicago has done, we find few metrical habits not to be found in the work of other poets. His favorite foot is the iambic; his most used line the pentameter; most of the lines have a pause at the end, and many are end-stopped; the cæsura usually comes at the end of a foot, and since most of the feet are iambic, the cæsura is generally of the masculine type. Even the irregularities in his verse are for the most part of the ordinary types found to a greater or less degree in the work of all poets, as his most used stanzaic forms are the common quatrain and the sonnet.

The individual quality of his verse is revealed, however, by the discovery that not a single poem in Lanier's collected work, no matter how short, is without substitutions of feet, though in a few poems the substitutions are so rare that the general effect is one of regularity. In many poems there are many lines in which all the feet are different from each other, as the lines: "And ever my heart through the night shall with knowledge abide thee"; "Beautiful glooms, soft dusks in the noon-day fire"; "Affable live-oaks, leaning low."

In like manner, the length of the lines in many of his poems varies considerably. Such lines as: "Yea, the Stream of the Light shall give off in a shimmer the Dream of the Night forlorn" and "As a silver-wrought garment that clings to and follows the firm sweet limbs of a girl" are predominantly anapæstic, and represent not the familiar fourteen-syllable line but a line of forty-two *possible* syllables, a length which, according to Mr. Saintsbury,[12] even Swinburne never attempted. But even these lines can be satisfactorily accounted for by classical scansion. It is Miss Brown's conclusion that "Lanier's use of the foot and verse . . . shows, not so much the creation of new elements, as the effective and varied marshalling of old forces." Lanier's advocacy of what must seem to many extreme radicalism in verse is like the intellectual radicalism of the well-born conservative—admirable for the tolerance that it reveals, and the more admirable in that it is not used as an excuse for or justification of radical actions on the part of the advocator.

As a matter of fact, had Lanier followed his own theories more closely, we should find in his verse something more akin to the metrically eccentric work of many present-day writers; and had he followed his theories to their logical conclusion, he would have printed his poems with the typic scheme expressed in musical notation at the beginning of the poem, but he never proposed doing this in spite of his statement that it might some day be done;[13] nor did he ever go so far as to give directions for the reading of his verse, as Vachel Lindsay did, though Lanier must have felt as strongly as Mr. Lindsay, that poetry is to be read aloud, that except when it is read aloud it can hardly be said to exist. In spite of his passionate defense of form in *The Science of English Verse* and elsewhere, and the faith in form as the necessary philosophic positive of negative chaos,[14] Lanier revealed no genuine interest in any one form save the sonnet. Great as is the variety of the stanzaic forms he used, he never wrote—nor even mentioned in *The Science of English Verse*— ballades, rondeaus or villanelles; of the stanzaic forms which he used, only the simple quatrain and the sonnet were used with any frequency. His thought was apparently in advance of his practice, as he himself seems to have realized.

On the other hand, it is more than likely that Lanier's theory followed his practice: he was, in spite of his interest in all sciences, artist first and a student or professor of technic afterwards. The year of the writing of his treatise on prosody marks no turning point in his career. "Sunrise" and "The Marshes of Glynn" are companion poems, the one written in 1880, the other in 1878; nor is the latter metrically very different from "The Symphony" or "Corn"; and foreshadowings of both these latter poems are to be found in even earlier poems, especially in the songs for "The Jacquerie" and in "Her bright soul burned in her dusky eye," which dates from 1866. In spite of the many references in his letters to the freedom he was allowing himself in verse and the theories governing that practice, we are forced to the conclusion that Lanier would have written as he did had he never given theory a conscious thought. That the theory he did evolve was consistently in advance of his practice is merely further proof that it was theory—the fine-spun speculations of the intelligent scientist who understands that what has not yet been discovered may soon be familiar, that what is not now done may at some later date be a common occurrence, of the man who, in short, realizes the distinction between the actual and the possible, but grants the reality of both.

§ 4

ONE WEAKNESS of Lanier's system of musical annotation is that, without each verse-note recorded and the time set by a fixed symbol, as in music, readers must always differ in their interpretations of the sound schemes of poems. Even Lanier's own poem, "The Revenge of Hamish"—presumably one of the poems he did not care to print until he had educated an audience to appreciate them, a poem Lanier expressly states to have been written as an example of the logaœdic dactyl, and therefore in 3-rhythm, is said by Professor C. W. Kent to be written in 4-rhythm. In his discussion of the difficult rhythm of five against seven, the form of the classical Japanese ode, Lanier expressed his belief that the Japanese odes are really in 3-rhythm. "But," he added, "it is more than possible that my own strong expectation of finding this rhythm, based upon the universality of the form in all European rhythmic effort, may have prejudiced my ear to hear it."[15] It is thus that, with differing prejudices, we must all reach different conclusions.

The corresponding weakness in Lanier's practice is that verse conceived as music must be interpreted faithfully, and we can, after the most careful and prolonged study, only approximate faithful interpretation. It may be that, with Lanier to read his verse, we should find new beauty in the long musical passages of his poems, and a music more genuine than that which comes from profuse use of rhyme—double and even triple rhyme, identical and internal rhyme—alliteration and onomatopœia, and of refrains, the words of which are too often meaningless. As it is, too many passages in his poems—such as the dawn passage in "Sunrise"—seem but romantic poetry gone mad, the words and phrases twisted and distorted out of real meaning, the sentences as uncertainly constructed as if there were no pretence that they are sentences. Even to the most sympathetic reader many passages in Lanier's poems, long after they have been found to have meaning and rhetorical coherence, seem utterly devoid of the spontaneity that we expect of great music as well as of great poetry.

That this should be so, one feels more and more as one studies the life of Lanier, is due not to failure to master the arts of music and poetry, but to the fact that he confused the technic of the arts as surely as he confused the function. All who heard him play his flute testified to his exquisite, apparently artless artistry. Sometimes he wrote poetry as he played: and the result is simple and memorable, for his gifts of imagery and ideas and language were great. Too often he wrote poetry with the echoes of his flute ringing through his mind: and the poetry he wrote then is too much like the music of the virtuoso, or the product of the goldsmith or jewel-setter—detailed, careful, dainty, delicate, lovely: artistic but not art. In a word, the effect is too apparently striven for. "It strikes us," a critic once remarked of Lanier, "that nobody who talked as much and as eloquently about his art as Lanier did could ever have accomplished much that was really great."[16] Perhaps this is true. Perhaps Lanier's very desire to write his treatise on prosody, to be connected with Johns Hopkins, is evidence that he was fundamentally a scientist rather than an artist, an expounder of art rather than a creator of it.[17]

§ 5

LANIER's influence on others must, in any case, be sought in the two fields: his influence as a poet and his influence as a writer on prosody. His direct influence on other poets has, as a matter of fact, been negligible—or most evident in the work of poets whose own work was negligible. It is significant that of the many poets who have addressed poems to his memory only Paul Hamilton Hayne, Miss Lizette Woodworth Reese, Father Tabb, and Hamlin Garland are at all well known, and of these poets Hayne was older than Lanier, and nationally known before Lanier began to publish; Miss Reese and Father Tabb are too original to show much influence;[18] and Mr. Garland, whose early poetry does reveal the influence of Lanier, is himself known not for his poetry but for his prose fiction. Furthermore, of the many poems written to Lanier,[19] not one is of any great merit. Lanier, unlike Keats, Shelley, Wordsworth, and many other poets—and in spite of the untimeliness of his death and the loveliness of his character—has not inspired a single memorable poem. The fault, one would like to believe, is in the peculiar quality of his verse, not in the personality of the man. As a poet, Lanier falls too much out of the main current: his excellencies are too individual and he was too much removed, in poetic practice as in life, from his contemporaries and from those who came after him. His undoubted influence is to be observed in the work of only one poet of originality and strength: Richard Hovey did for a while reveal in noteworthy work the influence of Lanier, and he seemed even to Mrs. Lanier worthy to inherit her husband's laurel crown,[20] but we now see that his poetry is a little less than what we thought it was, and it is, by and large, even more neglected than that of Lanier. Lanier may have influenced Francis Thompson,[21] but the evidence is as yet scanty. An influence on the poetry of Miss Millay is possible, but not at all certain. Suggestions of imagist technic in Lanier's verse suggest but do not prove an antecedent for the poetry of Ezra Pound, Richard Aldington, and H. D.

Lanier's influence as a theorist is, however, of real importance. "He seems," wrote the critic of the *Nation* in 1888, "a poet of the future, the herald of better things to come from the pens of those who are inspired by the ideas that animated him." And Mme. Blanc, at the end of an able critical article in the *Revue des Deux Mondes*, has written: "others after him will explore the land of which he had only a glimpse. They will escape the perils of discovery and substitute, perhaps, their glory for his, as Americus did for Columbus." *The Science of English Verse* is full of suggestive truth even where there is accompanying error, filled with ideas that still have the power to stimulate and to inspire others, as they did the young Hamlin Garland,[22] though the decisive battles for freedom in poetic form have been long since won. Looking back now we can see that Lanier as well as Whitman must be recognized as a leader of the attack upon the citadels of the past, the one calling to his standard those who would overthrow form altogether, the other those who would master form and create new, freer, and still more beautiful forms. For in spite of inaccuracies and the mistaken judgments expressed in *The Science of English Verse*, Lanier did much more to clarify his discussion of English prosody than merely to ask "a few challenging questions."[23]

He demonstrated beyond dispute the musical nature of poetry; he showed that time, whether strict musical time or time of a freer order, is the basis of rhythm; and he defined the little understood use of silences in verse. Writers on prosody were quick to recognize the value of his writing. In a paper on "Quantity in English Verse" appearing in the *Transactions* of the American Philological Association for 1885,[24] Professor Thomas D. Goodell pointed out that Lanier first recognized the resemblance between classical and modern meters while defining the differences; Professor F. B. Gummere published the same year his *Handbook of Poetics* in which, without reference to Lanier on this point, however, he asserted that "Time is . . . the chief element in Poetry, as it is in Music and Dancing,"[25] repeating the key doctrine of Lanier's treatise. In an article on "Principles of Criticism" in the *Atlantic Monthly* for November of that same year, Edward Rowland Sill, a mediocre poet himself but an able academic student of poetry, repeated the opinion he had previously expressed to Gilman that Lanier's book was "the only thing extant on [the] subject that is of any earthly value,"[26] saying: "it is the only work that has ever made any approach to a rational view of the subject. Nor are the standard ones overlooked in making the assertion."[27] At the Johns Hopkins celebration of Lanier's forty-sixth birthday, on the occasion of the presentation of the Keyser portrait bust, Albert H. Tolman, a former pupil of Lanier's, declared in a paper he thought fit to reprint later, when his own fame had been achieved: "Quietly disregarding the learned rubbish that had accumulated, he studied our verse as a set of present phenomena of the world of sound. Lanier sought to explain verse as a present fact. . . . So long as man's heart beats are separated by equal intervals, he will never distribute accents without reference to time."[28] And Mr. T. S. Omond, from the perspective of another century and another continent, has written: "Criticism must yield to praise so far as fundamentals are concerned. It is Lanier's glory to have brought these finally to light. Temporal relations are shown by him essential to verse; whether or not we accept his reading of these matters comparatively little. The 'new prosody' takes in his book a step which can never be retraced. . . . to many the book came as a revelation. . . . The name of Sidney Lanier is imperishably associated with [the great advance of prosodic science in the eighth decade of the nineteenth century]; he led its triumphant attack upon the fortresses of prejudice and superstition. If he made mistakes, they may well be forgotten in view of his great achievement. He showed, once for all, where the foundations of true prosody lie, for which reason 1880 must always be memorable in the annals of [the] subject."[29]

In *The Science of English Verse*, after expressing the opinion that the rhythmic but unmetric verse of Shakspere's later dramatic monologues should be printed "without the deceptive line-division" Lanier adds: "Particularly in using the rhythm

$$\frac{3}{8} \ \flat \ \flat \ \flat \ | \ \flat \ \flat \ |$$

in English verse, a certain finicalness attaches to a regularity of line-grouping: while if it be employed without lines, but merely in great masses of unlined prose, the effect is noble in the highest degree. A development of English rhythm lies, I feel sure, in this direction." Looking back over the poetic development of the last fifty years, it seems certain that Lanier's prophecy has come true, and that the liberalizing effect of Lanier's teaching, if not the example of his own poetic work, prepared the way for the splendid achievements of others in free verse and polyphonic prose. Mme. Blanc has indeed discussed his significance as a precursor of Verlaine and Mallarmé and "all those who compose in verse symphonies, variations, romances without words, canticles, and scales"; and Professor G. L. Swiggett has suggested his influence on René Ghil, a poet who, like Lanier, also wrote a treatise on the poetic art, though there is no certain line of influence connecting Lanier's work with that of any of these French poets. But in American literature there is surely to be traced an influence of Lanier's theory on the verse of such different poets as Ezra Pound and Amy Lowell,[30] poets whose work has been from the first accompanied by much intelligent theorizing.

In comparison with the earlier poetry of Whitman or the later free verse of Stephen Crane, such poems as Lanier's own "Marshes of Glynn" and "Sunrise" seem somewhat conventional, but when they are compared with the work of those poets listed and discussed in so representative and inclusive an anthology as, for instance, Sladen's *Younger American Poets: 1830-1890*,[31] they are found to have a freedom of movement and a beauty of song not to be found in the work of contemporary poets. And this beauty and this power came not from any radical break with the past but from an intelligent combination of the best the past had to teach with the best the present revealed of the promising future. "Fresh beginnings," writes Professor Lowes in his *Convention and Revolt in Poetry*, "are excellent stimulants to a jaded world, but a defective method of progression. The great constructive element in both life and art is the dealing of genius with the continuity of tradition. . . . Cut the connection with the great reservoir of past achievement and the stream runs shallow."[32] Where eager progressiveness of ideas and conservatism of form are happily blended, when innovation and tradition are perfectly balanced, development is healthy, sane, and fruitful. In *The Science of English Verse*, the manual Lanier prepared to enable us to read with better understanding the great poetry of the past, he pointed the way that, as we now see, the poetry of the future was to take. A treatise that does this must be given permanent place alongside those of Sidney and Peacock, Wordsworth and Coleridge, Shelley and Poe on the art that lost none of its dignity in being reduced to a science, the art of poetry.

CHAPTER EIGHTEEN

PROSPERO'S LOVE

§ 1

TO SAY OF him as Professor Mims does that "Among American poets Lanier has the same place with regard to the teaching of English that Lowell and Longfellow have in the study of [other] modern languages,"[1] is not to exaggerate at all. But Lanier's Johns Hopkins lectures were—by request of President Gilman—designed not for scholars but for a miscellaneous audience. In answer to Lanier's letter of July 13, 1879, a letter in which Lanier discussed in detail his plans for the course of lectures he was to begin that fall, Gilman had written: "There is a miscellaneous company, including some persons of very high cultivation; many of general liveliness of mind and good purpose; and a very few specialists,—who like to attend the *Hopkins Hall* lectures. These lectures attract attention to our work, cause it to be talked about among educated people, quicken many minds not able to quicken themselves; and help many of our own young men who are working in different departments of study to keep up an interest in literature, history, etc. These 'Hopkins Hall lectures' ought to be carefully prepared,— but they should give general views, not minute criticisms, or facts, or very abstract philosophy. . . . After it is known what you can give and how attractively you give it,—I think you will not be without earnest followers.

"I think your aims and your preparation admirable. I can make no suggestions upon these points. I only desire that in the form of presentations, you may be ready to adapt yourself to such circumstances as will develop themselves; and that you will not expect or attempt *too much the first year* lest we all be disappointed."[2]

That Lanier took Gilman at his word is suggested by the report on the course made by a graduate student at Johns Hopkins[3] who, on November 16, 1879, wrote to his parents: "The course is not at all profound . . . and the attendance of University men is constantly diminishing. Lanier is quite a pleasing speaker, but he is making the course altogether too popular and transcendentally poetical." Aware, however, of Gilman's warning to Lanier, we should not read the published lectures expecting more than Lanier ever intended giving.

§ 2

IN MR. HENRY LANIER's preface to the volumes of Shakspere lectures, *Shakspere and His Forerunners*, published in 1902, the statement is made that "This work contains two sets of Shakspere lectures delivered by Mr. Lanier in Baltimore during the winter of 1879-80, one at Johns Hopkins University, the other to a class of ladies at Peabody Institute." The statement, it would appear, is somewhat inaccurate, but it is difficult now to get at the facts. The course at the Peabody Institute, as we have seen, was given in the winter of 1878-79, though it may have been repeated the following winter. The lectures at Johns Hopkins on "English Verse, especially Shakespere," were given on Tuesdays and Fridays, October 28 through December 19, 1879.[4] "The author," Mr. Henry Lanier adds, "did not revise these hastily written lectures, and they were penned under heavy stress of the illness that was closing in upon him, and with no idea of their inclusion in a book. But . . . the material fell together with merely a little pruning of repetitions and of matters elaborated in *The Science of Verse.*"

Internal evidence confirms Mr. Lanier's statement that the lectures are from more than one course. The statement made in the second chapter on the metrical tests of the chronology of Shakspere's plays that "this rhythmic accent test occurred to me last summer while writing a work on English verse" undoubtedly refers to the writing of *The Science of English Verse* in the summer of 1879, and so dates Chapter XXI as of the Johns Hopkins course, and the three final lectures on *A Midsummer Night's Dream, Hamlet*, and *The Tempest* seem to follow the plan that Lanier proposed in his letter to Gilman of July 13, 1879. But the reference in the final chapter to his essay on Bartholomew Griffin as being but recently published fixes the final chapter—or at least one part of it—definitely as of the Peabody course, for after going the rounds of the editors this essay had been sold for publication, in March, 1879, to the *International Review*.[5] It is altogether possible, and even likely, that Lanier used notes of the first course for lectures of the second, making impromptu such changes as were necessary, but the lectures as they have been given us seem designed rather for an audience of women, such as he met at the Peabody Institute, than for the mixed class of graduate students that he met at Johns Hopkins.

Our conclusion must be that the Shakspere volumes, with four chapters on prosody omitted, preserve almost completely the lectures that Lanier gave in 1878-79 at the Peabody Institute, and that his first course of sixteen lectures at Johns Hopkins probably consisted of a repetition in less detail of most of the material he had already used in *The Science of English Verse* and a repetition, possibly with enlargements, of the last five lectures, on the metrical tests of Shakspere's plays and on man's relation to the supernatural, to man, and to nature, as given in *Shakspere and His Forerunners*.[6] But in spite of the fact that in preparation these lectures antedate *The Science of English Verse*, discussion of the lectures on Shakspere most properly comes after discussion of the work on prosody, which, we may repeat, is based on the material of the four omitted lectures.

§ 3

IN THE first of the lectures Lanier lists, with the breathless enthusiasm of a boy counting his agates, poetic forerunners and contemporaries of Shakspere, little stars whose radiance—the figure is Lanier's—is obscured in the bright light of Shakspere's day; and to those who say there is not time to read these poets he asserts with the zeal of a convert, "after you have read the Bible and Shakspere, you have no time to read anything until you have read these." And this enthusiasm for "these old artists," he quickly reveals, is his reverence for the religion of "loyal love" and of honor to womanhood which they have given us. The admission prepares one to expect much quotation from the love poetry of the period, and should remind us of Lanier's own poem "The Symphony." In the later lectures on George Eliot we shall find Lanier recurring again to this idea and enlarging on it, and referring to the world—the world of the 1870's in America even—as "a universe in which love is the organic idea." But some preliminary training in the technical principles governing the poetic art, in the science of verse, Lanier adds, returning to his main subject, is necessary to the proper under-

Ode

To Johns Hopkins University.

How tall among her sisters, and how fair, —
How grave beyond her youth, yet debonair
As dawn, 'mid wrinkled Matrons of old lands
Our youngest Alma Mater modest stands!.
In fair brief cycles round the punctual sun
Hath she, old Learning's latest daughter, won
Such grace, such stature, and such fruitful fame
~~From far the sages saw, from far they came;~~
(Howbeit she was ~~though~~ born
Unnoised as any the stealing summer-morn)
~~From far the sages saw from far they came~~
They came and ministered to her,
Led on by soaring-genius'd Sylvester
— By him that loosed the knot great Newton tied
And flung the door of Fame's strong temple wide
As favorable fairies thronged of old and blessed
The cradled princess with their several best,
So, gifts and dowers meet
To lay at Wisdom's feet

standing of the treasures of English poetry, to the understanding of Shakspere as well as of Wyatt, Griffin, Lyly, Fletcher, Daniel, Spenser, Drummond—in short, to the understanding of any poetry that goes by the name.

Lanier saw Shakspere as Carlyle saw him—as a hero, a type of manhood at its best; and the mood in which he approached his study was one of hero-worship, his purpose to reveal the greatness of a great man. The scholarly building up of background is to humanize Shakspere, to reveal him as the product of a heritage, and as an important contributor to the heritage of which Lanier himself, his contemporaries, and future generations are heirs. Therefore, after drilling his listeners thoroughly in English metrics in order that with the equipment of a technical knowledge they might better understand the literature they were about to study, Lanier proceeded to trace certain moods and conceptions and attitudes from early Saxon times to the time of Shakspere. His approach to Shakspere is, accordingly, for at least three-quarters of the published volume, oblique, but his method is singularly effective in making Shakspere stand out strongly against his environment, as, in approaching a building from various points of view we come finally to see round it and to see it whole, and to realize suddenly the complete beauty of it.

He compared, for example, the *Address of the Soul to the Dead Body* with *Hamlet* to show the gradually developing attitude of Englishmen toward the supernatural; and *Beówulf* with *A Midsummer Night's Dream* to show the developing, changing, softening attitude toward nature, introducing also selections from Gawain Douglas and Thomas Sackville and the pseudo-Chaucerian poem *The Flower and the Leaf*. The effect of the comparison is to make very clear the lack of restraint in the presence of nature that was characteristic of the Elizabethans and of Shakspere especially, and the ennobling effect of the freer attitude on man.

It was hard for Lanier not to be didactic, but he was never more attractively didactic than in the Shakspere lectures. In this penultimate paragraph of the third chapter, for instance, we have in prose what is almost a condensation of "The Marshes of Glynn," a paragraph of which "A Ballad of Trees and the Master" is a simplification: "Day by day we find that the mystic influence of Nature on our human personality grows more intense and individual. Who can walk alone in your beautiful

Druid Hill Park, among those dear and companionable oaks, without a certain sense of being in the midst of a sweet and noble company of friends? Who has not shivered, wandering among these trees, with a certain sense that the awful mysteries which the mother earth has brought with her out of the primal times are being sucked up through those tree-roots and poured upon us out of branch and leaf in vague showers of suggestion that have no words in any language? Who, in some day when life has seemed *too* bitter, when man has seemed *too* vile, when the world has seemed all old leather and brass, when some new twist of life has seemed to wrench the soul beyond all straightening,— who has not flown, at such a time, to the deep woods, and leaned against a tree, and felt his big arms outspread like the arms of the preacher that teaches and blesses, and slowly absorbed his large influences, and so recovered one's self as to one's fellow-men, and gained repose from the ministrations of the Oak and the Pine?"[7] And the chapter ends, in an echo of Wordsworth, with this sentence: "For to him who rightly understands Nature she is even more than Ariel and Ceres to Prospero; she is more than a servant conquered, like Caliban, to fetch wood for us: she is a friend and comforter;[8] and to that man the cares of the world are but a fabulous *Midsummer Night's Dream*, to smile at—he is ever in sight of the morning and in hand-reach of God."

This indirect approach to Shakspere allowed Lanier to make important matter out of a discussion of such a subject as "Some Birds of English Poetry," the title of the fourth chapter, in which he gave his own almost complete translation—partly metrical—of *The Phœnix* and quoted Dunbar's *Twa Gentil Birdis* and Shakspere's *The Phœnix and the Turtle* entire. Lanier read well, we know, and probably his reading carried interpretation and, indirectly, commendation to those who heard him, but the reader of the printed lectures reaches the conclusion that his comments are altogether too meager, lost as they are in a mass of text and inconsequential matter. As a matter of fact, over one-fourth of the two volumes is given to quotation of entire poems and long scenes—sometimes entire acts—from plays. Lanier's method as a critic is a valuable one, however, whether employed in the classroom or through the medium of the printed page, for it makes one's listeners and readers form judgments of their own. Lanier's juxtaposition of Anglo-Saxon poems,

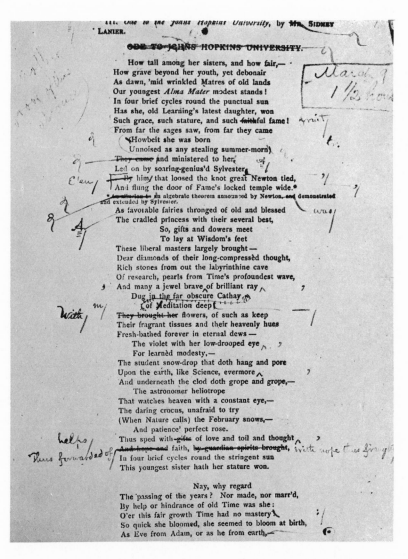

Part of the corrected proof of Lanier's "Ode to Johns Hopkins University." Courtesy of the John Hopkins University Library.

Middle English poems, and poems by Shakspere and his contemporaries makes critical thought inevitable. A phrase or a
sentence points the direction that, it seemed to him, thought
should take.

Two lectures on women—one on "Women of English Poetry
Down to Shakspere," the other on "The Wife in Middle English
Poetry"—complete his review, if such it may be called, of the
literary background of Shakspere. Again, the lectures consist
almost entirely of readings—from *Elene*, from the Towneley play
The Voyage of Noah, from Chaucer's clerk's tale of patient Griselda,
from Shakspere's *Love's Labour's Lost;* but these lectures are
undoubtedly from the Peabody Institute series, and were probably not included in the Johns Hopkins series, or if included were
greatly abridged. However, they serve a purpose in the scheme
of either series, for they make clear a changing attitude toward
women in English literature, an understanding of which prepares
us for the four lectures on the sonnet, in which Lanier quotes
freely from the various series of sonnets written in glorification
of love and women at the period of England's glory when—and
it seemed to Lanier a most significant fact—a woman sat on
the throne.

In these four chapters, which begin with a brief discussion
of the development of the English language until it became an
instrument capable of expressing the most "personal and holy"
matters in the musical Italian sonnet form, we have probably
the essence of the projected but never completed volume on
English sonneteers. Unsuccessful as he himself was in writing
unquestionably great sonnets, Lanier loved the form[9] because
to him each sonnet seemed a private letter from the poet to the
reader, bringing the two into the most intimate literary relation
possible, and because the Elizabethan sonnets were all—almost
without exception—concerned with love. He pauses in his discussion of the sonnet to discuss the manliness of this love, but
he knew of course that the range of the sonnet's power is not
limited to the expression of love and the glorification of the
beloved. "You can pray in a sonnet," he wrote, "or praise
equally well; . . . [so] it suits equally well as a form for expressing the most intense emotion of the strong man who after years
of bitter struggle at length triumphs over opposition." And in
his lectures he read four of his own Columbus sonnets to prove
that sonnets may "sound the whole gamut of human emotions,"

from the idle play of a lover's fancy to the intense emotion of his idealized Columbus at the hour of the discovery of the western land. This discussion of the English sonneteers leads directly, of course, to a discussion of the sonnets of Shakspere, and—finally— to a discussion of the growth of Shakspere's character that Lanier finds revealed in the sonnets and in the plays.

But this building up of background—this approach to Shakspere and to an understanding of Shakspere from every possible angle—is not yet complete. Lanier would not only have us read Shakspere understandingly and with a correct knowledge of meter but also with a correct knowledge of the pronunciation, and the next two lectures are given to a discussion of "Pronunciation of Shakspere's Time," based on Ellis's *Early English Pronunciation*. Characteristically enough, Lanier, always able to see the forest as well as the trees and eager "to accomplish as many ends as possible with a given means" proceeds, in his reading of passages from *The Two Gentlemen of Verona* in the old usage, to continue the discussion of constancy and forgiveness in friendship begun in his discussion of the sonnets, and not actually dropped until the final discussion of *The Tempest* in the last sentence of the last lecture. So likewise in his discussion of "The Music of Shakspere's Time," Lanier carries the idea that life, as well as music, depends on the principle of opposition and of antagonism, an idea which he had expressed eleven years before in his poem "Life and Song." Midway in Shakspere's career, in the second or what Lanier calls the Real Period—the period in which *Hamlet*, *Lear*, *Macbeth*, and *Timon of Athens* were written—antagonism came; but Shakspere conquered it and ordered it to sweet music. So the plays of the third—or Ideal—period, *Cymbeline*, *A Winter's Tale*, *The Tempest*, and *Henry VIII*, breathe "of reunion after absence, of forgiveness of injuries, of heavenly grace." Shakspere drew his opposition to harmony; he converted his antagonism into ravishing sounds.

In the original scheme of the 1878-79 course that Lanier gave at the Peabody Institute there were to have been, as we have seen, besides Lanier's twenty-four lectures fourteen by other lecturers on such subjects as "The State of Natural Science in Shakspere's Time" and "Religion in Shakspere's Time";[10] these other lectures were not given, but the four lectures by Lanier on "The Domestic Life of Shakspere's Time" touch briefly on

the subjects of the omitted lectures. They are, of course, the
most comprehensive of all the lectures and reveal most succinctly
the unlimited intellectual curiosity of Lanier's mind. In the
second of the four he gives a truncated narrative consisting of
ten pages of his own invention of the life of young Will Shakspere
at Stratford, artfully constructing it from contemporary material
and historical facts. The narrative is given to show how with
a little imagination the wealth of facts and of contemporary
chronicle might be made to bring the daily life of "those marvelous
centuries" in which Shakspere lived, completely before our
eyes; but it lacks altogether the obviousness of mechanical
construction and possesses the complete charm of perfect fiction.
One wonders, nevertheless, if it was intentionally or unintentionally that Lanier has Shakspere in 1575 reading Marlowe's
Tamburlaine, which was not written until at least a dozen
years later.

These lectures on the domestic life of Shakspere's time include
some long passages from Laneham's account of the Kenilworth
revels, from Heywood's play of *The Four P's* from Latimer's
sermons, and from Sackville and Norton's *Gorboduc;* the lecture
on the doctors of Shakspere's time includes quotations from
early medical books and from Shakspere's plays in which reference is made to medicine and to doctors. Finally, in the twenty-
fourth lecture (Chapter Twenty) we are back to the subject with
which Lanier began his course: English verse—and especially
Shakspere's.

Pages 186-224 and 295-96 of *The Science of English Verse* are
repeated with only slight modifications as Volume II, pages
203-51 of *Shakspere and His Forerunners*. In neither discussion of
the metrical tests to determine the chronology of Shakspere's plays,
however, does Lanier contribute anything original to the investigations of Fleay, Ingram, and other scholars; but his explanation
has the virtue of being lucid and comprehensive and interesting.
Here as well as anywhere is to be found the measure of Lanier's
success as a popularizer of academic knowledge.

The chronology established by the checking of facts with the
metrical analysis of Shakspere's plays, Lanier used for the larger
purpose of approaching Shakspere the man through his plays,
and he assigns the plays to three periods, the period 1590-1601,
the Bright (or Dream) Period, or the Period of Carelessness;
1601-08, the Dark (or Real) Period, or the Period of Bitterness;

24

1608-13, the Heavenly (or Ideal) Period, or the Period of For-giveness; and through the plays he traces Shakspere's meeting with opposition, his overcoming it, and his final achievement of forgiveness, which is wisdom, in the plays of his last creative years. Incidentally, Lanier interprets the metrical tests philo-sophically as a test of growth from formalism through chaos to true form, and the lectures end as they began with a discussion of form—in life and in art.

For Lanier artistic advance was almost unthinkable unless accompanied by, occasioned by, moral advance. For his discus-sion of Shakspere's growth as man and artist Lanier repeats from his seventh lecture a diagram we shall find him using again in *The English Novel.* A man's view of the world reaches upward, to God; downward, toward nature; and out, to his fellow-man. It is Shakspere's growth in these directions that Lanier traces through typical plays of the three periods, through *A Midsum-mer Night's Dream, Hamlet* and *The Tempest.* The metrical tests have revealed that Shakspere's progress as an artist was to-ward "a more artistic management of oppositions"— the artistic oppositions of regularity and irregularity, rhyme and blank verse, strong-endings and weak-endings, normal accents and abnormal accents, etc., in verse. So also in our study of these three plays we find Shakspere advancing "in the artistic manage-ment of those moral oppositions which make up human life as these esthetic and physical oppositions make up verse." Lanier insists altogether too much on the careful balancing of opposi-tions—finding it also in the characters of the plays as Valentine against Proteus, Theseus against Hippolyta, Lysander against Hermia, and enmity of Montague and Capulet against love of Montague and Capulet; but his interpretation of Shakspere's growth is one that has become popular. There is hardly a reader of *Hamlet* who must not at some time have felt that the moral uncertainty, the bitterness, the questioning, the despair of Hamlet is moral uncertainty that the author himself must at some time have known; and most teachers and critics of Shakspere find in Prospero a delineation of Shakspere himself and the breaking of the staff a symbol of Shakspere's farewell to the stage.

In the third chapter, on "Nature in Early English and in Shakspere," Lanier had already said: "To keep ourselves simple and pure, to cultivate our moral sense up to that point of insight that we see all Nature alive with energy, that we hear the whole

earth singing like a flock of birds, yet so that we remember
Death with Mr. Darwin, so that nothing is any more commonplace, so that death has its place and life its place . . . is not
that a modern consummation of culture?" So in *The Tempest*
Lanier finds Shakspere rising to the plane where he can look
with tolerance upon "this Janus-faced Nature, one face life, one
face death." He had emerged, as the race emerges, "from what
we may call the barbarism of youth into what we may similarly
call the civilisation of maturity"; and we find Shakspere at the
end "accepting the moral laws of opposition—instead of blindly
fighting them, as so many of us do in so many various ways—and
using *them* in heavenly ideals of behaviour."[11]

And at the end, repeating again, but in each repetition driving
his point home with more force and constantly clarifying our
understanding of Shakspere the man, he repeats: "Surely the
genius which in the heat and struggle of ideal creation has the
enormous control and temperance to arrange and adjust in
harmonious proportions all these esthetic antagonisms of verse,
surely that is the same genius which in the heat and battle of
life will arrange the moral antagonisms with similar self-control
and temperance. . . . Surely, in fine, there is a point of mere
technic in art beyond which nothing but moral greatness can
attain. . . . In short, . . . it is the poet who must sit at the
centre of things here, as surely as some great One sits at the
centre of things Yonder, and who must teach us how to control,
with temperance and perfect art and unforgetfulness of detail,
all our oppositions so that we may come to say with Aristotle, at
last, that poetry is more philosophical than philosophy and more
historical than history."[12]

§ 4

THE INEVITABILITY of Shakspere in our heritage Lanier slighted
perhaps in his lectures, but comment would have been superfluous, and Lanier's own poems acknowledge the debt magnifi-
cently both for himself and for his readers. Had Shakspere's
characters and Shakspere's message not passed completely and
perfectly into our language many of Lanier's finest metaphors—
metaphors drawn from Shakspere not as from a book but as
from nature—would be unintelligible, and such a poem as Lanier's
exquisite "Marsh Song—At Sunset,"[13] written during the winter
of 1879-80, would be absolutely meaningless. But the "Marsh

Song," with its magical adjectives, is indeed one of the clearest, most comprehensive of all Lanier's poems, needing no explanation.

Lanier turned his prose into poetry with ease, and at least one other poem comes bodily from the Shakspere lectures, the poem "Opposition,"[14] which appeared in *Good Company* (Springfield, Massachusetts) in the issue for January, 1880. Taking a line from his elegy in honor of Bayard Taylor, written probably a full year previously, and remembering undoubtedly his own interpretation of a line from *The Taming of the Shrew*,[15] he embodied in a poem which so eclectic an anthologist as Mr. Conrad Aiken has chosen as the one poem by Lanier for his modern *Anthology of American Poetry* the philosophy implicit in *The Science of English Verse* and stated explicitly in these Shakspere lectures.

> Of fret, of dark, of thorn, of chill,
>   Complain no more; for these, O heart,
> Direct the random of the will
>   As rhymes direct the rage of art.
>
> .   .   .   .   .   .
>
> Of fret, of dark, of thorn, of chill,
>   Complain thou not, O heart; for these
> Bank-in the current of the will
>   To uses, arts, and charities.

If we are to find philosophy in Lanier's poetry it is here, rather than in the pseudo-ballad "How Love Looked for Hell"[16] or even in "Sunrise" that we must find it. For Lanier this principle of opposition, of Form against Chaos, of Good against Evil, of Love against Selfishness, of Design against Accident, of Belief against Scepticism, is the fundamental principle of creation, so manifest that the definition of evil as the absence of good, as he seems to suggest in "How Love Looked for Hell," is untenable. The idea comes in part from Poe's *Eureka*, in which from the simple postulates of attraction and repulsion Poe develops his "enormous idea" of the course of creation as "the rhythmic beating of the heart of God."[17] It comes in part too from Spencer, who "has formulated the proposition that where opposing forces act, rhythm appears, and has traced the rhythmic motions of nature to the antagonistic forces there found, such as the two motions which carry the earth towards, and away from, the sun and so result in the periodicity of the earth's progress, and others."[18]

With Lanier, however, the idea is developed into a philosophy capable of explaining all the phenomena of life. So we have paired off Form and Chaos, Generalization and Particular, Altruism and Egoism, Love and Selfishness, Good and Evil, Birth and Death, barriers to a lane over which life passes, and all art is made to depend upon this principle of opposition or antagonism.[19] Music, for instance, is the vibration caused by the opposition of a longitudinal and a transverse force on a stretched string; or, as Lanier phrased it, "two forces, the one acting athwart the other." And modern music, the new music of Lanier's new day, he conceived as the vibration resulting from the antagonism of Italian melodic music and German harmonic music, the one glorifying the individual and the known, the other glorifying humanity and the unknown.[20] We recall of course the early poem "Nirvâna" with its listed opposites, a poem in which Lanier sought a Nirvâna that meant escape. But the philosophy expressed in "Opposition" is not a philosophy of escape: rather, it is one of rhythmization, of the transverse force of the human will acting upon the longitudinal strain of the natural instincts of man, and bringing about his "etherealization." It is a philosophy of reconciliation, and of moral harmony, a philosophy, perhaps, of compromise, but the more practical and acceptable for being so.[21]

But no matter how much Lanier insists upon the idea of opposition, and repeats it, and develops it, it is not with him merely a philosophic idea, but a religious one. He came upon it not by study of the works of philosophers—who but confirmed him in his beliefs—but through faith in the traditional body of Christian teaching and out of his own observation of life and the effort to reconcile his views of a beneficent universe to his own intense sufferings. His wisdom is not theoretical, philosophic wisdom, but the profound, practical wisdom of the deeply wise practical man. It is this wisdom that permeates the Shakspere lectures and that makes them, apart from and beyond their value as lectures on Shakspere, so important for the student of Lanier.

§ 5

FOR THOUGH Lanier does not say in these published lectures what he has not said elsewhere, he says here (as if the lectures were letters, which he wrote with equal ease and freedom) freshly and spontaneously what he says more formally, more self-consciously elsewhere, and in such a way that even reading the two volumes we feel something of the personal magnetism all his listeners felt when he spoke from the platform.

His appearance at this time Gilman described as striking. "There was nothing eccentric or odd about him, but his looks, manners, ways of speech had distinction. I have heard a lady say that if he took his place in a crowded horse-car, an exhilarating atmosphere seemed to be introduced by his breezy ways. He was not far from five feet ten inches in height, slight in figure with jet black hair, pallid complexion, bright restless eyes and a long flowing beard which gracefully fell upon his breast. His motions were alert and nervous, his speech gentle and refined, his dress careful and his gloves of the nicest fit, but there was nothing finical in all this, not even the suspicion of Bohemia, and in the days of his greatest need, he was always a gentleman in appearance and dress. [A] rare combination of gentleness and intellectual brightness [and a] sunshiny and sympathetic smile . . . illuminated his face. [Of him] one said, 'He looks like Moses'; another, 'He looks like Christ.' A German physiologist simply said 'Tuberculosis.' "[22]

One who heard the Peabody Institute lectures and some at least of the Johns Hopkins lectures also, has described the effect that Lanier produced from the platform: "His voice, though distinct, was never elevated above a moderate tone; he rarely made use of a gesture; certainly, there was no approach to action or to the adaptation of his voice to the varied characters of the play; yet many scenes which I have heard him read I can hardly believe that I have never seen produced on the stage, so truly and vividly did he succeed in presenting them to my imagination. At the time I used to wonder in what element lay the charm. Partly, of course, in his own profound appreciation of the author's meaning, partly also in his clear and correct emphasis, but most of all in the wonderful word-painting with which, by a few masterly strokes, he placed the whole scene before the mental vision."[23]

One of Lanier's students, Professor Waldo Selden Pratt (since become distinguished as an authority on ecclesiastical music), who attended the lectures on "English Verse" and the ten expository readings from Chaucer and Shakspere that Lanier gave in February and March, 1880, and was often at Lanier's home during the first half of 1880, has given an even more interesting account of Lanier as a teacher, and of the attraction he had for his students: "It is curious . . . how little I remember of the substance of the course. But somehow I gained a distinct impetus in thought and feeling that has been a life-long possession. Much was due to the fact that after the lectures . . . he and I frequently, almost habitually, walked home together, as we lived in somewhat the same region. Here again, I cannot recover what we talked about. But the general sense of contact with a rare and choice spirit has always remained. Mentally, he had an almost startling keenness and a grasp that was not so much philosophical as intuitive. He had no pride of knowledge, but an insatiable desire to know and understand. And spiritually there was something that seemed unique in the quality and texture of his nature that exhaled in all he said and did, in his judgments and opinions, in his impulses and enthusiasms. At the time I simply felt rather vaguely the impression of his intermingled strength and gentleness, his earnestness and mirth, his reverence and mischief, his aspiration for himself and his self-expenditure for others. All these contrasts in his nature did not become clear to me till later, as I came to know his poetry and as I grew better able to analyze my own experience with him."[24] Elsewhere Dr. Pratt has written of Lanier's essential youthfulness of mind, saying "the more I think of it, the more I recognize that his soul was incapable of aging. . . . This absolute freshness of heart and spirit seems to me to have been one of the highest notes of Mr. Lanier's genius."[25]

§ 6

IT WAS THE "freshness of heart and spirit" in Lanier's discussion of literature that made his lectures vital and significant. "It has several times occurred to me," he wrote President Gilman March 16, 1880, "to ask if I might not be of further service to you in providing instruction for the *under*-graduates of our

Collegiate Department in Rhetoric, Sentence-building, English
Composition, Punctuation, and the like, with practical exercises
in Essay-writing. I believe this forms part of the 'Course' in
every college: and I have recently seen some shrewd strokes at
Harvard for turning out graduates who could not write a
passable English letter. All the instruction in my special line,
so far, has been quite advanced.

"Perhaps I should repeat that I gave the last of my series of
ten readings on Monday night; and that I had a pleasant meeting with the Science-class yesterday afternoon at four, in Professor
Morris's room."[22] Such a letter reveals that Lanier possessed
what the average teacher all too often lacks, an enthusiasm for
his work, an eagerness to be of the greatest possible service to
his pupils. Much of this enthusiasm is conveyed to one who
reads the published lectures.

But something more than enthusiasm Lanier put into his
lectures. It is his deep, wise, undeviating love for his fellow-
man. Seeing in Prospero's forgiveness of his enemies the symbol
of Shakspere's own farewell to public life, Lanier wrote: "this
Prospero, is he who, having his enemies in his power, . . . has
greatened beyond ridicule, has enlarged beyond revenge, has
learned the truth of true love, the dignity of man toward his
fellow, the wonder and miracle of forgiveness—in fine, the true
ideal behaviour and relation of man to his fellow-man." And
if, tracing in Lanier's published work the growth of his character as Lanier traced in Shakspere's plays the growth of Shakspere's character, we ask what these lectures signify, one answer
only is possible: Lanier in tracing the moral growth of another
artist revealed that he himself had grown beyond indignation,
sensitiveness, and remonstrance, to full and perfect forgiveness,
as, in the old Greek idea, the spectator at a tragedy achieves
the purification of the hero.

We should, then, for our own ennoblement even more than
for our understanding of Lanier, or Shakspere, read these lectures.
But one word of warning should be kept in mind as one reads.
Preserved as these lectures have been in but incompletely revised
notes never intended for publication, edited under circumstances
not the most fortunate, and printed without adequate proof-
reading, they are not as Lanier would have wanted them given
to us. As a matter of fact, the critical horror at the erroneous
ascription of the illustrations that were added to the elaborate

first edition of *Shakspere and His Forerunners* must have caused many to approach with prejudice the text for which alone, and that not entirely, Lanier was responsible. Had he himself prepared the lectures for publication he might have corrected many errors; others, however, the limitations of his scholarship would have prevented his observing; and physical weakness would surely have interfered with the thoroughness of his work as it did in the proof-reading of *The Science of English Verse*. But had he himself prepared the lectures for publication they would have lost in formal rewriting much of their charm of spontaneity. We have only to compare the references to Poe's *Eureka* in *Shakspere and His Forerunners*[26] with the similar reference in *The Science of English Verse*[27] to see how, in formal rewriting, the lecture material becomes less interesting; how, in divorcing the idea from the personal experience in which in *Shakspere and His Forerunners* it is embedded, Lanier made it less telling; how the significance of "this rhythmic idea" loses inevitability.

Mr. Henry Lanier states that in preparing the Shakspere lectures for publication he attempted to prune them "of repetitions and of matters elaborated in *The Science of Verse*," but were all matters repeated in *The Science of English Verse* and in separately published essays deleted, there would be left only disconnected fragments of the Shakspere lectures. As it is, they represent a rich quarry, the quarry of Lanier's scholarly studies, out of which came not merely *The Science of English Verse* and parts of the lectures on "The Development of Personality" (*The English Novel*) but also much in the prefaces to the books for boys, in such essays as "The Death of Byrhtnoth" and "The Physics of Music," and even in some of the poems. They may be considered as a mass of notes, recording not only Lanier's reading and his varied interests, but his personal experiences and his religious attitude toward life. And it is these references to personal experiences—in Macon, in Brunswick, in Florida—these repetitions of ideas found in the letters, in the poems, in *Tiger-Lilies*, in the essays, these revelations of character, which constitute, for the student of Lanier's work, the main interest of *Shakspere and His Forerunners*, and its charm.

CHAPTER NINETEEN

A FINER FIBRE

§ 1

THE SHAKSPERE lectures are, however, in quite another way of a fabric with Lanier's other work. As his letters and poems are often marred by verbal infelicities, by his apparent inability (as Professor Mims observes) to discover the inevitable word, and by the lack of simplicity that his use of strange and inappropriate words produced, so his lectures are marred at times by conceits, inaccuracies, hasty generalizations, needless repetitions, verbal extravagances, and a tendency —in his own phrase—to "embarrass with riches," and most of all by a fondness for "bringing together people and books that never dreamed of being side by side,"[1] for like Novalis's pupil Lanier saw nothing alone but found significance where significance is not always apparent and is often actually absent. To put it in a phrase, he was not, from the academic point of view, scholarly and academic. But this may be forgiven where enthusiasm is so abundant. The outpouring of the riches of Elizabethan literature is like the rush of the tide into the marshes, breath-taking and beautiful in its unrestraint.

In reading the lectures we must remember Lanier's implied reference to himself as an enthusiastic interpreter, and the statement, quoted above, in his letter to Mrs. Fields à propos criticisms of *The Science of English Verse:* "I have no more claim to 'scholarship' than to the throne of England. . . ." Lanier was essentially not a scholar, though with experience, further study, and time in which to polish and correct, he might have become one; but he did much to inspire students to achievements that were impossible for himself. How correctly Lanier grasped the principles of scholarly study is apparent to anyone who reads the published lectures.

In his lecture to a class of women on "The Wife in Middle English Poetry" we find him audaciously proposing that the members of his class undertake the study of the transmutation of all words remaining to us from the Anglo-Saxon. How he would have rejoiced if he might have known that the scheme he then suggested was at the time actually under way in England, but extended to cover not merely words of Anglo-Saxon origin but all the words of the English language, a scheme carried out in so thorough a manner that it was brought to completion only half a century later with the publication in 1929 at the Clarendon Press of the last volume of *The New English Dictionary.* Lanier's achievements must be measured in part at least by the high, reverential regard in which he held scholarship. "The Man," says Carlyle, "is the spirit he worked in, not what he did but what he became."[2] Lanier's attitude toward scholarship is clearly revealed in the lectures and in the "Ode to Johns Hopkins University" which he read on Commemoration Day, Monday, February 23, 1880.[3] It is not one of Lanier's best poems, but it is an able one, and it indicates, as the lectures do, not only his appreciation of the works of others and the great love he had for the institution with which he had become identified, but also his sane and healthy attitude toward the profession he had embraced.

Whatever his aims and his efforts, however, his achievement was dearly bought. One feels in the work that Lanier produced this year the weariness to which he confessed in the letter that accompanied the copy of *The Science of English Verse* presented in May to E. C. Stedman. "To snatch a moment from the frightful bread-and-meat work which has owned me so long," he had written. Even *The Science of English Verse* was in a way bread-and-meat work. But it is nothing short of miraculous how much bread-and-meat work of a high quality and how much real poetry Lanier produced during the last two years of his life.

§ 2

OF THIS bread-and-meat work the most time-consuming, and therefore the most exhausting for Lanier, was the boys' books— "pot-boilers all,"[4] disguise the fact as he did in his enthusiastic introductions—which he prepared at intervals in 1879, 1880, and 1881, on which he was working during the last month of his life. The first of these, *The Boy's Froissart,* appeared in November, 1879, the first of Lanier's books to bear the imprint of Charles Scribner's Sons. Designed for the Christmas trade, and to appeal to the current taste for the medieval which had affected even juvenile literature, *The Boy's Froissart* proved so successful—going into two additional printings with a total of 4,500 copies in 1879 alone—that another volume, *The Boy's King Arthur*, was commissioned for publication in November, 1880. The plan that then developed, much to Lanier's delight, was to issue one book a year in a series to be called "The Boy's Library of Legend and Chivalry." In his last letter to Hayne Lanier mentioned "another book I've just sent on, to continue the series with, next Christmas," probably *The Boy's Mabinogion*, the introduction to which he prepared in June, 1881, at his camp in North Carolina. And then, as if in fear of quick-coming death, he prepared still another volume, *The Boy's Percy*, which even had he lived would not have been published sooner than it was, in November, 1882; and he left incompletely edited when he died *The Boy's Monstrelet* and *The Boy's Gesta Romanorum*, besides an edition of the Paston letters to inaugurate a similar series for girls.

Before 1900 thirteen thousand copies of the *Froissart* were sold, of the *King Arthur* 12,900, of the *Mabinogion* 5,500, of the *Percy* 3,800.[5] The figures reveal what Lanier and his publishers should have known, indeed probably did know—that boys would take to Froissart and Malory but it would be more difficult to persuade boys to read the *Mabinogion* or to find pleasure in Percy's old ballads, and that the series could not be continued indefinitely. But the four books, fully illustrated, well printed on heavy paper and with attractive title-pages in black and red, and bound elaborately in green bindings rich with gold, are attractive books, well designed as gift books (the original price of the volumes was $3.00 each) in the best contemporary manner. That contemporary taste approved of the matter and the format is indicated by the notice of the *Froissart* in the *Nation*, Lanier's *bête noir* among the journals, which said: "That boy will be lucky who gets Mr. Sidney Lanier's 'Boy's Froissart' for a Christmas present this year. There is no better and healthier reading for boys than 'Fine Sir John'; and this volume is so handsome, so well printed, and so well illustrated [by Alfred Kappes] that it is a pleasure to look it over";[6] and by the review in the Philadelphia *Times* which praised Lanier's work as editor and the appearance of the volume upon which, the reviewer said, "The publishers have lavished fine paper, presswork and binding."[6]

But contemporary opinion is usually least critical and least accurate when it is most enthusiastic, as Lanier himself—and from experience of an opposite sort—knew. These books, which were greeted with such acclaim in a day when little attention was paid to the creating of beautiful books for children and the very idea of the series was something of a novelty, must seem to us of the present day curiously stodgy books to present to adolescents, in spite of the perennial charm of much of the material they contain. Coming to them from a study of Lanier's lectures on Shakspere and the elements of English prosody, we recognize immediately their chief defect—indeed, we take them up expecting to find them what they prove to be, a sort of substitute for the scholarly editions of old classics Lanier had tried in vain to persuade publishers to undertake. As we examine them we see that they are, from the point of view of an age wise in the ways of juvenile reading tastes and interests, not books for boys at all but books for precocious young men. For us they are most interesting because of what they reveal of Lanier's scholarly interests and practices, and of his curious misconceptions of adolescence.

For his *Froissart* Lanier did not use Lord Berners' translation of the *Chronicles* nor even a modernized version of it, which one would expect him to have used, but the more modern translation by Thomas Johnes, published in 1802-05, a translation that lacks the charm of the older one without being more accurate.[7] But a modernized version of Berners' translation had not been made available by 1879, and it would have taken far more of Lanier's time to prepare one than could profitably be given to the collecting of "connected stories which show . . . as many of the historic figures of Froissart as possible."

Lanier's volume is actually about one-ninth the length of the original, and much of the material is rearranged chronologically to give better sequence. Most of the space is given to stories of the campaigns that led up to the battles of Crécy and Poictiers, the accounts of the battles, and to the accounts of the uprisings of the peasants, the Jacquerie in France, and Wat Tyler's Rebellion in England; and forty pages are given to Froissart's account of the crusade against the Saracens. Indeed, as one contemporary critic[8] complained, Lanier's book was not an abridgment of Froissart's *Chronicles* nor a winnowing of wheat from chaff, but an arbitrary selection, with far too many battle passages.

The footnotes that Lanier supplied to explain gaps in the text, to supply dates and additional information, to condemn the somewhat dubious morality of chivalry, and once to encourage possibly lagging interest by stating that more exciting things were to come, are not beyond the comprehension of the "young reader" for whom the work is intended; but it is doubtful if the young reader—assuming that boys still read Froissart's *Chronicles*, and in Lanier's edition—take any interest in comparing specimens of modern English with old English and old French, in the description of the battle of Crécy, or care a rap whether the words be "every word . . . Froissart's" or not. The introduction is quite definitely of more interest to a mature reader than to a young reader and of most interest to the student of Lanier. The discussion of chivalry, of Malory, and of the growth of the Arthurian legends from Wace, Layamon, De Borron, and Walter Map; the mention, though brief, of Chaucer, Langland, and Wyclif; and the insertion of Chaucer's ballade on "Lak of Stedfastnesse"—all this must seem to the young reader to have very little to do with Froissart. And whatever the reading of Froissart may have meant to the boy Lanier, it is doubtful if other boys, as they read the chronicles, think of the increasing difficulty of being a good knight nowadays and of "the strict payment of debts; . . . the purity of the ballot box; the sacred and liberal guaranty of all rights to all citizens; the holiness of marriage; the lofty contempt for what is small, knowing and gossipy." Nevertheless, Lanier's desire in editing Froissart and the other volumes of the series was to help boys to be more manful men—"To speak the very truth; to perform a promise to the uttermost; to reverence all women; . . . to be constant to one love; to be fair to a bitter foe; to despise luxury; to preserve simplicity, modesty, and gentleness in heart and bearing." To Lanier the way to knighthood in the fourteenth century and the way to knighthood and love in the nineteenth century seemed essentially the same.

§ 3

WHEN IN the records of knighthood Lanier found what seemed to him unknightly, he did not hesitate to excise it. In the introduction to *The Boy's Mabinogion* (a selection from Lady Charlotte Guest's translation) he wrote: "as in the other works of this series, the original text is scrupulously preserved, except occasionally to hasten the long-lagging action of a story,—in which case the interpolation is always placed in brackets,—and except where the demands of modern reserve required excision"; and in the introduction to the *Percy:* "Each ballad is given here exactly as it stands in the original except that the spelling has been modernized and such parts cut away as cleanliness required." But in the *King Arthur*, in the introduction to which he made no such explanation, Lanier excised as freely as—indeed more freely than—in the *Mabinogion* and the *Percy*. In this volume, for instance, Lanier never admits that Galahad was Launcelot's son by Elaine, or Modred Arthur's son by his sister, and his obscuration of these facts, so essential to the old story, robs it in Lanier's version of much of its fine tragic quality. The love of Tristram for Isolde and of Launcelot for Guinevere is likewise obscured as much as possible; the drinking of the love potion in the former story is not mentioned at all, and in the latter Guinevere's stinging rebuke when she discovers Launcelot sleeping with Elaine—"False traitor that thou art, look thou never abide in my court, and not so hardly, thou false traitor knight that thou art, that ever thou come in my sight"—is explained by the statement that "a certain enchantress had wrought that Sir Launcelot seemed to have shamed his knighthood [and] the queen was nigh out of her wit, and . . . she writhed and weltered as a mad woman"—all of which is a sheer perversion of the truth of the old story which many a boy has read in the original, as he has read the unexpurgated versions of Shakspere's plays and the Bible, without being harmed.

But the excisions for cleanliness' sake in the *Percy* are most amusing, and most inconsistent of all. In the ballad of "Edom O'Gordon," for instance, the two lines

> This night shall ye lie within mine arms,
> Tomorrow my bride shall be

are omitted, and the stanza in which they occur is reduced by the omission to two unrhymed lines (though the omission is not indicated); but in the ballad of "Valentine and Ursine" the queen's statements concerning her pregnancy, the phrases "labor strong" and "childbed pains" and even the priest's proffer of "odious love" are allowed to remain. Surely "modern reserve" would have counselled omission of the obstetrical details.

Such omissions, whatever the motive, are hardly consistent with the modern scholarly ideals of "the scrupulous fidelity of the editor to his text"[9] upon which Lanier laid so much stress, and on this point it is interesting to compare with Lanier's four volumes the one-volume *Age of Chivalry* by Thomas Bulfinch (in the original edition of 1858 or in the 1884 revised edition of Edward Everett Hale) which Lanier's volumes almost exactly parallel; or to compare Lanier's *King Arthur* with the abridged version of Malory designed especially for boys that Sir Edward Strachey issued in 1868, and which Lanier seems to have used as the basis of his own edition. Neither Bulfinch nor Strachey nor Hale felt it necessary to obscure for boys the stain upon chivalric legends of the actual relations between the sexes which, for the strict moralist, the rapturous idealism of chivalry cannot justify or excuse. Strachey and Bulfinch, in this and in other ways, follow the ancient texts far more literally than Lanier did.

Such omissions can, however, be forgiven Lanier, for the scholar is always expected to use his own judgment in presenting moral questions and even the editors of the "Loeb Classics" series are sometimes so little daring as to translate the Greek original into Latin instead of into English. But Lanier's texts, in spite of his attempts to indicate all his own summaries and interpolations by the use of brackets and his repeated statement that every word not in brackets is the author's, are not accurate if we judge by strictly scholarly standards; and the brackets and the italicized words have the effect of cluttering the page without correctly indicating all changes and omissions and without helping the reading.

§ 4

IN HIS introductions Lanier discusses other matters that boys must consider also just a little unnecessary: for instance, in the preface to the *Froissart*, the discussion of Malory and the development of the Arthurian legend. This is repeated, of course, in the preface to the *King Arthur*, and expanded with quotations from Geoffrey of Monmouth, and from Layamon; and as in the *Froissart* Lanier gave passages in old French and old English, so here he gives an extract in old French from Walter Map's

THE

BOY'S KING ARTHUR

BEING

SIR THOMAS MALORY'S HISTORY

OF

*King Arthur and his Knights of the
Round Table*

EDITED FOR BOYS WITH AN INTRODUCTION

BY

SIDNEY LANIER
EDITOR OF "THE BOY'S FROISSART"

Illustrated by Alfred Kappes

NEW YORK
CHARLES SCRIBNER'S SONS
743 AND 745 BROADWAY
1880

Title-page of "The Boy's King Arthur," the sixth and last volume
of Lanier's work published before his death. (In the original the
initial letters of the main title appear in red.)

25

La Queste del Saint Graal, and another in the original Middle
English from Layamon's *Brut,* with glossarial notes. But matter
that is misplaced in the one case is certainly developed in too
great detail in the other. Not even in the Johns Hopkins lectures
had Lanier touched on more recondite matters.

In the introductions to the *Froissart* and to the *King Arthur,*
Lanier's criticism of his authors is of only a general sort, and
chiefly a commendation of their virtues—not of style, but of
attitude. In the introduction to the *Mabinogion,* however, he
ventures upon literary criticism, comparing the *Mabinogion* with
Malory's *Morte Darthur* and pointing out "the constant presence
in the latter of a certain reasonable restraint, a sober proportion,
a sense of the supreme value of law, even in the most apparently
lawless excursions"—a sentence that might have been taken
from the Shakspere lectures or the lectures on the English novel.
"It would be going far beyond proper bounds," he adds, "to
discuss here how this subtle feeling for the beauty of restraint,
this underlying perception of the artistic necessity of law and
order, has quietly reigned, not only over the advance of English
literature, but has been also the moving spirit, the perpetual
King Alfred, of the whole of English development in general."
And he comments again on the necessity of this appreciation of
law in our own country: "may I not add, if only as one of those
utterances which a boy sometimes profitably remembers though
at first dimly understood—the love of Law beyond all laws
would seem to be particularly vital in a republic; being a principle so comprehensive, that at one extreme, in contact with
certain tendencies, it flowers into that sense of proportion, of
the due relation of all parts of the universe to the whole, which
is the artist's largest perception of beauty, and is the main outfit
of genius in constructing Mabinogion, in literature, in all art;
while at the other extreme, working with certain other tendencies
of character, the same love of Law is at once the root of decorous
behavior on the part of the private citizen, and of large statesmanship on the part of the public official." It was impossible
for Lanier to consider art and morals, literature and life, as
separate subjects; and never could the necessity be greater, he
thought, of making clear the vital oneness of the two than in
books for boys. The brightest thing in the whole *Mabinogion* was
for him the story of Taliesin, with the "almost adoring reverence"
which it reveals of the Welsh for the Bard, the Poet.

§ 5

But it is undoubtedly in this, the third volume of the series, that Lanier loses touch most completely with his young readers. The comments on "the intense feeling for color" and the "almost Oriental luxuriance of tint" in the *Mabinogion* must be lost on them; and the mention of Matthew Arnold and Keltic magic, the directions for the pronunciation of Welsh words, are certainly for the more mature—one might almost say the more educated—reader alone. Of the four books, however, the *Percy*, as even the sale figures would indicate, holds less enjoyment for boys. Boys—boys of the age for which this book was intended, boys of twelve to sixteen—seem to care little for poetry, and of all poetry least for such ballads as Lanier gives. The introductory account of Percy's discovery of the famous folio manuscript and of the poetic revolution signified by the date 1765—the year of the publication of Percy's *Reliques*—and the discussion of Percy's reprehensible conduct in rewriting the ballads, and publishing his versions as genuine, is somewhat beyond the comprehension and interest even of the typical college freshman, and to the young boy can seem only words, words, words.

"It is remarkable," wrote the critic of the *Nation* on the first appearance of this volume, "that [Lanier's] prose style could not accommodate itself to young minds; at least we cannot imagine how differently he would have composed his introduction, had he been addressing adult readers." Remembering the style of the Shakspere lectures and of the essays on scholarly subjects we must admit the justice of the *Nation's* criticism. Recalling the essays on "The Death of Byrhtnoth" and "John Barbour's Bruce," intended without doubt for young readers, we are forced to add that the weakness in the books and the essays that Lanier prepared for boys lies not only in the style. Lanier, we are told, was greatly loved by boys and girls, and it is amazing that he should have failed so signally in producing work that could interest them.

The ballads that Lanier gives in the *Percy*—and he gives them for the most part as they appeared in the *Reliques*—are hardly even well chosen: two, "The Friar of Orders Gray" and "Hardy-knute," are, as Lanier well knew, spurious, and "The Nut Brown Maid" is not properly a ballad. Several of the ballads on historical subjects and fighting, for which he has a preference, such ballads as "Sir Andrew Barton," "Mary Ambree," and "The Winning of Cales," are late, and lack the fine quality of the older ballads, of "Edward," for instance, which Lanier gives, and of "Sir Patrick Spens,"¹ which he strangely omits. His preference is for the long historical ballads, and he gives fewer ballads on love, and two only of folklore and superstition, and no humorous ballad save the satirical "Guy and Amarant" of Samuel Rowlands. His choices, by and large, are not the popular choices of anthologists nor the careful choices of most lovers of old ballads, and they are a little difficult to explain. The selections from the older literature which he included in his Shakspere lectures reveal better taste and a keener perception of enduring qualities.

§ 6

WHAT LANIER does give in the four volumes is a series of fine narratives of battle and adventure which overcome successfully the weight of scholarly matter with which he encumbered them. Read in the proper chronological order, indicated in the introduction to the *Froissart*, and not in the order of publication, they afford an excellent survey of the growth of chivalry and of chivalric ideals, and of the final decay of morals and manners when "the ideals of knighthood begin to be lowered . . . by the temptation of ransom," and war itself becomes a trade. They present, moreover, to the modern boy what Lanier was so eager to present, the highest, purest ideals of chivalry, ideals which, whatever their relation to reality, many directors of youthful education still hold it good for a boy to have. Boys of today probably do not willingly read the *Mabinogion* or Percy's ballads, perhaps not even Froissart's *Chronicles*, though Lanier could with some truth say in 1880 that "a thousand persons are familiar with at least the name of Froissart to one who ever heard of Malory."¹⁰ But boys of today do read the finest of all the tales of chivalry, the tales of the *Morte Darthur*, which Lanier himself helped greatly to their present popularity. For these boys Lanier's own volume of selections remains in print, in the form in which he himself saw it and in an edition made bright by the pictures of N. C. Wyeth; and Lanier's edition of the text remains on the official list of approved texts and recommended books issued by the American Library Association.

For mature readers the books have an interest they must lack for boys. The introductions are undeniably interesting and thoroughly readable. The texts themselves are full of good things. Lanier tells in one of his letters how he picked up a volume as it came fresh from the printers and—familiar though it was by reason of the preparation and the proof-reading—conned page after page with pure delight.[10] If we read these books to understand better the man who found such pleasure in them, for the light they throw not merely on his scholarship or on his critical development but on his life, we see that they were designed obviously for just such boys as he wanted his own boys to be and such a boy as he himself had been—a clean, honest boy with the ideals of "a very manful man," keenly aware of his duties to society and of his heritage of a great tradition.

"You are doing a right good service by suggesting such old, sound stories to the readers of our younger generation," Gilman wrote to him, "—and you seem to me yourself a valiant knight, fighting against ill health and other opponents, a fight for all that is noble and inspiring."[11] It is this Lanier, the fighter, boy archer, soldier of the Confederacy, advocate of democracy, and battler against disease, that boys will always be able to understand and love, even though they lay aside with impatience the editions of the old authors that he prepared especially for them.

CHAPTER TWENTY

LARK OF THE DAWN

§ 1

BUT IN considering together the four books for boys, ignoring the fact that work on them extended from 1879, possibly from 1878, through the last days at Camp Robin in the early fall of 1881, we have overlooked some interesting work on which Lanier was engaged while the manuscripts of the *King Arthur*, the *Mabinogion* and the *Percy* remained yet unfinished.

First, there were the translations from Anglo-Saxon and Middle English poetry contained in the Shakspere lectures, in *The Science of English Verse*, and in separate essays, but undertaken not so much as part of his academic work—not even as an integral part of his treatise on prosody—as for his delight in the labor. The translations, made most likely with some assistance from his distinguished colleague, Professor A. S. Cook, have been called noteworthy;[1] for us they are at least interesting.

Besides the purely literal, interlinear ones, the translations are of two sorts, those made with the emphasis on the content and those made to indicate to ears unfamiliar with the language of the original something of its beauty and power. Those of the first sort are in prose, of dignified words and cadences, and, though pedestrian, are able enough. The translations of the second sort are the more interesting, though not always the more successful. The brief fragments from *Beówulf*[2]—as readable a translation as has yet been made—are of the second sort; in the translation of *The Phœnix*[3] we have examples of both sorts. The metrical part does, it is true, preserve to some extent the rhythm and the alliteration of the original, but it is not in itself able poetry. On the other hand, Lanier did not mean it to be considered for its own merits. "I have kept the translation as nearly literal as possible," he said. It is to his credit that he reproduced as well as he did the rhythm and the meter, suggesting at the same time the idioms of the language.

Part of the translation of "The Battle of Maldon"[4] we have in two versions.[4] In the unfinished essay on "The Death of Byrhtnoth"—an essay that is a frank plea for the intensive study of Anglo-Saxon literature for the fuller appreciation of the strength of language and vigor of emotion of our later literature—Lanier translated the first hundred lines of the poem with a view to reproducing "the send and drive of the rhythm"; the next eighty-five and the last sixteen lines he translated into unmetrical prose, but with a more accurate reproduction of the order of words, the vocabulary, and the poetic embellishments of the original. In both the metrical and the unmetrical portions of the translation line arrangements are ignored, but so successful is Lanier in reproducing the meter that even the untrained ear must notice the break between the two portions, buried within a paragraph though it is:

"Waded the war-wolves west over Panta, recked not of water, warrior vikings. There, o'er the wave they bore up their bucklers, the seamen lifted their shields to the land. In wait with his warriors, Byrhtnoth stood; he bade form the war-hedge of bucklers, and hold that ward firm to the foe. The fight was at hand, the glory of battle; the time was come for the falling of men that were doomed."

Lanier was a careful translator, deeply appreciative of the peculiar qualities of the poetry he was translating.[5] Whatever light an investigation of his translations may throw on Lanier as a poet, it is not without value in revealing in still another way the conscientiousness with which he undertook scholarly investigation.

§ 2

GROWING also out of his scholarly studies were the "Songs of Aldhelm," "half-jotted down" by October 20, 1878.[6] In the course of his studies Lanier had come upon this old Saxon bishop, Bede's senior, who wrote in his native language poetry which King Alfred greatly admired. None of Aldhelm's English poems is extant, but his Latin works survive, and Lanier—searching for English authority for his pronouncements on English prosody—began his introductory summary of prosodical history with

citation of Aldhelm's "Epistola Ad Acircium." Then, with growing interest, he turned from Aldhelm's essay on verse, to con-
jectures of what Aldhelm's own verse may have been. He noted,
with some show of faith, Grimm's conjecture that *The Phœnix*
may have been written by Aldhelm.[7] He may have observed
from the Latin poems that Aldhelm was a careful stylist, more
interested perhaps in the style than in the subject matter of
his poems.

In the eleventh of the Peabody Institute Shakspere lectures,[8]
delivered in February, 1879, Lanier spoke of Aldhelm as "a
name which stands at the head of our drama as well as of our
poetry, a name heard but little, yet to me distinguishing by
far the most fascinating figure in the history of English poetry
before Chaucer: I had almost said before Shakspere," and he
called Aldhelm "that beautiful soul," and—in the preface to
The Science of English Verse, written a year later—"the Father of
English Poetry."[9] Aldhelm, it is clear, had been idealized by
Lanier and turned into a symbol. The symbol, critics have
pointed out, represents poetic authority, and so stands for one
of the sturdiest cravings of Lanier, but Aldhelm is for Lanier
a symbol of another sort also: the symbol of the poet as a leader
of men, correcting their errors, calling them to worship, and
commanding their respect.

He is for Lanier not the bishop, the monk, or the scholar, but
the poet standing on the bridge, singing to the merchants as
they hurried, heedless of church services, about the town. So
in one of the poem outlines Aldhelm is made to rebuke the
merchants who say they have no time to listen to idle dreams:

> "Till ye hear me, ye have no time
> Neither for trade nor travelling;
> Till ye hear me ye have no time to fight nor
> marry nor mourn;
> There is not time, O world,
> Till you hear me, the Poet Aldhelm,
> To eat nor drink nor to draw breath.
> For until the Song of the Poet is heard
> Ye do not live, ye cannot live."[10]

"The Songs of Aldhelm"— Lanier's unpublished and unfinished

volume—is probably represented, in the collected poems, by seven poems grouped as street-cries, all of them poems of rebuke or remonstrance, or assertions of the power of poetry in life. The seven are "Remonstrance," "The Ship of Earth" (dating from 1868, but with the first two stanzas of that version omitted), "How Love Looked for Hell," "Spring and Tyranny" (renamed simply "Tyranny"), "Life and Song," "To Richard Wagner" (in a modified version), and "A Song of Love,"[11] the last an exquisitely simple lyric, restrained in metaphor, but clearly suggesting Lanier's ideas of the place of love in life. To these seven poems he prefixed two introductory stanzas[12] which may be freely paraphrased thus: In spite of the noise and confusion of modern life, nature remains a source of comfort and an assurance of the peace into which the confusion must be resolved. In these "Street-Cries" Lanier is the interpreter of nature and the prophet of peace to a generation more vainly busy than that of Aldhelm, and more foolishly convinced than his that the songs of the poet are idle dreams.[13]

§ 3

OF INTEREST to Lanier still, of course, and still absorbing much of his thought if not any longer a great deal of his working time, was that other poem of protest against the deadening, decivilizing forces in the social structure, "The Jacquerie."[14] It was a poem dreamed of in his youth as a memory of Froissart, given poetic form and shape over more than a decade of years, influenced, conditioned, and changed by the reading of Michelet's *Histoire de France* in Texas and full research in the ample library of the Peabody Institute, but left unfinished at Lanier's death— an interesting fragment sketched by a hand that had learned much of the novelist's art since *Tiger-Lilies* and much concerning the writing of verse, richly suggesting how fine a narrative poem Lanier might under favorable conditions have produced. The first chapter of the published fragment—beginning with four lines in rhyme but quickly changing to blank verse that never moves gracefully—dates possibly from 1868, but other parts of "The Jacquerie," particularly Chapter II, seem to date from a later period. "A Song of Love," published posthumously, is said by Mrs. Lanier to have been designed as one of the songs of the fool in "The Jacquerie," and to have been given its final form in 1879. The fragment as a whole probably represents the revision and reworking of thirteen years rather than the work of any one year.

Nothing that Lanier ever planned was quite so dear to him as this long poem, which should be not only a novel in verse but an indictment of Trade. Nothing perhaps remained more persistently in his mind, but during these years what leisure Lanier found from rehearsals and concerts and lectures and classes and his new job of editing had to be given to further study at the library and to the writing of prose articles. He had precious little time for poetry.

§ 4

THE PROSE of these last years met with little success. It is doubtful if Lanier received any more than the most nominal fee for his musical criticism that appeared in the Baltimore *Sun* of January 31, 1880.[15] The paper called "The Death of Byrhtnoth" was still unsold and it remained unpublished until seventeen years later when it appeared in the *Atlantic Monthly*, which under the editorship of Scudder and Page showed a disposition to pay honor to Lanier dead which under Howells it had denied to Lanier living. The fragmentary "Legend of St. Leonor," taken from the *Acta Sanctorum* and planned as part of an essay on "The Relations of Poetry and Science," was published in 1885,[16] the essay "How to Read Chaucer" in 1891, and "John Barbour's Bruce" in 1897. The last essay of any importance that Lanier himself saw published was the essay on "The New South" (written in February, 1880) which appeared in *Scribner's Monthly* for October, 1880.[17]

In this essay Lanier compared the social and economic significance of the large-scale farming of the West with the small farming of the post-bellum South, drawing his information from "a mass of clippings" from Georgia newspapers which he had been collecting for several years. "The quiet rise of the small farmer in the Southern States" since 1860 with the consequent improvement in the products raised, the organization of library societies and of amateur dramatic clubs in rural districts, the growth of the public school system for whites and blacks, etc., said Lanier, was "the notable circumstance of the period, in comparison with which the noisier events signify nothing " The predictions that he made have by and large proved true; his idea that intellectual and social progress depends upon economic progress has been accepted; and his intelligently liberal attitude toward the relations of Negroes and whites reveals Lanier as one of the real leaders of the new South. But his essay on small farming seems to have been inspired not only by a study of contemporary conditions but also by the contrasting picture of large farming in England three centuries before which his scholarly studies had shown him, and to which he devoted one-third of his article, making rich use of the materials republished by the New Shakspere Society, quoting liberally from statistics, from the Lenten sermons preached in 1548 by Bishop Latimer,[18] in which the good bishop described the evil situation of the yeoman and agricultural laborers caused by the sudden rage for sheep-raising and the destruction of the small farms, from More's *Utopia* and from statutes of the reigns of Henry VIII and of Elizabeth.

Into his essay any number of things can be read. Lanier underrated the development of manufacturing in the South, but recent events have raised serious doubts concerning the benefits of the existing industrial system in the southern states. Large farming too often produces overproduction; the plight of cotton planters in 1930 and 1931 has given ample evidence of the attendant dangers. Diversified farming means self-sufficiency, and newspaper accounts of the suffering of so many southern farmers in the winter of 1930-31 emphasized the failure of these farmers to attempt to raise more than one crop and the willingness to buy from dealers what they themselves should have raised and preserved. But Lanier was not so much a prophet or an astute student of an agricultural problem so enormous that it is essentially a problem of civilization, as he was a son of Georgia, burning with a deep and reverent love for his boyhood home. His economics may have been false, his proposed program ultra-conservative and impractical. But his affection is not to be questioned, and this after all, rather than economic theory, justifies the essay. The melancholy tone of the last paragraph reveals this fully: "it is," he wrote, "because many of [the blissful mountain ranges of the southeastern states] are actually virgin to plough, pillar, axe, or mill-wheel, while others have known only the insulting and mean cultivation of the earlier immigrants who scratched the surface for cotton a year or two, then carelessly abandoned all to sedge and sassafras, and sauntered on toward Texas: . . . that these lands are, with sadder significance than that of small farming, also a New South."

It is significant and pleasing that in this last published essay there should be epitomized all the important interests of Lanier's life—the ideals of personal conduct that he expressed in "The Symphony," the political ideals expressed in "Retrospects and Prospects," the economic interests revealed through a series of poems culminating in "Corn," the scholarly interests of his last years, the passionate loyalty to the southern soil, the intelligent but equally passionate loyalty to southern society—the southern scheme of things and manner of life, the intelligent conviction concerning the necessary disappearance of the color-line from the economic and political life of the South, and the religious idealism of all his poetry and all his music—of all his thought. For small farming, as Lanier envisioned it, must, by improving the economic condition of men, improve their moral condition; and moral growth in personality was, as he intimated in the Shakspere lectures and as we shall find him saying quite clearly in *The English Novel*, the essential fact of modern life. "The New South," it should also be pointed out, is a restatement in prose of a faith and a program stated nine years before in the poem "The Homestead."

§ 5

THE POEMS of this year are chiefly occasional pieces, little versified thoughts of no consequence, expressed however with charm and grace. Among these are the posthumously published and uncollected Valentine poem to Miss Lucie Browne; the untitled lines (called in the collected poems "Ireland") which he contributed to an art album published in May, 1880, to raise money for the relief of the Irish famine;[19] the sonnets "To My Class, On Certain Fruits and Flowers Sent Me in Sickness" and "On Violet's Wafers, Sent Me When I Was Ill," written during the serious illness of December, 1880, and January, 1881;[20] and the epigrammatic lines "To Dr. Thomas Shearer."[21] Even the Johns Hopkins ode is an occasional poem. But three or four other poems of the greatest merit, of undeniable beauty and power, were also written in 1880, so that the year made memorable for English prosody by the appearance of his *Science of English Verse* is memorable also in the life of Lanier. It is the year of the writing of "Individuality," "The Crystal," "A Ballad of Trees and the Master," and—chief poem of all—"Sunrise."

The first of these poems, "Individuality,"[22] reveals more fully than any other of Lanier's poems his interest in scientific theory and the effect of his scientific studies upon his thought. References to physical science we have observed from time to time in his work, from *Tiger-Lilies* through the essays on the physics of music and of verse to the Shakspere lectures. In Baltimore he had actually done some scientific experimentation, working on problems connected with sound, and he had used for a period of several months a microscope lent to him by Mrs. Sophie Bledsoe Herrick, Lowell's Baltimore friend, for the study of natural objects. "He plunged in with all the ardor of a naturalist, not using the microscope as a mere toy, but doing good hard work with it."[23] Finally, out of much study and grave deliberation he was to declare in "The Legend of St. Leonor," using a figure from the old legend of the *Acta Sanctorum:* "The scientific man is merely the minister of poetry. He is cutting down the Western Woods of Time; presently poetry will come there and make a city and gardens. This is always so. The man of affairs works for the behoof and use of poetry. Scientific facts have never reached their proper function until they merge into new poetic relations established between man and man, between man and God, or between man and Nature." Conversely he might have declared that poetry never fulfills its proper function of elevating man morally unless it grows out of a deep understanding of the relations of man with man, man with God, and man with nature. But poetry, he would have added, states truths of which science may not yet be aware.

The relation of his scientific studies, and his thought on scientific matters, to the poem "Individuality" is made clear in a letter to J. F. Kirk of June 15, 1880, sent with the poem. "I have been studying science," Lanier wrote, "biology, chemistry, evolution, and all. It pieces on, perfectly, to those dreams which one has when one is a boy and wanders alone by a strong running river, on a day when the wind is high but the sky clear. These enormous modern generalizations fill me with such dreams again.

"But it is precisely at the beginning of that phenomenon which is the underlying subject of this poem, 'Individuality,' that the largest of such generalizations must begin, and the doctrine of evolution when pushed beyond this point appears to me, after the most careful examination of the evidence, to fail. It is pushed beyond this point in its current application to the genesis of species, and I think Mr. Huxley's last sweeping declaration is clearly parallel to that of an enthusiastic dissecter who, forgetting that his observations are upon dead bodies, should build a physiological conclusion upon purely anatomical facts.

"For whatever can be proved to have been evolved, evolution seems to me a noble and beautiful and true theory. But a careful search has not yet shown me a single instance in which such proof as would stand the first shot of a boy lawyer in a moot court, has been brought forward in support of an actual case of species differentiation.

"A cloud (see the poem) *may* be evolved; but not an artist; and I find, in looking over my poem, that it has made itself into a passionate reaffirmation of the artist's autonomy, threatened alike from the direction of the scientific fanatic and the pantheistic devotee."[24]

"Individuality" is, unfortunately, not a very good poem in spite of its high thought and a few truly lyrical stanzas: the passion of Lanier's reaffirmation of the artist's responsibility produced only a few fine lines. The poem is too long and the misplaced accents rob it of the rhythmical beauty that might have helped to redeem its other faults. It is, to state the charge more briefly, labored; and without the letter to Kirk we do not find interpretation easy. The letter, however, guides us to the key verse:

> What the cloud doeth
> The Lord knoweth,
>   The cloud knoweth not.
> What the artist doeth,
> The Lord knoweth;
>   Knoweth the artist not?

The cloud, that is to say, may be explained as a physical phenomenon; the artist cannot be so explained, for the artist possesses free-will.

> Awful is Art because 'tis free.
> The artist trembles o'er his plan
>   Where men his self must see.
> Who made a song or picture, he

Did it, and not another, God nor man.

. . . . . .
Each artist—gift of terror!—owns his will.

This then is individuality. But the whole tendency of scientific teaching is against the doctrine of individuality and individual responsibility; so Lanier—in a generation before studies in psychology had tended to lessen still further the responsibility of the individual for his own actions—rebelled against science. The poem ends:

> Pass, kinsman Cloud, now fair and mild:
> Discharge the will that's not thine own.
> I work in freedom wild,
> But work, as plays a little child,
> Sure of the Father, Self, and Love, alone.

That Lanier should have rebelled against science and rejected the theory of physical evolution as it is applied to man, in spite of his ardent advocacy of science in other matters, need not surprise us. As his generation understood the theory—indeed, as Spencer and Huxley explained it—the import was materialism and, by consequence, atheism. Furthermore, the theory of evolution implied biological predestination, and to Lanier all these notions were abhorrent. But his gesture of defiance of the scientific trend of things is a gesture only, a brave but futile attempt to preserve in the face of the advance of science and its revelations of unalterable laws his faith in the integrity of the human personality and in the redeeming fact of love.

§ 6

THIS FAITH is expressed again in another poem written about this time, "The Crystal,"[25] a poem Lanier succeeded in selling, though "Individuality" went unsold and remained unpublished for a full year after his death. As in "Retrospects and Prospects," "Clover," the Johns Hopkins ode, and elsewhere, Lanier here lists the names of the great whom he reverenced and loved, but here, as he has not done before, he names the great not to praise them unreservedly but to indicate the defects that reveal their common manhood. Shakspere, for instance, is forgiven weaknesses which others must often have felt without always labeling:

> Juliet's prurient pun
> In the poor, pale face of Romeo's fancied death;
> .   .   .   .   .   Henry's fustian roar
> Which frights away that sleep he invocates;
>
> .   .   .   .
> Too-silly shifts of maids that mask as men
> In faint disguises that could ne'er disguise.

But the forgiveness is not only of literary defects, or of insufficient morality. Sometimes it is of blind teaching:

> So Buddha, beautiful! I pardon thee
> That all the All thou hadst for needy man
> Was Nothing, and thy Best of being was
> But not to Be.

Thus for one reason or another are named for forgiveness and characterized in phrases that have been called "sudden electric flashes"[26] the great whom Lanier loved: Shakspere, Homer, Socrates, Buddha, Dante, Milton, Æschylus, Lucretius, Marcus Aurelius, Thomas à Kempis, Epictetus, Behmen, Swedenborg, Langley (Langland), Cædmon, Emerson, Keats, and Tennyson.[27] These are great, but each possesses a

> little mole that marks
> [Him] brother and [his] kinship seals to man.[28]

It is only Christ who is perfect beyond forgiveness:

> But Thee, O man's best Man, O love's best Love,
> O perfect life in perfect labor writ,
> O all men's Comrade, Servant, King or Priest—
> What *if* or *yet*, what mole, what flaw, what lapse,
> What least defect or shadow of defect,
> What rumor, tattled by an enemy,
> Of inference loose, what lack of grace
> Even in torture's grasp, or sleep's, or death's—
> Oh, what amiss may I forgive in Thee,
> Jesus, good Paragon, thou Crystal Christ?

But there is something here that justifies us in refusing to accept "The Crystal" as an invocation of the Christ of the Churches, of the Christ of Christian theology, as Christian theologians would have us accept the poem. For it is Jesus as the perfect man, the great exemplar of Christian teachings, not God nor of God save as all men may be of God, that Lanier apostrophizes. Lanier's theology was altogether too simple and reasonable to admit a trinity or a duality of divinity. This fact, which is more evident in his poems than the essays on Lanier by Christian ministers would lead one to suspect, seems to have been appreciated by at least one minister who knew him, for such indeed seems the implication of the statement of the Reverend William Kirkus, rector of the Protestant Episcopal Church of Saint Michael and All Angels, Baltimore, who preached Lanier's funeral sermon. Writing for the *Christian Churchman* in the very month of Lanier's death Kirkus pointed out that Lanier's reverence for science, his contempt for sectarian disputes, his great honesty, and his rebellion against the Calvinistic training of his youth, "kept him somewhat apart from what is considered formal orthodoxy." But he was, Kirkus added, "a truly godly man. Few men, indeed, had firmer belief in the living power, the perpetual gracious presence, of the Eternal Father."

§ 7

BORN AND BRED, like Herman Melville, "in the bosom of the infallible Presbyterian Church," Lanier had of course once been perfectly orthodox in his thinking. But he possessed the true Protestant's passionate, relentless sense of personal responsibility, and he was, moreover, a man of original genius. He rebelled, therefore, as strongly as Melville against the narrowness of Calvinistic theology and the complacent mediocrity of contemporary Christian practice.[29] And his rebellion against organized Christianity had of course an effect upon his conception of God, and upon his personal relations to divinity.

Lanier's Christ of the later years is not the Christ of theology, nor is he actually a religious figure. In one of the poem outlines Lanier reveals the final end of his thinking:

"The Church is too hot, and Nothing is too cold. I find my proper Temperature in Art. Art offers to me a method of adoring the sweet master Jesus Christ, the beautiful souled One, without the straitness of a Creed which confines my genuflexions, a

26

Church which confines my limbs, and without the vacuity of the doubt which numbs them. An unspeakable gain has come to me in simply turning a certain phrase the other way: the beauty of holiness becomes a new and wonderful saying to me when I figure it to myself in reverse as the holiness of beauty. This is like opening a window of dark stained glass, and letting in a flood of white light. I thus keep upon the walls of my soul a church-wall rubric which has been somewhat clouded by the expiring breaths of creeds dying their natural death. For in art there is no doubt. My heart beat all last night without my supervision: for I was asleep; my heart did not doubt a throb; I left it beating when I slept, I found it beating when I woke; it is thus with art: it beats in my sleep. A holy tune was in my soul when I fell asleep; it was going when I awoke. This melody is always moving along in the background of my spirit. If I wish to compose, I abstract my attention from the thoughts which occupy the front of the stage, the *dramatis personae* of the moment, and fix myself upon the deeper scene in the rear."[30]

Christ to Lanier is not God made man, but the Jewish Jesus— than whom there has been no "man more dear and friendly and helpful and strong and human and Christly."[31] He is not God to be worshipped, but an ethical figure to be admired and adored. For the scientist, He sets the goal for spiritual evolution; for the artist, He is the artist of conduct; for the democrat, He is the brave, democratic hero; for the poet, He is a symbol, without which our poetry would be the poorer.

It is as a perfect democrat that Jesus appears in "The Crystal" but it is as symbol of mankind that He appears in another poem of Lanier's last year, "A Ballad of Trees and the Master."[32] The "ballad" is apparently only a versification of the story of Gethsemane, told with the simplicity of true art, but attentive reading reveals that the moral of the poem is not the meekness of Christ nor Lanier's tender love for Him: as in most of Lanier's poems, it is the healing effect of nature on the troubled spirit.[33] The poem is a ballad of trees and the master, not of the master and trees, certainly not of the master alone. It is, therefore, not so much a Christian poem as a pagan one, a poem of kinship with nature, as one realizes even more when one reads it in connection with the pantheistic "Sunrise" for which it was intended originally as an interlude. It was into the woods that Lanier went continually to escape the desolating sense of defeat that contact with society brought; it is into the woods that he goes again as death approaches, into remembered woods of the Georgia seacoast where he receives, in ecstasy, the inspiration for the poem that is his supreme poetic vision.

§ 8

AND DEATH was stealing softly upon him now, not to be fought off again. The opening of the year 1880 had found him seriously ill: the routine of giving eight lectures weekly—two public lectures at the university or two to university classes,[34] and six at private schools—and attending rehearsals and concerts of the orchestra, to say nothing of keeping up his private literary work, was a severe drain on his insufficient reserve of strength, and though he soon recovered from his January illness, his walking remained slow and difficult, and he suffered a relapse toward the end of May.

On July 19 he wrote to a friend: "It is now nearly six weeks that I've had a villainous fever, which has finally become the disgust of my doctor and the opprobrium of all medicine. Nothing seems to have the least effect on it. If it goes on it must result in overturning the fundamental concepts of philosophy: for it is apparently without cause and without end,—though it certainly had a beginning,—and it is self-existent,—though a parasite.

"Day and night it remains, calm, inexpugnable. I am satisfied that nothing ever acquired a state of existence so wholly imperturbable and elevated beyond the powers or the prayers of men,—except perhaps one of the grand gods of Lucretius, whose nature

Ipsa suis pollens opibus, nihil indiga nostri,
Nec bene promeritis capitur nec tangitur irâ.

"In truth this last line seems almost allegorical, in this connection; for *bene promeritis* may well enough symbolize the mild homœopathic suasives with which my Fever had been appealed to; while *ira* admirably represents the heroic doses of allopathic truculence with which it has been fought; but with the former *nec capitur*, with the latter *nec tangitur*.

"Seriously, I've been ill enough; and your imagination is all I can rely on—for words are here simply exasperating—when I tell you that about three weeks ago, thinking a change might help me, I managed to crawl down to Charles Street Station and *went* to New York,—and took to bed as soon as I reached the hotel, there,—and tossed thereon for four days with a fairly flaming fever,—and finally had to crawl back to Baltimore, without having accomplished a single stroke of business, without having seen a single picture or friend, without having heard a single crash of the horns and violins,—for which I longed unspeakably."[35]

On the 21st of July, having sent his sons to a farm in Virginia, Lanier went with his wife and her father to West Chester in search of quiet and rest. Here on August 14 was born the Laniers' fourth child, Robert. In a letter to Richard Malcolm Johnston Lanier announced the birth of the new baby, admitting at the same time his own ill-health. But with his characteristic gaiety he made even now a pun: "This mean, pusillanimous fever which took under-hold of me two months ago is still *there*, as impregnably fixed as a cockle-burr in a sheep's tail. I have tried idleness, but (naturally) it won't *work*." And, convinced still that the illness was curable, he added: "I get up every day and drag around in a pitiful kind of shambling existence. I fancy it has come to be purely a go-as-you-please match between me and the disease, to see which will wear out first, and I think I will manage to take the belt, yet."[36]

But the shadow of death has fallen now across all that he does, in spite of this brave boast. To a friend he confesses in a letter of September 5: "I was so ill during the time we were together on Wednesday evening—I really thought I would fall on the floor, and busied myself with picturing the scene, detailing the curious faces and so on, and regretting in advance the trouble it was going to give you—that I postponed until a better time many questions I wanted to ask. . . ."[35] However, he returned alone to Baltimore the middle of September to resume his studies in preparation for his third course of lectures at Johns Hopkins.

He interrupted his studies to prepare a textbook of selections from Chaucer and Shakspere, hoping through the publication of the book to increase his income, to provide a textbook for his own course on Chaucer and Shakspere, should he give it again, and to make available to young students an anthology that should open to them beauties of literature that are too often closed mysteries. The projected volume—like the earlier projected Chaucer volume—came to naught, but three papers constituting an introduction to it have bre peenserved and published.[37] A

reading of them will suggest reasons why the book was rejected
and will also throw light on Lanier's work as a scholar.

In the Shakspere lectures we have followed Lanier's interpretation of Shakspere's character on the basis of evidence
presented by placing three plays in chronological order. In his
textbook Lanier proposed reprinting these three plays and with
them three works of Chaucer: the knight's tale of Palamon
and Arcite, to be studied in conjunction with *A Midsummer
Night's Dream;* the pardoner's tale of the three robbers, to be
studied in conjunction with *Hamlet;* and the clerk's tale of patient
Griselda, to be studied in conjunction with *The Tempest.* The
purpose of such a comparative study was to reveal Shakspere
as man and artist and Chaucer as man and artist, and—though
Lanier does not state these other aims here—to help the student
arrive at a comparative estimate of the two as men and as
artists and gain some idea of the change in status of man as
an individual since the Middle Ages. Lanier planned to add
copious footnotes to the texts.

But the choice of the three plays as typical of the three periods
of Shakspere's life is an arbitrary choice on Lanier's part, representing his own preferences among the plays; and the choice
of the three stories by Chaucer depends entirely upon the previous
choice of plays. Furthermore, the conclusions presented seem
not so much to have been drawn from the plays and stories
chosen as the plays and stories to have been chosen according to pre-
conceived ideas. This is, of course, legitimate in a lecture course
or essay, in which the lecturer's or the essayist's personality is
of as much interest as the factual matter that he presents. But
it was almost audacious of Lanier to have expected other teachers
to accept his views unquestioningly and to use a textbook that
allowed no deviation from them. Such a textbook as Lanier was
preparing could have been used with success and profit to the
class by Lanier alone; and the expense of issuing such a work
for the limited number of pupils who studied with Lanier would
have caused any publisher to decline to publish it.

The introduction reveals, however, not only Lanier's lack of
perspective on his own method of teaching but the superficiality
of much of his scholarship, the inadequacy of his scholarly
methods. For we have here little discussion of Chaucer and
Shakspere, but much discussion of Shakspere and little of Chaucer.
The moral views of Shakspere, the artistic structure of his plays,

and the actual dates of the plays are discussed in considerable
detail, much as in *The Science of English Verse* and in the Shakspere lectures, but there is no discussion of Chaucer's moral
views on art, and no suggestions even for determining the chronology of his works to be studied. Perhaps such studies should
not be and cannot be made; but if so, Chaucer and Shakspere
should not be studied together in the way that Lanier suggested.
The introduction to his ill-conceived textbook confirms our
opinion that Lanier was too prone to make flashy generalizations, in what one critic has called his "drolly American self-
confident fashion of making a dash at difficult speculations that
have long exercised the minds of theorists, as if these questions
had never been raised before."[38]

The same critic added, however: "But the fairness of his
intentions often almost justifies his audacity, and one delights
in the ardency of [his] spirit and the courageousness of his questioning, even when one is least able to accept his conclusions,"
and with this we must agree. If we have not quarreled more with
Lanier's method and taken issue more ardently with his conclusions, it is because in the work in which we have found both
most fully revealed—the Shakspere lectures—we have also
found much that is so genuinely delightful and fine that we
have forgiven easily and ignored much in the act of forgiving.
The same conclusions presented more succinctly and more baldly,
as in this introduction, offend us more.

§ 9

WORK ON this textbook was an interruption in Lanier's work
in preparation for the lectures of the coming winter lecture
course. Time for other such bread-and-meat work he also found,
for he prepared an article on King Arthur for *St. Nicholas'
Magazine*,[39] a summarization of material he had included in the
preface to *The Boy's King Arthur* and of certain incidents from
the story. The article was supposedly designed to give some
account of Sir Thomas Malory's book which would bring it
before minds younger than those for whom the introduction to
The Boy's King Arthur was intended, but publication of it in the
December number of the Scribner owned *St. Nicholas' Magazine*
was also a move planned by the Scribners to encourage the
sale of the book. The article is the sheerest kind of bread-and-

meat work, a piece of no importance save for the recompense it brought Lanier.

But he found time also, in spite of such work and the laborious reading of English novels in preparation for a course that, as originally planned, was to have included a discussion of contemporary novels also, to write to his old friend Hayne: "I have been wishing to write you a long time and have thought several letters to you. But I could never tell you the extremity of illness, of poverty, and of unceasing work, in which I have spent the last three years; and you would need only once to see the weariness with which I crawl to bed after a long day's work—and often a long night's work at the heel of it,—and Sundays just as well as other days,— in order to find in your heart a full warrant for my silence. It seems incredible that I have printed such an unchristian quantity of matter,—all, too, tolerably successful,— and earned so little money; and the wife and the four boys—who are so lovely that I would not think a palace good enough for them if I had it—make one's earnings seem all the less. . . .

"For six months past a ghastly fever has been taking possession of me each day at about twelve M., and holding my head under the surface of indescribable distress for the next twenty hours, subsiding only enough each morning to let me get on my working-harness, but never intermitting. A number of tests show it not to be the 'hectic' so well known in consumption; and to this day it has baffled all the skill I could find in New York, in Philadelphia, and [in Baltimore]. I have myself been disposed to think it arose purely from the bitterness of having to spend my time in making academic lectures and boy's books—pot-boilers all— when a thousand songs are singing in my ear that will certainly kill me if I do not utter them soon. But I don't think this diagnosis has found favor with any practical physician; and meantime I work day after day in such suffering as is piteous to see."[40]

He had reached at this time that stage of development of his poetic powers when he could compose spontaneously and well, and when a poem that had to be written seized him he would, in spite of pot-boilers and ill-health, give it form. For at least one poem, "A Ballad of Trees and the Master," was written thus. Mrs. Lanier has described the circumstances: "It was cold November weather. . . . I was to go out for a little while to see a friend who was also ill. He urged me to go. As I went to change my house-dress for a warmer one, he began to write on a sheet of paper. I had been gone from the room perhaps fifteen or twenty minutes. When I came back he handed me the paper, saying, 'Take this to her and tell her that it is fresh from the mint.' It was 'The Ballad of Trees and the Master,' just as we have it without erasure or correction."[41]

§ 10

THE SUFFERING Lanier experienced at this time shows plainly in the finely molded face of the bust Mr. Ephraim Keyser made of him. Keyser, a native of Baltimore who had for some time worked in Rome, had returned to Baltimore to execute several commissions. One day Lanier went with his friend, J. R. Tait, to Keyser's studio, and Keyser, seeing him for the first time, was so impressed by the beauty of his head and the fineness of his personality that he begged Lanier to pose for him. The bust, completed in ten sittings of an hour each,[42] is of all portraits of Lanier the most satisfying; it portrays Lanier as he was at the period of his highest development as man and artist. Suffering shows in the face; but victory also—the victory of one who has met and conquered all opposition and is ready to face death as courageously as he had faced life.

His illness increased to such an extent that he was confined to his home and to bed. In December he was no better; his fever maintained an almost constant maximum of 104°; but it was during this illness, while he lay all but extinguished by the fierce fire of this fever, and with so little strength in his arms that he could not lift food to his lips, and his hand had to be propped to the level of his adjustable writing desk, that he pencilled in delicate, almost illegible script the superb "Sunrise."[43]

The restlessness and the burning of his fever pervade the lines; it is into the dream-troubled sleep of illness, no restful, natural sleep, that the clean nature odors of marsh and forest and sea come as something stronger than memories, less resistible than reality, to trouble Lanier and to waken him. But the sleep is stranger, more troubled even than the sleep of illness and of fever; it is surely the sleep of life, and awakening is to the freedom of all-releasing death.

> I have waked, I have come, my beloved! I might not
>   abide:

I have come ere the dawn, O beloved, my live-oaks,
>   to hide
>   In your gospeling glooms,—to be
> As a lover in heaven, the marsh my marsh, and the
>   sea, my sea.

There is no Wordsworthian reverence of nature here, for Wordsworth never knew such ecstasy or such a sense of the humanity
of nature. This is nature worship pure and simple, and unquali-
fied adoration of kinsmen trees, leaves, birds, marsh, and sea,
which only just escapes the blighting touch of the nympholeptic
longing apparent in "Corn" and in "The Symphony." The
language in which it is expressed lacks perhaps the musical
beauty of "The Marshes of Glynn," but there are in "Sunrise,"
as in "The Marshes," beautiful lines and beautiful rhythms,
passages superbly onomatopœic. The rustle of the leaves is in
the lines

> Ye lispers, whisperers, singers in storms,
> Ye consciences murmuring faiths under forms,
> Ye ministers meet for each passion that grieves,
> Friendly, sisterly, sweetheart leaves;

but in the twelve-line passage beginning "Oh! what if a sound
should be made!" there is the magnificence of silence, caught, by
paradox, in perfectly attuned phrases. And as in "The Marshes"
Lanier conveyed perfectly the hush, and then the noises of water
and air at sunset, so here he transcribes the sounds of the breaking of silence, the "low multitudinous stirring" swelling until—
all the voices of nature singing together—it ushers in the sun.

But it is no divided allegiance that the worshipper here swears:
the divinity to which Lanier makes obeisance is Divine Heat,
giver of life, worshipped from of old, but saluted neither by
Akhnaton nor by St. Francis more rapturously than by Lanier.

> Good-morrow, lord Sun!
> With several voice, with ascription one,
> The woods and the marsh and the sea and my soul
> Unto thee, whence the glittering stream of all morrows
>   doth roll,
> Cry good and past-good and most heavenly morrow,
>   lord Sun!

O Artisan, born in the purple! Workman Heat,
Parter of passionate atoms that travail to meet
And be mixed in the death-cold oneness, . . .
.   .   .   .   .   .

Thou chemist of storms, whether driving the winds
    a-swirl
Or a-flicker the subtiler essences polar that whirl
In the magnet of earth—yea, thou with a storm for a
    heart,
Rent with debate, many-spotted with question, part
From part oft sundered, yet ever a globèd light,
Yet ever the artist, ever more large and bright
Than the eye of a man may avail of; manifold One.

But the poet leaves us not with the thought of sunrise but with
that of sunset, or—to interpret literally—the end of life and the
sunrise of death:

I must pass from thy face, I must pass from the face of
    the Sun.
.   .   .   .

But I fear not, nay, and I fear not the thing to be done;
I am strong with the strength of my lord the Sun:
How dark, how dark soever the race that must needs
    be run,
                I am lit with the sun.

"Sunrise," in spite of all the faults of execution, of distracting
metaphor and of deceiving rhythm, is, as one critic has said,
"marvelous for its enraptured joyousness of spirit and the glorious
effulgence of a living dawn, pictured in the very presence of
death."[44] It is furthermore the very apotheosis of Lanier's poetry
and with its rapturous embrace of the sunrise the very apotheosis
of Lanier. But to see in "Sunrise" only this and the paganism
of Lanier's adoration of nature is to miss the social gospel not
only implicit but explicit, the message that makes "Sunrise" a
companion piece to "The Symphony," a chant for a new day
more characteristic of Lanier than "The Marshes of Glynn."
For the sun is not only the source of light and heat and life, and
the symbol—in Swedenborgian sense—of the soul's immortality;
the sun is also surety of a golden earthly day yet to be, architect,

builder and bondsman of a perfected social structure. Eleven years previously in the Furlow College commencement address Lanier had asked: "Has God failed you?

"The dawn that broke in glory upon this morning denies it: yonder sun that hangs upon His right hand in heaven denies it; and to-night, the faithful stars, with a myriad silver voices, will deny.

"When these fail you, religion will fail you. Until then, you have naught to do but smile at those absurd birds of evil, who, having found some decaying carcass of a sensation, straightway begin to flap wing boisterously through the air, and to screech out that the world is dead."

"Sunrise" ends on the same note of faith:

> Oh, never the mast-high run of the seas
> Of traffic shall hide thee,
> Never the hell-colored smoke of the factories
> Hide thee,
> Never the reek of time's fen-politics
> Hide thee,
> And ever my heart through the night shall with knowl-
> edge abide thee,
> And ever by day shall my spirit, as one that hath tried
> thee,
> Labor, at leisure, in art, till yonder beside thee
> My soul shall float, friend Sun,
> The day being done.

"Sunrise" is inferior in execution to "The Marshes of Glynn," and by no means a perfect poem, but it is a great poem, great as any in our American literature, and like Milton's "Lycidas" a poem to serve as a test by which to distinguish the true lover of poetry. Seldom before had Lanier sung so passionately and with such beauty of phrase and rhythm and with such conviction as he did here, nor was he to do so again. In comparison with the largely conceived "Sunrise" two poems that Lanier published in 1881—a new version of "Eternity in Time"[45] and "A Sunrise Song"[46]—seem feeble and of little consequence. Into the longer poem he had put all the strength illness had left him; to poetry he had little left to give.

CHAPTER TWENTY-ONE

A ROPE THROWN OUT

§ I

FAILING though his strength was, dying even then as we know him to have been, Lanier began the preparation of the lectures to be delivered as his third course of lectures at Johns Hopkins. A few he wrote out himself, but as his strength grew less he dictated the others to his wife. The excitement created by his impatience to begin the course caused a false appearance of improvement in his health, but on the day he first ventured out to test himself for the approaching task, there was an abrupt and complete change. Too weak now to walk, he had to be driven to and from the lecture hall in a closed carriage, and he had to sit while he read his notes: it was unthinkable that he should stand. Sometimes to those who heard him it seemed as if his life would go out even as he read, and they listened, we are told, with a sort of fascinated terror, wondering, fearing . . . Afterwards, in the carriage bearing him home, as he sank back exhausted on the pillows, the struggle for breath increasing, it seemed to Mrs. Lanier as if the end were truly at hand.[1] Slowly, undeniably, he was dying, and these lectures, buoyant though they are, like all his lectures, with optimism and with faith in the future, and revealing no signs of weakening health, are his testament and his farewell.

The title that Lanier himself gave the course was "From Aeschylus to George Eliot: Twelve Studies in the Modern English Novel as a Development of the Greek Drama,"[2] but the course was probably known from the first even to those who attended the lectures as "The English Novel" or "The Development of the Modern English Novel."[3] It is important, however, that we remember Lanier's own title for the course, for it suggests better than any other could the thesis he sought to develop—the development of personality in literary art—and the intimate connection of these lectures with the lectures on Shakspere and on Shakspere and Chaucer. This course was to treat in a general way the thesis developed specifically in relation to Shakspere in the others, and was designed, undoubtedly, less as a new course than as a continuation of the other two.

As originally planned the course was to have consisted of twenty lectures, but President Gilman, alarmed by the rapid exhaustion of Lanier's strength, had tactfully suggested that a shorter course would fit in better with the whole schedule of university lectures, and the number of lectures had been reduced to twelve. The change in scheme explains, Mrs. Lanier suggests, Lanier's failure to develop in detail certain subjects which he stated in his first lecture that he would develop, but the number of lectures had been reduced before the course was started; nor is Mrs. Lanier's further statement that the death of George Eliot "occurring in the middle of the course further modified the plan by urging Mr. Lanier to concentrate upon her work the remaining six lectures"[4] to be accepted, for the reason that George Eliot had died December 22, 1880, before the course was begun, and it is inconceivable that Lanier should have remained long unaware of the fact. As one reads the lectures and notes Lanier's strong expressions of disgust for the "classic" English novelists—Richardson, Fielding, Smollett, and Sterne— and his grudging admission of even Thackeray's qualities, one is persuaded to believe that it was with disgust that he suddenly decided to devote no more time to "this muck of the classics" or even to the other modern novels he had announced for discussion—Henry James's *American*, Howells's *Undiscovered Country*, Cable's *Grandissimes*, and Collins's *Moonstone*[2]—but to devote the remaining lectures and the last of his strength to a final glorification of his adored George Eliot, whom he admiringly ranked as the greatest of all English artists, greater even than Shakspere. Whatever single title we give the lectures proves inadequate to describe the contents exactly: the subtitle that Mrs. Lanier gave the revised edition of the lectures, published in 1897, "A Study in the Development of Personality," is perhaps most satisfactory. The lectures are not properly integrated. Only the idea that the modern personality, developing in an atmosphere of science as well as of art, is infinitely richer than the personality of ancient man, holds the lectures together at all.

§ 2

THE FIRST lecture of the course, announced for Wednesday, January 12, 1881, had, because of Lanier's health, to be postponed for two weeks, until January 26. In it Lanier states that whereas in his first course at Johns Hopkins he had discussed verse-form in general and analytically, he now intends to discuss a prose-form—the novel—in particular, and sympathetically, "from the point of view of literary art rather than of literary science"; and that he intended doing this by tracing certain lines of thought: first, "the enormous growth in personality which our time reveals when compared, for instance, with the time of Æschylus"; second, the simultaneous rise of modern music, modern science, and the novel; and, third, the necessity of "the wonderfully free and elastic form of the modern novel" for the clearer expression of the complexities of the modern personality. Fourthly, he added, he intended giving "copious readings from some of the most characteristic modern novels, in illustration of the general principles brought forward." The rest of the first lecture he devoted to a discussion of early English prose and to a discussion of reasons why it developed so much later than English poetry.

The second lecture begins with a discussion of literary form and an impassioned defense of form which, though fairly elaborate, can be stated briefly. Viewed scientifically or from the point of view of orthodox Christianity, the world today represents a reduction to form of chaos; in fact the whole universe is really "a great congeries of forms of motion," as the study of the atom has taught us, and the substance of things is not to be understood without a knowledge of the forms. The knowledge of these forms is Science; the creation of beautiful forms is Art; and Religion is "the faith in the infinite Form-giver and in that infinity of forms which many things lead us to believe as existing, but existing beyond any present correlative capacities of our senses. . . . Life is the control of all these forms to the satisfaction of our human needs." Form in poetry is essential, in spite of Whitman's arguments to the contrary, and study of the science of English verse is a study of the forms in which English verse has been and may be written. So also is form in prose essential, for "the relation of prose to verse is *not* the relation of the *formless* to the *formal;* it is the relation of *more forms* to *fewer forms*. It is

Sidney Lanier. Bronze bust at the Johns Hopkins University. Modeled by Ephraim Keyser nine months before Lanier's death.

this relation which makes prose a *freer* form than verse."

But hardly is the second lecture with this defense of form as form under way before Lanier is off his subject, and almost the whole of the second and third lectures is devoted to a general discussion of the relation of science to art, and to a specific consideration of the theories "(1) that science will destroy all poetry, all novel-writing and all imaginative work generally; (2) that science (as Walt Whitman would have it) will simply destroy the old imaginative product in its stead; and (3) that science will absorb into itself all imaginative effort (as Zola believes) so that every novel will be merely the plain unvarnished record of a scientific experiment in passion," repulsively unbeautiful. The lectures in which Lanier discussed these three theories must be for many readers the most interesting of the series. In contradiction of the first theory he cites the interest in science of Tennyson, Goethe, George Eliot, and Shakspere; but in discussing the second theory, Lanier goes off on still another tangent, and instead of refuting Whitman's prediction that the poetry of the future would be democratic poetry and different in form from the poetry of Tennyson and his contemporaries, Lanier discusses Whitman's theory of democracy and opposes to the brawny democrat of Whitman's poetry the democrat of his own conception, a democrat of weak biceps but of strong purpose and brave resolve. These passages are excellent as courageous, candid but unbiased, criticism of Whitman, and excellent too for what they reveal of Lanier, but we have wandered far from the topics of primary consideration, and we have yet to consider—and refute—the theories of Zola before we can proceed, in the fourth lecture, to a discussion of Lanier's first thesis, that there has been a tremendous growth in personality from the time of Æschylus to the time of George Eliot.

In two lectures—the fourth and the fifth—Lanier does develop this thesis, and develop it ably. He shows in a series of well chosen passages from the *Prometheus Bound* of Æschylus that there was no indication of growth in personality in the gods or in men and no realization on the part of Æschylus or his Prometheus of the richness and infinity of the variety in every man's ego. If objection is made it must be that the solitary example of one Greek play cannot be accepted as sufficient study of the ancient drama. In Shelley's *Prometheus Unbound*, Lanier finds, there is an "intenser instinct of personality" and a modern devotion to detail, but the "modernness"—the word is Lanier's—is unconscious, for Shelley "was penetrated with modern ideas . . . as a boy would be, crudely, overmuch, and with a constant tendency to be extravagant and illogical." It is Bayard Taylor's *Prince Deukalion* that Lanier chooses as an example of conscious modernness in the detailed wealth of description, of nature and of human nature, and in the realization of the as yet incompletely achieved growth in spiritual stature of man. Modernness, Lanier asserts, is the realization of human individuality, and progress, he implies, is in proportion to the development and appreciation of individuality in human society. Plato would have suppressed individuality;[5] Zola ignores it in forcing man to submit without reserve to the commands of science; and Whitman—if we are to believe the interpretation that Lanier gives the 32d section of the "Song of Myself" rather than Lanier's previous assertion, in his letter to Whitman, of Whitman's emphasis on personality—scorns it, believing that animals in their passivity know a contentment that man, toiling with the activity that his personality permits and demands of him, does not know. Lanier, jealous of his individuality and dreading the emptiness of a Nirvâna, the conception of which he now correctly understands, and unwilling also to admit the possible extinction of God's chief handiwork, the human soul, rebels against such doctrines. He concludes: "I have been somewhat earnest—I fear tediously so—upon this matter, because I have seen what seem the greatest and most mischievous errors concerning it, receiving the stamp of men who usually think with clearness and who have acquired just authority in many premises." But Lanier's apology is unnecessary; one does not expect a preacher to apologize for the passionate sincerity of his sermon.

In the sixth lecture Lanier does discuss, though briefly—and with little of "the concrete instance" that he repeatedly promises—his second thesis, one presented long before in *Tiger-Lilies*, that modern science and the modern novel begin simultaneously. But after devoting some twenty pages to the discussion of ancient and modern science—with an impressive array of famous names—and six pages to ancient and modern music, Lanier dismisses the novel with the paragraph: "And so finally, with the first English novel of Richardson in 1739-40, we have completed our glance at the simultaneous birth of modern science, modern music, and the modern novel."

In the eighth lecture, after a lecture devoted exclusively to George Eliot and her message, he does return to discuss briefly the "classic" novels, but, with his standards of sense impressions, his inability to distinguish between the surface impression of a book and the deeper, less concrete impression that comes from subtler, less obvious forces within it, he has no praise for any novels that appeared before *The Vicar of Wakefield*, and little for those that appeared thereafter until the time of George Eliot. The novelists between Goldsmith and Eliot, even Scott and Dickens—whom he admitted he liked, and thought worth reading—are hardly more than mentioned by name, though three pages are given to an entertaining discussion of Erasmus Darwin's absurd poem, *The Loves of the Plants*.

But the chapters on George Eliot (his third thesis, concerning the modern novel as the typical vehicle of modern literary art, he never develops except indirectly; and the only extract from a modern novel by an author other than George Eliot is a passage from Henry James's *Daisy Miller*), are much more than merely entertaining. To a generation that has forgotten George Eliot or that remembers her as the author of a book of required reading in high school, there could be no better introduction to her full-blooded, vigorous work than Lanier's praise of her. To speak of her work as a rose the roots of which reach into "the unsavory muck" of the eighteenth-century novel, or to say in Tennysonian metaphor that the publication of *Scenes from Clerical Life* came "with no more noise than that of a snow-flake falling on snow" is of course not to win—by style at least—the modern reader, either to George Eliot's work or to Lanier's criticism of it. Nor has the course of events since 1881 convinced the reader of today of the essential goodness of man or that love is "the organic idea of moral order," the lesson that Lanier finds most encouraging in George Eliot's work. But when Lanier discusses her work in detail he almost convinces one that she was what he believed her, the greatest of English, indeed to him of all novelists, greater than Dickens in that while she burned with an even greater intolerance of the evil in society, she did not like him describe a corrupt society satirically and from a purely destructive point of view, but with the "loving or constructive view" which the great artist must ever hold. She is even greater than Shakspere, Lanier asserts, for Shakspere never drew a true repentance while George Eliot (working in the freer form of the novel, to

27

be sure) created many characters who, like Gwendolen Harleth, undergo a complete metamorphosis of character. George Eliot, according to Lanier, more than any other of our writers, understood the infinite variety of the human ego and believed in the possibility of remolding and completely changing human personality.

What Lanier, with his interest in science, would have made out of George Eliot's novels after mastering the principles of modern psychology is a matter for speculation. Lanier was quite capable of misunderstanding scientific principles, as when he asserted that "many of George Eliot's characters appear like living objections to the theory of evolution. How could you, according to the theory, evolve the moral stoutness and sobriety of Adam Bede, for example, from . . . his drunken father and querulous mother?" The discoveries of modern psychology suggest that Shakspere's characters are more true to life than George Eliot's are without proving the truth of Lanier's contention that the world today is better able to understand and to appreciate repentance as depicted in art, with its implication that man is fundamentally more moral now than he was in Shakspere's day. But certainly there is truth in Lanier's contention that the literature of today reveals more love of man for man than did the literature of the past. Putting aside the question of George Eliot's greatness as a novelist, we can agree with Lanier that a "stimulus of human love . . . radiates from all her works." It is for this stimulus that we should read her novels.

"In love, and love only," he had asserted, "can great work that not only pulls down but that builds be done; it is love and love only that is truly constructive in art." "And in life," he would have added. In the last lecture of his last lecture course Lanier asserts once more, as he had in *Tiger-Lilies*, his faith in love as the source of all happiness. Through the entire body of Lanier's work we can trace this idea of the necessity to love, but the meaning of love has now become spiritualized and extended greatly. It is not earthly love, no longer even the love of Christ's commandment, nor Pauline charity. Nor is it, as Josiah Royce explained Lanier's teaching, love that denies the existence of evil. Rather is it love as the culmination of his theory of the etherealization constantly taking place in man, love as understanding tolerance, scientific truth, the solution of opposites, the one sure expression of the divine will, Christian love made into a philosophy and offered as a rational system for the solution of all problems that confront the individual and society. Indeed, Lanier has grown so far as to assert that of Christ's two commandments—to love the Lord with all our heart and to love our neighbor as ourself—the second is the essential one. If we love our neighbor whole-heartedly, and grow in that love, our personality may well be trusted to settle for itself the status of its relation to the Lord.

§ 3

WHEN LANIER wrote as he writes in the best parts of *The English Novel*, well and wisely, he invites comparison with Emerson. The separate lectures, often as apparently formless and as carelessly planned as the essays of Emerson, are worthy of more attention than they have received. *The English Novel* as a whole does not bear comparison with certain later essays on the art of fiction. Perhaps, indeed, no one lecture is wholly of value. Lanier's study is not a technical or an analytical one. There is, in the discussion of the novel as a form, much that is actually valueless. Lanier failed in making subtle differentiations: he confuses truth and beauty hopelessly; he reveals a distorting preference for the mystical to the actual; he lets the enthusiastic idealism in his thinking distort facts for him—as when he describes the first appearance of Effie in *Silas Marner*, a ray of sunlight illuminating her head, though George Eliot had set the scene at twilight with snow and clouds. But Lanier's work was pioneer work: he was the first American to indicate the necessity for the study of the novel as a form of literature, worthy of serious thought. And passages in Lanier's volume, little essays complete in themselves, reveal a keen critical insight and a high purpose. What he said of Whitman, of Shakspere, and of Shelley is well and kindly said, and worth reading. One cannot read Lanier's critical writings without feeling a challenge and accepting it; often a reconsideration of the work of an author in the light of his comments will lead one to agree with Lanier.

This is more true, perhaps, in *The English Novel*, of the comments on Whitman, Shakspere, and Shelley than it is of his comments on George Eliot, to whom Lanier gives greater space, making her glorification almost a predetermined result. For in speaking of George Eliot his enthusiasm weakens his arguments; it is too apparently excessive, and comes not from analysis but from infatuation which carries him to the point of inconsistency. His criticism of her is, moreover, too much conditioned by the spirit of the time in which George Eliot wrote and Lanier lectured: it is Victorian criticism of a Victorian novelist, and our standards today are different. But to call George Eliot and Sidney Lanier Victorian is to condemn neither, and in the work of Lanier we have the Victorian spirit, with much of its blindness and many of its limitations, but with all of its candor and courageous optimism. *The English Novel*, a series of lectures capable of stimulating the mind of anyone who reads them, has been too quickly forgotten, and in our college courses on modern literature—courses of which Lanier's course was one of the earliest prototypes—it is too readily ignored.

Unfortunately the publication of these lectures came under circumstances more inauspicious than those that attended the later publication of the lectures on Shakspere. The manuscript was prepared for publication shortly after Lanier's death by his friend Professor William Hand Browne of Johns Hopkins at a time when Mrs. Lanier was too ill to be consulted on any point. The mistakes of the first edition, Mrs. Lanier wrote in her preface to the revised second edition, resulted "some from the copyist's unfamiliarity with the feeble handwriting and others from the editor's uncertainty regarding Mr. Lanier's final wishes at various points." But a careful examination of the two texts reveals that most of the omissions from the earlier edition of any significance or importance are passages in which Lanier made it perfectly clear that, differ as he did from Whitman, he admired the poet and found delight in his poetry. One paragraph which is found in the second but not in the first edition repeats almost verbatim Lanier's letter to Whitman written three years previously, but one may be forgiven for reprinting it; and one may be certain that Lanier not only out of justice to Whitman but out of his regard for literary accuracy and his solicitude for truth would wish it. It throws new light on what Lanier said in taking issue with Whitman's prophecy concerning the poetry of the future to know that he had prefaced his discussion with the statement: "Here let me first carefully disclaim and condemn all 'that flippant and sneering tone which dominates so many discussions of Whitman. While I differ from him utterly as to every principle of artistic procedure; while he seems to me the most stupendously mistaken man in all history as to what constitutes true democ-

cracy, and the true advance of art and man; while I am immeasurably shocked at the sweeping invasions of those reserves
which depend on the very personality I have so much insisted
upon, and which the whole consensus of the ages has considered
more and more sacred with every year of growth in delicacy;
yet, after all these prodigious allowances, I owe some keen
delights to a certain combination of bigness and naïvety which
make some of Whitman's passages so strong and taking, and
indeed, on the one occasion when Whitman has abandoned his
theory of formlessness and written in form he has made *My
Captain, O my Captain* [*sic*] surely one of the most tender and
beautiful poems in any language."[6]

In his prefatory note to the 1883 edition Professor Browne
admitted "the omission of a few local and occasional allusions."
The examination of textual differences seems to indicate that
Browne suppressed Lanier's favorable allusions to Whitman because he thought to spare Lanier the shame of having defended
the author of *Leaves of Grass*. The saintly Lanier and the vile
Whitman! But the difference between the two is chiefly a matter
of emphasis, and the contrast exists only in the minds of idolators
of the one and the too rabid defenders of the other. The passages
on Whitman are among the best in *The English Novel* and Mrs.
Lanier's restoration of them in the 1897 edition should have
alone been sufficient to have called for a revaluation of the
importance of Lanier as a critic.

§ 4

BUT IN *The English Novel* as in the Shakspere lectures it is not
so much Lanier the critic as Lanier the man who interests us.
And if we remember as we read that within five months from
the time of the last lecture Lanier's earthly career was to end,
we must inevitably be the more impressed by the tremendous
bravery of the man who, pale of face, sat "not very reposefully
in his professorial armchair" reading "from dainty slips of MS.
in a clear, penetrating voice full of subtlest comprehension but
painfully and often interrupted by a cough" his testament on
truth and beauty while his audience listened with a kind of
terror, wondering if he would leave the lecture hall alive.[7] He
is the democrat of his own description, boldly proclaiming the
importance of man as man, whether he be weak or strong, poor
or wealthy, powerful or obscure; tracing the development of

personality and individuality from the time of the Greeks to his own period, in which, it seemed to him, some true understanding of Christ's message had been achieved.[8] He is the type of democrat without whom a republic cannot be built, for "a republic is the government of the spirit; a republic depends upon the self-control of each member; you cannot make a republic out of muscles and prairies and Rocky mountains: republics are made of the spirit."

A visitor at one of his lectures, Frances E. Willard, president of the Women's Christian Temperance Union, spoke to him of her enjoyment of his lecture and of a "mission" she was about to undertake among the Negroes of the South. "We are all striving for one end" was Lanier's comment on her proposed work, "and that is to develop and ennoble the humanity of which we form a part."[7]

CHAPTER TWENTY-TWO

ASPIRO DUM EXPIRO

§ 1

IF WE ACCEPT the distinction that Lanier himself made between poetry and verse, between technic and inspiration, and extend it to make poetry mean the expression in rhythmical but not necessarily metrical language of high and beautiful thoughts, of imagination and emotions, we find some of Lanier's best poetry of the last years in his prose work and in the little fragments in which he noted ideas to be elaborated at times of greater leisure into poems. In long passages in the Shakspere lectures; in his description of the "gracious land" of the South in his essay, "The New South"; in his lectures on the development of personality, we find poetic thoughts expressed in rhythmic prose of a higher order than the more labored, cloying prose of *Tiger-Lilies* or the early essays. Experience had matured him; hardships had developed a keener sense of reality and of appropriateness; and approaching death, perhaps, or wisdom, had brought spiritual calm. In Lanier's last letter to Hayne he wrote, *à propos* a poem by Hayne in the current issue of a southern magazine, "I fancy that I perceive a *clarified* quality in your later verse which shows a distinct growth in you. The plane of art seems higher and quieter, and the air purer." So in Lanier's poetry also, the art is higher and quieter, but the quietness is the quietness of ecstasy, tremulous with vision.

But there is also to be discerned in Lanier's work of these years evidence of impatience, the impatience that comes from frustration. "If only there were more time, how superbly fine and beautiful I could make this," one imagines him saying of all that he wrote; or else, in bitterness, "Here is art, and none will admit it."[1] So great, indeed, was the impatience that finally he remonstrated with God himself. In a poem outline that must belong to the last year of his life he cried:

O Lord, if thou wert needy as I,
If thou should'st come to my door as I to thine.
If thou hungered so much as I
For that which belongs to the spirit,
For that which is fine and good,
Ah, friend, for that which is fine and good,
I would give it to thee if I had power.
For that which I want is, first, bread—
Thy decree, not my choice, that bread must be first;
Then music, then some time out of my struggle for bread
     to write my poems;
Then to put out of care Henry and Robert, whom I love.
O my God, how little would put them out of care!

But God seemed as unwilling, or as impotent, to help him as man—man, in the guise of editors, to buy his work and, in the guise of doctors, to cure him of his disease. Still he worked on, undertaking a variety of tasks the very list of which, included in a letter written sometime during the spring of 1881, is audacious: "My lectures take all my time, and I cannot write you. I had not thought they would be so laborious, but I find the numerous illustrations of antique thought and habit require a great deal of research, and each lecture is a good week's work for a well man. And when I contemplate the other things I am waiting to do, many of them half done, to-wit: (1) my 'Hymns of the Marshes,' nearly complete, whereof you have the 'Marshes of Glynn' and the little song of 'Trees and the Master'; (2) my 'Clover and Other Poems,' now quite ready for the press; (3) my 'Credo and Other Poems,' a thick volume, all in memoranda, ready to be written out in a few weeks; (4) my 'Choral Symphony,' for chorus and orchestra, being my 'Psalm of the West,' with music; (5) my 'Symphony Life,' in four movements—first, childhood; second, youth; third, manhood; fourth, old age; (6) my 'Symphony of the Plantation,' being the old and the new life of the negro, in music; (8) my 'Girl's Paston Letters,' now in my desk, half prepared; (9) my 'Boy's Monstrelet,' also in desk, ready to arrange; (10) my 'Boy's Gesta Romanorum'—when I contemplate these, now lying upon my hands in actual forms of one sort or another, without daring to think of books merely projected, I fall to wondering whether I have any business or right to wait, whether I had not better go and borrow five

thousand, ten thousand dollars—which could so easily be repaid
in five years (the copyrights of the 'Boy's Froissart' and 'King
Arthur' would have done it if I had not been obliged to sell
them), and put myself in heaven at once, with nothing but
poetry to write and two years of freedom from slavery to butcher
and baker."[2]

§ 2

A QUARTER of a century after Lanier's death the marsh hymns
that he had completed were brought together in a single volume,
enriched by photographs taken near Brunswick, Georgia, in the
marshes of his poems.[3] But surely to "Sunrise," "Individuality,"
"Marsh Song—At Sunset," and "The Marshes of Glynn" should
have been added "A Ballad of Trees and the Master," planned
as the prayer whispered by the leaves to come after line 53
of "Sunrise," "Pray me a myriad prayer." And to these poems
might also have been added "Between Dawn and Sunrise,"[4] a
brief draft for a hymn of the marshes found among Lanier's
papers after his death, and one of the *Poem Outlines*[5] undoubtedly
intended also as a draft for a marsh hymn. In all these poems,
even if only in a single phrase, is to be found the suggestion of
space, of wide horizons and great sweeps of sea and land, that
is most characteristic of Lanier, and of which the sea-marsh is
fitting symbol.

The poems to have been included in the volume to be called
"Clover and Other Poems" are all given in the collected *Poems*
issued in 1884. The substance of "Credo and Other Poems" is
indicated by some fifteen of the poem outlines published in
1908.[6] Like the poem "Remonstrance," the poems in "Credo"
were to be attacks on orthodoxy and on creeds, an expression
of Lanier's life-long attack on the stultifying formalities of worship
and of belief. The other works listed in the letter probably never
achieved more form than "Credo and Other Poems"; of these
works no fragments have been published, if preserved. What
fragments remain of other schemes for prose and poetry that
were in his mind in the last years have been published in *Poem
Outlines*.

Not all the fragments collected in this volume are "poem
outlines." Some, as we have seen,[7] are but the seeds of poems;
others, it is true, are poems in embryo—the form already developing;[8] still others are poems in the final stages before com-

position is finished—some stanzas already developed in meter and rhyme, some lines perfectly polished.[9] One certainly, "What am I without thee?"[10] seems a completed poem, though composed in a manner more characteristic of Whitman than of Lanier. But many of the fragments are epigrams,[11] of which only one is in verse;[12] some are ideas for development in prose rather than in verse;[13] two are merely quotations, copied for future use;[14] many are expressions of ideas in finished prose, leaves from a diary never brought together, or paragraphs dropped from the lectures.[15] The fragments gathered in the volume are said to date from all periods of Lanier's life, but most come surely from the last months. In some of these we find him threshing out to a final solution the problem of selfhood—the individuality of man, sacred and not to be violated by union with other self, or with God.[16] And in the last there is evidence of the ultimate, tranquil acceptance of universal human experience. The song of a bird in the hills at daybreak fills the world of light with such beauty of music that there is left neither "Heat, or dry longing, or any indictment of God, or question."[17] Mundane facts no longer have significance: "Birth and death were before aught else that we know was";[18] from one we go to the other, and what availeth all our disputation and confusion?[19]

§ 3

THE LECTURE course was over by the middle of April,[20] but it seemed as if each day a special miracle had been wrought to enable Lanier to accomplish his work. Often unable to speak above a whisper in the mornings, when the lectures began his voice, clear and resonant, could be heard by the farthest away listener. At the end of April he went of necessity to New York to confer with his publishers concerning the publication of the additional volumes in the "Boy's Library of Legend and Chivalry." His health was now so bad, however, and he was so feeble that Mrs. Lanier wrote to his former student, W. S. Pratt, now in New York, saying that her husband lacked the strength required for the trip, begging him as one her husband loved to meet him and to watch over him as best he could. "I found him at the St. Denis," Professor Pratt wrote later, "and we had dinner together. I now know how completely he deceived me as to his condition. With the intensity and exaltation often

Mary Day Lanier. From a photograph made shortly after Lanier's death.
Courtesy of Mr. Sidney Lanier Eason.

characteristic of the consumptive, he led me to think that he was only slightly ailing, was gay and versatile as ever, insisted on going somewhere for the evening 'to hear some music,' and absolutely demanded to exercise through the evening the rights of host in a way that baffled my inexperience completely. Only just as I left him did he let fall a single remark that I later saw showed how severe and unfortunate, probably, was the strain of it all."[21]

Eight years before, when he left San Antonio, Lanier had been told that he had at best five years to live if he persisted in leaving Texas; and he had decided that he would rather have five years among libraries, music, and friends than ten or twenty years without these things in Texas; and for eight years now he had enjoyed them and fought off his disease. His bold effort to deny his true condition and to prolong the years of grace still further had not succeeded, and now at last he was to drink death's stirrup-cup. Within a few days Mrs. Lanier had to be called to New York, so serious was her husband's condition. The doctor pronounced tent life in a pure, high climate to be the last hope. Plans for spending the summer at Rockingham Springs, Virginia, were hastily cancelled, and Clifford Lanier was informed of his brother's condition and asked to make arrangements for camping near Asheville, North Carolina, in the Alleghany Mountains in which Lanier had spent that memorable summer of 1860.

Before proceeding to the camp, however, it was necessary to stop in Baltimore and there Lanier called on President Gilman to say goodbye but also to make arrangements for his lectures the next winter. As once before when he had been ordered to Florida, he could not believe he might die before his books were written. The brief interview with Gilman in the middle of May, 1881, is typical of his life. "His emaciated form could scarcely walk across the yard from the carriage to the door," Gilman wrote. " 'I am going to Asheville, N. C.,' he said, 'and I am going to write an account of that region as a railroad guide.[22] It seems as if the good Lord always took care of me. Just as the doctors had said that I must go to that mountain region, the publishers gave me a commission to prepare a book.' 'Goodbye,' he added, and I supported his tottering steps to the carriage door, never to see his face again."[23]

§ 4

ON RICHMOND HILL, three miles from Asheville, the tents were pitched and floored under the supervision of Clifford Lanier; the camp was named Camp Robin after the youngest Lanier child, now almost a year old. Lanier began immediately to collect material for the guidebook. On the monthly salary that the commission provided he and his wife and baby were able to live quite comfortably. Bread-and-meat work had proved a Samaritan's gift. The writing of the book would be easy, allowing time for other matters. The manuscripts of the *Mabinogion* and the *Percy* could be finished now (they were, indeed, sent to the publishers during the first month in camp); he could prepare lectures for the course of readings in the less familiar plays of Shakspere announced for "early in the next academic year" at Johns Hopkins.[24] There was time too for the things that interested him beyond their remunerative value—for playing the flute (the flute playing that helped his lungs so much and quieted his heart) and for scientific investigation. He wrote President Gilman requesting the use of scientific apparatus from Johns Hopkins that he might study "the so-called no-frost belt on the side of Tryon mountain."[25] Best of all, there was time for poetry—but the thoughts, the conceptions, the rhythmic phrases came in such profusion that none was finished: he could not, before the flood of his inspiration, conquer and restrain in the channels of form any part of it; and he could only jot down or dictate to his wife the outlines that, he was still sure, he would one day develop.

We have in the volume of poem outlines notes for a volume to be called "Hymns of the Mountains, and Other Poems,"[26] but far more interesting are a number of uncollected ones dating from these last days.[27] The title given to one little group holds for all. They are "Songs Against Death," for each poem reveals the tremendous struggle of life to conquer, the effort of the will to live supporting and giving strength to the dying body. In one he sings:

> Death lieth still in the way of life
> Like as a stone in the way of a brook;
> I will sing against thee, Death, as the brook does,
> I will make thee into music which does not die.

In another, with a realization that death, whatever it may
mean, cannot mean Nirvâna:

> As the woodpecker taps in a spiral quest
> From the root to the top of the tree,
> Then flies to another tree,
> So have I bored into life to find what lay therein,
> And now it is time to die,
> And I will fly to another tree.

But still he could not believe that the time had actually come
for him to die. "Never think I shall die," he said one day to
his wife. "Give me a stimulant to bring me back when you
see me fail."[28] So certain indeed seemed his improvement at
one time that his brother returned to Alabama, though in July
Lanier's father and step-mother came to join the encampment,
to be of what help they could.

The improvement, however, had been but temporary, and as
weeks passed and no real improvement came it was decided to
test the lower altitude and milder climate of Polk County.
Accordingly, on August 4, Lanier and his wife started on a
carriage journey across the mountains, Lanier reclining in his
invalid's chair which was fastened to the carriage. In Asheville
Mrs. Lanier had found friends of her parents whom she had
not seen for twenty years, Mr. and Mrs. George Westfeldt, and
now, on their way to Polk County, to give Lanier a rest from
the fatigue of the journey and to cement the friendship, they
stopped for a visit with the Westfeldts at their home, "Rugby
Grange," in the valley of the French Broad River. Westfeldt
had come as a boy from Sweden to America and had made a
fortune as a merchant in Mobile, New Orleans, and New York;
after the Civil War he and his family had lived in Europe and
had only recently returned to the United States. Meeting Westfeldt for the first time in Asheville Lanier had instinctively
recognized in the older man the kinship that wisdom gives to
great souls. To the large soul of the maturer, calmer man he
felt his own soul irresistibly drawn. "I have been searching all
my life for the father of my spirit," he had said to his wife, "and
I have only found him now."[29] At the home of the Westfeldts,
such a home as, long ago, he had described in *Tiger-Lilies*,
Lanier felt himself to be living at last the ideal existence of that

early dream; and we have a picture of him coming in at sunset and walking down the long southern drawing room to a large western window where he stood looking across the valley to Mount Pisgah, and then, as the sunset glow deepened into twilight, sitting down at the piano with his face to the window, pouring out his soul in sorrow and joy and pain and hope and triumph. It was the last time his illness allowed him so much exertion.[30]

§ 5

THIRTY miles farther on by carriage they went, over the mountains to Lynn in a sheltered valley where the climate is tempered by a curious current of warm air that moves along the slope of Tryon Mountain. Here, at Lynn, the final fever attacked him, and there was no going back. He himself must have known that it was to be the end. Clifford was summoned by telegraph, and he and his father moved the equipment of Camp Robin to Lynn. If it was now only a matter of time, Lanier was ready. Had he not sung:

> Look out, Death: I am coming.
> Art thou not glad? what talks we'll have,
> What memories of old battles.
> Come, bring the bowl, Death; I am thirsty.[31]

And had he not written in a little note on *Hamlet:* "Death, my God! it is the sweetest and dearest of all the angels to him who understands."[32]

But even now he rallied again, took interest in his work, dictated some poem outlines,[33] spoke of rewriting *Tiger-Lilies*, talked of his college days at Oglethorpe. Looking back to that time Lanier may well have asked if life had been worth the effort, and answering that question and restating his faith in the god of nature, he paid tribute to the man whose influence had meant so much, his teacher, James Woodrow.[34] He was, Lanier said, the strongest and most valuable stimulus of his youth, and he added: "I am more indebted to Dr. Woodrow than to any living man, for shaping my mental attitude toward nature and life. His spirit and method had a formative influence on my thought and fancy in all my literary work."[35]

Clifford Lanier, deceived by hope and pressed by cares of

business, planned to return to Montgomery. On August 24 he said goodbye. Lanier sat astride the easy-loping pony that, with the brief recovery of strength he had begun to ride daily, and his brother went away again believing that an indomitable will was once more triumphing over death. Five days later Lanier's father and his step-mother departed also. Only his wife remained with him.

The next day, August 30, there came a change. Lanier knew for certain now that in spite of all his brave attempts to fight off death, he was dying. Perhaps indeed he was weary of fighting, and lacked the will to keep on. But the thought of death could bring neither regret nor sorrow. Once he had declared "Birth is but the folding of our wings";[36] the unfolding of them would be a wonderful experience. And yet, while life lasted, he would sing. Feeble and dying, too weak to hold a pencil, but still awake to every emotion that sunrise had to offer, he dictated the words:

> I was the earliest bird awake,
> It was a while before dawn, I believe,
> And somehow I saw round the world,
> And the eastern mountain top did not hinder me.
> And I knew the dawn by my heart, not by mine eyes.

It was his last poem.

A few days later Mrs. Lanier sent a letter by stage across the mountain advising the Westfeldts of her husband's alarming relapse, and on September 6 young Gustaf Westfeldt rode the thirty miles on horse-back, his saddle bags packed with medicine and provisions, to see how Lanier was.[37] He found that the tent-camp had been abandoned, and Lanier had been moved to a neighboring farmhouse.[38] He was far gone, propped in an adjustable invalid chair which had been wheeled to the window of his room, which commanded a full view of the valley, then in the full luxuriance of late summer. His breath came feebly, and he spoke only by snatches, but he talked cheerfully, and most of all of George Westfeldt. "Send him my 'Sunrise,'" he said, "that he may know how entirely we are one in thought."[29]

§ 6

Young Westfeldt stayed that night at Lynn, and the next morning, Wednesday, September 7, 1881, a warm morning bright with full sunshine, he carried a few morning glories, picked from the porch of the farmhouse, into Lanier's room. They were his favorite flower, Lanier said, thanking Westfeldt, and—indicating the view from his window—he spoke of the profusion of nature in the valley. The view he called his compensation. The sunlight, flooding the valley and penetrating the room in spite of the swaying vines that screened the window, must have made him think of his own hymn of adoration and of the lines

> But I fear not, nay, and I fear not the thing to be done;
> I am strong with the strength of my lord the Sun:
> How dark, how dark soever the race that must needs be run,
> I am lit with the Sun.

He grew increasingly weaker, and Mrs. Lanier, remembering his admonition, offered him a drop of cordial. "I can't," he gasped, and did not speak again.[28] Young Westfeldt remained, but besides these three there was no one else in the room. Lanier died at 10 A. M.

CHAPTER TWENTY-THREE

ACHIEVEMENT

§ I

IT IS NOT without significance that Lanier's body was carried to Baltimore rather than to Macon for burial. Lynn, where he died, is much closer to Macon than to Baltimore. and in Macon his mother and his grandparents had been buried. But Macon he had left as in exile, and in Baltimore he had won recognition for his music, his poetry, and his scholarship, and there he had found the peace that victory over opposition gives. Either because of his own request, or at the command of Mrs. Lanier, who would have known his wishes respecting the matter, burial in Baltimore was decided upon, and to Baltimore the body was accompanied by Mrs. Lanier, Clifford Lanier, and the father, Robert Sampson Lanier.

It is also significant that Lanier, wishing even in death to perform some service to science, had requested that an autopsy be performed to determine the cause of the malady that had baffled so many physicians.[1] No autopsy was performed, however, and after funeral services at the Church of St. Michael and All Angels the body was carried to Greenwood Cemetery to be deposited temporarily in the Turnbull lot. But what was done then has been allowed to remain. The body lies where it was first buried,[2] and over the grave there was erected sixteen years ago a boulder of pink and black Georgia marble bearing on a bronze plaque his name and dates and the line from "Sunrise" "I am lit with the Sun," with a hieroglyph of a sunrise. So in Baltimore, the one in the heart of the city, the other in the quietness of the park-like cemetery, rest Edgar Allan Poe and Sidney Lanier, chief American poets from the South, and, with Whitman, greatest and best of our national poets.

§ 2

BUT LANIER, unlike Poe and Whitman, has not yet come into
his own. An excellent critical article by Mme. Blanc, packed
with translations of his best verse, appeared in the *Revue des Deux
Mondes* in 1898; an enthusiastic review of his poetry had appeared
in the London *Spectator* in 1890 and an appreciation by Richard
Le Gallienne appeared in the London *Academy* in 1900. His poems
and other of his works had already been brought out in English
editions and had called forth several favorable reviews in London periodicals, and his work was, it is said, admired by Robert
Bridges.³ But Lanier's name and his verse are not widely known
abroad, and even in America—in spite of some excellent critical
notices, which began to appear during his own lifetime—he is
known for what he was to only a partial extent, and he remains,
both as poet and as man, somewhere on the border line of obscurity and esteem, his qualities deeply appreciated by earnest
lovers of poetry, his name known to the public at large—even
to a part of the public that should know better—chiefly as that
of the author of a jingling poem about a southern river with
an Indian name.

That this should be so is due, perhaps, more than to anything
else, to external circumstances that are purely fortuitous. He
wrote poems so unlike the familiar poems of the day that critics
were without standards by which to judge his work. He left no
disciple, he founded no school. His direct and most evident
influence has been chiefly on minor poets. His fame among
American poets—a fame symbolized in 1900 by the inclusion of
his portrait with those of Bryant, Longfellow, Lowell, Whittier,
Emerson, Holmes, Poe, and Whitman in the frontispiece to
Stedman's *American Anthology*—has been eclipsed, on the one
hand, by the growth in appreciation of Whitman and the emerg-
ence from obscurity of Emily Dickinson and, on the other, by
the appearance of a bright legion of new singers. Lost between
two periods, younger by many years than any contemporary
poet worthy to be ranked with him save Emily Dickinson, older
in years, less understandable in manner, and cut off earlier in
his career than any poet of the next generation, Lanier is a
solitary figure in American letters—as solitary in his immortality
as he was in life, for he hungered in vain after the society and
friendship of literary men and women, belonged to no literary

circle, enjoyed the stimulating criticism and conversation of only such second-rate men of letters as Hayne and Taylor, and was during his creative years periodically exiled to dull frontier towns and uninteresting resorts by the fruitless search for health.

It is possible also that the circumstances under which his work has been collected and published have had much to do with the limited extent of popular appreciation of Lanier. His poems—on which his lasting fame must depend—have not passed into anthologies as freely as have those of other poets, and there has never been a volume of selected verse that should do for his fame what the volume of collected verse, with its mixture of good and bad, of finished poems and immature verse, could never do. And it is possible that much that has been written about Lanier has hindered rather than assisted the growth of appreciation of his work. Critical estimates, even the most generous, have not, by and large, been of a sort to win him admirers.

By most of his contemporaries and by the poets of the older generation he seems to have been ignored, and the volumes of memoirs and collected letters that appeared in the nineties and the first decade of the present century contained, with few exceptions, no references to him. The one contemporary figure of prominence among the writers of New York and New England who really admired Lanier and revealed a genuine understanding of what he was attempting—E. C. Stedman—admired "the man and his artistic spirit and mould" more than he did his work, and for that reason declined to edit the poems with a memoir.[4] Though the memoir prepared by Dr. William Hayes Ward is in many respects excellent, it is certainly inferior to what Stedman, in spite of his disagreement with Lanier's theories of poetry, would have written. It lacked, moreover, the power of attracting readers that anything written by as eminent a critic as Stedman would have had, and it emphasized in Lanier's work qualities neither demanded nor looked for in poetry today.

This latter fact is also true of several laudatory articles on Lanier by Thomas Wentworth Higginson, who fastened on him the epithet of "the Sir Galahad of American literature." A score of lesser critics have followed Ward and Higginson in presenting a picture of Lanier which, as our reading of his life has shown, is, without being absolutely untrue, certainly distorted by idealization. He was a normal, vital man, a splendid type of the nineteenth-century American, representing what our traditions at their best can develop.

For another erroneous, or mistaken, conception of Lanier, Stedman, who did so much for Lanier's fame in discussing critically his work, seems responsible. Answering Aldrich's objection to the inclusion of a portrait of Lanier instead of Halleck or Taylor in the frontispiece to his *American Anthology* Stedman wrote: "There are *seven* New England poets (including Bryant, and the engraved grave of Emerson) represented on my frontispiece and title-page. My book purports to be a *National* exhibit. Without Lanier, the South had only Poe. And Lanier's their next best boast among their dead poets; moreover, many lovers of poetry, of more or less 'importance in their day,' invest him and his work with ideal attributes. As for me, my view of him is carefully set forth in the 'Poets of America' and twice in the 'Nature of Poetry'—in the lectures which I delivered in Baltimore to his immediate adherents. In substance that view is precisely like yours—that he was essentially a musician. But he was an intellectual one, and also was a lyrist in words, as his shorter ballads, etc., show. Poe aimed at *melody* in verse, and succeeded. Now, Lanier *aimed* at 'harmony,' at 'thorough-bass': he tried to be a metrical Bach or Beethoven, to make verse do what *only* music can do. In this he ignored Lessing's law that no one of the fine arts *can* fully do the work of any other. Of course he failed, but if he had lived I think he would have done something fine, while trying after his impossible end—just as the alchemists founded chemistry while trying to transmute base metals into gold. *I* don't care for spasmodic and rhetorical measures, like those of Lanier's 'Sunrise,' etc. . . . But as a national anthologist I needed Lanier, and not Halleck or Taylor, for that frontispiece, and believe that you will conclude that my argument is sound."[4]

Such an attitude, generous as it was, has amounted to damning with faint praise. Stedman, in the decade and a half following the death of Lowell, was America's ranking man of letters, and his reputation gave his opinion—or, and worse, an abridgment of it—currency, and the conception of Lanier as a brilliant if somewhat one-sided man of letters, a misguided poet pursuing an unattainable ideal, writing verse to fit theories, and falling short of success in the very poem that posterity will undoubtedly consider his greatest, has passed into the textbooks on American

literature, by which the opinion of even the educated majority
is molded. It is still echoed—and Omond's saner pronounce-
ment on Lanier's theories, which necessitates a revaluation of
his poetry, is lost somewhere in the waves of the Atlantic.

Deliberate disparagements of the poet have also appeared—
and though Lanier has suffered from neglect, and from excessive
laudation, and from misconceptions of his character and that of
his work, he has suffered most from such inadequate and unsympathetic estimates as that of Edmund Gosse, who let himself
be prejudiced against Lanier by the effulgent admiration of the
Baltimore people for him. In an article contributed to the *Forum*
for October, 1888, Gosse asked the question "Has America
produced a great poet?" and proceeded to answer it by considering, in order, Lanier, Longfellow, Bryant, Emerson, and
Poe. Poe he thought the best of the lot; Whitman's existence and
poetry he practically ignored. Of Lanier he wrote:

"Reading [the poetry of Lanier] again with every possible
inclination to be pleased, I find a painful effort, a strain and
rage, the most prominent qualities in everything he wrote.
Never simple, never easy, never in one single lyric natural and
spontaneous for more than one stanza, always concealing his
barrenness and tameness by grotesque violence to language and
presposterous storm of sound, Lanier appears to me to be as
conclusively not a poet of genius as any ambitious man who
ever lived, labored, and failed. . . . I persist in thinking that
["Corn," "Sunrise," and "The Marshes of Glynn"] are elaborate and learned experiments by an exceedingly clever man,
and one who had read so much and felt so much that he could
simulate poetical expression with extraordinary skill. But of the
real thing, of the genuine traditional article, not a trace. . . .
I find him on all occasions substituting vague, cloudy rhetoric
for passion and tortured fancy for imagination, always striving,
against the grain, to say something prophetic and unparalleled,
always grinding away with infinite labor and sweat of his brow
to get that expressed which a real poet murmurs, almost unconsciously, between a sigh and a whisper."

§ 3

THERE HAVE, of course, been some excellent studies of Lanier,
impartial but generous, sane but appreciative. Unfortunately
few of these have achieved wide circulation, and none has

been quite of the sort to do for Lanier what inclusion of his verse in Stedman's anthology did—to rank him definitely and defiantly with the great, so that future studies might be in defense or in dispute of his position, but might dispense with the effort to reveal it. Two of the best of these studies, those of C. W. Kent and Dr. Clyde Furst, are lost in the files of learned periodicals; Baskervill's, included in a two-volume work on southern writers, has never become widely known; and Professor Mims's biography, because of the author's self-imposed limitations, stops short of an attempt to estimate Lanier's final place among men of letters. The best of all studies of Lanier is a study of the man, not of his work—the sketch of Lanier in Gamaliel Bradford's *American Portraits*. Perhaps the most sympathetically and generously appreciative estimate of his poetry is the too brief essay by John Macy in his *Spirit of American Literature*, a book curiously dated by the omission of any reference to Emily Dickinson and the single reference to Herman Melville, and by the spirited protest against esteem of Charles Brockden Brown and William Gilmore Simms to the neglect of Mark Twain.

Macy also protested against esteem of Bryant to the neglect of Lanier, and he sought to make up for the neglect of historians of American literature who had given a chapter to Bryant and only a page to Lanier by giving a chapter to Lanier and merely making mention of Bryant in the chapter as the author of the "Water Fowl," a fine poem by a lesser lyricist. As to Lanier's place in American literature, Macy entertained no doubts: "Three volumes of unimpeachable poetry have been written in America," he asserted, " 'Leaves of Grass,' the thin volume of Poe, and the poetry of Sidney Lanier. It is treading on treacherous negatives to say that there is not a fourth fit for their society; yet I believe that to make an adequate fourth one would have to assemble in an anthology the finest poems from . . . many gardens whose beauty is a splendid and consoling denial that the race of singers is dead or shall ever die till man dies." And some years later Macy made mention of Lanier in his *Story of the World's Literature*, in the last paragraph of the story: "After Whitman most American verse is an anticlimax. But any good anthology will contain some of the curiously compact and half-expressed verses—yet fully expressed in their mode—of Emily Dickinson; delicate elfin verses by Louise Guiney, . . . ; the 'homely' verses of James W. Riley; the poems of Thomas Bailey

Aldrich, with their thin excellence; and a poet much greater
potentially than his ill health and a hundred difficulties permitted
the Muse to realize in him, Sidney Lanier: you shall go far even
in the 'major' poets for anything more sweepingly gorgeous than
Lanier's *Marshes of Glynn* and *Sunrise*."

It is this quality of magnitude in Lanier's poetry and in his
character that must finally win him widespread recognition, not
merely as a poet but as an American of the finest Jeffersonian
stamp, motivated in all that he did by a great love for his fellow
men and a desire to help them, and not merely as an American
but as a man who has done for many what Mr. Hamlin Garland
has so beautifully confessed he did for him, come to him un-
heralded and unknown, exalted him, transformed him, and taught
him the essential lesson of life as of art, the lesson of freedom
within law. Lanier died, we must remember, at thirty-nine, at an
age reckoned young, and his poetic career had lasted only seven
years. In his art we have noticed a constant improvement, increasing skill in the handling of rhythms, improving taste in the
choice of words and the creation of metaphors, growth from
redundancy and ornateness, through tempestuousness and tur-
gidity, to the stark objectivity of "The Revenge of Hamish,"
the artless simplicity of "A Ballad of Trees and the Master,"
and the enraptured beauty of "Sunrise." In his character—as
revealed in his letters and his prose—we have observed a corresponding growth, steady and certain, his sympathies constantly
enlarged by art, his faith in man and society and God deepened
and intensified by the hurts and the suffering man and society
and—for sometimes it seemed indeed as if divinity were testing
him as it had Job—God had caused him.

§ 4

As a MUSICIAN he had unquestioned talent, perhaps even genius
as a performer, and he was too sincere in all that he did ever
to have become a mere virtuoso. He said once: "My flute is my
faucet; it lets out just what I have put in. If I can become beautiful, the soul running through my flute will be beautiful also."[5]
So, with only an innate talent for playing and a heart full of
love, he, "a raw player and a provincial withal, without practice, and guiltless of instruction," quickly took his place among
skilled and experienced musicians, won their admiration and
respect, and elicited from the great Patti the compliment: "He

reveals to me a world of soul sweeter than music. I cannot sing; he has made my music smell musty."[5] Had he confined his activity entirely to music, or, indeed, had music paid him a living wage that would have made it possible for him to give to music the major portion of his time as he gave the major quantity of his affection, he might have become great in reputation as a musical performer—and remained to posterity a memory, the tradition of a singing voice, utterly lost.

But because it was not economically possible for him to be solely a musician, and because nature had endowed him with a variety of gifts, Lanier attempted much more, finding outlets in a number of creative ways for the tremendous energy which his weak body contained and only a most uncertain hold on life supported. Possessed of a naturally inquisitive mind, and stimulated by the scientific activity of the age in which he lived, Lanier was on the way to making some genuinely useful scientific discovery, some improvement in the flute, some observation of natural phenomena. His respect for science led him naturally to seek to discover—if such existed—laws of poetical construction, analogous to laws of sculpture and painting and architecture and other arts known from ages past. In his investigation he was successful, and his proposition that time is the basis of rhythm has become accepted as the fundamental law of metrical and poetical structure. One may wish that the book in which he set forth the principles of his investigations and his conclusions were a more finished piece of work, like Harvey's book on the circulation of the blood and Darwin's on the origin of species, at once a literary and a scientific classic, but the final triumph and vindication of his conclusions is the vindication of his work. It is the idea, more than the book, that is significant.

It was as a scientist, of course, analyzing and dissecting, discovering adherence to or deviation from natural laws, that Lanier undertook his work as a critic. In this he was particularly successful, for to power of analysis was added in him the intuition of the artist; and his acute critical judgments, happily expressed in memorable phrases, are little masterpieces of their kind. Of Poe he said "The trouble with Poe was, he did not *know* enough. He needed to know a good many more things in order to be a great poet."[6] Of Shelley: "In truth, Shelley appears always to have labored under an essential immaturity: it is very probable that if he had lived a hundred years he would never have become a man: he was penetrated with modern ideas, but penetrated as a boy would be, crudely, overmuch, and with a constant tendency to the extravagant and illogical: so that I call him the modern boy."[7] Of Swinburne: "He invited me to eat; the service was silver and gold, but no food therein save pepper and salt."[8] Of William Morris: "He caught a crystal cupful of the yellow light of sunset, and persuading himself to dream it wine, drank it with a sort of smile."[8]

With time to work out critical principles, to fill in the gaps in his knowledge, to correct by study and research his hasty generalizations and mistaken assertions, he might have become a critic of prominence and importance. Actually he made amazing mistakes, which give one every right to speak of the "calm bigotry"[9] of his attitude; but his characterization of Thackeray as a "low-pitched satirist"[10] is no more mistaken than Thackeray's famous estimate of Swift; and important critics have gone wrong in betting on less important novelists than George Eliot. Lanier's published lectures are filled with admirable passages of criticism, so fine that they more than make up for other passages which as criticism are only unlicensed enthusiasm. On the whole they are acute and suggestive, as are most of his essays. And in at least one of the essays in which Lanier attempted a formal critical analysis of the work of one man, the essay on "Paul H. Hayne's Poetry," he produced criticism which, no matter how enlarged or amplified, must remain in principle unchallenged.

Lanier's defects as a critic are enthusiasm, lack of catholicity of judgment, and didacticism. Enthusiasm is of course a quality in a critic not to be despised, a quality that has often done notable work in turning appreciation toward a neglected writer. If enthusiasm led Lanier frequently to unbalanced judgments, it thus led most of his contemporary critics, for romantic criticism, knowing no fixed criteria, does not always achieve sound conclusions; as in the work of Pater, romantic criticism of art often becomes worthy art without being important criticism. But lack of enthusiasm is a defect less easily remedied than abundance of enthusiasm: without enthusiasm no critic ever conveys his feeling to others; Lanier, with increasing wisdom and growing seriousness, would probably have checked naturally much of the enthusiasm of his southern temperament, an enthusiasm which is excessive often because it is, in the sense of the word that Lanier used in reference to Shelley, boyish.

Lack of catholicity of judgment is a more serious defect in a critic, but catholicity is often a mark of uncertainty, and Lanier knew what he knew, knew what was true and what was to be preached in the gospel of beauty it was given him to deliver. He is to be more admired for his honesty in voicing his dislike of the novels of Fielding and Richardson—his contempt for "this muck of the classics"—than other critics who, with insipid and pious references to classics, seek to ignore or justify much that is truly foul and vulgar. If Lanier erred, he erred on the side of righteousness. That he could be fair, that he could praise for one quality what he must condemn for another and could find beauty where ugliness and vulgarity are also present, is proved by the earnest, impartial discussion of Whitman in *The English-Novel*.

Lanier's chief defect as a critic is his didacticism, a quality to be expected in one whose favorite occupation, whose professional ambition, was teaching. Believing passionately in the holiness of beauty, and that the artist's equipment is God-given, free though the artist is to do with it as he will, and convinced that his business in life, the thing that justified his existence, was to make poems, Lanier could not have been other than a religious poet. It is not, as we have seen, that Lanier is a theological poet, or necessarily a Christian poet; nor is he, in the strictest sense of the word, a mystic. Of Lanier's religious spirit Ward wrote: "The intense sacredness with which Lanier invested Art held him thrall to the highest ethical ideas."[11] He could not escape this thralldom: he could not judge the work of others by any other standard than that by which he worked and by which he judged his own work. To the young artist he said: "unless you are suffused—soul and body, one might say—with that moral purpose which finds its largest expression in love— that is, with beauty, truth, wisdom, goodness, *and* love, abandon the hope that the ages will accept you as an artist."[12] The idea of "Art for Art's sake" was intolerable to him. Borne on the wings of the great bird Purpose, he could not have sung as earth-bound poets may of temporal and amoral delights, as he could not tolerate the naturalistic, unbeautiful art of Zola. "Lanier," continues Ward, "was saturated with [the beauty of holiness.] It shines out of every line he wrote. It is not that he never wrote a maudlin line, but that every thought was lofty." Is it any wonder that he spoke at times almost contemptuously of his contemporaries who seemed blind to the truths taught by religion and for him proved by science, timid men more afraid "of doing something wrong or unpolished"[13] than of the damnation of oblivion reserved for those who fail to accept the gospel offered them? If he postulated moral earnestness in the work of others, he himself labored in the most sincere, unselfish spirit of revealing the good and reviling the evil, singing God's praises and doing God's work.

The misfortune is not, therefore, that Lanier's work as a critic was characterized by such qualities—for critics of all sorts are needed and critics of Lanier's type fulfill a useful function—but that his work as a poet should possess the same characteristics. Intoxicated by enthusiasm, he who shrank from any revealment of the external facts of his life in his poetry made such outpourings of the thoughts in his soul that many lines he wrote are almost embarrassing to read. Such entire lack of reserve in spiritual matters, such frank disclosures of sacred intimacies in his uxorious life with nature, affect the reader as Whitman's frankness and lack of reserve in physical matters affected his first readers; it is like the unguarded candor of adolescence, which arouses our sympathy without enlisting our respect: one sympathizes for Lanier rather than with him—and the enjoyment of poetry depends upon a community of feeling between poet and reader, not an antagonism.

Lack of catholicity of judgment led him, moreover, to persist in his own way of writing, contrary to the advice of even the most friendly critics. "We must yield something to custom," Taylor reminded him, "just as we wear horrid stovepipe hats."[14] But Lanier, who wore not only stovepipe hats but a beard because it was the custom, and sat miserable and disconsolate during a dinner given in his honor because he had had to come on from a lecture in a business suit, there being no time to change,[15] yielded no more than was absolutely necessary to the customs of the day in poetry. If it could be said with justice in 1888 that "to some he seems like a poet of another age discoursing on modern themes,"[16] with how much more justice may this be repeated now. By the language of even his best verse Lanier is dated, dated—in spite of the persisting modernness of his essential ideas—as belonging to an era for which we of today have little sympathy. His poetry is Victorian poetry, for the language is the lush language of sentimentalism, and sentimentalism combined with didacticism is an almost inescapable blight to any poem.

Much of the didacticism in his poetry, like the enthusiasm of his criticism, may be traced, however, to his state of health. Cut off by it rather than by temperament or by desire from the conventional activity of daily life, he lived so exclusively in a world of artistic speculation and scientific questioning that things spiritual came to be more familiar to him than things material, and moral facts to be taken for granted as much as physical facts are. And though he did consciously work in an attitude of moral earnestness, many of the didactic statements are as undeliberate as breathing. He was, Professor H. M. Jones asserts, and one must agree with him, "an abnormally spiritual man," but because he was it is unfair and unprofitable to judge his works by canons that deny the essential healthiness of spirituality. The famous line with which "The Symphony" ends, "Music is love in search of a word," Professor Jones calls "eminently false . . . not the utterance of a large and healthy spirit"; but to others than Professor Jones it must seem eminently true, the perfect definition of the kind of music that perfect spirituality alone justifies.

Fortunately, however, Lanier, with the inconsistency of men of genius, often produced poetry—not the major portion of his poetry, but much of it—marred neither by superabundance of enthusiasm, nor verbal conceits and awkwardnesses, nor by strained fancies, nor by a didacticism offensive to the average reader. The contemplation of nature endowed him—if only temporarily—with something of the largeness and beauty of nature, so that his best work is what we call natural—simple and easy and spontaneous. Tortuous though the sentences may appear in "The Marshes of Glynn," the tortuousness is that of forest patterns; the sentences are as unstudied as the subject is original and unborrowed. Nor is the exquisite simplicity of his several descriptions of sunset a studied simplicity. It is as if Lanier, in the presence of nature, lost his own identity and became only an instrument on which nature played, an instrument capable of the most precise rendition of nature's harmonies.

The suggestion is of course contrary to Lanier's own belief, expressed in "Individuality" and elsewhere, that the genius is not one through whom God works but one who takes the tools God gave him and then does his work. Lanier himself might have explained the difference in quality between verse of this sort and other verse by using the metaphor of the faucet that he used in explaining his flute-playing: his best verse, he would have said, was good because it was written when he himself was at his best morally. He believed, we are told,[5] that great music is but the rhythm of a great personality, one living in accordance with the laws of nature, or—for the terms we use to express the idea are less important than the idea they express—one living as the greatest of poets, the crystal Christ, the poet of conduct, has shown us how to live.

It is for his life, therefore, more than for his poetry, and for his poetry as a revelation of his life, that Lanier has appealed and must appeal to posterity. It is as impossible to dissociate Lanier and his best verse as it is to dissociate Wordsworth and "The Prelude," or Mrs. Browning and the "Sonnets from the Portuguese," or Francis Thompson and "The Hound of Heaven," or Whitman and the "Song of Myself." It is highly personal poetry, the more enjoyable for being so. We are all at heart hero-worshippers, and we need nothing more than contact with heroes—with great men. For hero-worship is good for the soul of the worshipper; it transfers to him something of the quality of the hero, and aids his moral growth as a man. The more carefully we study Lanier's life, the more are we confirmed in an impression of the fineness of his character and the potential greatness of his accomplishment, and the more valuable does the revelation that he made of himself in his poetry become.

We cannot, however, ignore the fact that in emphasizing Lanier's fineness of spirit and nobility of utterance, praising a few poems and overlooking many, we are being timid and refusing to answer the question, Was Lanier a great poet? "Let my name perish," we must remember him as writing to his wife, "—the poetry is good poetry and the music is good music, and beauty dieth not, and the heart that needs it will find it."[17] And, "I know, through the fiercest tests of life, that I am in soul, and shall be in life and utterance, a great poet."[18] Only the realization of his ability gave him the strength to toil on, notwithstanding sickness and want, the misapprehension of the critics, and the neglect of the public. Keats, Shelley, Wordsworth, and other great poets have left evidence of their own awareness of the inevitable verdict of posterity upon them. Was Lanier, in asserting his claims to greatness, also a prophet?

Aside from the fact that like many men who have never pretended to be professional poets he wrote a few poems that have become popular and that will live, does Lanier appear in the body of his work a true poet, an authentic *vates?*

Gamaliel Bradford quotes from Lanier's letters an interesting characterization of a New York musician with whom Lanier once played flute duos: "while he has taste enough to like the best music, yet there is a certain something—a flame, a sentiment, a spark kindled by the stroke of the soul against sorrow, as of steel against flint—which he hath *not,* and the want of which will forever keep him from penetrating into *the deepest* of music."[19] This, says Bradford, is true of Lanier as a poet: he chose the most promising, the most poetical subjects, but the battling spirit so characteristic of the man, so evident in the letters and the lectures, is not in his poetry. And Bradford is right: what Lanier achieved he achieved all too seldom: there is in his poetry so little of the natural magic that is the supreme felicity of great poets, though so much in his work just fails of achieving this magic, this poetic perfection—as if Pegasus leapt but could not soar.

§ 5

IN THE first place, Lanier had so "little of the wine of success and praise, without which no man ever does the very best he might," as he himself said in speaking of what would have been of inestimable service to Timrod's poetic ability,[20] but this of course is not the only reason for his failure. A clew to Lanier's failure to achieve the unfailing spontaneity of utterance which distinguishes good poetry from bad, which alone makes for what George Moore calls pure poetry, is afforded by certain of the so-called poem outlines, which examination proves to be very literally that. Those given in the volume of *Poem Outlines* on pages 2, 49, and 81, for instance, are so much like prose summaries of poems made as an academic exercise that one is forced to the conclusion that they are just the reverse—drafts for poems, sketched in exact detail. The conclusion is strengthened by the outline dating from August, 1881, given in the same volume on page 119. Here is an outline for a sonnet, conceived in the Shaksperean mold, with two lines actually in iambic pentameter. Confirmatory evidence that these are indeed first drafts

for poems comes from a lecture delivered before the New Century Club of Philadelphia in 1891 by Professor R. E. Burton,
a careful student of Lanier's work and his first bibliographer.[21]
Though a musician with an instinctive feeling for rhythm,
Lanier seems to have lacked the lyrical ability capable of sustained utterance: he did not, as Professor Burton pointed out,
think his poetical thoughts in appropriate verse form, save in such
an unusual case as that of "A Ballad of Trees and the Master."
The fact that so many of his poems seem to be the distillation of
passages of his prose, seems also to suggest the necessity of thinking his work out for content before putting it down in form.

It is not, then, that Lanier, harried by ill-health and the
necessity of writing prose for bread when he yearned to write
poetry for joy, lacked the time to revise his work; the defect
lies in the fact that he should have had to revise as much as
he did. Only in the case of a few of his poems is it possible to
study several versions and subsequent revisions; usually the
changes in text are improvements, but usually too they are more
numerous than they should be. As Professor Mims pointed out,
Lanier's statement concerning Swinburne may be applied equally
well to Lanier himself: "It is impossible in reading this strained
laborious matter not to remember that the case of poetry is
precisely that where he who conquers, conquers without strain."[22]
If we lack direct evidence of successive manuscript versions,[22a]
we have in his letters ample evidence of the care Lanier expended
upon his poems. The result of this care, as we have seen, is too
often a studied effect; the poetry, for all the rich qualities Lanier's
irradiating imagination gave it, is more epigrammatical than
truly lyrical.

This tendency toward epigrammatic writing, finding expression in fancies and similes, spoils such poems as "The Bee"
and "Clover," poems nobly conceived and not lacking in high
poetic lines. The tendency, become a fixed habit, manifests
itself even in "Sunrise," in the figure of the beehive from which
the "star-fed Bee, the build-fire Bee, . . . the great Sun-Bee,"
emerges each morning. Had music and poetry been truly wedded,
so that their offspring were the child of love and not of chance,
or had Lanier been more of the artist and less of the scientist,
such lines as those which mar the very climax of "Sunrise"
would never have been written.

Another clew to the reason for Lanier's failure, in spite of his rich poetic endowment, his knowledge of prosody, and his musical ability, remains for the psychologist to develop. Lanier in 1861, at the age of nineteen, a youth of good family, well educated, gifted as a musician and apparently also as a poet, not robust of health but certainly perfectly healthy, looked forward to several years of study in a German university and then to such an academic and literary career in America as Longfellow, after studying in Germany, was already enjoying, and to a life darkened by no financial cares. When the Confederacy was established his future seemed even brighter, for now it would be closely identified with the brilliant future that seemed certain for his native Georgia and for the new nation. War at first meant no end to his dream. There were romantic days in the saddle and romantic nights under the stars, and fighting was only a rumor, a news dispatch.

Then events took another turn. The romantic aspect of the war changed suddenly: Lanier went into battle, into prison. He came out broken in health. The Confederacy collapsed, and with it his dreams. From one point of view the rest of Lanier's life, coinciding as it did with a period of political reconstruction, was spent in an attempted spiritual and physical reconstruction, a vain effort to regain health and to achieve, in spite of the complete change in the political and social scene, the success and the rewards that the future offered in 1861. He did not altogether fail in the attempt, but what he achieved is far different from what he sought. If we contrast, for instance, "The Tournament: Joust the First," written possibly in 1862, at the latest in 1867, and at either date before he had awakened to complete realization of the wreck of his hope, with almost any poem of the last years save the "Evening Song" and "A Ballad of Trees and the Master," we see what effect the years of reconstruction had on his work: the early poems so smooth and easy in versification, so simply and beautifully lyrical, the later poems so rarely simple and lyrical, so often involved in thought and meter, in language and in metaphor—and between them days and nights of painful effort to justify by theory what he did by instinct. We are reminded inevitably of the apologetic[23] literature that came from the pens of southern political and military leaders during this same period.

He never achieved, it is unlikely even that with regained health and a longer life he would ever have achieved, the bright promise of his youth. The poet's career, especially in Lanier's conception of it, must be a social one, and to Lanier society became a symbol of the opposite of God, and he found genuine happiness only in nature and in art. But his hectic joy in his abandonment to nature and to music is one of his weaknesses: these masters, that gave him strength and courage to live, took payment, as it were, for their gift in shutting him off from the understanding, the appreciation, and the sympathy, of the majority of his fellow men. Viewed thus, his career as a poet appears but the wreck of a career, though a career of unusual promise.

He was, we must admit, no more a great poet than Georgia, or any other southern state, was a great state, or the United States a great nation during the period in which Lanier lived. That he did write some great poetry is no more to be wondered at than that the United States produced some great art, arrived at noteworthy achievements in the sciences, during the same period. And greatness we cannot deny to the best of Lanier's poetry, that golden residue left at the bottom of the crucible of his bitter experience, whether we judge it in relation to Milton's dictum that poetry should be simple, sensuous, and impassioned, or Wordsworth's statement that poetry is the spontaneous overflow of powerful emotions, or Poe's definition of poetry as the rhythmical creation of beauty, or Whitman's insistence that the spirit of an American poet must respond to his country's spirit. Lanier possessed if only to a limited extent the poet's natural endowment of melody, a lyric quality which he believed a heritage from the court-musician Laniers, that is indeed—whatever the line of descent—said to be a characteristic of most of the men of his blood. He had, moreover, a splendid intellect, one which if frustrated in fullest development was yet alive to the problems of his age and his country, of man and nature, and of man in nature. And he had deep compassion, deeper than that of any other American poet. "Every man is as good as his best" was one of his favorite sayings.[24] The songs that are his best—"Sunrise," "The Marshes of Glynn," "Corn," and a few others, the "Evening Song," "Opposition," "A Ballad of Trees and the Master," "The Stirrup-Cup," and "The Revenge of Hamish"—have the enduring qualities of originality and of his rare endowment, and the perfection that the true artist, not out of his knowledge but out of the wisdom that comes of pain, gives to his creation.

§ 6

THERE IS of course more melody, more perfect rhythmical beauty in his early master, Poe, more vigor and strength in Whitman, but no more magic in either, and no more of the ecstasy that all true poets must know, the ecstasy expressed in Phineas Fletcher's line "Ah, singing let me live and singing die." Longfellow's poetry is more learned and more finished, more carefully thought out and better executed; Emerson's often possesses a simplicity which limitation of skill gave him and which the confusion of talents too frequently denied Lanier. But Lanier's poetry often reveals a depth that Longfellow's never reveals, and a beauty that Emerson—whom in ethical qualities Lanier was most like—never achieved. If his flight was less sustained than that of either Longfellow or Emerson, his ability to soar less certain, he did nevertheless fly higher. He knew the high poetic heavens that Poe and Whitman knew, and that these three alone among American poets have known.

Compared with British poets Lanier seems of course much less great. Whitman is no very strange fellow for the company of Wordsworth: Poe's poetry survives comparison with that of Coleridge, Shelley, and Keats. But in spite of the largeness of his themes and his proneness to grapple with intellectual problems, there is not in Lanier much similarity to Tennyson, with whom he has been most often compared, nor, in spite of the beauty and the unconventionality of his verse, with Swinburne, who loved musical meters as passionately as he; nor is there much resemblance between his bright, sunlit poetry and the lovely melancholy verse of Keats. The only British poets with whose work that of Lanier seems to have a great deal in common are poets of a lower order, such poets as D. M. Dolben and Francis Thompson, poets who like Lanier seemed to have been denied by fate the opportunity of bringing their powers to the fullest development.

Such a comparison is, however, unnecessary and, when made, a little ridiculous. Just as Whitman is different from Wordsworth, and Emerson from Carlyle, so is Lanier different from any English poet with whom comparison might be made. The differ-

"The Master Light of All Our Seeing." From a painting made in 1893 by Annibale Gatti (1828-1909), inspired by Lanier's poem, "The Crystal"; now in the Library of the Johns Hopkins University. Lanier stands between Browning and Tennyson in the lower right-hand corner.

ence is in the essentially American quality of his poetry. In the marsh hymns he introduced a new theme to our literature, revealing the beauty of the apparently drab and colorless marshes. "In 'Corn,'" said John Macy, "for once an American poet strode into our splendid native golden fields and sang what his eyes saw, and deeper, what the harvest of the fields can be for man." Lanier's poetry is as indigenous to our soil as the corn, as beautiful and as indispensable to our life. "There are in Lanier," G. W. Cable once wrote John Muir, "such wonderful odors of pine and hay, and salt sands and cedar, and corn, and such wonderful whisperings of Eolian strains and every outdoor sound—I think you would have had great joy in one another's personal acquaintance." It is a great joy—for no quieter phrase will describe it—that the lover of our forest and sea-shores, our hills and our marshes, finds in reading Lanier's poetry.

It is, moreover, the essentially American quality that makes Lanier's protest against capitalism so different from the protests of an English poet with whom, because of his love for the beautiful things of the past and his eagerness to give such things to the men of the present, he is sometimes compared—William Morris: an American quality in "The Symphony" may be difficult to define and impossible to illustrate by quotation, but it is there, as inescapably there as it is in "The Psalm of the West," where it is more apparent. It is this American quality that will perhaps prevent any very general appreciation of Lanier's poetry abroad, for his poetry is at once less descriptive of America—and therefore less easily appreciated—than that of Whitman, and more distinctly American than that of Poe. His appeal must ever be to those who love America, love the bright warmth of the sun on her broad fields, and understand the American spirit. One may well paraphrase the song of the good angel in his Centennial cantata and say that so long as we shall love true love, and truth, and justice, and freedom, and God, and our fellow men, admire bold criticisms and hold brave hope in good to come, no matter how dark the present may be, the name of Lanier—in whose poetry these virtues are manifest—shall shine, and his fame glow.

§ 7

FOR HIS best prose less can be claimed than for his best poetry. "If, instead of ten volumes of prose," wrote Professor Mims, "there could be selected his best work from all of them, there would still be a residue of writing that would establish Lanier's place among prose writers of America."[25] But prose writers do not survive by such volumes of selections, and there are not among Lanier's essays—even if we consider the separate lectures as essays—enough successful ones on subjects of enduring interest to make up a volume not of fragmentary selections but of separate, self-contained pieces of finished work, a volume that would measure up to Lanier's own ideal of a scholarly book. And so all of Lanier's prose, the good and the bad, the finished and the unfinished essays—of which latter it may even be complained that all too many have been published—must survive together for the light they throw on his life, and, in spite of the suggestive value of certain of the essays to special students, for that only.

But even as a revelation of the man, Lanier's formal prose will never take the place of his personal letters. For Lanier was an excellent letter writer and, except in the letters to his wife and his brother, where he let himself go completely, the faults of his poetry are for the most part absent, as are the faults of his other prose. In them—especially in the letters written after 1869—is to be found Lanier's prose style at its best, with its clearness, fluency, eloquence, beauty, reflecting well the resiliency of his mind. And in them also is to be found what all too often is missing in the more formal prose, a delightful playfulness, humor not made up entirely of puns, animated, excited talk about himself and his work, and an unconscious delineation of his character more complete than any a biographer might produce.

Indeed, a volume of his best letters placed in chronological order would make unnecessary any biography and embarrass by its excellence any writer who should attempt to prepare one. Such a volume, with its revelation of a character as beautiful as its type is rare, of the genuinely poetic temperament illustrated in a man who with Promethean spirit defied discouragements, might achieve a fame and circulation independent of any interest in Lanier's poetry, as Johnson is known through Boswell's biography, Gibbon through his autobiography, Saint Augustine through his confessions, Amiel through his journal, to many who have not read and will never read the formal writings of the same men.

In his letters more clearly than in his poetry we see Lanier for what he essentially was, more than poet, more than musician,

a fighter, like Browning, marching breast forward, to greet the
unseen with a cheer. He lived, says Bradford, in a spiritual
whirlwind, until it snuffed him out; if ever a man died fighting,
Lanier did. He fought not only against disease and circumstances,
but the very limitations of the human personality, striving unceasingly to penetrate the depths of the soul, to discover the
last secret of the human mind that should reveal beyond all
doubt the relation that it bears to God. Thought was to him
as it was to Lucretius a despotic master, which gave him no
rest. Bradford calls him a splendid intelligence wearing itself
out for futile results, but the results do not seem so futile, for
it is given to few men to attain the wisdom and the conviction
that Lanier achieved, the belief that overmasters doubt, the
complete lack of fear of the thing to be done—the strength to
face death as if it were but a sunrise. In the light of Lanier's
achievement as a man, his achievement as poet or scholar becomes a matter of small significance.

§ 8

OF MAZZINI Lanier wrote: "He loved duty like one of the
iron souls of the North, and he loved love with the ardor of a
Southern temperament." Of Lanier himself we may say the same
thing. Lacking though physical strength was, and sensitive and
reserved though he appeared to be, Lanier had a fiery temper,
and when he was aroused to anger he would, as the expression
goes, have dared the devil himself. A Baltimore tradition tells
how Lanier forced the conductor of the Peabody Orchestra at
rehearsal to apologize to the pianist for overly harsh words
addressed to her.[26] As a champion of the rights of the poor
against capitalism Lanier displayed the same righteous indignation and the same courage. Nor was he afraid to say to southerners—brothers to himself in sensitiveness as by nativity—things
about southerners and their attitude toward the Negroes which,
had they not been ignored, must have made him unpopular and
cordially disliked.

It would have been difficult, however, for any reason actually
to have disliked Lanier. The thorough manliness of his character,
the natural charm of his presence, his extreme consideration of
all people at all times, his undeviating championship of what he
believed to be right in the face of all opposition, his uncompromising attack on evil—these are qualities that made him as man and

citizen outstanding and worthy of admiration. They are qualities that have given life to figures of legend and fiction, and immortality to such men as Sir Philip Sidney and General Lee.

They are qualities that give immortality to Sidney Lanier also; but in addition to them he possessed a quality that our heroes too often lack. All who knew him remembered him for his infectious sense of humor, his buoyant merriment. A son has described him as "quick, electric, flashing, full of jokes and gaiety."[27] Expressions of melancholy, and of despair, in his writings are too rare to be significant, and occur only in personal letters, as records of fleeting moods. Anyone who has read his lectures recognizes the truth of Mrs. Lanier's remark that "He bubbled over with merriment."[28]

This sense of merriment more than anything else saves him from too heroic immortality and makes him one of the busy world of ordinary men and everyday things, which was his chief concern, from which his interests seldom wandered far. Because he was and is one of us, a living figure of our own world, we need to know him, and so long as he becomes known to us for what he was, so long as he becomes known not merely to some but to all who love and cherish the American spirit and our great men, it matters little whether we find him in his poetry or in his letters, or in the tradition that lingers, or in the beautiful face of Keyser's bronze bust. It is only essential that we come to know him: until we have, discussion of his final rank as a poet is somewhat futile, and after we have, it appears unnecessary. We shall forgive him then, as he forgave others, the more or less, the "little mole of defect" in even his best work, and we shall elevate him from the rank of the uncertainly talented, in which he as a poet remains, to companionship with the great, the great not merely for what they did, but for what they became—and for what they have the power to do for others.

BIBLIOGRAPHY

COLLECTED PROSE AND POETRY

1867

Tiger-Lilies. A Novel. By Sidney Lanier. . . . New York: Published by Hurd and Houghton, 459 Broome Street, 1867.

1875

Florida: Its Scenery, Climate, and History. With an Account of Charleston, Savannah, Augusta, and Aiken, and a Chapter for Consumptives; Being a Complete Hand-Book and Guide. By Sidney Lanier. With Numerous Illustrations. Philadelphia: J. B. Lippincott & Co.

1876

Florida: Its Scenery, Climate, and History. With an Account of Charleston, Savannah, Augusta, and Aiken; a Chapter for Consumptives; Various Papers on Fruit-Culture; and a Complete Hand-Book and Guide. By Sidney Lanier. With Numerous Illustrations. Philadelphia: J. B. Lippincott & Co. 1876.

1776-1876. By Appointment of the U. S. Centennial Commission. *The Centennial Meditation of Columbia.* A Cantata for the Inaugural Ceremonies at Philadelphia, May 10, 1876. Poem by Sidney Lanier, of Georgia. Music by Dudley Buck, of Connecticut. New York: G. Schirmer, 701 Broadway.

Poems. By Sidney Lanier. Philadelphia: J. B. Lippincott & Co. London: 16 Southampton St. Covent Garden. 1877.

1879

The Boy's Froissart: Being Sir John Froissart's Chronicles of Adventure, Battle and Custom in England, France, Spain, etc. Edited for Boys with an Introduction by Sidney Lanier. Illustrated by Alfred Kappes. New York: Charles Scribner's Sons, 743 & 745 Broadway. 1879.

1880

The Science of English Verse. By Sidney Lanier. . . . New York: Charles Scribner's Sons, 743 and 745 Broadway. 1880.

The Boy's King Arthur: Being Sir Thomas Malory's History of King Arthur and His Knights of the Round Table. Edited for Boys with an Introduction by Sidney Lanier, Editor of "The Boy's Froissart." Illustrated by Alfred Kappes. New York: Charles Scribner's Sons, 743 and 745 Broadway. 1880.

1881

The Boy's Mabinogion: Being the Earliest Tales of King Arthur in the Famous Red Book of Hergest. Edited for Boys with an Introduction by Sidney Lanier, Editor of "The Boy's Froissart" and "The Boy's King Arthur." Illustrated by Alfred Fredericks. New York: Charles Scribner's Sons, 743 and 745 Broadway. 1881.

1882

The Boy's Percy: Being Old Ballads of War, Adventure and Love from Bishop Thomas Percy's Reliques of Ancient English Poetry, Together with an Appendix Containing Two Ballads from the Original Percy Folio MS. Edited for Boys with an Introduction by Sidney Lanier, Editor of "The Boy's Froissart" and "The Boy's King Arthur." With Fifty Illustrations from Original Designs by E. B. Bensell. New York: Charles Scribner's Sons. 1882.

1883

The English Novel and the Principle of its Development. By Sidney Lanier, Lecturer in Johns Hopkins University; Author of "The Science of English Verse." New York: Charles Scribner's Sons. 1883.

1884

Poems of Sidney Lanier. Edited by his Wife. With a Memorial by William Hayes Ward. . . . New York: Charles Scribner's Sons. 1884.

(Some copies contain an errata slip inserted between pp. x and xi.)

1891

Poems of Sidney Lanier. Edited by his Wife. With a Memorial by William Hayes Ward. . . . New Edition. New York: Charles Scribner's Sons. 1891.

(This edition includes seven poems not given in the previous edition: p. 152, "A Sunrise Song"; p. 153, "On a Palmetto"; p. 154, "Struggle"; p. 155, "Control"; p. 156, "To J. D. H."; p. 157,

1897
"Marsh Hymns. Between Dawn and Sunrise"; p. 158, "Thou and I.")

The English Novel: A Study in the Development of Personality. By Sidney Lanier, Lecturer in Johns Hopkins University; Author of "The Science of English Verse." Revised Edition. New York: Charles Scribner's Sons. 1897.

1898
Music and Poetry: Essays upon Some Aspects and Inter-Relations of the Two Arts. By Sidney Lanier. New York: Charles Scribner's Sons. 1898.

1899
Bob: The Story of our Mocking-Bird. By Sidney Lanier. With Sixteen Illustrations in Color. New York: Charles Scribner's Sons. MDCCCXCIX.

Letters of Sidney Lanier. Selections from his Correspondence, 1866-1881. With Portraits. New York: Charles Scribner's Sons. 1899.

Retrospects and Prospects: Descriptive and Historical Essays. By Sidney Lanier. New York: Charles Scribner's Sons. 1899.

1902
Shakspere and His Forerunners: Studies in Elizabethan Poetry and its Development from Early English. By Sidney Lanier. Illustrated. [In Two Volumes.] New York: Doubleday, Page & Co. 1902. (There was a limited edition of 102 numbered copies printed on Van Gelder handmade paper.)

1904
The Lanier Book. Selections in Prose and Verse from the Writings of Sidney Lanier. Edited by Mary E. Burt. Illustrated. Charles Scribner's Sons: New York, Chicago, Boston.
(This little volume contains "The Story of a Proverb" ["To him who wears a shoe, it is as if the whole earth was covered with leather."], pp. 3-19, and "King Arthur and his Knights of the Round Table," pp. 23-35, not reprinted elsewhere.)

1908
Poem Outlines by Sidney Lanier. . . . New York: Charles Scribner's Sons. MDCCCCVIII.

1916

Poems of Sidney Lanier. Edited by his Wife. With a Memorial by William Hayes Ward. . . . New Edition. New York: Charles Scribner's Sons. 1916.
(This edition includes two poems not given in the editions of 1884 and 1891: p. 222, "Our Hills"; p. 223, "Laughter in the Senate.")

UNCOLLECTED POEMS

"Civil Rights." *Herald* (Atlanta, Ga.), 1874 [according to Callaway]; *Telegraph and Messenger* (Macon, Ga.), October 29, 1874.

"The Dove." [First version.] *Atlantic Monthly* LXXIV, 186. August, 1894; *Letters*, 44-45.

"The Homestead." *Southern Farm and Home*, August, 1871, p. 92.

(?) "Now bends the lily, like a nun at prayer." *Thorn-Fruit*. By Clifford Lanier. New York, 1867. P. 43.

"Oh, Life's a Fever and Death's a chill!" *Independent* LXI, 1095. November 8, 1906; *Some Reminiscences . . . of Sidney Lanier*. By G. H. Clarke. Macon, Ga., 1907. P. 19.

"On the Receipt of a Jar of Marmalade." *New Castle* (Virginia) *Record*, April 11, 1891 [according to Callaway]; *Southern Writers*. By W. M. Baskervill. Nashville, Tenn., 1899. Vol. I, p. 147. (The version used in this biography is from Mrs. C. N. Hawkins, of Brooklyn, N. Y., for whom the poem was written, and who owns the MS.)

(?) "Sea-Foam." *Round Table* IV, 88. September 8, 1866.

"A Song." By Sidney and Clifford Lanier. *Southern Magazine* IX, 127. July, 1871.

"Steel in Soft Hands." (One stanza only.) *Sidney Lanier*. By Edwin Mims. Boston, 1905. P. 93.

"To ———." ("Her bright soul burned in her dusky eye.") *Mid-Continent* VI, 86. May, 1895; *Sun* (Baltimore), February 3, 1929.

"To Beethoven." (Sonnet.) *Independent* XLIX, 1489. November 18, 1897.

"To G. H." *Independent* LXI, 1095. November 8, 1906; *Some Reminiscences . . .* Pp. 17-18. (MS., Washington Memorial Library, Macon.)

"To J. L.———." *Round Table* III, 443. July 14, 1866; *Independent* XLVI, 849. July 5, 1894.

"To Lucie." *From Dixie*. Richmond, 1893. P. 39.

"To Miss Charlotte Cushman. (With a Copy of 'Corn.')." *Charlotte Cushman*. By Emma Stebbins. Boston, 1879. P. 268. (MS., Harvard College Library, AL 2327.15.5*.)

" 'To "The White Flower" of The English Novel.' Written in 1878 but printed in 1890 by L. Prang (Boston) on an illustrated Christmas Card." [Not seen; description quoted from Callaway.]

UNCOLLECTED PROSE

(See also Bibliographical and Critical)

"Annual Address Before the Furlow Masonic Female College, Delivered June 30th, 1869." *Catalogue of the Trustees, Faculty, Alumnæ and Students of Furlow Masonic Female College, Americus, Ga., 1868-1869.* Macon, Georgia: J. W. Burke & Co., Stationers, Printers and Binders. 1869. Pp. 19-30. Reprinted, with an introductory note by Jay B. Hubbell, *American Literature* II, 385-404. January, 1931.

"Devil Bombs." Unpublished essay, quoted in part by Mims, *Sidney Lanier*, pp. 45-47.

"How to Read Chaucer." *Independent* LXIII, 1748. November 26, 1891.

"Letter to Mr. J. F. D. Lanier, a banker of New York, giving an account of the Laniers in Europe and of their coming to America; privately printed, Baltimore, April 2, 1879, pp. 17." [Not seen; description quoted from Callaway.]

"Mazzini on Music." *Independent* XXX, No. 1543, pp. 3-4. June 27, 1878.

"Memorial Address (Extemporaneously Delivered and Later Reduced to Writing) at the Georgia Bar Association's Memorial Exercises for Judge Eugenius Nisbet, a Member of the Supreme Court of Georgia." *Telegraph* (Macon, Ga.), February 2, 1927. (MS., Washington Memorial Library, Macon.)

"Peace." *Southern Magazine* XV, 406-10. October, 1874.

"Robert E. Lee: In Memoriam." *Stratford on the Potomac. By Ethel Armes. And Address on Robert E. Lee. By Sidney Lanier. . . .* Publishers: William Alexander, Jr., Chapter, United Daughters of the Confederacy: Greenwich, Connecticut. MCMXXVIII. Pp. 5-8. (Quoted in part by Mims, *Sidney Lanier*, pp. 50-52.)

"A Scheme for a Course in English Literature." (Extract from a letter to President Gilman, of Johns Hopkins.) *Independent* XXXVIII, 325-26. March 18, 1886.

"The Story of a Proverb: A Fairy-Tale for Grown People." ("I was as a treasure concealed; But I loved, and I became known.") *Lippincott's Magazine* XXIII, 109-13. January, 1879.

"The Texas Trail in the '70's." *Outlook* CV, 582-85. November 15, 1913. (MS., Henry E. Huntington Library and Art Gallery, H M 7971.)

460 BIBLIOGRAPHY

"The Three Waterfalls." *Scott's Magazine* (Atlanta, Ga.) IV, 599-604, 679-83. August, September, 1867.
"What I Know About Flowers." *Sunday School Times* (Philadelphia) XXXVIII, 739. November 21, 1891; *Southern Churchman* (Richmond, Va.) XCIV, II. February 23, 1929. (The two versions differ slightly. MS. in possession of Mrs. William McKay, Hendersonville, N. C.)

UNCOLLECTED POEM OUTLINES

"As the woodpecker taps in a spiral quest." *Century Magazine* XXXII' 377. July, 1886.
"Death lieth still in the way of life." *Century Magazine* XXXII, 377. July, 1886.
"He passed behind the disk of death." *Century Magazine* XXXII, 377. July, 1886.
"I was the earliest bird awake." *Constitution* (Atlanta, Ga.), October 19, 1890; Baskervill's *Southern Writers* I, 226.
"The Lord's Romance of Time." *Sunday School Times* (Philadelphia) XXXV, 50. January 28, 1893.
"O Lord, if thou wert needy as I." *Southern Bivouac* n. s. II, 664. April, 1887; Baskervill's *Southern Writers* I, 190.
"One in Two." *Century Magazine* n. s. XII, 417. July, 1887.
"Two in One." *Century Magazine* n. s. XII, 417. July, 1887.

UNPUBLISHED LETTERS OF LANIER

1863. April 6. To Mrs. C. C. Clay. Duke University Library. (Quoted in part in *A Belle of the Fifties*. By Ada Sterling. New York, 1905. Pp. 200-01.)
1867, August 6. To Mrs. C. C. Clay. Duke University Library.
1867, August 21. To Hurd and Houghton, Publishers. In the possession of Dr. T. O. Mabbott, of New York City.
1868, December 2. To Charles and Caroline Weed Campbell. Wesleyan College Library (Macon, Ga.).
1872, March 2. To Paul Hamilton Hayne. Author's collection.
1874, November 5. To E. C. Stedman. Henry E. Huntington Library and Art Gallery.
1874, November 15. To Judge Logan E. Bleckley. Henry E. Huntington Library and Art Gallery. (Contemporary copy; quoted in part in *Select Poems of Sidney Lanier*. Edited by Morgan Callaway, Jr. New York, 1895. Pp. xlvi, 65.)
1875, January 3. To Mrs. S. M. Boykin. Washington Memorial Library (Macon, Ga.).

1875, June 16. To Edward Spencer. Johns Hopkins University Library. (The Lanier-Spencer letters deposited in the library of the Johns Hopkins University are the property of Mrs. C. S. Hayden, daughter of Edward Spencer.)

1875, December 17. To H. W. Longfellow. Craigie House (Cambridge, Mass.).

1876, February 12. To Edward Spencer. Johns Hopkins University Library.

1876, February 12. To Mrs. S. M. Boykin. Washington Memorial Library (Macon, Ga.).

1876, May 23. To Clifford Lanier. Henry E. Huntington Library and Art Gallery. (Contemporary copy; different parts are quoted in *Literary Life* [Cleveland], April, 1885, and Mims's *Sidney Lanier*, pp. 171-172.)

1876, August 15. To A. H. Dooley. Author's collection.

1876, August 15. To Edward Spencer. Johns Hopkins University Library. (Quoted in part in "Sidney Lanier and Edward Spencer." By E. P. Kuhl. *Studies in Philology* xxvii, 475-76. July, 1930.)

1876, October 17. To Gibson Peacock. Harvard College Library.

1877, June 25. To an unknown person. In the possession of Mr. Kenneth Rede, of Baltimore.

1878, July, 28. To D. C. Gilman. Johns Hopkins University Library.

1878, August 24. To J. F. Kirk. Harvard College Library. (Contemporary copy.)

1878, November 1. To Edward Spencer. Johns Hopkins University Library.

1879, January 8. To H. W. Longfellow. Craigie House (Cambridge, Mass.).

1879, February 5. To D. C. Gilman. Johns Hopkins University Library.

(1879. Undated letter.) To Edward Spencer. Johns Hopkins University Library.

(1879 ? Undated letter.) To H. W. Longfellow. Craigie House (Cambridge, Mass.).

1879, June 17. To E. C. Stedman. Yale University Library.

1880, February 10. To an unnamed publisher. Pennsylvania Historical Society.

1880, July 19. To W. S. Pratt. In the possession of Dr. W. S. Pratt, of Hartford, Conn.

1880, May 30. To Mrs. James T. Fields. Henry E. Huntington Library and Art Gallery.

1880, September 5. To W. S. Pratt. In the possession of Dr. W. S. Pratt, of Hartford, Conn.

MUSIC BY LANIER

Danse de Moucherons (Gnat Symphony). The first sheet of the MS. is reproduced in *The American Spirit in Letters*. (Vol. xi, "Pageant of America" series.) By Stanley Thomas Williams. New Haven, 1926. P. 256, ill. No. 667. An inscription reads: "To Henry C. Wysham. December 25, 1873. With the warm & friendly wishes of Sidney Lanier." The second sheet is reproduced in the present volume, opp. p. 174.

Huldegung der Britischer Nation. By Labitzky. Part for 3d. flute arranged by Lanier. (*Circa* Autumn, 1861.) MS. reproduced in *Sidney Lanier*. By Edwin Mims. Boston, 1905. Opp. p. 134.

Il Balen. From *Il Trovatore.* Air and Variation for Flute, with Piano Accompaniment. By the late Sidney Lanier. Copyright 1888 by A. G. Badger. [No imprint.]

A Little Song-Gem. *Love That Hath Us in the Net.* Words by Tennyson. Music by the Gifted Poet and Musician Sidney Lanier. New Orleans: Published by A. E. Blackmar & Co., 220 Camp St. [Copyright May 5, 1884.]

Wind-Song. (Composed *ante* October 29, 1874.) MS. reproduced in the present volume, opp. p. 184.

No other music by Lanier is known to have been printed. He is known, however, to have composed *Field-Larks and Blackbirds* (*ante* February 28, 1873); *Longing* (February 7, 1874); *Swamp Robin* (*ante* October 6, 1873); a musical setting for "My Life is Like a Summer Rose" by R. H. Wilde; a setting for the "Song of Love and Death" from Tennyson's "Launcelot and Elaine" *circa* 1862); and *Sacred Memories* (*ante* July 13, 1868). *See also* this volume, p. 424.

BIOGRAPHICAL AND CRITICAL

(The list that follows contains titles of only those books and articles that have been used in the preparation of this study. Titles of works consulted but found to be not useful or unimportant are numerous, but are not given here. Titles marked with an asterisk are works containing letters or parts of letters by Lanier not reprinted in the collected *Letters.*)

Abernethy, J. W. *Southern Poets.* New York, 1904. Pp. 3-34.

Allen, Alfred. "Reminiscences of Sidney Lanier." *Mid-Continent* VI, 81-86. May, 1895.

Anonymous. [A note on *Sidney Lanier*. By M. E. Gates.] *Critic* n. s. IX, 245. May 19, 1888.

———— [A note on a lecture by R. E. Burton before the New Century Club of Philadelphia.] *Poet-Lore* III, 369. 1891.

———— "The Death of Sidney Lanier." *Johns Hopkins University Circular* No. 12, 168. December, 1881.

———— [Obituary.] *Nation* XXXIII, 216. September 15, 1881.

———— [Obituary, with notice of commemorative meeting at Johns Hopkins University, October 22, 1881.] *Nation* XXXIII, 394. November 17, 1881.

———— [Sidney Lanier.] *Critic* XXI, 45. July 24, 1897.

———— "Sidney Lanier." *Independent* LX, 109-10. January 11, 1906.

———— [Sidney Lanier.] *Nation* LXXXII, 60. January 18, 1906.

———— "The Book of a Hero." *Outlook* LXXXI, 650-52. November 18, 1905.

———— "Sidney Lanier's Place in American Poetry." *Current Literature* XL, 36-38. January, 1906.

Baskervill, W. M. "Some Appreciation of Sidney Lanier." *Dial* XVIII, 299-301. May, 1895. (Not referred to in the notes.)

*———— *Southern Writers: Biographical and Critical Studies*. Volume I. Nashville, Tenn., 1899. Pp. 137-298.

Bentzon, Th. [Mme. Blanc.] "Un Musicien Poète. Sidney Lanier." *Choses et Gens d'Amerique*. Paris, 1898. Pp. 171-233. (Reprinted from *Revue de Deux Mondes* CXLV, 307-41. January 15, 1898.)

Blankenship, Russell. *American Literature as an Expression of the National Mind*. New York, 1931. Pp. 430-32.

Bourgeois, Yves R. "Sidney Lanier et Le Goffic." *Revue Anglo-Americaine*, Juin, 1931. Pp. 431-32.

Boynton, Percy H. *History of American Literature*. Boston, 1919. Pp. 349-58.

Bowen, Edwin Wingfield. *Makers of American Literature*. Washington, 1908. Pp. 348-70.

Bradford, Gamaliel. "Sidney Lanier." *American Portraits: 1875-1900*. Boston, 1922. Pp. 59-83.

Brown, Pearl Elizabeth. "A Study of Sidney Lanier's Verse Technique." (Unpublished master's thesis, University of Chicago, 1921.)

Browne, William Hand. *Sidney Lanier*. Memorial Address read before the meeting at Johns Hopkins University, October 22, 1881. Privately printed.

464 BIBLIOGRAPHY

———— "Sidney Lanier." *From Dixie* . . . Richmond, Va., MDCCCXCIII. Pp. 40-51.

Burton, Richard E. *Literary Leaders of America*. Chautauqua, New York, 1903. Pp. 296-309.

[Cable, G. W.] *George W. Cable: His Life and Letters*. By Lucy Leffingwell Cable Bikle. New York, 1928. Pp. 94, 214.

Cady, Frank W. "Sidney Lanier." *South Atlantic Quarterly* XIII, 156-73. April, 1914.

Callaway, James A. "The Imprisonment of Sidney Lanier." *Telegraph* (Macon, Ga.), February 3, 1916. (Referred to but once in notes.)

*Callaway, Morgan, Jr. *Select Poems of Sidney Lanier*. Edited with an introduction, notes, and bibliography. New York, 1895.

Calvert, George H. "Sidney Lanier." *Golden Age* V, No. 24, 4-5. June 12, 1875.

Carman, Bliss. "Poetic Fragments by Sidney Lanier . . ." *Times* (New York) *Saturday Review* XIII, No. 42, 606. October 24, 1908.

*Clarke, George Herbert. *Some Reminiscences and Early Letters of Sidney Lanier*. With an introduction by Harry Stillwell Edwards. Macon, Ga.: 1907.

*[Clay, Mrs. Clement C.] *A Belle of the Fifties. Memoirs of Mrs. Clay, of Alabama*. Put into narrative form by Ada Sterling. New York, 1905. Pp. 197-99, 201.

Davidson, James Wood. *Living Writers of the South*. New York, MDCCCLXIX. Pp. 319-24.

Dewey, Thomas Emmett. . . . *Poetry in Song, and Some Other Studies in Literature*. Kansas City, Mo., 1907. Pp. 46-73.

*Ethridge, Willie Snow. "Stories of a Fair-Haired Lad." *Telegraph* (Macon, Ga.) *Sunday Magazine*, February 3, 1929.

Foerster, Norman. *Nature in American Literature: Studies in the Modern View of Nature*. New York, 1923. Pp. 221-37.

*Franklin, Fabian. *Life of Daniel Coit Gilman*. New York, 1910. Pp. 241-44.

Fraser, A. M. "James Woodrow: 1828-1907." *Library of Southern Literature*. Atlanta, 1907. Vol. XIII, pp. 5957-63.

French, Samuel G. *Two Wars: An Autobiography*. Nashville, Tenn., 1901. P. 157.

Furst, Clyde. "Concerning Sidney Lanier." *Modern Language Notes* XIV, 197-205. November, 1899.

Garland, Hamlin. *Roadside Meetings*. New York, 1930. Pp. 144-53.

Gates, Merrill Edwards. "Sidney Lanier." *Presbyterian Review* VIII, 669-701. October, 1887. (Reprinted, the lines reset and the number of pages reduced, as *Sidney Lanier*, in pamphlet form.)

Gilman, D. C., editor. *The Forty-Sixth Birthday of Sidney Lanier*. Baltimore, 1888. (Contains the papers, poems and letters read at the Johns Hopkins memorial meeting, February 3, 1888.)

—— "Pleasant Incidents of an Academic Life." *Scribner's Magazine* XXXI, 614-24. May, 1902.

*—— "Sidney Lanier: Reminiscences and Letters." *South Atlantic Quarterly* IV, 115-22. April, 1905.

Gosse, Edmund. "Has America Produced a Poet?" *Questions At Issue*. London, 1893. Pp. 78-81. (Reprinted from *Forum* VI, 176-86. October, 1888.)

Graham, Philip Edwin. "Lanier's Reading." *University of Texas Studies in English*, No. 11, 63-89. 1931. (An incomplete but interesting list of books read by Lanier, containing, however, several gross inaccuracies.)

Griggs, Edward Howard, editor. *Sonnets to Sidney Lanier and Other Lyrics by Clifford Anderson Lanier*. Edited with introduction. N. Y., 1915.

*[Hankins, Virginia W.] "Some Memories of Lanier." *Southern Bivouac* n. s. II, 760-61. May, 1887.

Hearn, Lafcadio. *History of English Literature*. Hokuseido Press: Kanda, Tokyo, Japan, 1927. Vol. II, pp. 870-71.

Henneman, J. B. "The Biography of Sidney Lanier." *Sewanee Review* XIV, 352-57. July, 1906.

Higginson, Thomas Wentworth. *Contemporaries*. Boston, MDCCCXCIX. Pp. 85-101.

—— "Sidney Lanier." *Chautauquan* VII, 416-18. April, 1887.

Holliday, Carl. *History of Southern Literature*. Washington, 1906. Pp. 343-55.

Horder, W. Garrett. "Sidney Lanier and His Poetry." *The Quarto: An Artistic, Literary, and Musical Quarterly for 1896*. London, 1896.

Hovey, Richard. "The Laurel. An Ode: to Mary Day Lanier." *The End of the Trail*. New York, 1908. Pp. 3-16.

Hubner, C. W. *Representative Southern Poets*. Washington, 1906. Pp. 15-54.

Huckel, Rev. Oliver. "The Genius of the Modern in Lanier." *Johns Hopkins Alumni Magazine* XIV, 484-503. June, 1926.

Jones, Howard Mumford. "Sidney Lanier." In *American Poetry*. By Percy H. Boynton. New York, 1918. Pp. 670-75.

Kaufman, Matthias S. "Sidney Lanier, Poet Laureate of the South." *Methodist Review* LXXXII, 94-107. January, 1900.

Kell, John McIntosh. *Recollections of a Naval Life*. Washington, 1900. Pp. 296-97.

Kent, Charles W. "A Study of Lanier's Poems." *Publications of the Modern Language Association of America* VII, No. 2, 33-63. 1892.

Kirkus, Rev. William. [Obituary.] *American Literary Churchman* I, No. 4, 34. November 1, 1881.

Knight, Lucien Lamar. *Georgia's Landmarks, Memorials and Legends.* Atlanta, Georgia, 1914. Vol. II, p. 604.

*Kuhl, Ernest P. "Sidney Lanier and Edward Spencer." *Studies in Philology* XXVII, 462-76. July, 1930.

*Lanier, Clifford. "Reminiscences of Sidney Lanier." *Chautauquan* XXI, 403-09. July, 1895.

*—— "Sidney Lanier." *Gulf States Historical Magazine* II, 9-17. July, 1903.

—— *Sonnets to Sidney Lanier.* New York, 1915. (See Griggs, E. H.)

—— *Thorn-Fruit.* A Novel. New York, 1867.

Lanier, Henry Wysham. *Selections from Sidney Lanier. Prose and Verse.* With an introduction and notes. New York, [1916.]

*Lanier, James F. D. *Sketch of the Life of J. F. D. Lanier.* (Printed for the use of his family only.) Second Edition, 1877.

Lanier, Mary Day. "George Westfeldt, the Friend of Lanier." *Symposium* (Northampton, Mass.) I, 13-14. October, 1896.

Le Gallienne, Richard. "Sidney Lanier." *Attitudes and Avowals.* New York, 1910. Pp. 342-50. (Reprinted from *Academy* [London] LVIII, 147-48. February 17, 1900.)

Lindsay, Nicholas Vachel. "1906. First Begging Trip. Being in Florida, Georgia, and on to Kentucky, to Jett, near Frankfort." (Unpublished manuscript diary, in the possession of Mrs. Lindsay.)

Litz, Francis A. *Father Tabb.* Baltimore, 1923.

Lovett, Howard M. "Georgia's Intellectual Centre in the Sixties." *Confederate Veteran* XXXII, 97-98. March, 1924.

[MacClintock, W. D.] [Report of a lecture on Lanier by W. D. MacClintock at Chautauqua, New York, July, 1893.] *Critic* n. s. XX, 95. August 5, 1893.

McCowan, Hervey Smith. "Sidney Lanier, The Southern Singer and His Songs." *Self-Culture* (Akron, Ohio) X, 398-400. January, 1900.

Mabie, Hamilton Wright. "Sidney Lanier." *Outlook* LXXI, 236-39. May 24, 1902. (Reprinted from "The Poetry of the South." *International Monthly* V, 201-23.)

Macy, John. *Spirit of American Literature.* New York, 1913. Pp. 309-23.

Marble, Earl. "Sidney Lanier." *Cottage Hearth* IV, 141-42. June, 1877.

Mayfield, John S. *Sidney Lanier in Texas.* With introductory note by the late George Edward Woodberry. Dallas, MCMXXXII.

Miles, Dudley. "The New South: Lanier." *Cambridge History of American Literature.* New York, 1918. Vol. II, pp. 313-346.

*Mims, Edwin. *Sidney Lanier.* Boston, 1905.

Monroe, Harriet. "Rhythms of English Verse." *Poets and Their Art.* New York, 1926. Pp. 268-84.

More, Paul Elmer. "The Science of English Verse." *Shelburne Essays.* First Series. New York, 1906. Pp. 103-21.

Moses, Montrose J. *Literature of the South.* New York, 1910.

Newell, T. F. "Lanier's Life at Oglethorpe College." *Constitution* (Atlanta, Ga.), February 27, 1894. (Reprinted, Baskervill's *Southern Literature* I, 149-52, 153-55.)

*Northrup, Milton Harlow. "Sidney Lanier. Recollections and Letters." *Lippincott's Magazine* LXXV, 302-15. March, 1905.

Oliphant, Jean. "Wesleyan College Presents Sidney Lanier, Flutist." *Wesleyan Alumnæ,* January, 1925, pp. 4-9.

Omond, T. S. *English Metrists.* Oxford, 1921.

Page, Curtis Hidden. *Chief American Poets.* Selected Poems . . . with Notes, Reference Lists and Biographical Sketches. Boston, [1905.] Pp. 691-95; 650-51.

Painter, F. V. N. *Poets of the South.* New York, [1903.] Pp. 81-101; 227-34.

Pattee, Fred Lewis. *History of American Literature Since 1870.* New York, 1915. Pp. 22, 271, 274-88.

Perine, George C. *Poets and Verse-Writers of Maryland.* Cincinnati, 1898. Pp. 263-67.

*Phelps, William Lyon. "Fifty Years of Lanier." *Journal* (Atlanta, Ga.), July 6, 1931.

Rede, Kenneth. "Lanier's 'Owl Against Robin.'" *American Collector* III, 27-30. October, 1926.

Reese, Lizette Woodworth. "The Spirituality of Lanier." *Johns Hopkins Alumni Magazine* XIV, 482-84. June, 1926.

Roberts, Frank Stovall. "The Lanier Brothers, of Georgia." *Confederate Veteran* XXVII, 376. October, 1919.

Royce, Josiah. *Spirit of Modern Philosophy.* Boston, 1892. Pp. 442-45.

Scherer, James S. B. *The Holy Grail.* Philadelphia, 1906. Pp. 73-114.

Scott, W. J. "Life and Genius of Sidney Lanier." *Quarterly Review of the Methodist Episcopal Church, South,* n. s. V, 157-71. October, 1888.

Short, J. Saulsbury. "Sidney Lanier at Johns Hopkins." *Johns Hopkins Alumni Magazine* V, 7-24. November, 1916.

Simnds, Arthur B. *American Song.* London, 1894. Pp. 122-25.

468 BIBLIOGRAPHY

Sladen, Douglas. "An American Rossetti." *Literary World* (London) n. s. XLVIII, 378-79. November 17, 1893.

Snoddy, J. S. "Color and Motion in Lanier." *Poet-Lore* XII, 588-70. 1900.

Snyder Henry Nelson. *Modern Poets and Christian Teaching: Sidney Lanier.* Cincinnati, [1906.]

Spann, Minnie. "Sidney Lanier's Youth"; "Sidney Lanier's Manhood." *Independent* XLVI, 789, 821-22. June 21, June 28, 1894.

*Starke, A. H. "Sidney Lanier and Paul Hamilton Hayne: Three Unpublished Letters." *American Literature* I, 32-39. March, 1929.

*———— "William Dean Howells and Sidney Lanier." *American Literature* III, 79-82. March, 1931.

Stebbins, Emma. *Charlotte Cushman.* Boston, 1879. Pp. 268-69.

*Stedman, E. C. "The Late Sidney Lanier." *Genius and Other Essays.* New York, 1911. Pp. 250-53. (Reprinted from *Critic* I, 298. November, 1881.)

[————] *Life and Letters of Edmund Clarence Stedman.* By Laura Stedman and George M. Gould. New York, 1910. Vol. II, pp. 115, 154, 279.

———— *Nature and Elements of Poetry.* Boston, 1895.

———— *Poets of America.* Boston, 1885. Pp. 449-50.

Strong, Augustus Hopkins. *American Poets and Their Theology.* Philadelphia, 1916. Pp. 371-418.

Swiggett, Glen Levin. "Sidney Lanier." *Conservative Review* V, 187-92. September, 1901.

Taylor, Bayard. "A Picture of the Opening Ceremonies [of the Centennial Exhibition]." *Tribune* (New York), May 11, 1876.

[————] *Life and Letters of Bayard Taylor.* Edited by Marie Hansen-Taylor and Horace E. Scudder. Boston, 1884.

Taylor, Marie Hansen. *On Two Continents.* New York, 1905. Pp. 258-59.

[Thayer, William R.] *The Letters of William Roscoe Thayer.* Edited by Charles Downer Hazen. Boston, 1926. Pp. 26, 34, 36.

———— "Sidney Lanier and His Poetry." *Independent* XXXVI, 742-43. June 12, 1884.

Thorpe, Harry Colin. "Sidney Lanier: A Poet for Musicians." *Musical Quarterly* XI, 373-82. July, 1925.

Turnbull, Frances Litchfield. *The Catholic Man: A Study.* Boston, [1890.]

*Van Nosdall's List of Books for Sale. April 5, 1929: "Letter of Lanier to E. C. Stedman, [May, 1880]; June 2, 1929: "Letter of Lanier to the Editors of *Scribner's Monthly,* September 25, 1876."

Varnedoe, J. O. "Sidney Lanier: An Appreciation." *Georgia Historical Quarterly* II, 139-44. September, 1918.

Ward, William Hayes. "Four Poems." *Independent* XLIX, 933. July 22, 1897.

*——— "Memorial." *Poems of Sidney Lanier.* . . . New York, 1884. Pp. [xi]-xli.

Wayland, John W. *Sidney Lanier at Rockingham Springs.* Dayton,Va., 1912.

Weirick, Bruce. *From Whitman to Sandburg in American Poetry.* New York, 1924. Pp. 73-84, 93.

Wendell, Barrett. *Literary History of America.* New York, 1900. Pp. 481, 495-99.

West, C. N. *Brief Sketch of the Life and Writings of Sidney Lanier.* Savannah, Ga., 1888.

Westfeldt, Gustaf R. *Fifteen Minutes with Sidney Lanier.* New Orleans, 1915.

*[Whitman, Walt.] *With Walt Whitman in Camden.* By Horace Traubel. Boston, 1906. (Subsequent volumes: New York, 1908; 1914.)

Wiggins, Robert Lemuel. *Life of Joel Chandler Harris.* Nashville, Tenn., 1918. Pp. 70, 80, 127.

Wilkinson, William C. "One More Homage to Sidney Lanier." *Independent* XXXVIII, 1261. October 7, 1886.

Willard, Frances E. "Notes of Southern Literary Men and Women." *Independent* XXXIII, No. 1709, 3-4. September 1, 1881.

Willcockson, Ruth. "Rhythmical Principles and Practices of Sidney Lanier." (Unpublished master's thesis, University of Chicago, 1928.)

Williams, Stanley. "Sidney Lanier." In *American Writers on American Literature.* Edited by John Macy. New York, 1931.

Wills, George S. "Sidney Lanier—His Life and Writings." *Publications of the Southern History Association* III, 190-211. July, 1899. (Contains a full, accurate bibliography.)

Wilson, Heileman. "The Genius of Sidney Lanier." *Fetter's Southern Magazine* II, 11-16. February, 1893.

Wood, Clement. *Poets of America.* New York, 1925. Pp. 12, 68-81, 94, 382.

Woolf, Winfield. "The Poetry of Sidney Lanier." *Sewanee Review* X, 325-40. July, 1902.

——— "Sidney Lanier as Revealed in His Letters." *Sewanee Review* VIII, 346-64. July, 1900.

Wysham, Henry Clay. "Sidney Lanier." *Independent* XLIX, 1489-90. November 18, 1897.

SELECTED REVIEWS OF LANIER'S PUBLISHED WORK

Boy's Froissart.
Academy (London) XVII, 194. March 13, 1880.
Scudder, H. E. "Holiday Books." *Atlantic Monthly* XIV, 130. January, 1880.
Boy's King Arthur.
Academy (London) XIX, 7. January 1, 1881.
Scudder, H. E. "Books for Young People." *Atlantic Monthly* XLVII, 122-23. January, 1881.
Boy's Mabinogion.
Dial II, 182-83. December, 1881.
Boy's Percy.
Academy (London) XXIII, 237-38. April 7, 1883.
Nation XXV, 468. November 30, 1882.
Centennial Cantata.
Nation XII, 247. April 13, 1876; XXII, 336. May 25, 1876.
Apthorp, W. F., *Atlantic Monthly* XXXVIII, 122. July, 1876.
English Novel.
Dial IV, 40-41. June, 1883.
Harper's Magazine XLVII, 798-99. October, 1883.
Literary World (Boston) XIV, 204-05. June 30, 1883.
Nation XXXVII, 38. July 12, 1883.
Penn, Arthur. "Sidney Lanier on the English Novel." *Century Magazine* XXVII, 957-58. April, 1884.
Stoddard, F. H. "The Ideal in Literature." *New Englander* XLIII, 97-104. January, 1884.
Florida.
Literary World (Boston) VI, 116. January, 1876.
Nation XXI, 277. October 28, 1875.
Letters.
Dial XXVIII, 55. January 16, 1900.
Music and Poetry.
Critic n. s. XXXI, 365-66.
Burton, R. E. "Sidney Lanier's Essays." *Book Buyer* XVIII, 144-45. March, 1899.
Poem Outlines.
Poet-Lore XIX, 482-87. Winter, 1908.
Poems. 1877.
Harper's Magazine LIV, 617-18. March, 1877.
Newell, R. H. "The Music of the South." *Daily Graphic* (New York), January 22, 1877.

Taylor, Bayard. *Critical Essays and Literary Notes.* New York, 1890. Pp. 312-14. (Reprinted from the *Tribune* [New York], November 21, 1876.)

Poems. 1884, et seq.
Critic n. s. III, 3-4. January 3, 1885.
Literary World (Boston) XVI, 40-41. February 7, 1885.
Nation XXXIX, 528. December 18, 1884.
Spectator (London) LXV, 828-29. December 6, 1890.
Browne, Francis F. "Sidney Lanier." *Dial* v, 244-46. January, 1885.
Chamberlain, D. H. "Poems of Sidney Lanier." *New Englander* XLIV, 227-38. March, 1885.
Thayer, William R. "Lanier's Poems." *Independent* XXXVI, 1609. December 18, 1884.
———— "Sidney Lanier's Poems." *American* (Philadelphia) IX, No. 228, 167-68. December 20, 1884.

Science of English Verse.
Literary World (Boston) XI, 227. July 3, 1880.
Nation XXXI, 310-11. October 28, 1880.

Shakspere and His Forerunners.
Athenæum (London) No. 3943, 649-50. May 23, 1903.
Nation LXXVI, 401. May 14, 1903.
Outlook LXXIV, 476-77. June 20, 1903.
Brooke, C. F. Tucker. "Deceptive Illustrations." *Dial* LI, 245-46. October 1, 1911.
Few, W. P. "Sidney Lanier as a Student of English Literature." *South Atlantic Quarterly* II, 157-68. April, 1903.
Greenslet, Ferris. "Lanier's Lectures on Shakspere." *Atlantic Monthly* XCI, 266-67. February, 1903.
Payne, L. W., Jr. "Sidney Lanier's Lectures." *Sewanee Review* XI, 452-62. October, 1903.
Tolman, Albert H. "Shakespere Criticism and Discussion." *Dial* XXXV, 165-69. September 16, 1903.

Tiger-Lilies.
Atlantic Monthly XXI, 382. March, 1868.
Round Table VII, 396. December 14, 1867.

UNPUBLISHED LETTERS CONCERNING LANIER

Kirk, John Foster. To Gibson Peacock: January 16, 1875. Harvard College Library.
Lanier, Mary Day. To S. L. Eason: September 19, 1915. In the

possession of Mr. Sidney Lanier Eason, of Charleston, S. C.

—— To Mrs. James E. Fields: April 27, 1882; March 22, 1884. Henry E. Huntington Library and Art Gallery.

—— To Father Tabb: April 6, 1893; December 31, 1893. Author's collection.

—— To Dr. W. H. Ward and members of his family: March 23, 1891; November 20, 1900; March 4, 1902; October 26, 1909; August 13, 1910. Henry E. Huntington Library and Art Gallery.

Lanier, Robert Sampson. To Bayard Taylor: April 21, 1877. Cornell University Library.

Pratt, Waldo Selden. To his mother and father: November 16, 1879; February 1, February 8, February 15, March 7, March 29, May 12, May 17, 1880. In the possession of Dr. W. S. Pratt, of Hartford, Conn.

Taylor, Bayard. To Sidney Lanier: April 1, 1878. Cornell University Library.

—— To James Russell Lowell: November 1, 1875. Harvard College Library.

(Use has also been made of various other articles, reviews, letters and notices in newspapers—chiefly in the Macon *Telegraph* and the New York *Tribune*—and in the *Johns Hopkins University Circulars*, and of several souvenir programs containing information about Lanier. Sources for all such items are indicated in the notes if not previously in the text.)

PORTRAITS OF LANIER

Six photographs, one pen and ink sketch, and one portrait bust of Lanier are known to have been made before his death. They are as follows:

1. An ambrotype made in 1857. First reproduced—as an engraving on wood by T. Johnson: *Century Magazine*, n. s. V, opp. p. 803. (April, 1884). First photographic reproduction: *Symposium* (Northampton, Mass.) 1, No. 1. Frontispiece. (October, 1896.) Best reproduction: *Sidney Lanier*. By Edwin Mims. Boston, 1905. Opp. p. [26]. Reproduced in the present volume, opp. p. 24.

2. A *carte de visite* photograph taken about the close of the Civil War, showing Lanier in Confederate uniform. First reproduced: *The Lanier Book*. Edited by Mary E. Burt. [New York, 1904.] Frontispiece. Reproduced in the present volume, opp. p. 82.

3. In a group photograph made in 1866 or 1867. Reproduced: *Mid-Continent* VI, 83. (May, 1895.) Reproduced in the present volume, opp. p. 108.

4. A photograph made in 1870. First reproduced: *Letters of Sidney Lanier*, opp. p. 68. Best reproduction: Mims's *Sidney Lanier*, frontispiece.

5. A profile photograph (right view) made by Kuhn and Cummins, of Baltimore, January, 1874—the most familiar of all likenesses of Lanier. First reproduced—as a woodcut, in reverse: *Cottage Hearth*, June 1877, on the cover. (Reproduced thus in the present volume, opp. p. 294.) The best reproduction is that found in copies of the first edition of the collected *Poems*. New York, 1884. Frontispiece.

6. A full face photograph made by Kuhn and Cummins, of Baltimore, probably at the same time as the photograph previously described. First reproduced—as a woodcut: *Harper's Weekly* XXV, 653. (September 24, 1881.) First reproduction as a photograph: *Mid-Continent* VI, 81. (May, 1895.) Reproduced in the present volume, opp. p. 194.

7. A pen and ink sketch showing Lanier as a member of the Wednesday Club, made by Dr. Volck, a dentist of Baltimore, in 1878. Reproduced photographically in the Wednesday Club Album. Reproduced in the present volume—from the copy of the Album in the Johns Hopkins University Library, opp. p. 284.

8. A bronze bust by Ephraim Keyser, modeled about nine months before Lanier's death. First reproduced: *Mid-Continent* VI, 85. (May, 1895.) Reproduced from a new photograph in the present volume, opp. p. 414.

All other known likenesses of Lanier (oil paintings, engravings, busts, etc.) apparently derive from one or another of the portraits listed above.

NOTES

Bibliographical information concerning first and subsequent printings of collected poems and essays is given in connection with the principal mention of the title.

Bibliographical information concerning first and subsequent printings of uncollected poems and essays is not given in the notes as this information is included in the preceding bibliography of Lanier's work.

Lanier's letters to Gibson Peacock, Bayard Taylor, Paul Hamilton Hayne and to Mrs. Lanier and Bayard Taylor's letters to Lanier, are, with few exceptions, included in the volume of collected *Letters*. Accordingly, note references for quotations are omitted where the date and name of person addressed are mentioned in the text, though exact references are given for quotations from unpublished letters or letters printed elsewhere than in the collected *Letters*.

References to titles in the Bibliography are, as a rule, in the case of Lanier' own work to short title of volume; in the case of articles or books on Lanier to name of author only.

CHAPTER ONE

1. Eccentricity of academic judgment is revealed in the characterization of Lanier made by Mrs. Lucy Lockwood Hazard [*The Frontier in American Literature* (New York, 1927), p. 47]: "the decadent effusions of Southern dilettanti,—the pseudo-classical, pseudo-European poetizings of Timrod, Hayne, and Lanier, whose writing, thin and imitative, belongs entirely to the academic side of literature and has no connection with the author's geographical or social habitat." But this is more than academic eccentricity for it indicates absolute unfamiliarity with the work of each of the three authors named, especially of the work of Lanier whose best work springs from the Georgia soil and who wrote, moreover, a considerable number of dialect poems on topical themes.

2. *Southern Statesmen of the Old Regime* (New York, 1897), pp. 119-20.

3. *Autobiography of Joseph LeConte* (New York, 1903), pp. 60, 112.

4. Macon *News*, February 3, 1929, p. 3.

5. Clarke, 12.

6. Mims, 14. The Lanier genealogy is discussed by Lanier in two published letters to J. F. D. Lanier and reviewed at length by Mims, and summarized briefly in the present volume, Chapter xiv, pp. 286-87. The tradition that connects the Lanier family with that of George Washington is discussed and refuted in a series of articles in the *William and Mary College Quarterly*: iii, 71-74. July, 1894; iii, 137-39. October, 1894; iv, 35-36. July, 1896. For abstracts of wills of English Laniers see the *Virginia Magazine of History and Biography* xxviii, 340-42; xxxii, 260-63. Mr. W. G. Stanard, Secretary of the Virginia Historical Society, discussing the possibility of tracing Lanier's descent to the Laniers who were court painters and musicians under Henry viii, Elizabeth, James i and Charles i, writes (letter to the author of July 13, 1932): "there is no proof but some probability."

There is confusion in the records of later generations as of early ones. Mr. Henry Lanier gives the line of descent as John (1633-1719), the emigrant; Sampson, m. Elizabeth Washington; Sampson; Buckner; Sterling; Robert Sampson; Sidney. A cousin of the poet gives the line thus: John; Thomas, m. Elizabeth Washington; Sampson; Buckner; Robert Sampson; Sterling; Robert Sampson; Sidney.

7. Friendship had begun, it is said, even earlier, while R. S. Lanier was a student at the Virginia Military Institute. Portraits supposedly of Sidney Lanier's parents were reproduced in the Macon *News*, Sunday, February 3, 1929, p. 3. The picture of Mrs. Lanier is from a daguerreotype or tin-type, and is a blurred reproduction. The picture of R. S. Lanier is obviously from a miniature. It shows a handsome man with the firm mouth and prominent nose characteristic of Sidney Lanier. But the collar and the cut of the hair suggest a dandy of an earlier generation. R. S. Lanier was born September 22, 1819, and died October 20, 1893; Mrs. Lanier was born December 14, 1822, and died May 22, 1865.

8. *National Cyclopedia of American Biography* III, 535.

9. In the obituary notice in the *Report of the 11th Annual Meeting of the Georgia Bar Association* (Atlanta, 1894), quoted in Mims, 15.

10. To Northrup, May 12, 1866. All letters to Northrup appeared in *Lippincott's Magazine* for March, 1905, and are usually referred to in the notes by date only.

11. The "Lanier Cottage" on High Street, Macon, was not marked as the birthplace until 1912. In a paper read before the Macon History Club in 1913, Mr. Harry Stillwell Edwards spoke of it as "the house generally accepted as [Lanier's] birthplace." Mrs. W. A. Hopson and Mrs. Granville Connor, lifetime friends of Lanier and residents of Macon, insist that Lanier was born on Second Street, opposite the present location of the Alexandria School, and lived only briefly on High, perhaps for ten years at most. The most reliable Macon tradition is certainly against accepting the High Street House as the birthplace, though the present Macon attitude is to abide by the evidence of the tablet. The uncertainty and the attempt to obscure it are typical of the difficulties besetting the biographer of Lanier.

12. The description of Lanier's birthplace is based on information gathered by E. Prickard Karsten which appeared in a newspaper article published in a Macon newspaper in 1924. Clipping in the Lanier collection of the Washington Memorial Library, Macon.

13. Atkinson, C. Prescott. "Clifford Lanier." *Library of Southern Literature* VII, 3021.

14. The appearance of this house in 1869 is described by Mr. Harry Stillwell Edwards in the paper referred to in note 11, above. But the Laniers' occupancy of the house terminated some time during the Civil War.

15. Lanier, C. A., "Reminiscences of Sidney Lanier." *Chautauquan* XXI, 404.

16. In a letter to Sidney Lanier Eason, September 19, 1915. See also *The Lanier Book*, 128: " 'The Lanier family,' says the poet's wife, 'was one where love ruled.' "

17. Lanier, C. A., *Chautauquan* XXI, 403.

18. Mims, 18. In *The Lanier Book*, 128 Miss Burt quotes Mrs. Lanier as saying: "Mr. Lanier always spoke of his sister with deep reverence, calling her 'the violet' or 'my violet eyes.' He said of her: 'My sister never drifted from her native shore, which was heaven.' "

19. Lanier, C. A., "Sidney Lanier." *Gulf States Historical Magazine* II, 10.

20. *Ibid.*, 11

21. Clarke, 13.

22. *Letters*, 95.

23. Clarke, 12.

24. Mims, 24.

25. Lanier, C. A., *Chautauquan* XXI, 405.

26. Mr. Henry W. Lanier states (*Selections*, ix): "His mother taught him the notes on the piano, and he promptly passed on this new knowledge to John Booker, a musical negro barber of the neighborhood (who later had a famous troupe of darky minstrels which toured this country and Europe.)"

27. *Augustus Baldwin Longstreet* (New York, 1924), p. 69.

28. Clarke, 14.

29. *Chautauquan* XXI, 404. There is no other evidence that Lanier's middle finger was unnaturally short, but self-consciousness of his deformity may explain the tightly clenched fists in the two pictures that we have showing his hands.

30. Lanier, C. A., *Chautauquan* XXI, 404-05.

31. To R. M. Johnston: August 28, 1880. Mims, 324.

32. Ethridge.

33. Clarke, 14. *Cf. Shakspere and His Forerunners* II, 78: "the man knows not love who has not loved at eleven."

34. Hayne's single critical article on Lanier was first published in "A Poet's Letters to a Friend." *Critic* n. s. V, 77-78, 89-90. February 13 and 20, 1886. It appears also in the volume of collected *Letters*.

35. To. Mrs. S. M. Boykin: February 12, 1876. MS. Washington Memorial Library, Macon.

CHAPTER TWO

1. Lanier, C. A., *Gulf States Historical Magazine* II, 10.

2. Roberts.

3. W. A. Hopson, of Macon.

4. Lanier, C. A., *Chautauquan* XXI, 4c6.

5. This description is quoted by C. E. Jones in his *Education in Georgia* (Washington: Government Printing Office, 1889), pp. 79-83.

6. Thalian Hall was erected by the Thalian Society of old Oglethorpe University shortly before Lanier entered Oglethorpe. The first and second stories are divided into eight rooms—each having a fire place— and were used by the students. The third story was in one large hall with as many fire places as the floors below, and was used by the Thalian Literary Society for meetings and social affairs. Lanier's room—a second story room in the southeast corner, possibly not occupied by him until his second (Junior) year at Oglethorpe—was restored in 1930 as a memorial to Dr. H. D. Allen, founder of Allen's Invalid Home, which now occupies the site of the old campus. The room contains relics of Oglethorpe, including two books, *Greyslear: A Romance of the Mohawks* and *Didactics*, by Robert Walsh, from the Thalian Society Library and a *Book of Poetry* (Philadelphia: Presbyterian Board of Publications, no date) presented by Lanier to Mrs. Dollie Whitaker Hardeman when she was a school girl. The furniture is of the period; books by Lanier are kept in a cabinet that once belonged to President Talmage.

The site of old Oglethorpe has been marked with a stone which contains the cornerstone of the original main building erected in 1837. Dr. Talmage's home was occupied by Dr. and Mrs. Allen until 1921, when fire destroyed it.

I am especially indebted to Mrs. H. D. Allen, Sr., for information and pictures that make possible this statement concerning the scene of Lanier's college career.

7. Mims, 27-28.
8. Snyder, 14.
9. Mims, 31.
10. Varnedoe. *Georgia Historical Quarterly* II, 139-44. The ambrotype was made in 1857. In the picture the badge of the Thalian Literary Society is clearly discernible on the left lapel of Lanier's coat.
11. *Poems*, xxxix. All references to *Poems* (without date) are to the volume of collected poems, in the editions of 1884, 1891, 1916—or any of the reprints.
12. Ethridge, Willie Snow. "When Sidney Lanier was a Boy." Sunday Magazine of the Baltimore *Sun*, February 3, 1929, p. 11. Except for the incident quoted here, and the inclusion of an uncollected poem (see this work, Chapter IV, note 18, p. 482), this article is merely a condensation of the article by Mrs. Ethridge listed in the Bibliography.
13. Marble.
14. A somewhat different version of this affair is recorded by Mr. H. W. Lanier (*Selections*, xi). Lanier seems, in this account to have provoked the attack himself—though unintentionally—by teasing or raillery. His repentant adversary is said to have become his devoted nurse.
15. Mims, 31-32.
16. Baskervill, 149-51.
17. Mims, 32.
18. *Poems*, xii.
19. Allen. But see also Chapter III, note 62.
20. Byron is quoted by Lanier only once, in *Tiger-Lilies*, p. 194; Wordsworth in *Tiger-Lilies*, p. 29, but later also.
21. Cf. with this passage from "Aurora Leigh" Lanier's own poem "Barnacles."
22. Cf. "long-drawn Systole and long-drawn Diastole" in *Sartor Resartus* (Book II, Chapter III) and Lanier's use of the phrase, obviously a well-liked one, in *Shakspere and His Forerunners* II, 328, and in the sonnet "On a Palmetto."
23. However, Lanier seems never to have appreciated or attempted to understand Goethe. Mims remarks (p. 345): "Homer, Dante, and Goethe were but little more than names to him."
24. In the *Education of Henry Adams*, Chapter IV: "Harvard College, 1854-58," we read: "The literary world then agreed that truth survived in Germany alone, and Carlyle, Matthew Arnold, Renan, Emerson, with scores of popular followers, taught the German faith. The literary world had revolted against the yoke of coming capitalism—its money-lenders, its bank directors, and its railway magnates. [The satirists and idealists] turned to Germany because at that moment Germany was neither economical nor military, and a hundred years behind western Europe in the simplicity of its standard. German thought, method, honesty, and even taste, became the standards of scholarship. . . . All serious thought was obliged to become German, for German thought was revolutionizing criticism."
25. See *Music and Poetry*, 95, and *The English Novel*, 124.
26. Carlyle, "Novalis."
27. *Shakspere and His Forerunners* (referred to hereafter as *SHF*) I, 54.
28. Lanier could have read *Henry of Ofterdingen* in English in the Cambridge (Mass.) edition of 1842 (reprinted New York, 1853), selections from Novalis in Mrs. Sarah Austin's *Fragments from German Prose Writers* (New York, 1841), and in Carlyle.

29. *Tiger-Lilies*, 29.
30. Lecture III.
31. *Tiger-Lilies*, 35.
32. Henry James. *Works* (New York Edition) II, vii.
33. Lanier, C. A., *Chautauquan* XXI, 405-06.
34. Lanier, H. W., *Selections*, xi.
35. Untraced newspaper article on Clifford Lanier by Judge Walter Jones.
36. Fraser. See also P. E. Graham, "James Woodrow, Calvinist and Evolutionist." *Sewanee Review* XL, 307-15. July-September, 1932.
37. Baskervill, 153.
38. *Florida*, 210.
39. Northrup describes the exercises and quotes from the commencement program. The diploma awarding Lanier the degree of Bachelor of Liberal Arts hangs in the office of President Thornwell Jacobs of modern Oglethorpe, the gift of Mrs. Lanier. It is reproduced in *The Oglethorpe Book of Georgia Verse* (Oglethorpe University Press, 1930), opp. p. 160.
40. Lanier, C. A., *Chautauquan* XXI, 406.
41. Mims, 35.
42. *Tiger-Lilies*, 16-17.
43. "Lucrezia Borgia," an opera in three acts by Donizetti, first produced in 1834.
44. *Letters*, 85-86.
45. Mims, 30.
46. *Poems*, xiii.
47. Mims, 38.
48. Woolf, "Sidney Lanier as Revealed in His Letters." Stated on the authority of Mr. Woolf's father, a student at Oglethorpe at the time Lanier was there.
49. Lanier, C. A., *Chautauquan* XXI, 406.
50. *Poems* (1884); note on "The Mocking Bird," p. [243].
51. *Poems*, xiv.
52. Northrup.

CHAPTER THREE

1. *Tiger-Lilies* [119]-20.
2. Mims, 27.
3. *Tiger-Lilies*, 115.
4. Northrup, "Sidney Lanier," *loc. cit.*, 303.
5. Mims, 46-47.
6. In Mims, opposite p. 134, is a photograph of a musical score written by Lanier. In ink is written: "Huldegung der Britischer Nation. Labitzky. 3rd Flute. Arran. by S. C. Lanier"; and in pencil "C. E. Campbell, Dec. 1861. in camp at Norfolk."
7. Except where other sources are acknowledged, the details of Lanier's military experiences are taken from the long letter to Northrup of June 11, 1866, *loc. cit.*, 307-9.
8. Spann, "Sidney Lanier's Youth."
9. Hankins.
10. *Thorn-Fruit*, 21.
11. *Ibid.*, 34.
12. To Judge Bleckley: October 9, 1874. Mims, 153.
13. Quoted by Browne, *From Dixie*, 40.
'4. French, 157.

15. Cited by Mims, 49.

16. Lindsay.

17. Lanier, C. A., *Chautauquan* XXI, 407.

18. See unpublished letter of Mary Day Lanier to W. H. Ward: October 26, 1909. Henry E. Huntington Library and Art Gallery, H M 7749. See also *The Lanier Book*, 131, and *SHF* I, 55—on being cold.

19. Clay, 198.

20. MS., Duke University Library. (Quoted incorrectly in Clay, *A Belle of the Fifties*.)

21. Clarke, 15-16.

22. Hankins.

23. *Op. cit.*, 123.

24. *Op. cit.*, 31.

25. What slight information I am able to give concerning Ginna (Virginia) Hankins comes from Clarke's *Reminiscences* and the confessedly biographical *Thorn-Fruit*, supplemented by a brief account of Miss Hankins contained in a letter of June 15, 1930, from my aunt, Mrs. G. A. Hankins, of Williamsburg, Virginia, whose husband (and cousin) was a second cousin of Ginna Hankins. Ginna Hankins is buried in Hollywood Cemetery, Richmond, Virginia.

26. *Op. cit.*, 42.

27. *Op. cit.*, 43.

28. See Lanier, C. A., *Chautauquan* XXI, 407.

29. The other poem given in *Thorn-Fruit* (p. 91) might well, and with equal reason, be ascribed to Lanier, but neither the circumstances of its introduction nor the style of the poem suggests Sidney Lanier's authorship; it is probably by Clifford Lanier.

30. Clarke, 17.

31. It is hardly necessary to point out marks of resemblance, in vocabulary and in ideas, between this poem and the one previously quoted.

32. *Poems*, (1884), 222.

33. I quote from the version given by Clarke; the punctuation differs slightly from that in the collected *Poems*.

34. Professor Clarke's guess is that it "was no doubt appended to Mr. Hopson's copy . . . by way of a carried over comment or reference that would be understood and responded to by the poet's friend."

35. Clarke, 19. This part of Lanier's letter had already been published in a note in *Poems* (1884), 246.

36. Clarke, *loc. cit.* If this date is correctly given—and there is no reason to doubt it—the introduction of Lanier to Bacon's Castle must have occurred in the late summer or early fall of 1863, so that for at least a year he lived in proximity to Miss Hankins. All the verse here discussed probably dates from 1863.

37. The Laniers themselves had been stationed between Franklin, in Southampton County, and Suffolk in the spring of 1863. Clifford Lanier, writing to Mrs. Clay, on April 17, 1863, asked her to "write to us, directing care General French, Franklin, Virginia." Hopson had probably been transferred from Fort Boykin.

38. Lanier, C. A., *Chautauquan* XXI, 407-08.

39. It is interesting to note that Lanier probably read some of these books in editions printed in the Confederacy. *Macaria* (by the author of *St. Elmo*) was a new novel first published in 1864; *Les Misérables* was published in translation in Richmond in 1863-64.

40. Mims, 55-56.

41. January 18, 1864. Mims, 56.

42. *Cf. Thorn-Fruit*, Chapter xii.

43. Mims (49 ff.) places this experience in 1862, but I feel that the later date is the more acceptable. Quoted in part by Mims, the address was first published entire in 1928. See Bibliography, Uncollected Prose.

44. *Op. cit.*, 169-73.

45. At least the Irish major in *Thorn-Fruit* says this, pp. 57-58.

46. *Thorn-Fruit*, 61.

47. Wilmington fell January 15, 1865—and with it the last hopes of the Confederacy.

48. Lanier, in a letter to Ginna Hankins. *Southern Bivouac* ii, 760.

49. Clarke, 21-22.

50. Clarke, 22-23, 25. The last page of the letter ("Stormy Petrel" to the end) is given in facsimile on p. 24. The signature is "I am yours [*sic*] Own, S. C. L."

51. So Lanier, in his letter to Northrup, names the boat; and Clarke, Mims, and others follow him. But in both the articles by Clifford Lanier listed in the Bibliography the name of the boat is given as the "Annie."

52. *Chautauquan* xxi, 408. But probably quoted by Clifford Lanier from Browne, *From Dixie*.

53. Mims, 58-59.

54. Recollections of a survivor, in an undated clipping from the *Confederate Veteran*, 192-.

55. Litz, 22.

56. Callaway, J. A.

57. See *War of the Rebellion* (Washington: Government Printing Office), Series 2, Vol. vii, pp. 448-50.

58. *Poems* (1884), 224.

59. *Round Table* iii, 443. July 14, 1866; *Poems* (1884), 225.

60. *Cf. Thorn-Fruit*, 40: "Mark's salute to the spring, suggested by Heine's 'Frühlings Grüss.' " This statement by Clifford Lanier suggests that the poem may have been written not in prison but at Fort Boykin. The note in the collected *Poems* (1884) reads: "Point Lookout Prison, 1864."

61. *Tiger-Lilies*, 123-24.

62. This episode of Lanier's rescue from death is recorded by Mr. Alfred Allen, who quotes the "little mother's" own account of it, heard from her at a resort hotel. In recent letters to the author both Mr. Allen and Mr. Henry Lanier confessed that they had forgotten the name of the lady. But I am informed by Mrs. E. H. Clopton, a first cousin of Sidney Lanier, that the lady was Mrs. Mattie Montgomery and that her daughter was named Ella.

63. Lanier, H. W., *Selections*, xviii.

CHAPTER FOUR

1. Northrup, *loc. cit.*, p. 308. Professor Mims gives versions of the letters to Northrup that have been corrected "to conform to the original copies."

2. But *cf.* Mims, 58: "To this prison life Lanier always attributed his breakdown in health."

3. *Thorn-Fruit*, 98.

4. *Ibid.*, 102.

5. Originally published as "Wedding Bells," *Independent* xxxvi, 1057. August 21, 1884. Reprinted as "The Wedding," *Poems* (1884), 223.

6. "In those days," writes Mrs. G. A. Hankins, a contemporary of Ginna, "a soldier friend did not mean so much, as he might be 'here today and gone tomorrow.' " It is perfectly possible that I have read altogether too much into the evidence we have of Lanier's love for Ginna Hankins; and it may be of no significance that Clifford Lanier's hero, Mark Wilton, marries Lucy Pegram, who is quite definitely Ginna Hankins. Lanier and Miss Hankins remained friends throughout his life, and continued to correspond with each other.

7. *Independent* xxxvi, 1057. August 21, 1884; *Poems* (1884), 233. But the two poems are not grouped together in the collected *Poems*.

8. *Poems* (1884), 230. The footnote reads "Georgia, September, 1865."

9. Lanier, C. A., *Chautauquan* xxi, 408.

10. Modern Oglethorpe, at Oglethorpe (near Atlanta), Georgia, perpetuates the name and ideals but not the charter of Lanier's alma mater.

11. So Northrup gives the name; but Mrs. H. D. Allen, Sr. (née Whitaker) informs me that the oak referred to stood on the lawn of her uncle, Mr. J. C. Whitaker, and spells the name with a single "t."

12. Mims, 76.

13. Those who are unable to consult a file of the *Round Table* may find lengthy excerpts from several editorials reprinted in Mims, 76-78.

14. Letter to Northrup of May 12, 1866, *loc. cit.*, 305; *Tiger-Lilies*, 17.

15. Hankins.

16. *Cf.* Tennyson's "Maud," Part i, iii: "Passionless, pale, cold face, star-sweet on a gloom profound."

17. The uncertainty of Lanier's authorship makes it wise to attempt no interpretation of this poem. In defence of his authorship, I can only say that each rereading convinces me the more of it, and that it is a good poem, quite worthy of inclusion in his collected work. Against his authorship should be cited the fact that all of the poems undoubtedly by Lanier, both signed and unsigned, appeared in the column headed "Literariana"; this poem did not. But the fact may be without significance, one way or the other. Lanier's first signed contribution to the *Round Table* was "The Tournament" (Joust First), in the issue for June 8, 1867.

18. This poem is given by Mr. Alfred Allen, on the authority of "Ella" herself. It is also given in an article by Mrs. Willie Snow Etheridge, previously cited (Chapter ii, note 12), with the introductory note: "Lanier wrote another poem to G. H., so the old friends of Lanier believe, but the poem has never appeared in any of his published works. They do not vouch for its authenticity, but they like to repeat it, and say with knowing smiles that Sidney wrote it." In this version line 13 omits "dark" and line 18 is omitted entirely. Lines 10 and 11 obviously belong together, as a single line.

19. Judge Clopton had removed from Alabama to Macon in 1844. Clifford Lanier, as we shall see, married Judge Clopton's daughter Wilhelmina. Her brother, Edward Hunter Clopton, married Lanier's first cousin, Virginia Eason, daughter of Mrs. Wilhelmina Ligon Lanier Eason, of Charleston, S. C. Judge Clopton himself married in 1887 the widow of Senator Clement C. Clay, Mrs. Virginia Tunstall Clay, whom Sidney and Clifford Lanier had accompanied to Virginia in 1863.

20. September 26, 1866. Mims, 73-74.
21. June 11, 1866.
22. *Letters*, 121.
23. June 29, 1866.
24. To Northrup: December 16, 1867, *loc. cit.*, 311.
25. *Retrospects and Prospects*, 29.
26. July 28, 1866.
27. Mims, 78.
28. There is no "Dedication" in *Tiger-Lilies*. The Preface is dated September, 1867.
29. MS. in possession of Dr. T. O. Mabbott.
30. Mims, 14.
31. Mr. Charles Lanier died in 1923 at the age of eighty-nine. For a portrait see *Independent* LXIII, 1551, December 26, 1907; or *World's Work* X, 6714, October, 1905.
32. For information concerning J. F. D. Lanier see, among other sources, his autobiography, referred to in the Bibliography, and *The James F. D. Lanier Home: An Indiana Memorial*. By G. S. Cottman. Issued by the Department of Conservation of the State of Indiana, 1928.
33. April 16, 1867. Mims, 79-81.
34. Unpublished MS., Duke University Library.
35. On the subject of Lanier's candidacy see Mims, 91.
36. December 16, 1867.

CHAPTER FIVE

1. See *Thorn-Fruit*, 21; and this work, Chapter III, p. 45.
2. The name Thalberg is a translation into German of Montvale—the name of Sterling Lanier's Tennessee resort. But it is also the name of a musician distinguished in Lanier's day, Sigismund Thalberg, who visited the United States in 1857. Of him Liszt said: "Thalberg is the only artist who can play the violin on the piano."
3. But compare the Furlow Academy commencement address, quoted this work, Chapter VII, pp. 137-38.
4. *Cf.* also Lanier's statement in his letter to Northrup of June 11, 1866: "I like friendship better than all things else in the world." *Loc. cit.*, 307.
5. In the *Round Table*.
6. *Tiger-Lilies*, 106, 107, 125; and see the references to Novalis in the letter to Hopson of September 15, 1863; *Retrospects and Prospects*, 7-8; *Music and Poetry*, 95, 201; *English Novel*, 124; etc. See also, *ante*, Chapter II, p. 29. And *cf. SHF* I, 53-54.
7. *Cf.* the essay, "Mazzini on Music"; *post*, Chapter XV, pp. 318-19.
8. Pattee, 277.
9. Mims, 81-82.
10. This character—in Wilkie Collins's novel *Armmadale*—so soon lost her popular identity that Professor Mims let pass the erroneous spelling "Lydian Guelts" (Mims, 82) which President Snyder "corrected" to read "Lydian guilts." (Snyder, 40).
11. See Bibliography, Reviews.
12. Other equally obvious parallels between the two novels are numerous. *Cf.*, for example, the episodes of the deserted ladies, and the rôles played by their maids. Professor Pattee, however, considers the similarity not very great.
13. Longfellow, *Hyperion* (Prose Works, Boston, 1882. Vol. II), 43.
14. Wiggins, 80.

CHAPTER SIX

1. "To Wilhelmiha." *Manhattan Magazine* IV, 380. September, 1884; *Poems* (1884), 232. A sonnet by Clifford Lanier, "Wilhelmina. A Portrait," published in the *Century Magazine* XXIV, 192 (June, 1882), refers to another Wilhelmina, sister of R. S. Lanier.

2. Lanier, C. A., *Chautauquan* XXI, 409. Quoted entire as given.

3. Lanier's friend Campbell preserved the letter written by Lanier on the occasion of his wedding. Mr. Vachel Lindsay, who saw this letter in 1906, wrote of it then as "an ideal one-page wedding letter," but in conversation with the author in September, 1929, he described it as drippingly sweet, "like a ripe peach."

4. In his letter to Mrs. Clay of August 6, 1867, Lanier refers to his fiancée as "Miss Mamie Day"—Mamie being the name by which she was affectionately known to her family. In later years he almost invariably referred to her as "May." The earliest published photograph of Mrs. Lanier (1873) is that given in Mims, opp. p. 98.

5. Oliphant.

6. "Sketches of Sidney Lanier and His Life in Macon," by E. Prickard Karsten; unascribed newspaper clipping in the Lanier collection of the Washington Memorial Library, Macon. See Chapter I, note 4.

7. A letter of October, 1866. *Letters*, 65.

8. Lovett.

9. A letter written by their father, R. S. Lanier, to Clifford Lanier, June 23, 1878, quoted by Griggs (see Bibliography) illuminates the situation described in the preceding paragraph: "What you say relative to the distinction other men have won in the world brings to me an almost painful sense of your sacrifices. I do indeed daily think of you as a hero, who has had the courage to repress aspirations for distinction, with the view of benefitting others. On the notion that what could not be well helped most be borne (for you and I have been environed with circumstances hard to deal with) I have reluctantly acquiesced in your continued uncongenial vocation. But the fact of acquiescence was only possible, first on the idea that you were thereby rendering important aid to dependent relatives, and second, in the hope that every succeeding year would somehow bring about a change. . . . I have not been without fear that in the midst of your brave work you have had moments of repining."

10. Mr. C. P. Roberts to Mr. Vachel Lindsay.

10a. Mrs. Lanier died December 29, 1931, at the home of her son, Charles Day Lanier, Greenwich, Conn., after an illness of eight years; age eighty-seven.

11. Clarke, 26.

12. Mims, 97.

13. Mims, 92.

14. Mims, 94.

15. *Retrospects and Prospects*, 31.

16. *Independent* XXV, 1201. October 11, 1883; *Poems* (1884), 209.

17. *Round Table* VII, 124. February 12, 1868; *Poems* (1884), 93—as "Tyranny."

18. *Round Table* VII, 236, April 11, 1868; four stanzas quoted by Mims, 93 (1905); *Poems* (1916), 223.

19. *Poems* (1916), 222.

20. *Scott's Monthly Magazine* VI, 873. December, 1868; *New Eclectic* IV, 248. February, 1869; *Poems* (1884), 213.

21. "Our Hills," concluding lines.

22. Mims, 96.

23. Program preserved at Wesleyan College; reproduced in facsimile in *History of Alpha Delta Pi*. . . . Edited and compiled by Jessica North Macdonald . . . Ames, Iowa, 1929. Pp. 338-40. "Sacred Memories" is said to be and probably is an original composition.

24. *Letters*, 65-66.

25. March 15, 1869.

26. Lanier surely meant May, 1870—that is, the following year.

27. *Letters*, 222. The MSS. of the letters to Hayne published in the collected *Letters* are now in the Duke University Library.

28. So Mrs. Lawrence Turnbull told Mme. Blanc (Th. Bentzon). See Bentzon, "Un Musician Poète."

29. The Preface is dated October, 1869.

30. *Round Table* VII, 60. January 25, 1868; *Poems* (1884), 234.

31. The date given in the *Round Table*. In his letter to Northrup of December 16, 1867, Lanier does not even mention his approaching wedding.

32. *Independent* XXXVI, 545. May 1, 1884; *Poems* (1884), 236.

33. *Independent* XXXVI, 833. July 3, 1884; *Poems* (1884), 218.

34. *Century Magazine* XXXII, 377. July, 1886; *Poems* (1891), 156. J. D. H. was James DeWitt Hankins, a younger brother of Virginia Hankins.

35. *Southern Magazine* IX, 127. July, 1871; *Poems* (1884), 215.

36. Part I, *Round Table* V, 365. June 8, 1867; *Living Writers of the South*, 322; in "The Psalm of the West," *q. v.*; *Poems* (1884), 226-27. Part II, *Round Table* VI, 13. July 6, 1867. *Poems* (1884), 227-29.

37. "Betrayal," *q. v.*, was published in 1875; the three songs together in *Poems* (1884), 204-06.

38. "May the Maiden" has been set to music by Lawrence and Blackman, Mary Carmichael, John Alden Carpenter, and Mrs. K. Hill. With the "Evening Song" and "A Ballad of Trees and the Master" it has been most popular of Lanier's songs with composers.

39. *Round Table* VI, 61. July 27, 1867; *Poems* (1884), 219.

40. *Round Table* VIII, 329. November 14, 1868; *Poems* (1884), 89.

41. The capital letter indicates a line of different length, either shorter—as here— or longer than the rest.

42. There are several references to the lotus in poems of this period of interest in oriental themes; but the lily replaces the lotus in the later, revised version of one of the poems—"June Dreams in January." See below, Chapter XII, p. 249.

43. *Poems* (1916), 221, note 1.

44. *Round Table* VIII, 157. September 5, 1868; *New Eclectic* III, 250. October, 1868; *Scott's Magazine* VI, 718. October, 1868; *Poems* (1884), 94.

45. Privately printed on a single folded sheet, dated September 27, 1868. (The only copy I have seen is that belonging to Mr. Sidney Lanier Eason, of Charleston, S. C., great-grandson of Sterling and Sarah Fulwood Lanier.) Reprinted *Poems* (1884), 207-08.

46. *Lippincott's Magazine* XXXI, 58. January, 1883; *Poems* (1884), 214.

47. *Round Table* VIII, 281. October 24, 1868; *Poems* (1884), 221.

48. The first half, in a revised version, appeared as part of "The Psalm of the West," *Lippincott's Magazine*, July, 1876; the poem in the earlier version appeared first in the *Independent* XXXVI, 1121. September 4, 1884. Reprinted, *Poems* (1884),

237-40. I accept the date of composition given by Mrs. Lanier—1869—but it should be observed that the story told in the poem is truer of a later date, possibly January, 1874, or January, 1875.

49. In Mrs. Turnbull's novel, *The Catholic Man*, the hero Paul (Lanier) offers the first part of "June Dreams in January" as his own composition under the title of "A Southern Night Song." Perhaps Mrs. Turnbull knew of a publication of the poem under this title—but the version given is that used in "The Psalm of the West."

50. The titles are given by Mims, 96-97.

51. See Chapter III, p. 43.

52 *Southern Magazine* VIII, 288-90, 446-56. March, April, 1871; *Retrospects and Prospects*, 1-33.

53. There are few allusions to sculpture or painting in Lanier's poetry, and the allusions in his prose—as in the essay "From Bacon to Beethoven"—always seem forced. Lanier lived of course in a period that not only produced abominable sculpture, painting, and architecture, but that seemed to prefer of the art of the past that which was equally abominable. Lanier's knowledge of the arts, save the arts of music and poetry, was limited and his taste was undeveloped, and in no way superior to that of his period.

54. *Southern Magazine* X, 172-82. February, 1872; *Music and Poetry*, 95-114.

55. Starke, "Sidney Lanier and Paul Hamilton Hayne." The MSS. of the letters here first published are in the author's collection.

56. *Round Table* VI, 312. November 9, 1867; *Living Writers of the South*, 322; *Poems* (1884), 235.

CHAPTER SEVEN

1. Mims, 99.

2. Mims, 115.

3. Author's Macon notes.

4. See the uncollected poem outlines "One in Two" and "Two in One."

5. See in this connection the letter to Hayne of June 10, 1873, given by Starke, "Sidney Lanier and Paul Hamilton Hayne."

6. The phrase occurs again in the Centennial cantata, l. 50. See Chapter XII, p. 245.

7. Macon *Daily Telegraph*, April 27, 1870; Macon *Daily Telegraph*, April 27, 1887; *Retrospects and Prospects*, 94-103.

8. Mims, 103.

9. See Chapter III, pp. 59-60.

10. This address was first published in the *Sunday School Times* for November 21, 1891, with the following note: "A Sunday School address, delivered at a spring festival in or about 1868"; published again in the *Southern Churchman* for February 23, 1929, with this note: "Sunday School Address, written by Sidney Lanier for Master McKay, May 1, 1873." There is no doubt that it was written for William McKay, but the date of composition—or delivery—is uncertain.

11. *Letters*, 244.

12. *New Eclectic* VI, 294-96, March, 1870; *Poems* (1884), 210-12.

13. Mims, 281.

14. *XIX Century* II, 708. February, 1870. See Chapter XX, p. 45, note 54.

15. Said to have been printed in a Georgia newspaper in 1869, the first publication known to me is that in *Poems* (1884), 180.

16. *Poems* (1884), 175.

17. Joseph Clisby, editor of the Macon *Telegraph and Messenger*, had written edi-

torials advocating the planting of corn.

18. *Independent* xxxvi, 321. March 13, 1884; *Poems* (1884), 169.
19. *Letters*, 228.
20. Letter of February, 1870, quoted by Baskervill, 194.
21. *Letters*, 228-29.
22. *Letters*, 68.
23. *Independent* xxxv, 385. March 29, 1883; *Poems* (1884), 217.
24. *Letters*, 69.
25. Ethridge.
26. *Letters*, 70.
27. *Letters*, 71.
28. Mims, 115. R. B. Bullock was (1868-1871) reconstruction governor of Georgia, the leader of "a carnival of public spoliation," and Hall was one of his henchmen.
29. In a letter to Hayne of March 2, 1872 (unpublished MS. in the possession of the author) Lanier complains of the "swirl of business I've been tossed (*'Jactatus undis'*) for the past thirty days and nights."
30. This letter is given in Mims, 112-14, but I follow the fuller version of the Henry E. Huntington Library MS. H M 7084, a copy of the original made probably by Miss Susy Ward, showing slight changes from Mims's version. One page is missing from the Huntington MS.
31. Mims, 117.
32. On February 14, 1931, a tablet commemorating Lanier's residence in Texas was unveiled in the ballroom of the Menger Hotel, the gift of the Texas Division of the United Daughters of the Confederacy. The rooms occupied by Lanier (Suite No. 64) are described in a newspaper article of recent date, copied in the Boston *Transcript* from the San Antonio *Evening News:* "The suite consists of two high-ceilinged and spacious rooms joined by the old-type curtained archway. The living room has two immense old-style windows, wide as large doorways, which reach from the floor almost to the ceiling. They open onto the balcony which overlooks the famous Alamo Plaza. . . .

"Between the windows is a tall wall-mirror which extends from the floor to a height of almost nine feet. In a corner is an original old marble-topped smoking table belonging to the suite of furniture which, with but few changes, remains the same as that used by the poet when he made his home there. . . .

"The four posts [of the old solid mahogany four-poster canopied bed] which support the canopy are about nine feet in height and the level of the bed itself is three feet above the floor. . . .

"Beside the bed is a small table with carved legs which is also a part of the original set. Opposite the bed on the inside wall of the bedroom is a built-in liquor cabinet with huge mirror-doors.

"An ancient mahogany 'chest of drawers' occupies a conspicuous place in the opposite corner of the bedroom."

(Clipping sent me by Mr. Robert P. Eckert, Jr.)

CHAPTER EIGHT

1. Mayfield, 19. Mr. Mayfield has gathered—and thrice published—most of the available information concerning the three months Lanier spent in Texas.
2. Mims, 117.
3. Mims, 5.

4. Details of Lanier's residence in Texas are to be gleaned from his essay "San Antonio de Bexar."

5. The manuscript is in the Huntington Library. The signature to the letter is "Otfall," and a note, possibly in Mrs. Lanier's hand, reads "Pen Name, for newspaper publication, in Texas." On an accompanying sheet of paper is written in Lanier's hand "Marietta, Ga. Sep. 3rd 1873."

6. *Southern Magazine* xiii, 83-99, 138-52. July, August, 1873. Reprinted, slightly condensed, in *San Antonio de Bexar: A Guide and History.* Compiled and edited by William Corner (San Antonio, 1890), pp. 68-91; in full, *Retrospects and Prospects*, 34-93.

7. Mims, 118.

8. *Letters*, 74 n.

9. *Ibid.*, 71-72.

10. *Letters*, 73.

11. *Poems*, xix.

12. Lanier, C. A., *Gulf States Historical Magazine* ii, 14.

13. Lanier, C. A., *Chautauquan* xxi, 409.

14. Mr. Mayfield (p. 26), states that Lanier returned to Georgia by way of Dallas, where in the hotel lobby he lectured on poetry and read some verses to a group of people who had gathered about him.

15. Knight.

16. *Letters*, 236.

17. Browne, *Johns Hopkins University Circular No. 12*, 168.

18. The fact that Colonel R. M. Johnston was not paid for the Dukesborough tales that he contributed to the *Southern Magazine* [see his *Autobiography* (Washington, 1900), p. 72] leads one to suspect that other contributors might also have received no compensation. If Lanier did receive compensation the amount was probably never very great.

19. *Letters*, 74.

20. Wysham.

21. *Letters*, 74-75.

22. The details of this and the three paragraphs following are unless otherwise identified taken from *Letters*, 75-82.

23. "It is unfortunate that he left no compositions to indicate a musical power sufficient to give him a place in the history of American music." (Mims, 141.) For music by Lanier, see Bibliography. Published music by Lanier has not been noted by other biographers or critics. Even the article on Lanier in Grove's *Dictionary of Music and Musicians* makes no mention of his compositions.

24. Lanier's own letter of February 23, 1873, suggests that his music was realistic in character; but to call it realistic is not of course to call it imitative. Lanier's essay "From Bacon to Beethoven" contains some interesting remarks on programme music, and a denial of the possibility of actually imitating the sounds of nature; and his friend Wysham has described "Field-larks and Black-birds" as an interpretation, without imitation, which suggested the wild surroundings of the woods and fields.

25. *Poems*, xx-xxi.

26. Mims, 126-27.

27. *Letters*, 239.

28. Lanier, H. W., *Selections*, xxiii.

29. Wysham.

30. *Letters*, 84-85.
31. *Letters*, 77.
32. Foerster, 238.
33. Mims, 142.
34. *Letters*, 98.
35. *Letters*, 85. See this work, Chapter II, pp. 35-36.
36. *Letters*, 88.
37. *Letters*, 88-89.
38. *Letters*, 97.
39. *Letters*, 93.
40. *Letters*, 95.
41. Spann, "Sidney Lanier's Manhood."
42. *Poems*, xxxi f.
43. Baskervill, 212-13.
44. Stedman, *Poets of America*, 449.
45. Letter to President Gilman, January 29, 1888. *Forty-sixth Birthday of Sidney Lanier*, 25.
46. Wysham says that his eyes were bluish grey, and that even at this time his beard showed signs of grey. His fingers were long and tapering, his hand delicate but not thin. He seemed tall but actually he was less than six feet.
47. *Ca.* February 7, 1874. *Letters*, 94-95.
48. *Letters*, 98. The first page of the MSS., reproduced in *The Pageant of America* (New Haven, 1926) XI, 256, is inscribed: "To Henry C. Wysham. Dec. 25, 1873. With the warm, friendly wishes of Sidney Lanier."
49. Baskervill, 270.
50. New York *Evening Post*, March 6, 1874, p. 1; *Poems* (1884), 107.

CHAPTER NINE

1. Now Mrs. J. N. Nisbet of Macon, daughter-in-law of the Judge E. A. Nisbet concerning whom Lanier delivered a memorial address.
2. Author's Macon notes. But the story has been printed several times in Macon newspapers.
3. *Century Magazine* XXIV, 838-39. October, 1882; *Poems* (1884), 71-73.
4. *Poems* (1884), 244.
5. "Recollections of F. H. Gottlieb," Macon *Telegraph*, February 3, 1929.
6. *Letters*, 238-40.
7. Macon *Telegraph and Messenger*, May 31, 1874. Another performer at this concert was Mrs. James Monroe Ogden (née Lamar).
8. Czurda, a native of Breslau, Germany, had come to Georgia during the war. Lanier, it will be recalled, had for a while played regularly on Tuesday nights with Czurda and Mrs. Boykin.
9. The answer to "the age he preferred" is given in Mims, 311; the answers to the other questions in Miss Burt's *Lanier Book*, 134. It is possible that they do not belong together.
10. Author's Macon notes. The account of Lanier's stay at Sunnyside has been incorporated in several local newspaper articles, the information derived as here from Mrs. J. N. Nisbet.
11. This episode has also been recorded by J. M. Kell. For Kell see Bibliography.

12. To Northrup, September 1, 1874, *loc. cit.*, 314.

13. *Letters*, 100.

14. Mr. E. P. Kuhl states (*Studies in Philology* xxvii, 467, note 2): "Mr. Walter Damrosch told me in 1926 that his father, who befriended Lanier, had received many delightful letters from the poet. Unfortunately a warehouse, in which the furniture of the Damrosches was stored, burnt to the ground. Mr. Damrosch, throwing both hands into the air, said with feeling—'And all those beautiful letters went to ashes.'"

15. *Life and Letters of George Eliot*. By J. W. Cross (London, 1885), p. 277.

16. *Scribner's Monthly* x, 239-40. June, 1875; *Poems* (1884), 177.

17. Professor Callaway (*Select Poems*, 67-70) discusses at length the origin of the plot, the similarity to an episode in *The Gilded Age*, by Mark Twain and Charles Dudley Warner, and the method of the Laniers' joint composition.

18. The exception is Professor F. L. Pattee.

19. So the late Professor C. A. Smith assigned the honor. *Cambridge History of American Literature* ii, 353.

20. *Op. cit.*, ii, 354.

21. Mims, 186.

22. *Retrospects and Prospects*, 121-24.

23. *Scribner's Monthly* xii, 142. May, 1876; *Poems* (1884), 167.

24. *Letters*, 107.

25. Callaway, *Select Poems*, 60; Mims, 153-54, gives a longer version of the same letter. But the letter is given in full in a contemporary MS. copy, Henry E. Huntington Library and Art Gallery, H M 7082. Callaway, 61, quotes Bleckley's answer.

26. See Kuhl, "Sidney Lanier and Edward Spencer," and Starke, "William Dean Howells and Sidney Lanier"; see also this work, Chapter xv, p. 316.

27. Kuhl, *Studies in Philology* xxvii, 466.

28. *Poems*, xxii-xxiii.

29. Foerster, 229.

30. Baskervill, 195-96.

31. *Cf.* Tennyson's "Maud," Part i, x, v; and Carlyle's *Heroes and Hero-Worship*, Lecture i: "For if we will think of it, no time need have gone to ruin, could it have found a man great enough," *etc.*

32. See note quoted by Baskervill, 256.

33. The passage, "A Great Man Wanted," was first printed in the *Acorn* (La Paix, Md.; edited by Edwin L. Turnbull), June, 1887, and reprinted in the *Critic* vii, 309. June 18, 1887, and elsewhere. More of the letter is given in Callaway, *Select Poems*, xlvi, 65. The fuller transcript given here is taken from a contemporary, manuscript copy in the Henry E. Huntington Library and Art Gallery, H M 7083.

34. *Lippincott's Magazine* xv, 216-19. February, 1875; *Poems* (1877), 9-19; *Poems* (1884), 53-59.

35. MS., Washington Memorial Library, Macon.

36. Mims, 308.

CHAPTER TEN

1. For Kirk's answer see Harvard College Library MSS., Am 177 F. The MSS. of the letters to Peacock given in the collected *Letters* are also in the Harvard College Library, the gift of W. R. Thayer, the friend and protégé of the Peacocks.

2. Kuhl, *Studies in Philology* xxvii, 464.

3. *Letters,* 109.

4. *Lippincott's Magazine,* xv, 677-84. June, 1875; *Poems* (1877), 20-38; *Poems* (1884), 60-70.

5. *Southern Magazine* xvi, 40-48. January, 1875; *Music and Poetry,* 197-211.

6. Starke, *American Literature* i, 35-36.

7. Lindsay.

8. Mims, 160.

9. *Martha Washington Court Journal.* First Edition. Baltimore, February 22, 1875. P. 1, column 4. (Published on the occasion of a tea-party held by the Ladies of the Martha Washington Tea-Party to raise money for certain Baltimore charities.) *Poems* (1884), 113.

10. To Edward Spencer: June 16, 1875. Unpublished MS., Johns Hopkins Univeristy Library.

11. *Letters,* 113.

12. Unpublished MS., Johns Hopkins University Library.

13. *Cf.* Tennyson's "Maud," Part i, i.

14. *Cf. Poems Outlines,* 10.

15. *Cf. SHF* i, 71 f.

16. *Cf. Music and Poetry,* 35.

17. *Thorn-Fruit,* 13.

18. Letters, 66.

19. Page, 693.

20. *Cf. The Literature of Ecstasy.* By Albert Mordell (New York, 1921), p. 178: "Even Whitman stopped short of championing economic liberty," *etc.*

21. *Letters,* 14.

22. See, among other sources, the letter to Edward Spencer of June 16, 1875, referred to in note 10 above.

23. For Lanier's answer see Mims, 184-86.

24. *Letters,* 121.

25. See the references to his dress coat in a letter to Charlotte Cushman, quoted in Mims, 301; and see this work, p. 220.

26. *Lippincott's Magazine* xvi, 341-42. September, 1875; *Poems* (1877), 79-82; *Poems* (1884), 74-76.

27. *Letters,* 126.

28. *Letters,* 19.

29. *Letters,* 129.

30. Quoted in part by Kuhl, *Studies in Philology* xxvii, 475-76. MS., Johns Hopkins University Library.

31. Unpublished MS., Henry E. Huntington Library and Art Gallery, H M 7978.

32. October 5, 1875. MS., Yale University Library. Published in the Atlanta *Journal* of July 6, 1931, in a short article by Professor William Lyon Phelps entitled "Fifty Years of Lanier."

33. This paragraph is omitted from a letter to Taylor of February 7, 1877, appearing in *Letters,* 184-85. A transcript of it has been furnished me by Mr. E. R. B. Willis from the copy of the letter in the Taylor collection, Cornell University Library.

34. *Lippincott's Magazine* xviii, 554-55. November, 1876; *Poems* (1877), 83-86; *Poems* (1884), 77-79.

35. Taylor, *Life and Letters* ii, 675.

36. So I was told in June, 1929, by Longfellow's daughter, Mrs. Annie Allegra Longfellow Thorpe, who served as her father's secretary about the time of Lanier's visit.

37. December 17, 1875. Unpublished MS., Craigie House, Cambridge.

38. Unpublished MS., Harvard College Library, Am 765.

39. In *The Forty-Sixth Birthday of Sidney Lanier*. Edited by D. C. Gilman.

40. *Letters*, 134.

41. *Letters*, 241.

42. *Letters*, 135.

CHAPTER ELEVEN

1. *Letters*, 131-32.

2. *Literary World* VI, 116. January, 1876.

3. *Letters*, 241.

4. February 12, 1876. Unpublished MS., Washington Memorial Library, Macon.

5. *SHF* I, 165; and "How to Read Chaucer"—uncollected essay.

6. *Boy's King Arthur*, xxi.

7. *Cf. SHF* II, 267.

8. *Some Highways and Byways of American Travel*. By Edward Strahan, Sidney Lanier, Edward A. Pollard, and others. Profusely illustrated. Philadelphia: J. B. Lippincott & Co. 1878.

9. It is perhaps unnecessary to point out the pun—one of the "sallies of wit" that won contemporary admiration.

10. Dr. F. W. Peterson of the University of Illinois College of Medicine, in a radio talk from station WLS, November 20, 1929.

11. *Lippincott's Magazine* XVII, 37-51, 172-83, 283-301, 409-27. January-April, 1876; *Retrospects and Prospects*, 136-228.

12. *Letters*, 23.

13. *Lippincott's Magazine* XVII, 375. March, 1876; *Poems* (1877), 91-92; Stebbins's *Charlotte Cushman*, 268-69; *Poems* (1884), 44. (MS., Harvard College Library, AL 2327. 15. 5*.)

14. *Scribner's Monthly* XI, 64. November, 1875; *Poems* (1884), 80.

15. *Lippincott's Magazine* XVII, 89. January, 1876; *Poems* (1877), 89-90; *Poems* (1884), 81.

16. *Poems*, xxvii.

CHAPTER TWELVE

1. Why the refusals is not known. Lowell delivered a long original ode at the Fourth of July exercises at Taunton, Mass.

2. *Letters*, 136.

3. Baskervill, 200-01.

4. *Letters*, 138.

5. *Letters*, 139.

6. *Letters*, 141-42.

7. What Lanier meant by "color" is explained adequately in *The Science of English Verse*, *q. v.*; and see Chapter XVI, p. 335.

8. *Cf.* in a letter to Peacock: "As simple and candid as a melody of Beethoven's." *Letters*, 24.

9. *Letters*, 142-43.

10. *Letters*, 143. Peacock's MS. copy of the cantata text is preserved in the Harvard College Library, A L 2327. 15.5*. The text given in *Poems* (1884), 249-51, follows the Schirmer text.

11. *Letters*, 142.

12. *Letters*, 144.

13. *Op. cit.*, 24.

14. Mims, 169.

15. *Letters*, 27.

16. Mims, 169-70.

17. *Letters*, 159.

18. *Letters*, 160.

19. *Letters*, 165-66.

20. *Letters*, 162, 164-66.

21. *Letters*, 151. See Chapter XIII, pp. 254-55.

22. *Letters*, 28-30.

23. *Poems*, xxv; *cf. Poem Outlines*, 11.

24. *Letters*, 167.

25. See, for instance, *Letters*, 158-59, and Mims, 170—the latter quoted above, pp. 238-40. *Cf.* this volume, p. 224.

26. Gilman, *South Atlantic Quarterly* IV, 116. See also Taylor's account of the performance in the New York *Tribune* of May 11, 1876.

27. New York *Tribune*, May 20, 1876, page 8, columns 1-2; *Music and Poetry*, 80-90.

28. Mims, 178-79.

29. James R. Randall, author of "Maryland, My Maryland," at this time editor of the Augusta *Constitutionalist*. See Lanier's *Florida*, 255.

30. James Barron Hope?

31. Copied from the Henry E. Huntington Library and Art Gallery MS. H M 7085, contemporary copy. See Unpublished Letters in Bibliography for previous publication of excerpts.

32. Baskervill, 207-08.

33. *Lippincott's Magazine* XVIII, 39-53. July, 1876; *Poems* (1877), 39-78; *Poems* (1884), 114-38.

34. *Independent* XXXV, 897. July 19, 1883; *Poems* (1884), 139.

35. *Letters*, 146.

36. But Lanier always intended to give his ode a musical setting. See letter of 1881, quoted in Chapter XXI, pp. 242.

37. *SHF* I, 179 ff.

38. Mims, 179-80.

CHAPTER THIRTEEN

1. *Letters*, 114.

2. Mims, 163-64.

3. *Letters*, 152-54.

4. *Letters*, 154.

5. *Scribner's Monthly* XII, 543. August, 1876; *Poems* (1884), 50.

6. Taylor, *Life and Letters* II, 691.

7. See Chapter X, p. 219. The two ("Red" and "White") were published together, *Lippincott's Magazine* XV, 587. May, 1876; *Poems* (1877), 93; *Poems* (1884), 52. A holograph MS. version of the first in the Harvard College Library (MS. Am 177 F) differs considerably from the published version.

8. *Lippincott's Magazine* xviii, 371. September, 1876; *Poems* (1877), 94; *Poems* (1884), 106. A contemporary MS. copy in the Harvard College Library (A L 2321. 15. 5.) has textual differences.

9. Unpublished MS., in the possession of the author.

10. Letter to E. C. Stedman: June 17, 1879. Unpublished MS., Yale University Library.

11. *Lippincott's Magazine* xvi, 711. December, 1875; *Poems* (1877), 87-88; *Poems* (1884), 205.

12. *Poems* (1877), [5]; Stebbins' *Charlotte Cushman*, 269; *Poems* (1884), 43.

13. *Letters*, 34, note 1.

14. *Letters*, 168.

15. *Letters*, 156.

16. The fact of the friendship is established by a letter of November 23, 1877, from Hayne to Dooley. Unpublished MS., in the possession of the author.

17. *Lippincott's Magazine* xli, 643-45. May, 1888; *Music and Poetry*, 1-24.

18. *Scribner's Monthly* xix, 897-904. April, 1880; *Music and Poetry*, 25-46.

19. *Independent* xxx, No. 1527, p. 1. March 7, 1878; *Poems* (1884), 19-22.

20. *Cf.* the similar lists of names in *Retrospects and Prospects*, 9; "The Crystal"; "The Stirrup-Cup"; Johns Hopkins ode; *The English Novel*, Ch. vi, and various letters.

21. *Van Nosdall's List of Books for Sale*, No. 300. June 2, 1929.

22. But see Ward's article in the *Independent* for July 22, 1897. He speaks of his "delighted amazement" in receiving the poem in 1876, the first of Lanier's poems submitted to the *Independent*.

23. *Harper's New Monthly Magazine* lv, 439. August, 1877; *Poems* (1884), 23.

24. See the letter to Gibson Peacock of October 17, 1876. Unpublished MS., Harvard College Library, Am 177 F.

25. *Letters*, 35.

26. The incident has been described by Mrs. C. N. Hawkins (now of Brooklyn, N. Y.) in a letter to the author, April 17, 1929. Mrs. Hawkins also contributed the version of the poem given here.

27. *Letters*, 181.

28. *Lippincott's* xix, 91. January, 1877; *Poems* (1884), 151.

29. In New York, on January 26, 1877, Taylor and Stedman heard the poem sung to the setting by Dudley Buck, which Buck himself played. "It is simply superb!" Taylor wrote of the poem, or of the music, meaning probably both together.

30. *Galaxy* xxiii, 394-95. March, 1877; *Poems* (1884), 98.

31. *Letters*, 189.

32. *Letters*, 176.

33. *Cf. Poem Outlines*, 35.

34. *Cf.* Chapter xvii, pp. 350-51.

35. *Scribner's Monthly* xiv, 28. May, 1877; *Poems* (1884), 45.

36. *Letters*, 185.

37. *Lippincott's Magazine* xix, 355. March, 1877; as "Tampa Robins" *Poems* (1884), 28.

38. In the original version the following stanza occurs between present stanzas 2 and 3:

> These were to sweeten thee with song;
> The blood of heroes made thee strong.

What heroes! Ah, for shame, for shame!
The worthiest died without a name.

And line 3 of stanza 4 (3) reads: "If death such dear distillment be." The change to " 'T is thy rich stirrup-cup to me" is certainly not an improvement.

39. *Lippincott's Magazine* xx, 493. October, 1877; *Poems* (1884), 83. *Cf. Poem Outlines*, 14, 85. "The Bee" was rejected by Howells, of the *At'antic*. See *Letters*, 185 ff.

40. The jessamine was "the tutelar flower" of his old courting days, when he had wooed Mary Day under the golden, over-hanging vines; "our first love-making was achieved in the overhanging presence of its vines." Letter from Lanier quoted by Mrs. C. N. Hawkins in a letter to the author, April 17, 1929.

41. *Letters*, 185-86.

42. *Letters*, 189-90.

43. *Poems*, xxxv.

44. *Galaxy*, xxiv, 161. August, 1877; *Poems* (1884), 27.

45. *Cf. Poem Outlines*, 55.

46. *Scribner's Monthly* xv, 380-81. January, 1878; *Poems* (1884), 149.

47. *Letters*, 190.

48. *Lippincott's Magazine* xx, 115. July, 1877; *Poems* (1884), 26.

49. Letter of 1872, quoted in Chapter vii, p. 158.

50. *SHF* i, 83-84, note 3.

51. The phrase, Mother Earth, is recollected from the early poem "Our Hills."

52. *Independent* xlxii, 1265. August 27, 1891; *Poems* (1891), 153.

53. *Frank Leslie's Sunday Magazine* ii, 72. July, 1877; *Poems* (1884), 142.

54. Lanier does not identify the soul of the individual with the soul of God, or the whole, as Emerson does; he expresses only a sense of kinship.

55. February 3, 1929.

CHAPTER FOURTEEN

1. *Letters*, 194.

2. *Letters*, 42.

3. *Letters*, 196.

4. Those that I classify thus occur on pages 9, 12, 16, 21, 32, 36, 37, 46, 61, 63, 64, 65, 66, 74, 78, 82, 87, 89, 91, 92, 110; I add also the uncollected fragment, "One in Two." Subsequent references to the volume of *Poem Outlines* are to *PO*, followed by the number of the page on which the outline occurs.

5. *PO*, 9.

6. *PO*, 61.

7. *PO*, 63.

8. *PO*, 91.

9. See *Our Todays and Yesterdays*. By Margaret Davis Cate (Brunswick, Ga.: Glover Brothers), pp. 224-25. But in a letter to the author of June 12, 1931, Mrs. Cate stated that her information came from several elderly ladies whose memories were perhaps at fault in saying that "The Marshes of Glynn" was read aloud at a meeting of a literary club in Brunswick in the spring of 1875. See also *The Golden Isles of Georgia*. By Caroline Couper Lovell (Boston, 1932), p. 272.

10. *Letters*, 40.

11. Unpublished MS., Cornell University Library.

12. *Letters*, 44.

13. In the *Sonnets to Sidney Lanier* by Clifford Lanier three sonnets only are dated: February 20, 1875; March 16, 1875; and March 17, 1875. But eight of the eleven given were written during Sidney Lanier's lifetime.

14. The Laniers occupied a flat at 55 Lexington Street (now 2 East Lexington) and had their dinner sent to them from a restaurant in the same building.

15. Litz, 33-34.

16. Spann, "Sidney Lanier's Youth."

17. See Litz, 140.

18. "At Lanier's Grave"; "Ave Sidney Lanier"; "Greeting to Sidney Lanier"; "In Touch"; "Love's Hybla"; "My Star"; "To the Forthcoming Poems of Sidney Lanier"; "To Lanier's Flute"; "To Sidney Lanier"; also "The Captives," inspired by their prison friendship.

19. Letter from Mrs. Lanier, quoted by Litz, 55.

20. Mrs. Lanier's letters are usually addressed to "Dearest Jonathan"; or so at least are those letters in the possession of the author.

21. Lanier and Browne often played flute duets together. To Browne Lanier bequeathed the flute that he had used as a member of the Peabody Orchestra. After Lanier's death Browne performed several editorial services on Lanier manuscripts.

22. Mme. Blanc (Th. Bentzon) described a painting in Mrs. Turnbull's home: "Mrs. Turnbull exhibits a glorified Lanier, crowned with his ultimate immortality. He appears in a symbolic picture, ordered by this American art patroness, from the Italian painter Gatti, where are grouped all the great geniuses of the past, present, and future,—the latter emerging vaguely from the mists of the distance, and including a number of women. This innumerable multitude of the *élite* of all ages encircles a mountain which is dominated by Jesus Christ; and from this figure of Christ emanates the light which Mrs. Turnbull has caused to be shed upon the figures of the picture, with more or less brilliancy according to her own preferences. Designating a tall, draped figure who walks in the front rank of the poets, the lady said to me: 'This is Sidney Lanier'; and when I, despite my admiration for the poet of the marshes, ventured to offer a few modest suggestions, she went on to develop the thesis, that what exalts a man is less what he has done than what he has aspired to do."

This painting, "The Master Light of All Our Seeing," is now the property of the Johns Hopkins University, the gift of Mr. and Mrs. Turnbull. Reproduced opp. p. 450.

23. Ethridge.

24. *St. Nicholas's Magazine* IV, 468-72. May, 1877; *The Lanier Book*, 3-19. MS., Henry E. Huntington Library and Art Gallery, H M 7997.

25. *Letters*, 193.

26. Uncollected.

27. See Chapter VII, note 6.

28. Mr. Mayfield (p. 33, n. 24) states: "I have a note, the origin of which escapes me, that Lanier received twenty-five dollars from his banker cousin for this work." The MS. copy of Lanier's letter reproduced in facsimile by Mr. Mayfield (p. 25) is quite obviously not in Lanier's handwriting.

29. *Scribner's Monthly* XVI, 140. May, 1878; *Poems* (1884), 105.

30. *Galaxy* XXIV, 652-53. November, 1877; as "To Richard Wagner," *Poems* (1884), 95-96.

31. See especially *Letters*, 68, 106.

32. Lanier is said by Professor Mims (p. 140) to have completed a translation of Wagner's *Rheingold*. His intention of making a translation he stated in a letter of November, 1874. *Letters*, 106.

33. *Appleton's Journal* n. s. III, 568. December, 1877; *Poems* (1884), 163.

34. I have not been able to trace this magazine or any version of the poem earlier than that given in *Poems* (1884), 152-60. See *Letters*, 47, 48.

35. *Letters*, 229-34.

36. *Independent* XXXV, 1601. December 20, 1883; *Poems* (1884), 24-25.

37. Chapter VI, notes 20, 44.

38. *Letters*, 201.

39. See Chapter XII, p. 252.

40. *Letters*, 198.

41. Kuhl, *Studies in Philology* XXVII, 465.

42. *Letters*, 49.

43. A curious variant of this letter in which the servant is "a colored gentleman" is given by Huckel, *Johns Hopkins Alumni Magazine*, XIV, 491. (June, 1926.) That letter is probably not an erroneous copy of the letter quoted here but another written at the same time, and illustrative of Lanier's peculiarly tenacious memory. But "gentleman" is probably a copyist's error.

44. *Letters*, 49-50. 33 Denmead Street is now 33 Twentieth Street. Sometime between August 24 and October 20, 1878, the Laniers moved to 180 St. Paul Street (now 1022 St. Paul), and sometime before December 1, 1879, to 435 North Calvert Street. From the latter house Lanier was buried, and there Mrs. Lanier lived for some months after his death.

CHAPTER FIFTEEN

1. *Letters*, 206.

2. *Letters*, 208-09.

3. Baltimore *Sun*, May 28, 29, 30, 1878; *Music and Poetry*, 70-79 (condensed). Lanier's friend Edward Spencer was the chief editorial writer of the *Sun* and probably secured the assignment for him.

4. In the *Autobiography* of R. M. Johnston, p. 128, reference is made to a neighboring plantation owner, Major Edgworth Bird. How Lanier, a Georgian, met Mrs. Bird, another Georgian, in Baltimore, need not be asked.

5. Mims, 206.

6. Franklin, 244.

7. Gilman, *South Atlantic Quarterly* IV, 117.

8. This is explicitly stated by Gilman in an article on Lanier contributed to the *Pathfinder* (Sewanee, Tenn.) I, No. 3, pp. 2-5. September, 1906.

9. *English Novel*, 47.

10. The original publication I have not located. The German text is given in *Poems* (1884), 101.

11. Unpublished letter, MS. Cornell University Library.

12. *Letters*, 214.

13. *Letters*, 208.

14. Traubel, *With Walt Whitman in Camden* (1906), 208. This letter is given in fascimile opposite p. 208. It had been previously published in Traubel's magazine, the *Conservator* VII, 122 (October, 1896), with derogatory comment.

15. Thayer, *Letters*, 32.

16. *PO*, 41. *Cf. PO*, 54, with Whitman's prophecy that the priests shall pass away, Preface to *Leaves of Grass*, 1855.

17. *Lippincott's Magazine* XXI, 439. April, 1878; *Poems* (1884), 85.

18. Said by Mrs. Lanier to have been first published in the Baltimore *Gazette* (date not given). The only publication known to me is that in *Poems* (1884), 102.

19. *Independent* XXX, No. 1552, p. 1. August 29, 1878. *Poems* (1884), 103.

20. *Independent* XXXIV, No. 1757, pp. 1-3. August 3, 1882. *Bob, the Story of Our Mocking-Bird*, 1899 (see Bibliography). Reprinted in *The Lanier Book* (109-24) and *Selections* (128-42).

21. The incident upon which Lanier based his poem is related in Chapter III, which appeared in the February, 1878, issue of *Harper's Magazine* (LVI, 412-13).

22. *Appleton's Journal* n. s. V, 395-96; November, 1878; *Poems* (1884), 33-38. For a recent French criticism of the poem see M. Bourgeois's article listed in the Bibliography.

23. Also represented in this anonymous collection was a poet whose literary début was not to occur for more than a dozen years—Emily Dickinson. Her poem "Success" had been sent against her wishes by her friend Mrs. Helen Hunt Jackson whose novel, *Mercy Philbrick's Choice*, was one of the earlier volumes of the series. Other poets who contributed were Thoreau, Bayard Taylor, G. H. Boker, Christina Rossetti, W. E. Channing, Mrs. James T. Fields, James T. Fields, R. R. Bowker, Aubrey de Vere, Bronson Alcott, and Celia Thaxter.

24. . . . *A Masque of Poets. Including Guy Vernon, a Novelette in Verse.* Boston: Roberts Brothers, 1878.

25. *Letters*, 58. Contemporary reviews of the volume expressed similarly derogatory opinions.

26. *Masque of Poets*, 88-94; *Poems of Places*. Edited by Henry Wadsworth Longfellow: *America. Southern States*. Boston, 1879, 252-57; *Poems* (1884), 14-18.

27. The phrase "favor of God" occurs in Lanier's translation of "The Phœnix," *SHF* I, 84.

28. See Chapter IX, pp. 189-90, and references given in Chapter IX, note 26. Lanier did not reciprocate by ignoring Howell's work. *The Undiscovered Country* was announced for consideration in the original scheme of Lanier's second Johns Hopkins lecture course.

29. *Atlantic Monthly* XLIII, 410. March, 1879. There is, of course, the possibility that this review, though listed as being from the Editor's Office, is not the work of Howells.

30. At least in Longfellow's letter book, preserved at Craigie House, there is a record of a letter to Sidney Lanier, January 3, 1879. The MS. of Lanier's answer is at Craigie House.

31. *PO*, 19; *cf.* also *PO*, 17.

32. *Century Magazine* XXV, 819-20. April, 1883; *Poems* (1884), 86.

33. Unpublished letter. Contemporary MS. copy, Harvard College Library, Am 177 F.

34. See, among other sources, Lanier's letter to Gilman of July 28, 1878. Unpublished MS., Johns Hopkins University Library.

35. See Chapter XX, pp. 391-93.

36. As "The Proper Basis of English Culture," *Atlantic Monthly* LXXXII, 165-74 August, 1898: as "The Death of Byrhtnoth," *Music and Poetry* (1898), 136-58. Left unfinished by Lanier and completed by Dr. W. H. Browne.

37. *Letters*, 214.

38. *Music and Poetry*, 212-48.

39. *Letters*, 54-55.

40. See the letter to Edward Spencer of November 1, 1878. Unpublished MS., Johns Hopkins University Library.

41. *Letters*, 215.

42. Lanier's letter of formal acceptance of "the invitation . . . to lecture" is preserved in the Johns Hopkins University Library, an unpublished MS. letter to Gilman, dated February 5, 1879.

43. Spann, "Sidney Lanier's Manhood."

CHAPTER SIXTEEN

1. Mims, 204-05.

2. Franklin, 243.

3. To Edward Spencer: undated. Unpublished MS., Johns Hopkins University Library.

4. Lanier pays tribute to Sylvester in the Johns Hopkins ode. According to Mr. H. E. Shepherd ("Southern Poets." *Confederate Veteran* XXVII, 450-51. December, 1919), Sylvester referred to Lanier as "this great poet."

5. *Science of English Verse* (referred to hereafter as *SEV*), iv.

6. Mims, 239.

7. *Letters*, 55.

8. *Scribner's Monthly* XVII, 642-43. March, 1879; *Poems* (1884), 39-42. MS., Henry E. Huntington Library and Art Gallery H M 7977.

9. Some time, however, was given to genealogical research. See Chapter XIV, pp. 286-87.

10. See Mims, 245, 265-67.

11. *Independent* XXXVIII, 325-36. March 18, 1886. *Cf.* Mims, 261.

12. Gilman, *South Atlantic Quarterly* IV, 117-18; also Mims, 252-57.

13. *Cf. SHF* I, 165.

14. *Op. cit.*, pp. 165-70, 219-20.

15. The trip referred to in the letter to Stedman cited below, note 17.

16. See the undated letter preserved at Craigie House. This letter could not date from the time of Lanier's visit to Boston in 1875 and must be the letter that Longfellow answered (according to his own Letter-Book) June 5, 1879.

17. Unpublished MS., Yale University Library.

18. *Bob*, 1899, prefatory note.

19. *Scribner's Monthly* XXII, 453-54. July, 1881; *Poems* (1884), 47-49. Mr. Kenneth Rede, of Baltimore, owner of the manuscript, has published an interesting article on the curious textual variations.

20. In a letter to Professor Wayland. Wayland, 23.

21. Lanier undoubtedly taught in some schools in Baltimore. Ward (*Poems*, xxviii) says: "In October he opened three lecture courses in young ladies' schools." There are many occasional references to this work in articles on Lanier, and the sonnets

given in *Poems* (1884), 146, 147, are evidence of his having taught a class of girls: the Johns Hopkins class—as distinguished from the lecture group course—was composed of young men. But the often repeated statement that Lanier taught at Colonel R. M. Johnston's Pen Lucy School for boys is unconfirmed. There is—strangely—no reference to Lanier in Johnston's *Autobiography* (in spite of Lanier's services to Johnston as literary adviser and his friendship), and though exact dates are not given, Johnston's statements about his school suggest that by this date (1879) he had closed his school, because of the falling off in attendance after his conversion to Roman Catholicism, and was merely taking classes in his home. Lanier, of course, may have served him as assistant in this.

22. According to Ward (*Poems*, xxvii), *The Science of English Verse* was begun and finished in the six weeks spent at Rockingham Springs. In an unpublished letter to Mrs. James T. Fields (MS., Henry E. Huntington Library and Art Gallery, H M 2874) written May 30, 1880, Lanier stated that "the book was planned and written from beginning to end during the five weeks of my last summer's vacation." But it quite definitely grew out of lectures already written and it must have received some additional touches before the writing of the preface in February, 1880.

23. The sentence quoted comes from the Shakspere lectures (*SHF*, 1, 16) but the idea is repeated several times in *The Science of English Verse*. It may be mentioned here that in the published lectures "color" is throughout spelled in the English way, as are several other words.

24. *Music and Poetry*, 47-69.

25. *Galaxy* xix, 835-42. June, 1875.

26. *SEV*, xi.

27. My own understanding of this rhythm is the result of an explanation made by Professor W. M. Patterson, author of *The Rhythm of Prose* (New York, 1916), whose patience and kindness deserve more than this brief acknowledgment.

28. Quoted in *The English Novel* (1897), 65.

29. Mr. Llewellyn Jones observes ("Free Verse and its Propaganda." *Sewanee Review* xxviii, 384-95. July-September, 1920) that "if blank verse were actually in three-eight time—as Lanier asserts—*Paradise Lost* would be slightly more suggestive of a waltz than it is." The remark almost annihilates the whole of Lanier's system. Stressed syllables are likely to be held a little longer than others, but not *twice* as long—in the exact mathematical relations of musical notes; but this Lanier must have known, whether he stated it or not. His treatise is theoretical, his references all to the relative time and not to the absolute time required to pronounce English words. See the following paragraph.

30. Logically, of course, the accent does fall on "som-"; but as Mr. Omond observes, "his habit of letting accents come irregularly in successive feet seems destructive of true analysis."

31. Lanier wrote "typic" or "typical" without discrimination.

32. *Cf.* Lanier's remarks about the holiness of beauty. See Chapter xxiii, p. 442.

33. *Cf. PO*, 17.

34. *English Novel*, 33.

35. *English Novel*, 33; *cf. Letters*, 59.

CHAPTER SEVENTEEN

1. The Longfellow copy is at Craigie House, the Hayne copy at Duke University; copies sent to Stedman and Salem Dutcher, of Augusta, Georgia (see *Florida,* 257, and *Letters,* 241) have been listed for sale in book-dealers's catalogues; the copy sent George H. Calvert is in the Redwood Library, Newport, R. I.

2. Quoted in part by Stedman in "The Late Sidney Lanier." *Critic* I, 298. November 5, 1881; in part in *Van Nosdall's List of Books for Sale* No. 292. April 5, 1929.

3. Stedman, *Life and Letters* II, 154.

4. *SEV*, xv.

5. *Letters,* 60.

6. *SEV*, 57, note I.

7. Letter of May 30, 1880. MS., Henry E. Huntington Library and Art Gallery, H M 2874. See Chapter XVI, note 22.

8. *English Novel,* 32, 35.

9. *SEV*, 57.

10. *Letters,* 113.

11. Foerster, 235-36.

12. Saintsbury, *Manual of English Prosody* (London, 1910), p. 383.

13. *SHF* I, 28.

14. *English Novel,* 59.

15. *SEV*, 133.

16. *Critic* o. s. XXI, 45.

17. Lanier's interest in form emphasizes his kinship with other southern poets; the New England poets were for the most part interested more in the matter of poetry. But Lanier of course was greatly interested in the message—matter—of all art.

18. Tabb acknowledged a debt to Lanier. See Chapter XIV, pp. 282-83.

19. The list is too long to give here. I have collected some four dozen, by twenty-eight different authors.

20. Hovey's poem "The Laurel" is dedicated to Mrs. Lanier and the tribute to her husband is only incidental. In "Richard Hovey: A Biographical Study" (unpublished master's thesis, University of Chicago, 1922), Miss Lillian Mabel Funk states that Hovey met Mrs. Lanier at Farmington, Conn., in 1888. "Hovey was always a great admirer of Lanier and more or less consciously a disciple of his poetic creed and practice. At Farmington Mrs. Lanier was so deeply moved with Hovey's genius that she publicly honored him by presenting him with a laurel wreath which had once been bestowed upon her poet-husband. Hovey she believed capable and worthy to carry on Lanier's work; and the laurel wreath was not merely an honor, but also a charge to fulfill the promise which Hovey's genius gave of poetic achievement." Hovey published his poem "The Laurel" the following year. But Miss Funk quotes from an autograph manuscript sent by Hovey to E. O. Grover to be used in preparing an article on him for the *Dartmouth Literary Monthly* of June, 1894, in which Hovey states: "At Farmington I met Mrs. Lanier, widow of the late Sidney Lanier, and she presented me before I left with a wreath of laurel which had been sent her from the South." The question of Lanier's influence on Hovey belongs rather to a study of Hovey than to a study of Lanier. Here it may be pointed out, however, that though the verse of "The Laurel" is suggestive of that of Lanier, it is rigidly metrical, couched in the form of a Pindaric ode.

21. The question of Lanier's possible influence on Francis Thompson (see also p. 450) is perhaps the most fascinating of the many unsolved problems suggested by a study of Lanier. Mr. John Macy, writing in 1913, said: "A blood brother to Lanier's 'Sunrise' is Francis Thompson's 'Ode to the Setting Sun.' . . . These poems have much in common, opulence, splendour of metaphor and an amazing virtuosity in metrical matters. . . . If Thompson did not know the poems of Lanier, it is a case of predetermined affinities which the accidents of circumstance cheated of the earthly fulfillment of meeting. Have they some common earlier master I do not know? Or is identity of these powerful metaphors less striking than I find it?

THOMPSON: Whether man's heart or life it be that yields
Thee Harvest, must thy harvest fields
Be dunged with rotten death?

LANIER: Mulched with unsavory death,
Grow, Soul! unto such white estate,
That virginal-prayerful art shall be thy breath
Thy work, thy fate."

Mr. Clement Wood has pointed out the analogy of lines in "Sunrise" with lines in Thompson's "Ode to the Setting Sun."

THOMPSON: If with exultant tread
Thou foot the Eastern sea,
Or like a golden bee
Sting the West to angry red.

LANIER: The star-fed Bee, the build-fire Bee,
Of dazzling gold is the great Sun-Bee
That shall flash from the hive-hole over the sea.

Other similarities of metaphor, thought, and meter, are abundant. There is no mention of Lanier in Mr. Everard Meynell's *Life of Francis Thompson* (London, 1913), in which he does discuss Thompson's indebtedness to other writers. But Thompson, through his friendship with Mrs. Meynell, the friend of Tabb, may have been familiar with the poetry of Lanier.

Brought to my attention too late for anything more than brief mention here is an unpublished master's thesis in the library of Boston College by Sister M. Agatha, O. P.: "A Comparative Study of Francis Thompson and Sidney Lanier" (1932).

22. See the tribute paid Lanier by Mr. Garland in *Roadside Meetings* (New York, 1930), pp. 144-53.

23. Miss Monroe, in *Poets and Their Art*, p. 266.

24. Volume XVI, pp. 78-103.

25. *Op. cit.*, 135.

26. Mims, 353.

27. "Principles of Criticism." *Atlantic Monthly* LVI, 673, note 1. November, 1885.

28. "Lanier's Science of English Verse." Reprinted, *The Views About Hamlet, and Other Essays* (Boston, 1904), pp. 105-13.

29. Omond, 202.

30. Copies of Lanier's books, some of them marked, are in the collection of books left by Miss Lowell to the Harvard College Library.

31. Published in New York, 1891; the volume contains as appendices a summary of President M. E. Gates's article on Lanier (see Bibliography) and an article by Mrs. Turnbull.

32. *Cf.* with this Lanier's own statements on technic: *PO*, 7, 17.

CHAPTER EIGHTEEN

1. Mims, 261.
2. Franklin, 241-43.
3. Dr. Waldo Selden Pratt.
4. *Johns Hopkins University Circular* No. 1, 1. December, 1879.
5. VI, 284-98. Reprinted (1883) as suppl. to Grosart's ed. *Poems of Bartholomew Griffin* (1876); and in *Music and Poetry*, 115-35. Grosart said, "Anything more admirably sympathetic is seldom to be met with."
6. See *The English Novel*, 32.
7. *Cf. SHF* II, 310.
8. This part of the sentence is repeated verbatim, II, 316.
9. See also the prose fragment "The Sonnet," given in Clarke's *Reminiscences*, [28].
10. Mims, 210.
11. The repetition of ideas and of actual sentences in this lecture—*cf.*, e. g., I, 73, lines 28-31, and II, 310, lines 27-31—are evidence that these last three chapters, as they are given in *Shakspere and His Forerunners*, possibly without the summary of the course—pp. 312 ff.—may indeed be from the Johns Hopkins course and not from the Peabody course: it is hardly likely that Lanier would have deliberately used the same figurative sentence twice in the same course unless his memory, an unusually keen one for remembering and reusing phrases, sometimes even whole sentences, led him unconsciously to repetition. But it seems more than likely that the repeated matter represents a revision of the matter in its earlier form.
12. *Cf. SEV*, iv, and *PO*, 1.
13. *Our Continent* (Philadelphia: A. W. Tourgee, editor) I, 4. February 15, 1882; *Poems* (1884), 13. *Cf. PO*, 12.

In *A History of English Literature*, II, 870-71, Lafcadio Hearn says of this poem: "Short as it is, I take this poem to be the very best thing that the author ever wrote; but, of course, it is only a very light poem. Here some of the verse is certainly defective but the choice of adjectives is almost magical; and the beauty of the composition is the grotesque art of the first line of the three stanzas. Those three lines prove that the writer might have become one of the very best of poets if he had not died quite young, after years of sickness."

14. *Good Company* (Springfield, Mass.) IV, 444. January, 1880; *Poems* (1884), 51.
15. See *SHF* II, 60.
16. *Century Magazine* XXVII, 733-34. March, 1884; *Poems* (1884), 89-92.
17. *SEV*, 249; *SHF* II, 328.
18. *SEV*, 250.
19. *Cf.* Lanier's poems "Struggle" and "Control."
20. See "Mazzini on Music."
21. *Cf. PO*, 20, 31, 58, 86.
22. Gilman, *South Atlantic Quarterly* IV, 120.
23. Mims, 228-29.
24. Letter from Dr. Pratt to the author, September 6, 1932.
25. Mims, 258-60.
26. *SHF* II, 328.
27. *SEV*, 249.

CHAPTER NINETEEN

1. *SHF* II, 305.
2. *Sartor Resartus*, Book II, Ch. x.
3. *Johns Hopkins University Circular* No. 4, 38-39. April, 1880; *Poems* (1884), 108.
4. *Letters*, 244.
5. Sales figures are taken from Professor Wills's admirable bibliography.
6. Excerpts from journalistic reviews of the books are to be found in other volumes of the series, as advertising matter.
7. See Lanier's own comparison of the two translations, *Music and Poetry*, 141-42.
8. The reviewer of *The Boy's Froissart* in the *Atlantic Monthly*—H. E. Scudder.
9. *The Boy's Percy*, xxi.
10. Mims, 327.
11. Franklin, 244.

CHAPTER TWENTY

1. Payne, "Sidney Lanier's Lectures."
2. *SHF* I, 46-48.
3. *SHF* I, 83 ff.
4. *Music and Poetry*, 152 ff.; *SEV*, 149-50, 178. The quotation used is from *Music and Poetry*, 155.
5. See the penultimate line of the fragmentary "Song of Aldhelm" (*PO*, 50)—obviously an attempt to represent Anglo-Saxon alliteration in modern English verse. Perhaps the poem was intended as a faithful reconstruction of Aldhelm's thought in a close approximation to Aldhelm's language.
6. *Letters*, 215.
7. *SHF*, I, 77.
8. I.e. *SHF*, Chapter VII. The reference occurs I, 163.
9. *SEV*, v, note 1.
10. *PO*, 50. See also *ibid.*, 70.
11. *Century Magazine* XXVII, 659. February, 1884; *Poems* (1884), 97.
12. *Poems* (1884), 86.
13. See *SEV*, 265.
14. *Poems* (1884), 183-203.
15. Baltimore *Sun*, January 31, 1880, p. 1, col. 7; as "Two Descriptions of Orchestral Works." *Music and Poetry*, 68-69.
16. *Independent* XXXVII, 1627. December 17, 1885; *Music and Poetry*, 91-94.
17. *Scribner's Monthly* XX, 840-51. October, 1880; *Retrospects and Prospects*, 104-35.
18. *Cf.* Lanier's use of material from Latimer's sermons in *SHF* II, 127 ff.
19. *The Art Autograph*. New York, May, 1880, plate 10. (Published by the Art Interchange to raise money for the fund organized by the New York *Herald* for relief of the Irish famine.) Lanier's poem—reproduced in a facsimile of the manuscript—is on a page with "The Relief Ship at Twilight" by Helen Hunt Jackson and opposite the page containing "The Album Fiend" by Oliver Wendell Holmes and "Arbutus" by J. G. Whittier. Reprinted, *Poems* (1884), 148.
20. Published together, *Independent* XXXVI, 1409. November 6, 1884; *Poems* (1884), 146-47.
21. *Poems* (1884), 112.
22. *Century Magazine* XXV, 222-23. December, 1882; *Poems* (1884), 10-13.
23. Mims, 314-15.

24. Mims, 316-17.

25. *Independent* xxxII, No. 1650, 1. July 15, 1880; *Poems* (1884), 29-32.

26. Ward, "Four Poems."

27. *Cf.* with the characterizations here *PO*, 111.

28. I cannot agree with Professor H. M. Jones in finding in this poem the "fastidious air of a spiritual amateur," nor the "syrupy patronage . . . of a very young clergyman." The sentence quoted,

little mole that marks
[Him] brother and [his] kinship seals to man,

defines Lanier's own sense of imperfection, and of kinship with other artists, rather than any sense of superiority to them.

29. It is altogether possible that a realization of the inconsistency of Christian teaching and of Christian practice in tolerating slavery and in waging war served to inaugurate Lanier's rejection of orthodox Christianity.

30. *PO*, 104-05.

31. *English Novel* (1897), p. 296. *Cf. PO*, 76.

32. *Independent* xxxII, No. 16073, 1. December 23, 1880; *Poems* (1884), 141. And see note, *Poems* (1884), 245.

33. *Cf. PO*, 13, 30, and especially 112.

34. Ward (*Poems*, xxviii) says ten, but implies that the Hopkins Hall lectures and the class lectures ran concurrently.

The following announcement was made in the *Johns Hopkins University Circular* No. 2, p. 18 (January, 1880): "Readings in English Literature. Mr. Sidney Lanier, Lecturer in English Literature, will give ten expository readings of Chaucer's Knight's Tale and Shakspere's Midsummer [*sic*] Night's Dream in connection, beginning in the middle of January. . . .

"This course is intended only for the members of the University, and especially for those whose principal studies are directed to other subjects, and who have consequently but little time at command for English Literature.

"The aim of the lecturer will be to awaken an interest in the poems under review solely as works of art. The course will embrace a wide range of considerations bearing upon this end.

"The instructor will take pleasure in giving three or four preliminary sessions to students unacquainted with Fourteenth Century English, for the purpose of familiarizing them with the archaic forms of Chaucer."

In a letter of September 27, 1897, to Professor G. S. Wills (Unpublished MS., University of North Carolina Library), President Gilman called this course "Art of Expression," and stated that it was given "twice weekly, beginning March 13, 1880." But Dr. W. S. Pratt, who attended the lectures, states that they began the week of February 8, 1880. Is it possible that Gilman, forgetting the course on Chaucer and Shakspere, refers to another course—one Lanier proposed in the letter to Gilman of March 16, 1880, quoted pp. 374-75 above?

35. To W. S. Pratt. Unpublished MS. in possession of Dr. Pratt.

36. Mims, 324-25.

37. *Independent* xLIII, 1337-38, 1371-72, 1401-02. September 10, 17, 24, 1891; *Music and Poetry*, 159-96. The papers may have been prepared somewhat earlier, *circa* January, 1880. See the letter of February 10, 1880, to an unnamed person (unpublished MS., Pennsylvania Historical Society) and the *Johns Hopkins University Circular* No. 2, p. 18—the announcement of a course quoted in note 34 above.

38. *Critic* n. s. XXXI, 365-66. April, 1899.

39. "King Arthur and His Knights of the Round Table." *St. Nicholas' Magazine* VIII, 9-93. December, 1880; *The Lanier Book*, 23-35. MS., Henry E. Huntington Library and Art Gallery, H M 7996.

40. *Letters*, 243-45.

41. "A Festival Program to Honor Sidney Lanier . . . Sunday, August 15, 1926, at 4 P. M. in Calvary Episcopal Church, Fletcher, N. C."

42. I am indebted for this information to Mr. Ephraim Keyser, and his letter to me of July 30, 1930.

43. *Independent* XXXIV, No. 1776, 1. December 14, 1882; *Poems* (1884), 3-9. See Mrs. Lanier's account of the composition of this poem in *Selections*, 164, note 16.

44. Abernethy.

45. *Independent* XXXIII, No. 1683, 1. March 3, 1881; *Poems* (1884), 46. Called in this version, "A Song of Eternity in Time."

46. *Independent* XXXIII, No. 1691, 1. April 28, 1881; *Poems* (1891), 152.

CHAPTER TWENTY-ONE

1. *Poems*, xxviii-xxix.

2. *Johns Hopkins University Circular* No. 8, p. 99.

3. Wayland, 27.

4. Prefatory note to the 1897 edition of *The English Novel. The English Novel* has been published twice, as hereafter explained, but neither text is wholly satisfactory. The 1897 text is fuller, but in quoting I have used the 1883 text, except where use of the 1897 text is indicated, as being—in composition and punctuation—more characteristic of Lanier.

5. *Cf.* "Nature-Metaphors," *Music and Poetry*, 113-114: "the open-eyed observer of our era must decide that all those important institutions of society which depend for their well-being on spiritual strength and knowledge and loving sympathy, are now far in advance of the best olden times. Any one who will compare the idea of marriage, for instance, as developed in Plato's *Republic*, with the idea of marriage as developed in Tennyson's *Princess*, will satisfy himself on this point. The age which proceeded on Plato's idea must have been at bottom a barbarous age, no matter what products of intellectual culture may have sprung from it."

6. *English Novel* (1897), 45. See Mrs. Lanier's letter to the *Nation* (XXXVII, 183. August 30, 1883) expressing regret at the omission of this passage from the 1883 edition of *The English Novel*. Dr. Browne feared "some false interpretation of it"; publication of it in her letter was against his wishes but with his sanction: Mrs. Lanier felt that "without it a complete expression of Mr. Lanier's views upon [Whitman and his poetry] would be wanting."

7. Willard.

8. See *The English Novel*, 55.

CHAPTER TWENTY-TWO

1. See *PO*, 11, 28, 49.

2. Baskervill, 220-22.

3. *Hymns of the Marshes*. By Sidney Lanier. Illustrated from nature by Henry Troth. New York: Charles Scribner's Sons, MCMVII.

4. *Independent* XLIII, 625. April 30, 1891; *Poems* (1891), 157.

5. *Op. cit.*, 3.

6. *PO*, 4, 5, 6, 27, 43, 47, 54-55, 56, 60, 71, 98, 99, 120. To these I would add, as material intended for the projected volume, the outline given on page 114, because of the evidence of the prose fragment, "The Legend of St. Leonor," and that given on page 108, because of its similarity to that given on page 5.

7. Chapter XIV, note 4.

8. I classify thus those given on pages 2, 3, 4, 14, 18, 23, 25 26, 27, 45, 49, 52, 62, 76, 79, 81, 88, 95, 109, 116-117, 119, and the uncollected fragment "The Lord's Romance of Time."

9. *PO*, 24, 56, 57, 83, 85, 113, 114.

10. *PO*, 116. The "beloved" of this poem is probably Mrs. Lanier, for in spite of the metaphors and the similarity of the thought to thoughts concerning God as expressed elsewhere, this seems hardly to be a poem of metaphysical dialectics. Also addressed to Mrs. Lanier seem the fragments "Thou and I," "Two in One" and "One in Two" (the three published together in the *Century Magazine* XXXIV, 417. July, 1887—the first reprinted in *Poems* (1891), 158) in spite of the suggested problem of self-hood—the theme of other of the *Poem Outlines*.

11. *PO*, 34, 38, 42, 52, 75, 84, 90, 93, 96, 100, 102. "Struggle" and "Control" (*Century Magazine* XXXI, 572. February, 1886; XXXII, 62. May, 1886; *Poems* [1891], 154-55) are surely verse epigrams also. They belong in *Poem Outlines* rather than in *Poems*.

12. *PO*, 100.

13. *PO*, 8, 22, 97, 107.

14. *PO*, 39, 47.

15. *PO*, 48, 54-55, 58 (second half), 67, 80, 104-05, 106.

16. *PO*, 1, 72.

17. *PO*, 118.

18. *PO*, 120.

19. Poems by Lanier not mentioned in the text are: (1) "Souls and Rain Drops." *Lippincott's Magazine* XXXII, 117. July, 1883; *Poems* (1884), 216; (2) "Struggle." See Chapter XVIII, note 19, and note 11 above; (3) "Thou and I." *Century Magazine* XXXIV, 417. July, 1887. *Poems* (1891), 158.

20. Originally announced to end on Saturday, March 26, the schedule of lectures may not have been followed closely because of Lanier's uncertain health.

21. Mims, 330-31.

22. For the Associated Railways of Virginia and the Carolinas.

23. Gilman, *South Atlantic Quarterly* IV 121.

24. *Johns Hopkins University Circular* No. 11, 151.

25. Mims, 333.

26. *PO*, 1, 118, 120.

27. The first three of the Uncollected Poem Outlines listed in the Bibliography. *Cf.* with them *PO*, 83, 101, 120.

28. Gilman, *South Atlantic Quarterly* IV, 121.

29. Lanier, Mary Day, *loc. cit.*, 14.

30. Spann, "Sidney Lanier's Manhood."

31. *PO*, 101.

32. Baskervill, 223.

33. *PO*, 118, 119, 120.

34. *Poems*, xiii.

35. Dr. J. W. Flinn, "Dr. James Woodrow." Columbia, S. C., *State*, Charleston, S. C., *News and Courier*, January 18, 1907. Reprinted in *Dr. James Woodrow As Seen By His Friends.* (Columbia, S. C., 1909), pp. 4-32.

36. *PO*, 84.

37. Westfeldt.

38. Different views of the house at Lynn, N. C., in which Lanier died are to be found in the *Mid-Continent* VI, 86 (May, 1895) and in *The Lanier Book*, opp. p. 140.

CHAPTER TWENTY-THREE

1. So R. S. Lanier wrote his son's friend Northrup.

2. Efforts have been made to have the body removed to Rosehill Cemetery in Macon, but Mrs. Lanier has definitely stated her opposition to all such plans. A picture of Lanier's grave is in *Johns Hopkins Alumni Magazine* V, opp. p. 23 (Nov., 1916).

3. Horder.

4. Stedman, *Life and Letters* II, 279.

5. McCowan.

6. *Poems*, xxxv-xxxvi.

7. *English Novel*, 99.

8. *Poems*, xxxviii.

9. *Literary World* (Boston) XIV, 204-05. June 30, 1883.

10. *English Novel*, 189.

11. *Poems*, xxxvi.

12. *English Novel*, 280.

13. *Letters*, 176.

14. *Letters*, 190.

15. Mims, 302.

16. *Nation* XLVI, 118-19.

17. *Poems*, xxiii.

18. *Poems*, xxii.

19. *Letters*, 78.

20. *Florida*, 235.

21. *Poet-Lore* III, 369.

22. Mims, 366.

22a Most interesting evidence of this sort is given in an article appearing just as this book went to press, Dr. John C. French's "First Drafts of Lanier's Poems," *Modern Lang. Notes*, Jan., 1933. It concerns "Individuality," "Marsh Song—at Sunset," "Credo and Other Poems," and the Johns Hopkins Ode.

23. It is perhaps unnecessary to remark that I use the word in its Latin sense.

24. Huckel, *Johns Hopkins Alumni Magazine* XIV, 491.

25. Mims, 343.

26. Mims, 309-10. Wysham described Lanier's eyes as "more spiritual than dreamy—except when he was suddenly aroused, and then [they] assumed a hawk-like fierceness."

27. Mr. H. W. Lanier, *Selections*, viii.

28. Huckel, *Johns Hopkins Alumni Magazine* XIV, 490.

INDEX

The first page-number following the title of a poem, essay, or musical composition by Lanier refers to the bibliographical reference, though in the case of collected poems and essays the note number on the page indicated must be consulted.

Titles following the name of an author are in most cases of works known to have been read by Lanier.